Handbook of Motion Picture Production

HANDBOOK OF MOTION PICTURE PRODUCTION

WILLIAM B. ADAMS
Associate Professor
Department of Theater Arts
University of California, Los Angeles

Line Illustrations by Len Keennon

A WILEY-INTERSCIENCE PUBLICATION
JOHN WILEY & SONS, New York • London • Sydney • Toronto

Library of Congress Cataloging in Publication Data:

Adams, William B
Handbook of motion picture production.

"A Wiley-Interscience publication."
Bibliography: p.
Includes index.
1. Moving-pictures—Production and direction.
I. Title.

PN1995.9.P7A3 791.43'02'32 76-51818
ISBN 0-471-00459-6

Printed in the United States of America

10 9 8 7 6 5 4 3 2 1

To

ELODIE KEENE

Preface

This is a guide for the would-be film producer, for the lone filmmaker, and for those somewhere in between the two. Regardless of the kind of motion picture you intend to produce—high-budget, low-budget, studio-made, or individually made—the basic skills are the same. This book describes most of the tasks involved.

Most books on filmmaking have been organized around the chronology of film production. They imply that making a film is comparable to stringing beads together: start with the idea bead, put on the script bead and a number of other beads in chronological order, and finish with the negative-cutting bead. Some books, built around the work categories set up by the craft unions, imply that filmmaking comprises a number of separate activities: acting, directing, writing, photographing, editing, designing, scoring, and so forth, and that workers in those areas can limit their work to their specialties just as they could if they were making automobiles or sewing machines. This idea is common today, although practicing filmmakers have long since learned that all film elements are operative to some extent at every point in filmmaking, which is the process of integrating these elements horizontally, vertically, forward, and backward throughout the course of the production. Currently, the teaching of filmmaking is of course no less integrated than the process itself. As a consequence, books that are based on production chronologies, work categories, and encyclopedias are of little value in both the teaching of filmmaking and in filmmaking itself. I have avoided the string-of-beads theory, the job categories, and the encyclopedics and have instead tried to indicate that filmmaking occurs in several dimensions simultaneously.

Much of this manuscript embodies the experience, ideas, and attitudes of Kenneth Macgowan, Edgar Brokaw, Norman Dyhrenfurth, Floyd Crosby, Charles Van Enger, Curtis Courant, George Travell, Palmer Schoppe, William Shull, Lynne Trimble, Colin Young, and other faculty members during the exciting early years of the UCLA film school. Their learning and experience have been passed along to succeeding generations of faculty and students. I am indebted to Edgar Brokaw for allowing me access to his amazing fund of personal knowledge and expertise; to Len Keennon, who drew the illustrations and whose work in both film and teaching are reflected in them; and especially to Elodie Keene, filmmaker extraordinary, whose hard work and professional advice made the completion of this book possible.

WILLIAM B. ADAMS

Santa Monica, California
January 1977

Contents

Handbook of Motion Picture Production

ONE

Production Phases

Although filmmaking can entail an almost unlimited number of tasks and operations, certain basic steps are common to all films; yet there is no absolute set of rules and procedures to follow. Every film, every filmmaker, every set of working conditions is unique in some way, and the process must be modified to fit the circumstances. The large production company employs hundreds of specialists and builds expensive sets. The small producer may use a crew of five or six and a simple set or two. The lone filmmaker, working with one helper, does everything himself. Regardless of the degree of complexity and expense of your particular undertaking, the basic tasks of filmmaking must be done by someone, no matter what his job title may be. These tasks fall into three stages, as follows:

1. Preproduction
   Writing
   Preproduction planning
2. Production
   Picture shooting and sound recording.
3. Postproduction
   Editing
   Sound recording (music and effects)
   Final editing
   Mixing
   Titles and opticals
   Negative cutting
   Composite printing

Production here means the actual shooting, or photography, although the whole job of making a film from start to finish is obviously production.

PREPRODUCTION

The preproduction process includes everything you must do before you can begin shooting the picture. Depending on the type of film you are making and the type of producer you are, production involvement varies widely. Basically you need a plan and careful preparation before you can start, and the plan begins with a central idea that can be developed into a script. For a feature entertainment film, you usually start with either a story or a synopsis of one. For a documentary, you select a particular phase of actual life. An educational film starts with certain information or attitudes. Business and industrial films deal with aspects of a particular business. And experimental and avant-garde films often start with the desire to express a mood or merely manipulate visuals. Film ideas, stories, and information must be arranged verbally in the form of a script, which then becomes the basis of a definite plan for shooting and completing the picture.

The script then goes to a production manager, who breaks it down and isolates every person, prop, special effect, and item needed to get the shooting done. He also gives copies to specialists—set design and construction, camera, props, wardrobe, special effects, transportation—and each analyzes the script and makes a detailed list of the requirements for his specialty. With all this information on hand, the production manager prepares a production schedule and a budget.

Although we usually think of film for a picture as coming from the shooting unit, there are actually three sources of film: (1) film shot for the picture during the scheduled production period; (2) animation and art work; and (3) stock film from the film library. Decisions about what use to make of film from these three sources are generally made during the writing and production planning stages. As you edit the film, however, you may discover places where animation, artwork, or stock footage can save you money or enhance the film's effectiveness. Most feature films consist predominantly of originally produced footage, but it is not unusual for them to include either an occasional stock shot of an interesting location or animated titles. Documentaries tend to use a greater amount of library film, while educational and technical films use footage from each source in varying amounts depending on the information or process to be depicted.

Preproduction planning is usually quite formal, specific, and comprehensive, and the company adheres rigidly to a script and a detailed shooting schedule. The production manager plans every move in advance. For example, say that on July 10, scenes 10, 11, and 36 of a script are to be shot on location at the Lazy-Y ranch. Needed—in addition to the director, production staff, and actors—are twenty horses, thirty extras, production crews, trucks, buses, meals, rest rooms, and all the necessary camera, grip, and sound equipment. All must be notified, confirmed, and transported. The amount of paperwork—memos, orders, receipts, letters, requests—and man-hours of planning are staggering. Without such preliminary work, a production of any complexity at all will collapse before it ever gets started.

In contrast, shooting may be quite informal, as with the lone filmmaker shooting an unstaged documentary-oriented film. In this situation, tortuous preproduction planning need not be carried out just because "that's the way they make movies." Obviously, it is possible to go scriptless into the world equipped only with camera and film, shooting whatever strikes your interest and later making something of it in the editing room. Yet even this seemingly casual method entails starting with a plan—the plan to shoot in a random way. You cannot escape the necessity to preplan to some extent: how much film to carry, where to go first, what equipment to take for contingencies, what tentative schedule to follow, what sort of action to look for, how much money to carry, how big a crew to use, and so on. If your subject matter does not permit a formal schedule, you can analyze your working conditions and be ready for all contingencies.

Anyone in the film business to make a living or even a lot of money will have to pay especially close attention to preproduction planning, for often it is in this stage that the line is crossed between profit and loss. Paradoxically preproduction planning does not end with the beginning of shooting but continues through completion of the film. A film in production must be closely monitored at every stage to determine exactly how the money is holding out and where the major problems will probably occur.

Production planning consists of analyzing the script, isolating essential details, designing the production, preparing the budget, setting up the shooting schedule, hiring people, and keeping track of the budget and the progress of the production.

PRODUCTION

Production is the actual shooting of the picture and involves most of the familiar specialties and techniques—acting, directing, camera, sound, and special effects. The director and his crews stage, enact, and record on film all the action the script requires. Successful shooting will depend to a great extent on how carefully the preplanning has been conducted and how promptly everyone and everything arrive at the right place at the right time.

Shooting

On location or on the set the camera photographs the action and the recorder records the sound. This is called *double-system shooting*—that is, sound and action are recorded on separate pieces of equipment and remain on separate pieces of film from this point on until the final print of the finished picture. All film production, with the exception of news reporting and unstaged events, is done in double system which, because of the separation of sound and action, allows complete flexibility in editing and creating sound tracks.

In *single-system shooting,* the sound is recorded in the camera on the picture film at the time of shooting. The result is a picture negative with the sound track recorded along the edge on a thin magnetic stripe. Since this makes editing extremely inflexible, single-system shooting is used only when the subject matter is more important than the quality, as in news events and political speeches.

During shooting, the camera is loaded with either negative or original reversal film on which the action is exposed. The accompanying sound is recorded on quarter-inch tape on the sound recorder. At the end of the day's shooting, the cameraman sends the exposed negative to the laboratory to be developed. After developing the laboratory makes a positive print of the negative, which is called the "daily print." The combined prints are referred to as "dailies," or "rushes." Every day, the editor, director, and cameraman look at the dailies from the previous day's shooting. These prints are then sent to the editing room to become the editor's workprint.

After the dailies have been printed, the lab sends the *negative/original* (see p. 159) to the vault to be stored under controlled humidity and temperature conditions for use later in the negative cutting room.

The sound track of the day's shooting must also go to the editing room to be edited along with the picture, but since it is on quarter-inch tape it is first sent to the studio to be transferred to sprocketed magnetic film.

POSTPRODUCTION

Postproduction includes everything necessary to complete the picture after it has been shot. Although there is an understandable tendency on the part of those unfamiliar with filmmaking to assume that when the shooting is over the job is done, this is far from the truth. Film financing and planning based on this assumption easily lead to disaster. After all shooting is finished, a film is about 25% complete: the workprint must be edited; sound effects have to be recorded and built into sound tracks; music must be selected, scored, and edited to the workprint; and all the sound tracks—music, dialogue, sound effects, narration—have to be combined into a single track. Titles must be designed and photographed and optical effects made. The negative has to be cut and matched to the workprint, and final composite prints made in the laboratory.

Since it comes as an anticlimax, it is easy to bog down in postproduction. During shooting, everyone is fresh and excited; afterward, the psychological advantage is gone, and it requires extra effort to maintain the momentum.

Editing

In the editing room the editor manipulates, or edits the workprint and the sound track to arrive at a final version of the film that reflects that intent of the script. His task is one of selection. The length of this workprint is many times the length of the completed picture, and it is the editor's job to select certain shots and pieces of shots from the workprint and assemble them so that they tell the story or create the desired impression. He edits the workprint of the *visuals* and the *principal sound track* simultaneously. For a narrated film, it would be the narration track. For a lyric or rhythmic film, in which music and visuals are integrated, the principal track would be the music. Usually the principal sound track is either dialogue or narration.

The editor's job is one of constant viewing, selecting, rearranging, evaluating, and rearranging again. He continually handles and works with all film shot for the picture and is responsible for making a coherent picture out of the mass of film produced during shooting.

Interlock Screening

During editing, as has been discussed, the sound and the picture are on separate strips of film. One of the requirements of editing is the handling of the two strips so that they are always synchronized, or "in sync." Film editing machines are designed with two separate "heads"—one for action and one for sound—that can be operated separately or quickly and easily locked together to hold sound and picture in a perfect in-sync relationship. When picture and sound are played back in this way, we speak of running a picture "in interlock." Until the time that the final print of the completed film comes out of the lab, sound and action can only be seen and heard together on the editing machine in interlock, or on the screen by means of interlock projection. In the latter method the projectionist threads each sound track—there are often more than one—onto separate magnetic playback machines. Then he threads the picture in a projector. Playback machines and projector are electrically interlocked—that is, they are wired to start at exactly the same instant and run at exactly the same speed, thus maintaining picture and sound in sync.

When the editor gets the workprint edited into its first version, he screens it in an interlock projection session. Here the editor, producer, and director can observe the progress of the picture. Here too they make suggestions and try to agree on all changes, since alterations are relatively simple at this stage. Later, when sound effects and music have been added, changes can become quite costly, even prohibitive.

Music and Sound Effects

After the editor has revised the workprint it is ready for music and sound effects to be incorporated. The sound studio uses sound effects from its library as well as actually creating and recording effects, which are then used to build complete sound effects tracks to fit the edited workprint. Since very few sound effects recorded at the time of shooting are usable—they may be too loud or too soft; there may be too much interference from other noises; they may not sound right—almost all the sounds you hear in a film have been painstakingly recorded by some hardworking technician and carefully synchronized to the picture by the editor.

Frequently two kinds of music tracks are used in motion pictures: an originally composed score or a track consisting of already recorded library music. If an original score is to be written, the composer views the edited workprint, takes down the footage and time of each sequence, and notes any special effects that may be needed. He then composes the score, which is recorded by musicians according to precise timing or to the picture itself screened in the recording studio.

If the score is not to be original, there is a large and varied body of "canned" music available in libraries. The music cutter selects several different pieces and then edits them to the workprint. As in picture editing, he uses parts of musical numbers, rearranges their position, and mixes portions of many different numbers together. A good music cutter can synthesize a track so skillfully that few viewers ever suspect the music was not composed especially for the picture. Like the sound effects tracks, the music tracks must be synchronized with the edited workprint.

Often two pieces of music—or two sound effects—must overlap one another, but physically two pieces of film cannot be spliced together overlapped. Instead they must be put on separate strips of film and mixed together later. Since music, sound effects, and voice frequently overlap many times in a film, a picture with even fairly simple sound will have from four to ten sound tracks in the editing stage. A film with complex sound may have twenty or more sound tracks, all of which must ultimately be mixed together on one track.

Mixing

In preparing for sound mixing the editor makes up a cue sheet for each sound track, indicating the exact footage where a sound is to come in or go out, to be made soft or loud, or to be combined with sound from one or more of the other tracks. The editor measures footage from a start mark at the head of the edited workprint. Each sound track has its own start mark corresponding to and synchronized with the mark on the workprint. In the mixing session—which is actually an interlock projection of the workprint and all the tracks—the sound man, called the mixer, sits at the mixing console which has a separate volume control for each sound track. He watches the film as it is projected, refers to the cue sheets, and controls the volume of each track. Meanwhile the resulting sound is being recorded on a single track. Since the mixer is provided with a footage counter set to zero on the workprint start mark, he can determine from the cue sheet, as the picture runs through, which effects and music are coming up on which channels. The editor may also have cued the tracks with "streamers," diagonal lines about four feet long marked on the workprint.

The mixing console has a large number of controls: the main volume controls, banks of equalizers and filters to alter the frequency characteristics of any desired channel, a footage indicator, the dB meter, various other meters, and an intercom system that links the studio, the projection booth, and the machine room. If there are between ten and twenty tracks, the mixer cannot possibly adjust the level of them all, since he has only the usual human complement of hands. The object of having many tracks is to separate the different effects so that each can be preset at the level at which rehearsal proves it to be most effective. For complicated jobs, there may be assistant mixers to handle subsidiary tracks. The head mixer is responsible for dialogue, music, and perhaps the two main effects tracks. The fewer the tracks the greater the mixer's difficulties, since he must continually alter his levels, fading from one track to another, always keeping one eye on the screen and the other on the dB meter. An expert mixer working under these conditions develops the bravura of a virtuoso pianist. He is a peculiar, and valuable, combination of technician and artist.

Several practice run-throughs of the picture and its tracks let the mixer get the feel of the whole film. Any mistakes made during the recording require additional run-throughs until it is perfect. If the mixer cannot handle the complex tracks with sufficient speed, the tracks may have to be altered or another mixer may be needed to assist. A difficult reel will require many rehearsals before the crew is ready for a "take," and often several takes may be necessary before the producer is satisfied.

The final mixed track (also called the *composite magnetic track*) will be on magnetic film. But before this track can be used in making the composite print of the picture, it must be transferred onto photographic film in the form of a negative. This is called the *optical negative sound track,* and is made by the laboratory when it receives the magnetic mixed track from the mixing studio.

Titles and Opticals

When the negative cutter starts to match the negative to the workprint, he must have on hand the negative for the titles and all optical effects that are to be in the picture. Thus, soon after editing starts the titles must be designed, printed, and photographed and all the optical effects must be planned and made. It is wise to start work on titles very early in the production, and on opticals as soon as the editor knows their position in the picture. Both procedures take time, and completion of the film is delayed and costly if the titles and opticals are not ready.

Negative Cutting

Once the editor's final cut of the film has been approved and the mix is under way, the workprint and the negative from the vault go to the negative cutter who matches the negative exactly to the workprint. He breaks the negative down and winds each separate scene onto a core. Since the workprint was printed from the negative, there is a corresponding scene in the negative for each scene in the workprint. The cutter sets aside all such negative scenes and splices them together in exactly the same length and order that they appear in the workprint. This job must be done with extreme care under the most scrupulously clean conditions, since even the slightest damage to the negative is permanent and affects the quality of the final image. Tiny particles of dust actually scratch the negative and oil from the skin etches it. The negative cutting room is dustfree, with carefully controlled temperature and humidity, and the negative cutter wears clean white gloves as he works. Since the negative is irreplaceable and represents the entire investment of the producers, the necessity for its protection cannot be overemphasized.

The assembled and spliced negative, called the conformed negative (since it conforms to the workprint), then goes to the laboratory for composite printing.

Composite Printing

The composite print of the picture is a single strip of film on which are printed both the picture and the sound track. To make the composite print, the lab exposes both the conformed negative and the optical negative sound track onto one piece of film. The appearance of the resulting composite print is a series of pictures, or frames, with a narrow sound track running beside them for the length of the film. The first composite print to come out of the lab is called the first answer print, or the first trial composite print, and is viewed by the laboratory technician, producer, and director to observe the accuracy of color balance and printing light intensities. If these are not satisfactory, a second answer print, or second trial composite, may be struck with corrections. Sometimes a film goes through several answer prints before the desired quality is achieved. When an acceptable answer print is approved by all concerned, the subsequent prints, known as composite release prints, are made for release to theaters.

SUMMARY OF PRODUCTION STEPS

1. **Writing.** The writer prepares a script from a story or idea.
2. **Production Planning.** The production manager breaks down the script, prepares a budget and production schedule, and keeps track of the production's progress.
3. **Shooting the Picture.** The director stages the action along the lines of the script. The cinematographer photographs the action, and the sound director records the dialogue.
4. The cinematographer sends the exposed negative film from the camera to the laboratory for developing and printing.
5. The sound director sends the dialogue sound tape to the sound studio for transfer to magnetic film.
6. The laboratory develops the negative and makes a workprint from it. This workprint is sent to the film editor.
7. The laboratory puts the negative in a vault until it is needed.
8. The sound studio sends the magnetic sound track—now on sprocketed film—to the film editor.
9. The editor edits the picture and the principal sound track.
10. The editor conducts an interlock screening of the workprint for the director, the producer, and the sponsor.
11. The sound effects editor selects and records sound effects to fit the edited workprint. The composer composes and records the musical score.
12. Music and sound effects cutters cut the music and sound effects tracks to match the edited workprint and dialogue track. The editor then makes final adjustments.
13. The editor sends the edited workprint and all the edited sound tracks to the mixing studio.
14. Under the producer's supervision, the mixer and his assistants mix all tracks into one magnetic track while watching the picture.
15. The mixing studio sends the mixed magnetic track to the laboratory to be made into an optical negative track.
16. The workprint goes to the negative cutter.
17. The vault sends the camera negative to the negative cutter.
18. The optical department sends the negative of the titles and optical effects to the negative cutting room.
19. The negative cutter cuts the negative and conforms it to the workprint.
20. The conformed negative and the optical negative sound track are sent to the laboratory to be used in making the first trial composite print (answer print).
21. The laboratory screens the first trial composite print for approval.
22. Release prints are sent out to theaters.

TWO

Conventions

There are no such things as "good" or "bad" films; there are only effective and ineffective films. If what you produce is visually successful, you have made a good film. To make exactly the film you want requires a mastery of the medium and its conventions, which means learning all the techniques, methods, tricks, gimmicks, and skills of filmmaking and being able to use them in any way necessary to achieve the desired effect. Don't restrict yourself by espousing a particular school of filmmaking—never using a dissolve because "the dissolve is philosophically wrong," or making your entire film in one continuous shot because "reality has no cuts in it." If you must work this way, however, bear in mind that you limit your effectiveness as a filmmaker when you restrict yourself to a cult that designates "acceptable" and "unacceptable" techniques.

DEFINITION

A *convention* is a general agreement about basic principles. Perspective in drawing and painting is a highly sophisticated convention that we have all agreed upon as representing depth. In a photograph perspective is automatic, but it is still a convention. Although we find it hard to believe that photographic perspective is not self-evident to all people, anthropologists have discovered that to the unsophisticated untrained eye a photograph is a flat thing with no depth to it. Thus, until we have learned the convention of converging lines, a still photograph is not interpretable. We who have been accustomed to perspective from birth take it for granted, but we nevertheless had to learn to understand it. In the same way the motion picture, although it looks real, is a highly conventionalized piece of symbolism. Its conventions may seem self-evident to our sophisticated eyes, but film symbolism can be understood only by audiences educated to those conventions.

When we look at a movie, we sit in a large room surrounded by visible people all looking in the same direction. On the wall facing us is a two-dimensional picture projected from a window in the wall behind us. The action of the screen is accompanied by music from some orchestra apparently nearby, and we often hear sound effects unlike anything in real life. The action jumps from place to place instantaneously—from day to night, from reality to fantasy, from present to past. In no other art form are so many concessions made to credibility. Yet we do ignore the artificiality and accept the conventions of the motion picture. This is an important consideration when attempting new ways of expression on film. Normally, violating a convention causes confusion and misunderstanding in an audience, as, for example, in Fellini's great film 8½ in which he used the CUT instead of the conventional DISSOLVE to go from scenes portraying reality to those depicting fantasy. At that time, audiences, had been conditioned to a DISSOLVE in such a situation and simply did not understand what was happening. As more filmmakers began using the CUT in this way, however, audiences eventually became accustomed to the technique and a new convention came into being.

The conventions of film, then, are those working principles that audiences accept as believable. A convention has a life—it comes into existence and is accepted initially by only a few viewers. As the convention becomes established, it becomes meaningful to all. In time it may become a hackneyed cliche, rejected by audiences as laughable and old-fashioned. This is the general progression of taste in any art. A pattern of conventions becomes stifling to the artist and he seeks new ways to express himself. At first the public does not accept the artist's new techniques, and a period of terrible misunderstanding follows. When people talk about the meaninglessness of art, its immorality, and its political radicalism they are really indicating that they do not understand because they have not yet entered into an agreement about exactly what the new techniques mean.

Creativity in every art form is intimately related to the invention of new techniques and new modes of expression. Mastering a craft means mastering its conventions. But becoming an artist means being able to use these conventions creatively and then devising new ways of expression which may in turn become conventions.

Conventions are not static although some, such as canvas in painting and matching continuity in film, appear to be almost eternal. Inevitably conventions change, reflecting, of course, the changes in society and culture. Conventions are absolute rules only to the bureaucrat and the unimaginative filmmaker. The creative person instinctively takes conventions for what they truly are—a point from which to deviate. Following are some of the principal conventions of the motion picture:

CONTINUITY

All motion pictures fall into two categories: continuity films and noncontinuity films. A continuity film or scene is one that depicts a literal presentation of real life in believable, realistic chronological order. This is the continuity of the conventional dramatic feature film in which we see actors going through a series of actions that appear real and seem to be taking place in real time. The audience gets the feeling that the camera is watching actual events as they occur. All movements "match." When we see an actor in a MEDIUM SHOT reach for a gun on a table and we immediately follow with a CLOSEUP of his hand picking up the gun, the action in the CLOSEUP must look as if it were a continuation of the movement in the preceding MEDIUM SHOT. The speed and direction of the movement in the two shots must be identical—they must match. Another scene: As a woman opens a door and exits, we CUT to a shot on the other side of the door showing the continuation of her movement. The movements of both the door and the woman in the second shot must appear as an uninterrupted continuation of the first shot. If the matching is skillful, we may not even be aware that we have gone from one shot to another. Yet another example: We see a CLOSEUP of a man who turns his head to the right and speaks. We then see a CLOSEUP of a woman who turns her head to the left and smiles, and we believe that the woman is responding to the man.

The intent of continuity is to create in the audience a feeling that real action is occurring in real time. Essential to this type of film are the traditional conventions of matching action, matching screen direction, and matching set elements. Matched continuity has been a characteristic of narrative films for so long that many people both in and out of the film business have mistakenly come to accept it as the immutable law of motion pictures. Yet there is more to making effective films than following rigid logical continuity.

In the dramatic narrative film, matched continuity is the essential technique that produces the *illusion of reality*. It is the film equivalent of

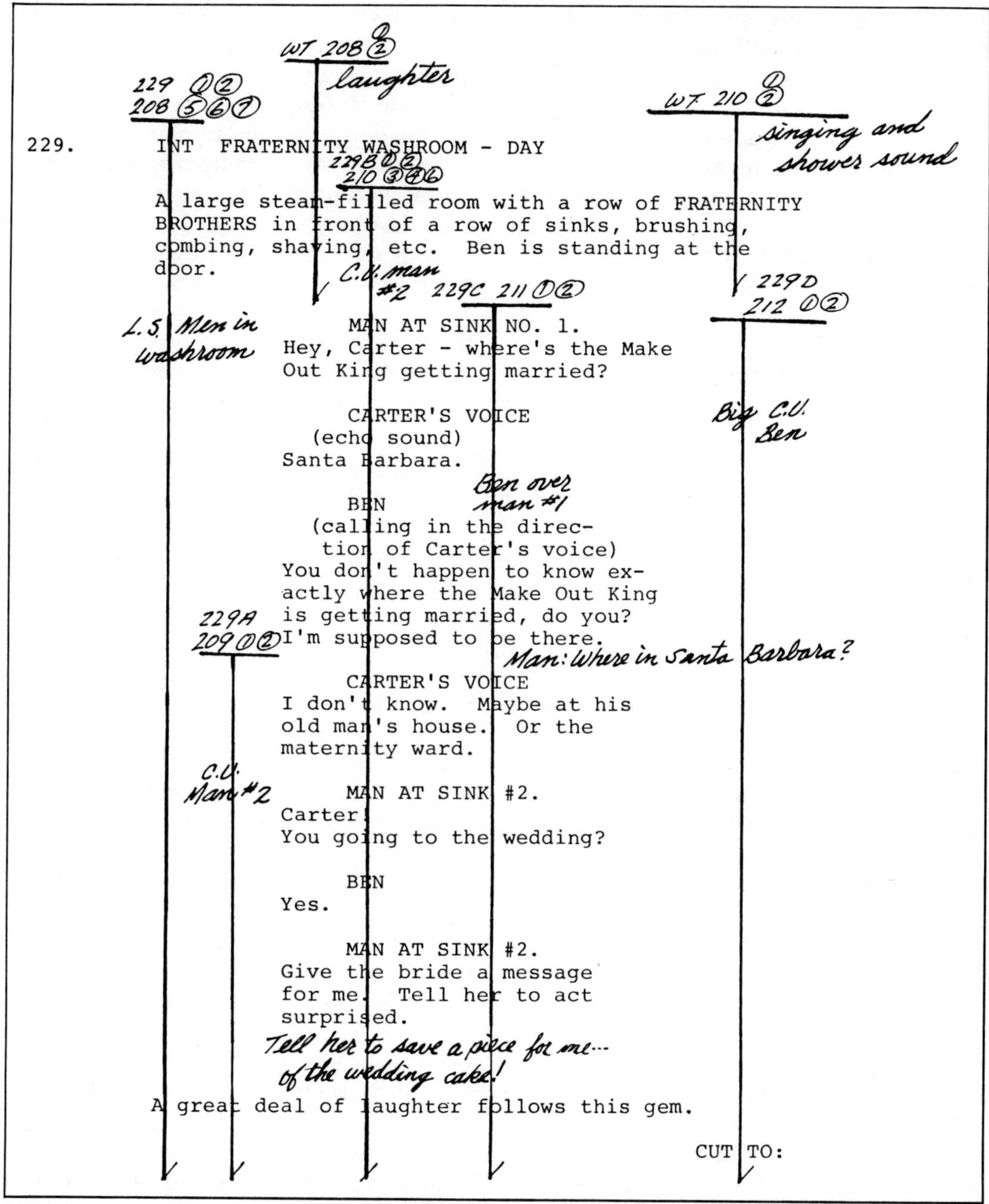

229. INT FRATERNITY WASHROOM - DAY

A large steam-filled room with a row of FRATERNITY BROTHERS in front of a row of sinks, brushing, combing, shaving, etc. Ben is standing at the door.

MAN AT SINK NO. 1.
Hey, Carter - where's the Make Out King getting married?

CARTER'S VOICE
(echo sound)
Santa Barbara.

BEN
(calling in the direction of Carter's voice)
You don't happen to know exactly where the Make Out King is getting married, do you? I'm supposed to be there.

Man: Where in Santa Barbara?

CARTER'S VOICE
I don't know. Maybe at his old man's house. Or the maternity ward.

MAN AT SINK #2.
Carter!
You going to the wedding?

BEN
Yes.

MAN AT SINK #2.
Give the bride a message for me. Tell her to act surprised.

Tell her to save a piece for me... of the wedding cake!

A great deal of laughter follows this gem.

CUT TO:

Fig. 2.1. Excerpt of script page of "The Graduate" as marked by the script supervisor at the time of shooting.

Daniel Defoe's "minuteness for verisimilitude," or scrupulous attention to all the details that make the reader feel he is reading a believable story that could be "real." In film, minuteness for verisimilitude consists not of exhaustive descriptive writing but of excruciating attention to matching visual details such as set geography, dress, decor, props, speech, and movement.

In its worst sense continuity means following all action through all its steps and can result in seemingly endless screen time spent merely to get characters from one place to another. For example: A man leaves his office. We see him go out the door, down the hall, into the elevator, out of the elevator, into the street, into a cab, ride across town, get out of the cab, pay the driver, walk across the sidewalk, and enter a building. All this is done in matching shots to make it look "real." Although this description is exaggerated perhaps, it characterizes the mindless use of matching continuity seen in too many motion pictures.

The page in Fig. 2.1 is from the shooting script of *The Graduate,* a typical narrative continuity type feature, written by Calder Willingham and Buck Henry. The lines and markings on it were made by the Script Supervisor during the actual shooting of the scene. Each line running vertically through the text represents an actual shot made during the filming. The length of the line indicates how much of the scene was included in that shot. Below is a summary of shots made in that scene. Notice that the master scene is Number 229. (For a description of the master scene, see p. 110) Each vertical line on the shooting script represents a different angle of that same scene and is numbered as an alphabetical subdivision of the master scene number.

Sc. 229. This is the Master Scene. A FULL VIEW shot. It plays through the entire script scene.

Sc. 229A. CLOSEUP of #2 MAN. Repeats the action of the scene from CARTER'S VOICE to the end of the scene.

Sc. 229B. MEDIUM VIEW. Repeats the action of the entire script scene.

Sc. 229C. CLOSEUP of MAN AT SINK #1. Repeats the whole script scene.

Sc. 229D. CLOSEUP of BEN. Repeats the whole script scene.

In each shot the director repeated the action exactly as it had been done in the master scene, so that in editing he could use any part of any shot and still match the master scene. He paid great attention to details to ensure that the action in each shot exactly repeated and matched the action of the master scene. This was done to create the impression of real events happening in real time, the essence of the continuity film.

DYNAMIC FILM

The noncontinuity film is often referred to as the *dynamic film.* It is distinct from matching continuity and is usually identified with documentary and fantasy. Its basic characteristic is that its continuity does not depend on matched dialogue and action for the illusion of reality, but relies on the associative effect created by certain visuals put together in a particular way. A dynamic sequence often consists of a series of nonmatching shots which create a dominant impression as a unit. A classic example of this technique is the Odessa steps sequence from *Battleship Potemkin.* Here Eisenstein shot many separate and unmatched shots of people as they panicked down the steps before the advancing soldiers. When these ostensibly unmatched shots were edited together, they conveyed dramatically the panic, terror, and brutality of the situation.

Examine the script page (Fig. 5.6) of a dynamic sequence from Pare Lorenz's film *The River.* Here are eight shots, all involving forests but unrelated in matching continuity. Clearly these shots are not supposed to be occurring concurrently in a specific forest, and the axe is not cutting the exact trees we see falling. Yet the sequence makes a coherent generalization about the relationship of indiscriminate logging and the growth of the United States.

In dynamic shooting, you must be able to take apparently unrelated shots and assemble them to create a total effect. It is not enough to shoot a series of beautifully framed and composed still shots (though "motion" may be present) and splice them together. A dynamic sequence consists of a combination of shots related visually in some way, even though the meaning may initially be clear only to you, the filmmaker. As the sequence progresses, the audience begins to perceive the relationship of the visuals and the meaning inherent in their juxtaposition.

THE ILLUSION OF REALITY

Even though we know that a motion picture is artificial and a compilation of conventions, we insist upon believability. We want to believe that what we are seeing could happen. This doesn't mean that we won't accept fantasy or make-believe in a movie. But what we see has to be believable within its own context. Creating the illusion of reality results in believability.

In a continuity film, reality is achieved through believable performance, matching action, realistic sounds, and the apparent realism of the surrounding scenes. If an action takes place in a street, we look for believable action in the background—people walking past in all directions as if on their regular daily business, cars and vehicles passing as they do in real life, and the street sounds of engines, horns, whistles, and footsteps. An audience is caught up in your continuity scene to the extent that you build a film environment of believability.

The high-budget film producer creates his illusion of reality by literally attempting to recreate reality itself. He rents a city street, ropes it off, and hires special officers to keep people out. He may hire hundreds of extras to act like pedestrians and to drive rented automobiles up and down the street. Even with all this, the illusion of reality is not yet guaranteed. It depends on the ability of the director to handle these diverse elements so that they give the appearance of reality. We have all seen films in which no expense has been spared to create all the trappings of reality, and yet the film looks fake. Obviously the filmmaker missed the essence of what makes a scene look genuine.

To create the illusion of reality, you must first understand what constitutes believability. You must see, evaluate, and remember. As you go about your daily routine, notice what is taking place. How do people talk and react to each other? How do they move? On the street, who stops and looks in windows? How do pedestrians avoid one another? In an office, what is happening? What makes it sound and look like a real office? Who comes in and goes out, and with what frequency? What is the essence of believability? Often it is not the obvious but the many little things that are elusive—a personal mannerism, a certain way things move in the wind, the particular way people carry out the regular business of living—that make for the illusion of reality. And finally, it all comes back to the perceptions of the writer and the director.

The illusion of reality is not confined to real-life, continuity-type films. Fantasy in the form of fairy tales, science fiction, mind trips, ghost stories, and other supernatural happenings require an air of reality to be believable. To make fantasy believable, you must lay a groundwork of reality so that all that follows seems the consequence of perfectly natural events. The portrayer of good fantasy sometimes resorts to Defoe's minuteness for verisimilitude, whereby even the most insignificant details of a situation are painstakingly described to create a climate of believability. In *The Wizard of Oz,* the film begins in a real-life way. Dorothy's life on the farm is presented as true, real, now. The tornado that transports her into the Land of Oz as well as the events leading up to it are terrifyingly real. Once the illusion of reality has been created, the audience will go along with the fantasy that follows. Science fiction films go into excruciating scientific detail, laying the realistic groundwork for trips to other planets, invasions from space, journeys into the fourth dimension, and so on.

Notice how the illusion of reality is created in diverse types of performances—films, television, stage, radio, and sales pitches by various performers, raconteurs, liars, lecturers, politicians, and school teachers. Whether his audience comprises thousands or merely one, the performer first creates the illusion of reality. Although we know full well that a performance is not "real," if it creates the illusion, we agree to accept it as a believable convention.

Actual reality has nothing to do with film reality. The filmmaker's task is to understand the difference between the two. Shooting the "real thing" is no guarantee that the result is going to look real or appear believable. Don't hesitate to build sets or to use actual places for locations. Feel completely free to rearrange things, manipulate lighting, invent sound effects, and use any and all devices that serve to achieve the result you desire. Only what the audience believes is important. If you want reality in your film, you have to create the illusion of it, and this requires you to work at two levels, as follows:

1. Decide what elements must go into your scene to contribute to its believability and its illusion of reality.
2. Plan and execute the production with skill and meticulous care so that your shots actually convince your audience.

With the above in mind, consider a scene from the film *Lost Weekend* (see Chapter 3.) The director staged the scene in an actual New York street. The actor playing the part of the drunk staggered down a Greenwich Village sidewalk while a hidden camera photographed him from a moving truck. No one in the scene except the actor knew that a movie was being shot. Passersby, if they thought about it at all, believed that the drunk was real, and they went about their business in a normal way. On the screen the scene was believable and "real."

On the first level, the director decided that strong believability would come from using a real street and its normal pedestrian traffic. He felt the illusion of reality would be greater with real pedestrians instead of extras. On the second level, the shot had to be planned and executed effectively. The mere fact that a "real" situation was used would not of itself make the scene appear real. Intense planning and site selection were involved in setting up the scene. The particular section of sidewalk used had to be selected carefully to show exactly what the director wanted. The actor had to be rehearsed in the action not only for his part but for the camera crew and the camera car driver. Consider the work that went into rigging the truck so that a hidden camera could follow movement on the street without attracting attention. The scene would have been ruined had passersby spotted the camera in the truck—people looking at the camera, waving, giggling, and pointing at the actor. The right time of day had to be determined so that traffic flow did not interfere. Obviously movie lights could not be used, so the shot had to be scheduled for the time of day when the available light was adequate. Using a real street and real passersby worked only because the production details were meticulously planned and executed.

A popular television serial has a time machine that can transport people backward or forward in time. The illusion of reality results from the machine's scientific aspect. As a time machine it looks genuine, with complicated controls, a complex instrument panel, impressive servomotor sounds, and a computer readout. It is presented as scientifically genuine, and even though audiences know that both the machine and the story are make-believe, they accept them as believable. If, however, the time machine were an obvious cardboard mockup with dials crudely painted on it, audiences would instantly reject both story and machine as "fake."

THE FRAME

In the normal process of living you see the world around you as an entire related scene making visual sense. Time is continuous, and events occur in a logical sequence before your eyes. Standing on the street corner, you can plainly see the location of buildings, the intersection of streets, the movement of cars and people, and you understand the physical relationship of all these things to each other. You may single out any object or person in the world around you and examine it in detail while still maintaining a grasp of the relative location of everything as a whole. But when you put life on film, you lose this overall relationship—you look at life through a small frame. Everything inside that frame has now lost its natural relationship to the surrounding world. A shot on the movie screen has meaning only with reference to itself, to the shots that preceded it, and to the shots that will follow. The audience has no conception of the larger scene from which it came. Your task as a filmmaker is to select shots and sounds from life, frame them in a particular way, and put them together into an entity called a motion picture. For example: An audience sees a CLOSE SHOT of a man saddling a horse. All it sees in the frame is part of the man, part of the horse, and maybe a small piece of fence in the background. From this information alone the audience doesn't know where the scene is taking place, what is happening, or why the man is saddling the horse. But if the audience hears sounds that seem to be coming from around the man, it receives a good impression of what is going on. It hears the sounds of leather, spurs, horses, and voices of men saying such things as, "I'll go along the river; you two scout the edge of the hills." Another voice says "Hurry up! He's got a head start already." The audience infers that a posse of some kind is forming and is about to pursue someone. Yet at the time of shooting there may have been no one else in the scene and the voices could have been put on the sound track later. Thus all these sounds enable the audience to "see" things that are not actually on the screen.

An audience cannot know instinctively what is supposed to be going on outside the frame unless you show it. As filmmaker, you see what is in the frame as well as everything else outside it. You know where things are. When you select items and put them in a frame, however, they lose all connnection and relevance to the actual surrounding area. Combined with other shots made in other places, these items can become something completely different from what they actually are.

VISUAL THINKING

One way to start seeing the world through a frame is to do just that. Carry a director's viewfinder and look at life as you go about it. Through the viewfinder, look at as much of life as you can. Examine every part of your world, animate and inanimate, from every conceivable point of view. Frame objects and people so closely that they become abstract. Frame on people and follow them as they walk and move. Follow moving cars and trucks. Look at things close, medium, and long, and begin to think of what you have inside the frame as completely unrelated to what is outside it. Then create relationships. Follow a pedestrian, perhaps, as he crosses the street, then CUT to a policeman. Although in reality the two may be completely unaware of each other, by placing them in sequence you have implied a relationship. Look at all aspects of the world around you as isolated bits of life that you can reorganize any way you wish. This is the essence of visual thinking.

Begin to analyze the way you look at things. For example, assume you have just entered a busy café. In a booth near the cashier sits a lone girl studying quietly. She is absorbed in her work, although the activity and noise around her are almost excruciating. In real life, you would usually take in the whole situation at a glance. You would hear the noise, see the bustle, and be amused at the girl studying. Put this total scene on film, however, and the overall impression that the live spectator receives is lost. On the screen an overall shot would not tell the story. The girl would be lost. As a filmmaker, your job is to direct the audience's attention to successive details of the scene. You could do this with a series of shots approximating the way you would look at the real situation. First, you take in the whole café and observe that it is extremely busy. Next, you glance at the cash register as it rings up a ticket. You see a busboy noisily clearing dishes from a table. A group of people in a booth are laughing and talking. Loud noises come from behind the kitchen door, through which comes a waitress carrying a tray full of food. You watch the waitress as she threads her way through the tables and passes the studying girl. Your attention focuses on the studying girl while the waitress continues on out of your sight. You are amused at such concentration in the midst of chaos. In this quick appraisal of the café, you have formulated a movie sequence. You have done a director's job. Translated to script form, your observation of the café and the girl might look like this:

INT BUSY CAFE DAY

FIRST LOOK WIDE VIEW CAFE

The cafe is full and busy. There is noise everywhere. PEOPLE are waiting for tables and booths. BUSBOYS are madly trying to clear vacated tables. WAITRESSES are going at top speed, trying to take care of too many people.

SECOND LOOK CLOSE VIEW CASH REGISTER

The CASHIER's HANDS keep the register working almost continuously as they slam checks into the posting slot, make change, and slam the register drawer.

THIRD LOOK CLOSE VIEW BUSBOY

The BUSBOY is clearing a table for four at which seven people sat. He is hurrying and making a great clatter.

FOURTH LOOK MEDIUM VIEW DINERS IN BOOTH

SIX DINERS in a semicircular booth. They are talking and laughing loudly as they eat.

FIFTH LOOK WIDE VIEW DOOR TO KITCHEN

We see BUSBOYS and WAITRESSES bustle in and out the door. Loud clanging and banging comes from the kitchen along with loud orders and commands. WAITRESS comes through the door from the kitchen carrying a huge tray at shoulder height. We FOLLOW HER as she threads her way down one aisle and turns down another. As she passes a GIRL sitting alone in a booth, we HOLD on the GIRL. She is studying, oblivious to the noise and chaos around her.

Change the *looks* to *shots,* and you have a script—a written record of how you looked at this particular slice of life.

It is also possible to make each shot in a different place and then combine them. You could shoot the cash register in EXTREME CLOSEUP in any empty café, with an actor's hands going through the action. The busboy shot could have been made in another city six months earlier. You could stage the noisy diners in a booth built on a sound stage. And you could take a CLOSEUP shot of the girl studying in a booth anywhere. Eliminate the FOLLOW SHOT of the waitress, to eliminate showing the whole café. Edit all the shots together in sequence, add café sound effects, and your audience will assume it is all occurring simultaneously in the same café.

There are an infinite number of ways of looking at things around us. Some people instinctively examine the world around them from changing points of view. Some have to work at it, and others, with perfectly good eyes, can't see at all. There is nothing new in this world except the way different people see it. To be a filmmaker, you have to be able to see. Look at your world through a frame and force your perceptions into new channels. Since the camera can record only through a frame, you should start learning early to "see" through one.

THE CUT

The CUT is an instantaneous transition from one shot to the next. Physically you make a CUT by splicing the tail of one shot onto the head of another shot. The effect on the screen is such that at one moment you see one image and the next instant you see another. It is an immediate and sometimes violent change of scene without any softening or preparation in the mind or eye of the audience. Yet if the filmmaker selects the shots correctly and makes careful CUTS, an audience may even be unaware that a change of image has been made.

The CUT is the most common transition in motion pictures, and occurs, according to convention, between shots that take place simultaneously. This has made possible the creation of the illusion of real-time sequential continuity action. If an audience sees a shot of a girl bound hand and foot, then a CUT to a shot of a burning fuse followed by a CUT to a shot of a man driving a car at desperate speed, the accepted meaning is that all three actions are happening at the same time. An audience will further assume that the three pieces of action are related—that the girl is in imminent danger of being blown up and the man is driving to her rescue.

THE DISSOLVE

The DISSOLVE is a transition from one shot to another that indicates a change of place, time, or psychological condition. We see it on the screen as one scene fading out with the following scene simultaneously fading in over it. For about two seconds we see both scenes on the screen at the same time. Traditionally this means either skipping backward or forward in time, changing location, or going into fantasy or memory. In noncontinuity and abstract films, the DISSOLVE is often used only for its visual effect.

Audiences have become so accustomed to the DISSOLVE as indicating a change of place, time, or psychological condition that such changes without DISSOLVES between them are often confusing. Traditionally, to go into the past, you would slowly DOLLY IN to a CLOSEUP of a woman's face and, to the accompaniment of ethereal music, DISSOLVE TO a shot of a little girl. Audiences know immediately that the girl is the woman when she was a child. To show a student going from Los Angeles to Paris, you would show her heading for the airport, DISSOLVE TO the plane's takeoff, then DISSOLVE TO the plane landing in Paris. In the 1960s, however, Fellini used the CUT instead. Early avant-garde filmmakers had happily ignored all the conventions, but up until Fellini the direct transition from reality to fantasy was unheard of in the feature film. In *8½*, for example, we see Guido sitting in an outdoor cafe with his wife. This is reality. Then, without a DISSOLVE or shaky music, we CUT directly into Guido's fantasy. He fantasizes that his wife and his mistress are friends, when actually they are enemies. We see the mistress enter and sit at a nearby table. Guido's wife goes to the mistress and we see them as great friends—which of course is only Guido's fantasy. To an audience accustomed to the traditional DISSOLVE convention, the scene is meaningless and confusing. To an audience more alert to new ways of expression, the scene makes complete sense.

To the present time, the DISSOLVE has been necessary for audiences to accept such transitions as believable. Audiences raised in the completely literary culture of the first half of the twentieth century needed the DISSOLVE in a film to take the place of the writer's words, "Twenty years later . . ." or "Dear reader, let us turn back to that time long gone . . . ." Although most people today do not require such literary devices to make motion pictures believable, most movie audiences probably still expect a DISSOLVE between scenes to show change in time, place, or conditon.

The DISSOLVE is a softening effect. It makes the transition from one shot to the next seem smooth, easing the shock an audience feels when it is too quickly jerked from one image to another. Whether to use the DISSOLVE or not depends on the way you work and what you believe will be effective. Sometimes using a DISSOLVE instead of a CUT helps to maintain the pace you have carefully established. In continuity editing, your audience may not be aware of CUTS if you have planned, photographed, and edited the action so that the flow of movement seems unbroken. But in a dynamic sequence of shots where you do not have the flow of physical continuity, CUTS may sometimes break the pace and feeling you set up. The DISSOLVE helps speed, slacken, or maintain pace to suit your purpose. It will take the film from one scene to another smoothly even though the scenes may differ in content, composition, and speed of movement. You can control the effect of the DISSOLVE by carefully selecting shots that either match or contrast in movement, mass, or color.

FADES

The FADEOUT and the FADEIN are self-explanatory transitions. A FADEIN is just that—starting from a black screen, the picture gradually comes up to full brightness in two seconds. A FADEOUT goes in the opposite direction—the normal picture darkens down to black. Traditionally the FADES are used in three situations: a FADEIN at the beginning of the picture, a FADEOUT-FADEIN between sequences, and a FADEOUT at the end of the picture.

Although at one time it was unthinkable to start a film or end one without a FADE, today many films begin on a direct CUT from a black screen and end on a CUT to black. A FADE indicates a marked change in time, place, or mood. Styles notwithstanding, use the FADE as you see fit to achieve the desired effect.

THE WIPE

Wipe is a generic term referring to any one of various transitions usually produced optically, such as the incoming image that appears to push the other image off the screen, the film that seems to flop over exposing another image on the other side, or the image that explodes on the screen revealing another image behind it, and so on. Obviously it is a trick effect that generally calls attention to itself, and is especially successful in slick promotional films and in movies where an impression is created through technical virtuosity. The WIPE has been used mostly in theater previews of coming films and in television commercials, where shock and hard-sell techniques are considered valid. Thus audiences generally tend to accept wipes as artificial, but this is not a hard-and-fast rule. If you see a way to use the WIPE as a transition creating the desired effect, use it. If it does not work, it is merely a poor transition.

SCREEN DIRECTION

Screen direction is simply the direction in which things seem to be going or facing on the screen. Remember that the audience is always in one place looking at that fixed frame up on the screen that represents the world. The only orientation that exists is that of the frame; you, the filmmaker, must supply the audience with the information that tells it which direction is which. In a movie the camera represents the audience's eyes, and when you direct a film you are pointing the eyes of the audience at whatever you want them to see. If a person on the screen looks to the left, an expectation of what he is looking at is set up in the audience. If it then sees a shot of another person looking to the right, the audience gets the impression that the two persons are looking at each other. Thus, by the use of direction, a relationship is established between two isolated heads. This is the basis of screen geography, or the apparent arrangement and location of the places and things seen in a film. The geography inside the frame has nothing to do with the actual location where the film was shot.

In the motion picture all directions are stated in terms of the position of the camera, which is the position of the audience's eye. The right-hand side of the picture as seen from the audience is called camera right, or screen right. The left side of the picture is camera left, or screen left. In the legitimate theater the directions are opposite, but the stage has finite dimensions of depth, length, and width. In the motion picture the frame opens onto the world, where things change constantly. The only reference points in the movie are the camera and the audience, both of which are in the same position relative to the frame.

Since the audience can see nothing outside the frame, and it understands only what is put there for it to see, you must create all directions. In shooting a scene you are free to move the camera at will. While directing a scene in a room you might shoot toward one wall, then move across the room and shoot back toward your original camera position. You may then end by shooting scenes from many different parts of the room. This means that you have changed screen direction many times for your audience. On the legitimate stage, the audience always sees the room from one point of view only, but a movie audience may see action in the room from any point. For example: The audience sees a scene looking toward a table. Then it sees a shot looking from the table back across the room in the direction where the camera was placed initially. Consider what happens on the screen when you make such a camera move. In the first shot, looking toward the table, one of your actors crosses the room from camera left to camera right. Then, if you move the camera across the room looking back from the table and shoot another angle of the same scene, your actor will be moving across the room from camera right to camera left. Although he is still moving in the same direction in the room, in relation to the camera he is going in the opposite direction. This is important because the audience sees things only relative to the camera. To the audience, a CUT from the one shot to the other would look as if the actor had suddenly reversed his direction.

Start thinking in terms of camera right and camera left. Use the viewfinder to help. The world you are putting on film does not remain fixed in direction. Every time you move the camera, you set up a new set of directions. Part of the craft of directing consists of controlling screen direction so that the audience is always oriented in the direction you desire.

Everything except a solid color ball has a direction, and putting a frame around anything establishes a direction. All direction is related to the frame, which represents the point of view of both the camera and the audience. In real life you can look at a person from any position and still maintain your orientation as to where that person is in relation to you and the room you are in. On film, however, when the position of the camera is altered the orientation of the audience changes.

Screen direction is the essence of the illusion of reality in a *continuity sequence,* which depends for its believability on the impression that things are happening on the screen just as they would happen in real life. Assume that you shoot a scene in which an actor reaches into a drawer for a pistol. First, you shoot a MEDIUM SHOT in which he opens the drawer and reaches into it. Then you change the camera angle and shoot a CLOSEUP of his hand going into the drawer, so that your audience may see in detail what he is doing. To maintain a feeling of smooth continuity, you would shoot the two shots so that the action in the CLOSEUP seems to be an uninterrupted continuation of the movement in the MEDIUM SHOT. The action of the CLOSEUP would have to repeat the action of the MEDIUM SHOT and be moving in the same direction on the screen. When this type of action is shot correctly and the CUT made at the proper point, the transition seems almost nonexistent. In fact, some audiences will not even be aware that you have made a CUT from MEDIUM SHOT to CLOSEUP.

Now suppose you shoot the action described above (the hand reaching into the drawer) with mismatched screen direction. The MEDIUM SHOT is the same as above, but this time you move the camera around to the other side of the desk. By moving the camera around, you change the screen direction of the movement of the hand. In the MEDIUM SHOT the hand reaches (as before) into the drawer with a movement from left to right, but in the CLOSEUP the hand is moving from right to left. In a realistic continuity sequence, a mismatch like this is enough to destroy the illusion of reality. Although this does not, however, mean that all movement in a film must go in one direction—a monotonous prospect indeed. As the director you should be constantly aware of direction relative to the camera and make certain that changes in direction do not interrupt the illusion of reality or the particular feeling you are trying to induce in your audience.

Acceptance of the fact that shots separated by CUTS are occurring simultaneously, combined with screen direction, makes it possible to create a scene that an audience will accept as representing real-time continuous reality. In the example given earlier of the man reaching into the drawer, the CUT between the two shots told the audience that the MS and the CU were happening sequentially at the same time. The matched screen direction indicated that the CU was another view of the same movement. The end result is the illusion that real action is taking place on the screen.

A scene in which two or more persons are talking to each other depends largely on proper screen direction for believability and smooth flow. The audience has to feel that the characters are talking *to* each other. Such a scene can be established by showing them first in MEDIUM SHOT—a MAN facing screen right, a WOMAN facing screen left. If you go into a closer shot, they should be seen in the same relative position—each still looking in the same direction as in the MEDIUM SHOT. Now go to a CLOSE TWO SHOT, in which we see the woman full-face as if we are looking at her over the man's shoulder. She is still on the right-hand side of the frame facing left. She says something to him and, as he replies, CUT to a CLOSE SHOT of the MAN as if we are looking over the woman's shoulder at him. He should still be on the left-hand side of the frame facing right. If you reverse the actor's positions after having thus oriented your audience, you can create an abruptness which confuses the audience and momentarily diverts attention from what the actors are saying.

Another problem of screen direction occurs in dialogue scenes when only one person at a time is seen on the screen. The audience sees a CU of a character speaking and then it sees a CU of another character answering. Since individual CLOSEUPS do not have a built-in reference to one another, it is up to the director to maintain their relative directions. For example, two women are talking: The FIRST WOMAN looks screen left and speaks. When the SECOND WOMAN answers, if she is looking screen right, it will appear that she is facing the FIRST WOMAN. If the SECOND WOMAN faces screen left when she answers, it will appear that she is looking away from the FIRST WOMAN.

After a scene has been shot, you may find it necessary to make pickup shots, that is, shots of one or more actors to add or change lines. To make these shots usable in the original scene, you would have to remember which way other actors were facing initially. As an isolated instance this does not seem too difficult, but when you are involved in shooting an entire film out of continuity it becomes a mental feat to remember all your screen directions and keep them straight.

Another consideration in dialogue screen direction occurs in shooting a group of people talking. A person says something to one of the others, who answers; a third person adds a comment; a fourth then speaks to the original speaker, and the second speaker responds to the first. The characters in such a group continually change their speaking direction. If the director or editor is to maintain a logical scene geography, he must think carefully. Although the problem may be simplified by keeping the camera in one place and shooting the entire scene in one sustained shot, this leads to monumental boredom and negates the flexibility of the motion picture. Thus your task is to shoot CLOSEUPS, TWO-SHOTS, and GROUP SHOTS that maintain direction and provide a feeling of logical continuity. Each position relative to the others must be memorized and each CLOSEUP shot so that each person looks as if he is talking to the person to whom he is supposed to be talking. Practice directing this kind of scene on paper by outlining a situation such as a group of people engaged in conversation around a table. Plan each shot and move the camera around so that you get various angles and closeups. Number the characters and decide on their speaking order. For example: #1 speaks, #3 answers, #1 nods, #4 speaks, #5 disagrees, #2 cuts in, #3 interrupts. Sketch a frame for each shot you would make, showing the direction each person is facing. When you are finished, you will have blocked out an entire dialogue scene for shooting—a necessary prerequisite for any film you may direct. Making such a plan is more time consuming than you may suspect at first, but it will take even longer if you try to do it at the time of shooting. There will be periods when you will be forced to create such scenes on the spot, but make every effort to plan them in advance. Changes during shooting may cause you to revise a whole scene, which means reblocking on the set. In this kind of situation the director's mental computing capacity is pushed to its limit, since not all scenes consist of simple conversations. Movement of the camera, the actors, and inanimate objects in addition to the direction of dialogue may need to be taken into account.

STAGE BUSINESS

Stage business is action that actors perform with their hands and bodies during a scene. Eating, disassembling a bomb, opening a safe, performing an operation, writing, making coffee, are all examples of stage business. Depending on what is being done and how important it is to the sense of the film, business has to be watched carefully in relation to screen direction. Usually the direction of business follows the general direction of the main action, but you must be careful that the credibility of the whole scene is not ruined by a small discrepancy. The problem usually occurs in matching CLOSEUPS, as in the example mentioned earlier of the hand reaching into the drawer. Since matching CLOSEUPS of business are usually shot at some other time than the main scene, it is easy to forget the exact kinds of movements and their directions. The solution is to keep a careful record of how business was transacted. Sketches and photographs indicating direction and other details of stage business are valuable for this purpose. Normally it is the script supervisor's responsibility to keep such records. (See Script Supervisor, Chapter 3.)

In such events as stampedes, mob scenes, and battles, there is usually a direction the action must take. A mob, like a cattle stampede, is obviously a single mass moving in a particular direction and may be capricious in changing its direction. Usually a battle is waged by two opposing sides facing each other.

When a stampede begins, it is important to show that the herd is stampeding en masse in one direction. The direction is probably unimportant except to indicate the early impression of a large mass moving as one. This entails showing different shots of the herd going in the same screen direction until you have established positively the idea of this directional movement. Once the basic direction is set, you can then indicate the mindless indirection of a stampede through movement in any screen direction. The same method may be employed in editing a mob scene.

Battle scenes traditionally have two opposing forces that immediately provide two built-in directions, left and right. And although you may want to mix the direction of the actual infighting, you should still maintain a left-right directionality so that audiences may determine which side is winning. A classic example of battle screen direction is the scene in Laurence Olivier's film, *Henry V,* where the French cavalry attack the British yoemen. We see the French constantly moving from right to left, intercut with shots of the waiting British always looking from left to right. This directionality is maintained until the British fire their arrows into the French. Then we see a frontal view of the French, after which screen direction no longer exists, as the two forces engage in the chaos of personal combat.

Screen direction helps the audience remember the direction leading to a destination. A chase is the most common destinational type of action. The good guy is chasing the bad, and both should be going in the same direction to maintain the idea of a chase. When the direction of one is altered without changing the direction of the other, the impression is created that the two are running toward each other. If for example, a man being chased runs across the screen from left to right and actually runs out of the right-hand side of the frame (Fig. 2.2*A*). In the next shot, if you pick him up as he comes in the left-hand side of the frame, the audience gets the feeling that his running is continuous in the left-right direction. If you were to CUT to the next shot in which he were running right to left, it would appear as if he had suddenly changed direction and were running into the arms of his pursuer (Fig. 2.2*B*).

Suppose you want to show a girl on a galloping horse going somewhere. If she gallops out of frame right, on the next shot she should come in from frame left (Fig. 2.2C). If she goes out of frame in the lower left-hand corner, in the next shot we should see her come in the upper right corner of the frame (Fig. 2.2*E*). When you maintain screen direction this way, audiences understand it to mean an uninterrupted directional movement. Actually, when you direct a chase, a ride, or a journey, you make many individual shots of action having little or no relationship to each other. Yet combined in terms of conventional screen direction, they result in a unified, uninterrupted continuity.

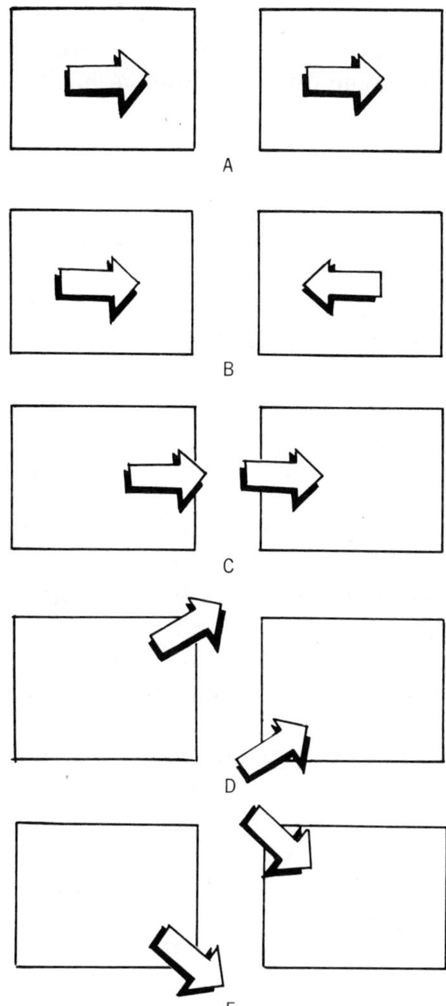

Fig. 2.2*A*. Successive shots in which the action of each is going in the same direction and gives the impression of realistic movement in that direction.
Fig. 2.2*B*. Successive shots in which the action of each is in opposition to the other and gives the impression of conflict, approach, or collision.
Fig. 2.2*C*. Action going out of one side of the frame in one shot and coming in the opposite side of the frame in the next shot gives the impression of realistic lineal continuity.
Fig. 2.2*D*. Action going out of one corner of the frame in one shot and coming in the diagonally opposite corner in the next shot gives the impression of realistic continuity.
Fig. 2.2*E*. Action going out of one corner of the frame in one shot and coming in the diagonally opposite corner in the next shot gives the impression of realistic continuity.

SOUND

Another convention in motion pictures is the use of sound. There are three kinds of sounds in life: voice, music, and sound effects. These sounds are also found in motion pictures, where they are usually stylized, distorted, and rearranged. We find them believable because we have accepted them as conventions.

Some purists and critics mistakenly maintain that only the visuals are important, that the best motion picture is one without sound. Actually the motion picture is a combination of the two elements, and even the "silent" movies of the old days were not silent. From the very beginning, the impulse was to put sound in movies. Elaborate musical scores were composed for silent motion pictures and were played during screenings by live organists or pianists. Sometimes full orchestras were used. Every early theater had its piano or organ player who provided a musical sound track to the silent picture. Although some dramatic motion pictures were remarkably effective in telling stories purely through visuals, the mere absence of sound did not make them better pictures. The sound in motion pictures impresses audiences far more than they are consciously aware. Most propaganda motion pictures, notably *The March of Time* and the propaganda motion pictures of Nazi Germany, rely more on narration and sound to carry their message than on the picture. Often the visuals in a movie show one thing while the narration or the dialogue indicates the opposite, but the audience will remember what is said rather than what is seen. Thus the audience ascribes what is said to what it has seen. Shut the sound off during any motion picture and, by its absence, you will realize just how important it is.

Sound can evoke powerful feelings and reactions because, unlike the visual images of the movie itself, it gets help from the listener's imagination. When a listener hears a sound or a combination of sounds, his imagination is triggered into visualizing the things he has associated with those sounds in his past life. The result is often a reinforcement of the movie's visuals far beyond the superficial meaning of the sound itself. Consider, for example, a shot of a woman about to cross a freeway. We see only the woman and not the freeway. Depending on the kind of sound used, the audience will create its own mental image of the traffic. The off-screen sound of constantly screaming passing cars and trucks will evoke the image of a dangerous freeway facing the woman. The mild sounds of an occasional passing car will evoke in the audience an impression of a quiet, safe roadway, and the audience will be convinced that the woman in the scene is reacting to the sound the same way they are although she may remain impassive. Using sound this way ranges from the obvious, as in this example, to the sophisticated use of subliminal sounds to evoke all sorts of feelings, emotions, and impressions.

Visuals do not stimulate a viewer to imagine other visual images. The only image the picture evokes in the mind of the viewer is the picture itself. In contrast, sound sets up all kinds of evocations in the viewer's imagination that augment the visuals on the screen. This psychological quality of sound is well known and is used to great effect by makers of horror movies, science fiction movies, and disaster epics. Recall the effect sound had in *Earthquake,* or in some good horror or ghost movie you have seen. Consider how ineffective a science fiction movie about space would be if there were no unusual sounds. Listen carefully to sound in the movies you see and learn to identify its effect in contrast to that of the visuals. The point here is not to make an esthetic conclusion but to say to you, the filmmaker, that sound is far more important to the effectiveness of your film than you may suspect initially.

Dialogue

Dialogue is a convention, and we believe conversation on the screen that we would never believe in real life. Listen to the way people talk in real life and on the screen. There is a difference. On the screen sentences are worked out, pronunciation is clear, each exchange of dialogue is structured to arrive somewhere, and a character always gets to say what he is supposed to say. In real life people don't talk this way. Their sentences are chaotic—they start, stop, change the subject, stutter, and mumble.

It is neither good nor desirable for characters in movies to talk exactly as they do in real life. In a film, as in a play, dialogue must help tell the story. Mumbling and senseless gabble, realistic though it may be, only confuse the audience. Over the years we have come to accept the artificiality of screen dialogue as a believable convention. The aim of dramatic dialogue is to sound real rather than to be real. This does not mean that dialogue should not be made both real and believable. However, you do not get believable dialogue merely by recording real talk and putting it into your script.

Listen to people talk. When you consider everything most people say, you will notice how many extra words, phrases, and false starts there are. Consider ways to eliminate extraneous matter and retain the essence of what is said. If you waste words you risk losing the attention of your audience. In the limited frame of a motion picture, it is the synthesis that counts.

Narration

Narration is a voice on the sound track apparently coming from somewhere off screen. It is called *voiceover narration*—and is the familiar voice we hear in educational films, sales films, commercials, and TV documentaries. We have come to accept this disembodied voice as having authority, and in motion pictures it tells us exactly what is right and what is wrong. In the United States almost all of us have been subjected to films from kindergarten through college. In all that time we have been given information and guidance by that familiar disembodied voice. A whole generation has been taught to believe in a voice—the voice of an authoritative being, either a man or a woman—but absolutely right and unanswerable. It has become the voice of God.

It is important to know that audiences tend to believe what a narrator says. When visuals on the screen appear confusing or disjointed, you can feel an audience straining for guidance. Then you can feel the relief when the narrator's voice comes on to straighten things out. What does this mean to the filmmaker? It means you have a ready-made audience that is disposed to believe anything you tell it. Although every preposterous thing you say in a film will not always be believed without question, the narrator is an authority to an audience.

Thought-Voice

Another convention is narration used as a *thought-voice*. That is, a character's thoughts are stated by an off-screen voice to indicate what he is thinking. On screen, he is not speaking through his lips, but the audience hears his voice saying what is going on in his mind. It is the soliloquy of the stage translated into film. This device includes supernatural voices and letter-writers. In the old days of movies, when a character read a letter we were always shown a CLOSEUP of it to read while music filled the time. Today, with fewer people able to read rapidly, and with the poor legibility of writing on the TV screen, an off-screen voice reading the letter is a believable and acceptable convention.

Music

Music accompanying dramatic action in a movie is a convention. Although the action is supposed to be real and every effort has been made to make a scene realistic and believable, audiences not only accept music but take it as intensifying the reality of a scene. How fake can you get? How much farther from reality than to hear a musical score while people are going through tense dramatic situations? It requires a considerable stretch of the imagination to accept such a combination as believable, but we do. In no other art form is music used this way. Since we always think of a motion picture integrally with its score, when you plan a sequence or a film, you immediately begin to imagine the kind of music you want with it. Audiences will accept all kinds of action and dramatic scenes with the appropriate mood-building music along with it. This situation has been parodied many times in comedy routines, where a tender love scene is taking place in a beautiful secluded spot while we hear the sound of a full symphony orchestra playing sweet music off screen. It seems laughable when exaggerated, but this is exactly the way music is used. To be effective, the music must be appropriate; if it is not, the scene is destroyed. When you accept the idea that music contributes in an important way to the effectiveness of your film, the need for intelligent, creative musical choices becomes obvious. Music often works on audiences without their knowledge. Although they may not recall whether the music was good or bad, they remember that they did or did not appreciate its effect.

Sound Effects

Sound effects contribute far more to the realism and believability of a motion picture than most people, including filmmakers, imagine. Sound effects in film are not exactly like real-life sound effects, but we have accepted the convention of movie sound effects. Notice the sound of two men fist-fighting in a film. The hits sound more like two pieces of wood striking together than those in a real fight. In real life, a blow with force enough to sound like a movie blow would undoubtedly kill a man instantly. Frequently the true sounds that real things make do not sound believable on film. Thus real sounds need not be used, since our only concern is making sound effects seem believable to an audience.

Sound effects augment the illusion of reality much more than voice and music. A single step on pavement, the crunch of heavy shoes in gravel, the clink of a coin on a glass counter top, the muffled click of a purse snapping shut, are some of the sounds that create in an audience the feeling that what is seen on the screen is "real" and therefore believable.

Sound effects are not merely those sounds that occur at the time of shooting—they are carefully selected and specially recorded for each particular scene. Although some sound effects that occur during shooting may be usable, they must frequently be created just as the action of a scene itself is created.

CAMERA MOVEMENT

It is a convention that the camera is the human eye, and the screen before us shows what it sees. Learning to use *camera movement* effectively requires learning how you see. People don't go through life with their eyes fixed steadily ahead. There are an infinite number of ways of seeing things, and movement lets audiences see in ways they have never seen before or in unaccustomed ways. Thus the camera moves in closer to a person, we feel we are moving with it. The camera PANS from left to right, and we see the scene as if we were moving our own eyes from left to right. We take this for granted, but people do not naturally accept camera movement in this way. Research has shown that so-called primitive people seeing motion pictures for the first time react quite differently from what might be expected. Some actually believe that the person on the screen is being blown up like a balloon when the camera moves into a CLOSEUP, or that a PAN shot is a long picture being pulled horizontally across a screen-shaped hole in the wall. Audiences understand only what they have learned, and today sophisticated audiences have learned that camera movement represents the audience point of view. Along with the camera, the audience is moved in, out, through, or around the action of a movie. The moviemaker's task is to guide the eyes of the audience into seeing what he wants them to see, from whatever point of view he chooses. When the camera moves, even in the most unlikely way, we feel that our own eyes are moving. Camera movement represents a changing point of view, a flexibility we do not always realize in life. As spectators in real situations we are not able to see the world around us from the changing point of view of a moving camera. Theoretically it is possible for a person to observe life from the end of a moving boom or from the top of a water tower, but it is not usual. Camera movement (like camera placement) gives us a chance to examine the world from points of view that we may never have access to.

We achieve movement during a shot by swiveling the camera on its mount, by moving the camera mount itself, or by changing the optics of the lens. Such moving shots are indicated by the following designations: PAN, TILT, DOLLY, CRANE, ZOOM, FOLLOW.

Pan and Tilt

The PAN is horizontal movement of the camera, left or right, and the TILT is vertical movement up or down—both from a fixed position. PAN and TILT roughly simulate the movement of your head when you move it left and right or up and down, but the effect is not quite the same. Although most people assume that the camera in a PAN or a TILT shot sees things the way a person does when he moves his head, it does not. Amateur movies often consist of a constant panning and tilting of the camera (the garden hose technique) to include every aspect of a scene. On screen this resembles an incoherent waggling of someone's unselective imagination. Promiscuous PANS and TILTS often result in boring films and may even be painful to the eyes, since you cannot look at anything in detail while your eyes are moving. Try panning your head slowly without stopping. You cannot read printing or register visuals, except vaguely, without stopping your eyes. Perhaps they stop only for a fraction of a second, but they must stop to see and to understand. Some people have developed the ability to register details in one quick eye pass, but they still do it in many quick stops. When you look at the outside of a building, you do not study it while your eyes are moving but in static pieces one at a time. First you look at the whole building. Then your eye picks out one small detail after another, dwelling on each as long as its interest holds. Of course, you PAN and TILT your eyes as you go, but this is only a means of getting from one static detail to the next. You don't really absorb what is in between. In translating your visual inspection of the building to the camera, you would make a series of static shots of the details of the building, each shot separated by CUTS. You might PAN or TILT from one detail to another but not necessarily to take in detailed information. If the PAN or TILT is slow enough—and this is where the moving eye and the moving camera differ—a viewer may actually examine details within the slowly moving frame.

PAN or TILT only when you have a reason. This doesn't mean that you must be able to provide a written rationale for your shot, for if you "feel" a situation calls for a PAN there is a good reason. But do not PAN simply because you think it's time to or becaue you think it would make you appear professional. The amateur PANS and TILTS his camera all over Europe because he doesn't want to miss anything. Consequently, he misses everything.

There are several generally accepted conditions under which to PAN or TILT: to follow a moving person or object; to move from detail to detail; and to show a particular point of view. Do not consider these inviolable. If a shot does what you want it to do, feel free to violate every rule in the book.

Following a Moving Person or Object

Not only does following allow you to stay with your subject, it also allows you to change angles, subject, and screen direction. If you PAN and TILT with a character walking toward the camera, he will move from a LONG SHOT into a CLOSEUP as you follow him. Obviously, as an actor walks, you must PAN the camera to keep him in frame. You also may have to TILT simultaneously, since even if the subject stays on one plane, as he gets nearer the camera you must TILT to keep him vertically in frame.

By panning and tilting you can change subject matter and establish relationships at the same time. Refer back to the example discussed earlier in which you looked at the busy café and the studying girl. You framed your shot on the waitress and PANNED with her until she passed the girl at the table. At that point the camera stopped and let the waitress go out of frame, HOLDING on the girl. (See p. 13.)

Moving from One Detail to Another

On the screen, the audience cannot see things overall as is possible in real life. If you want your audience to see several details in a scene, you should show each detail in turn. This ability to move in close to a person (or object) and isolate him from his surroundings is one of the qualities that makes an effective movie. To emphasize a relationship between two things, PAN or TILT from one to the other. For example: we see a CLOSEUP of a MAN's HANDS smoothing the dirt around a plant in what appears to be a garden plot. The CAMERA HOLDS on the hands long enough to establish the situation, then it PANS to a CLOSEUP of a nearby COILED RATTLESNAKE. The impact of this shot introducing the snake is much stronger than that of a MEDIUM SHOT, in which we see both the man and the snake at the same time. Use of the PAN or TILT in this way allows precise control of a scene's dramatic effect. You can make your audience react at exactly the moment you desire. A more complex PAN/TILT reveals several items or conditions one after the other, for example, a slow PAN around a room. Start with a static CLOSEUP of a rumpled jacket thrown over the back of a chair, and PAN and TILT the CAMERA to a pair of scuffed shoes and dirty socks thrown on the floor. As the PAN continues, we see in turn books dumped on the couch, three or four scattered magazines, and an ashtray overflowing with half-smoked cigarettes. Although we have not yet heard or seen anyone, we have been given some idea about the kind of person who lives there. If the PAN/TILT is not too fast, the audience will have time to examine each part of the scene carefully. As your moving shot reveals one thing after another, the audience's imagination begins to work, and you can induce a more intense reaction than when you show everything simultaneously. You are in control of your audience.

Dolly

To DOLLY means moving the camera either toward or away from the subject. It gets its name from the wheeled cart, or dolly on which a camera may be mounted. Dollies range in complexity from a simple flat bed with four wheels to the complex crab dolly with four fully rotatable wheels and a hydraulically operated boom arm. A dolly is an extremely useful camera mount, particularly on floors and flat areas where it allows you to move the camera into any position. The arm lets you move the camera from near the floor up to about seven feet high. (See Camera, Chapter 7.) More important, however, it makes it possible to move the camera during a shot. (For further discussion of the dolly shot, see Script, pp. 106.)

A ZOOM shot, like the DOLLY, is movement toward or away from the subject except that it takes place optically in the lens. The camera itself does not move. (For a further discussion of uses of the ZOOM shot, see Script, p. 106.)

A crane is a wheeled camera mount similar to a dolly but larger. Cranes range in size from oversized dollies to large truck-size vehicles. It has a boom, or crane with the camera mounted on the end of it. You can get very smooth movement on a crane, and you can position the camera as high as forty or fifty feet, or down to ground level. (See Script, pp. 107.)

Follow Shot

In a FOLLOW SHOT, the camera moves along with a moving subject to keep the subject the same relative screen size for the duration of the shot.

Moving Shot Structure

Plan a moving shot to give yourself the greatest flexibility in editing. That is, shoot more than just the segment of action you think you will use. Think of a moving shot as having a three-part structure: (1) a static beginning, (2) a moving middle, and (3) a static ending. Say you want to follow an actor along the street. Start the shot on the street, the actor not yet moving. Then, camera running, have the actor start his move. As he moves, PAN the camera with him keeping him in frame. When you have followed him as far as you want him to go, stop the PAN and *hold,* having him stop his move or go on completely out of frame. Then shut off the camera. This applies to almost every moving shot no matter what the subject—race car, galloping horse, or passing fish. You may not need all the footage, but it may be usable. Do the same on any shot in which the camera moves even though the subject is static: hold on the beginning framing for a longer time than you plan to use, then follow the action to the end framing and hold it also longer than you think you need. What you have then is a shot that meets your basic needs yet gives you two additional shots if you need them. Although every moving shot cannot be made this way, whenever it is possible it works to your advantage.

CREATING NEW CONVENTIONS

In every art form the artist is the first to become bored with old techniques, he tries to express himself in new and different ways. At first exposure, people are usually confused. It takes time for audiences to grasp new forms for communicating ideas. But eventually they do, and another phase of style begins. Consider the different styles in the history of painting. Each had its phase of turmoil and misunderstanding, but audiences always discovered eventually what the artists were trying to say.

If your new ideas are not immediately accepted, don't be discouraged. Although these innovations may be terribly exciting to you, working in the medium, others simply do not yet understand. They will eventually, but you must give them time. For example, a simple technique such as using a CUT instead of a DISSOLVE led many people to the conviction that movies were senseless, disjointed, and self-indulgent. When true, this charge is not because a CUT is used in place of a DISSOLVE. The audience always lags behind the artist in proceeding from ignorance to sophistication. If you wait for them to catch up, you let them dictate your rate of growth. Thus in the end your audience will pass you by. Always try to push the limits of their understanding a little.

Only a few of the most fundamental conventions have been discussed here. There are many more, for everything in a movie that makes sense to an audience is the result of some kind of basic agreement about meaning. Try to understand all the conventions and use them freely to achieve the result you want. Be open: don't use or reject a convention merely because it is or is not fashionable. Use or devise anything and everything to suit your purpose. Create your own conventions.

THREE

The Production Unit

The production unit is the technical group responsible for converting a script into a length of uncut film. There is no such thing as the ideal unit. In the past, when movies were made only by big studios, it was possible to list the members of a typical crew and assign to each a clearly specified task recognized as the domain of a particular job specialty. But today film production is no longer the exclusive domain of a few major studios. Equipment is available to all. Laboratories, sound studios, and optical houses are open to the independent producer at the same price as for the major company. Thus anyone with an idea and money can produce a film. Only in certain craft guild productions—as in most feature films, the surviving studios, and television—is the strict occupationally specialized hierarchy adhered to.

Films are produced by the most diverse companies imaginable. At one end is studio feature production with its unions, sound stages, and big budgets; at the other is the lone filmmaker doing his own camera work, recording his own sound, editing his own film, and even selling his own completed prints. In between are the thousands of small, medium, and large groups turning out every kind of film from pornography to industrial sales. Thus to say that a motion picture production unit is made up of just so many people doing just so many jobs would be academic and completely misleading.

Today descriptions of the people who work on films are still limited mainly to the feature film. For the most part encyclopedias describe film production as it was conducted in the 1940s. Some of it is still done that way because there are still studio-type productions. Yet there are many ways of making a picture. Making a film is the process of completing a certain number of tasks. How these tasks get done and how many people are used depends on the kind of picture being made and the conditions—financial, physical, and aesthetic—involved in making it. In filming production under union limitations, every task involved in filmmaking has been minutely delimited and placed in a category. Only certain designated people may perform each task. For example: an assistant director may not move a lamp; a grip may not move a potted plant; the script girl may not press the camera switch.

In nonunion filmmaking the various tasks are also carried out by specialists, but there is a flexibility in job categories that makes it possible to work with smaller, more versatile crews. Job categories represent work to be done, and who does the work is important only in relation to the type of production being made. Thus any job may be done by anyone capable of doing it—the editor might be the sound man during shooting; the entire crew might load and unload the equipment. A crew of four or five indiscriminately might do anything and everything to shoot the picture regardless of classification.

The following list contains those jobs roughly representative of the crew required for a film made under union conditions. A feature made in a large studio, involves hiring and directing the crew described here. For our purposes, these job classifications provide a good breakdown of the kinds and extent of jobs to be done in making a film. In any film *someone* must do the work implicit in these classifications. The assistant director may be the "chief honcho," the prop man may be "the one who gets all the things we need on the set." Terminology is not binding, but it is convenient. Consider this list as a working detail of the tasks required to make your film. Rather than structuring your production unit to fit the list, reconstruct the list to fit your production.

FILM CREW

A PRODUCING CREW

- Producer
- Production Manager
- Director
- Assistant Director
- Script Supervisor

B CAMERA CREW

- Director of Photography
- Camera Operator
- Camera Assistant

C SOUND CREW

- Mixer
- Boom Operator
- Sound Assistant

D GRIP CREW

E ELECTRICAL CREW

F SUPPORT CREWS

- Set construction
- Properties
- Set decoration
- Makeup
- Hairstyling
- Wardrobe
- Special effects
- Scenic artists
- Drivers
- First aid
- Painters
- Carpenters
- Laborers
- Greensmen
- Projection
- Animal handlers
- Accounting
- Secretarial
- Legal

PRODUCING CREW

Producer

The word "producer" has long been the subject of many jokes, and the job has been looked on as a nebulous sort of thing, something other than a serious position. Actually, the producer is the boss. He is the one who usually controls the money, buys the story, hires the writer and director, makes the big decisions, and worries about what is going to happen. A producer's primary aim is making money, and this comes ahead of making what he thinks will be a good picture. He needs a peculiar combination of business sense and aesthetic discrimination. The producer's job starts with finding a script, which is followed by getting the money and making the picture. Essentially, his specific responsibilities are detailed in Chapter 4, "Production Management." Unless on a very small budget, he hires production specialists to do the actual paperwork and figuring, but remains close to the work at every minute. In a small-budget picture, the producer may do all the breakdown and planning himself.

There are all types of producers with various kinds and levels of responsibility. Major film companies, for example, sometimes assign a producer to a picture to represent the company and oversee the production according to company policy. In this case the producer is the boss, who is representing a bigger boss. Independent producers, who raise money wherever and whenever it can be found, are the absolute bosses over their productions. Although some producers even use their own money to make pictures, this is rare; for an old maxim of the film business warns, "Never make a film with your own money."

A gathering of all the successful producers of films, would undoubtedly yield as diverse a bunch of varmints as could be imagined. Despite external impressions, however, many characteristics are common to all. The desire to succeed prevails. This ensures a constant, unrelenting drive toward the final goal, the completed film. It involves doggedly attending to details, checking on other people seeing to details, anticipating major problems before they occur, refusing to accept defeat, and keeping track of everything every step of the way. Thus the successful producer is a positive person who is capable of making decisions. Although no one can make the right decision every time, an executive must make more right decisions than wrong ones. Decisions must be made clearly and rapidly, without falling into the trap of seeking constant counsel and delaying until the time for suitable action is past.

The next most prevalent producer quality is the ability to pick the right person for the right job, which also entails willingness to go along with the one chosen even though he or she may do some strange things. A director chosen by a corporate personnel officer under normal business hiring standards might undoubtedly look the part, but he would not be a director. People—artists, technicians, professionals—and their talents determine the quality of the finished film. The successful producer is one who finds and hires the right people and then gets them to do their best work. Summing up, then, the producer is the person who decides to make a picture, finds or puts up the money, chooses a story or script, hires all the people involved, worries through every phase of production and if all goes well, gains awards, fame, status, satisfaction, and profit.

Production Manager

The production manager carries out the detailed tasks of the producer; in small productions he may actually be the producer. The job is to see that all production planning (as detailed in Chapter 4) is carried out.

Director

The director is the person solely responsible for converting the script into a film. No matter how brilliantly the writer has visualized his ideas, most of them cannot be expressed as the script prescribes and must therefore be presented in some other way. Also, the physical materials—sets, locations, actors—will often suggest various modifications to the script. A skillful director takes advantage of these opportunities yet never loses sight of the overall line of the script. The final responsibility for each setting, for the pace and action of the scene that takes place in it, and for dovetailing each scene into those that precede and follow it are the director's domain. In consultation with the cinematographer, he must decide on each camera position and must rehearse the action until it is perfect. He must have enough overall grasp of detail to fasten onto the smallest piece of action in front of the camera and make something significant of it. The art of direction cannot be taught, though a few rules of thumb may be set down. The best way to learn direction is to observe people and life diligently and to direct and edit films.

Those who attempt to delineate the director's tasks, usually specify the conventions and mechanical means for achieving these tasks. They say that to be a director you must learn about screen direction, matching action, framing, composition, and so on. Although such things are certainly part of the director's bag, direction involves much more. Directing entails putting ideas and visuals together in a way that makes aesthetic sense. Thus a director should be sensitive to people and to life; he must be able to visualize; he must have skill in dealing with people; and he should be a first-rate communicator.

Matching action, continuity, dynamic cutting, and so on are the concern of everyone, involved in filmmaking. Writer, editor, production manager, cinematographer, and grip should all understand the basic conventions, which will be discussed in a separate chapter. Here, it will suffice to indicate some of the ways a director may proceed in making his film.

There are as many kinds of directors as there are pictures. Directing a feature dramatic film is not exactly like directing a documentary. The director's job differs depending on whether his money or someone else's is at stake. In a theatrical feature the director will have a entire crew of technicians and production specialists. In a smaller production he may be the cameraman, the writer, and the editor combined. Between shots he may be required to help build the sets and carry equipment. Thus the duties of a director cover a wide range from opulent overseer to hardworking laborer.

The first requirement for a director is the ability to see. As he looks at anything—a street scene, a group of people at a table, a car backing out of a garage—his curiosity and perception should cause him to reconstruct each scene in many different visual ways. There are an infinite number of ways to look at something, and what makes a film interesting is the way its director chooses to see the things that are in it. Since there are no new subjects in this world or this life, it is only the particular way an artist sees a thing that makes it interesting or significant.

Directing is creating the raw material that will be edited into a film, the raw material being the mass of shots exposed on film. The director must understand that all this raw material has to be combined in a compatible way. Therefore, the way materials are conceived and shot directly affects their combination and cohesiveness. Many an editor has cursed the director for shooting scenes and shots that would not go together. A competent director will edit the film in his head before shooting and as the shooting progresses.

As was mentioned earlier, the conditions under which a director works will vary widely. He may be working with a full crew composed of specialists in many fields, or he may be working with only a cinematographer and a sound mixer with each of them performing the necessary labor to get the picture shot. Whether he is involved in a collossal production or a one-person show—the director's tasks generally fall into three categories as follows:

1. Major responsibilities
2. Procedure during shooting
3. Contribution to editing.

Director's Major Responsibilities

INTERPRETING THE SCRIPT

What makes a director individual is the way he interprets the script. That is, how does he visualize the finished production from reading the script? There are "directors" who actually have no point of view regarding what they do. Such directors add nothing of themselves to the film, but are merely high-paid starters who shout "action" and "cut" at appropriate times. Every script needs interpretation, yet there is more than one interpretation for any given script. You may see a particular script as a serious statement with humorous overtones. Another director may see the same script as a comedy with serious implications. Still another may consider it vacuous slapstick.

Interpretation refers to the individual way a director sees and understands the story or subject he is going to put on film. If it is a documentary on air pollution in the cities, who does he consider to be the villain—voracious industry or the apathetic public? In a film facts never speak for themselves; they are only instruments to be used to reveal the point to be made according to the way the director presents them. Thus to make a good film, the director must have a point of view. He must know his characters inside and out and know why they act as they do. If the director cannot answer all the questions the script poses, such indecision or ignorance will be evident in the finished film.

A script must be read and reread to determine its content and to visualize how it will look inside the frame. The director may find that certain ideas or visuals do not work for him, in which case he may have to rewrite certain parts of the script. If he is also the producer or the writer, this may be a simple matter. But if someone else's approval is necessary, he may require long discussions to convince the writer, producer, or sponsor that rewriting will improve the picture. Such discussions, even when they prove futile, are often beneficial since they may result in greater insight about the intention of the script.

At this stage the director should read the script over several times until he understands it thoroughly. He should visualize every shot and direct the picture in his mind until it becomes as vivid to him as if it were on the screen. Thus when he proceeds with the actual direction, he is prepared to change everything. Preplanning the film is necessary and valuable, but if the director remains inflexible and sticks slavishly to his original plan just because it is the plan, his film will probably be stiff and boring.

DESIGN THE PRODUCTION

The design of a film does not necessarily coincide with an artist's conception of it. Design refers to the tone or quality of its presentation—its inherent character. We can say that a film has a personality or character, and the appearance of its sets, costumes, lighting, dress, types of buildings, as well as its pace, all form part of what we call design. On the obvious level are certain stereotype designs. A musical comedy is usually done in high-key lighting with lots of color in the costumes and the sets. Mysteries are somber and low-key. But there is more to design than merely reinforcing the stereotype.

If you were to direct a feature film on a large budget, you could undoubtedly have a number of sets built just for the film. You would work with a production designer who would design the sets, specifying in detail exactly what they should be right down to the type of curtains, furniture, style of architecture, wallpaper, and outside coloring and landscaping. The director would try to use only those sets consistent with the mood, story, and pace of the film. To make a smaller picture on a lesser budget, he would still design the production by determining the kinds of locations and sets, the clothes the actors will wear, the kind of lighting necessary, and so on. Design is a misleading word because it has the overtones of "art." Yet whenever the director determines what the actors, sets, and locations are going to look like, he is designing the film. It is possible to hire a production designer to plan the entire production, accompanied by sketches, detailed renderings of sets, costumes, furniture, and blueprints. This work must be done to some degree on any film. If you build a set, you have to decide how it is to be built, what style, what kind of wallpaper, what kind of windows, how big, what shape, how furnished, how new, how old. Taken together, these considerations constitute design. If actual homes and buildings are used, the process will still involve selecting the proper places based on the director's specifications. This too is design.

CHOOSING LOCATIONS AND SETS

Looking for and choosing locations and sets to shoot in is really an extension of design because these places are selected on the basis of how well they will fit into the director's concept of the film's mood or decor. But scouting locations is not normally referred to as designing. Part of the director's job is to go out and find the locations and existing sets he wants. Large film companies have special people whose only task is to scout locations and keep a list of those found suitable. Although he may hire someone to do the initial scouting to find a number of places that fit into what he wants, the director must approve and decide on the final choice.

When the director first decides to make a film, he undoubtedly has a mental picture of the milieu in which the action will occur. Frequently he cannot make a firm shooting plan until he has selected the right locations. Perhaps the action takes place in an alley. He may have to spend days or even weeks prowling about cities to find the right spot. He may find an alley that is better, or maybe he doesn't really know what the alley should look like, but will keep looking until he finds the one that works. He might even end up building an alley.

If the director plans to make more than one film, it may be helpful to keep a morgue file of good locations. Every filmmaker has a mass of future films in his head, each one usually involving some sort of interesting or suitable location. He should take still photos of possible places to put in a film someday and keep a record of where they are.

After a location or set has been chosen, the director should explore any obstacles that might make it difficult or impossible to shoot what he wants. Suppose he finds exactly the right room in a house. It may look like what he wants, but perhaps he is planning on a certain lighting setup and the ceiling is too low for the lights to fit. Maybe the sun will have changed its position by the time he shoots, making that perfect window backlight impossible. The cinematographer and production manager should be included when locations are selected. It is futile to find the perfect set and not be able to use it.

CASTING

Casting is far more important to the success of a film than most people, including some directors, suspect. An actor, meaning anyone in a film whether professional or not, is the focal point of the audience's attention. People are fascinated by people, and it is the human aspect that makes anything succeed or fail. In a sense, casting is a part of film design. A person who is not right for the film is not right even though he may be the greatest actor in the world. Miscasting causes more failures than almost any other element in filmmaking, so do not cast lightly or hastily. Do everything you can to find the right actors, who may not necessarily be professional actors. You may be doing a documentary, a technical film, or an art film in which you do not want to use professionals. Still, you must choose who will be in the film, and you should choose even more carefully. A miscast professional actor can sometimes carry a film pretty well because of sheer virtuosity, but it is never just right. A miscast nonprofessional may lead to disaster.

To a certain extent, every character in a film is a stereotype. Perhaps not the obvious, melodramatic stereotype typified by the sleepy Mexican, the villainous Italian, and the ugly American, but one with enough visual qualities to identify him with the type of part he is playing. Think of all the great performances you have seen and try to recall one in which the actor did not look the part he was playing. One Hamlet does not resemble another, yet each one looks like the Hamlet he is portraying. You may reason that people in real life do not always look their parts, but they do. Incongruous as a fat lifeguard or a skinny Sumo wrestler may seem, when they do exist in real life they are believable. Yet reality is not always achieved by casting a skinny Sumo wrestler to play the part of a skinny Sumo wrestler. When he has to play himself, he becomes an actor. And he no more knows how to act himself than he knows how to do any other professional task with which he is unfamiliar. Thus he is an expert in being himself, not in acting himself. This does not mean that nonactors should not be cast in documentaries and nontheatrical films. Putting professional actors in such films often adds a false quality that is quite obtrusive. A nonactor can give an impressive performance doing what he customarily does. A skinny Sumo wrestler acting out what he does normally is much different from the same wrestler playing the part of some other Sumo wrestler acting out fictitious events. Therefore when using nonactors, have them perform actions that they do routinely as a part of their jobs or avocations.

How do you find actors? They are everywhere. Some sources include the following:

1. Casting companies
2. Daily contacts
3. Little theaters and community theaters
4. Films and television
5. Open casting

Casting Companies. Every city with theater and film production, has independent casting agents who may be easily located through the telephone directory or by inquiries. They keep lists and photographs of all professionals indicating their types, age, specialties. For a fee, they will help find actors, set up auditions, and generally do what needs to be done to cast a film.

Daily Contacts. Be constantly on the lookout for possible actors. Everywhere you go, watch people and make notes about types, characteristics, and possibilities.

Little Theaters and Community Theaters. There are over 15,000 amateur and professional theater groups in the United States today, and each one has some fine actors. Many of these theaters are thoroughly professional and provide good training for both young and old actors. Go to plays put on by these groups and look for actors for your film.

Films and Television. Notice all the actors in the films you see. The size of the part is not necessarily an indication of the quality of the actor. Some of the finest actors play only bits. Remember names; agents and casting agencies can locate whomever you want. Television is a good source because so many young actors are hired to play bit parts on series programs and then are rarely or never used again. Some of these people are excellent.

Open Casting. To conduct open casting, make a public announcement that you are available to all comers for auditions. This will result in many aspirants and may turn up some surprisingly good people. Often, however, the sheer volume of people who show up makes this method extremely time consuming and exhausting. In cities where there is a lot of film and theater activity, open casting can result in so many applicants that it is literally impossible to interview everyone without some kind of preselection. Of course, when you apply preselection to casting, it is by definition no longer open.

When casting, give each applicant ample opportunity to show what he can do. A good actor grows in a part as he understands it more and feels it, and you may easily miss the one who is just right for your film by dismissing him too quickly. Some truly great actors have been unable to appear even adequate on a first reading. It is up to the director to be able to recognize something inside a person that will come out as a fine performance. Do not confuse slickness with good acting. As pointed out in Chapter 6 on Narration, a radio announcer is trained to deliver a slick, smooth performance on unfamiliar copy. Although when compared to an actor on a first reading the announcer may sometimes sound excellent, as the part develops and the show proceeds the announcer type rarely changes, while the actor grows in the part and enhances it.

In casting the aim is to find the actor who can best give the desired performance. Such an actor can rarely be found through superficial questioning. Although you will in time develop individual techniques and procedures for selecting actors, proceeding from an initial interview through a reading and a screen test is a workable method.

Interviews. An interview will tell the director whether the prospective actor is the physical type he needs. An initial judgment can be made on the basis of voice, mannerisms, and general appearance. Do not dismiss an actor too quickly. Get him to relax, and ask him questions that will encourage him to talk unselfconsciously. Since jobs are important to actors, they are often understandably tense on interviews. An attempt to impress sometimes results in affected speech and manners. Underneath the affectation, however, may be the actor you require, and it will pay you, sometimes handsomely, to get to the real person. Casting on the basis of superficial appearance alone is done by bad directors and advertising agencies.

Readings. If the applicant passes the interview, try him out in a reading. Have him read a scene from your film or from some play or screenplay of enough substance to give him a chance to show his talent. If you have him read dialogue, get competent actors to read the other parts. If you have already cast some of the parts, have these actors read with him. Again, make the actor feel relaxed so that he shows you what he can really do. Also use other materials for reading—narration, poetry, newspaper clippings—anything that may provide insight into the actor's range and capability.

Screen Test. One of the characteristics of film is that people usually do not look the same on the screen as they do in real life. Depending on the standards you apply, some people look worse, some look better, and very few look the same. In the film industry the term "photogenic" has been used to refer to those people who "look good" on film. In the past a person whose photograph looked like the romanticized version of the ideal hero or heroine was considered to be photogenic. Happily, this approach is becoming outmoded, but you cannot really tell what your actor is going to look like on film until you take pictures of him. This is the purpose of a screen test, and is extremely valuable.

For the screen test choose a scene that you think will show you what the actor can do. Treat it as if it were a real scene being shot for your film. Rehearse and direct the actor and do everything you would normally do to make the scene a success. Get good actors to play any other parts in the scene since they bring out the best in others. Mediocre actors hurt the performance of every other actor in the scene and thus say little about the ability of the person playing opposite them.

After the screen test has been shot, edit it with all the care you would give to a production scene. Try to make the scene work, then view it. It is valid only if you have given your actor all the direction and help you can. If you have set up the screen test as a sort of obstacle course for the actor to "pass," it will tell you nothing. Do not assume that if an actor does well in a bad situation, he will do better in a good one.

LAYING OUT THE SHOOTING PLAN

We constantly hear of directors who never work from a script, creating freely and easily as they go along. Regardless of the mythology surrounding any director, however, there is no such thing as a film made without a script. A script always exists—even if only in the directors's head—at some point in the production. It is said that Godard made *Weekend* without a script. Perhaps he did not carry along a written stack of papers labeled "script," but he had decided at some point what he was going to do and he communicated this to others. In *Weekend* there is a sequence in which hundreds of automobiles are stalled in earth's ultimate traffic jam and hundreds of others lie wrecked and burning along the sides of the road. Assume that he created this scene without a script, that he walked out to a random location with his crew, stood for some time looking keenly and speculatively about him and then called for automobiles, actors, props, burning cars, and special effects. The reaction? The production manager would respectfully point out to the director that it would take him a little while to round up the extras for the scene; the prop man would respectfully point out that it would take a little time to round up the automobiles needed in the traffic jam; the special effects man would respectfully point out to the director that it would take him a little while to rig the crashed and burning automobiles. Then the director and his staff would return to the hotel and wait for the scene to be rigged and deployed. It is ridiculous to assume that Godard would proceed in this manner. At some time previous to the shooting he obviously formulated the scene—at least in his mind—sufficiently to request ahead of time the necessary cast, extras, props, special effects, and scene deployment. This constitutes a script, untyped perhaps, but nevertheless a script.

It is possible and often desirable to direct scenes without slavishly following a detailed script. You may gather the actors and develop a scene as it goes along, but you must have a clear idea of what you as the director want to achieve. To wander into the world without a plan, followed by a caravan of crews, cast, extras, technicians, props, costumes, and equipment just in case they are needed is clearly unworkable.

You will probably find it feasible to start with a detailed plan derived from the script. The worst directors follow the plan and the script to the letter. The best directors follow the plan and the script but change and modify as the situation develops. A scene rarely if ever is produced exactly as it is written (see Figs. 5.7 and 5.8), and the director must be sufficiently perceptive and willing to take advantage of on-the-set influences and happy "accidents." After planning a scene carefully, you may find that when the actors are assembled on the set a whole new way of doing the scene presents itself. This means working out the scene as it goes along, formulating new movements, reediting the scene in your head, even rewriting the dialogue as you go along. Although this method is often referred to as "shooting without a script," it is completely different from walking out into the world equipped only with a crew and bubbling genius.

To make your directing plan, you should already be thoroughly famililar with the script and have arrived at your interpretation of it. Also, you should have cast and directed each scene in the script in your mind. The next step is to set all this down on paper so that you will have a guide, and the people concerned will have something to go by in setting up and supplying the items you want.

1. Make plan sketches of all sets and locations. These may either be elaborate and to scale or they can be rough, depending on the director's personality. On each one indicate the course of the action; for example, *A* enters here, crosses to here, encounters *B* at this point, and so on. Indicate desired camera positions. You may wish to plan with a viewfinder on a scale model of the set. If you intend to shoot in actual locations, go to them and plan and walk through the action with a viewfinder.
2. List scenes, closeups, and reaction shots in the order you intend to shoot them with a brief identifying description of each. This list serves as your working shooting guide and as a quick reference to your progress.
3. Make a storyboard consisting of a sketch of

each shot or camera angle. You may or may not find this useful. One famous director, who made many successful but dull films, is said to have directed his films by faithfully following the storyboard made by his sketch artist down to the exact number of people shown in each sketch, mob scenes included. Actually the real director of this man's films was his storyboard artist. You may want to go this far in setting up your film, but there is a real danger inherent in relying too much on a storyboard. Since it consists of static pictures, a storyboard can depict only one instant of any action. But a motion picture is not a record of single instants; it is a record of motion, both visual and psychological, that cannot be frozen and still remain the same medium. The essence of film is its progress from one point to another—how do you get from one storyboard picture to the next? This *how* is the art of the director. Anyone can set up a well-framed, beautifully composed scene. But where the scene goes from there and how it relates to all the scenes that precede and follow it depends on the director, who must be able to understand and visualize motion. The hazard of following a storyboard is that the film may turn out to be a series of still tableaux accompanied by words or other kinds of sounds. A storyboard is not a motion picture and cannot be made into one because the essence of film occurs between frozen moments.

4. Edit each scene in your mind. Visualize the completed scene and determine how many shots and angles you will need to get the desired result. Remember that a scene rarely turns out exactly the way you visualize it, and allow yourself creative leeway by shooting it so that it may be edited in several different ways. Assume, for example, that you are going to direct the short scene from *The Graduate* shown in Fig. 3.1. The director made this scene in five shots. He knew how he wanted the scene to play on the screen, but shot it with such flexibility that it could be assembled in the editing room in many different ways. The following are the shots he made:

Sc. 229. LONG SHOT. Master shot framed on the row of men at the sinks. The entire scene is played from this angle with BEN'S VOICE calling in from OFF SCREEN.

Sc. 229A. CLOSEUP MAN #2 at sink. The last half of the scene is played from this angle with CARTER'S VOICE and BEN'S VOICE calling in from OFF SCREEN.

Sc. 229B. BEN as seen over the shoulder of the man in the shower. BEN enters the door and the whole scene is played from this angle with all the other VOICES calling in from OFF SCREEN.

Sc. 229C. MEDIUM SHOT of BEN seen over MAN #1 at the washroom sink. Beginning with MAN #1's line, the rest of the scene is played from this angle with the other VOICES calling in from OFF SCREEN.

Sc. 229D. BIG CLOSEUP OF BEN. Beginning with the voice of MAN #1, the rest of the scene is played from this angle with the other VOICES calling in from OFF SCREEN.

As you can see, the director staged and shot the scene twice in its entirety and three times partially. Each shot overlaps and repeats the action of the others, making it possible to edit the final version several ways. Also, while he was set up with all the actors, and showers, and running water, the director called for the recording of *wild sound,* or nonsynchronous sounds of running water, singing, and the like. These wild tracks are indicated on the script supervisor's script as slate numbers *WT229* and *WT229B*. Figure 3.2 shows the script version of the scene, as marked by the script supervisor, to indicate how much each shot covered. Note that new lines of dialogue added at the time of shooting have been written in. There are now several options for cutting this scene. You could establish the setup with Sc. 229 (see Figure 3.3). LONG SHOT MEN IN WASHROOM, and then cut to Sc. 229D CLOSEUP BEN for the remainder of the scene. Or you could cut in and out of any of the scenes at almost any spot you feel is best. This approach of covering a scene from several angles and overlapping the action is the fundamental part of directing that allows the director great creative flexibility. After shooting there are so many influences affecting the end result—pacing, sound effects, interpretation, rearrangement, special effects—that to tie down the final version in the shooting is to lose part of the capability of

```
229.      INT  FRATERNITY WASHROOM - DAY

          A large steam-filled room with a row of FRATERNITY
          BROTHERS in front of a row of sinks, brushing,
          combing, shaving, etc.  Ben is standing at the
          door.

                         MAN AT SINK NO. 1.
                    Hey, Carter - where's the Make
                    Out King getting married?

                         CARTER'S VOICE
                      (echo sound)
                    Santa Barbara.

                         BEN
                      (calling in the direc-
                       tion of Carter's voice)
                    You don't happen to know ex-
                    actly where the Make Out King
                    is getting married, do you?
                    I'm supposed to be there.

                         CARTER'S VOICE
                    I don't know.  Maybe at his
                    old man's house.  Or the
                    maternity ward.

                         MAN AT SINK #2.
                    Carter!
                    You going to the wedding?

                         BEN
                    Yes.

                         MAN AT SINK #2.
                    Give the bride a message
                    for me.  Tell her to act
                    surprised.

          A great deal of laughter follows this gem.

                                                  CUT TO:
```

Fig. 3.1. Excerpt of script page from *The Graduate* before shooting.

film. And this approach applies equally to documentary and other kinds of film. Pare Lorentz, in laying out his plan for shooting the logging sequence for *The River* (Script, p. 93) did not merely make the shots we see in the script. He shot many different kinds of logging and timber scenes that were never included in the finished picture. Although he had decided ahead of time on a way he though the sequence should be assembled, he shot it in a similar way to that of the director of *The Graduate*—with enough overlapping and matching coverage to allow him the option of editing the scene several different ways.

5. Rehearse the actors. Because of the nature of motion picture production, rehearsals are not usually as lengthy or as concentrated as those for the legitimate stage. In the theater it is assumed that several weeks of rehearsal are a part of the actor's commitment to the show; and each actor, no matter how small his part, must be present at every rehearsal and every performance. In films, however, there are rarely long, sustained scenes. Actors in small parts do their bits and are gone.

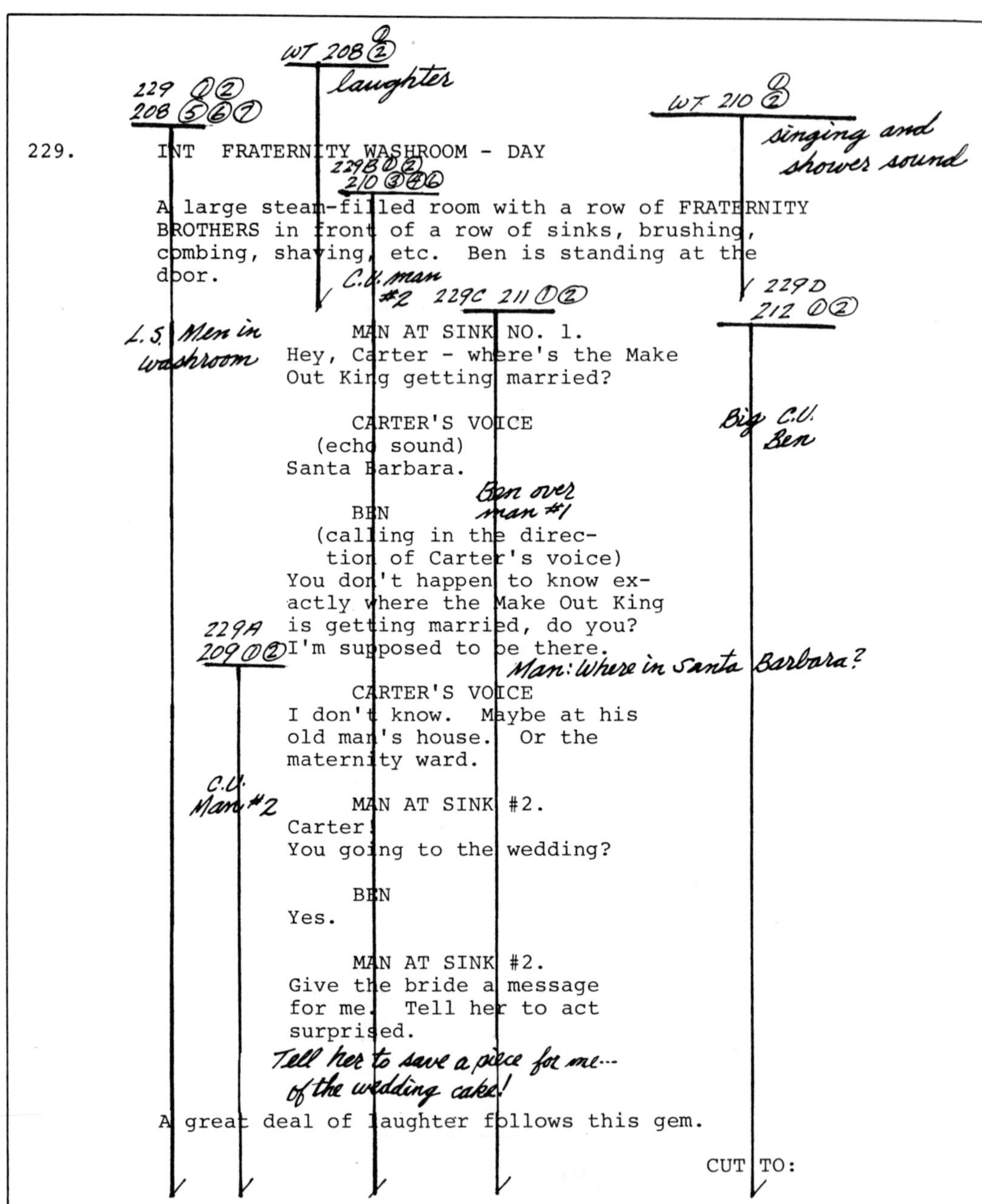

229. INT FRATERNITY WASHROOM - DAY

A large steam-filled room with a row of FRATERNITY BROTHERS in front of a row of sinks, brushing, combing, shaving, etc. Ben is standing at the door.

MAN AT SINK NO. 1.
Hey, Carter - where's the Make Out King getting married?

CARTER'S VOICE
(echo sound)
Santa Barbara.

BEN
(calling in the direction of Carter's voice)
You don't happen to know exactly where the Make Out King is getting married, do you? I'm supposed to be there.

CARTER'S VOICE
I don't know. Maybe at his old man's house. Or the maternity ward.

MAN AT SINK #2.
Carter!
You going to the wedding?

BEN
Yes.

MAN AT SINK #2.
Give the bride a message for me. Tell her to act surprised.

A great deal of laughter follows this gem.

CUT TO:

Fig. 3.2. Excerpt of script page from *The Graduate*, as marked by the script supervisor at the time of shooting.

The press of getting the production under way is such that there is usually not much rehearsal time. Also, it is physically difficult to arrange rehearsals for a film. The best rehearsals are done on the actual sets and locations, but since these are often widely separated, it can prove difficult to transport the actors.

Motion Picture Situations

Unlike the legitimate stage, motion pictures deal with situations ranging from carefully scripted dramatic action to unplanned one-time live events. Rehearsal means something different for each kind of production. In some cases it in-

SCRIPT SUPERVISOR'S NOTES

6-2
SCRIPT SCENE 229
SLATE 208

Take				Notes
1	Com	Print	38	35mm Long shot Master to row of men at sinks. Ben O.S. calls in to group and they answer him.
2	Com	Print	34	
3	Inc	Nga	04	
4	Inc	Ngd	25	
5	Com	Print	42	
6	Com	Print	39	
7	Com	Print	40	

6-2
SCRIPT SCENE 229
SLATE WT 208

Take				Notes
1	Com	Print	10 (laugh)	WILD TRACK OF LAUGHTER AND OF TOWEL SNAPPING
2	Com	Print	12 (towel snap)	

6-2
SCRIPT SCENE 229A
SLATE 209

Take				Notes
1	Com	Print	15	4" CLOSE TO #2 Man at Sink.
2	Com	Print	14	
3	Inc	Ngd	10	
4	Com	Print	15	
5	Com	Print	15	
6	Com	Print	15	

6-2
SCRIPT SCENE 229B
SLATE 210

Take				Notes
1	Com	Print	37	35mm Reverse over man in shower to see Ben enter, speak to men.
2	Com	Print	40	
3	Com	Print	38	
4	Com	Print	36	
5	Inc	Nga	32	
6	Com	Print	39	

6-2
SCRIPT SCENE 229B
SLATE WT 210

Take				Notes
1	Com	Print	12 (singing)	WILD TRACK SINGING AND SOUND OF SHOWER RUNNING
2	Com	Print	16 (shower)	

6-2
SCRIPT SCENE 229C
SLATE 211

Take				Notes
1	Com	Print	30	4" Med to Ben over #1 Man in wash room.
2	Com	Print	35	

6-2
SCRIPT SCENE 229D
SLATE 212

Take				Notes
1	Com	Print	28	4" Big Close to Ben
2	Com	Print	28	

Fig. 3.3. Script supervisor's notes for the scene in Fig. 3.2, as typed at the end of the day's shooting.

volves only the camera, in others only the actors, in still others, both. There are five basic situations:

1. Dramatic continuity
2. Staged documentary
3. Documentary
4. Live interview
5. Extempore
6. Accidental

DRAMATIC CONTINUITY

This is the scene containing written dialogue memorized by actors, in which action is carefully rehearsed and blocked out. The written and rehearsed scene has been the staple of the entertainment film for many years. It is designing the action to fit the camera with the aim of making the scene appear as if it were happening in real life. Even though the script supervisor keeps track of matching and continuity, the director must be alert to matching and should constantly plan ahead for what has been shot and what he plans to shoot. Do not underestimate the mental concentration necessary to direct continuity scenes so that they appear believable.

Another problem in directing dramatic continuity involves the skill of good actors and the ineptness of poor ones. Trained actors read dialogue with a smoothness that passes for real talk, but which is not real. Pay close attention to how things are said in dramatic films and you will find that the characters are speaking with sophistication but with little reality. Although people in real life do not talk the way people in movies do, it is desirable in this kind of scene to create the illusion of reality. Most dramatic continuity scenes are artificial and stylized, but audiences have accepted this convention so completely that they rarely notice its lack of reality. Sometimes dedicated directors and actors strive to go beyond the superficial slickness of the written scene, and occasionally one of them succeeds. This dissatisfaction with "Hollywood" quality led to the precursors of the modern film such as *cinema verite* and the underground film of the 1960s.

STAGED DOCUMENTARY

This is the shooting of real people—not actors—in actual events over which the director had control. Often it is the reenactment of a real situation using as actors the people who actually do the work. The staged documentary includes such films as Flaherty's *Nanook of the North,* Wright's *Song of Ceylon,* and most industrial, technical, and sales films. The central elements in this type of documentary are first a process or sequence of operations, and second, the people who customarily carry out the operations in real life. This means that the director must first understand thoroughly what is happening and how to work with nonactors. In preparation for shooting the igloo-building sequence, Flaherty first had to understand the process of igloo building. Then he had to get Nanook to act—to do what he normally would as he built an igloo. And this is essentially the problem in every staged documentary: learn the process, then get the actual people to perform their jobs realistically.

Working with nonactors is not difficult if you do not try to make them do things they cannot, such as act. When told to do something that he does not normally do, the untrained actor invariably becomes stiff and awkward. He is self-conscious and does not really understand the reasons or need for doing what has been asked of him. The result is always disastrous. The director can, however, get excellent performances from nonactors by making them feel at ease and asking them to do only what they normally would. A milling machine operator doing his job before the camera is usually far more realistic than an actor playing the part of a milling machine operator. Start by asking the nonactor to show you exactly what steps he goes through as he does his job. As he explains and shows you, begin to arrange shots and edit in your mind. Let him know what you are doing, why you shoot closeups and repeat action from different angles. You may be surprised at how quickly nonactors understand what is required of them for the camera.

A nonactor is believable when he is at ease. The director can help him to relax only if he is able to relate to people as human beings. Flaherty was successful with Eskimos because he liked and understood them. Consequently they responded to him with warmth and believability. Arrogance, conceit, arbitrariness, or curtness of manner will instantly alienate the nonactor and cause him to appear awkward. Perhaps he will go through the motions because he has been hired or because his employer insists, but his spontaneity, and therefore his believability, will be effectively suppressed. Remember that each person is an expert in his own job and deserves respect for it.

DOCUMENTARY

This refers to shooting one-time events that were not set up merely to be photographed. In contrast to continuity directing, which involves planning the action to suit the camera, the shooting of nonrecurring events can be said to require planning the camera to fit the action. In this case the camera is allowed to watch and to record on film whatever it can in the best way it can. For example, the subjects in a street scene or a carnival may not be aware of the camera. Or they may be aware but indifferent, as in nonrecurring events such as meetings, political campaigns, boat or rocket launchings, athletic events, and so on. The problem for the director here is to anticipate everything. Preplanning is the key to success in this type of shooting. Construct the entire and exact course of events in advance. Plan camera and microphone locations, movements, and changes in plans. Give explicit written instructions to each camera operator, sound director, technician, and helper. Actual events wait for neither man nor camera, so be ready ahead of time with prepared plan and equipment in order and keep ahead of what is happening. Obviously you cannot do retakes on actual nonrecurring events, but you can plan your shooting so that the film covers the action from more than one point of view. One way to achieve this is to use multiple cameras. Assign a cameraman to get long shots and establishing shots. Assign another to get CUs, medium shots, reaction shots, and other pertinent shots that may be used in editing the final film. Since events such as the Olympic Games and rocket launches, for example, cannot be reenacted, assigned cameramen should cover several different aspects of the proceedings as they occur. At a later time you can reenact and shoot atmosphere scenes and routine operations related to the main, nonrecurring event.

Though dynamic editing, as distinct from continuity editing, is used in all kinds of films, it is usually identified with documentaries. Its basic characteristic is that structural continuity does not depend on matched dialogue and action. Rather, its meaning lies in the effect created by the particular relationship of seemingly unrelated shots. The classic example is the Odessa steps sequence from *The Battleship Potemkin.* There Eisenstein shot many separate and unmatched shots of people as they panicked and retreated down the steps before the advancing soldiers. When these shots were edited together, the total effect was unified and powerful. The problem of the director is to make each shot say something by itself and still contain an element that further develops the main idea when combined with one or more other shots. Consider the logging sequence in *The River* (see Script, p. 93). Although all its shots could have been made in the same forest, edited together they create the impression of lumbering operations over a vast area. One tree begins to fall; then we cut to another shot of another tree falling. Before this tree hits the ground, we cut to still another falling tree. Together, these shots suggest a constant and unrelenting program of deforestation.

In documentary shooting, the director must be able to see and shoot scenes that will relate to each other in terms of the intent of the total film. It is not enough to shoot a series of beautifully framed and composed still shots (even though movement may be present) and splice them together. A dynamic sequence consists of a combination of shots related visually in some way, even though this relationship may not be clear initially to anyone but the director.

LIVE INTERVIEW

This is a documentary situation set up specifically for making a film. It includes interviews, panel discussions, and various group activities. Although they do not follow a written script, the participants know that what they are doing is primarily for the camera. The director's task is to determine camera placement and movement and to get the participants relaxed and in the right frame of mind. He may expect them to respond to the camera as if it were another person in the group, or he may want them to act as if the camera were not there.

EXTEMPORE

Impromptu acting began in live television shows of courtroom situations. The actors were briefed about who they were, what the situation was, and what course of action they were to follow. Without memorizing lines, each actor played his part as if he were the real person, using whatever words he needed to carry out his role. The lawyers were real-life lawyers hired as actors and given cases to plead before the camera as if the situation were real. Under a good director, this approach is quite workable in motion pictures. Set up a situation and tell each actor who he is supposed to be and what he is supposed to be doing. Then let the actors work out the scene while the camera is running. There are disadvantages to this method: it can be costly because of the retakes involved, matching can be difficult, and not all actors and directors can function in this way. When used effectively, however, it can yield some startling results, particularly since editing gives the director the prerogative of eliminating and rearranging. Although memorable moments in scenes are sometimes created by the spontaneous responses of good actors to lines in the dialogue, be aware that actors generally ad-lib in clichés.

ACCIDENTAL

This type of motion picture situation is similar to the impromptu type except that not all the actors know what is happening. Most of them do not even know they are in a scene. This occurs when you send an actor into a real-life situation and record the interaction with a hidden camera. One of the first well-known successful uses of this in feature films was in *The Lost Weekend,* in which Ray Milland, as the alcoholic, staggers along a New York street in search of a pawnshop. A hidden camera in a panel delivery truck follows his progress. He is unshaven, dirty, disreputable looking, and looks like any other Greenwich Village drunk. No one on the street suspects that he is anything other than what he appears to be, and the scene carries a feeling of reality and believability that could never be achieved on a staged street with extras playing the parts of pedestrians. The little accidental actions of people that are genuine responses to life as far as they are concerned help create a measure of reality rarely found in a staged scene.

Although the director can get some very interesting and sometimes surprising footage by this method, there are inherent dangers. He is legally liable if anyone is hurt or inconvenienced, or if property is damaged. One director instructed an actress to faint on the sidewalk on a city street. In the resulting excitement one of the bystanders was hurt, and the producer was sued and charged a large bill for the time of police, ambulance crew, and equipment. The footage was excellent, but probably not worth the price paid.

Director's Procedure During Shooting

The director is responsible for the progress of shooting. He may depend on others to get sets built, equipment in order, and everything arranged, but it is the director who determines whether or not the camera rolls. If he says nothing, everyone does nothing. If he engages in conversation, the crew waits until he is finished. If he takes three hours for lunch, the crew waits for his return. In addition to formulating, interpreting, and visualizing, the director's job is to tell people what to do. Following is a list of sequential actions for the director to take during shooting:

1. Line up the shot. This includes all the fiddling around that goes into getting the scene ready to shoot. Although visitors to movie sets are always impressed by the seeming chaos and confusion, this is the nature of setting up a scene. To keep the situation from degenerating into actual chaos, all concerned must diligently keep the aim in mind—preparing a scene for shooting. This applies to every kind of film, whether it entails dramatic sound-stage shooting or pure documentary. No production works according to a set of rules, so the individual director has to adapt his way of working to the demands of the situation. However some sort of rational approach to lining up a shot can make things go more quickly and smoothly than otherwise:

(a) Tell the cinematographer where to place the camera. Describe the action and the effect you want. Even though you may have worked out most of these details in advance, you are still responsible for saying, "Let's begin here."

(b) Inform the sound director what the action is to be. Determine what changes in the action may be necessary to get adequate sound.

(c) Explain to the actors precisely what you want them to do. Do not assume that an actor knows what to do and where to move. Much valuable time is wasted when the director fails to communicate positively with his actors. Say to an actor, "Start here." Indicate the spot by standing on it or marking it. Then go through the action detail by detail until you are sure that the actors know what is expected of them.

(d) Check your action, framing, and movement by looking through the camera. A shot is recorded only in the way the camera sees it. You cannot tell what a scene will look like on film by looking at it from any other point of view.

(e) Go through a camera rehearsal. This is a rehearsal acted out as if the camera were running. It gives the director, the cinematographer, the sound crew, grips, and everyone technically concerned a chance to see if everything is set up properly and runs smoothly. Do this as many times as you deem necessary.

2. Think of every shot in terms of action, continuity, screen direction, pacing, timing, length, and its purpose in both the sequence and the film. Anyone can set up a scene and shout "action" and "cut," but only a director can plan the action so that it carries out the purpose and interpretation of the film. Shoot so that scenes may be edited more than one way. Overlap the action on different angles of the same piece of action. Start the action ahead of the point where you intend the scene to begin and run it past the point where it is to end.

3. Stand behind the camera during the take. Only from this point of view can you tell how the scene is going. A scene viewed from a position away from the camera may look satisfactory, even though through the lens it may be worthless. Since the director must make the decision to keep or reject the scene, he should stand where he can tell what is going on. A tendency of beginning directors is to stand between the camera and the action, a little to one side. From this point of view you might as well be a visitor to the production rather than the one in charge of it.

4. Remember inserts, closeups, and *cutaways*. Although you may not have planned for such shots, always be ready to shoot any action that will provide flexibility in editing. Cutaways are extra shots of faces, reactions of people, or bits of unplanned action that can literally save your picture in the editing room.

5. Make decisions and compromises. After the shot, check with camera and sound and decide whether to retake the scene or print it. Once you have decided, call for the next setup and get on with the show. Do not be easily discouraged from getting what you want, but be prepared to make compromises. Cinematographers are just like other people in that they are sensitive about their work. Sometimes, when asked to set up an unusual shot, a cinematographer may say that it cannot, be done. The director must be able to tell whether the cinematographer is merely backing off or is serious. Not many things are impossible to do. Often it is purely a function of money and time—how much are you willing to spend to achieve the effect you want?

Above all, as a director, learn how to work with actors and to communicate with them.

Assistant Director

The assistant director is the organizer for the shooting unit and is responsible to the production manager. The job involves ascertaining that everything and everyone is at the right place at the right time. This includes almost everything discussed in Chapter 4 ("Production Management"). The assistant director makes it possible for the director to concentrate on directing, and the job must be carried out aggressively, efficiently, and doggedly, as follows:

1. Break down the script and prepare all lists and shooting schedules. (See Chapter 4.)
2. Notify all cast and crew about each day's shooting schedule and requirements by preparing and posting call sheets and work orders. Make arrangements for them to be on the set, and see to it that they are there.
3. Be sure that everything needed at the time of shooting is on hand or has been ordered—cast, crews, props, special equipment, shooting permits, transportation, and so on.
4. Take charge of the shooting unit. Keep the crew moving. Keep them quiet when necessary. Avoid unnecessary conversation.
5. Set up and direct background action involving extras. Assign people to control crowds, including the hiring of special police where needed.
6. Maintain the daily production report.

7. Keep an up-to-date list of everyone's name, address, and phone number. Keep a running check on where people can be reached.
8. Watch what is going on and be prepared for all contingencies.

Script Supervisor

The script supervisor holds the master script and keeps a record of the shooting. Like the assistant director, the script supervisor does organizational work, freeing the director to handle the creative end of the shooting. The script supervisor is the director's memory of what needs to be done, what has been done, what angles were shot, what the position of props were at the end of each shot, what scene numbers are to be used, and everything else the director needs to know. The script supervisor is constantly at the director's side, and on all but the most simple production he is indispensable.

Before shooting begins, the script supervisor must become completely familiar with the script, its story, the characters and their names, the locale, the chronology, special effects, and all requirements both specific and implied. He does not actually have to memorize the script, but when he has read and reread it and analyzed and dissected it he may find that it is firmly printed in his mind.

Mark the script so you can tell at a glance what the requirements of each page are as to night or day, special effects (such as rain, lightning, breakaway furniture), costumes and clothing, and the physical condition of both actors and objects. Break down the script (see Chapter 4) and make a quick-reference index, including the following:

Scene numbers
Names of sets
Locations
Time and weather conditions that affect clothing, makeup, props, cast, or sets.
Special props, vehicles, equipment, animals, etc.
Special effects

Also, make lists of requirements whenever they appear useful or necessary. These might include bits and extras, wild tracks to be recorded, pickup shots not called for by the script, insert shots, changes affecting the physical condition of the actors, clothing or sets, and anything else pertinent to the specific situation.

Script Supervisor's Responsibilities

RESPONSIBILITY TO THE PRODUCER

Provide the producer with a record of the shooting progress in the form of scenes shot, script pages covered, screen time, camera setups, and any other information requested. This information is recorded on a daily production report, usually kept by the assistant director. He may also be asked to keep a daily log (see Fig. 4.7), if necessary. A detailed minute-by-minute log of the day's shooting is impressive only if it serves a useful purpose.

RESPONSIBILITY TO THE DIRECTOR

As the on-the-set assistant to the director, the script supervisor keeps track of the almost endless details essential for making a good motion picture. He is involved with the director in rehearsals and in shooting.

Rehearsals. Keep a record of the action as it is staged by the director for any scene that is complicated enough for either the actors or the director to forget a move or a line. Such a record includes the camera movement that has been planned for all master scenes and covering angles. Note changes or additions in the dialogue or departures from the script. Be alert.

Shooting

1. Begin by examining the set or the location. See that props and other items called for in the scrip are in the scene. Make a note of the exact position of windows, shades, and draperies, for matching within the sequence being shot and for matching to exteriors or interiors to be shot later. Note which way doors open, and check all signs on doors, windows, and walls to see that they comply with the script and are spelled correctly. Note any weather or lighting conditions that will have to be matched.
2. Determine the slate number, which is the scene number to be photographed and recorded, and give it to camera and sound. The master scene is usually the numbered scene, with

all pickups and covering angles carrying the same scene number with letter designations, for example Sc 229, 229A, and so on. This is important because it gives the editor a continuity line and tells the director what pickups relate to which scene (see Figs. 3.1, 3.2).

3. Make a diagram of each shot, showing camera angle, position of actors, direction and extent of movement. This information is essential for retakes or additional coverage, particularly at a later date.

4. For each take make a note of scene length in seconds, whether the take was complete or incomplete, the reason that it is incomplete, and a brief description of the shot including the lens used (see Fig. 3.3).

5. Make a note of all action for matching purposes. Observe the gestures of actors and where such gestures occur relative to specific words in the dialogue. Keep track of the direction of movements, exits, and entrances, and on which words of dialogue they occurred. Note the handling of props—which hands were used, lengths of cigars and cigarettes, levels of liquid in glasses and bottles, and food consumed. Record the sequence and disposition of movement in such actions as the putting on and removal of garments, parachute harnesses, and the like. Also take note of the sequence and movement in the assembly or dismantling of any structure or device, and the operating sequence of any machine or process. Check all entrances and exits through doors and windows—whether closed or open, and if open, how far. Observe the position of actors and the position of their hand props; coats on or off, buttoned or unbuttoned; hats, gloves, eyeglasses, and so on.

6. Read off-screen dialogue or narration during rehearsals and shooting.

7. During the shooting of a scene, check the dialogue for correctness. Record errors and changes and call them to the director's attention.

8. Advise both camera and sound personnel of the takes to be printed, and double-check the list at the end of the day's shooting.

9. On pickup shots and covering angles, decide on the slate number and make sure that each shot matches the master scene at the starting point.

10. For matching, keep a file of polaroid still photographs of sets, props, hair, makeup, wardrobe, or any other items that seem necessary.

RESPONSIBILITY TO THE EDITOR

The script supervisor must supply the editor with a script that is an accurate record of the scenes as shot. When the action or dialogue has been changed, retype the necessary pages incorporating the changes. If there are song-and-dance routines, type them and insert them in the script in the proper continuity. On the blank page opposite each scene, type a description of every shot, listing slate numbers and all pertinent information on each take (see Fig. 3.3). Include any instructions from the director to the editor. Line each page of the script, showing how much as covered by each shot (see Fig. 3.2).

The script supervisor is usually indispensable. Some kind of record must be kept on any production no matter how small or uncomplicated. The crew may not be large enough to include a script supervisor who does only the one job, but a full-time, efficient professional is a worthwhile investment.

CAMERA CREW

The camera crew is responsible for operating the camera and seeing to it that the director gets what he asks for, flawlessly exposed and perfectly composed. Achieving this can entail the operation and supervision of much highly specialized and sophisticated equipment. Depending on the kind of production involved, the camera crew may consist of one man or many. The camera crew is listed below as having several distinct jobs in separate categories. In a feature production, the crew will consist of at least four people. As the type of production changes the composition of the camera crew also changes, but the kinds of jobs that have to be done remain essentially the same.

Director of Photography

The director of photography is responsible for the conduct and quality of the picture's photography and for all decisions about camera and lighting. He may or may not operate the camera depending on the kind of production involved. The following are his main responsibilities:

1. Takes charge of the camera crew and is responsible for all photography.
2. Runs through the action, sets, and locations in advance with the director, and determines what equipment and skills are needed.
3. Orders all camera equipment and film.
4. Checks that all camera equipment is operating properly and that the camera crew is competent to operate it.
5. Lights all scenes, indoors and out, and determines the exposure.
6. Gives the director what he wants in the shortest possible time.

Camera Operator

The camera operator works the camera and is responsible for filming the scene in a professional manner. He frames the scene properly, follows the action, keeps the camera clean, and sees to it that focus and exposure are set and maintained properly. The job includes the following specific tasks:

1. Takes direct charge of the camera and its accessories.
2. Checks in advance that the camera is loaded with film and operating properly. This means that all batteries are charged to capacity; all accessory equipment is on hand; all film, filters, hand tools, tape, rags, clips—everything is loaded and ready.
3. Sets up the camera on dolly, crane, tripod, shoulder pod, or wherever required. Levels the camera, checks its position, and is ready to shoot at all times.
4. Follows the action during camera rehearsals and makes all adjustments and settings needed to get the shot properly during the take.
5. Ensures that everything is set for the take: battery connected, power on, lens set for correct *f*-stop and focus, proper filter, magazine in place, film in the camera, lens cover off, shutter open, sync cable connected. No matter how small the oversight or mistake, if it results in a bad take or no take at all, the disaster is large.
6. Sees that all camera equipment is well guarded. Doesn't let any equipment get farther away from the camera than ten feet, unless someone is directly assigned to take care of it or it is locked securely in a safe place.

Camera Assistant

The camera assistant stands by the camera operator and aids in every way possible. He changes magazines and lenses, checks magazines and aperture for dirt, follows and sets focus and *f*-stop, measures distances, takes care of the equipment, keeps the camera report, and carries things. Additional assistants may be needed for such tasks as keeping the slate and camera report and loading magazines, depending on the size and requirements of the production.

Again, the separate jobs of cinematographer, camera operator, and camera assistant are often combined into one. The lone filmmaker will undoubtedly serve as the entire camera crew, while the director of photography for a large production almost never touches the camera. It all depends on budget and goals. Obviously the fewer the people, the more versatile the crew and the less the expense, although there is a practical size for every film. A four-man crew in a fast-moving documentary or cinema verité situation could conceivably be cumbersome to the point of inefficiency. A one- or two-man crew on a large studio production would be helpless. Thus the size of the crew must be fitted to the job.

SOUND CREW

Four basic tasks are necessary in recording sound on stage or on location: placement of the microphone, controlling sound level and quality, recording the sound, and rigging and running cables. Traditionally the film industry uses four technicians to do these jobs, but this many people are not always necessary or desirable. The character of the production determines the size of the sound crew. The job titles and responsibilities of the sound crew are discussed below.

Mixer

The mixer is in charge of the sound. He determines what equipment is to be used, how it is to be placed, and also advises the director about what needs to be done to get good sound. The mixer loads and unloads the recorder, operates it during shooting, sets the necessary volume levels, determines the quality and usability of the sound recorded, and maintains the sound report.

Boom Operator

The boom operator is in charge of physically locating the microphone and holding it during the take, keeping the microphone in the proper location or moving it, as specified by the mixer. When a boom is not used, the boom operator holds the microphone in position by hand or on a hand-held boom called a "fishpole."

Sound Assistant

The sound assistant's job consists of handling and taking care of the equipment: stringing cables, rearranging them, coiling them after use, and loading and unloading equipment as needed.

There are production in which all these functions may be carried out by one person, such as a documentary team of two—director/cinematographer and sound person—using a professional tape recorder carried on a shoulder strap. If it is necessary to put the microphone in position some distance from the recorder with greater mobility, a microphone assistant may be added. On a compact shooting unit doing sync scenes on a set, sound can be handled quite successfully, with a mixer operating the recorder and an assistant holding the microphone in the scene. Both of them share in rigging and striking: rigging is unloading equipment and setting it up; striking is taking equipment down and loading it. Consider the jobs mentioned above as an indication of *what* has to be done. Depending on the nature of your film, assign whatever people are necessary to perform these four tasks adequately.

GRIP CREW

The grip crew is in charge of all physical operations on the actual shooting. This includes materials, tools, sets, trucks, reflectors, ropes, scaffolds, rigging, dollies, and cranes. It is easy to overlook the fact that any shooting requires a tremendous amount of physical work merely to get things moved, put into place, and held together until a shot is over. When the director wants a tree branch hanging down outside a window, the grip crew finds a suitable branch, hangs it so it looks right and is secure enough not to injure anyone on the set, then takes it down after the shot is made. A grip is more than an ordinary laborer, he is a master of all trades and has sufficient physical stamina, knowledge of film production, and ingenuity to solve the many incredible problems that arise. Grip equipment includes tools for any kind of job, ropes, rigging, lumber, tape, hardware, nails, straps, levers, everything. No matter what the title, there must be someone on a motion picture crew to do the grips' skilled manual work. You may have the finest creative artists money can buy working on your film, but without grips they are dead weight. The following are grip jobs:

1. Rigging, maintaining, and striking sets, platforms, flats, walls, backings, and everything involved in set operation.
2. Operating, steering, and placing of all dollies, booms, cranes, and camera platforms. This includes laying or building tracks or making setups for camera movement.
3. In charge of all materials and equipment, other than camera, such as tools, sets, trucks, reflectors, ropes, scaffolds, building materials, and so on.
4. Loading, unloading, maintaining, and operating all grip equipment.
5. Standing by on the set to seee that neither the director nor the cinematographer has to do anything not directly connected with his own specific duties.
6. Starting early in the day, having an answer to every problem, operating at a dead run, and remaining cheerful in the face of all adversity.

A good grip crew anticipates every need before it occurs. If they see the cinematographer looking around quizzically, they deduce immediately that he needs a table and get one. If there is no table available, they build one. A grip takes pride that no one ever has to ask for something—he has already rigged it.

ELECTRICAL CREW

On a feature production the electrical crew is often large, particularly during shooting in sound stages and in setups where many lights must be used. The head electrician, called the gaffer, is in charge of the crew and is responsible for installing all the lights and for rough lighting the set after consultation with the director of photography. The director of photography makes adjustments and additions before shooting. The crew consists of the gaffer's assistant, lamp operators, and laborers. Whenever a generator is used, the generator operator is part of the electrical crew. Depending on the kind of production, a lighting crew may or may not be used. In a film that requires a great deal of complicated rigging of lights, the director of photography will probably want a gaffer to do the basic lighting. In smaller productions the grip crew can rig and operate the lights while the cinematographer does the lighting.

SUPPORT CREWS

The support crews include whatever technicians, experts, laborers, or consultants you need to get your shooting done. Filmmaking requires many different skills at various times—hairdressers, makeup artists, prop crews, wardrobe people, special effects, first aid, drivers, drapers, painters, laborers, carpenters, paperhangers, plumbers, horse wranglers, animal trainers, glassblowers, and so on. Whatever the need, the job has to be done. It is not necessary to adhere to the stratified categories of skills peculiar to the feature film industry of past years. Filmmaking today involves individuals who can do many tasks, not just one.

The size of a motion-picture shooting unit depends on the size of its budget, the kind of film being made, and the conditions under which it is being made. The smallest workable unit is the lone filmmaker working as producer-director-cinematographer. The lone filmmaker can make impressive films within certain limits, but shooting under more complex conditions while still maintaining professional standards of quality calls for elaboration. A workable group for small-unit operation consists of a director, a cinematographer and assistant, an assistant director, and a grip. If sound is to be recorded a mixer will have to be added and, depending on the complexity of the situation, a microphone assistant. If lighting is needed, one or more electricians may be necessary. For a slightly more elaborate unit, a second camera assistant, a script supervisor, and another grip will be needed. Thus, without exceeding the limits of a modest scale of production, a location unit may quickly expand from a basic five persons to eight or even twelve.

FOUR

Production Management

Planning, budgeting, and scheduling a motion picture are like planning a military campaign. You are faced with the logistic problem of routing an incredible amount of equipment, materials, and people to the right places at the right time. If some seemingly small item is neglected, the whole production may suffer and even collapse. The planning of moviemaking is called production management, and the best production manager is a person with both the ability and the inclination to organize details in a hard-headed, practical way. Creative people are often unwilling to undertake this prosaic task, but without it they quickly become trapped in a morass of unresolved details. Anyone who sets out to plan, schedule, and budget a motion picture, must be prepared to work with details, costs, percentages, estimates, extensions, and figures.

STAGES OF FILM PRODUCTION

Motion picture budgeting and scheduling are linked because costs cannot be figured until it is known how a picture is to be done and how long it will take to do it. In the process of budgeting, then, detailed schedules must be prepared for preplanning, shooting, and completion. The stages of film production are referred to as preproduction, production, and postproduction.

Preproduction	Production	Postproduction
Script	Staff and crews	Film editing
Producer	Actors	Electronic editing
Writer	Film	Sound effects
Director	Video tape	Music
Casting	Actual shooting	Optical effects
Production design	Developing/printing	Titles
Location scouting		Mixing
Shooting schedule preparation		Negative cutting
Budgeting		Answer print

Preproduction Planning

The biggest costs occur during actual shooting, or production, when you are paying crews and actors, and accumulating costs for equipment, film, laboratory, locations, sets, transportation, insurance, taxes, and overhead. Since the cost rises every day, try to work out all the problems in advance to reduce the shooting period to its most effective minimum. This is called, *preproduction planning.*

In the days of silent movies, pictures were sometimes shot "off the cuff," that is, without a script. Buster Keaton tells of starting feature-length movies without scripts and improvising as he went along. The silent-movie directors did pretty well, but the advent of sound complicated off-the-cuff shooting and today's high production costs killed it. Motion picture preplanning has progressed from a few notes on a shirt cuff to today's detailed checklists. To try now to shoot a picture of any complexity without some form of preproduction planning would be disastrous.

Budgeting is not easy, mainly because of the variables. Moviemaking is unlike other production activities such as automobile manufacturing, for example, in which the fixed cost of each part is known as well as the precise amount of time required for assembly. Motion pictures consist of elements whose effectiveness depends on the creative efforts of many people, and to date no one has figured out a way to determine in advance exactly how long it takes an artist to do a particular task. You can make a close estimate through experience and knowing the particular people involved, but the process is controlled by constantly changing conditions. The time required for setting up scenes, situations, and special effects, marshalling equipment and people, and making the many necessary arrangements depends on human moods, weather, creativity, doggedness, and luck. Your task in budgeting is to analyze all elements in light of your experience to arrive at a close approximation of what you are going to spend.

Contingency Budgeting

Unlike most other businesses, motion picture production involves elements that vary on a day-to-day or even a minute-to-minute basis. You may have everything planned and budgeted to the exact minute and penny, but there are so many uncontrollable and unpredictable variables in making motion pictures that you are always working in the shadow of disaster. Therefore you must be prepared for the unpredictable by use of *contingency budgeting.* This means increasing the total budgeted cost of a production by a fixed percentage of from twenty to forty percent. After the total cost of everything has been figured out, add twenty to forty percent of your total to the budget. The percentage you use will depend on the specific conditions, your experience, and your individual skill.

Contingency budgeting is peculiar to motion picture production, and you may have to be careful about how you refer to it. Those outside the movie industry do not understand budgeting for an undefined catastrophe, and conventional business people will often react to a thirty-five percent contingency as if company funds were being embezzled. Although it is difficult to hide a contingency if a client is entitled to a close inspection of the budget, be aware of the probable reaction and be prepared to explain the problem.

MOTION PICTURE COSTS

There may be thousands of items in a budget or very few, but there will always be more than you anticipate. The following list includes most kinds of motion picture costs:

Ideas
Stories
Scripts
People
Materials (film, videotape, construction materials, food, expendables, etc.)
Equipment (purchase and rental of cameras, grip equipment, sound gear, special effects machines, etc.)
Facilities (stages, studios, offices, editing rooms)
Transportation and trucking
Laboratory
Overhead (the cost of maintaining an organization)
Taxes
Fees
Insurance

These expenses are commonly arranged in twenty or thirty categories, beginning with the cost of the script and ending with the cost of the final print. These categories roughly approximate the sequential phases of moviemaking. The following budget checklist contains those expense items common to all production. Every company has its own budget forms that are more or less similar but vary with the kind of picture being made and the particular organization of the producing company. Rarely will all of these expenses be necessary in a single motion picture, but each one will appear at one time or another. Also, there are cost items not on this checklist that will arise constantly, but it would be

mercial, industrial—without a script leads to financial ruin. From an approved, detailed script, exact lists of every person, item, condition, and cost needed to do the job may be extracted. Without a script, estimates, plans, and schedules are based on supposition.

Determining Running Time

To make precise calculations about the cost of raw film stock, laboratory, prints, and sound studio services, you need an estimate of what the running time of the finished film will be. Compute running time by actually reading aloud and acting out the whole script with a stopwatch. Try to visualize both movement and pacing. A narrated film is generally the easiest to figure because the time for reading narration plus relatively simple adjustments for visuals provide a close estimate. Dramatic films may be more difficult to time since any given scene may range from very short to very long, depending on your director and actors, but you can come very close with practice and experience.

For most kinds of markets and uses, film length is clearly indicated because films fall into five categories that automatically determine the broad limits of running time, as follows:

1. Theatrical motion pictures. These are films intended for release to the entertainment movie houses and include feature dramatic films, some feature documentaries, and short subjects. Standard features traditionally run ninety minutes, but some prestige pictures run up to three hours. Distributors prefer features no shorter than eighty minutes, while theatrical shorts are rarely longer than ten minutes.
2. Films for television. These must be made to standardized lengths since both national and local TV programming are laid out in precise segments of time based on half-hour blocks. As a result, TV films must fit half-hour, one-hour, hour-and-a-half, or two-hour time slots including station breaks and commercials. TV commercials are usually made to run a few seconds up to one minute.
3. Special-use nontheatrical films. This includes mainly business, industrial, and promotional films whose length is clearly determined in advance by their sponsors since they usually have specific applications in mind. Many are intended for TV showing, which means that they must be in half-hour increments. Other industrial and business films are used in sales presentations, orientation sessions, and similar programs. In each case film length is established by the intended purpose of the program.
4. Educational films. These vary in length from two or three minutes up to feature length, but most must fit into a class period of no longer than forty to fifty minutes. Allowing time for the teacher's introduction and for discussion following the screening, ten to fifteen minutes is the general range for educational films.
5. Films without program time limitations. This includes many scientific films, documentaries, art films, so-called underground films, student films, and films made solely for personal interest or individual expression. Their length is determined by the filmmaker's personal involvement and finances. Since they are not tailored to fit any specific program, films in this category range in length from a few seconds to several hours.

If you are planning a film with no script or one that is a rambling personal expression, arrive at a general length of time for a working figure as, "twenty minutes or so," or "about feature length." The inexperienced person usually estimates film length about four times higher than it will actually be. Film is a compressing medium with the capacity for transmitting a tremendous amount of information in a very short time. So don't be surprised if your twenty-minute idea becomes a five-minute film.

The Level of Production

Any given scene or entire film may be made in a style ranging from simple and cheap to complex and expensive. The level of production you decide on directly affects the budgeting, and your decision depends on how much money you want to spend and how much apparent lavishness you want your film to have. For example, take a scene in which two people meet in a busy airline terminal, speak a few lines, and then go their separate ways. You can shoot the scene expensively, cheaply, or somewhere in between.

To shoot the scene cheaply, the following method may be used:

1. Send a small crew out to take an establishing shot of the airline terminal at its busiest. Or, if available, buy a stock shot of the terminal.
2. Rent a portion of the terminal or build a set that duplicates a part of it, and take fairly close shots of the two people meeting.
3. Edit the two scenes together so that they appear to be occurring at the same place and the same time.

To shoot the scene expensively:

1. Rent the entire terminal and fill it with several hundred extras.
2. Put the camera on a crane and move through the crowd until you pick up the two characters.

The latter method of shooting involves heavier expenses than the cost of the terminal, the extras, and the camera crane. Setting up such a large scene and making it work takes large crews and much time. The difference in cost between the two ways of shooting this scene could conceivably run to more than $100,000, yet in both the story content is exactly the same. The advantage of the expensive way is a lavishness and richness that may enhance the film's believability and impact. However, lavishness and expense do not necessarily make a good picture. Some of the best films ever made have been done simply, their excellence being the result of ingenuity, taste, talent, and ability.

Script scenes are written without any indication about how they should be shot. It is up to you as producer to decide the production level you want or can afford for your picture. The low-budget technique, described in the airline terminal sequence, of showing an establishing shot of an impressive scene and then cutting to closer shots that are seemingly in the same place is a time-proven method for creating the illusion of reality. Although film purists object to sets, substitute locations, and "cheated" scenes as not being "real," remember that actual reality has nothing to do with film reality. The proof is in the seeing, and believability is the test. If your scene is believable, the authenticity of the location is irrelevant. If the scene looks fake, it is a failure even though you may have used the real Taj Mahal, and the Kremlin, the real Gobi desert, or the real moon. No one can say whether it is better to make a high-budget or a low-budget motion picture. Whichever you make is up to you, but you must decide just how you intend to do it—high-budget, medium-budget, cheap, or downright miserly—to proceed rationally with budgeting.

To determine the production level, review the various elements on the following production level checklist and decide how you will handle each one:

Film versus videotape
Shooting ratio
Color vs. black-and-white
Music
Sound
Optical effects
Sets
Locations

Film versus Videotape

To shoot on film or on videotape is a question you must decide according to your budget, the kind of picture you are making, and how you work. Videotape, like film, is merely a medium on which a motion picture is recorded. But the process of motion picture production is exactly the same for each: there must be a script; the production must be planned, scheduled, directed, lighted, and photographed; the picture must be edited, mixed, printed, and released. If you are operating on a tight time/money schedule, it could conceivably pay to shoot on videotape. If you are a smaller producer or a lone moviemaker to whom a few days one way or the other does not mean saving several thousand dollars, it is less expensive and more convenient to shoot on film. Obviously, the lone filmmaker working with his own equipment can work less expensively and with greater freedom by shooting on film, especially 16mm.

Electronic shooting and editing equipment is available at high rental rates, so it must be used quite efficiently—shooting and editing the greatest amount of material in the shortest, most concentrated time. But at several hundred dollars per hour, it may be more economical to take more time in production than to spend a large amount of cash for electronic shooting and editing facilities. The advantages of shooting on videotape rather than film are as follows:

1. Less light is required under all conditions of shooting. This entails less lighting equipment, less power, fewer technicians, and greater speed in setting up with consequence lower costs.
2. Immediate replay. A take can be viewed by the director on the set immediately after it has been shot. This may eliminate returning to a set or location for retakes.
3. Long takes. Takes as long as thirty minutes can be made on tape. It may be argued that this is a serious aesthetic setback to the art of filmmaking, but in the hands of a good director this technique can be effective.
4. Decreased editing time. Editing time for a feature may be reduced by 50 percent or more.
5. Optical effects may be made during the editing. Even the most complicated optical effects can be integrated into the picture with very little additional time required.

The disadvantages of shooting on videotape include the following:

1. The short-run expense is that daily costs for camera equipment and editing facilities may be several hundred dollars per hour. The time saved does not always represent an equal cash benefit to the filmmaker.
2. Medium and long shots, particularly exteriors, may be inferior in quality to those shot on film. This implies alternatives such as limiting the production to close shots, accepting the poorer quality of longer shots, or shooting on both videotape and film and mixing them in the final version.
3. Loss of mobility. The electronic camera depends on a vehicle containing the videotape recorder (VTR) and the necessary electronic equipment. The camera is connected to the videotape recorder (VTR) truck by a cable, which is a handicap to speed and mobility.
4. The lone filmmaker and the very small crew cannot feasibly shoot electronically because of the large crew and equipment requirements.
5. For a release on film, the cost of transferring the tape version to negative film is high.

Shooting Ratio

When shooting on film, this is the ratio of the amount of film exposed during production to the amount of film used in the completed picture. The shooting ratio makes it possible to estimate accurately most of your laboratory and film costs because you are working with fixed figures. If your movie is to be 360 feet in length, and during production you exposed 1800 feet of film, your shooting ratio would be five to one (5 × 360 = 1800). If you know the final running time and you have decided on a shooting ratio, you can then calculate exactly what your film and laboratory costs will be. For example, consider four items that will appear in your budget: raw film stock, processing, workprint, and answer print:

Estimated running time: 360 feet
Shooting ratio: 5 to 1

Then:	Raw stock needed (360 × 5)	= 1800 ft
	Processing	= 1800 ft
	Workprint (90% of 1800)	= 1620 ft
	First answer print	= 360 ft

When you apply a per-foot cost of film stock and laboratory work to the above footages, you determine a firm total cost for those items. All other items in your budget that are priced by the foot can be computed on the basis of the shooting ratio.

When you shoot in videotape, the shooting ratio does not pin down your raw stock costs quite so neatly. During shooting, your rented tape might be used and bad takes might be erased; both of these would affect precise preproduction estimates of the shooting ratio. Videotape requirements should be estimated with respect to their intended use—buy, rent, erase. But the shooting ratio indicates a consideration even more critical than the amount of videotape or film to be used—time. Obviously, shooting at a ratio of 10:1 is going to take more time (money) than shooting at 4:1. Thus, the shooting ratio is an important indicator in your budgeting and scheduling calculations of both shooting time and requirements for film and videotape.

To arrive at a preliminary shooting ratio, carefully analyze the script or proposed film with respect to the following:

1. Lip-sync dialogue. This usually takes more film than silent scenes. Actors must deliver lines properly, performances must be correct, sound has to be recorded perfectly, and all movement of the camera and equipment must be silent. The high probability of mistakes means retakes and, in turn, more film in the camera. Consequently the ratio for shooting dialogue is higher than for silent or postrecorded scenes.
2. One-time events. Parades, games, festivals, explosions, races, rocket launches, boat launchings, fires, and so on happen only once. Getting them on film generally takes a high shooting ratio, and to get different angles you must often use more than one camera, sometimes many.
3. Complicated action. Complicated action increases the probability of multiple takes and a higher shooting ratio. Suppose you want the camera to follow an actor as he comes out of a store on a city street and walks down the sidewalk. He stops to light a cigarette obviously to avoid two men passing. He continues to the corner, where a car driven by a woman he recognizes skids around the corner and continues on its way. The camera moves in so that the actor is in closeup just after the car speeds by—all of this in one shot. The movements of the actor, the two men, the speeding car, and the camera must be precisely timed and coordinated. A slight mistake, and the whole action has to be done over. In such scenes you can expect retakes to increase the shooting ratio.

Various types of motion pictures fall into fairly predictable shooting ratio patterns. Feature films generally are shot at a ratio of about 15 to 1. This figure can go up or down depending on the lavishness or spareness of the production, or how complex the action or shooting conditions may be. Documentary films usually require a high shooting ratio. Even though many documentaries are made with postrecorded sound tracks, the photography of material and events not directly under your control results in a high shooting ratio. Students and novice filmmakers often assume, with disastrous results, that a documentary will be inexpensive to shoot. The footage required for a documentary can be staggering; and although every situation has its own peculiar requirements, don't be surprised at ratios up to 50:1.

Films with voice-over narration in which there is control of the scenes and the action can be done in the range 4:1 to 10:1, with the norm probably being 5:1. These are mainly industrial, business, and sales films, some educational movies, technical reports, and certain documentaries. Low-budget features, although they use lip-sync dialogue, often come within this range.

Color versus Black-and-White

The decision to use either color or black-and-white may be financial, aesthetic, or both. Color films are more salable since they are in greater demand by both theatrical and nontheatrical distributors and by television. But individual ideas seem to be suitable exclusively for one or the other. We say, "It's really a black-and-white story," or "It wouldn't be anything without color." Making a motion picture in color costs more, although the difference is diminishing as faster and better color film emulsions are perfected. The main considerations are as follows:

1. Color film raw stock, processing, printing, and optical effects cost more per foot than black-and-white film.
2. Color film requires color-balanced lights. To mix daylight and artificial light, as in shooting inside a house with sunlight coming in through the windows, window filters and mounting time are necessary.
3. Black-and-white film may be used successfully with a mixture of daylight and various kinds of artificial light.
4. Black-and-white film emulsions are generally faster than color, which translates into fewer and smaller lights, smaller crews, and less time.
5. Color on videotape is no more expensive than black-and-white. However, the problem of color-balanced lights applies to videotape just as it does to color film. (See item 2 above.)
6. Distributors are not interested in buying black-and-white films.

Base your decision on all the variables—economy, salability, ease of production, and aesthetics.

Music

The most expensive way to put music to a film is to hire a composer to provide an original score and then record it to picture in a studio with a full orchestra. The cheapest way is to buy library, or "canned" music and lay it in to the picture like so much decorator's molding. Between the two extremes are other acceptable choices, depending on the level of production you have chosen. (See Music Editing, Chapter 10)

Sound

The range here is between full sound effects and none at all. Sound effects in a picture never just happen. Whether the sound is a bird call, footsteps, the rustle of grass, a door closing, or the clink of keys, it must be recorded and put in sync with the visual. Full sound effects mean time for recording, selecting, sound effects editing, and mixing. (See Editing Sound Effects Tracks, Chapter 10)

Optical Effects

Optical effects are photographic effects that must be made in an optical printer. These include dissolves, fades, hold-frames, wipes, titles on a moving background, rollups, separation printing, and so on. They involve planning, setup time, the time of specialists, and film and laboratory costs. In 16mm film, dissolves, fades, and some superimpositions can be made in negative cutting at very little additional cost; but all other effects must be done by competent optical departments. Costs escalate quite rapidly. Some films, particularly those in world exposition exhibits, many science-fiction features, and theatrical trailers, depend almost entirely on optical effects. Other films exclude them entirely, relying on story, mood, concept, and nonspectacular appeal.

Sets

Elaborate sets and production value add impressiveness to a film but they can quickly become expensive. Very small sets—a part of a room, a corner of an airline terminal, an office—when used imaginatively, are effective, believable, and considerably cheaper than elaborate sets. Actual locations can be very effective and believable, but rental, lighting, crew transportation, and sound problems often add up to more money and time than the cost of building a set.

Locations

Taking a crew on location is expensive, and costs increase with distance and time. Although there are many strange and intriguing distant locations, be aware of the well-known Hollywood dictum: "A tree's a tree, and a rock's a rock—shoot it in Griffith Park."

SCRIPT BREAKDOWN

Script breakdown is the process of carefully analyzing the script, isolating every detail, and then grouping the details by category on breakdown sheets and production lists. On a large studio production, the production manager gives a copy of the final script to each department—art, camera, sound, grip, construction, music, wardrobe, makeup, props, electrical, special effects—and each makes its own breakdown and compiles a list of requirements for its own specialty. These lists are returned to the production manager who uses them as the basis for his preparation of the budget and the shooting schedule. On smaller productions the same lists need to be compiled, except that one or two persons may do all the work. Regardless of a picture's complexity or simplicity, whether it is to be shot on film or videotape, the process of breakdown is the same and is essential to budgeting and scheduling.

Scene Description

The *scene description* (Fig. 4.1) in the script gives the basic information you need for the beginning of a script breakdown. An adequate scene description should contain the following information:

Which scene
How we see the scene
Where it happens
When it happens
Who is involved
What is happening
Props being used

Breakdown consists of identifying and marking these elements individually. To break down the script, go through it page by page and do the following (see Fig. 4.2):

1. Isolate each numbered scene by drawing a heavy line across the page between each scene.
2. Underline the name of each set, stock shot, insert, or animation scene.
3. Put a circle around each cast, bit, and extra in each scene.
4. Underline each essential prop. This includes any property without which the scene could not be shot.
5. Underline wardrobe for each character if mentioned in the script. If not, make a note in the margin.
6. Analyze each scene carefully and, in the margin, make notations of items that will be needed but have not been called for in the scene description.

Analysis, the last step of script breakdown, is quite important since the script writer never includes in his scene description a detailed list of everything in the scene. He merely indicates the general atmosphere and gives his attention to the action and the dialogue. You must determine the exact number of specific items that have to be on the set or on location when the camera rolls.

Look at Scene 21 in Fig. 4.2. Anne is cooking and serving a meal. Specific cooking utensils and food are not mentioned in the script, but they have to be there when the scene is shot. Notations in the margin indicate that food and utensils will be needed. Before shooting, these will have to be broken down further into the exact amount and kinds of cookware, food, and tableware. These are essential props.

Production Lists

After you have gone through the script and marked and analyzed it, make up the production lists (see Figs. 4.3*A*, *B*, *C*, and *D*). Begin with a set list. Start at the beginning of the script, write down the sets by name, and number then consecutively. Although a set may appear several times at different places in the script, record it only once. For all subsequent scenes appearing on that set, note their numbers after the original entry, as in the following example:

Set List

1. BOAT INT Sc 3-4-5-6-22-23-24-76-91-114
2. ALEX's APARTMENT Sc 1-2-21-25-26-120-121-122-123
3. POLICE OFFICE INT Sc 23–125–126–127-243

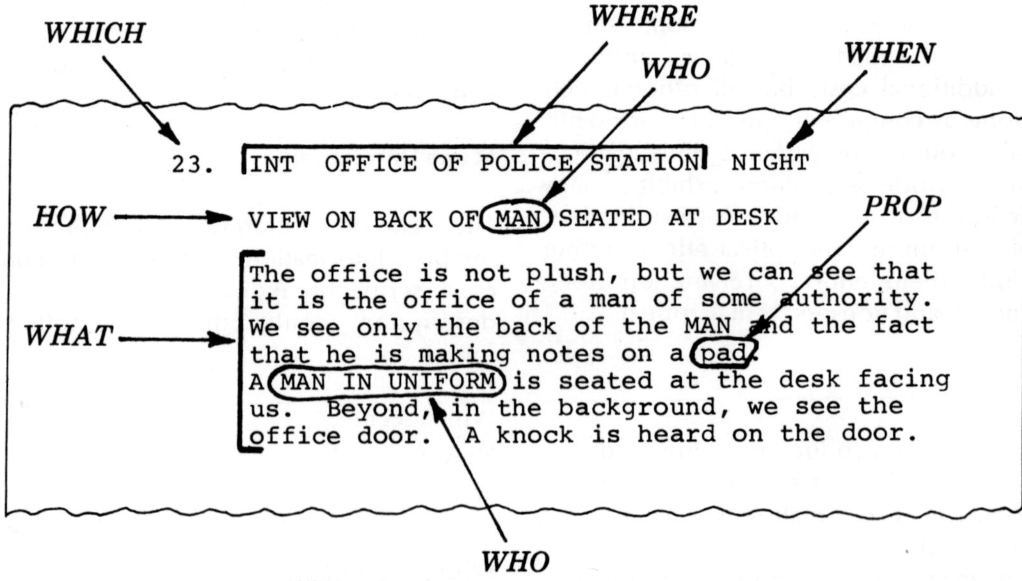

Fig. 4.1. M.P. The-information a scene provides.

EXT BEACH NEXT TO PIER DAY

BEACH CROWD
2 DOGS

17. FULL VIEW OF BEACH FROM PIER

Acres of scantily clad people lolling in the sun and disporting themselves variously. Surf, sand, sun . . . the whole bit. La Dolce Vita in full session.

18. MEDIUM VIEW OF ANNE MARK AND DAVID IN THE SURF

SURFBOARDS
EXTRAS
IN B. G.

MARK AND DAVID go through a complete pantomime of the elementary instructions for surfing, but we are too far away to hear them over the noise and the surf. After a short while, MARK and DAVID turn and wade to the shore leaving ANNE experimenting in the surf.

19. CLOSE VIEW ON ANNE ON THE SURFBOARD

We see her as she struggles and tries, in a very small bikini, to handle the surfboard. Finally she catches and rides a small wave.

20. CLOSE VIEW ON DAVID AND MARK AT THE CABANA

EXTRAS
WRESTLERS
BEACH CHAIRS
TOWELS
LOTION
WHISKEY BOTTLE

They are lolling against their cabana wall, all the usual beach paraphernalia about them. In the background there is gym equipment and a padded ring in which practitioners of the gentle art of Judo and Karate are working out. MARK touches DAVID and nods in the direction of the athletes with a "get-them" expression.

DISSOLVE TO:

INT ALEX'S APARTMENT EVENING

21. MEDIUM VIEW ON ALEX AND ANNE

ALEX, with a drink, is seated at a counter bar that separates the living room from the kitchen. ANNE is preparing dinner and during this sequence begins serving him. She sits down herself on the kitchen side, getting up from time to time to add things or tend to something on the stove.

COOKING UTENSILS,
PLATES, SILVERWARE
2 PLACE SETTINGS
PRACTICAL FOOD
COCKTAILS &
GLASSES.

ALEX
(sipping his drink) Well,
you got a lot of action today.

ANNE
Say, what is this?

ALEX is mildly surprised at the touchy response.

ALEX
I mean who is this "Red Rover?"
What the hell do you think I
mean?

Fig. 4.2. A motion picture script page lined and marked for breakdown.

When listing scene numbers, use dashes between numbers, not commas. Always list every individual number, never inclusive numbers. The notation 16-24 does not mean 16 through 24. It means 16 and 24. This method avoids any chance of ambiguity.

When you have gone through the script and extracted and listed all the sets and numbers of

```
CAST LIST

ANNE  17-18-19-20-21-40-41-42-43-50-52-61-64-75-76-77
      78-79-81-101-102-106-107-125-126-127-128

DAVID 17-18-20-44-45-46-47-48-49-53-54-62-108-109-110

MARK  17-18-20-50-64-65-66-67-68-69-70-108-126-127-155-
      183-184-185-186
```

A

Fig. 4.3*A*. Cast list of each character followed by every scene number in which the character appears.

```
ESSENTIAL PROPS LIST

Surfboard  17-18-19-20

ALEX'S pistol  108-109-110-111-112-113

Whiskey bottle  15-16-17-18-109-110-213-214

ROVER'S Wallet  4-5-6
```

B

Fig. 4.3*B*. Essential property list followed by the numbers of every scene in which props appear.

```
COSTUME LIST

ALEX   #1 Sneakers, jeans, jersey  2-3-4-5-6-50-51
          All scenes from 174 to end.

       #2 Sport shirt, slacks  84-85-86-92

ANNE   #1 Bikini  17-18-19-20-93-94-95-96

       #2 Cocktail dress  45-46-47
```

C

Fig. 4.3C. Costume list for each character by number, followed by every scene number in which it is used.

```
INSERT LIST

Scene 23  CU Alex's hand feels edge of glass
      29  CU Coin in Baldy's palm
      64  CU Pencil traces course on chart
      93  CU Emblem on Swift's lighter
      99  CU Compass heading NNE
     100  CU Red light on police car
     123  CU Elevator indicator
```

D

Fig. 4.3*D*. An Insert list of closeups that can be shot at one time without keeping the full production crew standing by.

the scenes occurring on them respectively, repeat the same procedure for other list headings: cast, essential props, and wardrobe. These are the principal lists necessary to make up the breakdown sheets and the shooting schedule. Depending on the nature of the action, you may have to make other lists related to scheduling and action on the set. For example, a special effects list is needed if the action calls for bullet splatters, breakaway windows or furniture, gun flashes, explosions, the breaking of bottles or glasses, or smoke, fog, or rain. You may also need a list of inserts, or closeups, that can be shot without the entire crew.

For the remainder of the budget information, analyze the script and make lists of requirements for whichever of the following apply:

Camera	Makeup
Sound	Set dressing
Grip	Music
Electrical	Painting
Construction	Special FX
	Miscellaneous

Breakdown Sheets

After you have broken down the script, analyzed it, and compiled lists, the next step is to transfer all this information to the breakdown sheet (Fig. 4.4*A*) This form has spaces for all the information relating to a particular group of scenes that can be photographed at the same place simultaneously. The set lists, together along with stock shots, inserts, and animation, indicate how many breakdown sheets you will have. Each entry constitutes a group of scenes to be entered on one breakdown sheet.

Each breakdown sheet contains that group of scenes taking place on the same set or location. Thus you have at your fingertips a distillation of everything you will need to shoot at any given time and place. As you plan your production, add items to the breakdown sheet that are pertinent to your own way of working and to the specific nature of your film. You will need at least the following information on each breakdown sheet:

1. The designation SET, STOCK SHOT, INSERT, or ANIMATION
2. Number of script pages represented
3. Cast
4. Bits
5. Extras
6. Essential props
7. Special instructions
8. Scene numbers and brief synopsis of each scene.

In the script sample in Fig. 4.2 each numbered scene has been isolated by lines; the cast, props, and wardrobe have been marked; and each scene has been analyzed for items not specifically called for by the writer. The first four scenes (Scs 17-18-19-20) all occur at the same location, so they are grouped together on one breakdown sheet entitled EXT BEACH NEXT TO PIER (Fig. 4.4*B*). Notice that on the same breakdown sheet, two later script scenes (Scs. 35-36) are included because they too occur at the beach location and should therefore be shot along with the others.

Although Scene 21, ALEX's APARTMENT (Fig. 4.2), is on the same script page as the beach scenes, it is entered on another breakdown sheet entitled INT ALEX'S APARTMENT (Fig. 4.4*A*) Also on the same sheet are other scenes that are widely separated in the script but which all take place in the apartment.

Go through the entire script and group all the scenes on breakdown sheets respectively according to the following headings:

1. Set. The name of the set or location where the scene is taking place.
2. Stock Shot. A shot or scene that does not have to be shot but is available in the stock film library.
3. Inserts. Closeup shots, such as a hand signing a letter or a key being inserted in a lock, that can all be shot at one time in a relatively small setup with a small crew.
4. Animation or Artwork.

The end result of compiled breakdown sheets will be a loose-leaf, detailed analysis of your script. You can then shuffle the pages at will and put them into the necessary order for planning, shooting, or pricing. Each related group of scenes can be budgeted and scheduled as a unit independent of the continuity or other parts of the script.

PRODUCTION TITLE MOMENT OF SANITY SEQ. ______ PAGE 1

DAY OR NIGHT NIGHT

NAME OF SET INT ALEX'S APARTMENT NO. OF SCENES 10

NO. OF PAGES ______

Extra Talent and Bits	Cast and Wardrobe Change	Scene Numbers and Short Resume of Action
	Alex #2 Sport shirt and slacks	21. Alex and Anne eat dinner
	Anne #3 Sport	40. Alex and Anne settle for night
	Rover #7 Wind-breaker	
	Raoul #1 Suit	171. Anne enters apartment
	Smith #1 Suit	172. Smith in chair DOLLY BACK Gunfight
		173. Anne kneels by Rover
		174. CU Alex
		175. CU Anne and Rover
		176. CU Anne
		177. FS Apartment
		178. MS Raoul enters
		179. CU Alex and Anne
		180. CU Raoul DOLLY BACK

EFFECTS
Bullet hits on wall
Brekaway lamp
Blood

MUSIC AND MISCELLANEOUS

CONSTRUCTION ESSENTIALS

ESSENTIAL PROPS.
Food
Utensils
Pistols -
Machine gun
Pillow
Table setting
Cocktail glasses

Enterprise Printers and Stationers
7529 Sunset L.A. 46, CALIF. Telephone: 876-3533 19

A

Fig. 4.4*A*. Script breakdown sheet for interior location sequence.

PRODUCTION TITLE	MOMENT OF SANITY	SEQ.	PAGE 1 of 1
		DAY OR NIGHT	DAY
NAME OF SET	BEACH NEXT TO PIER EXT	NO. OF SCENES	6
		NO. OF PAGES	1

Extra Talent and Bits	Cast and Wardrobe Change	Scene Numbers and Short Resume of Action
23 male bathers 30 female bathers	Anne #1 Bikini David #4 Trunks	17. LS Crowded beach - MOS 18. MS Anne, David, Mark in surf - MOS
8 children 6-12	Mark #2 Trunks and robe	19. CU Anne on surfboard - MOS 20. CU David, Mark on sand - MOS
8 men in Karate suits		
	David #6 Slacks and sweat-shirt Ben #1 Slacks and sport shirt	35. MS David and Ben at railing SND 36. CU David - SND

EFFECTS

MUSIC AND MISCELLANEOUS

2 poodles on leash
Dog handler

CONSTRUCTION ESSENTIALS

ESSENTIAL PROPS.

Suntan lotion
Beach towels
Transistor radio

Enterprise Printers and Stationers
7529 Sunset L.A. 46, CALIF. Telephone: 876-3533 19

B

Fig. 4.4B. Script breakdown sheet for exterior sequence.

Up to this point only dialogue scripts have been discussed, but the same approach applies to all kinds of scripts. Figure 4.5 shows one page of a technical report film script. In marking a narrated script such as this, isolate only the scene descriptions with lines, leaving the narration side of the page unmarked. Make the same kind of analysis, notations, and lists, and transfer the material to breakdown sheets. The scenes in Fig. 4.5 would break down on three breakdown sheets as follows:

Stock shots Sc 71
Engineer's office Scs 72-73-75
Inserts Sc 74

PICTURE	NARRATION
SHOOT IN BLDG #24. 71. LONG SHOT Design Group with men working at desks. STOCK SHOT IF AVAILABLE.	The successful accomplishment of all objectives on five consecutive orbital missions has also established the Shaman Missile and Space Division as a leader in the calculation of space trajectories.
USE ONE OF THE OFFICES IN ENGINEERING BLDG. 72. MED TWO SHOT Two engineers working at desk. They have a number of reports scattered on desk. DUMMY REPORTS → SHOOT WITH #73-75	The amount of effort which is required to plot a typical mission trajectory and its variables is not generally known. For example, each mission requires . . .
SHOOT WITH #72-75 73. CLOSE SHOT Engineer as he picks up booklets one at a time as they are named and drops them on desk. When he comes to the last one he opens it.	. . . a Basic Trajectory, a Mistake Analysis, Test Objectives, a Static Report, Time Study, Safety Study, and Probability Study.
74. CLOSEUP COMPUTER INPUT CALCULATIONS as Engineer makes them. INSERT.	While the use of computers plays a large part in conducting these studies, each problem and its ramifications must be thoroughly analyzed before it can be set up for computer calculation.
SHOOT WITH #72-73 75. CLOSE SHOT Above Engineer as he flips booklet open to check printout symbols. NEED ACTUAL REPORT.	Computation of the mission trajectory, for example, requires the consideration of more than one hundred parameters . .

Fig. 4.5. Split-page narration script lined and marked for breakdown.

Other scenes in the script may also belong on the above three breakdown sheets, but only those scenes from the script page in Fig. 4.5 are listed here.

Production Schedule

Preparing a production schedule means deciding how much time is to be spent on each thing that has to be done—preparing the set, shooting the scene, editing, recording, mixing, negative cutting. Lacking experience, you will probably find the most difficult task is estimating how long it takes to shoot a dialogue scene and how many such scenes you can reasonably plan on completing in a day. There is no set rule because scenes differ widely, but you can almost always be sure that more time will be required than you think. Even though the action of a scene may be quite short, the production crew may need a much longer time to work out the details of lighting, camera movement, microphone placement, and so on. Understanding this is essential to accurate scheduling. Consult freely with technical people.

All creative people do not work the same way—some are quick, some slow. One director may customarily shoot many takes and alternative scenes; another may usually do few retakes and no alternative scenes. Classically, actors range in temperament from steady to volatile, but each is predictable if you are familiar with his or her personality. Know something about the people you are dealing with. Also, there are endless conditions that will affect the time required to shoot a scene—waiting for a train to come by, waiting for traffic to be just right, waiting for just the correct sun angle. If it sometimes appears that all nature and society are deliberately conspiring to frustrate the filmmaker, remember Murphy's famous law—"If anything can possibly go wrong, it will,"—and do everything you can to anticipate and provide countermeasures to the imminent disasters.

Making up a production schedule requires familiarity with the process of filmmaking. Each film is unique, and you will be continually required to anticipate and solve new problems that are somehow related to the old problems you solved on other films. Develop a knack for analyzing a scene and approximating the way it will be set up and directed. Look, for example, at the script in Fig. 4.2. Here, Scenes 17-18-19-20 are all occurring at different parts of the same beach. Scene 17 is one wide shot of the beach filled with people. The director will conceivably pick a suitable spot and shoot without having to rehearse actors since he is shooting the actual documentary scene as it happens. Although the script calls for one shot, he will probably shoot one or more closer shots or even a second full view of the beach from a different spot. Bearing in mind how both director and crew work, estimate how long it will take to select the camera positions, to set up, and to shoot. A scene like this could reasonably be completed in one-quarter of a day, or two hours. But the time really depends on what the director plans to do with the scene—shoot it as called for or expand it into something more complex. Scene 18 almost certainly would not be shot from one camera angle as written. It is a master scene that the director will break down into several shorter shots. To estimate the time required, you will have to make an educated guess about how the director will do it. How long will it take to set and rehearse the action? Or has this been done previously? Will the surf be rough or gentle? This will definitely affect how rapidly the shooting goes. The level of production must also be considered. If the production is lavish, it may call for special items such as platforms built out into the surf, underwater cameras, booster arc lights, and so on. If the production is spare, it may even be shot without reflectors. Obviously more equipment and more technicians mean more time. Evaluate all these variables. Scene 19 is clearly a part of the action in Scene 18 and you would consider shooting it along with the various angles of Scene 18. In Scene 20, in addition to the two principal actors, David and Mark, there is important background action involving the wrestlers that must be set up and rehearsed. This scene is ostensibly simple, yet its staging and shooting can be quite complex since the foreground and background actions must work together. Again, the level of production along with your scene analysis will determine the time required for shooting.

Shooting Schedule

When you have decided how much time will be needed to shoot each scene, make up a shooting schedule. (See Figs. 4.6*A* & *B*). Include the following information:

Shooting date
Name of set or location
Numbers of the scenes to be shot
Brief description of the action
Where the scene is to be shot
Cast required
Costumes required
Number of script pages involved
Time allocated in fractions of a day.

SHOOTING SCHEDULE

PROD: THE GLOOMY MAGENTA MIDGET

Date and Date	Set or Location and Scene Numbers	WHERE LOCATED	Cast
FRI 3/26	INT WILSON LIVING ROOM NIGHT Sc 32-34 Bob has glass of beer -- Talks on phone 4 1/8 pages 1 day	Stage #4	Bob #4 Ellen #2
SAT 3/27	INT AEROSPACE PLANT DAY Sc 48 Men walking to their jobs 1 page 1/4 day	Acme Corp.	Bob #7 Will #2 Ed #2 Bogen #2
	EXT PLANT LUNCH TABLE AND PHONE BOOTH Sc 68-69-70 Men listen to radio during lunch. Bob calls Ellen 2 3/4 pages 1/2 day	Acme Corp.	Bob #10 Will #4 Ed #4
	EXT PLANT GATE DAY Sc 71-79 Bob walks thru gate, talks to Hank 3/4 pages 1/4 day	Acme Corp.	Bob #6, 3 Hank
MON 3/29	INT LOCKER ROOM DAY Sc 12-47-62-63-76-77 Bob arrives - Men talk about the game 4 1/4 pages 1 day	Stage #7	Bob #2,6,11 Will #1,2 Ed #1 Bogen #3,4
TUES 3/30	INT WILSON LIVING ROOM NIGHT Sc 49-50-54-58 Bob looks at news broadcast and leaves to go bowling 4 3/4 pages 1 day	Stage #4	Bob #8 Ellen #5 Skip #3

A

Fig. 4.6*A*. Motion picture shooting schedule.

SHOOTING SCHEDULE

PROD: MOMENT OF MADNESS

Day and date	Set or Location and Scene Numbers	Where Located	Cast
MON 6/16	EXT BEACH NEXT TO PIER DAY Sc 18-19 David and Mark teach Bella to surf 1/4 page MOS 3/4 day	Sundown Beach	Anne #1 David #4 Mark #2
	EXT BEACH NEXT TO PIER DAY Sc 17 Full view of the beach 1/8 page MOS 1/4 day	Sundown Beach	
TUES 6/17	EXT BEACH NEXT TO PIER DAY Sc 20 David and Mark on the sand 1/8 page SOUND 1/2 day	Sundown Beach	David #4 Mark #2 Extras
	EXT BEACH NEXT TO PIER DAY Sc 35-36 David and Ben at railing talking about the robbery 1 page SOUND 1/2 day	Sundown Beach	David #6 Ben #1

B

Fig. 4.6*B*. Motion picture shooting schedule for sequence broken down in Fig. 4.4*B*.

Carefully analyze the breakdown material for the special requirements of each block of scenes. The tide may be suitable for beach scenes only during four days of the month. Obviously, you will schedule such scenes for those four days, shifting other scenes to other days. Every film has individual peculiarities that can affect the order of shooting, and you should consider very carefully the total result when you assign the shooting day for a scene. In making up the shooting schedule, be guided by the following:

1. Shoot in script continuity only if possible and convenient.

2. Stay on one set or location until you shoot all the scenes that occur there. This is the fastest and most economical way to shoot (with certain exceptions). For example, if both the first and last scenes in your film occur on the same street corner, shoot the two scenes consecutively. An exception is the schedule in Fig. 4.6B, where shooting is scheduled to begin in the living room set on Friday, followed by shooting at the aircraft plant and the locker room on Saturday and Monday. On Tuesday, shooting is once again resumed on the living room set. The question arises; why break up the shooting on the living room set? Why not finish all the living room scenes before going on to the others. The answer involves time and money: the aircraft plant is only available on Saturday. Also, the characters, Will and Ed, appear only in the aircraft plant and locker room scenes. By shooting these two scenes on consecutive days, the two actors can be released from the payroll. Besides, no real problem is created by leaving and returning to the living room set—no expense is involved, since the set is left as is over the weekend and requires no rebuilding or rerigging.

3. Schedule the most expensive items for the shortest length of time. If you have a very expensive actor, on a weekly basis, it may save money to shoot all his scenes consecutively and get him off the payroll even though this means going

back later to several locations to shoot the scenes he was not in. The cost of going back may be less than keeping the actor on salary to sit on a set while the scenes he is not in are being shot. The same applies to the scheduling of expensive equipment or processes. Study the alternatives and arrive at the one most expeditious for you in time, money, convenience, or aesthetics.

4. Availability. The availability of actors, sets, locations, and equipment greatly influences the schedule. It is a fact of film production that you can't always get everything you need when you need it. The actor you want is available for only two weeks during the next six months. Your mountain lake location will be snowed in this year until the middle of June. The festival you planned to shoot has been postponed until next year. Since such conditions arising without warning can spell disaster, always check on availability before you make definite plans.

5. Weather. Shoot all exteriors first. If you shoot the interiors first and the weather turns bad, you will have to wait around—sometimes at great expense—until the weather is good again. Always have an alternate plan. For every exterior have an interior *cover set* ready so that you can shoot in case of inclement weather. This principle applies to any situation in which your shooting depends on something not entirely within your control. Cover yourself by having something else ready to be shot.

6. Preparation time. It takes time to build sets and miniatures, to prepare locations, and to conduct tests. Don't schedule something to be shot before it is ready. Confer with all the people involved and keep track of the status of everything.

Cost Computation

To compute costs you need to know three things: how many items (people, equipment, and supplies) you will have to pay for, how long the length of time each is to be used, and the unit price of each item. The shooting schedule indicates the length of time; and the production breakdown, consisting of breakdown sheets and production lists, shows how many items will be needed. The prices you must pay depend on the conditions under which you are making your film. If you produce under craft-union conditions, all wage scales and working conditions will be clearly specified by contract. (See *Hollywood Production Manual* in The Reading List). If you produce on a nonunion basis, costs will depend on whatever negotiations and arrangements you can make. Charges for equipment and facilities can be determined from the readily available price schedules of rental houses and studios.

Look at the breakdown sheet in Fig. 4.4*B*. From this you can develop a detailed list of budget items for the six scenes (17-18-19-20-35-36) on that sheet. Check the shooting schedule (Fig. 4.6*B*) against the breakdown sheet (Fig. 4.2). The Shooting Schedule shows that you will spend two days shooting most of the six scenes. The breakdown sheet tells you what cast and main items you will use.

Scenes 17-18-19-20 are marked "MOS," which means that they are to be shot silent. Scenes 35–36 are marked "Sound." Analyze all the scenes and their requirements to determine the necessary elements that have not yet been listed. As you proceed, you will find that the detailed budget list contains many more items than the breakdown sheet calls for. Although trucks are not mentioned in the script or on the breakdown sheet, you know that everything has to be hauled to the location. But before you can decide on how many vehicles will be needed, you must determine how much has to be hauled. Reflectors are not called out on the breakdown sheet, but you know that when you shoot outdoors they will be used, plus one grip for each reflector. Obviously you will have to feed and house people if they are going to be on location more than one day, and you have to transport them. Thus the task of budgeting and scheduling consists of relentless and painstaking analysis. Figuring everything possible for the six scenes, we arrive at the needs listed in Fig. 4.7. Notice that these needs fall within eleven of the twenty-four budget groups and apply only to Scenes 17-18-19-20-35-36.

When you have detailed everything you will need and how long you will need it, figure the cost of each item by multiplying its rate by the amount you need in days, weeks, or quantity (notice on the budget form [Fig. 4.7] the three columns—Quantity, Rate, and Totals). To help you compute costs, keep at hand copies of craft guild contracts and rate schedules, equipment rental and purchase catalogues, and price

Page No.
1.

TITLE MOMENT OF MADNESS PICTURE NO.

EXT BEACH NEXT TO PIER Scs 17-18-19-20-35-36 DATE PREPARED

ACCOUNT NUMBER	DESCRIPTION	DAYS, WKS, OR QUANTITY	RATE	TOTALS
2	PRODUCTION STAFF			
	Director			
	4 principal actors			
	1st Assistant Director			
	2nd Assistant Director			
	Script Supervisor			
	Note: Production Staff is on either salary or contract for the entire picture. Their costs will be added later to the total budget.			
3	CAST			
	53 Extras (bathers)	1 day		
	8 Children	1 day		
	8 Extras (wrestlers)	1 day		
6	LOCATION			
	Scouting (transportation, meals, and hotel for Director, Production Manager, and driver)	3 days		
	Hotel 32 people	2 days		
	Meals 32 people	2 days		
	Location rental	2 days		
	1 portable dressing room	2 days		
	1 portable rest room	2 days		
	2 drivers			
	1 contact man			
7	CAMERA			
	1 1st cameraman	2 days		
	1 camera operator	2 days		
	1 camera assistant	2 days		
	Camera equipment rental			
	Camera and accessories	2 days		
	Camera crane	2 days		

ENTERPRISE STATIONERS, HOLLYWOOD
NO. 88

Fig. 4.7. Requirements for cast crew, and location expenses for sequence broken down in Fig. 4.4*B*. Representative of large studio-type production.

Page No. 2.

TITLE MOMENT OF MADNESS PICTURE NO.

EXT BEACH NEXT TO PIER SCS 17-18-19-20-35-36 DATE PREPARED

ACCOUNT NUMBER	DESCRIPTION	DAYS, WKS, OR QUANTITY	RATE	TOTALS
8	GRIP			
	1 key grip	2 days		
	2 company grips	2 days		
	Grip truck rental	2 days		
10	SOUND			
	1 sound director	2 days		
	1 assistant	2 days		
	Sound equipment rental	2 days		
14	PROPS			
	1 Prop person	2 days		
	1 cabana	2 days		
	1 surfboard	2 days		
	1 transistor radio	2 days		
	Purchase: sun tan lotion, beach towels, beach chairs, dark glasses, canned drinks, etc.			
16	WARDROBE			
	1 wardrobe person	2 days		
	Rental: 8 karate constumes	2 days		
17	MAKEUP AND HAIRDRESSING			
	1 makeup person	2 days		
	1 hairdresser	1 day		
	Purchase supplies			
18	ACTION ITEMS			
	2 poodles	1 day		
	1 dog handler	1 day		
21	TRANSPORTATION			
	3 cars for staff	2 days		
	2 trucks (camera, sound, grip, props)	2 days		
	2 busses (crew and extras)	2 days		
	7 drivers	2 days		

ENTERPRISE STATIONERS, HOLLYWOOD
NO. 88

Fig. 4.7. *(Continued)*

schedules for raw stock, sound studios, stages, optical houses, and other services. The Budget outline in Fig. 4.7 (EXT BEACH NEXT TO PIER) includes only the basic requirements for shooting the six scenes involved. To arrive at the budget for the entire script, add the requirements of all other groups of scenes in the script to the postproduction estimates and the costs of staff, overhead, taxes, insurance, and licenses.

Although the budget analysis described above is based on a feature studio approach, the procedure for shooting the same scenes in a more modest way follows the same method. Assume you are an individual filmmaker shooting these scenes on a low budget. You will have to do the same things in a different way. For example, look at #6 Location on the list. For your film you must scout locations just as a large producer does, but you go by yourself and do your own driving. Also, during shooting you will not rent portable rest rooms and dressing rooms, but you must see to it that some kind of local facilities are available for your cast and crew. Overall a small producer cuts down on everything, relying on ingenuity, energy, talent, enthusiasm, persuasiveness, and luck.

POSTPRODUCTION BUDGETING

Up to this point only the costs involved in the shooting of the picture have been considered. Even though the production phase is responsible for your largest expenses, time and money are still needed to get the picture finished and into a composite print. The principal items included in postproduction are as follows:

Picture editing
Optical effects and titles
Sound effects editing and music editing
Mixing
Negative cutting

Picture Editing

Estimating picture editing time depends on the kind of picture being made and on whether it is edited electronically on tape or mechanically on film. Feature editing on film generally requires from two to three weeks per reel (one *reel* is ten minutes of screen time), including sound effects cutting, music cutting, mixing, and negative cutting. Thus for a film picture of nine reels (ninety minutes), the editing could take from eighteen to twenty-seven weeks.

Conventionally the film editor has an assistant as well as a music cutter, a sound effects cutter, and a negative cutter. On smaller productions one person alone may do all the editing and cutting. Without assistants to help with the routine mechanical tasks that make up the bulk of film editing, the job may take much longer to complete. Some pictures can be made faster than others. For example, a one-reel narrated industrial movie on film that has been shot strictly according to the script can easily be edited in about a week.

Optical Effects and Titles

Optical effects increase film editing time, since each effect must be planned, ordered, made up in the optical printer, checked, and laid into the picture, all of which is tedious and slow.

You may edit your picture electronically, even though it has been shot on film. In such a situation, after shooting, the laboratory transfers the film picture into a computer for editing. You may then edit the picture by electronically ordering the computer to assemble the visual information the way you want it. When editing is complete, the laboratory will transfer the edited picture from the computer back onto either film or videotape, or both.

Electronic editing is faster than film editing, and a feature movie may be edited in from two to four weeks (optical effects included) as against ten to twenty weeks for film. Although it seems that the only choice to make is electronic editing, there are other considerations beside time. In conventional terms, electronic editing facilities are expensive—several hundred dollars per day—while film editing facilities may run from less than fifty dollars down to almost nothing per day. Although electronic editing time is short, the high rental rate quickly brings the total cost up to and past that of a longer film editing period. The cost advantage of electronic editing accrues mainly to the producer of pictures made with interest-bearing capital. The financial advantage of completing the editing of a motion picture in three weeks, say, as opposed to eighteen or twenty weeks means earlier relief from interest-bearing loan payments and earlier returns from the box office. These advantages are worth paying a high rental rate for facilities.

Another advantage of electronic editing is that optical effects of even great complexity may be done in the computer at the time of editing at no extra expense other than editing time. This eliminates all the expensive, time-consuming operations involved in setting up and making optical effects on film.

Sound Effects Editing and Music Editing

Sound effects editing and music editing are done the same way for a motion picture shot on either film or videotape, and the costs are about the same. For film, the laboratory makes black-and-white duplicates of the editor's workprint or it makes black-and-white film transfers from the electronically edited picture. In both situations the sound editors edit the music and sound effects to fit the black-and-white film duplicate. The edited sound tracks then go through the mixing session with the edited workprint. After the mix, the mixed track may be transferred to either film or videotape.

Electronic editing is undoubtedly too expensive for the smaller producer or the lone film-maker since the saving in time may not offset the high cost of electronic facilities. If you work in your own editing room with your own equipment, you can afford to spend more time editing. Although your own time and labor are worth money, until they are worth the several hundred dollars a day that electronic editing costs, it is less expensive to work in film. In editing a picture under craft-union conditions, if you add up the costs for a film editor and assistant, film editing room, supplies, and optical effects, the total will probably be very close to the cost of editing the same picture electronically. But the difference in time required may be startling—twenty weeks, say, for film editing against two weeks for electronic editing. You must decide whether the time saved by use of electronic editing is worth the cash you must spend for electronic facilities.

Mixing

The speed at which *sound track mixing* progresses depends on the complexity of the desired effect and on the number of tracks. The quickest track to mix is one with a voice track—either dialogue or narration—accompanied by a music track and a relatively simple sound effects track. It takes longer to mix a track composed of several effects and music tracks that rely on intricate fades and combinations for their effectiveness. Time for mixing ranges from a half minute to three minutes of screen time per hour. (See Chapter 10.)

Negative Cutting

Negative cutting (see Chapter 11) consists of breaking down all negative scenes into individual rolls, listing edge numbers, and assembling the film negative to conform to the edited workprint. It is a purely mechanical operation and the time required for it depends on the availability of all negatives, the number of scenes to be cut, and the skill of the cutter. These things considered, negative cutting takes from one to three days per reel (ten minutes).

There is no way to determine exactly how long it will take to edit a picture. It depends on the kind of picture and its length, the amount of footage involved, and the complexity and number of sound tracks and optical effects. A mass of documentary material takes longer to coordinate than a dramatic picture with a fairly straight story line.

Sample Estimates

A routine sound track consisting of dialogue, library music, and a few sound effects is easier and faster both to edit and to mix. As you work with motion pictures, keep a record of how much time it takes to complete different kinds of tasks. Eventually you will build up a backlog of experience and information, so that you can budget almost to the minute and the penny. Until you have this experience, use the following estimates as a guide:

Film editing (including SFX and music): one half reel per week.

Electronic editing (plus SFX and music): three to five reels per week.

Mixing: Two minutes per hour.

Negative cutting: one half reel per day.

Remember that these are only working estimates subject to revision upward or downward depending on the picture, the operation, and the people involved. They are generalizations from which you may wish to deviate.

Budgeting does not end with a preproduction estimate but continues on through completion of the film. The flexible nature of moviemaking demands that you watch the progress of production carefully lest the costs quickly overrun the budget. Creative movie people—particularly art directors, production designers, and directors—tend to consider any expense worth the result; unhappily, however, all budgets, even very large ones, must be limited. Thus it is not creative abandon alone but sheer diversity that threatens the motion picture budget. Expenditures may accrue in several places at the same time. For example, while the laboratory bill is growing, sets are being built, locations scouted, supplies purchased, and sound recorded. Without careful monitoring, it is quite possible for all the money to be spent long before the end is in sight. Both producer and Production Manager must keep track of expenditures and see to it that the money lasts until the picture is finished.

Keeping Track of Expenses

To keep an accurate running account of what is happening during film production, the operation should be scheduled so that everyone knows at all times what he is supposed to do and where he is supposed to be. Although a complete shooting and production schedule is always prepared in advance, conditions in moviemaking change rapidly and often, necessitating constant reevaluation and rescheduling. You must have available accurate information at regular intervals about the progress of the film. This is done by means of the following:

Daily production meeting
Revised shooting schedule
Daily call sheet
Daily work order
Daily production report
Daily log
Weekly budget summary.

Daily Production Meeting

This meeting brings together all concerned department heads and the production manager to discuss the progress and problems of production and to make appropriate plans for the next day's shooting. Although the meeting may involve many people in a large studio or may consist or only one or two individuals on a small production, the purpose is the same: to plan for tomorrow's shooting on the basis of what is happening today.

Revised Shooting Schedule

If something has slowed down the shooting, scenes scheduled for today will have to be rescheduled for tomorrow. This in turn may mean that certain equipment must be held over for another day. The actor called for tomorrow won't be needed until the day after, and so on. As a result of this meeting, the production manager issues the next day's shooting schedule, call sheet, and work order.

Daily Call Sheet

This sheet lists all cast, bits, and extras needed for the next day's shooting. It should contain at least the following information: the actor's name, the name of the character to be played, wardrobe needed, where to report, and the time to report.

Daily Work Order

This is a list of the technical requirements for the next day's shooting. It specifies what crews (camera, sound, electrical, makeup, etc.), transportation, and equipment will be needed.

Daily Production Report

This is a detailed report of what has been accomplished during the day's shooting. It is compiled by the assistant director from his own notes and from those of the script supervisor. It should contain the following information:

Production name or number
Name of set
Date
Number of setups today
Number of scenes shot today
Total number of scenes in the script
Number of scenes shot previously

Total number of scenes shot
Number of script scenes left to shoot
Number of days in shooting schedule
Number of days to date
Number of days behind schedule
Number of days ahead of schedule
Time of today's shooting call
Time shooting started
Time lunch started and finished
Time dinner started and finished
Time shooting finished
Total footage shot today
Net footage shot today
Total footage shot to date
Net footage shot to date
Slate numbers shot today
Script scenes completed today
Number of extras used
Cast used: Time called; time arrived on set; time dismissed.

Daily Log

This is a minute-by-minute record of the day's work (Fig. 4.8).

As you see, the information on the daily production report provides a detailed running summary of how the shooting is going. It is the basic source of information for the daily production meeting. Again, the extent and completeness of this report depends on the kind of production involved. For a feature film or a large studio operation, a detailed report is essential for daily planning and adherence to the budget. On a smaller production, keeping a daily record is necessary but it might not be economical to spend the time necessary to compile such an all-embracing report. However, examine the log in Fig. 4.8. It records precisely how much time is required to set up a scene and light it, to rehearse the actors, to lay dolly tracks, to adjust lights, to shoot, and to do all the tasks required on the set. A file of such information is invaluable in estimating future schedules and budgets. The amount of information on the daily production report varies with every producing company, and you may find it more expedient to design a report form that is workable for your particular organization or accounting system.

Weekly Budget Summary

This type of report, a summary of all expenditures to date, may be issued weekly or as often as you see fit. Its purpose is to let you know what has been spent and how much has been accomplished. This enables you to make reasonable decisions about the future conduct of production. Should scenes be eliminated? Should more money be spent on other scenes? Should an elaborate set be made more simple? How many more extras will the budget allow? To make any and all such decisions affecting your film and its budget, you need to know exactly the status of your expenditures to date.

Keeping track of expenditures and the final summing is a job for an accountant. Tax laws, social security, and trust regulations create some stringent conditions for any person or company involved in producing films for profit. You must keep accurate records of all money transactions and should file periodically federal, state, and/or municipal reports. Since laxity in budget management and accounting can quickly lead to financial disaster, be sure to have the services of a business manager familiar with the hazards of cost accounting for a picture whose budget involves more than the cost of film and processing.

THE CARE AND FEEDING OF SPONSORS

The nontheatrical film in the United States is big business, and several thousand pictures are made every year in many fields—education, industry, sales, business, promotion, propaganda, government. Most of these are produced under contracts awarded to nontheatrical film producers on the basis of competitive bidding. For example, if the Department of the Interior wants a film on conservation, it invites nontheatrical producers to bid for the job. The contract is awarded to the qualified producer who says he can complete the film for the lowest price. Most nontheatrical film production is done on this lowest bid basis. Government agencies are required by law to accept the lowest bidder, but a few private firms base their selection of a film producer on what they believe to be ability, talent, and the probable excellence of the completed film.

The main difference between theatrical and

DAILY LOG PROD: #322 FALL OF NIGHT
Crew Call - 8:00 AM Director - 8:00 AM Shooting - 9:00 AM

Sc 131A	8:00-9:22	Setup equip. Lineup and light. INT BARN
	9:22-9:26	Place people
	9:26-9:43	Director explaining scene to people
	9:43-9:50	Adjust lighting
	9:50-9:55	Shoot 1 take
131B	9:55-10:04	Shoot 2 takes
131C	10:04-10:10	Move closer
	10:10-10:15	Shoot 2 takes
131D	10:15-10:20	Shoot 1 take
155A	10:20-10:25	Select setup
	10:25-10:43	Line and light
	10:43-10:45	Rehearse
	10:45-10:47	Shoot 1 take
155B	10:47-10:55	Rehearse
	10:55-11:10	Shoot 7 takes
155C	11:10-11:25	Shoot 8 takes
155D	11:25-11:30	Shoot 1 take
135A	11:30-11:40	Move closer
	11:40-11:42	Shoot 1 take
145A	11:42-12:07	Select setups
	12:07-1:07	Lunch
	1:07-2:05	Line and light reverse full shot
	2:05-2:20	Rehearse
	2:20-2:25	Shoot 1 take
145B	2:25-2:34	Shoot 3 takes
145C	2:34-2:40	Line and light
	2:40-2:45	Shoot 2 takes
133A	2:45-2:50	Select setups
	2:50-2:55	Line and light
	2:55-3:00	Shoot 1 take
133B	3:00-3:10	Line and light
	3:10-3:15	Shoot 1 take
133C	3:15-3:20	Line and light
	3:20-3:23	Shoot 1 take
133D	3:23-3:27	Line and Light
	3:27-3:30	Shoot 1 take
133E	3:30-3:36	Line and Light
	3:36-3:40	Shoot 1 take
133F	3:40-3:45	Line and light
	3:45-3:50	Shoot 2 takes
133G	3:50-3:55	Line and light
	3:55-3:56	Shoot 1 take
157A	3:56-4:02	Line and light
	4:02-4:06	Shoot 2 takes
143X1A	4:06-4:15	Line and light
	4:15-4:20	Shoot 1 take
136A	4:20-4:30	Select setup
	4:30-4:45	Shoot 9 takes
145D	4:45-4:55	Line and light
	4:55-5:00	Shoot 1 take
	5:00	Company dismissed

Fig. 4.8. A representative daily log of shooting, as kept by the script supervisor.

nontheatrical films besides subject matter is in the way they are financed and used. The theatrical feature is made with money supplied by some person or studio interested in speculating for profit. It is aimed at theater audiences that will pay money to see it. If the film succeeds, its producer and backers make a great deal of money. If it fails, they lose.

Nontheatrical Film

The nontheatrical film, which includes documentaries, educationals, publicity films, industrial, scientific, and other specialized films, is not made to yield money from box office sales. Educational films are usually made and financed by individual producers for possible profit from the sale of prints to schools. Other nontheatricals are paid for by firms or government agencies to be shown free to public, their purpose being propaganda, goodwill, or the sale of products. Some large companies and government agencies maintain their own film production units, but most of them hire nontheatrical producers to make their films for them.

Sponsor

The germ of the idea is the starting point. Usually it originates in the mind of someone who is not himself a professional filmmaker. It may originate with an individual or a group: the board of directors of a company, a commanding officer in the armed services, a school principal, the public relations officer in a government department, a member of a university faculty. This person or group of persons is known as the *sponsor.*

Let us say the sponsor engages you as the producer. Your task will be to carry out his ideas in an acceptable film and to make some money in the process. As producer, your association, if limited to a single film, will last three months to a year. During that time, all sorts of unexpected troubles may occur. The sponsor may dislike the script, and fail to reach agreement with you on it. The film may take much longer to produce than the contract allows. When it is finished, it may not meet the sponsor's expectations. It may even leave behind it a trail of legal action and unpleasantness. In this event the sponsor is likely to avoid films in the future. Remember that filmmaking is much more than a technical process. It is an assemblage of very human abilities and frailties; and even at its best, it is a precarious balance of uncertainties. On the other hand your relations with the sponsor may grow increasingly cordial, resulting in a successful film and future contracts.

Once the idea for the film is agreed on, the sponsor is almost certain to ask what it will cost. Since short films have been made for as little as a hundred dollars and as much as several hundred thousand, it is obviously impossible to take an average. However, on the basis of your experience and what you know of the sponsor's requirements, you should be able to quote a figure within twenty-five percent of the correct one. Afterwards, you will of course budget the picture accurately on the basis of the first script, and should then be within the limit of five percent above or below the actual cost. Sometimes the sponsor has a fixed ceiling, so that you can tailor the film to the known figure.

Producer

Nontheatrical producers range from one-man companies up to large organizations operating at almost the same level as feature film producers. You don't have to own a studio to bid on or be awarded a nontheatrical film contract since you can easily hire qualified people and facilities in the larger cities for any length of time you inquire.

As a nontheatrical producer you are a contractor, very similar to a building contractor, who undertakes to manufacture a motion picture according to a set of specifications for a fee. If you contract to produce a film for a sponsor, be sure that such specifications for the film are clearly understood by all parties concerned, and are in writing. Your profit is included in the fixed fee, and it can easily be consumed in reshooting and revising as a result of ambiguous specifications. Many a nontheatrical film producer has paid money out of his own pocket to make up for misunderstandings in the original agreement. When a sponsor publishes or sends out an invitation for producers to bid on a film, he usually includes specifications for what he expects.

Bid Requirements

Although bid requirements will differ with each sponsor, the following items are typical of what you as producer can expect when you bid on a film contract:

1. Basis of Award. The most common basis of award is the lowest price bid from a responsible bidder. A responsible bidder has the qualifications the sponsor deems necessary to do the job. Some government agencies consider a bidder responsible only if he can show that he has produced a minimum of five pictures of the type wanted of an acceptable quality. But the sponsor may establish what standards he will accept and from whom.
2. Bidder's Facilities. The bidder is required to provide the address of his facilities and to

describe them. A prudent sponsor will verify this information.

3. Script Conferences. The number and location of all script conferences between the sponsor and the successful bidder.

4. Completion Time. The exact day and date the completed film is to be delivered. Delays caused by circumstances not under the producer's control may be considered in negotiating a later delivery date.

5. Performance Bond. The producer is required to furnish a bond with surety in an amount equal to the contract price guaranteeing performance of the contract.

6. Changes and Additions. Any changes or additions to the picture must be authorized in advance by the sponsor's change order or a new contract. This means that the producer is responsible for added expenses unless the sponsor first gives approval.

7. Releases. The producer is responsible for getting all releases for people, locations, music, and stock footage. He must pay all music royalties and television clearance fees.

8. Ownership of Material. All of the stock footage, original, or negative photographed for or used in the picture, and all tapes, sound tracks, and transfers are the property of the sponsor. The producer has no right to duplicate or lend any original, negative, prints, outtakes, or trims. Of course, any agreement about the disposition of this material may be made between the sponsor and producer. For example, the producer may make the film at a lower price in exchange for all the footage not used in the final print.

9. Material to be Delivered to the Sponsor before Final Payment is Made. Although any agreement can be made, the sponsor usually specifies that he owns the following items:

(a) Workprint
(b) Conformed negative or AB rolls
(c) Composite magnetic sound track and optical negative track
(d) All tapes and transfers used to make the composite sound track
(e) All original outtakes and trims
(f) All workprint outtakes and trims.

10. Payment. A description of exactly how and when payment is to be made.

11. Film Specifications. The producer is required to make a picture that is of high photographic quality, technically accurate, and psychologically sound. Any part of the film that does not meet the highest standards of the motion picture industry can be rejected and the producer can be required to redo the work to meet the acceptable standard. The following should be made explicit:

(a) Purpose of the film
(b) Intended audience
(c) Film content
(d) Script: the producer must supply a preliminary script, a shooting script, the narrator's script, and the final script. Each version to be approved by the sponsor.
(e) The type of film to be used
(f) All crews must be professionally competent.

All of the above may appear overly meticulous, but detailed specifications and agreements are vital to the success of any contractual operation. The essence of nontheatrical film production is financial rather than aesthetic. The sponsor is interested in art, culture, and society only to the extent that they make him, his products, and his politics look attractive.

Submitting Bids as a Producer

As a producer bidding for a film contract, you must also put your bid in terms that unmistakably specify what you will and will not do for the money paid. It is common practice to submit a bid in letter form, repeating the sponsor's specifications along with your own, as follows:

1. Refer to the sponsor's bid request by name or number and state your bid price. Say that the basis for the price quoted is explained in subsequent paragraphs.

2. Describe the length, amount of animation and live action, and the type of film it is to be photographed on.

3. The producer (your name or that of your company) will supply facilities, equipment, personnel, and materials for the production of the following requirements:

(a) Script, to include one complete revision of the first draft submitted and one "polish" of such revision. Further revision will require more money. Without this limitation, it is possible to go on endlessly revising the script without payment.

(b) The producer will provide live action production including crew.

(c) Animation production. Specify that this applies only to simple animation such as backgrounds, cel overlays, wipe-offs, and cycles. If the sponsor wants straight-ahead or character animation, the high costs involved will necessitate separate negotiations.

(d) Music and sound effects. Specify whether the music is to be an original score or library music. Specify the number of musicians to be used, and indicate the extent and source of the sound effects.

(e) The producer will provide editing and rerecording.

(f) The producer will provide all processing through delivery of the first composite print.

4. List everything you expect the sponsor to furnish, such as production space and power, consultative and technical assistance, operating personnel who may appear in the film, demonstration and allied equipment, and any liaison with departments and personnel that may be involved.

5. Payment. Indicate how and when you expect to get paid for the job. Progress payments are generally accepted throughout the nontheatrical film business. Under this plan payment is often made in three equal, progressive installments. One-third is due and payable on approval of script and production planning, one-third on completion of shooting, and the final third on delivery of the first composite release print.

Basis of Bid Invitation

Many bid invitations are based on an approved script, and a copy is given to you as a bidder from which to develop your estimate. But you are frequently asked to submit a bid on a film for which the script has not yet been written. Although this is difficult, it can be done if the specifications are clear and airtight. If the film's limits are not spelled out definitely, costs can easily exceed the price you have agreed on, and you, as producer, may end up paying the difference.

At some time you will probably be asked how much you charge to make a film. As we have seen in the discussion on the level of production (see p. 53), it all depends on the kind of film. But potential film sponsors are usually not aware of or receptive to this fact. They generally understand better when you counter with another question, "How much does it cost to build a house?" Obviously, it all depends on the house. So it is with film.

Cost Estimate Categories

When you produce nontheatrical films, finding sponsors will consume a large part of your time. Your income consists of the profit from each film contract, so you will constantly be seeking new contracts before the old ones have been completed. This means that you will often have to quote prices on partially formulated ideas and idle suggestions. Most prospective sponsors want a ballpark estimate—a price in the range of what the film will actually cost, such as, "about four thousand dollars," or "between sixty and seventy thousand." But ballpark figures are dangerous because the film you envision may be entirely different from the film in the prospective sponsor's mind. In the schedule that follows, nontheatrical films are arranged into five categories according to the level of production and the probable cost range. This schedule permits both you and your intended sponsor to have the same film in mind as you discuss costs. Obviously these categories cannot be priced exactly, but they are helpful when you try to explain how much it costs to make a film. Also, the cost range for each category provides enough leeway to prevent you from committing yourself to a price that can't be met. Sometimes you can include minimum art work within the cost quoted; but extensive animation must always be budgeted separately. Costs are quoted on the basis of running time, with *one screen minute* as the basic unit. Complete production includes everything from script preparation through delivery of the final picture.

Category 1. Selection and editing of stock motion picture footage into a silent picture, including negative cutting and release printing. Generally applies to films used for displays, briefings, and other short-time uses. Sufficient research is included for the preparation of caption sheets or notes for speakers.

Cost Range. Up to $300 per screen minute.

Category 2. Research, script, and complete production of either a sound motion picture with postrecorded narration or a silent picture with subtitles. Generally, at least fifty percent of the completed film must come from existing stock footage. This includes limited interior lighting setups and exterior photography.

Cost Range. $300 to $600 per screen minute.

Category 3. Research, script, and complete production of a motion picture with post-recorded narration and sound effects. In some cases live sound may be included. This category generally applies to technical reports, proposal films, sales films, and high priority briefings.

Cost Range. $600 to $950 per screen minute.

Category 4. Research, script, and complete production of a sound and color motion picture. Includes music, detailed sound effects, and up to twenty percent live sound recording. This category aims at a high level of production value.

Cost Range. $950 to $2,000 per screen minute.

Category 5. The production of a complete, high production value motion picture for public relations, propaganda, public service, and top priority sales and promotion programs. Includes any and all production techniques as required.

Cost Range. Unlimited.

Remember that production costs are subject to constant change relative to inflation, availability of personnel and facilities, and subject matter involved. The cost ranges indicated for the five categories above serve as a starting point in estimating the relative complexity of different kinds of films.

When the producer and the sponsor first meet to discuss the outline, a meeting of minds is vital. If a hidden divergence of opinion already exists about the scope or purpose of the film, it may widen as production progresses, only to surface when a lot of money has been spent and it is too late to make any changes. Although the sponsor will normally read the script very carefully to safeguard his investment in the production, it is essential that he try to read it with an imaginative eye. The more original the film is to be, the more unconvincing the script may appear to the layman. It is difficult even for the filmmaker to equate written words with visual images, and it is practically impossible for a sponsor who tends to pay exclusive attention to the narration, which he mistakenly believes will carry the film alone.

Problem Production Stages

The sponsor is likely to cause trouble during three stages of production: on script approval, on screening dailies, and on approval of the edited workprint. At each stage the sponsor is in a position to make what he believes to be constructive criticism, and unless the producer maintains control, his motion picture is in danger of becoming an illustrated lecture on film. Often the sponsor, is a multiple entity. There may be colleagues on the board of directors, or public relations experts, or seniors in the government hierarchy, or fellow committee members, to consult and satisfy. However necessary it is to seek the opinion of such persons, the sponsor should realize that good films cannot be made by committees.

APPROVALS

Starting with the script, the producer should try to convince the sponsor that only one person be designated to give approvals. Sponsors have a disturbing tendency to invite opinions and criticism from many quarters. Only initially, in laying out the content and purpose of the film, are the ideas of the sponsor and his associates important. Later, particularly during shooting, the sponsor should not be in touch with the production unless you ask him to provide facilities and technical assistance.

SCREENING DAILIES

The next danger stage is the screening of dailies. Untrained people looking at dailies are unaware that everything is included in this first screening of each day's work: the shot that shows the actor scratching himself before the action starts; retakes from different angles; the runoff at the end of each shot; and all the fluffed lines and mistakes. The producer and the editor know that the parts they want are in there somewhere and that all of the unusable footage is a necessary part of shooting. But the untrained person looks at dailies as if he is seeing a completed picture. Obviously his reaction may be one of shock and terrible disfavor. He often wonders aloud, "Is that what all our money is going for?" Everyone claims to understand the raw quality of dailies and they always assure you they will make allowances in their judgment. But they don't understand and they don't know how to see beyond what is on the screen. Even experienced filmmakers find it difficult to see potential in someone else's dailies. If possible, do not let the sponsor see the dailies.

INTERLOCK SCREENING

The first interlock screening of the first cut of the picture is the next trouble spot. You must get the sponsor to approve of the picture at this stage and make whatever changes he wants before negative cutting. Whenever there is only one man to give approval, the situation is quite simple. Walt Disney always had complete, final, and individual approval over everything that was done in his studio. Other people were consulted sometimes, but the final approval came from one man alone. The most difficult situation for approvals is one in which a number of people have been assigned as an approval committee. This occurs frequently in the defense industry and in large corporations. Large bureaucracies are reluctant to have a single man make a decision, and often individuals with a great deal of authority in large firms are themselves reluctant to make decisions. The result is decision by committee; and usually the members of such approval committees know little about motion pictures. They wish to be consulted and heard, yet they will not say anything they think may offend or contradict anyone higher in the corporate or military hierarchy.

Immediately preceding an interlock screening, explain the situation carefully and then prepare the sponsors for what they are about to see. Explain that this is a workprint, the actual film that has been worked on in the editing room; that it has grease pencil marks on it to indicate effects; that it contains blank pieces of leader to take the place of torn or destroyed sections. Mention specifically that the pencil marks, slugs, and so on are standard throughout the motion picture business, and that it is necessary to see beyond the workprint and visualize the completed picture. Explain that at this point the picture only has narration, that the music and sound effects have not yet been added. The producer's task is to convince the sponsors that an interlock workprint is not the finished form, although they never really understand. They are usually amazed when they see the final product. The only thing that counts is the completed picture; and if you can achieve this goal without letting the approval committee destroy it, you have done a good job.

It is very disheartening to discover that those who have the authority to approve scripts and films are usually able to identify quickly the one aspect that makes a picture effective and demand that it be removed or changed. You may wonder why an executive or group of executives who apparently are having a picture made to further their own or their company's interests would intentionally destroy the effectiveness of their own film. It may be that what makes a picture effective is its inherent visual metaphor; and a metaphor in a motion picture, as in other works of art, is based on very subtle and delicate manipulations of the material. A probable reason that many executives, military men, and government officials are able to sabotage their own pictures is that they are rarely susceptible to metaphorical appeal. They are accustomed to dealing in broad melodramatic situations, with pictorial art and program music. They are attuned to the obvious and the usual, and a metaphor based on a subtle combination of images and sounds is beyond their understanding. They actually believe it is silly and meaningless; therefore they tell the producer to eliminate it.

DEALING WITH SPONSORS

Always try to deal with the highest ranking executive in the company or the highest ranking military officer. If you can get a president or a commanding general to make a decision, then all those below him in the corporate or military hierarchy will agree enthusiastically. It is extremely difficult to work with an executive or officer who does not have the authority to make a decision. He will never try to assess the facts as they are but rather as he thinks they will affect his superior's opinion of him.

Success in making sponsored films depends almost entirely on how well the producer can get along with sponsors. Since not everyone is suited to this kind of production, it is prudent to determine as soon as possible whether you and your sponsors are compatible. The principal source of frustration is that the sponsored film is a manufactured commodity and not a work of art. No matter how competent and talented you may be, you will have to make the motion picture that satisfies the person who is paying for it. If you are unwilling to do this, then some other area of filmmaking may be better for you. Feeding, caring for, and outwitting sponsors calls for tact, ingenuity, talent, hard work, and perseverance. The results can be, though not invariably, good films and tidy profit.

FIVE

The Script

This chapter deals with scripts, not writing, and does not pretend to make a writer of anyone. Kenneth Macgowan's observation on the teaching of writing is accurate and definitive:

> Nobody can teach you how to write . . . a teacher can only help you by pointing out occasional lapses, awkward repetitions of words, speeches that are not in character. He cannot teach you how to invent plots. He can only indicate flaws such as dullness, inconsistency, and anticlimax, and possibly suggest changes and developments that seem inherent in the material. A teacher cannot show you how to create characters. He can only call your attention to the stereotypes in your script and suggest the need for richer and more significant detail. He cannot give you that inherent sense of the dramatic . . . but he can show you how you may have bungled in organizing the material you have brought together. Above all, he can help you by sneering at your puerilities and platitudes, and trying to open your mind to the richness of human experience that lies all about you.

If you truly want to be a writer, you will write until you become one, and no obstacle will stop you. If you only fancy the idea of being a writer, the odds are against your becoming one even though you might take creative writing courses, study how-to-do-it books on writing, attend writing symposia, and join writing clubs. None of these help much; actually, they may hinder, for they take up time that could otherwise be spent in writing.

LEARNING FILM WRITING

The best way to learn film writing is to write a script, produce the picture from it, analyze what went right and what went wrong, and then repeat the process as many times as it takes to get the knack. Unhappily this method is rather expensive, but you must see your scripts produced in order to learn. Writing and making even a one-minute film is a practical and workable way to get experience. Read scripts and look at all kinds of films. Participate in as much film production as you can. Find out what works and what doesn't work, and why.

Putting a script into the "proper" form will not necessarily make it a good script, but just having a professional look about it may ensure that a prospective producer will at least riffle through the pages before he rejects it. Unfortunately, appearances mean more than they should in the film business. A good script submitted in an offhand, nonprofessional format is usually rejected out of hand, while a poor script in a professional format often is read and considered by responsible people. Motion picture scripts are generally paid for by people who have little aesthetic conviction and a diminished capacity for visualization. Consequently externals such as format, paper quality, and binding become important initially. These things alone won't sell a script, but like a neat suit of clothes and a shoeshine they will help get you into the producer's office.

There are as many kinds of scripts as there are films. If you are a lone filmmaker, the script you write to shoot and direct yourself will be far different from one written by a screenwriter for a director he may never see. John Cassavetes, an independent filmmaker of long standing, uses a script as a departure point for improvisation, revising the script with each rehearsal until the piece is set. If it makes sense to you, you can even write your script in occult symbols on bits of old wrapping paper. But when you set out to write a script that someone else is to pay for and other people must act upon, you should do it in a way that is unambiguous and readable. This is the rationale for standard script formats and notations. According to the kind of picture, scripts are laid out on the page in two ways: split-page script for narrated films, as in Fig. 5.1, and full-page script for dialogue films, as in Fig. 5.2.

PICTURE:	SOUND:
FADE IN	
1. EXT CALIFORNIA FOOTHILLS with pastureland in foreground.	Classical guitar music in a stately Spanish style extends through Scene 8.
CAMERA PANS LEFT across hills and pastureland and stops on a fine old California live oak tree in FULL FRAME.	
2. LONG SHOT EXT FOOTHILLS Two men on horseback ride slowly along the base of the hills in the distance.	
CAMERA PANS LEFT to a small herd of cattle in the distance being worked by two cowhands.	NARRATOR: One generation passes away and another generation comes, but the earth abides forever.
CAMERA PANS across pastureland to a country road.	
DISSOLVE TO:	Is there anything whereof
3. CLOSE SHOT SAGEBRUSH The sagebrush fills the frame.	it may be said . . .
CAMERA TILTS UP from the sagebrush to reveal the City of Los Angeles spread out in the basin below.	see, this new?
4. FULL FRAME SHOT OF FREEWAY INTERCHANGE. A composition of crossing overpasses. It is deserted - not a car in sight. A sign in the foreground reads, DO NOT ENTER.	It has been already of old time . . . which was before us.
5. CLOSEUP. SURFACE OF CONCRETE fills the frame. CAMERA TILTS UP to reveal a long eight-lane freeway completely deserted and empty of cars.	

Fig. 5.1. Split-page script for narrated films.

	Visual	Narration
6.	LONG SHOT EXT CALIFORNIA HILLS in background. CAMERA ZOOMS back to reveal a vast new housing tract in the valley foreground.	
7.	CLOSEUP EXT SECOND STORY WINDOW of 1890 mansion.	There is no remembrance of things past . . .
	CAMERA ZOOMS SLOWLY back, PANS to, and HOLDS on busy freeway in foreground with Los Angeles City Hall large in the center back-ground.	neither shall there be remembrance of things that are to come with those that shall come after . . . and there is no new thing under the sun.
8.	EXT LOS ANGELES STREET Cars pass left and right in close foreground.	I have seen all the works that are done under the sun, and behold . . .
	CAMERA PANS and TILTS UP to a full-frame shot of sign reading LOS ANGELES CITY LIMITS.	all is vanity and vexation of spirit.

Fig. 5.1. *(Continued)*

SPLIT-PAGE SCRIPT

Look at the script excerpt in Fig. 5.1. At a quick glance you can readily see the parallel relationship of the narration to the visuals. The left-hand column indicates visual scene descriptions and camera instructions, while the right-hand column indicates the text of the narration and other sound.

The script excerpt in Fig. 5.2 is a master scene from a feature film. (For a discussion of The Master scene, see p. 110) Scene descriptions and camera instructions extend the full width of the page, while the dialogue appears inset down the center of the page with the speaking character's name directly above his lines. The full-page form is the easiest to read to get a feeling of continuity because your eye goes steadily down the page, reading each speech and scene description as it occurs sequentially. In contrast, as you read the split-page format in Fig. 5.1, notice how difficult it is to maintain a feeling of continuity of picture and narration combined. Your eyes jump continually back and forth between the two columns. To understand the writer's intended relationship between images and sound in a split-page script, the reader must be capable of visualizing and willing to make the mental effort to "see" as he reads. Unfortunately most producers, sponsors, and technical advisors are unskilled in visualizing and invariably read only the words in the right-hand column, with the predictable reaction that something has been left out—which is perfectly true for them, since they have not "seen" the visuals as they read. Although you explain carefully that the visuals will supply the "missing" information, they rarely understand and invariably insist that more words be added to make the script clear and complete. Since more words mean the destruction of a good visual script, your aim should be to try to make it possible for a reader to read visually as well as verbally.

Compare and read the two script versions of the same sequence in Fig. 5.3 and Fig. 5.4. Notice how in the split-page script (Fig. 5.3) the picture column is easy to read and visualize through Scene 3 because there is no narration. As soon as the narration appears in the right-hand column at Scene 4, the problems of column switching and complete visualization begin.

FULL-PAGE SCRIPT

Sometimes it helps to put a narrated script into a full-page format to force a reader into reading scene descriptions as well as narration. Read the

```
220.     INT.  BEDROOM - STEPHENSON APARTMENT - NIGHT

         Al and Milly are dressing to go out to dinner.
         Al is struggling to button the collar of a
         semi-starched evening shirt.  Al is in an ugly
         mood.  He gives another heave to his collar,
         but he can't make it.  He turns to Milly,
         exasperated.

                        MILLY
              I suppose it would be all
              right for you to wear your
              uniform.

                        AL
              Anything but that!  Have you
              got a button hook?

                        MILLY
              There's one there on the
              dressing table.

         Al fishes around and finds the button hook.  He
         inserts it awkwardly through the button hole,
         hooks it on to the button, then gives a tremendous
         wrench, as though he were trying to boost a jeep
         out of a mudhole.  He almost strangles himself,
         but he buttons the collar.  He smiles painfully
         with relief.  He puts on his dinner coat.  But
         then the button bursts.  He curses silently.  Milly
         laughs.

                        AL

              I'll admit it's screamingly funny.

                        MILLY
              Let me tie your necktie around
              it anyway.  Nobody will know the
              difference.

         Milly starts to fix his tie and continues through
         the following dialogue.

                        MILLY
              Penny's going out dancing with
              Woody Merrill.

                        AL
              Who's he?

                        MILLY
              You know - Bill Merrill's son.


                                            (CONTINUED)
```

Fig. 5.2. Full-page script format. A Master scene from *The Best Years of Our Lives,* written by Robert E. Sherwood.

```
220.        (Cont.)

                              AL
                    Oh, yes.  Fine people, the
                    Merrills.  They're strictly
                    TCR - That means Top Credit
                    Rating at the bank.  Are his
                    intentions honorable?

                              MILLY
                    I doubt it.  But - they're
                    going to be properly chaperoned
                    by Fred Derry and his wife.

                              AL
                    Fred, eh?  Some chaperone!

                              MILLY
                    I think Peggy's crazy about him.

                              AL
                    Who - Merrill?

                              MILLY
                         (she finishes his tie,
                          then)
                    No - Fred.

               Al looks at her.

                              AL
                    Have you got any evidence to
                    support that amazing statement?

                              MILLY
                    No - just a hunch.

                              AL
                         (as if that settled it)
                    Oh!

               He turns away, and goes out of scene.  We HOLD
               on MILLY.

                              MILLY
                    But my hunches are pretty good.

                                                       CUT
```

Fig. 5.2. *(Continued)*

full-page version (Fig. 5.4) and notice how it might flow more easily for someone not accustomed to visualizing and forming image-sound relationships in his mind. When narration and scene description follow one directly below the other, it is difficult not to read everything. Your reader may not be able to visualize well, but in reading a full-page script he is usually less inclined to think of narration and description as not being related. Consequently he may not feel that something has been left out and thus will not insist on more words.

The full-page script for a narrated picture is useful only as an aid in getting an untrained script reader to read picture descriptions and camera instructions as well as the spoken words. For production, it is more workable and convenient to recast a full-page narration script into a split-page version.

Some sponsors, mainly the armed services and government agencies, will not accept a narration script in a full-page format. Many of these sponsors publish detailed specifications for script formats, and if you intend to do work for them you must conform to their requirements. Such sponsors are dedicated to mediocre films and will not let themselves be fooled into accepting a script that is visually sound.

KINDS OF SCRIPTS

Ideally, a script contains sufficient information for the production crew to turn it into a motion picture. Feature scripts and some educational and industrial scripts often give minutely detailed descriptions of action and sound, which are then produced according to a precise schedule. Other scripts, such as those for certain documentaries and art films, cannot be so specific because the subject matter cannot be controlled as easily. In the documentary shooting of one-time events—street scenes, riots, fiestas, floods—hardly anything can be controlled. Lighting, weather, actions of people, movement of vehicles must all be photographed as they happen without

FADE IN:	
PICTURE:	NARRATION:
1. LS MOON ROCKET ON LAUNCH PAD AT CAPE KENNEDY DAY	
There are no people visible. The sound is that of the pre-launch talk of the controllers over the intercoms.	
2. CLOSE SHOT MOON ROCKET ON PAD LOW ANGLE FEATURING ENGINES	
The low, close angle is to emphasize, when the engines fire, the magnitude of the power we are dealing with. The engines ignite, and as the rocket goes out of the top of the frame, we pick it up in a	
3. TRACKING SHOT ROCKET IN FLIGHT	
This shot is through a telephoto lens in slightly slow motion. The rocket climbs beautifully, shedding ice and flame.	
We see it climb forcefully. Then, THE ROCKET EXPLODES in flight.	
The CAMERA PICKS UP a big piece of hardware as it falls, seemingly endlessly toward the earth. We stay on the falling piece, but before it hits the earth, and before anything on earth comes into frame . . .	
DISSOLVE TO:	
4. MS EXT PIECE OF MOON ROCKET WRECKAGE	
It is lying in the wild terrain typical of the area around Cape Kennedy.	A moon rocket is a composite of many systems.
THE CAMERA SLOWLY PANS to the next nearby piece of wreckage. As the Narrator continues, we see more and more pieces revealed.	Each system and subsystem has to work exactly right the first time.

Fig. 5.3. Split-page script for narrated film.

	THE CAMERA STOPS on a particularly twisted piece of wreckage in CLOSEUP.	This space vehicle could have been wrecked by the failure of a single part among thousands . . .
5.	CLOSEUP ANOTHER PIECE OF WRECKAGE	by a miscalculation . . .
6.	CLOSEUP ANOTHER PIECE OF WRECKAGE	by sheer technological complexity, or by . . .
	CAMERA ZOOMS IN quickly to a TIGHT CLOSEUP as we immediately CUT TO:	
7.	EXTREME CLOSEUP OF FIBER SEEN THROUGH MICROSCOPE It is resting calibrated micrometer disc.	contamination! - - a piece of dirt so small it takes a microscope to see it.

Fig. 5.3. *(Continued)*

prompting or control. Consequently the documentary script writer is less specific about exact images, and presupposes that the director will resort to talent and ingenuity in covering unpredictable situations. Art films (and some documentaries) are often "written" in the editing room after the filmmaker sees what material he has shot. Such a film may have started with the filmmaker's feeling, say, that water in motion would make a good film. Initially his script might be no more than a few notes about the kinds of places to shoot, since the precise nature of his visuals is known only after they have been photographed. Regardless of the idea, however, the notes almost always have to be written into some form of script before you they can be transformed into a film. "Script," however, covers a wide variety of forms and stages. Each script, starting with an idea, may in turn become an outline, a synopsis, a treatment, and a shooting script. At each stage it will differ according to its purpose.

CONVENTIONAL DRAMA IN FILM

For over sixty years, most feature films have been built according to the rules of continuity that have prevailed on the stage for more than 2,000 years. Dialogue dominates action, and the feature script therefore concentrates on developing the story predominantly through what the characters say rather than through what the camera sees and how it moves. Since the beginning, feature film entertainment has presented stage dramas on film. There have been adjustments, of course, with dissolves, fades, and special effects, which make the conventional feature appear as if it really were a film instead of a play. But most feature films, even in the 1970s, remain largely stage-type dramas on film.

BREAKING CONVENTIONS

Up until recently, because of this dominance of conventional drama, it has been considered almost immoral to violate the literal flow of a feature film's strict lineal continuity in any way. But the motion picture is a perfect medium for visual abstraction and varying patterns of continuity; thus in the 1950s and 1960s talented directors began to develop the true possibilities of the feature film by using it visually in ways that early avent-gardists had briefly experimented with years before. In 8½ Fellini jolted feature audiences by going into and out of fantasy sequences on direct cuts—that is, without the mumbo-jumbo of cliché dissolves and ethereal music. Godard did away with the stodgy necessity for all sequential pieces of action to match each other exactly in point of time. For example, in *Breathless* we see the two lovers walking together in one part of Paris, then on a direct cut we see them days later somewhere else in Paris. The scene works, but to older undiences the transition is abrupt and confusing.

The first Hollywood feature film to make adequate use of the visual potential is *Rachel, Rachel,* written by Stewart Stern and directed by Paul Newman. It effectively violates sequential time through direct cuts both into and out of

```
FADE IN:

1.   LS   MOON ROCKET ON LAUNCH PAD AT CAPE KENNEDY    DAY

     There are no people visible.       SOUND is the pre-
     launch controllers over the intercoms.

2.   CLOSE SHOT  MOON ROCKET ON PAD  FEATURING ENGINES

     The low, close angle is to emphasize, when the engines
     fire, the magnitude of the power we are dealing with.
     The ENGINES IGNITE, and as THE ROCKET GOES OUT OF THE
     TOP OF THE FRAME, we pick it up in a

3.   TRACKING SHOT  ROCKET IN FLIGHT

     This shot is through a telephoto lens in slightly slow
     motion.  The rocket climbs beautifully, shedding ice
     and flame.

     We see it climb forcefully.  Then, THE ROCKET EXPLODES
     in flight.

     THE CAMERA PICKS UP a big piece of hardware as it falls,
     seemingly endlessly toward the earth.  We stay on the
     falling piece, but before it hits the earth, and before
     anything on earth comes into frame . . .

                                               DISSOLVE TO:

4.   MEDIUM SHOT   EXT  PIECE OF MOON ROCKET WRECKAGE

     It is lying in the wild terrain typical of the area
     around Cape Kennedy.

                           NARRATOR
               A moon rocket is a composite of
               many systems.

     THE CAMERA SLOWLY PANS to the next nearby piece of
     wreckage.  As the Narrator continues, we see more and
     more pieces revealed.

                           NARRATOR
               Each system and subsystem has to
               work exactly right the first time.

     THE CAMERA STOPS on a particularly twisted piece of
     wreckage in CLOSEUP.

                           NARRATOR
               This space vehicle could have been
               wrecked by the failure of a single
               part among thousands . . .
```

Fig. 5.4. Full-page version of the split-page script shown in Fig. 5.13.

```
5.    CLOSEUP  ANOTHER PIECE OF WRECKAGE

                          NARRATOR
                by a miscalculation . . .

6.    CLOSEUP  ANOTHER PIECE OF WRECKAGE

                          NARRATOR
                by sheer technological complexity,
                or by . . .

      CAMERA ZOOMS IN quickly to a TIGHT CLOSEUP as we immediately

                                                  CUT TO:

7.    EXTREME CLOSEUP OF FIBER SEEN THROUGH MICROSCOPE

      The piece of fiber is resting on a calibrated micrometer
      disc.

                          NARRATOR
                contamination! . . . a piece of dirt
                so small it takes a microscope to
                see it.
```

Fig. 5.4. (*Continued*)

stream-of-consciousness flashbacks and thought sequences. One short sequence in particular is a fine example of film's capacity for communicating visually. Rachel's dependent and demanding mother has just gone to bed for the night. The light is not yet out and Rachel is standing beside the bed with a glass of water and her mother's bottle of sleeping pills. Rachel is worried and distraught, over the way her own life is going; and though she loves her mother, her dependence and hypochondria are hard to cope with. In a MEDIUM SHOT we see Rachel standing beside the bed. Then on a CUT we see a TIGHT CLOSEUP of Rachel's hand stuffing sleeping pills into her mother's mouth. Then another CUT back to Rachel beside the bed as before. She quietly hands her mother one pill and the glass of water. The CLOSEUP of Rachel's momentary fantasy of stuffing the pills into her mother takes less than two seconds; yet we get a clear and impelling insight as to Rachel's mood and feeling. In a stage play or a traditional film, this information could only be conveyed verbally in a soliloquy by Rachel, or in an expository scene in which Rachel tells another character her feelings. These devices—soliloquy and expository scene—are stage conventions requiring many words and lengthy presentation time; and although both have their legitimate uses in film, the visual solution of depicting Rachel's state of mind by a quick look into her fantasy is more effective and artistically more appropriate to film.

RANGE OF FILM WRITING

As a film writer, your task is not only to master both the verbal art of the stage and the dialogue screenplay, but to go beyond and work with the real stuff of film—visuals. Film writing includes more than just the dramatic feature. It covers a wide range from dramatic dialogue to documentary to artistic abstraction to scientific description all with one central requirement—visualization. The raw material of film is the outside world—the land, the sea, people, and places. It is not the mental world of concepts and beliefs. As a writer then, you must be able to see and to write things that can be put on a screen.

UNSHOOTABLE SCENES

Film has at its command all the resources of sound, it is first and foremost a visual medium. Consequently a script should never be a mere literary construction of words with a list of shots added as an afterthought. The script excerpt shown in Fig. 5.5 is an example of the worst in scriptwriting. It is written in the style of a lecture or textbook, yet it cannot even be called an illustrated lecture since its visuals do not illustrate anything in the narration.

The main ideas of this script are all in verbal form; the shots that accompany them are merely a nondescript assemblage of visuals placed next to the narration which, in turn, is abstract and difficult for the listener to grasp. "Time immemorial," "framework on which a new American democracy would be constructed," "underlying principles," "philosophical idealism," "free enterprise system," "freedom," "justice," and "liberty," are words that film is poorly suited to convey. The script plods along at an unvarying pace, and unlike the reader of a book or newspaper, a film audience cannot go back and review a difficult passage again. It is a waste of good film to throw away its visual advantages by subordinating the picture to words in this way. The ear is easily wearied by a monotonous, sermonizing speech, and a film produced from this script would bore its audience to distraction.

Writers of bad films make the mistake of glibly selecting visuals that in some vague way are supposed to represent abstract words or statements. In the script excerpt shown, examine what the writer expects his visuals to do. Reexamine the first paragraph of narration: it is forty-six words long and states a nonvisual, intellectual concept.

1.

PICTURE:	NARRATION:
Painting of horse-drawn pioneer wagon train passing through a stately forest.	From time immemorial, the vast reaches of the United States wilderness were covered with unending forests of all kinds of wood -- wood that would someday be the framework on which a new American democracy would be constructed.
Scenes of construction and steel mills.	As the underlying principles of the industrial revolution began to be manifest in its full strength, the inroads on American resources became greater and greater, and the philosophical idealism of the free enterprise system burgeoned into a palpable consumption of apparently limitless supplies of raw materials.
Workers entering steel mill at start of day.	And through it all, the classic American espousal of freedom, justice, and liberty maintained its steady growth.

Fig. 5.5. Excerpt from a script exemplifying "unshootable" scenes.

As the underlying principles of the industrial revolution began to be manifest in its full strength, the inroads on American resources became greater and greater, and the philosophical idealism of the free enterprise system burgeoned into a palpable consumption of apparently limitless supplies of raw materials.

What is the audience doing during all this yammer? It is staring at a still picture. The visuals of this material are completely inadequate and unrelated. The narration resorts to abstract terms and rhetorical devices that have no visual counterpart or significance, and the result is a nonfilmic and ineffective sequence.

THE VISUAL SCRIPT

In contrast, a competent script is simple, concrete, and above all visual. It keeps interest alive by continuity of idea, and by narration, dialogue, random voices, sound effects, and music, all balanced against one another like the instruments of an orchestra. A good script is not the translation of a word idea into a visual idea. It is, rather, a visual idea in words that is translated back into visuals by the director and his camera so that it creates in its audience an attitude, feeling, or impression. A good example is the lumber sequence from Pare Lorentz's early American documentary, *The River* (Fig. 5.6). The statement he assigns to this sequence is that America's great stands of virgin timber were systematically ravaged in the 1800s to support this nation's westward expansion. In this sequence, Lorentz lets the visuals do the main work, with the words adding just enough to direct our feelings and to provide the little information we need. The shots of timber show us how magnificent this country's resources once were. In calling out the names of American trees, the narration evokes a nostalgic feeling for the past abundance of our lush forest lands. Virgil Thompson's score intensifies the impression of the American frenzy with a symphonic variation of "Hot Time in the Old Town Tonight." By the time this short sequence ends, we have formed a definite attitude and have received the information we need for later. For the audience then, the sequence is an experience rather than a rhetorical exercise.

PURPOSES OF A SCRIPT

A script, as a written description of a proposed motion picture, has two purposes: (1) to provide sufficient information for the production to be adequately planned and scheduled, and (2) to serve as a guide or plan for the director to follow as he shoots the picture. Often the script is referred to as a blueprint of the film, but this is inaccurate and misleading. A blueprint is a plan that specifies the exact final form of a product. You can determine exactly what a house is going to look like by examining the blueprints. Not so with a film. Everyone who works on a picture contributes something that affects the appearance of the final result. The writer's concept and formulation contribute the most. The director, since style, pace, and overal interpretation are his, has the next greatest influence. The editor, next in importance, assembles the director's material according to his own interpretation. During production, the skill, enthusiasm, and capabilities of technicians clearly influence the outcome; crew attitudes alone can mean either getting what the director has in mind or compromising. The environment also contributes—it rains or shines at the wrong time; high tension lines are in every direction; noises come from everywhere; the water is too cold; the sand is too hot—and each situation means an adjustment or change of some kind. Above all, scenes simply do not always work out the way the script says they will. For example, the *Rachel, Rachel* scene referred to earlier was written as shown in Fig. 5.7. As you can see, this script scene originally called for Rachel's fantasy to be an entire death scene including her pulling the sheet over her mother's face. Fig. 5.8 depicts the scene as it actually played on the screen.

As it turned out, the scene did not play best exactly the way it was written. But you cannot always tell how a scene will work until it has been rehearsed on camera, and sometimes not until it has been shot and gets into the editing room.

Although the journey from the page to completed film is long, and many strange things happen along the way, don't assume that a few hasty, underdeveloped notes will suffice for a shooting script. The best start toward a good picture is a complete script that represents exactly what you feel will be the perfect film. An old saying in the

PICTURE:	SOUND:
Mountain covered with dense stand of virgin timber.	(Music: symphonic - reminiscent of the American wilderness integrated under the following sequence)
DISSOLVE TO:	
SLOW PAN across another stand of magnificent timber.	NARRATOR: Black spruce and Norway pine. Douglas fir and red cedar. Hemlock and aspen.
DISSOLVE TO:	There was lumber in the North.
SLOW TILT up tall forest trees.	The war impoverished the old South, the railroads killed the steamboat . . . But there was lumber in the North.
CLOSEUP. Rough bark of tree trunk fills frame. Head of axe comes in, makes cut in bark, and swings out of frame.	Heads up! . . . Lumber on the upper river. (Sound: striking axe through cutting scenes)
Second swing of axe makes another cut and the big chip falls away.	Heads up! . . . Lumber enough to cover all Europe.
FULL SHOT. Tall pine starts to fall. As it is halfway down . . .	
CUT TO:	
CLOSE SHOT. Axe head bites several times into tree.	Down from Minnesota and Wisconsin. Down from St. Paul.
FULL SHOT. Tall fir starts to fall. Halfway down . . .	Down to St. Louis and St. Joe.
CUT TO:	
FULL SHOT. Another tree starts to fall. When it is halfway down . . .	Lumber for the new continent of Lumber for the new mills.
CUT TO:	
PICTURE:	SOUND:
FULL SHOT. Tall Douglas fir falling. We see it gain momentum until it finally slams down across a small river sending up a great fan of white water.	(Music: symphonic arrangement of "Hot Time in the Old Town Tonight" starts with the splash of the falling tree)

Fig. 5.6. A page from the cutting continuity script of *The River,* by Pare Lorentz.

```
83.    CLOSE SHOT  MOTHER'S HAND

       As RACHEL's HAND pours twenty or thirty sleeping
       pills into it from a bottle.

                          RACHEL
                 These should help you go sleepy
                 bye.

       PAN UP with Mother's HAND as she swallows the pills
       and follows it with a glass of water RACHEL gives
       her, which she drinks down noisily.  She dies.
       RACHEL pulls the sheet across her face.

84.    CLOSE SHOT  RACHEL

                          RACHEL'S INNER VOICE
                 I don't mean it!  If I think that way,
                 it's liable to happen . . .

       PAN as she bends to arrange her mother's pillows.
       The old lady helps her, very much alive.  Then, as
       RACHEL rests her against them, Mother takes her
       hand.
```

Fig. 5.7. Sequence from shooting script of *Rachel, Rachel,* written by Stewart Stern.

motion picture business is, "No one ever intentionally set out to write a bad script." So because you know your script will probably undergo some sort of metamorphosis, don't start it off with the handicap of having been sloppily thought out and casually put together.

SEQUENTIAL STAGES OF SCRIPT DEVELOPMENT

There are several sequential stages your material may go through as you develop it into a script. Since situations always differ, there are no absolute rules. But the predictable direction is from idea to completed script. Just how you get from one to the other depends on the kind of script it is, the organization you work for, and your own particular way of working. Some writers prepare an elaborately detailed plot outline before starting on dialogue and scene building. Others start off by writing the actual shooting script, letting the plot and dialogue develop as they go along. Each writer, has a method that works best for him. Rules are valuable only if you can profitably adapt them, or some part of them, to your way of working. The following four considerations are essential in some way to the writing of a motion picture script:

1. Idea: What do you want to say?
2. Purpose: Why do you want to say it?
3. Audience: Who do you want to say it to?
4. Script: How are you going to say it?

In the making of any film these four questions must be asked and answered, but not necessarily

```
MS   RACHEL STANDING BESIDE MOTHER'S BED

She is holding the bottle of sleeping pills and a
glass of water.  She looks at her mother, not moving.

CLOSE UP   RACHEL'S HAND FULL OF PILLS

The hand forces all the pills into Mother's mouth.

MS   RACHEL STANDING BESIDE THE BED

in the same position as before.  She gives one pill
to her Mother who swallows it with the water.
```

Fig. 5.8. The scene in Fig. 5.7, as actually directed by Paul Newman.

in the order given. The feature film producer starts with purpose, which for him is to make money. His next consideration is audience, and he looks for the largest ticket-buying audience available. He then goes back to the first question and searches for a story. When he has his idea, he turns to the final question—script—and figures out the way to make the film appeal to his preselected audience. In contrast, a lone filmmaker may begin with an idea that he feels has visual possibilities. His sole purpose may be self-expression, and he may not even consider an audience until after he has completed his film.

WRITING THE SCRIPT

These three considerations—idea, purpose, and audience—are actually the basic decisions you should make before you can proceed rationally to getting the script written.

Idea: What Do You Want To Say?

Every script has something to say. What is said may not be terribly important; in fact it may be quite insipid, but a film about anything has a basic idea. For a feature film it is usually a dramatic story, either the writer's original or one from a novel or play. An educational film starts with a subject to be taught. A training film demonstrates a skill or process. Whatever it is, you should be able to express briefly and simply what your film is about. A clear statement of your idea in the beginning makes it easier to develop the script later. Put your idea into a simple sentence or two: "A young man returns home from the Army and finds that his parents cannot accept the fact that he has changed." "The native beauty of Los Angeles has been destroyed by unscrupulous developers of industry and real estate." "Light reflections on moving water make beautiful patterns."

If you cannot make a straightforward statement of your idea, you probably will have difficulty in all successive stages. This does not mean that an idea has to be simple. On the contrary, a good idea is often complex, but initially it should be stated in its most simple and direct terms. This is not always easy, and requires you to think everything through carefully.

Purpose: Why Do You Want to Say It?

There are many reasons for wanting to make a film, and if you know what yours is, you have a better chance of succeeding. If your purpose is money, don't make a five-minute abstract study of light patterns. If you want to express yourself, don't make a training film on field-stripping a rifle. If you want fame, don't make technical films for an industrial firm. It is easy to trap yourself into thinking your purpose is something it is not. In some way every film is a personal involvement of its maker. When your film reaches the screen, inescapably a part of you is exposed for everyone to see. This may be less painful or frustrating if you know in advance why you are making the film and what you expect it to accomplish.

Audience: Who Do You Want to Say It To?

An audience is a group of people with a common point of view. There are many distinct and identifiable audiences, each with its own peculiarities, and each wanting the films it sees to be consistent with its tastes. A feature audience wants entertainment, but one of college age expects an entirely different film from that expected by a middle-aged audience. Movies made for small children are not enjoyed by teenagers. Businessmen do not like abstract films; church groups do not watch girlie films; and an audience of artists is not likely to appreciate a film on diesel engine maintenance. Ignorance of this elementary proposition has resulted in untold film failures. Whatever audience you are aiming at, to be successful you must start with a good understanding of its knowledge, prejudices, and beliefs.

How much does your audience know? If you present material that is over its head, it is confused; if you explain what is already knows, it is insulted. It is necessary, then, to assume a certain knowledge level. If you were to make a teaching film on physics for a high school class, you would be guided by the amount and kind of information mastered by high school students up to that time. A film on the same subject for physicists would be entirely different.

Audiences like films that support their respective prejudices and beliefs. To produce a successful film, you would normally make a thorough analysis of the nature of the people you are aiming at and then formulate a set of working limitations. Some filmmakers find it unacceptable to "cater" to an audience. This is understandable, since each person makes films for his own reasons. But don't be misled by the filmmaker who refuses to consider his audience and then becomes bitter when he is ignored at the box office. Audiences would prefer not to think deeply, and to get one to accept a new idea or a new way of visualizing requires that a filmmaker be a master of his medium. This is not to imply that you should never do things audiences don't understand. All new ideas in any art are at first understood and appreciated by only a few. If your innovations are not immediately embraced by all, don't be upset. The difficult trick is to perceive the difference between innovation and ineptitude.

If you want an audience to react, you must understand what it reacts to. Maybe you dislike audiences—some filmmakers do—and want to revolt them, confuse them, or even bore them to death. To do this successfully involves understanding the people you are aiming at. Most filmmakers, however, want to please audiences and simultaneously to present new ideas. This desire becomes a part of the problem of educating people gradually into accepting new expressions in art. It is important to know just how much new expression an audience will absorb before it closes its mind. The following checklist may be of value:

1. How much does your prospective audience know about the subject?
2. Is it liberal or conservative with regard to politics, art, morals.
3. What is its age group?
4. As a group, what are its notable prejudices?
5. Describe in detail the character and personality of a typical member of the audience.

You cannot truly understand people merely by going over a checklist, but it sometimes helps to get you started.

Script: How Are You Going to Say It?

After you have made the first three decisions—idea, purpose, audience—proceed with the physical work of getting together a script. This includes doing research, preparing an outline or synopsis, writing a treatment, and writing the shooting script. Not every script involves all these preparation stages, but they will be necessary at one time or another. Not all ideas and subjects can be handled in the same way. Dramatic stories, which include most feature films, do not generally require subject research, but may be readily stated in an outline and in a treatment. Documentary, industrial, educational, and other films that impart information require much research and careful outlining, but do not as a rule translate neatly into treatments.

Research

This involves finding out all about your subject. In motion picture writing and production, research is of three kinds:

1. The research conducted by the writer of a fictional script in developing his story. This would be the reading, traveling, investigation, and in a sense, the entire education of an author. It is not directly related to the process of scriptwriting in the sense that the other two kinds of research are. If, however, the script is set in a different historical period or if it deals with a very specialized sector of society, very meticulous formal research is required to make the script believable. Attention to detail and accuracy becomes very important.
2. Subject research conducted by the writer in preparing a nontheatrical film script. Whatever form it takes, the script of an information film must be solidly based on research. Once the idea has been approved, all the information in the film must be gathered and checked.
(a) Go through books, articles, film, catalogs, brochures—anything that will help you master the information, principles, and techniques to be depicted.
(b) Have a full discussion with all people concerned. If you are making a film for a sponsor, find out exactly what he wants or thinks he wants. Talk to technical experts, particularly the men who do the work. Shop foremen, mechanics, drivers, machine operators, leadmen, and working supervisors all can give you surprisingly more information than you will get from managers and office supervisors.

(c) Get a technical expert to write an explanation or summary of the subject.

(d) Visit all locations and talk to the people involved. Examine everything from all angles. Make mental and actual notes on visual situations and possibilities.

(e) Become familiar with all the conventional research sources. It you don't know how to use a library, learn. You may be surprised at the information a good library contains.

(f) For an educational film, talk to teachers, students, superintendents, audiovisual experts, and film distributors. Find out what constitutes a teaching film. Just calling a film "educational" does not make it so. Remember that adults buy the films that are shown to children.

3. Visual research. Motion picture research goes much further than the gathering of quotes and references, as is done in literary research. You are involved with visuals, and the gathering of visual references is necessary. Still pictures of all kinds and from all sources can provide visual ideas, and the respectability of the source is unimportant. A formal scholar would be arrogantly contemptuous of sensational exploitation magazines as a serious source of material, but for the film writer, any kind of visual stimulation and suggestion is valid and welcome. (see Recommended Reading)

(b) Outline. When you have conducted enough research to know what you are talking about, assemble the material in some sort of sensible order. A subject outline sometimes helps to organize the material and provides a guide to follow. Depending on how you work and think, an outline can be a help or a hindrance. Some writers find outlining a waste of time; others find it indispensable. For technical subjects or training films in which a definite and sequential body of information is presented, a content outline in the order of presentation is essential. Once you have worked out such an outline, the script is actually well on its way. Government agencies and the armed services require an approved content outline before work can begin on the shooting script.

(c) Synopsis. A synopsis is a condensed statement of a novel, story, screenplay, or some longer narrative. Often you will find it necessary to synopsize your material, particularly when you try to sell it. Sometimes a prospective producer will read a synopsis when he will not read an entire screenplay. Also, making a synopsis forces you into isolating the bare structure of your story, showing up redundancies, weak spots, and inconsistencies. You may resist making a synopsis because it seems difficult. But if you try selling your ideas and scripts, you will be asked to present both a one- or two-sentence synoposis and a single-page one. Your first reaction is that it can't be done—but it can if you set your mind to it. It seems difficult because you have developed your story through a lot of sweat and tears and to reduce it to a sentence or two seems like destroying it. Also, it is helpful to synopsize a story you are considering for production so that you can see the basic framework of what you intend to put on film.

The following are two synopses describing, in its entirety, John Steinbeck's novel *The Wayward Bus.* The first synopsis is in two sentences, the second is longer. Notice that only the action of the characters is described. Without expository description and dialogue, you can clearly see what will be going on film.

Synopsis #1. A group of diverse characters are traveling in an ancient bus that breaks down, forcing them to spend the night in a wayside garage-cafe. The next day they continue their journey until mounting tensions finally erupt and the Mexican driver deliberately bogs down on an old stagecoach road.

Synopsis #2. Rebel Corners once seceded a hundred acres and a blacksmith shop from the Union. Now it is a cafe-garage-bus station kept by Irish-Mexican Juan Chicoy, an intensely attractive and virile man of fifty, and his aging wife Alice. She is wildly jealous, given to raging tempers and occasional bouts of drinking. She is terrified that Juan will leave her for a younger woman, and Juan himself often wonders why he does not. On a morning soggy with rain, Juan repairs his ancient bus, Sweetheart, which broke down the night before with the passengers he was taking from the Greyhound stop to San Juan de la Cruz. The passengers have occupied his bed and those of Norma, Alice's helper, and the garage apprentice, Pimples. Pimples lives up to his name, a lad who is taking adolescence hard. Norma is a drab girl whose great love is Clark Gable. The passengers are old Van Brunt, prophet of doom; Mr. Pritchard, president of a medium-sized business; his wife who has relegated Mr. Pritchard's sex life to the nonexistent place it holds in her own heart and body; their daughter, Mildred who has had two affairs and now falls embarrassingly in love with Juan Chicoy. There is Mr. Ernest Horton, an ex-serviceman traveling for a novelty company. Before they get under way this morning, they are joined by a girl who is now using the pseudonym Camille Oaks. Camille is sex personified. Men fight over her and women hate her, though she longs for a feminine friend. Leaving Alice after a flaring rage, Juan takes his bus load, which includes Pimples and Norma, to discover that the river has arisen and the bridge is unsafe. He has had enough and decides to abandon bus and passengers and go back to Mexico. But Mildred Pritchard follows, and he returns to find that after being turned down by Camille, Mr. Pritchard has raped his wife and Mr. Van Brunt has had a stroke. Juan goes on as before.

From a synopsis, you can pick out and assemble each group of action that needs to be developed.

(d) Treatment. The treatment, like a synopsis, is a narrative statement of what the film is about, except that it is longer and more detailed. The advantage of a treatment is that it can be read comprehendingly by anyone, whether familiar with script terminology or not. If the script has to be approved by a producer or sponsor, it is easier for him to read and understand what the film is all about if it is in a treatment. The treatment can be flexible and as complete as you want to make it—include dialogue, if it seems appropriate, and narration. In treatment form, it is easy to see clearly if the purpose of the film has been considered and whether it is consistent with the nature of the audience selected. Most importantly, at this stage changes can be made easily without time-consuming script revisions.

If you can arrive at a clearly stated treatment, the task of writing the shooting script becomes much simpler. A full treatment consists of a narrative account of each sequence in the completed film. Here, you have worked out all the story details and progress of the action. Roughly one page of treatment converts into five pages of script. The following treatment excerpt is for the opening sequence of Stanley Kramer's film, *The Sniper*:

Beginning under the titles, we find Eddie alone in his cheap furnished room, suffering from almost unbearable emotional tension. Suddenly, as if he has given up a struggle with himself, he goes to a locked drawer, takes out a rifle with a telescopic sight. Turning off the room lights, he goes to a window, hides behind the curtains and trains the gun on a woman passing in the street below. He centers her on the hairlines of the sight, pans the gun with her, pulls the trigger. There is an empty click. The gun is not loaded. He puts it back into the drawer, locks it, sits down again, trying to calm himself.

This describes only *what* happens, not why or how. It is actually a skeleton shooting script lacking any details to fill it out. This piece of treatment became ten script scenes requiring a page and a half. Look at the script in Fig. 5.9 and see how the treatment relates to it.

This bit of action is complete within itself, it has a beginning, a middle, and an end. Its purpose is to tell the audience that Eddie lives alone, that he has a serious emotional problem somehow connected with women, and that this problem involves a barely suppressed tendency toward violence. A film script is a succession of such scenes, each presenting and developing the action we need to understand the story or whatever is being said. Sequences, as they are called, can be put together in any way you wish. Conventionally, features have always followed the rules of stage continuity, but this is not mandatory or desirable in films. Here is another treatment excerpt from *The Sniper*. Very sparely it indicates Eddie's action and the purpose of the sequence:

Eddie suddenly bursts into a drugstore, goes into a phone booth, makes a long distance call. He is trying to reach a doctor in charge of a psychiatric ward in a prison in another city. It is too late, the doctor cannot be reached. Eddie hangs up without giving his name or leaving a message.

With this information, you know what the scene has to accomplish, and you can proceed to develop it. The bones are here, but the flesh must be added. Look at the resulting script in Fig. 5.10, which was written from the above paragraph. Notice that it conveys the information called for; but in addition, it reinforces the implication in the opening sequence that Eddie's problem somehow involves women. During the phone call and the asking for change, the girl at the counter is prominent in the background and Eddie is constantly looking at her.

The above treatments are typical for either a short film or long features. Although these excerpts are for a fictional story, you can make a treatment of any idea that is visual regardless of its degree of abstraction or noncontinuity. If you cannot make a treatment of what you intend to put on film, perhaps your subject is a nonvisual one or you are incapable of visualizing.

(e) Shooting script. Although learning the mechanics of scriptwriting will not make a writer of you, it will make it easier for you to present your material to responsible people. A shooting script is a description of what you want others to see, so describe each scene and what happens in its simplest terms as you see it in your mind. Don't get involved with camera angles, lenses, and all the intensely technical things that sometimes appear to be obligatory in a script. Read the script excerpts in this chapter and you will see that they really are not very complicated. Since no director will following a writer's camera directions, tell it the way you see it, not the way you think some director wants it.

Although there are no set rules for script format, any professional can tell at a glance whether or not a script has been written by an

THE SNIPER

FADE IN:

TITLES OVER:

INT. EDDIE'S ROOM - DUSK

1 CLOSE SHOT THE BUREAU 1
EDDIE'S hands come into the scene and pull the bureau drawer open. They reach in and remove an M1 carbine with a telescopic sight attached. They turn the gun over and over very gently, like a mother fondling a child. Then Eddie reaches again into the drawer, takes out a soft cloth. He rubs the stock and barrel of the gun, gently cleans the lenses of the telescopic sight. The cloth is returned to the drawer, and Eddie brings out a single M1 cartridge. He holds it in one hand, cocks the gun, and pulls the trigger. There is a dry click. Then o.s. are heard the sound of two pairs of footsteps. Eddie's hands freeze. Then, as the TITLES FADE:

2 FULL SHOT STREET (SHOOTING THROUGH WINDOW) 2
Across the street a young man and woman, holding hands, have just reached an apartment house. As they stand dawdling there Eddie, the carbine in his hands, suddenly comes into the scene, sitting down on the bed among the scattered sections of a Sunday paper. He watches the young couple for a moment, then slowly brings the carbine up to firing position, steadying his aim against the window.

3 CLOSEUP THE TELESCOPIC SIGHT 3
SHOOTING ALONG the barrel of the carbine.

4 CLOSEUP MUZZLE OF THE CARBINE 4
It is very steady, hardly wavering.

5 LONG SHOT GIRL AND MAN (SHOOTING THROUGH TELESCOPIC SIGHT) 5
As they talk in the entry of the house. The crosshairs come slowly down until their juncture is at the base of her skull. As she leans over, smiling, and kisses the young man with her the juncture of the crosshairs follows her.

6 CLOSEUP EDDIE'S RIGHT INDEX FINGER 6
as it slowly tightens on the trigger.

Fig. 5.9. Script scene from one one-paragraph treatment referred to in text. (p. 98) From *The Sniper,* original treatment by Edna and Edward Anhalt, screenplay by Harry Brown.

2

7 CLOSE SHOT EDDIE 7
squeezing the trigger very, very carefully, holding his breath, almost absolutely motionless. Then he pulls the trigger all the way. There is a dry click: the carbine is not loaded.

8 LONG SHOT ENTRANCE OF HOUSE OPPOSITE (EDDIE IN F.G.) 8
The girl trots up the steps and disappears. The young man looks after her for a moment, then moves down the hill and o.s. Eddie slowly lowers the carbine. He stares out at the house opposite for a moment, then suddenly reaches up, pulls down the window, and turns back to face into the room.

9 MEDIUM SHOT EDDIE (SHOOTING FROM BUREAU) 9
He rises from the bed, crosses to the bureau, and puts the carbine back in the drawer. His eyes are wide; he is sweating a little. Almost automatically he locks the drawer, then holds the key in his hand and stares at it as though it -- or his hand -- had a life of its own. Then suddenly, with an expression of disgust, he hurls the key away. It clatters in a corner of the tawdry room. But Eddie continues to stare at his open hand.

10 CLOSEUP THE KEY 10
Where it lies in the corner. We hear the sound of footsteps and the slam of the door as Eddie hurries out of the room.

DISSOLVE TO:

Fig. 5.9. *(Continued)*

amateur. The suggested terminology and formats in the following pages are a basic vocabulary of scriptwriting. They will enable you to put your script into a professionally acceptable form—a form readily understood by people in the motion-picture business.

SCRIPT CONVENTIONS

A script is a word description of what will ultimately be on film. Often, many different people need to understand clearly what the script refers to, and as a result certain conventions have developed for conveying the following necessary information:

1. The location where the scene takes place.
2. The time of day when the action occurs.
3. Which scene (scene number).
4. The angle or point of view (POV)—how we see the scene.
5. Who is in the scene.
6. Description of the action and camera movement—what is happening.
7. Words spoken by actors and narrators.
8. Special effects directly related to the action.
9. The transition from one scene to the next.

Almost any comprehensible arrangement of the above information results in a usable script. Remember that script information is not for the director alone. Everyone concerned—production manager, designer, cameramen, grips, and all the specialists—depend on the script for material to act upon. It is a highly sophisticated form for indicating quickly and unambiguously the information required by a diverse number of people.

The script excerpt shown in Fig. 5.11 is in a professionally acceptable format, but this is not the only way to do it. As you read professional scripts, you will notice that although formats differ all of them obviously are arranged in a similar pattern.

1. The location where the scene takes place. This is the first piece of information we need—where are we? INT SMALL SHORT ORDER CAFE DAY. Put it in underlined capitals beginning at the far left margin so that it can be spotted immediately in a quick glance at the page. Do not number it. We understand it as being the place where the numbered scenes that follow it take place. INT (interior) and EXT (exterior) indicate the desired effect and not necessarily where the shooting will take place. This information is

INT DRUG STORE

19 There are three people in the drug store: a young woman at the drug counter (SANDY), a soda-jerk (SAM) behind the fountain directly across from her, and an attractive girl who is just finishing a malt. Eddie goes directly to a rack of telephone directories next to the booth and looks at the first page of one of them. He reaches in his pocket and takes out some change. Then, as he enters the booth and closes the door behind him, the girl slips off her stool and says good night to Sam as she leaves.

20 REVERSE ANGLE PHONE BOOTH IN F.G.
Eddie dials "Long Distance." In the b.g. the girl is paying her check at the drug counter. Then:

EDDIE
(into mouthpiece)
I want to get the State Prison at Huntersberg. No, I don't know the number.

Her check paid, the girl leaves the drug store. Sandy speaks across the room to the soda-jerk, her voice waspish, a little too loud, heard clearly through the glass of the booth.

SANDY
She always drink two malts?

SAM
Let her. It's good for business.

SANDY
Your business. Monkey business.

Eddie looks over at Sandy.

SAM
Ah, Sandy, what's the matter?

But Sandy doesn't reply. Lips pressed together, she busies herself near the cash register.

21 CLOSE SHOT EDDIE
looking at Sandy. The voice of the operator calls him back to the telephone.

EDDIE
What? . . . How much? . . Just a minute.

(CONTINUED)

Fig. 5.10. Script scene from *The Sniper,* screenplay by Harry Brown from a treatment by Edna and Edward Anhalt. (See p. 98 in text.)

```
22      FULL SHOT    DRUG STORE
        Eddie comes out of the booth and crosses to the cash
        register, taking a dollar bill out of his pocket.

23      MEDIUM CLOSE SHOT    AT CASH REGISTER
        Eddie holds out the bill to Sandy.

                                EDDIE
                  Could I have some change, please?

        For three or four seconds Sandy makes no move toward
        him, then, with a flick of her eyes toward Sam, her
        mouth still set, she takes the bill and rings up a
        NO SALE sign on the register.  While she is doing
        this, Eddie never takes his eyes from her face.  She
        hands him the change.

24      CLOSE SHOT    PHONE BOOTH
        As Eddie returns from the cash register and enters the
        booth, closing the door behind him.  He puts several
        pieces of change in the money slot of the phone.  Then:

                                EDDIE
                  All right. . . Hello? . . This is
                  Mr. Edward Asher.  I want to speak
                  to Doctor Gillette.  It's very im-
                  portant! . . . What?  Two weeks?
                        (impatiently)
                  Well, what's his number there? . .
                        (growing anxiety)
                  But I've . . . I've got to reach him.
                  I told you, it's very important . . .
                        (his voice goes
                                higher)
                  It's a matter of life or . . .
                  Listen, there must be a phone near
                  where he is . . .  Can't you . .?
                  Well, can you please tell me if . .
                  All right . . all right . .
                        (almost shouting)
                  ALL RIGHT!

        And he hangs up.  He remains there, his hand still on
        the now-dead receiver.  After a moment, he opens the
        door of the booth and starts toward the exit.
```

Fig. 5.10. (*Continued*)

particularly essential to the work of the production manager.

2. *The time of day when the action occurs.* This belongs on the same line with the location. It refers to the time of day—early morning, day, night, dusk—to be depicted in the scene. It not only sets the mood for the script reader but alerts the cameraman to the type of effect he will be asked to create.

3. *Which scene (scene number).* Each scene should be numbered consecutively to facilitate breakdown and the consequent manipulation of scenes during production. Sometimes you may want to maintain the same scene numbers on successive script revisions. That is, if you drop a scene, still carry its number in the revised script but mark it OMITTED. If you add a scene, say, between Scene 10 and Scene 11, mark it Scene 10A. This is helpful when you go through several script revisions and need to refer to scenes in earlier versions. You can easily determine that scenes have been omitted and when, which are new, and which are the same.

4. *The angle or point of view (POV)—how we see the scene.* The angle indicates the point of view from which we see the action, and point of view always represents the position of the camera. Thus, a HIGH ANGLE SHOT is one in which the camera is in an elevated position pointing down into the scene. In a LOW ANGLE

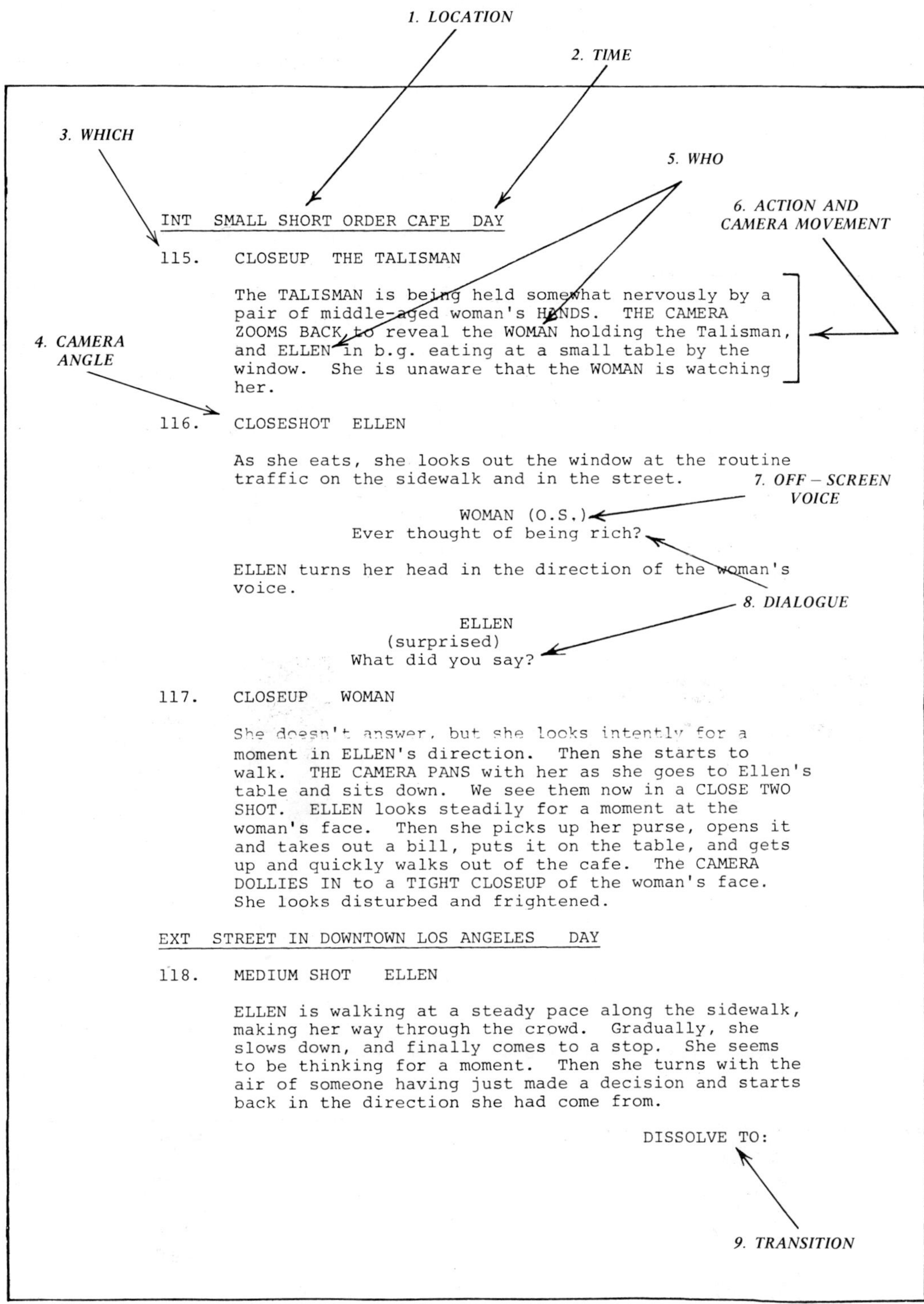

INT SMALL SHORT ORDER CAFE DAY

115. CLOSEUP THE TALISMAN

The TALISMAN is being held somewhat nervously by a pair of middle-aged woman's HANDS. THE CAMERA ZOOMS BACK, to reveal the WOMAN holding the Talisman, and ELLEN in b.g. eating at a small table by the window. She is unaware that the WOMAN is watching her.

116. CLOSESHOT ELLEN

As she eats, she looks out the window at the routine traffic on the sidewalk and in the street.

WOMAN (O.S.)
Ever thought of being rich?

ELLEN turns her head in the direction of the woman's voice.

ELLEN
(surprised)
What did you say?

117. CLOSEUP WOMAN

She doesn't answer, but she looks intently for a moment in ELLEN's direction. Then she starts to walk. THE CAMERA PANS with her as she goes to Ellen's table and sits down. We see them now in a CLOSE TWO SHOT. ELLEN looks steadily for a moment at the woman's face. Then she picks up her purse, opens it and takes out a bill, puts it on the table, and gets up and quickly walks out of the cafe. The CAMERA DOLLIES IN to a TIGHT CLOSEUP of the woman's face. She looks disturbed and frightened.

EXT STREET IN DOWNTOWN LOS ANGELES DAY

118. MEDIUM SHOT ELLEN

ELLEN is walking at a steady pace along the sidewalk, making her way through the crowd. Gradually, she slows down, and finally comes to a stop. She seems to be thinking for a moment. Then she turns with the air of someone having just made a decision and starts back in the direction she had come from.

DISSOLVE TO:

Fig. 5.11. A scene written in a professional motion picture script format. From *The Talisman* by William Adams.

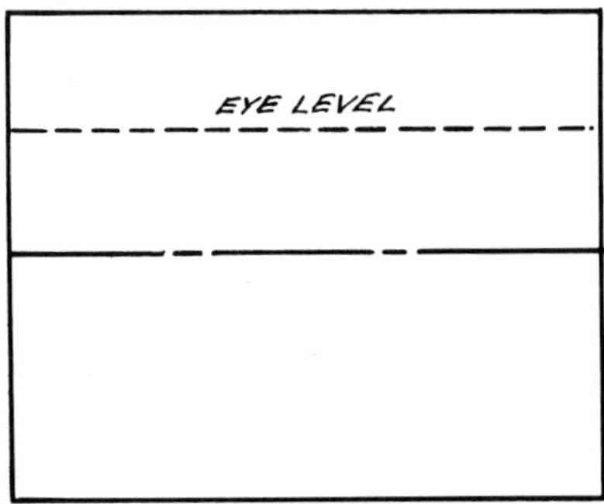

Fig. 5.12. In framing the human figure, the eyes usually appear close to the center of the top half of the frame.

shot the camera points up. The familiar terms for designating angles are those almost burlesque movie terms CLOSEUP, MEDIUM SHOT, LONG SHOT, and so on. These are definable within limits, but there is no absolute definition for each term. Every person working in films has his own understanding of them. It is fruitless to argue about what size shot CLOSEUP indicates. It means whatever the user intends it to mean. For scriptwriting, however, shot designations may be defined within useful limits.

To construct a working list of angle designations, start with the human head. Most motion picture shots of people usually frame the human head, with the eyes in the center of the top half of the frame (Fig. 5.12). Remember, this is not a rule but a working assumption from which to deviate. That which succeeds is successful; so if the effect you want requires your character's eyeballs to be resting on the bottom frame line, but all means put them there. For script designations, however, a usable set of terms has been devised based on the position mentioned above of the eyes in the frame. Regardless of whether the shot is a CLOSEUP or a LONG SHOT, eyes are usually in the same general area of the frame (Fig. 5.13*A*–*G*). In designating angles for the script, simply use terms that best explain what

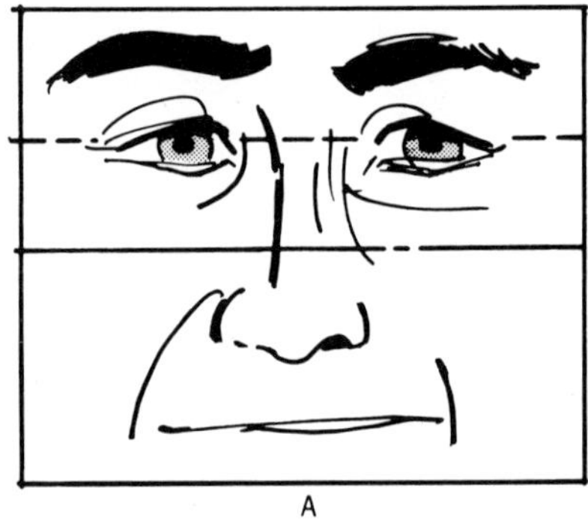
A

Fig. 5.13*A*. EXTREME CLOSEUP (ECU). With the eyes close to the eye line, the bottom frame line can be anywhere between the chin and the eyes. You could call this an ECU of a face; but a full-frame shot of one eye could be called an ECU of an eye.

B

Fig. 5.13*B*. CLOSEUP (CU) or TIGHT CLOSEUP. A full-face shot that may include the neck. Also called BIG CLOSEUP when the neck is in the frame, and a BIG HEAD CLOSEUP when the head alone is in frame.

C

Fig. 5.13C. CLOSEUP (CU). The bottom frame line can be anywhere between chest and chin.

D

Fig. 5.13*D*. MEDIUM CLOSEUP (MCU). The bottom frame line can be anywhere between the waist and the chest.

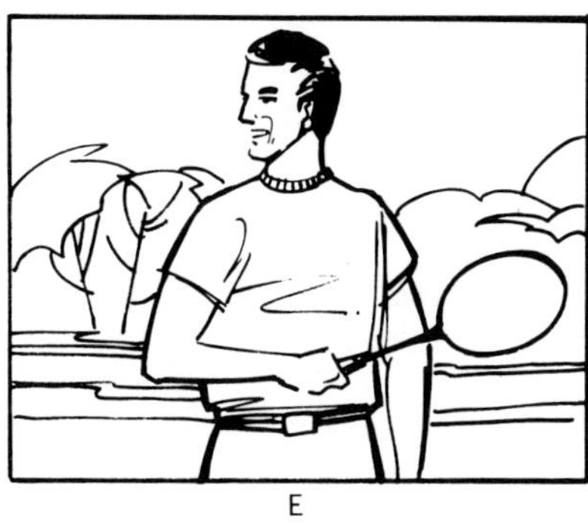

Fig. 5.13*E*. MEDIUM SHOT (MS). The bottom frame line can be anywhere between the knees and the waist. This sometimes is called a WAIST SHOT or a FINGERTIP SHOT, depending on where the bottom frame line hits.

Fig. 5.13*F*. FULL SHOT (FS). In this shot the full figure fills the frame from top to bottom.

Fig. 5.13*G*. LONG SHOT (LS). The figure or object is framed within a larger scene.

Fig. 5.13*H*. When a building fills the whole frame, *FULL SHOT BUILDING* is the usual designation.

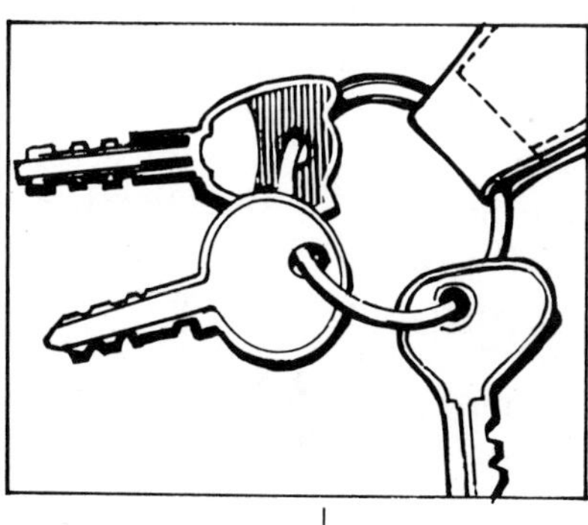

Fig. 5.13*I*. TIGHT CLOSEUP KEYS. A small object filling the frame is usually referred to as being in TIGHT CLOSEUP rather than in FULL SHOT.

you have in mind. Although such terms are neither binding nor final as to the way the picture will be handled by the director, they do provide a visual reference to the writer's intention. Always write them in capital letters.

Some writers prefer not to use such designations as CU, MS, and so on, because they mean very little at the script stage, particularly in dialogue films. Directors rarely, if ever, use the camera angles called for by the writer, so it probably is a waste of effort to "direct" the picture during writing. What is necessary is a clear

```
15.  WIDE VIEW OF BALLROOM

     A dance is in progress and the floor is filled to
     overflowing with bouncing, sweating people.

16.  VIEW OF BAR

     JOHN pushes his way through the crowd and orders
     two drinks.  As he waits, he is jostled by the crowd
     and almost pushed away from the bar.

17.  CLOSE VIEW ON JOHN

     as he pays for the drinks, picks them up.  He turns
     and works his way back through the crowd juggling
     the drinks.
```

Fig. 5.14. Rather than referring to the specific camera angle, the term *view* may be used to designate the general point of view of the scene.

statement of what we are seeing and what is being said. Another way of doing this is by indicating only what we see without specifying the angle and precise shot size, as in Fig. 5.14. Here, the writer has provided just enough scene information to let the reader know the area where the action occurs. He knows that the director will work out a visual sequence at the time of shooting. Regardless of the method you use for designating angles in the script, however, it will be acceptable if your directions are unambiguous and easy to understand.

5. Who is in the scene. It is important that we know immediately who is involved in the scene without having to search through the text to find out. Write each character's name in capital letters every time it is mentioned.

6. Description of the action and camera movement—what is happening. All action in a motion picture occurs from the point of view of the camera, which represents the eye of the audience. A description of the action can only describe what is seen, not what if felt, hoped for, or anticipated. Consequently, describe only what can be photographed—clearly, succinctly, and visually. The scene shown in Fig. 5.15 simply cannot be photographed. As it stands, the scene is a joke. How do you set up and photograph such things as "speculates on the alternatives," "feeling of remorse suffuses his whole being," "the consideration of what course to take?" In the revised version (Fig. 5.16) the description of the action becomes visual and thereby workable.

Camera movement is an integral part of action, so you should have a good idea of the effect any movement creates. The following are the basic movements and their designations. They occur only while the camera is running, that is, while the scene is played or photographed.

Dolly. This is the process of moving the camera either toward or back away from the subject. A DOLLY IN approximates the way your eye would see the scene while walking toward the subject. On the screen a DOLLY IN movement is in the direction from a LONG SHOT to a CLOSEUP, and the subject becomes larger in the frame. To move from a MEDIUM SHOT to a CLOSEUP, you would write, CAMERA DOLLIES IN TO CLOSEUP. Movement away from the scene is a DOLLY OUT, and the direction of movement is from CLOSEUP to LONG SHOT.

Zoom. The ZOOM, like the DOLLY, is movement toward or away from the scene except that

```
26.  MS  ALLAN BEFORE THE FIREPLACE

     As he stares into the fire, he speculates on the
     alternatives he had chosen and the ones he had
     rejected.  A deep feeling of remorse suffuses his
     whole being and leads him to the consideration of
     what course to take.  He clenches his fist tightly
     and turns as the CAMERA DOLLIES IN to a CLOSEUP.
```

Fig. 5.15. Script scene containing "unshootable" information.

```
26.    MS  ALLAN BEFORE THE FIREPLACE

       He stares into the fire for several moments.  Then,
       he clenches his fist tightly and turns as THE
       CAMERA DOLLIES IN to a CLOSEUP.
```

Fig. 5.16. Unshootable elements deleted from the script scene in Fig. 5.15.

it takes place optically inside the lens. The camera itself does not move. The cameraman makes a ZOOM shot by moving a lever on the lens, changing its focal length and creating apparent movement either in or not. The effect is quite different from that of a DOLLY shot in that a foreshortening of the scene occurs as the ZOOM approaches the CLOSEUP position. The resulting change in perspective is not always desirable.

A ZOOM has certain other characteristics: It is confined to a straight line—you cannot ZOOM IN to the corner of a building and then turn the corner. In a DOLLY SHOT, the camera would actually move to the corner and could make the turn; but in a ZOOM, the camera remains in one spot. Unlike the dolly shot, you cannot ZOOM IN to the edge of a canyon and then look over the edge, nor in to a person reading and look over his shoulder. The ZOOM is best used for special effects and for moving toward or away from scenes in situations where dollying the camera would be impossible, such as going into a CLOSEUP of a person on the opposite side of a busy street, or across a canyon, or up to a window on the tenth floor. The ZOOM makes CLOSEUPS possible in documentary situations.

Pan. Panning is movement of the camera horizontally from right to left or left ro right:

CAMERA PANS with GEORGE as he walks from the door to the gun rack.

Tilt. This refers to movement of the camera up and down. The camera is not raised or lowered in a tilt shot, but is swiveled from a fixed position:

CAMERA TILTS UP to the Talisman on the mantelpiece.

Crane. A crane shot results from the movement of the camera mounted on the end of a long boom. This gives the camera the capability of three-dimensional movement within the area reached by the radius of the boom. During shooting, the camera can be craned smoothly from a low to a high position at the same time as it is being moved horizontally or in or out.

As ELLEN climbs the stairs, CRANE HER UP to the first landing. When she stops, TILT DOWN TO the Talisman at the bottom of the staris.

The direction above combines two camera instructions. First, the camera is actually raised on the end of the crane boom to the height of the first landing. Then, with the camera remaining at that level, the cameraman points it downward to bring the Talisman into frame.

Follow Shot. A follow shot is one that follows a moving object—person, train, horse, automobile—by moving the camera along with it while maintaining a consistent framing. A typical follow shot would be one in which we stay with two people in CLOSEUP as they walk along the street talking to one another.

Two or more camera movements can be, and often are, combined during shooting. However, in the script it is less confusing to refer to only one movement at a time. Keep camera directions as simple and uncomplicated as possible—the script should not do the director's planning. Write camera movement instructions in capital letters.

7. Dialogue and narration. In a full-page dialogue script, insert the dialogue down the center of the page to quickly and easily distinguish it from the location and the description of the action. Label each speech with the speaker's name or designation in capitals centered on the page. Repeat this designation every time a direction separates one part of a speech from another even though it is obvious that the same person is still speaking (Fig. 5.17). If your speaking character is not in the frame, indicate this either by designating the voice as off-screen (O.S.) or simply as a voice (Fig. 5.18).

Instructions regarding the manner of a character's speaking or state of mind may be put in parentheses inserted between the character's

```
                    WILLIE
          This is the reason I came
          here so quickly . . .

He tosses the Talisman lightly in his hand a
couple of times.

                    WILLIE
          And this is the reason I'm
          going to stay.
```

Fig. 5.17. Speaker's name designated for dialogue following stage business.

name and his first line of speech (Fig. 5.19). Keep these instructions extremely short and use them only as indicators of mannerisms, mood, state of mind, or way of speaking. Longer and more detailed instructions belong in a descriptive paragraph separated from the lines of speech (Fig. 5.20*A*). This last speech with its instructions would be better written as shown in Fig. 5.20*B*.

8. Special effects and music. Since Writer and production people know that music and effects will be added to a film at the proper time, it is not necessary to indicate music and special effects unless they are an essential part of the action. Examine the opening scene in the excerpt from the *The Sniper* (Fig. 5.9). It is a CLOSE SHOT on Eddie's hands holding a gun, cocking it, and pulling the trigger. OFF SCREEN is heard the SOUND OF TWO PAIRS OF FOOTSTEPS. This last sound is obviously essential to the action, because it is the motivation for Eddie's hands to freeze. The other sound effects in the scene—drawer opening, gun being handled and cocked, trigger pulled—are implicit in the action and are not called for in the script because they will be added later as a matter of production routine.

In a split-page script, refer to sound effects and music in the narration column, as shown in Fig. 5.21.

9. Transitions. These are instructions—CUT, FADEOUT, FADEIN, DISSOLVE, WIPE—that indicate what the visual effect is to be when we go from one scene to the next. Traditionally each transitional effect has been accepted by motion picture audiences as having specific meanings.

FADEIN and FADEOUT. These effects usually begin and end a picture. In a FADEIN the picture starts with a black screen and gradually comes up to full visibility within two seconds. A FADEOUT occurs when the normal picture gradually darkens to a black screen.

CUT. A cut is an instantaneous change on the screen from one scene to the next. Conventionally this has been used between scenes and events that are supposed to be happening concurrently. Thus, if we see a shot of a woman sitting inside a house reading, and then the picture cuts to a shot of a man walking along the sidewalk, we conventionally assume that at the same time the woman is sitting the man is walking. CUT does not have to be written between

```
               WOMAN (O.S.)
     Ever thought of being rich?

               OR

               WOMAN'S VOICE
     Ever thought of being rich?
```

Fig. 5.18. Off-screen voice may be designated by words or initials.

```
                    ELLEN
          (surprised)
     What did you say?

                    MRS CAMERON
          (fanning herself)
     It's been warm today, hasn't it?

                    MR CAMERON'S VOICE
          (after a long pause)
     I see in the papers where it says taxes
     may be coming down next year.
```

Fig. 5.19. Extremely brief indications of characters' emotions may be made in parentheses within the dialogue.

```
HOMER sees that MR. CAMERON is without a match,
and jumps up.

                    HOMER
          I got a light, Mr. Cameron.

                    MR CAMERON
              (nervously he hastily lights
              his own match, giving Homer
              no chance to show what he can
              do)
          No, no!
```

A

Fig. 5.20*A*. Too much information included in the script dialogue.

```
HOMER sees that MR CAMERON is without a match,
and jumps up.

                    HOMER
          I got a light, Mr Cameron.

                    MR CAMERON
              (nervously)
          No, no!

He hastily lights his own match, giving Homer no
chance to show what he can do.
```

B

Fig. 5.20*B*. A more workable recasting of the script form in Fig. 5.20*A*.

each scene in the script where a CUT occurs since it is universally understood that every scene CUTS to the next scene unless some other transition is indicated. Sometimes, however, to emphasize the shock value or special use of a CUT, you may find it effective to write it in (See Fig. 5.6.)

DISSOLVE. An effect in which we see one scene fading out while the next scene fades in on top of it. For about a second we see both scenes on the screen at the same time. Conventionally the DISSOLVE means a change in time, place, or psychological condition. To show the passage of time into either the past or the future, one scene DISSOLVES TO another. Traditionally the DISSOLVE was mandatory for going into or out of fantasies, dream sequences, and the past and future. However, this structured use of the DISSOLVE is no longer an obligatory convention. The more visually sophisticated audiences of today need not be dealt with gently in transitions. Direct CUTS into and out of the past, the future,

PICTURE:	SOUND:
CLOSEUP. Rough bark of tree trunk fills frame. Head of axe comes in, makes cut in bark, and swings back out.	NARRATOR: Heads up! Lumber on the upper river. (SOUND of biting axe heard under MUSIC during tree-cutting scenes)
Second swing of axe makes another cut and the big chip falls away.	Heads up! . . . Lumber enough to cover all Europe.

Fig. 5.21. Indication of music and sound effectsf in a split-page script.

fantasy, dreams, and present reality are workable. Again, it all depends on what that filmmaker is trying to accomplish.

In a full-page script, transitions read best at the right side of the page between the scenes involved (See Fig. 5.4.) In a split-page script, put transitions in the left-hand, or picture column (See Fig. 5.3.)

Master scene. A master scene is a piece of action that takes place in one location and has its own beginning and end. It is represented in the script as one continuous action without closeups or other angles. Often only the dialogue is indicated in a master scene with all movement and subsidiary matching angles left to the later devices of the director. A motion picture is

```
90.       INT. PARRISH LIVING ROOM - NIGHT

          In contrast to the noisy, violent gaiety of
          Penrose Street, the Parrish living room is
          quiet and strained.  All we HEAR at first, is
          the irritating SOUND of Mr. Parrish scraping
          the bowl of his pipe.  Mr. Parrish, Mr. and
          Mrs. Cameron (Wilma's parents), Homer, Wilma,
          and Louella are sitting about, stiffly and ill
          at ease.  Cameron is rather stodgy, pompous
          man, and his wife is a mousy, fluttery little
          woman.  No one knows exactly what to say.  Al-
          though they try not to look at Homer's hooks,
          everything they say or do is dictated by their
          intense awareness of them.

                              MRS. CAMERON
                        (fanning herself)
                   It's been warm today, hasn't it?

          No one replies.

91.       TWO SHOT - HOMER AND MR. PARRISH

          The ANGLE is PAST Homer, TOWARD his father, who
          continues to scrape the bowl of his pipe.  He
          becomes conscious of Homer looking at him, and
          then becomes extremely self-conscious of his
          own hands.  He feels guilty about them, stops
          cleaning his pipe, and tries to get rid of his
          hands by folding his arms across his chest.
          OVER this, we HEAR:

                              MR. CAMERON'S VOICE
                        (after a long pause)
                   I see in the papers where it says that
                   taxes may be coming down next year.

          Mr. Parrish, who now has his arms folded across
          his chest, turns to Mr. Cameron, feigning profound
          interest.

                              MR. PARRISH
                   Is that so -- coming down, eh?

                              MR. CAMERON
                   Yep --

92.       GROUP SHOT

          Louella is staring at Homer's hooks.  She is
          quite honest in her curiosity.  Mr. Cameron, now
          that he has Mr. Parrish's ear, shifts pompously
          in his chair and then speaks:
                                                (CONTINUED)
```

Fig. 5.22. Script scene from *The Best years of Our Lives,* written by Robert E. Sherwood.

```
92.        (Cont.)

                         MR. CAMERON (Cont.)
              Well, I'll tell you -- as I see it
              -- we're headed for bad times in
              this country.  Of course, we're in
              the backwash of the war boom now,
              but the tide is running out fast.
              Next year, in my opinion, we'll
              see widespread depression and un-
              employment.
                    (he takes a cigar from
                     his vest pocket)
              Have a cigar?

                         PARRISH
              No thanks, Mr. Cameron.  I've got
              my pipe.

           He holds it up.

                         CAMERON
              Homer?  Didn't you contract the
              tobacco habit in the Navy?

           He smiles rather patronizingly at Homer as he
           offers him a cigar.

                         HOMER
              Just cigarettes, Mr. Cameron.

           Cameron bites off the end of the cigar and
           spits it elegantly into the fireplace.

                         MRS. CAMERON
                    (to Homer)
              Wilma tells us you were in the
              Phillipines, Homer.

                         HOMER
              Well - I was around there, Mrs.
              Cameron.  But I never saw any-
              thing.

                         MRS. CAMERON
              Did you meet General MacArthur?

                         HOMER
              No - I didn't get to meet him.

           Homer sees that Mr. Cameron is without a match,
           and jumps up.

                         HOMER
              I got a light, Mr. Cameron.
```

Fig. 5.22. (*Continued*)

generally a composite of many master scenes. Look at the master scene in Fig. 5.2. Its main purpose is to tell the audience that Peggy is in love with a married man. The secondary purpose is to give us a little insight regarding the characters of AL and MILLY. This master scene, a small entity standing by itself, is not broken up into camera angles, but runs straight through under the one scene number. It will probably not be shot this way, for the director may break it up into several different angles, and may play it quite differently from the way it is written. You may visualize exactly how the scene should be directed, but unless you are also the director, avoid writing any more than is necessary to make the meaning and intent of the scene clear.

Examine Fig. 5.22, the PARRISH LIVING ROOM. The writer has divided this master scene up into three numbered scenes, but they are not really camera angles. He does this to clarify his intention. Scene 90 is identified as the PARRISH LIVING ROOM—this establishes the setup. Scene 91—TWO SHOT HOMER AND MR. PARRISH—is not a suggested camera angle, but it is the writer's way of indicating that the relationship between Homer and his father at this moment is very awkward. In Scene 91, we then go back into a GROUP SHOT, which is really the same general shot as Scene 90, the opening shot. Obviously the director will not shoot this scene in three shots as in the script but will make several shots with closeups and reaction shots.

Figure 5.23 is a master scene, not broken down into matching shots. A director would undoubtedly prefer to work from this version.

Script writers sometimes do write master scenes that are broken down into several camera angles. If the writer is also the director, he will write the script in whatever form he considers most useful. Figure 5.24 is an example of a master scene written with closeups and reaction shots in a way it could conceivably be directed. But rarely can a writer successfully "direct" the picture in the script stage.

```
133        FULL SHOT - THE ENTIRE GROUP

                       JUVENILE
           We're only in town a couple of
           minutes and we've already drawn
           a crowd.
               (strolls over toward
                Inez)
           Hi there.  What's your
           name. . .?

                       INEZ
           Me?

                       JUVENILE
           Yeah . . .

                       INEZ
           Inez.

PORFIRIO and JESUS watch dumbly.

                       JUVENILE
           Inez.  That's a good name
           for a pretty girl.  How old
           are you?

                       MANUELA
           She's ten.

                       INEZ
           I'm going on eleven.

                       JUVENILE
           How would you like to marry
           me . . and go on the stage?

She pauses shyly for one split second to
size him up and think about it.

                       INEZ
           I would like it.

                       JUVENILE
           That's the girl.

                       MANUELA
                (whispering)
           Inez!  You can't.  You can't
           go away.  You've got to marry
           one of the boys from our own
           town.

                       INEZ
           But then I could be an
           actress.

                       MANUELA
           Do you think your mother
           would let you?

                       INEZ
           I'll ask her.
```

Fig. 5.23. Scene from *Juan,* by Flora Mock and James Fisher, as shown in Fig. 5.24, written as a master scene.

133. FULL SHOT - THE ENTIRE GROUP

JUVENILE
We're only in town a couple
of minutes and we've already
drawn a crowd.
(strolls over toward
Inez)
Hi there. What's your name . .?

INEZ
Me?

JUVENILE
Yeah . . .

INEZ
Inez.

134. CLOSE UP - JESUS, PORFIRIO

watching dumbly.

JUVENILE
Inez. That's a good name for
a pretty girl. How old are you?

135. TWO SHOT - MANUELA - INEZ

MANUELA
She's ten.

INEZ
I'm going on eleven.

136. CLOSE SHOT - JUVENILE

JUVENILE
How would you like to marry me
. . and go on the stage?

137. CLOSE SHOT - INEZ

She pauses shyly for one split second to size
him up and think about it.

INEZ
I would like it.

138. OVER SHOULDER - GIRLS IN F.G. - B.G. CAMERA
FAVORING JUVENILE

JUVENILE
That's the girl.

MANUELA
(whispering)
Inez! You can't. You can't
go away. You've got to marry
one of the boys from our own
town.

INEZ
But then I could be an actress.

MANUELA
Do you think your mother would
let you?

INEZ
I'll ask her.

Fig. 5.24. Same scene from *Juan* as shown in Fig. 5.23. This scene has been written with detailed camera angles.

SIX

Narration: Writing, Directing, Editing

The effectiveness of narration depends on how it is paced and how much is used. A continuously running current of words often causes your audience to "tune out" so that it neither hears what is being said nor sees what is on the screen. A constant, yammering voice on the sound track defeats its own purpose. Narration cannot say everything that needs to be communicated. If it could, there would be no need for visuals, and you would be in the prose business instead of the movie business.

PURPOSE OF NARRATION

Narration is more than a mere supplement to a picture because it can make effective a visual that might otherwise be meaningless. For example, in one sequence of Pare Lorentz's documentary, *The River,* we are shown slow pan shots of logged-out and burned-over mountains. The narrator says:

> Black spruce and Norway pine, douglas fir and red cedar. Scarlet oak and shagbark hickory . . .
>
> We built a hundred cities and a thousand towns . . . But at what a cost.

Although the words don't explain literally what the "cost" and the cause are, the pictures of the slashed and burned forests show us vividly how senseless progress has destroyed what once were magnificant stands of timber. In this example the words and pictures considered separately mean little, but together they make a statement. This narration is a near repetition of earlier narration in the film, where we see the mountains in their virgin forested condition. The resulting visual-verbal irony induces in the audience a strong emotional response to the wanton deforestation. The point is this: narration is not purely expository material to be put in the track whenever the audience is to be exposed to "facts." Instead, it should be used as an element that is integrated with visuals to yield a total effect.

EFFECTIVENESS OF NARRATION

Narration is most effective when a word or a phrase cues exactly to just the right picture. A frame or two in either direction may mean the difference between a workable and an unworkable film. Learn to experiment with narration.

Change its position relative to the picture and notice the change in effect. See how much of the narration you can eliminate and still have the film make good sense.

OBSTACLES TO GOOD FILMS

Producers and sponsors who are unable to visualize are the enemies of good films. They insist that film narration be detailed, explicit, and complete in its treatment of any subject. It does no good to explain that the visuals will carry the communication. They want it all said, and when such people are in a position to approve scripts, the resulting films are generally poor. Pare Lorentz was able to make *The River* into a great documentary because he was not encumbered by bureaucrats who had the authority to insist that he include all the "correct" information.

Narration is an integral part of the picture and there should be only enough of it to influence the audience in the right direction. Again, take *The River*. In the opening sequence we see a series of slow pan shots across mountains that are not burned but covered with virgin timber. The narration is spare:

> Black spruce and Norway pine, douglas fir and red cedar. Scarlet oak and shagbark hickory. Hemlock and aspen. There was lumber in the north.

The tree names coupled with the picture create a poetic and powerful image, and the audience responds with a feeling for the virgin American forests. Imagine the same visuals, timbered mountains, accompanied by an officially approved narration something like the following:

> Initially, the hills and mountains in the northern areas of the United States, extending from the eastern seaboard to the Rocky Mountains, were heavily forested with a variety of timber—hickory, spruce, pine, oak, and many others. . . .

This is no longer a powerful visual experience but a talky illustrated lecture. Unfortunately, most narrated films sound like this.

SCOPE OF NARRATION

Narration should not do all the work. Texts for newscasts, speeches, or brochures must be in complete, detailed sentences, since the written word here must convey the whole message by itself. In film, however, the narration can be no more than a word, a phrase, and occasionally a sentence to create, in conjunction with the picture, a unified and effective image. We often hear talk of the "purity of the image," which implies that since film is a visual medium it should exist without the adulteration of sound. This is nonsense. Sound at its best is an artistic effect blended with the picture in such a way that one without the other is insufficient.

Spare and telling narration works perfectly in a film whose visuals are strong and effective. However, in films having weak or virtually no visual quality, the narration must necessarily be explicit and complete, resulting invariably in a poor film. Talented film writers and directors for industry, government, and education despair of making truly good films for their sponsors simply because most of the sponsors insist that long, detailed narration texts accompany sequences of vaguely related visuals.

There are five main tasks involved in putting narration to film:

1. Writing narration
2. Selecting a narrator
3. Directing the narrator
4. Conducting the narration recording session
5. Editing narration.

Writing Narration (see Script, Chapter 5)

Writing narration involves a consideration of its requirements as they relate to accompanying visuals. This means being aware of and, if possible, being involved in editing the film.

Editing the prerecorded narration and the picture *simultaneously* results in the most effective film. But narration usually needs to be revised or added to after the picture is edited. When you write the narration before the picture is photographed, you may feel that it has been set down in the final and best possible form. Upon viewing the film, however, it will be evident that changes should be made. Although most narrated films conform slavishly to a script containing the "final" narration, both picture and narration influence each other as to how each should be done. The following is a workable procedure for integrating the writing of the narration with the shooting and editing of the film:

(a) Write the script so that the visuals and the narration are as final as you can make them.

(b) Shoot the picture according to the script, keeping the narration in mind. Be ready to change some scenes and add or delete others if you can see that their relationship to the narration will be improved.

(c) Revise and record the narration, being guided by the way the picture was shot.

(d) Edit the picture and the revised narration together. During editing, you may find that more changes in the narration are indicated.

(e) If necessary, rewrite the narration and record it again.

(f) Make the final edit of the revised narration and the picture.

Many producers, sponsors, directors, and editors consider this approach too tedious and time-consuming, which may explain why so many dull, illustrated lectures are continually being passed off as motion pictures.

If you do not wish to use a professional narrator for a preliminary track, record the narration in your own voice or have someone else do it who is reasonably competent in reading aloud. Use this "scratch" track to edit to the picture and as a basis for rewriting the narration. You can then record the new version with a professional narrator for the final version. A scratch track is convenient to make and inexpensive, but there is the danger that the timing and delivery of your scratch narrator are so different from those of your actor-narrator that your final narration won't fit the picture. To prevent this, you must be familiar with the style and pacing of the person who does your final narrating.

Again, do not require your narration to stand alone. Remember that the primary communication lies in the combination of picture and narration. Good narration does not intrude upon the audience but guides and suggests. For example, here is a typical scene from a narrated technical film. The visual is a particle of dust as seen through a microscope. Figure 6.1 shows how it was originally written. When read by a competent narrator, this bit of narration would take ten seconds. This short time is almost interminable on the screen, especially when we are viewing a single static shot. To prevent a dull, dreary scene, some narration must be eliminated.

PICTURE	NARRATION
Sc 23. MICROPHOTOGRAPH. Particle of dust as seen through a microscope.	This one is less than three-thousandths of an inch long, measured on the calibrated micrometer disc in the microscope. It would take twenty-thousand this size to cover a square inch.

Fig. 6.1. Unedited version of a scene in the script of a narrated film.

Examine the narration in the scene above. Since it is obvious that the particle of dust we see on the screen is "this one", cut out these two words. Eliminate "is," for by itself it means nothing. A film is not a specifications sheet, so we don't need to know that the particle is "measured on the calibrated micrometer disc in the microscope." If the audience is a technical one, it will see and understand the micrometer disc. If the audience is nontechnical, the statement is irrelevant. In a film, the phrase, "it would take," becomes nonsense, and "this size" is redundant. The deletable portions can then be lined as shown in Fig. 6.2. Yet it can be shortened further. "Less than" is really a rider insisted on by a technical advisor because he abhors generalizations. But film is a kind of generalization, not a medium for statistical reports. Also, we don't need the word "cover." This shortened version is shown in Fig. 6.3. The reading time for the narration is now down to four seconds. We see on the screen that the particle is in a microscope. We hear a significant piece of data—"three-thousandths of an inch"—and then our imaginations are quickly stimulated by verbal imagery—"twenty thousand to a square inch." With the narration at its original stupefying length, the audience would be very bored by the time the narrator gets to this last imaginative bit, and the effectiveness of the shot would be lost. Good films consist of few words and effective pictures. Thus the aim of written narration, as in any other form of writing, is to reduce the number of words to the barest minimum necessary.

~~This one is~~ less than three-thousandths
of an inch long, ~~measured on the micrometer~~
~~disc in the microscope.~~ ~~It would take~~ twenty
thousand ~~this size~~ to cover a square inch.

Revised, it now reads:

Less than three-thousandths of an inch
long. Twenty thousand cover a square inch.

Fig. 6.2. Partially edited version of the narration of the scene in Fig. 6.1.

PICTURE		NARRATION
Sc 23.	MICROPHOTOGRAPH. particle of dust as seen through the microscope.	Three-thousandths of an inch long. Twenty thousand to a square inch.

Fig. 6.3. Final edited version of the narrated scene in Fig. 6.1.

Several things to avoid in writing narration are quite obvious and diminish a film's effectiveness. The following techniques to avoid are insidious and should be recognized instantly.

1. Don't produce an illustrated lecture. This can easily be done by writing a complete verbal text and fitting pictures to it. Most industrial, governmental, and educational films are illustrated lectures that might as well be presented as slide lectures or in book form.

2. Don't start the picture several times. Almost everyone can think up a good opening sequence for a narrated film. It is relatively easy to write an impressive visual and verbal introduction, but after this the job becomes considerably tougher. Making an entire picture of nothing but opening sequences is an easy trap to fall into. It sounds like a film, looks like a film, and runs as long as a film—but it's not a film.

3. Don't use too many words. When you have too many words to be worked in, the narration often must run constantly and rapidly. This not only turns the film into an illustrated lecture, but also irritates the audience. As a rule of thumb, try using less than sixty words per minute of picture and let the visuals do more of the work.

4. Don't use long or compound sentences. Subordinate clauses constitute a verbal quicksand that quickly swallows an audience. Use fewer words and let the visuals work.

5. Don't use rhetorical devices and abstract terms.

6. Don't describe a scene that is not in the picture. The impulse to get "essential" information into a film often results in this senseless practice. It is the illustrated lecture carried to the point of filmic absurdity.

7. Don't withhold necessary information until the end of the scene. When you cut to a scene, let the audience know immediately what it needs for the scene to be intelligible. This situation usually occurs when the narration consists of long sentences with introductory phrases and subordinate clauses.

8. Don't tell the audience what the camera is doing. "We are now moving through the front door of the White House," the narrator says. But the audience is way ahead—it can see that the camera is moving through the door. If you can see what is happening, there is no need to describe it.

9. Don't use verbal or visual clichés. These are all those worn out phrases and images we know so well. Verbal cliches: "unlimited horizons," "in addition," "a beehive of activity," "bigger and better." Visual cliches: Pages blowing off a calendar, or clock hands speeded up, to show the passage of time; a low-angle shot of the villain; the glamor-lighted heroine; the company president seated at his desk saying a few words to the film audience; colorful, nonobjective images to indicate a narcotics "trip". Clichés make your work easy and your films dull.

10. Don't use statistics and figures. Sponsors continually insist on this kind of information, but no one listens to or remembers statistical material in a film. Occasionally a graphic comparison is effective in animation, but generally, statistics are a waste of time.

11. Don't be too commercial. Many business films overemphasize the name of the product and the company. This may work well in TV commercials, but in films it puts an audience on its guard and causes it to stop believing. Films that achieve the most impressive results in selling and propaganda rarely if ever mention the company name or its product directly.

12. Don't have the narrator read any of the printed titles.

13. Don't say the same thing in different ways.

14. Don't end a film more than once.

15. Don't use a "kettle-drum" finale. This is a terribly dramatic ending. It usually consists of a narrator's optimistic assertion about new horizons, embellished by improbable predictions for the future and accompanied by a ninety-piece symphony orchestra. The kettle-drum finale is a favorite of aerospace industry films, which usually end with a rocket rumbling into the blue while the music peaks in a crescendo of brass.

Selecting a Narrator

A narrator is an actor, not an announcer or someone with a good voice, or just a good speaker. Narrating is acting, and the finer the actor you get, the better the narration and the better the picture. The most mechanical and unconvincing narrations are spoken by radio announcers and news commentators. The best narrations are done by good dramatic actors, and the director who is sensitive to film will hire the finest actor available, regardless of the type of film being made—educational, documentary, or commercial.

In selecting the right narrator for the job, some facts should be known about radio announcers, television news commentators, and actors. Although all three types usually perform before audiences, each exhibits different characteristics. Radio announcers are the worst film narrators, but generally make the best impression on the first audition. They are trained to give a slick reading to unfamiliar copy, and usually have resonant, mellifluous voices. They know how to vary tone, accent, and cadence so that their voices always seem interesting. Although they have an air of absolute confidence, somehow they sound artificial. They are rarely able to change from this slick, phony, huckster style that lacks believability. Announcers sound impersonal, and the listener never has the feeling that a human being is speaking.

Television news commentators generally make slightly better film narrators than do radio announcers. They are a little more personal, which helps an audience feel that a human being instead of a robot is doing the talking. Occasionally commentators may perform well, but usually they are difficult to work with because of the nature of the job. A commentator attracts large faithful audiences because of his particular personality, and he generally misinterprets his popularity as evidence of dramatic ability. This may be fine for live TV, but is the worst training possible for film narration. Since the TV commentator tends to dominate the film, the most popular and successful commentators are usually the poorest film narrators unless they are playing themselves.

The actor, as was mentioned earlier, makes the best film narrator although he often gives the worst performance on a first audition. A good actor needs to think about his material and must be directed. With help from a good director, he is capable of a fine performance.

Directing the Narrator

Remember that the narrator is a person, not a speaking machine. He may appear, and probably is, composed and confident, but he will always feel some anxiety about his performance. He cannot guess the way you expect the job to be done, so be direct and explicit in explaining your requirements.

It is not necessary for the actor to memorize the script for off-camera narration. Actually, memorization usually works against you since more time (hence more money) is required, changes and variations are more difficult to make during recording, and the actor feels less relaxed.

Give the actor a copy of the *narration text* ahead of time so he can read it and get the feel of it, but don't give him the entire script. If he doesn't know exactly what the picture is about, his attempts at variant readings will often result in a performance that is even better than expected. Explain the style, pacing, and mood you are seeking. Perhaps a read-through aloud together will help, but the most productive work will be done in studio rehearsals in front of the microphone. Explain all exceptional pronunciations, uses of jargon, and occupational emphases. For example, in a current film about machine tools, the narrator uses the term "bar stock" several times, referring to a piece of metal bar used in the fabrication of various metal products. To those in the metal trades, the emphasis in pronunciation is on the "bar"—that is, BAR'-stock. In the film, the narrator pronounces it "bar-STOCK'," which immediately indicates to the film's specialized audience that the narrator knows nothing about the subject. Thus the believability of the film is destroyed. A narrator does not have to be expert in the subject of every film he narrates, but he must give that impression. It is the director's task to tell the narrator how to achieve a believable reading. A mistake in emphasis or pronunciation in the final track is the fault of the director. If the narrator continually misreads a word or phrase, the director must be aware of it and insist on retakes until the reading is correct.

Generally it is not helpful to show the narrator the film since he cannot visualize the finished product in the same way as the director. At this point the film is a long way from completion, and the nearest thing to the final result is your description of what the result will be. Explaining this to the actor is probably more valuable to him than showing him an unfinished film. Actors prefer a director to explain what he wants. There is, however, the danger that the director will say too much. The value of a good actor is that he himself adds to the performance or reading. Completely detailed instructions as to mood, inflection, accent, and so on serve to constrict the actor so that he is hesitant to move. A good director knows what to say, but he also knows when to stop saying it.

Conducting the Narration Recording Session

Setting up a narration recording session requires a studio or some suitable place to record. In or near a city that has recording facilities, it is simple to contact a recording studio and make a reservation. Provide the studio with the following information:

1. Date and time wanted.
2. Length of recording session. A rule of thumb in determining how much time you need is to multiply the reading time of the narration text by six. For a fifteen-minute narration allow one hour and a half for recording. This varies depending on the director, the actor, and the script, but it is a starting point.
3. Setup arrangement. This refers to the way you want the studio arranged. An actor seems to perform better and faster when he reads in a standing position with the script on a lectern before him, but you may prefer him to sit at a table. In either case, decide in which direction he should face—toward or away from the recording control booth.
4. Recording materials. The usual arrangement is to record the narration on quarter-inch tape master and then transfer it to magnetic film. Store the master tape for protection and use the magnetic film for editing.

At the recording session there should be scripts available for the narrator, director, and mixer. Some directors prefer the film editor to be present at recording sessions; others do not. Having the editor present helps him to become thoroughly familiar with the narration. Also, he can often detect mistakes and make suggestions that might otherwise be bypassed.

THE NARRATION SCRIPT

The narration script should contain only the text of the film's narration. (See Fig. 6.4.) Do not include camera angles, scene descriptions, sound effects, or other notations since they do not concern the narrator and only serve as distractions. Type the narration script, double-spaced, on white dull-finish paper. Make the lines short and centered on the page. Short lines make reading easier for the narrator and wide margins leave plenty of room for his notes. Do not let the last sentence on the page run over onto the next page. Number the pages clearly in the upper right-hand corner.

Some directors number the paragraphs consecutively for quick reference to any part of the script. However, it is best not to do this because numbers often subliminally impose a mechanical pattern on the narrator's reading. Any part of the script may be referred to quickly by indicating the page number and area, as "page twenty-three just below the center of the page." Many narrators unwittingly tend to treat numbered paragraphs as independent blocks when they should actually be considered a continuing flow.

Enclose each page of the narrator's script in a transparent glassine cover to eliminate the sound of wrinkling paper. Provide the narrator with a grease pencil to make notes on the glassine cover.

Before the recording session starts, be sure the narrator's station is set up. If he stands, check the lectern for sturdiness and adequate size. If the narrator sits at a table, see that the chair is silent. Have ashtrays, water, pencils, and paper at hand.

The best place for the director is in the control room next to the mixing console where he can hear the narrator's voice through the sound system, which is the way it will be heard on film. When you sit in the studio with the narrator, you hear his voice directly and not the way it is being recorded. From the booth you can talk freely to the narrator through a microphone installed for that purpose.

Begin the studio rehearsal by having the narrator read the script through aloud to get the feel of it. Listen to this first read-through from the control room, but do not make any comment unless the narrator asks for it. Usually on this first try the narrator will try out his voice. He may stutter, whisper, try several attacks on one word, make jokes, ask a question, and generally try to get in good voice. Don't criticize or direct at this stage. Let him relax. Finally, the narrator will want to try a serious read-through for volume and performance. Do not interrupt him on this one unless the interpretation is completely wrong. Take notes on this reading, and when he is through, give him your critique from the first paragraph to the end. Give the narrator time to make notes and accent marks on his script.

During both rehearsals and recording, let the narrator go through the reading without interruption regardless of fluffs and misinterpretations. After he has finished, give him your corrections and have him do retakes of portions that demand it. The reason for this is that the longer an actor goes without interruption, the more he gets the feel of the part he is playing. One moment he is stiff and artificial, the next he is rolling along with style and believability. He should do retakes of the parts that don't quite gel until he hits his stride. But remember that no matter how good a narrator is, he will find it difficult to give a strong, believable reading in the face of continual petty interruptions by the director.

Although the actor-narrator needs freedom to get into the part, he also must give the interpretation the director requests. Directing actors is a problem in human relations, and every good director has his own way of working. Obviously then, what succeeds for one may fail for another. Study yourself carefully and develop your own techniques for working with actors.

Ask the narrator to read only the text. Every time he has to note a scene or take number and dutifully announce it for the record, he is forced out of character. Instead, keep an accurate record on the director's script and let the narrator be free of bookkeeping. Follow the script as he reads. Listen very carefully, and note in the margin each passage that should be redone. Wait until he finishes to explain the mistakes and request retakes.

To indicate a retake of a narration section, write the next number opposite the passage in the margin (see Fig. 6.4.) For example, if take number one (T-1) is in progress, mark T-2 in the margin for each part you want the narrator to do a retake of. During the retake, if you want the narrator to redo it a third time, mark T-3 in the margin. When you get the reading you want, circle the take number of that take. Take designations in the script tell the editor that there are retakes at the end of the main body of the re-

Down the Yellowstone, the Milk, the White and Cheyenne. The Cannonball, the Musselshell, the James and the Sioux. Down the Judith, the Grande, the Osage and the Platte. The Skunk, the Salt, the Black, the Minnesota.

Down the Rock, the Illinois, and Kankakee. The Allegheny, the Monongahela, Kanawa, and Muskegon. Down the Miami, the Wabash, the Licking and the Green. The Cumberland, the Kentucky and the Tennessee. Down the Ouchita, Wichita, the Red, the Yazoo.

T-2

A Indicates that the passage is to be done again.

Down the Missouri, three thousand miles from the Rockies. Down the Ohio, a thousand miles from the Alleghenies. Down the Arkansas, fifteen hundred miles from the Great Divide. Down the Red, a thousand miles from Texas. Down the Great Valley, twenty-five hundred miles from Minnesota.

T-2
T-3
T-4

B Indicates the good take.

Carrying every rivulet and brook, creek and rill. Carrying all the rivers that run two-thirds the continent, the Mississippi runs to the Gulf.

Fig. 6.4. Good and bad takes noted on the film editor's copy of the narration script. Note the wide margins and short lines for easy readability.

cording. After the recording session is over, the studio should deliver the following items:

1. The quarter-inch master tape of all takes and retakes.
2. A magnetic film transfer of all takes and retakes.

Put the quarter-inch master tape in the vault for safekeeping and use the magnetic film transfer for editing.

Narration editing is often tedious and time-consuming. There is no quick way, so learn to experiment constantly: Cut out words and pauses; add words from other sentences; change the pace by changing the spaces between words; cut out coughs and "ands" and "ahs." Eliminate from the track anything that detracts from the effect you want to achieve. Combine, overlap, and displace. The narration track is viable and can be manipulated in the same way as visuals.

Whenever possible the editor should be at the narration recording session. This may not be possible or feasible on a large production, but the lone moviemaker or even the editor on a smaller production will of necessity be present. During the recording, the editor follows the script and takes notes. He advises the director about suggested retakes for run-on words and lines that later may be difficult to cut apart or rearrange. For example, take the following bit of narration:

Watches, rings, jewelry, and anything else that can carry contamination must be left outside.

As editor, you may feel that a pause might be useful after the word, "jewelry," but you cannot really be sure until you begin editing. If the narrator has read, "jewelryan danything" (which can be done by a competent actor without sounding sloppy), you might suggest that another take be made with clear separation between "jewelry" and "and." During editing you can easily arrange longer pauses between words, only if they are not actually run together. If they are, the words don't sound right when you cut them apart. Before the narration recording session is wrapped up, ask for "room tone," a recording of the ambient sound in the booth or room where the narration was recorded. (See Sound Effects Editing, Chapter 10.) This should be done in complete silence—only the sound of the empty studio. Room tone is used between segments of narration so that the silence in the pauses sounds like the silence originally recorded between the narrator's words. All silence is not the same, and indiscriminate blank film used between bits of narration will create a distinct and disturbing change in sound. Room tone recorded at another place or time may not be the same because the ambience of a room can change even when the furniture is rearranged.

PREPARATION FOR NARRATION EDITING

Since narration is customarily recorded on quarter-inch tape, the studio will make a transfer onto magnetic film to be used in the editing room. Two identical magnetic film transfers should be ordered and, before making any cuts in either, have the two sync coded together. (See Syncing Dailies, Chapter 10.) Sync coding the two narration tracks gives matching code numbers on the two tracks. Use one of these tracks for editing, and should any part of it become damaged, you can replace it with the correspondingly numbered section from the second untouched track.

For purposes of economy and time you may choose not to make a second copy of the narration; not everyone does. It is common practice to make only one narration transfer from the master tape and use it in both editing and mixing. This can be done if the track does not pick up undesirable noise during editing, or if you do not damage it. If the track survives editing unscathed, you are ahead of the game, although there is always the possibility that a major mishap will make the work track unacceptable for mixing. You can, of course, order a new track transferred from the master tape, but recutting it to the damaged track without code numbers is tedious and time-consuming.

SETTING UP NARRATION TRACKS FOR SYNC CODING

To sync code two identical transfers of the narration track, find the frame on each where the sound begins, as follows:

1. Play the first track in the sound reader or editing machine until you hear the first word on the track. Mark the first frame in which the first sound of the first word appears. This should be the same word for both tracks. Locate and mark the same frame on the second track.
2. Put both tracks in the sync machine with the marked frames in sync. Since the two tracks are identical, if you have marked the same frame on each, the tracks will now be in perfect sync. Roll toward the head and mark splice lines at the identical point on each track.
3. Splice at least twelve feet of single-perforated lightstruck leader on the head of each roll. (See start marks and leaders; Chapter 9.) Make these splices on the right-hand side of the sync machine, leaving the two tracks in the machine.
4. Roll to a point in the leader that is six feet from where you have spliced it to the sound track—approximately the midpoint of the twelve-foot leader. Make start marks on both leaders, indicate the desired code numbers, and identify the head of the leaders with your name and production. Mark one track "Narration," and the other "Narration Protection." (See Assembly of Sync Dailies, Chapter 9.)

5. Make out the lab order, specifying that the two tracks be sync coded as indicated on the leader.
6. Send to the lab for coding.

When the two sync-coded rolls come back from the lab, put one away to be kept clean and untouched. If you are careful, the track you edit will be satisfactory to use in the mixing session. Then after the mix you can erase the protection copy of the narration and reuse the film for another transfer.

NARRATION EDITING MATERIALS

When you begin narration editing, you should have the following materials at hand:

1. Two sync-coded transfers of the narration on magnetic film. Each of these rolls should contain the complete narration of the picture, fluffs and all, followed by the retakes of lines and sections.
2. A copy of the script of the film.
3. A copy of the narration text.
4. A sound report from the recording session to indicate the good and bad takes. This should be in the form of notes made at the recording session on the editor's or director's script.

ALTERNATE WAYS OF EDITING NARRATED PICTURES

There are three ways to put narration to a picture, and whichever one you choose depends on how good a finished product you require. The methods are as follows:

1. Edit the picture and the prerecorded narration simultaneously shot by shot.
2. Edit the picture into its final form, then lay the narration in to fit it.
3. Record the narration to the edited picture while it is being projected.

Picture and Prerecorded Narration Edited Simultaneously Shot by Shot

This method is usually the best because creative editing is possible. With both picture and voice on hand as you edit, you may select, rearrange, pace, and, and delete in any way you see fit. Actually, since narration is not literary, it should be treated as a distinct sound element of the track along with other effects and sounds.

1. Start by breaking down the narration into useful units—sometimes a paragraph, sometimes a sentence. Flange each piece into a roll and mark it for scene number and script page. Indicate whether it is a circle (good) or NG (bad) take. Remove all extraneous material between takes such as the talk between the director and the actor, mumbling, shuffling of feet, rustling of paper, and so on. Be careful to take out these unwanted sounds because they can be difficult to hear on an editing machine and may often appear as a complete surprise on the high-fidelity playback machines at the mixing session. Many an editor has been embarrassed in the mixing session to hear a stray "action" or "cut" in his final sound track.

Don't throw away bad takes. Listen to them carefully because sometimes the takes indicated as NG sound better in the editing room than they did at the recording session. Obviously some takes will be unusable, but takes that were redone because of nuances in interpretation may turn out to be the ones you want to use in the final sound track. Break down the picture into separate shots, and flange them into individual rolls marked as to scene and take number.
2. Arrange both narration and picture takes in script order on your editing table ready to be assembled.
3. Make up leaders for both picture and narration. (See Start Marks and Leaders, Chapter 9.) Making leaders at the outset is important. Don't start off with short temporary leaders because they will lead you into possible trouble later on. Make up leaders that will carry through the entire editing and mixing process. This means sufficient thread-up and sync leader, Society leader, the sync pop, and proper start marks. (see start marks and leaders, Chapter 9.) After you have made up the leaders, set them aside for the moment.
4. Workprint assembly. Now edit the movie. From the script, determine what shot should be first. Perhaps you have several options or several different angles of the opening scene. Try them in turn in your editing machine, and try out the

opening narration with the various shots and at various places relative to the picture. Be sure that you have not spliced or cut anything up to this point. Finally, decide which shot of picture is to be the opening one, mark the frame where you want it to begin, and splice this point to the picture head leader which you have already made up. Next, try out the first lines of narration against the picture. When you have decided what narration to use and at what point it should start, splice it onto the single-perforated head leader you have made up for the narration track. The narration will probably not start with the first frame of picture, so you will have to add room tone between the tail of the leader and the start of the narration. Continue in this way, building the picture and the narration together as you go.

The placement of narration relative to the picture is critical. A frame or two one way or the other can make a significant difference. For example, you can control the pace or apparent speed of the film by the way you position certain words in the narration. By allowing the narration to lag behind the picture, you may create a slow, boring pace; or you may create anxiety in your audience by running the narration up to the last frame of the scene or shot. Since the positioning of words must be exact, casually letting the narration fall where it may will defeat your purpose. Try for the best arrangement. Experiment. Notice the effect of small changes in the relative position of narration and picture.

Temporary Sync Marks

Since narration is not recorded in sync with the picture, there is no way of establishing sync until both narration and picture have been assembled and spliced in the proper relationship. This means that as you edit, you build up increasing footage that loses sync if it is taken out of the editing machine or the relative position of track and picture are shifted. Without sync marks you would have to go back to the head leader start marks and run through all you have edited to locate sync. To eliminate this inconvenience, place temporary sync marks on your sound and action at regular intervals. A good spacing for temporary sync marks is at the end of every other shot, or at the end of every lengthy shot. As you work, you will discover the best interval for temporary sync marks. Make temp sync marks by marking the picture with an "X" and the corresponding sound frame with the three sound sync lines. You may number them consecutively as you go, or use odd-shaped symbols if you lose track of numbers or get out of sequence.

Scratch Narration Track

You may find it too expensive to record the narration with a professional narrator, edit it, and then recall the narrator for additional lines and changes. Sometimes it is feasible to edit the picture with a scratch track, or narration recorded by someone other than a professional narrator. This could be the editor, the director, or someone else on the crew who has an appropriate voice. A scratch track has several disadvantages: voice quality and interpretation are not the same as that of the professional narrator, so the effect of the edited version may be different. Also, the timing may be quite different. The advantage of this method is that you can try out the narration and discover what changes or additions should be made, or if the narration really works. From this, you can rewrite and recast the narration so that when you go into the recording session you will get pretty much what you require. Further, you probably won't need additional recording sessions for retakes and changes (which means less money spent on recording). The best technique, of course, is to use the professional narrator to make both the scratch track and the final recording.

Lay Narration into Edited Picture

The next best method for adding narration to a film is to add it after the picture has been edited. This is the original way of putting narration to film, and most of the early narrated documentaries were done this way. Although a scratch track here is useful, you must be careful to see that the final narration by the professional narrator fits the timing of the scratch narration. Remember that the picture is already in its final form, and if the narration is too long there is nothing to do but lengthen the picture or rewrite and renarrate. Both these methods may be impracticable or impossible. Before making the final narration, make up a timing sheet indicating the running time in seconds for each section of picture for which narration is to be made. Then, during the recording session, be sure that the narrator does not run over or significantly under these times.

Record Narration to Projected Picture

This is the worst possible way to put narration to a film. Nonprofessionals believe this to be the only way it is done because a movie appears to be just that—a series of pictures with someone talking. The only possible advantage to this method is that it might conceivably save time in editing the sound track. In this method, the picture is first edited into its final form. Then the narration is tailored to fit into the running time of each scene requiring narration. At the recording session, the narrator sits in the studio, script in hand, while the picture is projected on the screen before him. As the picture rolls, the narrator reads the script and is recorded. The result is always substandard because the narrator has to give a flawless reading on one run-through. If he makes a fluff or a poor interpretation, the whole thing must be done over again. Further, how can he possibly give a good reading while trying to watch the film for cues? He cannot, so the director usually stands besides him and taps him on the shoulder to cue him on each paragraph. If you feel you must record narration this way, do so; but consider it an amateur method that will probably yield amateur results.

SEVEN

Some Aspects of Shooting

There are many different styles and tastes in photographing films and you are free to choose any one you prefer. You may favor the glamorous, artificial lighting of the movies of the 1930s; you may prefer the stark reality of cinema verité; you may choose the natural look of available light; or you may select a style that is in between or a combination of all of these. There is no one way to do motion picture photography; it depends on your individual feeling about what life looks like. If a location is dirty and dingy, you can make it look beautiful and romantic, or you can make it look real. Some cinematographers believe in recreating a thing on film as it really is rather than taking something ugly and making it beautiful. Others tend to put too much light on everything, and still others are inclined to make everything look low-key and moody. Some set up shots simply; others try for foreground objects and out-of-focus shots, extreme wide-angle and long-focus lenses, and high- and low-angle shots. Everyone has his own philosophy; but since there is an appropriate time and place for every kind of shot, the only rule in filmmaking is that whatever works successfully is the thing to do.

Shooting a film is not just loading the camera, taking a reading with the light meter, and then pressing the button. First, it is seeing the elements in a scene—the light, the shadow, the arrangement of objects, the mood, the feeling, the possibilities for saying what the photographer or the director wants to say. Only when you are able to see in this fashion, using imagination and keeping an open mind, can operating the equipment have any significance so that worthwhile results are possible.

Motion picture photography is not still photography. It is not photographing a series of separate pictures, although that is the way it appears when you look at a piece of motion picture film. It is the recording of movement. The camera is a surrogate human eye; and while the camera is running, you must assume that it is actually a part of your senses, an observing, participating human being. The camera is the eye of the audience.

This chapter will not review the elements of basic photography, for that has been done many times at great length and is readily available to all. Rather, the aspects of shooting a film that have not generally been described will be discussed. As a filmmaker, your task of getting the action onto the film is divided as follows:

1. Tools of shooting.
2. Analysis of the situation.
3. Logistics: determining what you need and how to get it to where you want it.
4. Shooting the picture: lighting, exposure, focus, and framing.
5. Disposition of the exposed film.

AMATEUR/PROFESSIONAL CAMERAS

There are four groups of cameras used in making 16mm films: amateur/professional cameras, professional silent cameras, professional sound cameras, and special purpose cameras. The amateur/professional cameras were manufactured as expensive home-movie cameras for well-to-do home-movie makers. They include such cameras as the Bell and Howell 70, the Bolex, the Eastman Cine Special and K-100, the Beaulieu, and the Cannon. These cameras are precise instruments, and much professional work has been done with them; but for full professional production work one or the other have certain limitations. The Bell and Howell, Bolex, and Cine Special are spring-driven and shot length is consequently limited to less than half a minute. All are built primarily for internal one hundred-foot film loads, and attempts to add external magazines for greater capacity are not always successful. Also, motors have been designed to be added as well as other modifications; but the end results are still not as versatile and rugged as professionally designed cameras. However, these cameras are excellent machines and may be used by the 16mm filmmaker to make highly professional films. Do not reject a camera just because it is not the latest professional model; do be prepared, however, to cope with problems of registration, parallax, limited running time for any one shot, lack of adaptability to other professional equipment, and a lack of ruggedness under a sustained, professional shooting schedule.

PROFESSIONAL SILENT CAMERAS

The second type, the professional silent camera is best represented by the Arriflex Model S (Fig. 7.1), the Mitchell 16, and the Maurer 16. These cameras are fully professional in design—that is, precision film movement, pin registration, electric motor drive, external magazine, with controls and features analogous to 35mm professional cameras. In fact, the Mitchell 16 is a scaled-down version of the 35mm Mitchell. These cameras are referred to as silent because they are not quiet and are used for silent shooting. All three of these cameras—Arriflex, Mitchell, and Maurer—are used in sound shooting, but each has to be mounted in a blimp when so used. Of these three cameras, the Arriflex S brought about great changes in 16mm production. The Mitchell and Maurer are heavy, studio-type cameras not suitable for hand-holding, and require a great deal of effort to move and set up. The Arriflex is small, light, and easy to hand-hold and move about, and is designed so that the operator can reach all controls during shooting. While the Maurer 16 and the Mitchell 16 are limited to studio-type operation, the Arriflex puts the 16mm filmmaker out into the world.

PROFESSIONAL SOUND CAMERAS

This category refers to precision professional cameras that are self-blimped and designed specifically to be used in shooting 16mm sound motion pictures. The predominant cameras here are the *Arriflex BL,* the *Eclair NPR,* (Fig. 7.2), and the Cinema Products CP-16. Fundamentally, these are the same as the silent cameras, with precision film movement, pin registration, external magazine, electric motor drive, and precision lenses. However, the Arriflex BL, the Eclair NPR, and the CP-16 operate at a noise level low enough for them to be used in sound shooting. The Eclair is a noiseless camera—that is, its mechanism has been designed to run quietly—while the Arriflex is self-blimped (Fig. 7.3), or insulated to prevent the internal noise of operation from excaping outside the camera body. The Arriflex BL, the Eclair NPR, or the CP-16 used in combination with a synchronous quarter-inch tape sound recorder, is the standard 16mm professional filmmaking tool.

SPECIAL PURPOSE CAMERAS

Equipment in this category is used for work involving high-speed and time-lapse photography, single-system shooting, animation, instrumentation photography, and underwater work. Although it is possible to install high-speed motors on standard production cameras, the maximum speeds attainable in this way are from 48 to not over 128 frames per second. These speeds are adequate for slow motion scenes involving people; but for extreme slow motion, as in special effects and scientific studies, much

Fig. 7.1 Arriflex S-16 silent camera.

higher frame speeds are necessary. Since production cameras are not built to withstand extremely high frame rates, specially designed high-speed cameras must be used. Be sure to get full information and instructions on setup and operation when using these cameras because focusing and framing are critical and are not always done in the same way as with a production camera.

Time-lapse photography consists of exposing single frames of motion picture film one at a time at predetermined intervals to compress a long-time action into a shorter time. The interval between exposures may be from a fraction of a second to several days. The result is that action is speeded up, the degree depending on the interval between exposures. A familiar example of time-lapse photography is a sequence of flowers growing from seed to full bloom in a few seconds, or the flowing of fog for several hours compressed into a sequence of two or three minutes, or the construction of an entire building compressed into five minutes. Many of the amateur type cameras can expose one frame of film at a time, making it possible to shoot limited time-lapse sequences. To do time-lapse photography with a professional camera, use special time-lapse equipment, which, through a special timing mechanism, exposes the film at the predetermined interval and triggers lights if so set up.

In single-system shooting, the sound is

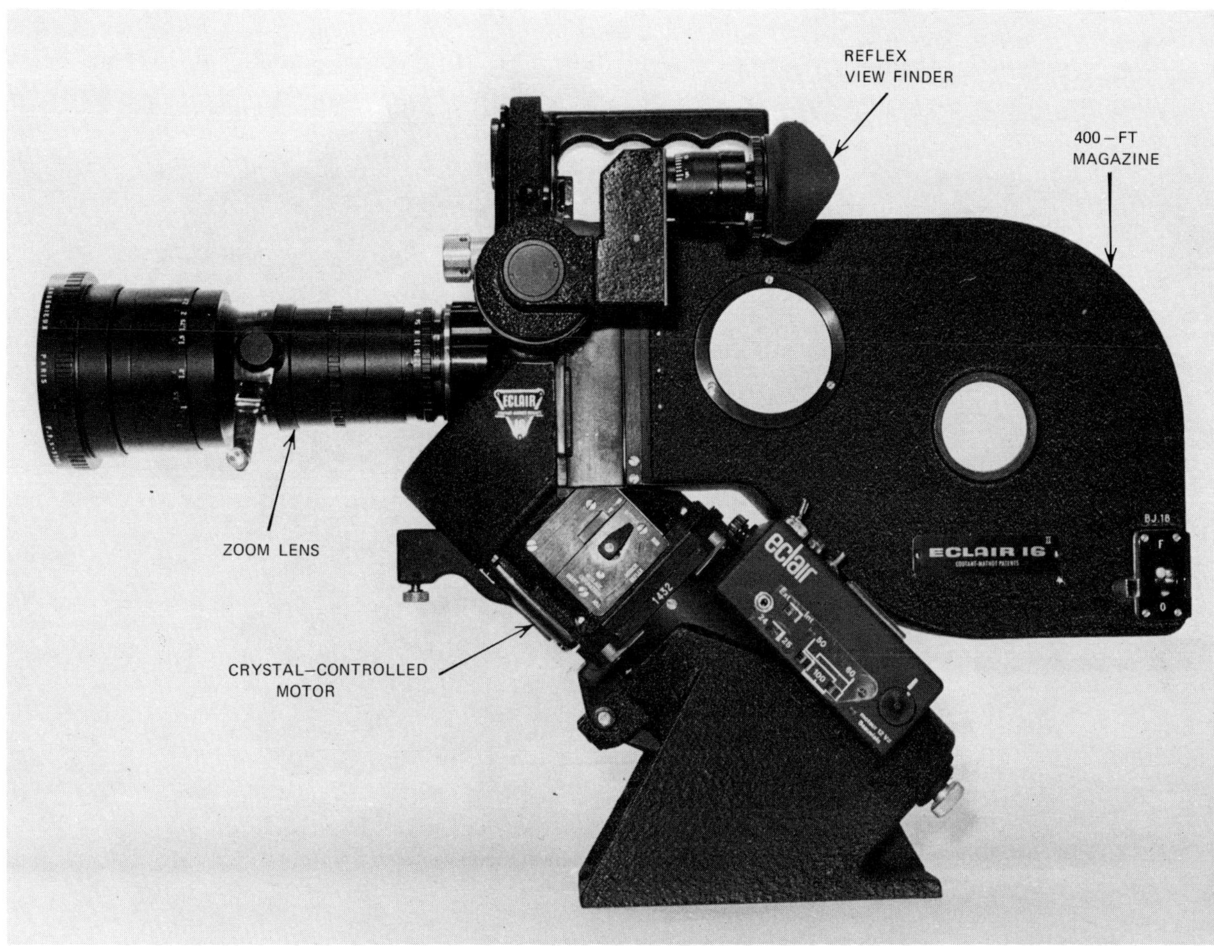

Fig. 7.2 Eclair NPR-16 noiseless camera.

recorded on the film in the camera at the same time the film is being exposed. The sound is recorded magnetically on a magnetic stripe laid down along the edge of unexposed reversal film. Subsequently the sound goes through the developing process along with the film. Single-system shooting requires a camera containing the recording device inside the camera body. The most commonly used single-system camera is the Auricon, although Cinema Products, Arriflex, Mitchell, and several others do manufacture single-system equipment.

Animation Cameras

Although it is possible to shoot simple animated sequences with a single-frame camera, good animation requires a special camera mounted on a special stand. The camera must be capable of precise exposure at any speed from single-frame up, and it must have a controllable shutter with precision registration and movement.

For underwater work any kind of camera may be used, but for obvious reasons it must be mounted in waterproof housing. There must be external controls on the housing by which the camera controls such as lens setting, focus, on-off, may be operated.

CAMERA CHARACTERISTICS

Basically a motion picture camera is simple. It consists of a light-tight box in which the film is positioned in front of an aperture, a lens to direct light through the aperture onto the film, an intermittent mechanism to move the film into position for each exposure, a shutter to block off the light while the film is being moved, a motor to drive the intermittent mechanism, a viewing

Fig. 7.3 Arriflex BL 16mm self-blimped camera.

system so the camera operator can see what is being photographed, and controls for operating the camera. Beyond this there are refinements.

The Arriflex 16S model camera illustrates the basic elements of the motion picture camera. (See Fig. 7.1) At the front is the turret with mounts for three lenses, any one of which may be rotated into the taking position in front of the aperture. The circular part of the camera body just behind the lens turret houses the shutter, a rotating disk with pie-shaped sections taken out of it. Behind this is the main body of the camera.

Inside the camera are the aperture plate and the pressure plate. The film rides on the aperture plate, which has a hole in it the size of the motion picture frame through which the light from the lens strikes the film. For loading the film, the pressure plate, which opens and closes like a door, holds the film steady against the aperture plate. At the edge of the aperture and pressure plates there is a *pull-down claw* and a *registration pin.* As the shutter rotates, its solid and open portions alternately pass in front of the aperture. When its solid portion is in front of the aperture plate, preventing light from passing through, the pull-down claw engages in a sprocket hole and pulls one frame of film into the aperture in taking position. At this point, the registration pin goes straight into another sprocket hole and holds the film absolutely steady as one of the open portions of the shutter passes the aperture, allowing light to hit the positioned frame of film. As the solid portion of the shutter again covers the aperture, the registration pin backs out of the sprocket hole, the claw once more pulls down another frame of film, and the registration pin goes in. The open portion of the shutter then comes past again, making another exposure. The cycle is repeated 24 times every second as long as the camera is running.

All professional cameras will produce sharp, precisely registered pictures, and it is not difficult to choose a camera for 16mm professional use. Whenever buying, renting, or using a camera, the following characteristics should be considered and compared.

Film Movement

When the camera is running, film must be moved one frame at a time for positioning in the aperture, and it must be held steady while the exposure is being made. The mechanism that does this is the film movement, which consists of the pull-down claw and the registration pins. All cameras have some kind of pull-down claw, and all professional cameras also have pin registration. During the exposure part of the film transport cycle, a metal pin moves into a sprocket hole and holds the film steady in exactly the same position as every other exposed frame was held. This ensures complete steadiness of the projected picture. Steadiness depends on precise registration; for even the tiniest difference in positioning from frame to frame during exposure results in a shaking picture on the screen that becomes worse as the screen size is increased. Super-8mm home-movie cameras and some of the more expensive 16mm semiprofessional cameras do not have pin registration, but the result is usually not noticeable because amateur movies are intended for projection on small home screens. Although some amateur cameras that lack pin registration can produce steady pictures, scenes intended to be spliced together that have been shot on two different cameras of this type may often show a displaced frame line when projected. If you plan to use a semiprofessional camera that does not have pin registration, make a test to determine whether the unsteadiness is acceptable or not. If conditions are such that you have to mix scenes shot on two or more separate amateur cameras, shoot a test roll in each camera and splice shots from one camera to shots from the others. If the frame line registration of the cameras does not match, a displaced frame line will show on the screen during projection. All 35mm cameras usually have two registration pins and two pull-down claws, one on each side of the film. The 16mm Mitchell, a scaled-down model of the 35mm Mitchell, has a double pull-down claw and two registration pins. Other 16mm cameras, such as the Arriflex and the Eclair, have a single pull-down claw and single registration pin on one side only, making it possible to use both single- or double-perforated film. Also, a movement in which a single pull-down claw stops briefly to act as a registration pin gives positive registration and steady pictures. Sharpness and steadiness of the image exposed in the camera have a direct relationship to the final image on the screen. High-speed shooting, special effects cinematography, optical printing, front and rear projection, and multiscreen presentations all have exacting registration requirements. The camera negative/original must be carried forward through masters, internegatives, separations, and release prints with the least possible deterioration so that good effects and steady pictures will reach the screen.

Viewing System

Two types of viewfinders enable the camera operator to view the scene while the camera is running: the *reflex viewfinder* and the *monitoring viewfinder.* In the reflex viewfinder, the camera operator sees the scene through the lens that is actually taking the picture; what is seen in the viewfinder is being photographed simultaneously. This is done mechanically by a mirror on the front of the rotating shutter that alternately reflects the incoming light from the scene to the viewfinder during part of the shutter cycle and then lets it pass through its cutout section and onto the film in the aperture during the other part of the cycle. This alternation occurs twenty four times a second, and the operator sees the scene twenty four times a second in between the times the film is being exposed at the same rate. The effect is that of looking at exactly what is being shot at the same time exposure is taking place. Not only does reflex viewing make it possible to see the scene exactly as it will be on the film, but it allows the focus to be set by eye when the viewer eyepiece is adjusted to the operator's eye.

Viewfinder

Reflex viewing is now inherent in the design of all modern professional motion picture cameras, but there are many older nonreflex cameras still available and in use throughout the world. These are fine, precision instruments, and you should be prepared to work with a monitoring viewfinder should the occasion arise. The monitoring viewfinder is attached to the outside of the camera and, since it is not in line with the taking lens, it does not see the scene framed exactly as the lens does. Consequently, the monitoring viewfinder must be adjusted for every position of the camera and subject so that the operator looking through it sees the scene framed just as it is framed on the film. The basic problem here is one of *parallax,* or the apparent displacement of the subject being photographed because the film and the viewfinder see it from two different points of view. If the external viewfinder is not aimed at what the lens is aimed, then the operator does not see what is being photographed. For the camera operator, dealing with and correcting parallax during shooting is an essential task. The monitoring viewfinder on professional cameras is often coupled to the follow-focus mechanism so that when the camera assistant changes focus to adjust for movement in the shot, the parallax of the viewfinder changes correspondingly.

Noise

Before sound it was not necessary that a camera be noiseless or even quiet, and motion picture cameras were originally designed without considering how much noise they made. With the advent of sound, it was obviously impossible to shoot dialogue scenes with overpowering camera noise in the background; and the first attempts to get rid of camera noise resulted in the building of large soundproof booths called "iceboxes," in which the camera and crew were installed and from which they photographed scenes through small windows. Clearly, the restrictions on camera movement and flexibility were unacceptable; so the standard Mitchell camera was modified to run more quietly, and a "blimp," or soundproof case was designed into which the camera could be mounted. Since a blimp can be put on a tripod or a dolly and moved as necessary, this was a great improvement over the icebox, but it was still cumbersome. Ultimately, cameras were self-blimped—that is, the camera body itself was so constructed that it did not transmit the clatter of moving parts and film. Most modern professional cameras are self-blimped, and those that are not may be used for sound shooting when mounted in a blimp. Note that *silent camera* does not mean noiseless *camera.*

SILENT CAMERA. A camera intended for silent shooting, that is, for shooting without sound. Though this type of camera makes noise and is not generally suitable for sound shooting, it may be used for sound shooting when mounted in a soundproof blimp. Examples: Arriflex S and M models, Mitchell 16, Maurer 16.

NOISELESS CAMERA. A camera designed so that its internal workings operate without making noise, or a camera that is self-blimped, that is, one with the soundproofing built into the camera body itself. It can be used for sound shooting, without being mounted in a blimp. Examples: Cinema Products, CP-16, Arriflex 16mm BL, Eclair 16mm NPR, Bolex 16 mm Pro, Arriflex 35mm 35BL, Mitchell 35 mm BNC.

Noise Levels

The following are the approximate noise levels of some of the most commonly used 16 mm professional cameras. These levels are customarily taken with the camera three feet from the microphone.

CP-16	26 dB
Mitchell 16 in a blimp	26 dB
Arriflex Model S or M in a blimp	27 dB
Eclair NPR	29.5 dB
Arriflex BL	31 dB
Bolex Pro	35 dB (5 ft)

In sound shooting, the amount of noise a camera makes determines its usability. Usually, a dramatic picture containing dialogue is shot in a stage or location where the ambient noise level is low; therefore, a very quiet camera is needed so that its noise level does not intrude on the low ambient level of the scene. Also, dialogue pictures generally include closeups that place the camera quite close to the microphone, thus increasing the possibility that camera noise will be picked up.

In documentary scenes where sound is being recorded, if the ambient noise level is greater than that of the camera, it is quite feasible to use, say, an Arriflex S. Often, even closeup shots in which the camera may be heard are used in many films and television documentaries. The reduced expense and ease of camera handling may often outweigh the advantage of using a noiseless camera. Much filming can also be done without sound, and many documentary pictures and scenes within dramatic dialogue films are shot silent with the intention of adding sound later. For filming to playback in 16mm it is not necessary to use a noiseless camera, since the sound has been prerecorded and is played back on the set only for cueing the actors. These considerations are vital because cost is important in every film, and it is generally less expensive to use a silent camera than a noiseless one.

Lens Mount

A lens mount is the mechanical arrangement by which lenses are attached to and removed from a camera. Since there is no universal lens, although the Angenieux zoom lens is often used as one, and since there is a limit to the number of lenses that may be carried in a camera turret at one time, lenses are removable so that a wide selection may be used. Since not all lenses fit all cameras, be sure that the camera you intend to use can accommodate the lenses you will need. Four kinds of lens mounts are generally considered standard:

"C" MOUNT. Also known as the Bell and Howell mount. This is a threaded mount, with female threads on the camera body and male threads on the base of the lens. The lens may be screwed into or unscrewed from the mount. Used on many types and makes of cameras.

ARRIFLEX MOUNT. Found only on Arriflex cameras. The lens slides into a short barrel on the camera and is held in place by spring-loaded pads that may be released for loading and unloading by means of two finger-operated levers. After long use, the springs holding the lenses in place may become weak, allowing the lens to move or even drop out of the mount. If heavy or very long lenses are used in this mount, they should be supported by a special bracket that attaches to the front of the camera.

CA-1 MOUNT. Found only on the Eclair camera. It is a deep bayonet mount, that is, a split flange on top of the lens fits into a long channel that provides sturdy support. To install a lens, slide the base of the lens into the barrel mount and twist it gently clockwise. To remove, untwist and pull out.

MITCHELL MOUNT. Found only on Mitchell cameras. This mount consists of a short barrel that slips into the camera body. Extending from the barrel is a flange with holes drilled in it through which the mount is bolted to the camera body. The base of a Mitchell lens is machined with two turns of a largeland thread which screws into the mount barrel. A set screw, or focusing lock, holds the lens firmly in the mount.

It is helpful to use a wide variety of lenses, and various adapters are available that make it possible to use lenses made for one type of mount in one of the other types. Adapters should be used only as a last resort because even the most minute discrepancy in the seating of a lens results in inaccuracy, particularly with wide-angle and zoom lenses. On the two-lens turret of the Eclair camera, it is common practice to fit one lens position with a CA-1 mount and the other lens position with either an Arriflex mount or a C mount. Thus a variety of lenses is available without the necessity of using adapters.

Treat a camera mount like any precision instrument. Be sure that the socket and the lens are clean and dustfree and that no scratches or abrasions are on the joining surfaces. A piece of dust on the raised portion of a metal scratch can affect the critical back focus of a lens and result in inaccurate seating and focusing. Regardless of the mount, use a support bracket for any unusually long or heavy lens.

Shutter

Most professional motion picture cameras operate with a shutter opening of 170° to 180° with a nominal exposure of 1/50 of a second at twenty-four frames per second. Actually a 180-degree shutter gives an exposure of 1/48 of a second, and a 170-degree shutter gives an exposure of 1/51 of a second; but for determining lens settings, 1/50 is generally used for openings between 170° and 180°. The difference is so small that it would be almost impossible to compute and calibrate. Arriflex cameras and the Eclair NPR have shutter openings of 180°: but the Arriflex shutter is fixed while that of the Eclair is adjustable, except while the camera is running. The Mitchell 16 shutter is variable from 0° to 235° with the camera running. Since a complete rotation of the shutter represents 360°, a 180° shutter is open half the time for exposure and closed half the time for the film to be advanced and registered. Although some shutters may be opened wider than 180°, the resulting shorter time for film movement and registration can be a threat to registration accuracy because of the shorter and faster action of the movement. At a shutter opening of 180°, there is a certain amount of blur in frames in which movement takes place. If you doubt this, closely examine individual frames of a piece of film on which some sort of action has been photographed—someone walking or running, or a car driving by. Many of the frames will be blurred; but on the screen the blurs will not be noticeable because they correspond to the blurs that we actually see in real life but don't notice consciously. This is one of the reasons that movement on film appears real to us. If the shutter opening is reduced, exposure time is also reduced, thus photographing less of the action and eliminating the blur effect. The overall effect is an apparent sharpness in the picture, but this is not actually so. We are seeing images that represent less of the action that is occurring, with a resulting stroboscopic effect—unpleasant choppiness or jumping of the image. A stroboscopic effect is most noticeable in shots of wagon wheels that seem to be going backward, or when the camera pans along vertical lines such as a picket fence. The jumping back and forth of pickets or vertical lines is unpleasant and sometimes even painful to the eye. What is lacking is the blur that makes movement appear normal to us, which is eliminated because with a smaller shutter opening or with a fast camera pan less of the action is photographed on each frame. The value of an adjustable or variable shutter is often overrated and misunderstood, and it is a mistake to assume that a camera lacking a variable shutter is inferior to one with such a shutter. Most amateur filmmakers consider a variable shutter quite valuable, for they customarily make fades and dissolves in the camera. But the professional filmmaker has no need for this, and would actually find it a handicap. A variable shutter is indispensable in animation and optical printing, but for almost all production filmmaking a shutter opening of much less than 180°is undesirable.

Camera Drives

A camera drive is the device that makes the camera operate. It may be a hand crank, a windup spring, or an electric motor. Although some of the earlier amateur cameras that have been and still are being used for some professional work, such as the Bolex H16 and the Bell and Howell 70, have spring-wound motors, all professional 16mm cameras in use today are driven by electric motors operating on either direct current (dc) or alternating current (ac). There are two types of camera motors according to their mode of operation:

Variable-speed motors, ac or dc; and constant speed motors, synchronous (ac only), governed (dc), and crystal-controlled (dc only)

Variable-Speed Motor

A variable-speed motor, also called a *wild motor,* is one in which the frame speed may be changed as desired. By turning a knob or control handle on a wild motor, it can be set to operate over a range usually from 8 frames per second to 24, and sometimes to 48 frames per second. A frame rate higher than 48 fps generally requires a special high-speed motor. There are many makes of wild motors, and a familiar one is the Arriflex 8-volt dc variable speed motor. The knurled knob on the rear of the motor controls a variable resistor that changes the voltage according to its position, and as the voltage is raised or lowered, the motor speeds up or slows down. Such a motor is inexpensive and simple and is excellent for all nonsynchronous or silent shooting, but it cannot maintain an exact speed when the load or the battery voltage changes. Even though you set its speed by the tachometer at 24 fps, it will not hold this speed within the tolerances needed for synchronous shooting. During a very long shot the speed of a wild motor may vary, since the drain on the battery causes it to drop slightly in voltage. When using a variable-speed motor, be sure to check its speed with the tachometer before or during each shot; but even though its speed varies during shooting, the variation is not noticeable on the screen in non-lip-sync scenes. Most narrated documentaries and educational films you have seen were shot with wild motors. There are both ac and dc (batteries) wild motors, but those operating on direct current are used more frequently.

Constant-Speed Motor

For synchronous sound shooting, a constant speed motor is essential. When used with a sync-pulse system, a camera motor must maintain a speed of 24 fps within a tolerance of ±1½ percent. If the frame speed varies more than this, normal sound-resolving equipment cannot make an in-sync transfer. It is possible to sync transfer some out-of-sync shots with a special resolver or by using a speed varier on the transferring tape recorder, but these should be resorted to only as emergency measures because they are expensive in both time and money and are not always successful. Even though you may be tempted to shoot sync sound with a wild motor carefully kept at a setting of 24 fps on the camera tachometer, don't do it. With little or no indication on the tachometer, the error can go as high as 6 to 10 percent and will certainly exceed ±1½ percent. For sync sound, three types of camera motors will operate at a constant speed: the synchronous motor, the governed motor, and the crystal-controlled motor.

Synchronous Motor

A synchronous motor runs in synchronism with the frequency of ac, which is 60 cycles per second in the United States. The motor's speed is controlled absolutely by the frequency. The most familiar example of a synchronous motor is the electric clock, which keeps accurate time because it can never run fast or slow. Its only error would be the small, long-term frequency changes in the power company's generators that are compensated for almost instantaneously.

The synchronous motor consists of a rotor containing a series of fixed magnetic fields and a stator of alternating magnetic fields. This is not especially significant for the filmmaker except that a fixed magnetic field cannot be created with alternating current; therefore direct current must be used to energize the rotor poles, while alternating current energizes the stator poles. As a consequence, a synchronous camera motor must have a power supply, usually in the form of a small metal box in the power cord line, which steps down some of the alternating current to power the stator and changes some to direct current to energize the fixed magnetic fields of the rotor. A synchronous motor requires a special cable with the power supply built into it.

Since 60 Hz current means 60 cycles per second, a sound camera runs at 24 frames per second. For every 60 cycles, the motor turns the camera exactly 24 frames. In the earlier days of sound shooting, a sprocketed sound recorder driven by a synchronous motor was used to record sound for pictures being shot on a camera that was also operated by a synchronous motor. Since both motors were plugged into the same 60 Hz line (or wall outlet), they both ran at the same speed, keeping both sound and picture in sync. Today we use quarter inch tape recorders to record sync sound, but the recorders do not use synchronous motors. A synchronous motor would not be effective because no matter how precise the speed of the recorder motor may be, tape speed would not necessarily be constant. Tape slippage, shrinkage, and stretching can effectively negate the constant speed of a recorder motor. To maintain sync today, we use the sync-pulse system, even though the speed of the tape is not the same as that of the camera and is not constant.

It is very simple to use a synchronous motor-driven camera and a tape recorder. There need be no connection between the camera and recorder as long as both take power from the same alternating current (all ac current in any one location comes from the same source). If the same ac current used to drive the camera is used as a sync reference in the tape recorder, the sync pulses put on the tape will correspond exactly to 60 cycles per second. This is accomplished by using a transformer plugged into the ac outlet to supply the reference frequency to the recorder. The transformer also steps down and rectifies some of the ac current so it may be used to drive the recorder, although this is unnecessary because the recorder may still be operated on its batteries while using the 60 Hz reference for sync pulse.

Governed Motor

A governed motor is the solution to running a constant speed motor on direct current. Lacking a supply of constant 60 Hz power on location, it is necessary to have a constant speed motor that operates on battery power. The governed motor powered by dc (which has no built-in frequency to control speed) operates within a tolerance acceptable for sound shooting. When quarter-inch, sync pulse recording was developed, the governed motor was designed to be used with it.

One type of governed motor works on centrifugal force, which opens contact points when the motor attains a speed of 24 fps. This shuts off the motor, which then slows down and allows the points to make contact again, speeding up the motor. The breaking and making of the contact points as the speed increases and decreases is held within an extremely small range so that the motor stays within the $\pm 1\frac{1}{2}$ percent error tolerance. Other, more sophisticated, governed motors operate by means of transistorized circuits that act as on-off switching devices. For sync shooting, the motor has a built-in sync-pulse generator to supply a 60 Hz sync signal to the recorder. A sync cable from camera motor to recorder must be used.

Crystal-Controlled dc Servo Motor

Servo is derived from the Latin *servus,* meaning slave. A servomechanism is a machine designed to carry out orders, which is just what a crystal-controlled camera motor does. It continually adjusts its speed according to instructions received from a control unit within the motor itself. The result is a dc constant-speed camera motor with the accuracy and reliability of a true synchronous motor and without the necessity for a sync cable connecting the camera and the recorder. It is based on the principle that a crystal oscillates at a constant frequency when a voltage is applied to it. The control unit continually compares the speed of the camera motor to the frequency of a built-in crystal oscillator, and if any speed variation occurs it sends a signal to the motor commanding it to slow down or speed up. This comparison and command occurs so rapidly that the motor speed remains constant. Operating on batteries (dc), the camera is highly versatile and independent of ac current, with a sync error of about ¼ frame over 400 feet of 16mm film. This is greater accuracy than the normal ac line frequency supplied by the power company.

For cordless sync, the crystal-controlled camera must be used with a tape recorder having a crystal-regulated sync pulse. A *crystal time-sync generator* may be attached to or built into a tape recorder, not to regulate the recorder's speed but to supply a 60 Hz sync-pulse signal to the tape. This signal may then be used for transfer to magnetic film.

Various cameras and recorders, each regulated by a crystal, may be used without sync cables and all will be in sync with each other without any limitation of distance or line-of-sight relationship. Depending on the make or type, a plug on the crystal-controlled motor allows an external reference frequency to be substituted for the crystal frequency. This allows the motor to operate in a selection of any one of the following different modes:

1. Ac synchronous operation. Plugging in an ac line substitutes an ac reference signal for the built-in crystal control signal. The motor then follows the ac line frequency instead of that of the crystal oscillator, and the camera will work in perfect sync with any equipment powered by ac synchronous motors, such as a sprocketed film recorder, a tape recorder using an ac reference, sprocketed studio playback machine, or other cameras.
2. Playback. Running a sync cable from a tape recorder into a crystal-controlled motor substitutes a sync-pulse signal prerecorded on tape for that of the crystal signal. The camera will then follow the recorder during playback, and picture and tape will be in sync.
3. Other external sync signals. The motor will follow any proper signal supplied by a conven-

tional sync-pulse cable from another camera, projector, or recorder.

4. Conventional cable sync operation. The crystal motor also generates a conventional 60 Hz sync-pulse signal that may be supplied through a sync cable to any recorder designed to receive a sync-pulse signal.

5. Variable speed. If a variable frequency source is substituted for the crystal frequency, the speed of the camera may be set at any desired speed with far greater accuracy than with any existing wild motor.

For a further discussion of sync shooting, see Chapter 8.

METHODS OF SYNC SLATING

Some form of slate is necessary in double system shooting to synchronize the sound and picture. (See Syncing Dailies, Chapter 10.) With sync-cable shooting, it is common, particularly in documentary work, to use a *bloop light* built into the camera and a tone oscillator built into the recorder, but this method does not work with crystal sync. The following are the most generally used methods of 16mm slating.

1. Conventional clapsticks. (See Syncing Dailies, Chapter 10.) This method uses the conventional slate with a hinged board attached to the top that may be slammed down to produce a loud bang. Scene identification is written on the slate, and at the start of each shot the slate is framed in the lens and photographed as the slate operator reads the scene identification and then slams the clapper down. The camera records the moving clapper and the recorder records the sound. Later, in the editing room, the editor matches the first frame showing the clapstick closed to the first sound of it on the track, putting the shot and its sound in sync. This is the simplest method of slating and provides full production, scene, and take information on both the sound track and on the picture.

2. Bloop and light slating. This is one form of automatic slating through a built-in bloop light in the camera and a built-in tone oscillator in the recorder. When the camera starts, a relay inside the camera closes and supplies power simultaneously to a bloop light that fogs the film and to an oscillator that puts a tone on the tape. When the camera gets up to speed, 24 fps, the relay opens and shuts off both the bloop light and the tone oscillator simultaneously. There are usually more frames of tone on the sound track than there are fogged frames of picture because the recorder reaches speed much faster than the camera. Therefore, since only the last frames of tone and bloop are in sync, synchronize the *last fogged frame of picture* with the *last frame of tone* in bloop-and-tone automatic slating. This type of automatic slating must have a sync cable connecting the camera and the recorder. With crystal sync there is obviously no cable connection, so there can be no bloop-and-tone sync. One of the other methods must then be used.

3. External light and oscillator tone. A small light may be mounted on the recorder, operated by a switch that also operates the sync tone oscillator in the recorder. At the beginning of the shot, or at the end while the camera is still running, the camera operator swings the camera to include the recorder in the frame. The recordist then closes the switch and both the light and the tone are energized simultaneously, providing a tone on the track and a light on the film that may be synchronized later. The recordist may also hold a numbered slate next to the recorder for scene and take information.

4. External sync device. This device works similar to the external light and oscillator tone except that the light and the tone-producing unit are housed in a small portable box or package that may be carried by hand or attached to the recorder. It consists simply of a small light and a buzzer or tone generator operated by the same switch. When the switch is closed, the light and buzzer go on simultaneously, the light being photographed and the tone being picked up by the microphone. As in the previous method, a numbered slate may be held next to the recorder for scene and take information.

5. Tapping the microphone. When an electronic slating source is either unavailable or inconvenient, a satisfactory sync slate may be made by the microphone operator holding up the microphone and tapping it before the camera. The sound of the tap and the picture of the action can be synced quite accurately. There is of course, no slate identification unless the recordist maintains some kind of numbered slate with it, but this method is usually used when the speed

of shooting dictated by conditions precludes preparing numbered slates for each shot.

6. Radio slating. This consists of a transmitter attached to the camera and a receiver in the recorder. When the camera starts, the bloop light in the camera flashes a number of frames and the radio transmits a tone to the recorder by way of the receiver. Both receiver and transmitter are very small and provide great flexibility for cordless shooting. On film the result is the same as with the conventional bloop and tone: the last fogged frame is in sync with the last frame of tone.

SELECTING A CAMERA

Primary considerations in selecting a camera are the kinds of jobs to be done, and these in turn will affect the decision of whether to buy or rent a camera. First, a camera with a precise, steady movement is necessary for any job, and this choice is relatively easy since any professional 16mm camera produces steady pictures. Shooting sound requires a camera that is blimped or noiseless. For sound stage shooting, or shooting on a controlled location setting, a heavier blimped camera may be acceptable; for shooting sound in a documentary or cinema verité situation, a light, noiseless camera capable of being easily handheld would be best. If you operate alone, you will need a lighter camera than if you shoot with a crew.

The professional cameraman working regularly at a variety of films would probably not benefit by buying a camera, since every shoot may require a different kind. One production may be a studio dialogue film; another, a TV commercial involving silent hand-held shooting; still another, high-speed shots of tennis players and so on. Since no one camera is designed for all these types of shooting, it is more feasible to rent a camera suitable to the film only for the shooting period. Many early Hollywood directors of photography owned their own cameras—some costing as much as twenty or thirty thousand dollars—although they always worked on the same kind of dramatic feature motion pictures requiring the same type of camera. The independent filmmaker involved predominantly with one type of film, such as documentaries or art films, may find it more convenient to own a versatile camera such as the Arriflex BL and rent specialized types of cameras and accessory equipment as they are needed.

To develop a basis for selecting a camera, first become familiar with the cameras on the market. Write to camera manufacturers for descriptive literature and specifications on all the professional cameras. Become familiar with the specifications of each, particularly with respect to the six characteristics discussed earlier, and visit rental houses and dealers to actually see and handle the cameras. Watch out for sales gimmicks, features that sound wonderful when described by a brochure or a salesman but which do not actually contribute anything special. One manufacturer, for example, stressed its camera's internal heating system, which is excellent if you plan to shoot in subzero temperatures; if not, the cost and extra weight are not worth it.

Use a camera before you buy it. It is helpful to rent a camera of the same model and shoot the type of material for which you will customarily use the camera to see how the footage turns out. Examine the weight, the feel, and the balance. Observe how you grip and hold it, and how the viewfinder is placed. Will it accept the various kinds of lenses and motors you will need? Is it rugged and versatile? The best camera is one that suits you best and can do the things you require most effectively.

In considering cameras for rental or purchase, don't be limited by fads. Occasionally, among filmmakers it has been fashionable to consider one particular camera-recorder combination or another as the only equipment to use. This is silly and self-defeating, since there is a wide range of camera equipment made and used for many years that is capable of turning out excellent pictures. The ingenuity and talent of the filmmaker often transcends the limitations of equipment.

Lenses

A lens is an optical device consisting of several elements, or pieces of special glass ground in a special way, that forms an image by focusing rays of light. The lens gathers in the light rays from the scene being photographed and focuses them onto a flat piece of film inside the camera. A thorough understanding of lens optics is not necessary to shoot good motion pictures, but anyone interested should certainly pursue the study in depth. In earlier times aberrations of lenses were generally uncorrected, so one had to be familiar with the physics of lenses to be able to compensate and use them correctly. Today, however, lenses used in motion picture work have become so refined that it is only important to know how to use them.

The amount of light a lens gathers is determined by its *aperture,* or diameter, and this amount of gathered light is further controlled by the iris *diaphragm,* a controllable opening inside the lens. Lenses are of fixed or variable focal length. A fixed focal length lens, referred to as a "hard" or "prime" lens, is manufactured with one permanent focal length, say, 25mm. Its aperture or its focus setting may be changed, but it remains a 25mm lens. A lens with a variable focal length is called a *zoom lens* and may be set to any focal length in its designed range, which usually extends from a wide-angle position to a long focal length position.

The lens is the eye of the camera, and therefore the eye of the camera operator, the director and, ultimately, the audience. But the lens does not see in the same way the human eye does, and it is a mistake to assume that what you see with your eye will be recorded by the camera lens in the same way. Among the numerous characteristics of lenses, the ones of primary concern to the filmmaker are angle of view, depth, resolution, and speed.

Lens Angle of View

This refers to the width of the horizontal area that a lens will see or take in. A *wide-angle* lens covers a relatively wide field of view, and a *long-focus* lens covers a narrower field. The human eye has a field of vision covering an arc of around 120°, with a slight fall-off at the extreme left and right edges. The widest angle lens, with the exception of special effects lenses, is about 50°. To shoot a scene that covers as wide a field of vision as you can see with your eye, even the camera with a wide-angle lens must be moved far back from the scene, which makes all objects in the scene appear much smaller and farther away than your eye sees them.

The lens that produces an image corresponding most closely to human vision is referred to as *normal.* For 16mm the normal lens is the 17½mm lens. For an 8mm camera, normal is 10mm; and for a 35mm camera, it is 35mm. A normal lens does not, of course, give the same width image that the eye sees, but it does give an image that closely resembles it in verticality, image size, and perspective. A picture shot through a lens with an angle wider than normal would seem to curve inward from the sides at top and bottom. Shot with a lens narrower than normal, the image would appear to lose perspective with both near and far objects becoming similar in size.

Focal Length

The *focal length* of a lens determines, or refers to, its angle of view, and is established by the distance in millimeters from the diaphragm of the lens to the *focal plane.* The focal plane is where the film is placed, and is the point at which the incoming rays come to a sharp focus. The diaphragm is the iris inside the lens that may be opened or closed to allow varying amounts of light pass through the lens. Short focal length lenses cover a wide-angle of view, and long-focal length lenses cover a narrow angle of view. These focal lengths are reflected in the actual lengths of the lenses themselves. Physically, wide-angle lenses are usually short—one or two inches—with a fairly large diameter, while long-focus lenses are longer, sometimes as much as two or three feet.

Lens Depth

Lenses of different focal length give images of differing aspect relative to depth or distance from the camera. This is true both in the apparent size of objects and in the sharpness of focus.

A long-focus lens does the same as a telescope in making far objects seem close, but it compresses everything from the distance to the foreground with a consequent loss of perspective (Fig. 7.4). This is called *foreshortening* and makes all the elements in the scene look the same size. An example of this would be a closeup of a football player on the near side of the field taken with a long-focus lens; in the background is someone the same size on the far side of the field—the feeling of perspective and distance has been lost. Shots of traffic taken with a long focal length lens make the cars appear jammed

Fig. 7.4 A long focal length lens foreshortens the scene and makes all objects seem jammed together and the same size.

together and in a far worse mess than they really are. Through a long focal length lens anything approaching the camera, say, a man running, does not appear to be getting any closer. We can see that he is running, but he stays the same size and in apparently the same place. A classic shot of this type is in the film, *The Seven Pillars of Wisdom,* in which a long lens was used to shoot a camel and its rider approaching from a long distance away in the desert. The foreshortening effect of the lens so compressed the heat waves rising from the desert sand that they created an intense wavering filter through which an indistinguishable black figure stayed the same size as it approached the camera. The total effect was one of extreme visual excitement and rising suspense.

A wide-angle lens does exactly the opposite: it expands a scene and makes the background appear much farther away than it really is (Fig. 7.5). Anything moving toward or away from the camera seems to be moving at a faster rate. Unlike the long-focus lens, the wide-angle lens can tolerate some camera shaking and movement

Fig. 7.5 A wide-angle lens makes a scene appear very deep, and background objects seem distant. These effects vary with the focal length of the lens.

without showing in the picture. This is one of the methods of obtaining good hand-held shots.

DEPTH OF FIELD

The range of image sharpness, or focus, varies with the focal length of the lens. This range is referred to as the *depth of field* and indicates the distance through which an object may be moved toward or away from the camera and still be in focus. As many a photographer sadly learns, not everything that the lens is pointed at will always be in focus. Under certain conditions almost everything, regardless of distance, may be in focus; but objects mainly in the close foreground and in the far distance will be out of focus. The length of the area in focus lying between close foreground and far distance is called the depth of field and depends on the focal length of the lens, the focus setting on the lens, and the *f*-stop. A change in any one of these—lens, *f*-stop, or focus setting—results in a different depth of field. As you examine depth of field tables (in American Cinematographer Handbook), you will see that as the lense diaphram is opened wider (i.e., the lower the *T*-stop or *f*-stop numbers), the smaller the depth of field. In shooting this means that when the lens is opened up to compensate for a low light level, the depth of field becomes small. With an abundance of light, you can close down the lens and gain a much greater depth of field.

Wide-angle lenses have an expanded depth of field, and long-focal length lenses have a narrow depth of field, and the manipulation of all these considerations enters into competent motion picture photography. Sometimes an expanded depth of field is desirable; other times only one part of a scene is required to be in sharp focus, with everything else closer and beyond slightly fuzzy. In situations where you want the focus to cover, say, the movement of an actress as she goes in and out of the in-focus area, either the camera operator or his assistant must "pull focus," which means changing the focus of the lens and thereby following the action, keeping the actress always within the depth of field of the lens.

Lens Resolution

This is the ability of a lens to distinguish between the small details of the object or scene being shot. The test for resolution consists of shooting a chart with horizontal and vertical lines printed on it. Portions of the chart contain lines that are printed progressively closer together. How well a lens can distinguish between lines that are very close together is a measure of its resolution. A lens with high resolving power can give a picture that clearly shows separate lines in a pattern where the lines are extremely close together. A low-resolution lens shows the same pattern not as distinct lines but as an overall gray mass. Obviously, a high-resolution lens gives sharp pictures, while a low-resolution lens produces soft pictures. Since different lenses of the same make and model may have different resolving powers, it is wise to test a lens before buying it. Other things that affect resolution are the resolution of the film being used and the kind and amount of filters used in front of the lens.

Lens Speed

Lens speed refers to the amount of light a lens transmits to the film and is usually expressed as *T*-stops or *f*-stops for the highest transmission value of the lens. That is, a lens whose widest opening is *f*/2.5 is referred to as an *f*/2.5 lens. A *T*/2 lens would be one whose widest opening is *T*/2.

f-Stops and T-Stops

The *f*-number indicates the amount of light supposedly transmitted to the film; the *T*-number indicates the amount of light actually transmitted to the film. The *f*-number is a numerical way of indicating the size of the diaphragm opening, from which it is inferred that a certain amount of light will pass through. However, this number is a geometrical calculation arrived at by dividing the focal length of the lens by the diameter of the diaphragm opening—it indicates only the diameter of the opening and not the actual amount of light being transmitted through that opening. As light passes through a lens, some of it is lost through reflection and some by absorption. Since these losses vary from lens to lens, an *f*-number does not mean the same thing for every lens. *T*-stops, on the other hand, are calculated by actually measuring the amount of light that passes through and comes out through the back of the lens. While the *f*-number is based solely on the light entering the lens without considering light losses within the lens, the *T*-number is based only on the light that is actually transmitted. *T*-numbers are valuable in that any given *T*-stop represents an exact amount of light regardless of the lens and its focal length. A lens marked only in *f*-stops may be sent to an optical house for electronic *T*-stop calibration and marking. However, it is possible for *T*-numbers to vary as the lens becomes older. With use, the coating on the lens becomes worn, some of the blackening inside the lens barrel may be lost, and surface scratches and abrasions inevitably appear. The effect of any or all of these is to reduce the transmission of light through the lens, thus reducing the effective *T*-number. To counter these effects, the *T*-stops should be recalibrated or checked occasionally.

Zoom Lens

The zoom lens is a variable–focal length lens available in several focal length ranges. By means of a lever or an adjusting ring on the lens barrel, a zoom lens may be set for any focal length within its range. Typical variable ranges for 16mm zoom lenses are from 12.5mm to 75mm, 9.5mm to 95mm, and 12mm to 120mm. Any focal length between the two extremes may be selected. Although not generally as sharp as prime lenses, well-designed and constructed zoom lenses such as the Angenieux and Canon lenses are used regularly in all types of professional work. Even when zooming is not done during shooting, it is extremely convenient and time-saving to use a zoom lens as a universal lens, selecting whatever focal length is desired for successive setups.

The internal assembly of a zoom lens is more complex than fixed lenses, and as a result more of the incoming light is absorbed and reflected. Consequently, *T*-stops should always be used on a zoom lens. Also, a zoom lens must be seated in the camera body with a high degree of precision. Unlike the hard lens, which is focused by being moved closer to or farther away from the film, the zoom lens is focused by movement of the front element only. There is only one position of the rear element relative to the film plane. If the zoom lens is not seated properly, because of dirt, damage, poor adjustment, misalignment, or carelessness, it will be out of focus. So be sure that the lens flange and the camera body are kept scrupulously clean and free of scratches and nicks.

FOCUSING

For focusing, a zoom lens should be set at its longest focal length position and at its widest aperture. With the focusing established at this position, you can then zoom back to the focal length you want the shot to start at. If focusing is not done this way, it is possible that the sharpness achieved at the wide-angle position will gradually deteriorate as you zoom to a longer focal length.

During a zoom, all parts of the image except that on the optical axis will shift to one side or the other. An object that is centered remains centered during the zoom in (Fig. 7.6). If you start on a wide-angle framing of an object that is slightly off-center, as you zoom in to a closer angle, the object will shift to the side of the frame on which it was originally off-center (Fig. 7.7). This may be compensated for by moving the camera, but there are situations in which you may want a static camera and a straight zoom back. Since it is difficult to determine the exact center of the frame in a wide-angle position, before shooting, center the object with the lens in the closeup position and then zoom back to the starting wide angle. If the camera is not moved later, centering is automatic during the zoom in. Even with the lens improperly seated, it is possible to have the image sharply focused at the longer focal lengths; but it will go out of focus when zoomed to wider angles.

Diopter Lenses

These are auxiliary closeup lenses that may be placed in front of a camera lens to shorten its focal length. In this way a prime lens may be used for extreme closeups without using extension tubes or bellows. A split diopter is actually a part of a diopter lens that may be used over a portion of a prime lens to bring both near and far objects into sharp focus at the same time. A diopter is a unit of measurement of the refraction power of a lens and is equal to the reciprocal of

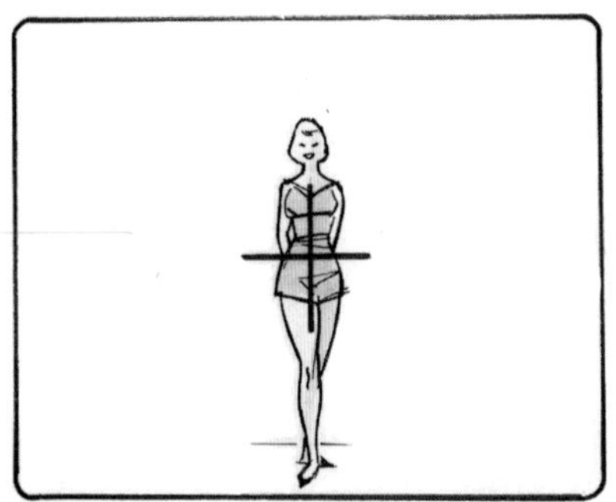

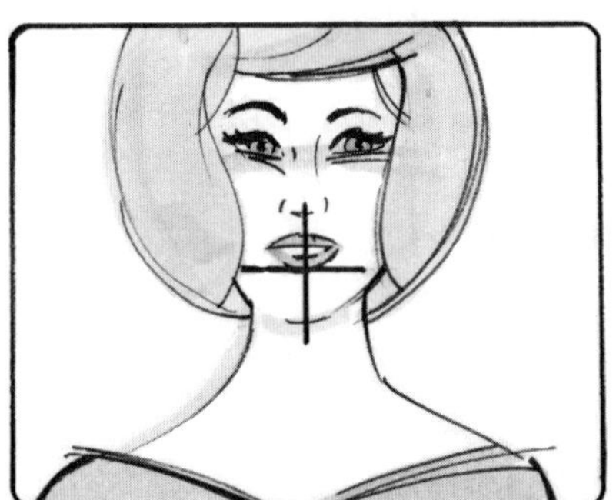

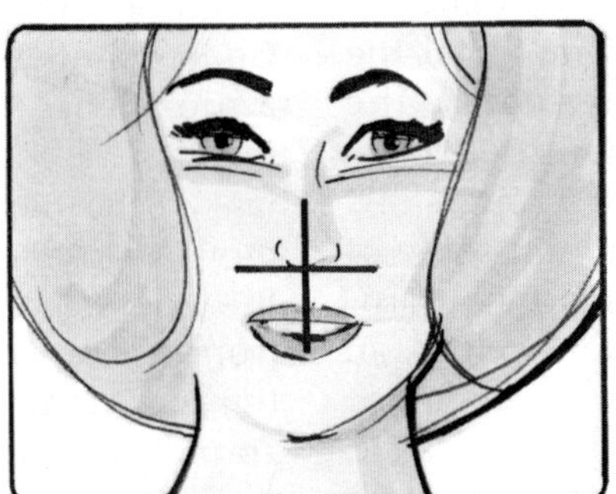

Fig. 7.6 Zoom lens object centering.

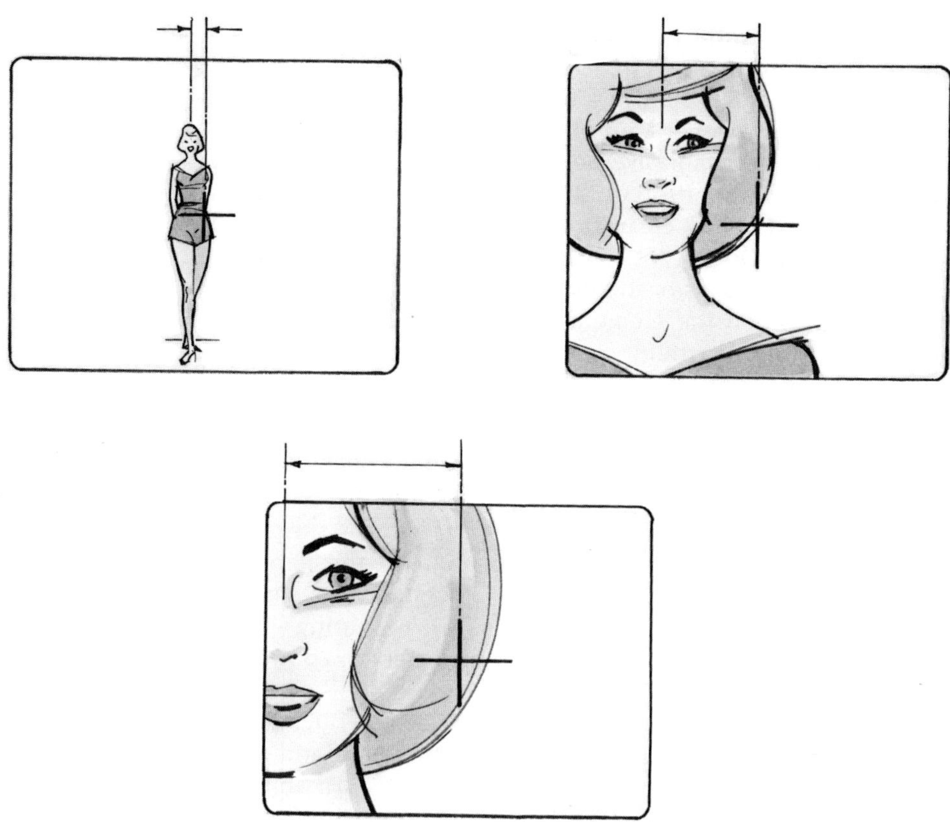

Fig. 7.7 If the object is off center in the wide-angle position, it goes farther off center during the zoom in. The amount is proportional to the zoom ratio of the lens. For a 10:1 zoom lens, the object will deviate ten times its original off-center distance over the full zoom range.

the focal length in meters. Diopter lenses are so-called because they are identified by such measurements as +1, +2, +3, +4, +5, +6. The lower the number, the greater the closeup effect. Higher diopter numbers are possible, but their quality is unsuitable for motion picture lenses. Diopter lenses are available in threaded mounts and series sizes.

Care of Lenses

A lens is a delicate device that determines the quality of the image on the film. It consists of a series of glass elements cemented together precisely to effect the proper transmission of light rays. All its elements must be maintained in an exact relationship to each other and to the film plane for a quality image to be photographed. Dirt, heat, and vibration destroy lenses, and it is your responsibility to see that lenses are exposed to them as little as possible.

It is better to prevent a lens from getting dirty than to clean it, for constant cleaning only hastens the removal of the coating on the front element that has been put there to cut down on reflective losses. Keep lens covers on both the front and rear elements whenever the lens is not being used, in a dust- and dirt-proof container. Often a lens may look dirty, but a puff from a bulb air blower or a few gentle sweeps with a sable hairbrush will get rid of most of the particles. Use only a brush made from sable hair—and don't ever touch the brush with your fingers or let it touch any part of your skin. Grease from the skin transfers easily to a brush and later spreads from the brush to the lens.

Dust on the lens does not affect the quality of the image but grease smears do. A fingertip smudge spreads body grease on the lens surface, and if left there, the acids in the human grease will etch the lens permanently, thereby reducing its resolution. Clean off fingerprints or other grease smears immediately with a piece of lens tissue and a first-quality lens cleaning fluid. Roll a piece of tissue and tear it in half to give a frayed cleaning tool. Do not use any other kind of cloth or paper—anything else is too abrasive and will scratch the lens surface. Put one drop of fluid on the end of the paper and gently clean the lens with a circular movement. Do not let any of the lens cleaner flow out to the edges of the lens because it will seep in between the elements and dissolve the cement holding them together. There may sometimes be a fingertip smudge on the lens that you cannot normally see. To detect this, inspect the lens surface with a magnifying glass, holding it at various angles to the light. At a certain reflecting angle, smudges become visible that are otherwise not immediately noticeable. Also, keep the flange surfaces of both lens and camera clean because even a small piece of dust or dirt can prevent the lens from seating accurately. Carry the lenses in cases packed in shock-absorbing plastic or foam rubber. Do not carry them in glove compartments or car trunks where all three evils—dirt, heat, and vibration—are inevitably present.

Lens Inspection

Any final determination of the soundness of a lens should be made by an optical laboratory or an optical technician, but when considering a lens for purchase, rental, or use, there is a systematic physical inspection you can make initially to determine the condition of the lens. Generally if a lens passes the following test, it is a good one:

1. Somewhere on the lens the manufacturer and lens type are indicated. This is a quick way of determining whether the lens was a good one when new.
2. Be sure its focal length and aperture are what you require.
3. Is it calibrated in *T*-stops, *f*-stops, or both?
4. Turn the focusing ring and the diaphragm ring, and move the zoom control through their full range of movement. If there is any play, dragging, roughness, looseness, or rattling, the lens should probably be checked by a laboratory.
5. Look into the front element, turn the diaphragm ring, and visually check the diaphragm for operation and for broken or missing pieces.
6. Check the front and rear elements for cracks or chips in the glass, which are indications of unkind treatment and probably call for a laboratory check. Tiny air bubbles in the glass may be ignored.
7. Look at the black coating on the inside of the lens barrel to determine whether it has flaked or chipped. If its light-absorbing ability has diminished, the quality of the image will be affected.
8. Are the lens elements still firmly mounted? Gently shake the lens, and if the elements rattle, it should be checked by a laboratory.
9. Inspect the flange—the rear surface that fits against the flange of the camera body—for any scratches or particles of dirt that may prevent it from seating properly. This is especially important in zoom lenses.

When buying a lens, first perform the above inspection and then send it to an optical laboratory for a complete bench test. Also, test it by shooting film, both scenes and resolution chart. No two lenses are exactly the same, even though they may be identical models made by the same manufacturer, and you may have to submit several lenses to a bench test before finally deciding which one to buy. Through careful selection and testing, it is possible to accumulate a complement of extremely fine lenses.

LIGHT

The basis of photography is light, and the cinematographer's art is concerned with modifying and controlling it. Light is found everywhere, but the filmmaker cannot always use it without altering its color, its intensity, or its quality. Such alterations are referred to as *light control* and are made at the lens with filters and at the light source with a variety of materials.

Light is a part of the electromagnetic spectrum and is made up of waves emitted from a source. The radiant energy of the electromagnetic spectrum is classified according to wavelength (Fig. 7.8), or the distance between the crest of successive waves. The shortest wavelengths, the cosmic rays, are so small that there are billions of

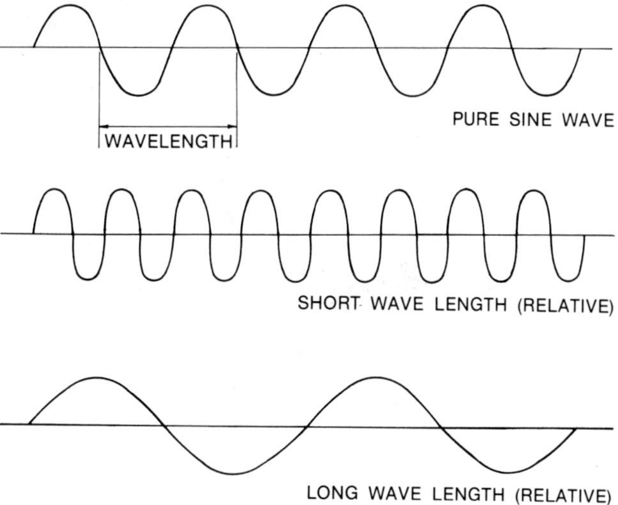

Fig. 7.8 The wavelength of energy in the electromagnetic spectrum determines the color of light.

waves to the inch; while the longest, electrical power waves, are several miles in length. The visible spectrum, the range of waves that the sensors in the human eye respond to, is a very small segment somewhere in the middle (Fig. 7.9). These visible rays graduate from violet at the short-wave end, through the blues, greens, yellows, oranges, up to red. The length of the waves varies from 320 nanometers (nm) (one millionth of a millimeter) at the violet end to 750 nm at the red end. White light, or light that we normally see as being white, consists of a combined balance of all these colors of the visible spectrum (Fig. 7.10). This can be demonstrated by refracting a beam of white light through a prism, which breaks up the light into separate colored beams. When white sunlight strikes droplets of water in the air, the droplets act as prisms and separate the white sunlight into its discrete component colors. The resulting rainbow is a graphic illustration of the visible spectrum, each color representing a specific wavelength of radiant energy. The white light of the sun is made up of all the visible colors in certain proportions—so much red, so much blue, and so on—which vary according to the sun's position and according to the condition of the atmosphere (Fig. 7.11). Other kinds of light, such as incandescent bulbs, arc lights, and fluorescents, give off light that is apparently white; and their

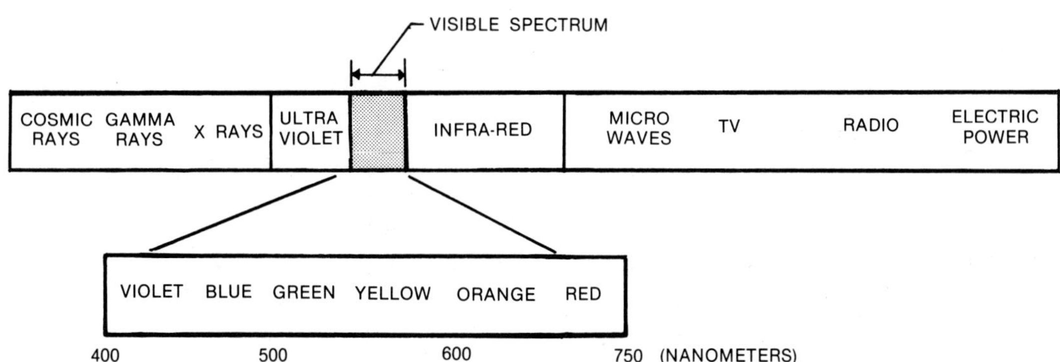

Fig. 7.9 A very small portion of the electromagnetic spectrum is visible to the human eye. This visible range extends from the short wavelength violets tothe longer wavelength reds.

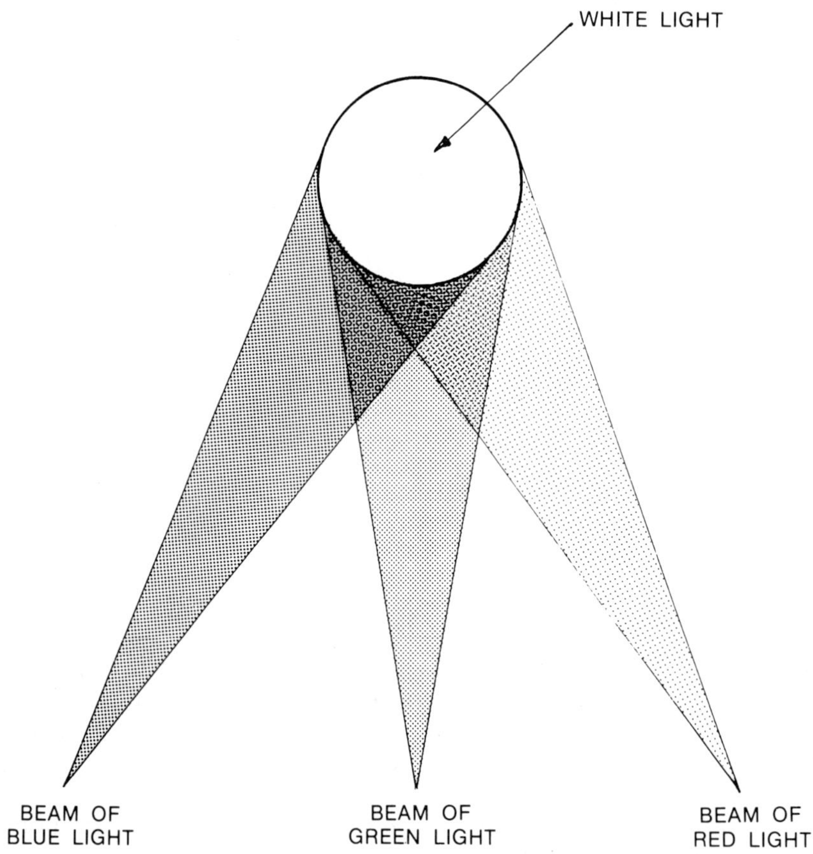

Fig. 7.10 The primary colors of light are red, green, and blue. When combined in equal amounts, they form white light.

light also contains all the colors of the spectrum in different proportions, both from each other and from the sun.

COLOR

Color is the word that describes an *imbalance* of visible radiant energy reaching the eye from objects and from light sources. A beam of light is unbalanced when it has, say, no blue wavelengths in it; and the remaining wavelengths—green, yellow, orange, and red—together form the combination that our eyes perceive as yellow. A piece of butter is yellow because when white light strikes it, it absorbs the blue light and reflects the others. Similarly, when white light

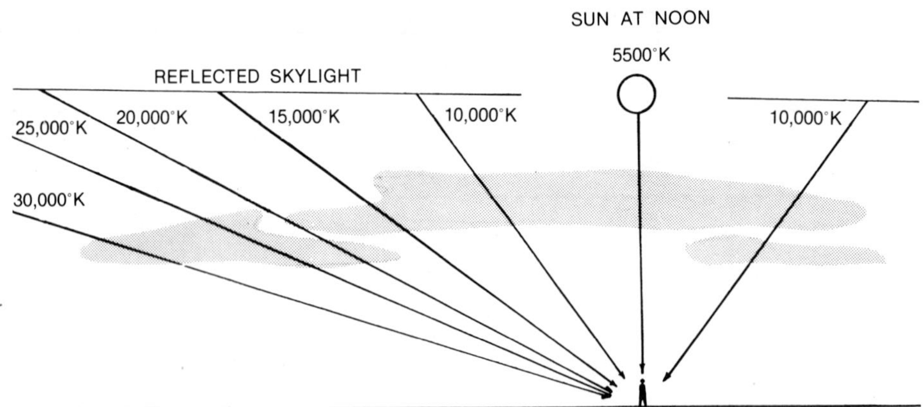

Fig. 7.11 The color temperature of skylight varies according to the position of the sun.

passes through a green filter, all wavelengths except green are absorbed and only the green wavelengths are allowed to pass through. Colored objects reflect or transmit some wavelengths more readily than others; consequently the colors we see are the result of radiant energy reaching the eye after being modified by the objects they have been reflected from or transmitted through.

Color of Light Sources

The color of light sources—electric lights, the sun, candles, carbon arcs, and fluorescent lights—is determined by the wavelengths of energy they emit. Every light source emits its own peculiar combination of spectral colors, and a light source giving off light that is relatively balanced in all the visible wavelengths looks white to the eye. Unfortunately for photography, all light that appears white to the eye is not white. The peculiar balance of colors in a light source affects film in a unique way, so that a slight imbalance that is not obvious to the eye can be quite noticeable to color film, and, to some extent, to black-and-white film.

Since film, unlike the human eye, is highly selective in its reaction to the colors contained in white light, color films are disigned to react correctly only to light sources with specific combinations of wavelengths. A type of film that gives faithful results under incandescent light renders a scene blue when used in sunlight. Conversely, a film that shows colors accurately in sunlight records scenes exposed under incandescent light in warm, reddish tones.

Kelvin Color Temperature

The two kinds of light that film must be balanced to are daylight (5500°K) and artificial light (3200°K). The exact color of the light in these two types is expressed as color temperature, which in turn is expressed in degrees Celsius measured from absolute zero (minus 273°C) on the Kelvin scale. All objects will give off light if they are heated; and, as the heat is raised, the color of the light emitted will change. A piece of iron turns a dull red when first heated; and as it gets hotter, its color changes to red-orange, then white, and finally blue-white. Similarly, the tungsten filament in an incandescent lamp changes color with changes in applied voltage. The more voltage applied, the hotter the filament becomes, and the bluer the light. When voltage is lowered, the filament becomes cooler and redder. Color temperature expressed in degrees Kelvin can be used to designate an exact color in any heated object. The following are Kelvin color temperatures:

800–2850°K	Reddish
3000–3350°K	Yellowish
3350–5000°K	Whitish
8000°K	Pale blue
60,000°K	Brilliant blue

Color Temperature of Light Sources

Any solid such as iron or tungsten, that radiates energy when heated, is called a *thermal radiator*. If the temperature becomes sufficiently high, the energy radiated may fall within the visible spectrum, in which case the solid becomes a source of light; but there is no relationship between the color temperature of a light source and its own temperature. Color temperature merely indicates the color of the light emitted, and the actual temperature of a glowing tungsten filament may be higher or lower than the numerical expression of its color temperature. The table shown below contains examples of apparent color temperature values. Although sunlight has many different color temperature values, depending on the time of day and condition of the atmosphere, photographic daylight is considered to have a color temperature of 5500°K, and daylight films are balanced to this value.

Photographic daylight	5500°K
Sunlight at sunrise	1800°K
Sunlight at noon	5400°K
Sunlight in midafternoon	4800°K
Sunlight in late afternoon	4300°K
Overcast sky	6500°K
Clear skylight	12,000–30,000°K
Motion picture incandescent light bulbs	3200°K
Photoflood bulbs	3400°K
Household light bulbs	
100–200 watt	2900°K
75-watt	2800°K
40-watt	2650°K

Candle flame	1850°K
Xenon arc lamp	6000°K
White-flame carbon arc	5000°K
High-intensity sun arc	5500°K
Warm white fluorescent	3000°K apparent
Cool white fluorescent	4200°K apparent
Daylight fluorescent	7000°K apparent

Although fluorescent lights are listed in the table, their color temperature is an apparent one since technically a color temperature designation can apply only to incandescent light sources, that is, light sources whose color is relative to its degree of heat or applied voltage.

As shown in the table, the higher the color temperature, the bluer the color; and the lower the temperature, the redder the color. Since the apparent color temperature of fluorescents does not indicate any specific color distribution, it is difficult to determine from their appearance or color temperature how they will affect color film. Manufacturers of fluorescent lights can supply information about what filters to use for color film. Such recommendations, however, are only the basis for actual camera tests, which is the only way to determine the best filter combinations.

Controlling the Color of Light

The color temperature of light used to expose film, whether indoor artificial light or outdoor light, must be the same as that of the film being exposed if faithful color rendition is to be achieved. For both 16mm and 35mm professional film production, indoor, tungsten-balanced film emulsions balanced at 3200°K color temperature are customarily used for both indoor and outdoor shooting. Consequently, since photographic daylight has been designated as 5500°K, there must be some degree of color temperature control applied to the daylight source. Actually, as can be seen from the comparative tables of color temperature (Fig. 7.12), daylight has an extremely wide range of color temperatures, that generally range between 5400°K and 6000°K, with 5500°K established as the fixed value.

Normally there are two kinds of light available in shooting: 3200°K incandescent light and 5500°K daylight. When shooting outdoors, sunlight may be converted to 3200°K by a daylight filter over the lens. The ones most frequently used are Harrison C-4, Eastman 85, and Gavaert CTO 12B. When shooting indoors with 3200°K lights, no filter is needed because the lights and the film are balanced for the same color temperature. When the two types of light are mixed, combination measures are needed.

INTERIOR SHOOTING

In shooting interiors with 3200°K tungsten lights mixed with daylight (5500°K) coming through doors, windows, or skylights, there are two choices: hang sheets or panels of a daylight filter (Harrison C-4, Eastman 85, Gavaert CTO-12B) over the windows or other openings, converting the incoming daylight to 3200°K color temperature. The second choice is to convert the tungsten light to 5500°K. The color temperature of one type of light must be changed to correspond to the color temperature of the other. If the two are mixed the daylight, which is extremely blue compared to the 3200°K of the tungsten lights, gives an objectionable blue cast to the scene. Four ways of handling this kind of situation are as follows:

1. Place sheets or hard panels of one of the daylight filters over the windows to convert the incoming daylight to 3200°K.
2. Put glass or plastic filters over the tungsten lights to convert their color temperature (3200°K) to daylight (5500°K) to match the light coming in through the windows. This is usually the least satisfactory method because filters for this purpose cause a significant light loss, reducing the overall level and consequently requiring more lights and power for exposure.
3. Use lights that have a dichroic coating on them, which gives them a color temperature of 5500°K to match the daylight coming in through the windows. Dichroic coatings cause less light loss than filters, but are quite fragile and wear off easily, causing the color temperature of the lights to swing toward red.
4. Shoot with a mixture of daylight and tungsten light. This can be done if the setups are such that the tungsten light can override the blue of the daylight, as in close shots. Some filmmakers like the effect of an extremely blue exterior seen through windows.

EXTERIOR SHOOTING

In shooting exteriors with daylight, the color temperature is not always at 5500°K, but varies greatly with time of day and condition of the atmosphere. Notice the various color temperatures of daylight indicated in Fig. 7.12. When shooting outdoors, it is common practice to disregard small changes in the color of daylight as the day goes on and to allow the laboratory to make color corrections later during printing. But if the shifts in color during the day are great, or color changes are aesthetically desirable, there is a range of filters that make small corrections in color temperature. These are the Harrison Light Corrector series (Fig. 7.12), the Eastman filters numbered 81 through 82, and the Gavaert CTO and CTB filters.

It is possible to use correcting filters effectively by judging the light based on the time-of-day scale and actual observation as described above; but for precise color temperature determination, a color temperature meter is essential. By comparing the relative values of blue and red in a light source, the meter arrives at a color temperature reading. Readings from the meter scale are converted to appropriate filter numbers.

Filters

A photographic filter is a colored piece of glass or gelatin placed at the front of the camera lens to change the color balance of the light passing through it. The principle of filters is based on the fact that white light is made up of all the colors of the spectrum, and that any one or combination of these colors can be augmented, reduced, or eliminated from a beam of light by being passed

Type of Light Source	Color Temperature	Harrison Light Corrector Disc required to convert the Light source to a color temperature of 3200°K
Skylight		
Very blue	30,000°K	C-14
Strongly blue	25,000°K	C-13
Quite blue	20,000°K	C-12
Fairly blue	16,000°K	C-11
Very bluish	13,000°K	C-10
Strongly bluish	11,000°K	C-9
Quite bluish	9500°K	C-8
Average shade (bluish)	8000°K	C-7
Light shade (fairly bluish)	7100°K	C-6
Average Daylight	6500°K	C-5
Overcast sky	6500°K	C-5
Photographic Daylight	5500°K - 6000°K	C-4
Sunlight at noon	5400°K	C-3
Sunlight in mid-afternoon	4800°K	C-2
Sunlight in late afternoon	4300°K	C-1
Sunrise	2000°K	B-7
Sunset	2000°K	B-7
Photoflood Bulb	3400°K	C-1/8
Household light bulbs		
150-250 Watts	3000°K	B-1/8
75-150 Watts	2900°K	B-1/4
40-75 Watts	2600°K - 2800°K	B-1/2

Fig. 7.12 Harrison Light Corrector Discs are filters that correct the color temperature of light sources to 3200°K. The proper filter may be estimated from this table, or it may be determined from a color temperature meter. If the difference is large, it is best to use the meter; if it is very small, the filters may be disregarded and correction applied later in the printing process.

through a particular color medium. The purpose of a filter is redistribution of the colors in light so that light of an exact, predetermined color combination exposes the film. Filters are used to correct color temperature, balance intensity, create mood and special effects, judge light distribution, and control density and color balance in printing.

Gelatin filter sheets are square and range in size from two inches to five inches. Glass filters, consisting of gelatin laminated between two pieces of glass, are both round and square and are available in many sizes. Filters are made with Type A and Type B glass. Type A glass is optical glass similar in quality to that used for lenses, and is used in exacting work such as microphotography and wide-aperture photography. Type B glass is not as precise, but is acceptable for normal photography. The following is a list of several categories of filters according to their application:

1. Neutral density filters (see p. 171).

2. Color conversion filters. These are filters used to change the color temperature of a light source so that it matches the color balance of the film being used. The most familiar use of a color conversion filter is that of converting daylight from 5500°K to 3200°K color temperature to match professional tungsten film. This is usually done by putting either a Harrison C-4, an Eastman 85, or a Gavaert CTO-12 filter over the lens. Color temperature changes such as this are relatively large, but additional filters—the so-called light-balancing filters—make small changes in color temperature that range from about 600°K per filter to less than 100°K.

3. Color compensation filters. These filters are used mainly in laboratory printing for the attenuation of the red, blue, or green components of the spectrum. They are also used to make slight color-balance changes in shooting and to correct for small variations in the color balance of specific emulsion batches. They are identified as the Harrison Color Compensation series, and the Eastman and Gavaert "CC" series.

4. Black-and-white-correction filters. Black-and-white film does not respond to light as the human eye sees it. Green, for example, appears lighter to the eye; and correction filters change the light balance so that the film is exposed at luminances close to those seen by the eye. A pale yellow filter is normal correction, and a deep yellow filter is strong correction.

5. Black-and-white contrast filters. These filters are used to separate colors that look different to the eye but the same on black-and-white film. For example, a red apple and its surrounding green leaves both look gray on film. A red filter over the lens holds back some of the green light, which underexposes the leaves, making them appear much darker than the apple. A green filter would switch this contrast around, making the apple darker and the leaves lighter. The whole range of filters can be used to create varying contrast moods on black-and-white film.

6. Haze filters. Haze is bluish and causes overexposure, diffusion, and reduced detail in both black-and-white and color film. The effect of haze is reduced on color film by ultraviolet filters and on black-and-white film by a pale yellow filter. These filters hold back some of the blue and reduce its exposure. Mist and fog are composed of white particles of water in the air and are unaffected by haze filters.

7. Tricolor filters. These are primary red, primary green, and primary blue filters used in making color separations.

8. Combination filters. Filters of this type combine neutral density with color conversion, black-and-white correction, or black-and-white contrast filters. Filters 85N3, 85N6, and 85N9, for example, convert daylight to 3200°K while reducing exposure by one, two, and three stops respectively.

9. Special effects filters. The various special effects filters alter the image in some way other than changing the color balance or luminance. A diffusion filter softens an image and reduces the harshness of hard lines and blemishes in the human face; star-burst filters turn highlights into star-pointed rays; split-field lenses allow effects to be made on part of the frame only; and contrast filters make it possible to rebalance the lighting ratio of existing light.

10. Fog filters. Fog filters are used to simulate natural fog by lowered contrast and a slight halo effect. Harrison Double Fog filters for color film create the fog effect without reducing definition or requiring an increase in exposure.

11. Polarizing filters. These filters are also called *pola screens*. A polarizing filter, or polarizing

the system fuse or breaker. Although each side of a three-wire extension may be protected by a 100-ampere fuse, the cables going to the lights may not be able to carry that much. It is possible to work well within the limits of the line fuse and still burn up or melt cables, with the consequent danger of fire and injury plus the loss of time in shooting.

FILM

Since there are many different kinds of film, the choice depends on which is best for the particular job. The ideal film would require no more than available light; it would render colors and contrast exactly as they are seen in real life; and the image would be sharp with clear and readable fine details. No film does all these things simultaneously. Extremely fast films record an image in a very dim light, but the image shows too much contrast with little or no gradation between light and dark, and detail is lost in the shadows. Some films produce images with contrast finely graded between dark and light, but they usually require a great deal of light. Films render color faithfully in either daylight or artificial light, but not in both. Good prints and dupes can be made from some films but not from others. Thus, one of the problems in using film is selecting the right one for the job it must do.

Film Base

Motion picture film consists of a strip of clear plastic material called the *base*, on which is coated a thin layer of material called the *emulsion*. The emulsion is the light-sensitive stuff in which the photo image occurs, while the base is merely a mechanical support. When you touch a piece of film, the main substance you feel is the base, which is much thicker than the thin and fragile emulsion. Emulsion cannot stand alone, and without the film base to hold it photography would be impossible. Cinematographers and laboratory workers often refer to film as "emulsion" because they are really concerned with characteristics of the emulsion.

When the emulsion is exposed to light, it undergoes a chemical change relative to the amount of light tht hits it; the greater the amont of light, the greater the changes. After processing, or development—a timed immersion in certain chemicals—the changes in the emulsion become permanent.

When a scene is photographed the different values of light reflecting back from the various parts of the scene are recorded on film. Some parts will be dark, others light, and still other parts will be somewhere in between. The camera lens transmits light from the scene to the film emulsion in precisely the same relative intensities as it appears in the scene. These different light intensities hitting the emulsion cause it to be exposed in the same relative proportion and in the same relative places as in the original scene. After the film is developed, the image resembles the original scene.

Motion picture film base is made of cellulose acetate, which is cotton treated with acetic acid. Until recently this base was made of cellulose nitrate, which is cotton treated with nitric acid. Both substances are satisfactory film bases, but cellulose nitrate is highly inflammable and is no longer used. Since older films still have their original cellulose nitrate bases, you should be aware of what you are handling. It is illegal to project nitrate films without specially built projection rooms. The two bases are usually referred to as "nitrate" and "acetate" films respectively. Acetate film is also referrred to as "safety film," and although it is flammable, it burns very slowly.

The photographic emulsion is a layer of gelatin in which are suspended millions of silver halide grains. Light that hits these grains affects them in such a manner that they change to metallic silver while the film is being developed. Also during development, the unexposed grains are washed completely out of the emulsion, while the exposed grains of the image are retained. In partially exposed areas only part of the grains wash away, so the whole range of light gradations in the scene is reproduced in the varying amounts of silver grains that remain in the developed emulsion. The greater the exposure, the greater the density of the silver grains remaining on the film. An overexposed negative becomes very dense—hardly any of the grains are washed away—and it looks very dark (dense), with little or no visible detail. In an underexposed negative, most of the grains are washed out in development, the negative appears very light, or "thin," and the resulting picture shows little or no contrast or detail.

Film Types

At first glance the catalogues of film types available from manufacturers such as Eastman and duPont seem confusing because of the great variety of films with a wide range of characteristics. But when these films are considered in different categories, their selection and use become clearer. Films are generally divided into the following five categories according to their use:

1. Camera films. These films are designed to be used in the camera for original photography.
2. Intermediate, or duplicating films. These films are used in intermediate stages as, for example, when printing dailies, duplicates, or release prints from camera originals. Intermediate films are designed with characteristics such as low contrast and low speed, which make them unsuitable for camera shooting or screening but produce an image that is best suited for making a print onto some other stock.
3. Sound recording films. These emulsions are used solely for sound tracks.
4. Television recording films. These emulsions are used to make recordings or kinescopes of pictures from television monitor tubes.
5. Release print films. These emulsions are used to make final prints of completed pictures. They yield the best image when projected.

Normally a filmmaker is concerned solely with selecting camera films. Choices among the other categories are made in the laboratory, depending on the method of reproduction chosen for a particular production. Only camera films are discussed here.

Film Processing

Basically, film emulsions are identified by one of two processes used in their development and printing: *negative/positive* and *reversal original*. These two processing methods result in different images at various stages of development. The final result in each case is a positive projectable image, but the process itself contains certain implications for deciding which one to use.

Negative/Positive

This is the conventional emulsion for both black-and-white and color motion pictures. When this emulsion is exposed, the areas of greatest exposure become the most dense (the more an area is exposed, the more silver grains are retained), and the areas of least exposure become thin and light. The resulting image on a piece of exposed negative film is negative, that is, the light areas in the original scene are depicted as dark and the dark areas are rendered as light. To get a correct image, a second strip of film must be exposed through the negative, and when this second strip is developed the result is a "positive," or *print*. If a third strip of film is exposed through this print, another negative, called a *duplicate negative*, results. Often a duplicate negative is used to make many final prints of a completed motion picture. This is done to protect the irreplaceable camera negative from scratches and general wear. Since the entire financial investment may be tied up in the camera negative, a dupe negative is often made when more than two or three prints of a picture are wanted. When the irreplaceable negative wears out, the investment is lost unless there is a duplicate negative for protection. Each subsequent duplication of the camera negative is referred to as a "generation." Thus, a print made from the camera negative is a *first-generation print*; the duplicate negative made from a positive print is a *second-generation negative*; the print made from a second generation negative is a *second-generation print*, and so on. The contrast of the image increases with each generation; and if duplicate negatives and positives are made in succession, eventually the image will have increasingly greater contrast and finally become a black-and-white silhouette. For this reason, an emulsion used as an intermediate positive or duplicate negative is designed to have inherently low contrast. That is, if an intermediate positive is projected on the screen, it appears very "flat," or lacking in normal contrast. It does not look "real." In making a duplicate negative from such a positive, however, the increased contrast that accompanies printing a photographic image brings the picture up to normal. Almost all 35mm motion pictures for theatrical release, both black-and-white and color, are made on negative/positive film stock.

Reversal

Reversal camera film becomes a positive image when developed. The lights are light and the darks are dark. Originally, reversal films were made so that home movies shot on the film that was actually in the camera could be projected. This saved the time and expense of having a print made for projection. Later, reversal films, especially in 16mm, became practicable for professional film production; and today a full array of professional 16mm emulsions is available. In the reversal process, the negative image is developed initially as in conventional negative/positive development. Then, instead of fixing the silver image and removing the undeveloped emulsion, the laboratory exposes the film to white light and redevelops it. The resulting image is positive. To make a print of a reversal *original*, a second strip of reversal film is exposed through the original and reversal processed as described above. Each generation consists of positive images instead of the alternate positive and negative images seen in the negative/positive process.

ORIGINAL

The reversal film used in the camera is referred to as *original* instead of negative. Even though its image is positive, the original is still the irreplaceable camera film and must be treated with the same care as a negative. The original should not be handled, and for editing, a reversal workprint should be made. Reversal films are intended for use in production in the same way that negative/positive films are used. Although the image is positive when projected, the original may not be any more rugged or immune to damage than a negative. There are, however, two or three high-speed 16mm color reversal films that are made as "shoot-and-show" films, that is, the original is intended for projection. Such films are used mainly by television news departments, since there is no need to use a news report original beyond the first broadcast. Reversal color films for this purpose are generally high-speed emulsions with a built-in contrast that looks normal in the original but becomes unacceptably harsh in subsequent prints.

NEGATIVE/ORIGINAL

Both the negative camera film and the reversal original camera film are irreplaceable and must be treated with extreme care. Camera film, that is, film that was in a camera and on which a picture was shot, will be referred to here as *negative/original*. The reason for this is that there is sometimes a tendency to handle reversal original film carelessly or to project it, the rationale being that since reversal yields a positive image, it cannot be damaged. This is not so. The reversal original is in the same position as a camera negative and should be treated as such. As used in this book, "negative/original refers to either a camera negative or a camera reversal positive, both of which are irreplaceable.

PRINTING METHODS

During printing the image of one strip of film is exposed onto another strip of film. This may be done in two ways: by *contact printing* or by *optical printing*. In contact printing, two pieces of film, the negative with its developed image and the raw stock onto which the image is to be exposed, are fitted together emulsion to emulsion and are run through a printing machine, or *printer*. As they pass by the printer aperture, light is beamed through to expose one film onto the other. The two strips of film run on the same sprockets. In *continuous-contact* printing, the two strips of film move continuously at a constant rate and are exposed as the two touching films pass the printer aperture. Since the two strips of film are moving during exposure, the possibility of slippage between them may result in a certain loss of resolution in the print. In *step-contact* printing, called *registration printing*, the two strips of film are fitted together just as in continuous-contact printing, only the printer stops and starts intermittently. Each frame is stopped at the printing aperture and held firmly in place by registration pins that move into the sprocket holes during exposure and then out, as the films are advanced to the next frame. Continuous-contact printing is used for almost all general workprinting and release printing. Registration-printing is used when extreme registration accuracy is required, such as in separation negatives and intermediate positives for optical effects.

Optical Printing

Optical printing consists of projecting the image from one piece of film onto another, unexposed piece of film, This is done in an *optical printer*, which is essentially a highly precise projector mounted so that it projects directly into the lens of a camera. The optical printer is used principally in making blowups, reductions, and for special photographic effects. Because of its precision in construction and operating control, it can make any combination of dissolves, fades, superimposures, reductions, blowups, and wipe effects onto any size film or type of stock.

In *continuous optical printing*, the projector and the camera are set to run at exactly the same speed, frame by frame, making it possible to produce reductions or blowups at a fairly fast rate. In *step-optical printing*, the projector and the camera move together frame by frame with a complete stop and registering during the exposure, as in step-contact printing. This is done in making optical effects.

Film is available in various widths, emulsions, sprocket hole sizes, and number of sprocket hole rows. Usually the filmmaker need not be concerned with the whole range of film types and specifications, since the differences depend on the type of work being done and are therefore important primarily to the laboratory.

FILM PERFORATIONS

Film *perforations* are the regularly and precisely spaced holes punched along the edge or edges of motion picture film. These holes are engaged by the teeth of various sprockets and pins by which the film is transported and positioned as it travels through cameras, processing machines, projectors, and other film-handling equipment.

A-Wind and B-Wind

All 35mm film has two rows of perforations, one along each edge of the film; while 16mm film comes with both single and double perforations. Since 16mm was originally an amateur film stock not intended to have a sound track, it was made with double perforations, one set along each edge. When 16mm film was judged suitable for professional sound pictures, one row of perforations was eliminated in release print stock to make room for the sound track. Although 16mm sound pictures are released on single-perforated stock, 16mm camera films are both double- and single-perforated. Film for use in 16mm single-system camers is single-perforated, with a magnetic stripe laid along the film's length on the side with no perforations. Unless you are shooting single-system sound, always use double-perforated 16mm film in the camera. Since film with a single row of perforations cannot be reversed end to end or flopped over without changing the relative position of its perforations, the terms *A-wind* and *B-wind* are used to indicate the way a roll of single-perforated film is wound. These terms are important primarily in the laboratory, where printing emulsion to emulsion requires that the proper wind of film be used. For the filmmaker, A-wind or B-wind is important only insofar as the correct wind is used when shooting single-perforated film, as in single-system sound shooting.

A roll of film comes from the manufacturer with the emulsion in. To identify A-wind or B-wind, hold the roll up in front of your face with the film coming off the top of the roll toward your right. If the perforations are on the side of the film closest to you, it is A-wind. If the perforations are on the side of the film away from you, it is B-wind. The normal camera emulsion position is B-wind. You may also use your hands to remember the winds. Clench both fists in front of you, palms facing each other with your thumbs toward you. Assume the palm to be the emulsion, the fingers to be the film pointing in the direction it unwinds from the roll, and the thumbs to be the sprocket holes. The left hand is A-wind and the right is B-wind.

SELECTING SUITABLE FILM

Film may be purchased from the manufacturer on cores or spools. Rolls of 16mm film 400 feet or more are availble on cores and are intended for magazine loading. Film on cores must be loaded into and out of the magazine in total darkness, either in a changing bag or a dark room. 16mm film also comes on daylight loading spools in lengths of 100, 200, and 400 feet. Not all magazines, the Arriflex for example, can accommodate camera spools since the take-up roll displaces the space left in the magazine as the feed roll becomes smaller. The word "daylight" in daylight loading spool can be misleading. The film is originally wound on the spool by the manufacturer with a side-to-side motion, so that alternate layers of film touch opposite sides of the spool. This helps prevent light from seeping through between the spool and the film. After the roll has been exposed, however, it is no longer wound this way, and light can easily penetrate the roll. For this reason, a daylight spool should always be loaded in subdued light and unloaded in total darkness. The practice of routinely unloading daylight spools in a changing bag or dark room may save the last shot on the roll from being flashed, otherwise the last ten or fifteen feet of the roll will be lost. Whenever possible, film on cores rather than spools should be used because spools are noisy in magazines and tend to create wear.

Obtain copies of motion picture film catalogs and price schedules from all the film manufacturers, study them, and keep them on hand for ready reference. Manufacturers of film stocks publish a data sheet for each emulsion they sell. The data sheets describe film characteristics, what the different types will do under varying conditions, and also contain recommendations for exposure, lighting, and development, as well as latitude, filter factors, resolving power, color balance, sensitometric curves, exposure index, and other information. Following the recommendations of the data sheets alone will not ensure perfect results, but they do present much valuable information.

Selection of the proper emulsion to use depends on what you intend to shoot, what the conditions are, and the result you desire to achieve. Experience, that is, actually shooting and observing the results, is the best way to learn how to select the correct film; but discussing with others what films can do, and reading data sheets and other information is also helpful. The main characteristics involved in the selection of a film emulsion are speed, latitude, grain, color balance, resolution, and contrast.

Film Speed

The speed of a film emulsion refers to its sensitivity to light. Film that is very sensitive to light, and therefore records an image when exposed to a small amount of light, is called "fast" film; one that requires a great deal of light to form an image is called "slow." If this were the only criterion, fast film would always be chosen because of its need for very little light. This in turn would mean that only small, lightweight lighting units would be required to light the actors and the set; the crew could be smaller and faster; actors would be more relaxed under less intense lights and would consequently give better performances; moving from one location to another would be faster and easier; time would be saved; and the total cost would be much lower. Yet fast film is not always the answer because the faster a film is, the more undesirable its characteristics may be, particularly its contrast and graininess.

The speed of film is indicated by its *exposure index*, which is a numerical indication of its speed in relation to other films. Exposure numbers are used with exposure meters calibrated according to the American Standards Association (ASA) speeds. American and British exposure meters are calibrated to ASA speeds, although there are other older numerical exposure systems, such as Weston and General Electric (now obsolete), and the DIN system currently in use in Europe.

Exposure Index

The exposure index for a film is indicated on the data sheet and on its container as an ASA number for both daylight and tungsten light—TUNGSTEN: ASA 100; DAYLIGHT: ASA 64. Do not assume that the exposure index for any film is absolute, for exposure index values stated in the data sheets have been calculated by practical tests. These values do indicate a starting point that may be modified by your own judgment based on your own tests and by the standards of the laboratory you use.

Film with exposure index numbers up to 50 are considered slow films; those with numbers from 50 to 80 are medium speed; and films with an ASA index of 100 or above are considered high-speed films. Since processing formulas and conditions differ with each laboratory, the actual speed of a film may not be the same for any two or more laboratories, although each laboratory attempts to maintain its own constantly uniform processing. When you plan to use an emulsion that is new to you, it is helpful to shoot a series of tests of several scenes at different speeds and have it developed and printed at the laboratory you intend to use. The resulting prints, related to your test exposures, will indicate the effective film speed to use for further shooting with processing to be done at that laboratory.

Latitude

Latitude is an inherent characteristic of film emulsion that determines the range of exposure it can handle. When a negative emulsion is exposed, the areas of greatest exposure become proportionately less dense. This relationship between density and exposure is represented by the *characteristic curve*, or graph of a film's density, in which the degree of density is plotted according to the amount of exposure. Such a curve for any emulsion is made by repeated exposure and development. A piece of the emulsion being tested is exposed at a low value, developed, and then examined in a sensitometer, an instrument which measures the density in the developed film. Next, a second piece of the same film is exposed at a higher value, developed, and also examined in the sensitometer. This process continues with successive pieces of film until an entire series of density and exposure values is obtained. These values are then plotted on the graph, the result being the characteristic curve of that emulsion. Theoretically, for each increase in exposure, there should be a proportional increase in density. And there is, but not over the whole range of exposure. In the plot of the sensitometric curve, the horizontal axis is the amount of exposure and the vertical axis is the amount of density (Fig. 7.15). Notice that the plot is curved at the bottom (the toe), is straight in the center (straight-line portion), and is again curved at the top (the shoulder). Exposure that falls within the straight-line portion will result in a correct image; but with an increase in exposure, the curve enters the shoulder where any such increase will not produce a proportional increase in density. Eventually the emulsion will record no further detail, no matter how great the exposure. Ideally, if the film represented in this curve were used for a perfectly exposed and detailed image, the exposure levels of the scene shot would fall between 2.00 and 1.00 (B and C) on the curve. Since each division on the exposure, or horizontal, axis represents about 3⅓ lens stops, this film would have a latitude of 3⅓ stops. Thus, if the brightest object in the scene were four stops brighter than the darkest object, the film could not be exposed so that both the brightest and the darkest objects would appear sharp and detailed. Either the brightest oject would be correct, and the darkest object underexposed; or, if the darkest object were correctly exposed, the brightest object would be overexposed.

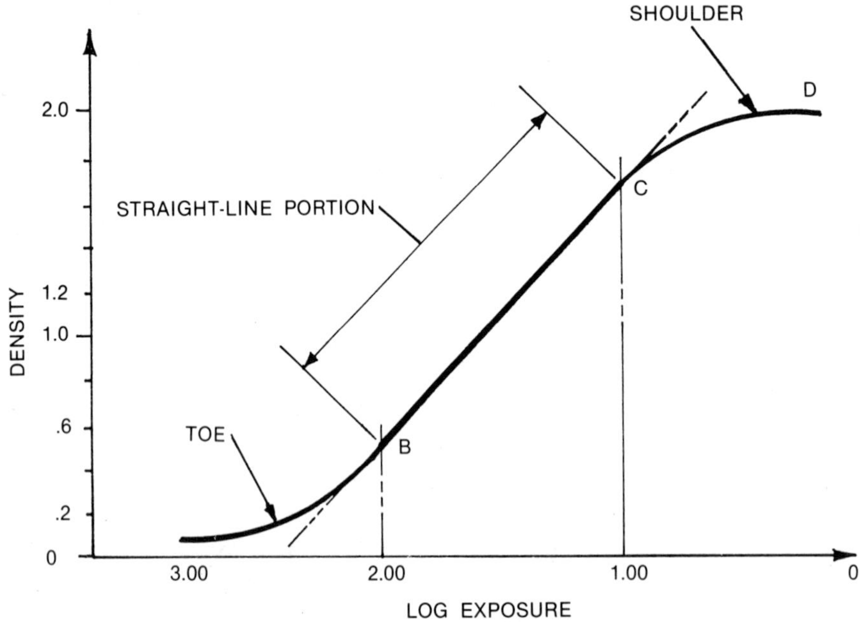

Fig. 7.15 Characteristic curve of film emulsion.

Be aware of the latitude of the film stock you are using, for this determines how you handle the lighting and shooting of scenes. In shooting a scene, of which part is in direct sunlight and part in the shade, meter readings will indicate how far apart the two areas are. If the latitude in the scene is greater than the latitude of the film, the scene cannot be shot as is without either overexposing or underexposing one of the areas. In such a scene, the latitude of the scene can be brought within the latitude of the film by using reflectors or booster lights to bring the level of the shade area up to within the latitude of the film. Either increase the light level of the shade with a reflector or cut down the intensity of the sunny area by blocking the sun with a scrim. Generally, negative films have a wider latitude than reversal films, which implies that in shooting with reversal film more fill light, either reflectors or lights, is necessary to bring the darker areas of the scenes to within the latitude of the film.

Although latitude can be scientifically described as being derived from laboratory tests, photography is basically a subjective matter. Personal taste and preference, the mood of the scene, and the taste of the audience for whom it is intended all determine how film is exposed. You should determine latitude by actual shooting tests and measure the results against your own taste.

Graininess

Photographic emulsion consists of a layer of gelatin in which millions of grains of silver halide are suspended. After exposure and processing, these turn into grains of metallic silver, which, like the half-tone printing dots in newspapers, appear continuous to the eye. Under certain conditions, however, these grains become visible as individual areas of differing density. You have undoubtedly seen films that have an extremely grainy appearance, while others look smooth and even. The graininess of an emulsion is determined initially by (1) the manufacturer when it is produced, and (2) by the developing process used in the laboratory. Generally, fast films have an inherently coarser grain than slower films, and the data sheet for each usually indicates whether it is a fine- or medium-grain emulsion. But other factors determine the graininess of a film and its subsequent print. Pushed development in the lab increases grain, as will nonuniformity in the temperatures of developing solutions. In large, uniform areas grain is more noticeable than in dark, shadowed areas, which means that development may be pushed in night and low-key scenes without the normal noticeability of grain. Since audiences become more quickly accommodated to grain than any other characteristic of a film, it is probably more important to consider the effectiveness of the film's message than to fret over grain.

Color Balance

Although color film renders scenes apparently as we see them in real life, it does so under special conditions. Thus it is necessary to use film that is adapted, or balanced, to the color of the light to which the film will be exposed. For accurate, or at least believable, color in professional motion pictures, the light source must be matched to the film. The following two conditions have become standardized:

1. Photographic daylight: 5500°K. Although sunlight color temperature varies widely, depending on time of day and atmospheric conditions, 5500°K has been established as the standard color temperature of photographic daylight. All professional daylight films are designed to be used in this color light.
2. Artificial light: 3200°K. Professional films for indoor use are designed to be used in light of this color temperature. All motion picture incandescent lights, both quartz and conventional types, emit 3200°K light when operated at 120 volts.

Professional *daylight film is manufactured to give correct color reproduction when exposed in daylight or light with a color temperature of about 6000°K.* Professional *tungsten film* is designed for correct color reproduction when exposed in light with a color temperature of 3200°K. Incandescent light bulbs rated at 3200°K are the standard incandescent light source in the motion picture industry. (See Light Control)

Obviously, if the light source is a different color from the color balance of the film being used, the picture is not going to look right unless something is done to correct the discrepancy. Such a correction may be made by placing a

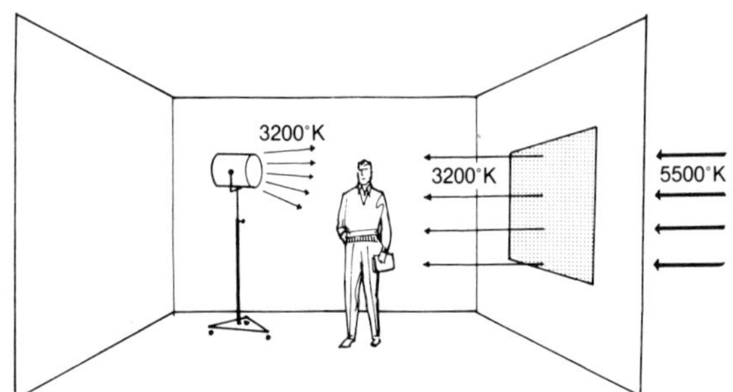

Fig. 7.16 A color conversion filter over a window changes the color temperature of daylight to match the motion picture light being used inside.

suitable filter on the camera lens or on the light source itself. Consider, for example, a professional 16mm color reversal film color balanced for tungsten at 3200°K. Normally, this film would be used indoors, using standard motion picture lighting units rated at 3200°K. But if this film were used to shoot outdoors in daylight, it would then be exposed in light that is approximately 6000°K. When light of 6000°K is compared to light of 3200°K, it contains a great deal more blue; so when 3200°K film is exposed with 6000°K light, the result is an extremely blue, unacceptable image. To use an interior film outdoors in daylight, a filter must be placed over the lens to change the color temperature of the light. This special filter (Wratten #85, Harisson C-4) prevents much of the blue component in daylight from passing through to the film. The resulting light that hits the film has been converted to 3200°K.

When shooting color, be aware of the color of the light being used for exposure. Both daylight and interior artificial light exist in many different colors depending on the time of day and local conditions. The many different filters available for both the lens and the lights make it possible to maintain precise control over the color of photographic light.

Resolution

Resolution, or resolving power, is the ability of a film to reproduce in fine detail the various parts of an image. We refer to an image as "sharp" (good resolution) or "soft" (poor resolution). The resolution of an emulsion is measured by successively photographing several test patterns consisting of alternate dark and light lines, different patterns having varying numbers of lines per millimeter. The ability of the film to distinguish these lines is stated as resolving power in lines per millimeter. Since the contrast between the lines themselves also determines the appearance of the final image, resolving power in lines per millimeter includes a statement about the contrast in the test pattern. The emulsion data sheets published by the film manufacturers indicate resolving power at different pattern contrasts along with the development used. Lenses, too, vary in resolving power, or their ability to distinguish between objects that are close together in a scene to be photographed. A good lens is sharp; a poor one is soft. Since sharpness in the final image depends on the resolving power of the film, the resolving power of the lens, the contrast inherent in the scene, and the developing process used, it is important to remember that no one element will provide good resolution.

Contrast

Contrast is a term indicating the variations of light and shade that lie between the light and dark areas of a scene. Imagine a scene in which an actor is standing in a garden on a dark night. The only light visible is a hard spotlight hitting him from one side. This would be an extremely high-contrast scene since only those surfaces or objects hit by the light would be visible. One side of the actor's face would be brightly lighted, while the other would be almost black. (Fig. 7.17*A*). Now imagine the same scene in normal daylight. The sun acts much the same as the spotlight but the reflected light from the sky now lights up the opposite side of the actor's face and the shadows so that we see the scene as normal (Fig. 7.17*B*). The contrast between darks and lights is softened by the sky light, with high contrast appearing only between a few very dark, shaded areas and nearby lighted areas. Again, imagine the same scene in a fog. There is no directional light; in fact, the light seems to be coming from everywhere, and no one area seems much lighter or darker than any other. This would be a low-contrast, or "flat," scene (Fig. 7.17*C*). The contrast of a film emulsion determines how it will reproduce these differences between dark and light objects in a scene, and is manufactured with different inherent contrast

Fig. 7.17*A* High contrast. Actor lighted with spotlight. Little or no gradation between light and dark.

Fig. 7.17*B* Normal contrast. In normal daylight, a scene contains a whole range of gradations from light to dark.

Fig. 7.17*C* Low contrast. Person in fog. The whole scene seems flat and gray.

responses. A film intended for copying line drawings or printing must have high contrast, that is, little or no gradations of gray between the black and the white. A film intended for making most kinds of motion pictures must reproduce all the tones between dark and light so that the final picture closely resembles the original scene. Contrast is related to the latitude of the film, the range between the light and dark objects it can reproduce faithfully. To bring the brightness range of a scene down to where the film can handle it, either more light should be thrown on the dark objects or some of the light should be blocked off the light objects, or both. The final contrast in any film is determined by all or any combinations of the following five conditions:

1. The contrast designed into the film. Camera films, both negative and reversal, are not intended for projection, but are designed instead for prints to be made from them. Since contrast increases with each generation of reproduction, camera films are designed with a low contrast below normal. When subsequent prints are made, the normal increase in contrast brings it up to what we call normal. For example, 16mm Commercial Ektachrome, a camera original not designed for projection, appears flat and unfaithful to the scene depicted when projected; but a print made from the same piece of film has the correct amount of contrast and appears normal. The 16mm Ektachrome news films, however, which are designed for projection, gain unacceptable contrast when printed.

2. The developing process. The kinds of developing chemicals used and the length of development time effect contrast: the longer the development period the greater the final contrast. The implication here is that any laboratory may turn out developed film with a degree of contrast different from that of any other laboratory. Be aware of the kind of work your laboratory does before you commit time and money to a production. Shoot tests and have them developed by the lab you propose to use.

3. The lighting contrast of the scene. Lighting a scene is essentially controlling contrast through controlling the amount of light applied to or shielded from objects or parts of the scene. A great deal of control is possible in determining the final result. (See Controlling Light Quality, p. 166.)

4. Exposure. This is closely related to lighting. (See Light Intensity p. 170) Underexposure produces a "thin" negative with low contrast. Overexposure produces a dense negative with high contrast. With reversal film, the result is the opposite: underexposure produces a dense reversal original with its consequent higher contrast, while overexposure produces a thin, washed-out original. In both negative and original, a thin emulsion is difficult to control in the printing since most of the grains have been washed away and there is nothing left to "bring up" by increasing the intensity of the printing light. A thin negative may be printed with some success, but little can be done to improve an overexposed 16mm reversal original.

5. The contrast of the photographed scene. Suppose you are shooting a scene involving actors in the desert on a bright clear day. The contrast between the shadows and the bright areas lighted by both the sun and the intense blue sky can be violently stark. Or an indoor scene may have sharply contrasting areas of white and black. Or you may want to shoot a two-shot of black and blond actors. Every scene has its own built-in contrast that may be altered either by changing the set itself or by lighting to reduce contrast. The greater the difference in intensity between dark and light, the sharper the contrast, as in the example of the scene described above.

QUALITY OF LIGHT

Regardless of its color or brightness, there are two conditions of light quality: hard and soft.

1. *Hard light* is directional, concentrated light coming from a single source and having all its rays roughly parallel to each other. The sun produces hard natural light just as a spotlight produces hard artificial light, The most noticeable effects of hard light are high contrast, a clearly defined shadow, and a strong indication of direction.

2. *Soft light* is diffused, unconcentrated light, apparently coming from many directions at once or from no direction at all. Artificial soft light is produced by unfocused bulbs, by light reflecting from a diffused matte surface, and by hard light shining through a diffusion medium such as cloth, paper, plastic, or a screen. Natural soft light is produced by sunlight shining through clouds on an overcast day or being reflected from the sky on a clear day. Skylight just before sunrise and just after sunset is soft, as is the light in full-shade areas such as a deep canyon or the shadow side of a mountain or a building. The principal characteristic of soft light is low contrast. It casts vaguely defined shadows or none at all, and seems to come from no single-point source.

In almost every real-life situation, people and objects are lighted by a combination of hard and soft light (Fig. 7.18*A–E*). In the home, a ceiling fixture or a table lamp is the hard source and constitutes the main, or "key," light. At the same time, light bouncing off the walls and ceiling constitutes the soft "fill" light. On a sunny day, outdoor light is a combination of hard sunlight and soft skylight. The hard, direct sunlight sharply delineates everything, and the soft reflected skylight fills in all the shadows. Controlling the the balance, or ratio, of these two kinds of light is part of the art of lighting for motion pictures; and the basic comparison to start with is a person or object lighted by the sun. Notice that the sun's hard light is the main light, or *key light* as it is called. It is hard, often harsh, and clearly indicates the direction from which it is coming. Not so obvious is the soft *fill light* emitted by the sky and apparently coming from all directions. This soft skylight coming from everywhere at once fills the cracks, creases, overhangs, and other shaded areas caused by the sun's direct, hard light. Sometimes, however, direct sunlight is so bright and harsh that the skylight is not able to fill in the shadows with the same intensity as the sun. The result is a high-contrast appearance, deep shadows under the eyebrows and chin, and facial wrinkles that show up as deep, dark lines. When confronted with this situation the cinematographer has to "fill in" the shadows with reflectors or booster lights. Even though an outdoor sunlit scene may appear correct to the eye, a reflector is usually necessary in filming to fill in faces and shadows because film is not as good at handling contrast as the human eye. We look at people outdoors in sunlight, and though we notice the shadows and lines, we still see them as reasonably normal. Film, however, accentuates the contrast between the light areas and the shadows so that sometimes little or no detail is visible in the shadow

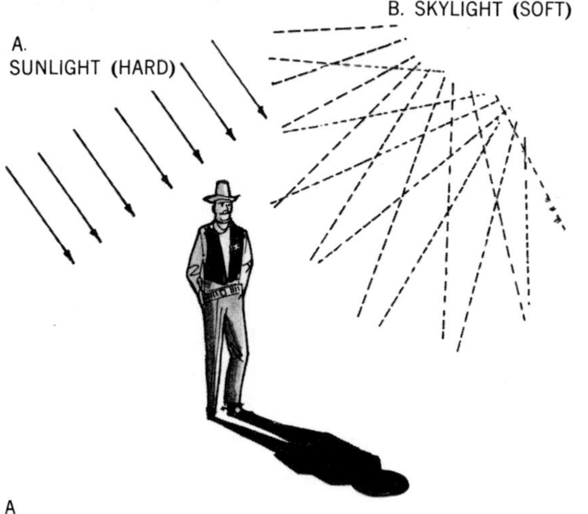

Fig. 7.18*A* Normal condition. Hard light from the sun, with shadows filled in by the soft light reflected from the sky.

Fig. 7.18*B* Normal condition indoors. Hard light from lamp, with soft light reflecting from walls and ceiling.

Fig. 7.18C Soft light only. The hard light of the sun is diffused into soft light when it passes through an overcast.

Fig. 7.18*D* Hard light only.

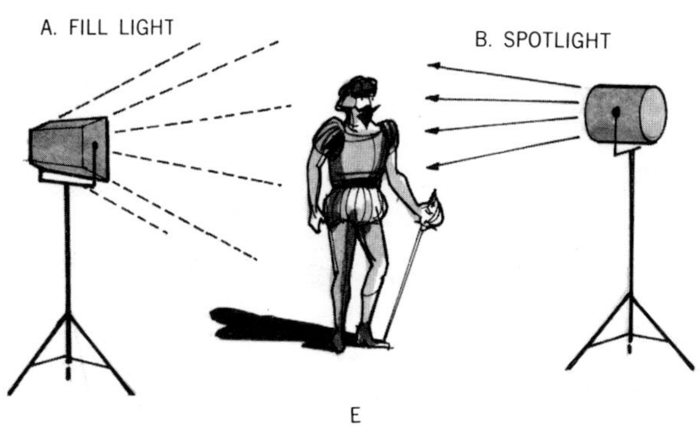

Fig. 7.18*E* Normal condition artificially created in the studio. Hard light from a motion picture spotlight. Soft light from a motion picture fill light.

areas—eyesockets are completely black and no features can be discerned on the shadow sides of faces.

CONTROLLING LIGHT QUALITY

Most motion picture lighting involves manipulating hard and soft light; and although there are occasions when a scene may be lighted either with hard light or soft light alone, most scenes are lighted with varying ratios of one to the other. In many situations, light from artificial lighting units, both spots and broads, is too hard and harsh, particularly with the multilamp units that are commonly used for interior lighting and exterior boost or fill. Two or more lights in combination and multilamp units both tend to create multiple shadows and harsh edges. Diffusion is used to smooth out harsh light to soft, nondirectional lighting without a significant loss in color temperature.

A light that produces hard light is referred to as a *spot*; one producing soft light is called a *broad*, which refers to its broad unconcentrated rays. A hard, direct spot, even when "filled" with soft light from a broad, creates a harsh effect, particularly on faces. So hard lights, though still maintaining their direct, focused quality, are often softened for a warmer, kinder effect. The quality of spots and broads is commonly modified by scrims, diffusion, reflectors, and filters.

Scrims

A *scrim* is a black cloth or stainless steel netting that is placed in front of the light to modify it (Fig. 7.19). As discussed under light intensity (p. 170), a scrim is used mainly to reduce the intensity of light without changing its color or quality. But a scrim does soften light to some degree. Although it is not primarily a diffusing medium, it does sometimes diffuse light sufficiently to kill an unwanted harshness. A rule of thumb is always to put at least a scrim over a spotlight used as a keylight on a person unless harshness is part of the mood effect of the shot.

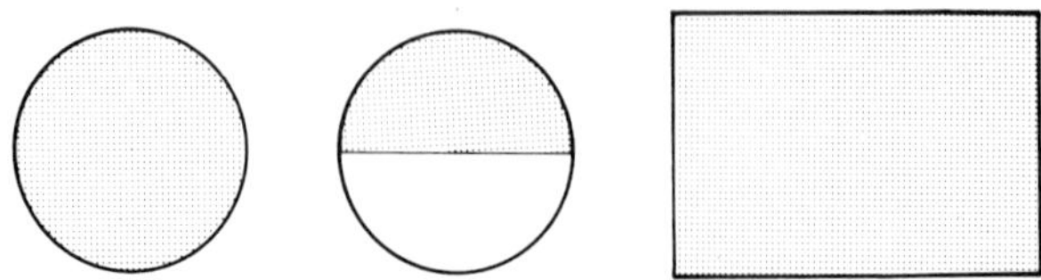

Fig. 7.19 Scrims are frames covered with wire or cloth mesh. Placed in front of a light, they soften the light quality and reduce its intensity.

Diffusion

Diffusion is anything placed in front of a light to break up its directional quality and hardness. Diffusion softens light, so that it appears to be coming from a larger light source than is actually the case; and shadows produced by diffused light are less distinct and have soft edges. Generally, scenes shot in color look more pleasing when photographed under diffused light (Fig. 7.20*A* and *B*).

The diffusion of light may be accomplished by reflecting it from a diffusing surface or transmitting it through a diffusing material; and over the years, almost every type of material imaginable

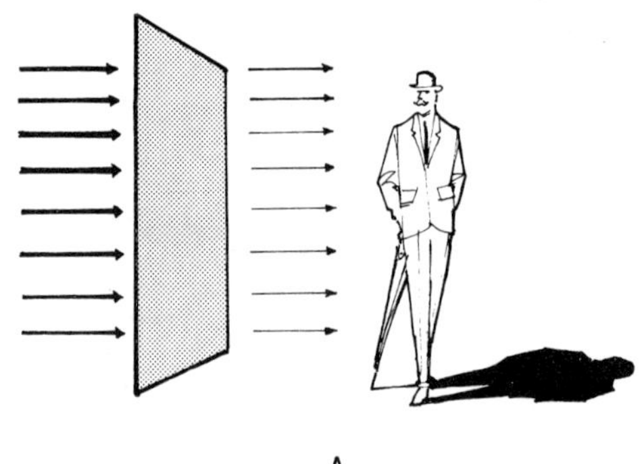

Fig. 7.20*A* A scrim reduces the intensity of the light and softens it slightly, but does not affect the shadow-casting characteristic.

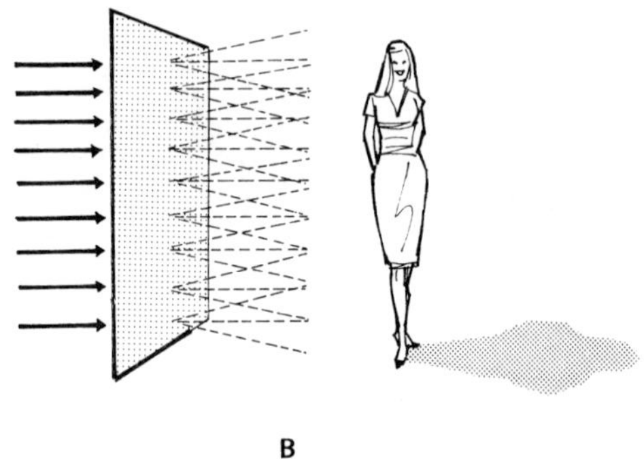

Fig. 7.20*B* Diffusion reduces the intensity of light. It also diffuses and softens light and softens the shadow cast, but does not change color temperature.

Light Position

Moving the light closer to or farther away from the scene changes the intensity accordingly. Although this is not possible with lights fixed to a catwalk or to a set wall, lights on stands can often by moved quite effectively. Outdoors, relatively small changes in the position of sun reflectors toward or away from the scene result in substantial changes in intensity.

Lamp Control

Spotlights and some nonfocusing lights are built so that the bulb may be moved forward and backward inside the lamp housing. The closer the bulb is to the reflector, the more concentrated, or "spotted," the light beam will be. In the spot position, the light covers a small area but is quite intense. When the bulb is moved close to the light's lens, or toward the front, the light becomes more "flooded" and less intense. Fine adjustments in intensity can be made in this way.

Dimmers

A dimmer is a variable resistor that reduces the voltage to a light, thereby reducing its intensity. Dimming works best for black-and-white film, but for color the reduction in voltage causes a reduction in the color temperature of the light with a consequent color shift in the image. However, judicious dimming with careful attention to color change can sometimes be done for color film. Even black-and-white film reacts adversely to dimming below a certain level because the reds predominate and tend to underexpose all other spectral colors in the scene.

Augmentation

Often, when shooting exteriors in deep shade or on heavily overcast days, the available outdoor light is insufficient. Reflectors and lights may be used to bounce sunlight into shaded areas; and if the sun is not shining, lights may be used (Fig. 7.28*A*). If power is available, regular studio lights

Fig. 7.28*A* Without the cluster of Mole-Richardson booster lights in the left foreground, the faces of the actors and the horse would be as dark as those in Fig. 7.28*B*. Sun reflectors or booster lights can be used with equal effectiveness in both situations.

Fig. 7.28*B* The sun lights this scene from the rear and a little to one side. This causes the actors in the jeep to stand out from the background, but their faces are indistinguishable in the shade. When the cinematographer is ready to shoot, the reflector in the right foreground will be tilted slightly downward to reflect sunlight into the actors' faces to make them appear distinct and unshaded as in Fig. 7.28*A*.

can be used. If not, there are battery-operated lighting units that provide limited-area lighting for short periods of time. Lights used in this way are called *booster lights* (Fig. 7.28*A*).

ANALYSIS OF THE SHOOTING SITUATION

In preparing for a shoot, adequate preparation is essential for an effective, economical shooting schedule. A motion picture shoot is often analogous to a combat situation: you try to anticipate every contingency, but when you get into the fight, the success of the operation depends entirely on your crew and the equipment you have brought. Anything forgotten or not considered—masking tape, film, furniture pads, a screwdriver, spare power cables, extra batteries—can result in complete defeat or at least in devastating loss of time and money. Develop your own checklist, using the following items as a guide:

1. Read the script and formulate a preliminary plan.
2. Go to each location or set and have the director describe in detail the action, mood, and intent of the scenes to be shot there.
3. Observe the natural lighting conditions. Where will the sun be during shooting: Can reflectors be used to reflect sunlight indoors, or can they be used at all?
4. Is power available, or will a generator be needed? How much power is available in volts and amperes? How far is the source of power from where the lights will be used? Compute the distance to determine how many electrical cables, feeders, and extensions are needed. To use the power, will a power company representative, custodian, or electrician have to be notified or hired? What permission is required to gain access to the power?
5. What local conditions might affect what has to be done? Check the condition of the terrain: trees, underbrush, sand. What kinds of vehicles

will access to the area accommodate? What kind of protection from the elements is needed? What kinds of camera mounts can be used in the area—dolly, crane, camera car?

6. What are the provisions for unloading and loading? Is there a loading dock? Is an elevator available? A freight elevator? How large? How wide is the stairwell?

7. For shooting in houses or buildings where there are large windows or substantial amounts of incoming daylight, determine how to handle the mix of daylight and artificial light. Can the windows be covered with color-converting filter material? Is it better to shoot with daylight-corrected incandescent lights and leave the windows unfiltered, or is it better to correct the window daylight to 3200°K and shoot with 3200°K lights?

8. What are the space limitations of the interiors to be used?

LIGHTING PURPOSE

The purpose of lighting in motion picture photography is threefold: to make all elements sufficiently visible to obtain the proper exposure on the film, to make a scene look the way the director or cinematographer wants it to, and to induce a particular feeling or mood. Both indoor and outdoor scenes must be lighted because film does not "see" things the same way the human eye does. Unlike the eye, film cannot make out a wide range between dark and light areas. The human eye has wide latitude; it can see and distinguish both very light and very dark objects simultaneously with great clarity of detail. Film has a narrow latitude in that it cannot render very light and very dark objects or areas faithfully at the same time. If you were to use a narrow latitude film to photograph a dark-skinned actor wearing a white shirt, by varying the exposure you could achieve either of the following, but not both:

1. Good skin tones and facial details with an overexposed, or "burned up," shirt.
2. A normal appearing shirt, with an underexposed face showing few or no facial details.

A still photographer may compensate for this difference by adding light to, or withholding light from, portions of the picture during printing; but the motion picture photographer cannot do this. To render accurately both dark and light on motion picture film, more light should be thrown on the dark areas or the intensity of light should be reduced on the light areas. In either case, the range of brightness from dark to light must be made to fit into the latitude of the film. This is one of the tasks of motion picture lighting both indoors and out.

Lighting for motion picture photography includes the use of several different kinds of lights, each traditionally classified as to how it is used. These include key light, fill light, back light, cross light, kicker, and eye light. Each of these lights is not used in every scene or shot, but only as needed according to the conditions and the setup. Traditionally, these lights are shown in one diagram (Fig. 7.29) as constituting the ideal lighting arrangement, but all these lights are rarely used at one time in this way. It is useful to consider each type of light in terms of what it accomplishes. Consider the subject to be an actor, although any object, even a whole set or scene, may be lighted the same as a person. The following are the lights and their characteristics:

Key Light

This light is usually hard and simulates the normal main source of light falling on a scene. Outdoors, in daylight, it is the sun; indoors it is the light from a lamp or ceiling fixture, or from a window. The key light is usually above and in front of whatever is being shot. Besides simulating natural light, key light concentrates the attention of the viewer, establishes the scene's mood, and provides a basis for the exposure. Depending on the light source simulated, the key light may come from any direction—early morning or late afternoon sun, a fireplace, a welding torch, or a TV screen.

Fill Light

This is a soft light coming from the general direction of the camera or from overhead. This is the general, diffused light, such as skylight or light reflecting from walls, that fills in the shadows created by the key light. Its broad, diffused source acts to fill creases and depressions to eliminate or diminish shadows. The greater the

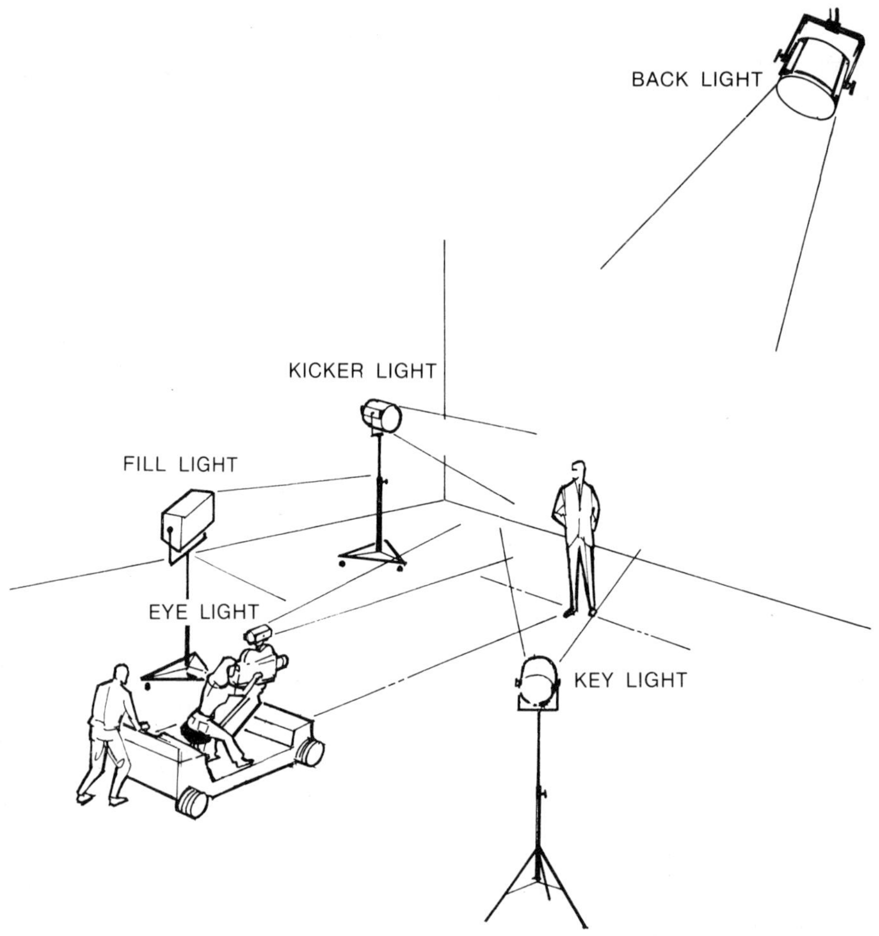

Fig. 7.29 Schematic arrangement of basic motion picture lights. Depending on the experience and taste of the cinematographer, this arrangement may vary widely. More than one light of each type may be used, and some may be eliminated.

intensity of the fill light, the more the scene is flattened out and *contrast* reduced. Contrast, or the range between dark and light in a scene, is determined by the amount of fill light used. A subject lighted solely with a hard key light shows extreme contrast: the side nearest the key light is bright and detailed, while the opposite, or shadow side is dark and indistinct. As you add fill light, the dark areas become lighter and the contrast between dark and light becomes less. The ratio between key light and fill light determines the "key" of a scene. *High key* indicates that the fill light intensity is close to that of the key light. In *low key* lighting, the fill light is much less intense than the key light. A ratio of 2:1, that is, the key light with twice the intensity of the fill, is high key. As the ratio of key to fill increases, say 4:1, the key becomes lower.

The key of a scene is related to the *latitude* of the film being used. Recall that latitude is the ability of a particular film to record detail in light and dark areas. Color film is normally narrower in latitude than black-and-white film; the ratio of key to fill for a color film might be 2:1, while that for black and white could be 4:1 for the same scene. The key of a scene is traditionally determined by its mood—high key for comedies and musicals, low key for mysteries and tragedies. Yet these conventions may be modified in any direction to fit the mood or meaning you are attempting to convey.

High and Low Key Lighting

The two extremes of lighting are high key and low key, and there is a whole range of gradations between the two. In a high key scene, the predominant tones are from gray up to white; in a low key scene, the predominant tones range from dark gray down to black with very few highlights. The highest key scene is created by placing the key light right next to the camera. This direct key light produces a single flat surface without texture; shadows are behind the subject and therefore are not visible to the lens. If the key light is moved to the side, the contrast increases and a lower key is achieved. As the key light is moved farther to the side, more shadows are produced by the modeling effect of the light, and the key of the scene becomes lower. The overall intensity of the scene has nothing to do with its key; instead, both placement of the key light and the ratio of key light to fill light determine key. The closer the key and fill are in intensity, the higher the key of the scene; the farther apart they are, the lower the key.

Kicker Light

This is a light coming from behind and from one side or the other of your subject. It "kicks" the subject out from the background and helps provide a feeling of depth and solidity. The use of this light ranges from directly to one side to almost in back. When used directly from the side, a cross light gives an edge to whatever is being lighted. In lighting furniture, for example, it gives a visible edge that otherwise would blend into the background.

Figure 7.30*A* shows the use of filler and kicker lights.

Back Light

This is a hard light that hits the subject from behind. Since it must not be seen in the shot, it is usually set high, but it may be placed directly behind the subject if no great movement is involved. A back light outlines an object so that it appears to stand out from the background, thereby helping to create the impression of depth or third dimension. Used without front lighting, the back light produces a silhouette. Back light hitting the back of whatever is being lighted, may be higher in intensity than the other lights, and does not need to be diffused as much.

Eye Light

This is a small light, capable of being focused and dimmed, that is placed very close to the camera or even mounted directly on top of it. Used at a subdued intensity, it gives sparkle to the eyes and makes the face and general limited foreground seem more alive. Since its position is quite close to the lens, any shadows the eyelight makes are behind the subject and therefore not visible. A light mounted in this way is often referred to as an "obie" or "bash" light (Fig. 7.30*B*). Eyes are the focus of a person's expression, and eyes without light look dead even when the light level is very high. To make the eyes significant, focus the lens on them sharply and use the eye light.

Lighting is done in two basic situations: in the studio and on location. Over the years, large lighting units have been developed to create any type and amount of light on a sound stage. Large carbon arcs can spread much light over large areas, and huge cone lights and broad arcs can supply incredible amounts of fill light. Yet with all this lighting facility, the trend—for reasons of both money and taste—is toward shooting on

Fig. 7.30*A* This TV set is keylighted with a 4000-watt lamp producing soft light (1). Fill lights (2) and (3) are 1000-watt soft lights. Kickers (4), (5), (6), and (7) are 1000-watt spotlights producing hard light. The actor's stop light is a 650-watt hard light (8). The window light (9) is a 1000-watt spotlight. Additional fill light is put into the set by spotlights (10) diffused through white silk.

Fig. 7.30*B* A "bashlight," "obie light," or "eye light." It may be used even when the camera is moving because its cast shadow is always behind the actor.

actual locations, where it is impossible to carry the massive and expensive units designed for studio shooting. As a result, lighting is now greatly involved with small lighting units from 500 to 2000 watts and a variety of reflective materials. Location lighting, regardless of whether the film is dramatic or nontheatrical, has become similar to conventional documentary lighting with all its attendant problems of limited power, small lights, minimum space for placing lights, general lack of technical conveniences, and the necessity for almost constant mobility.

BASIC LIGHTING POSITIONS

Unlike studio shooting, where it is relatively easy to place a light in any desired position relative to the action, location shooting entails a constant battle to place the lights where they can do an effective job. Fundamentally, however, the task of both inside and outside lighting is to illuminate the actor or subject from four positions, as follows:

1. A dominant directional hard light from roughly 45° to the side, to make shadows and give the subject shape. This is the key light and should simulate the motivating light source in the scene.
2. Soft fill light from almost directly in front of the subject, to fill in the deep shadows, create the desired key of the scene, and provide overall illumination.
3. A back light from high up behind the subject, to separate the subject from the background and provide depth to the scene. Since film is two-dimensional, objects without backlight often appear to be painted on the set wall.
4. A kicker light from the side to give the subject a feeling of substance or depth. Such a light adds a little more life and perspective to both the scene and the subject.

Location interiors frequently have low ceilings and no off-set space, so the problem of placing lights is sometimes a challenging one. Usually it is fairly simple to position the key light and the fill light, but putting a back light behind a subject high enough to be out of the scene requires ingenuity. Sometimes it simply cannot be done; but whatever the conditions, ingenuity can always affect an arrangement that is worked out. For example, several small lights may be hidden behind pieces of furniture and props to produce exciting results.

Outdoor Lighting

Outdoors, the problem is much the same except that there are no ceilings and probably no places to hang anything. Try to do the same with sun reflectors as with the four lights indoors. The sun may serve as either the back light or the key light, with reflectors doing the other three jobs. Use the soft side of the reflector for key and fill lights, and use the hard side for back and side lights.

Conventionally, the sun is used for key light outdoors and reflectors supply the fill. If power is available outdoors, booster lights may be used for fill, but reflectors are cheaper and faster. They do have drawbacks, however, the obvious one being that they need sunlight; on an overcast day or in a fog, a reflector is worthless. Reflectors must be continually adjusted because the angle of light changes and moves off the spot it is aimed at as the sun moves. As the day wears on, the color temperature of the sun and the reflected light shift toward the reds, which give faces a progressively warmer cast. Also, the large flat surfaces of reflectors catch the wind easily and often vibrate, which is visible later on the screen. Since wind also blows reflectors over, an untended reflector should not be left standing. A falling reflector can literally kill the person in its path.

Soft Lighting

Another way to light, rather than using the four basic positions, is to fill everything—set and actors—with soft light. Use only soft, diffused broad lights and take advantage of every white reflecting surface available. The resulting low contrast and gentle colors are exceptionally pleasing. The effect is similar to that achieved when shooting outdoors on an overcast day: there are no harsh shadows, and the light is even and soft. A variety of lights called *softlights* are designed specifically to provide a large amount of highly diffused light. There are also materials to further aid in the diffusion of light. Reflecting fabrics may be hung on walls and ceilings, and even pieces of white styrofoam sheets may be broken up and placed in reflecting locations. Polyester sheets augment diffusion even when hung in front of softlights. Another method of creating soft light is to cover a set at ceiling height with a diffusing material, such as Soft Frost, produced by Roscoe Laboratories; lighting from above then provides a soft, even field of light over the whole set. (See Fig. 7-21.)

Source Lighting

A third lighting method is *source lighting*. This process is used in working on location, where the natural light of the location is augmented by artificial lights to give the appearance that the available light is lighting the scene. A representative situation would be one in which much of the light is coming in through large windows. This light is assumed to be the key light, and tungsten lights are set so that both their direct and reflected light go in the same direction as the window light. This may be done by mounting lights above the windows and bouncing them off the ceiling into the room, or shining them through sheets of diffusion. Other lights may then be placed at various positions in the room to sidelight or backlight people and objects for depth and modeling. For an interior at night, the source would probably be a table lamp or an overhead fixture. This approach, of having the light in the scene come from the direction of whatever would produce the main source in real life, is particularly feasible today with the existence of lightweight lighting units and the wide range of diffusion materials available.

Good motion picture shooting cannot be accomplished by a formula. It depends on the taste, perception, and experience of the filmmaker, and there is no substitute for continual shooting and analysis.

DAY-FOR-NIGHT CINEMATOGRAPHY

There are three conceivable ways to shoot outdoors for nighttime scenes:

1. Shoot at night with whatever light is available.
2. Shoot at night using studio light.
3. Shoot in the daytime in full sunlight, making certain modifications that will create a nighttime effect. This is called *day-for-night* shooting.

Most professional cinematographers prefer to

shoot night scenes at night, using whatever studio lights are needed to achieve the desired effect. This is not always practical or even possible, particularly in westerns and other kinds of pictures that require large, open areas. Also in smaller locations, the cost of even a few lights and extra technicians is often prohibitive.

The difficulty in shooting exterior night scenes at night is that nighttime light is usually neither strong enough nor of the proper distribution to provide adequate exposure. Sometimes studio lights can be used to augment actual nighttime lights, but this works only for small areas such as limited street scenes, dark alley shots, and other places where practical lights may already be part of the scene. It is feasible to studio light closeups and medium shots outdoors at night, but there aren't enough lamps and technicians to cover half a county.

Shooting a night scene in full sunlight involves the following:

1. Filters to darken the sky, add contrast, and darken skin tones.
2. Underexposure to produce the "darkness" of night.

Night Effect

What is a night effect? The way to understand and master a technique such as day-for-night shooting is to observe. Study actual nighttime situations and decide exactly what conditions must be simulated or recreated. In a real situation on a dark night, little is visible even to a participant in the situation. On film, such a scene comes out pitch black. Since the purpose of a picture is to be seen, however, in nighttime shots some source of light is always assumed, usually the moon.

Study an actual night situation, say, two people standing under a tree with moonlight streaming down on them. What do you see?

1. The sky is dark.
2. The scene is contrasty, that is, there is not much gradual shading from dark to light.
3. Faces are visible as soft highlights, and show less contrast than the scene as a whole.
4. There is little visible detail in the dark areas (but there is some).

Day-for-Night Conditions

The object of the game is to recreate these conditions by shooting in the daylight with the sun standing in for the moon. This is called day-for-night shooting, and is done by *filtering* and *underexposing* the whole scene in such a way that a night time effect is created. Ideally, the following conditions should exist:

1. A blue sky.
2. Bright sunlight.
3. Some sources of shadow.
4. Action staged so that actors and objects can be lighted from behind and from the side.

Since ideal conditions are rare, the sky may sometimes be a thin blue, even white; sunlight may be weak; and sometimes the best staging for action may not be the best staging for lighting.

Everything discussed so far applies to both black-and-white and color photography, but there are many techniques that do not apply to both. They will be considered in turn.

Day-for-Night in Black-and-White

Probably the most characteristic quality of night is a dark sky. On black-and-white (BW) film, a red contrast filter will darken a blue sky—only a blue sky, not a white one. A deep blue sky can be darkened with a light red filter, while a pale blue sky needs a darker red filter. The selection of the proper red filter depends on the depth estimate of the blue of the sky.

You will recall that BW panchromatic film, although sensitive to all the colors in light, is most sensitive to blue light. That is, BW panchromatic film does not "see" things in the same way that the human eye does. When we look at a rich blue sky, white clouds stand out clearly in contrast. But the same view photographed on BW film records the blue sky and the white clouds at about the same intensity, resulting in a picture of white clouds blending into a white sky. Since the BW film is more sensitive to blue than our eyes are, the blue sky overexposes and becomes white. A red filter darkens a blue sky by reducing the amount of blue light that gets to the film. This results in underexposure and consequent darkening.

Another effect of the blue sensitivity of black-

and-white film is that faces and skin tones come out darker than our eyes see them naturally. Human skin contains quite a bit of red, which the film translates into darker than normal tones. A red filter corrects this and lightens facial and skin tones, and simultaneously darkens a blue sky. To counteract the blue-sensitive effect, filters are used to correct the light striking the black-and-white film. A red filter allows more red light and less blue light to reach the film, so blue objects (skies) photograph darker, and red objects (faces) photograph lighter. The greater such *correction,* the darker the sky (blues) and the lighter the sunsets and faces (reds). The procedure for shooting day-for-night on black-and white film is as follows:

1. Place a red filter over the camera lens to darken the sky and increase the contrast. The filter generally used is a Light Red (Harrison 83P or Eastman 23A). In addition to darkening the sky, it makes faces appear lighter. In long shots, where skin tones are not central to the scene, the red filter alone is sufficient.
2. In closer shots, where faces are seen, a green filter must be added to the red to darken the skin tones and generally soften the effect. Otherwise, faces will be pasty or chalky white. Also, the filter lightens green foliage, permitting more detail in such shadow areas. The most commonly used green filter is an Eastman #56 Light Green. The combination of #23 Red and #56 Green (Harrison 76U) is made specifically for day-for-night shots on black-and-white film.
3. Underexpose the scene from 1½ to 2½ stops. This brings the total light level of the scene down to an approximation of real nighttime.

Generally, the best day-for-night filter is the combination of #23 Red and #56 Green. Depending on the conditions and on your own preference, however, you may use any combination of red, green, or neutral density filters you wish. Constant observation, testing, and evaluation will enable you to arrive at various suitable combinations for differing conditions and effects.

Filters

The following are some common red and green filters for use in day-for-night combinations:

Reds

#23 Orange. Very slight overcorrection, lightens faces.

#23A Light red. Medium overcorrection. Lightens faces. Darkens sky and creates marked contrast between clouds and blue sky. Used with #56 when faces are in scene.

#25 Red. Heavy overcorrection. Blue sky very dark. Faces will be very light.

#29 Deep red. Extensive overcorrection. Makes blue sky and water black, faces chalky white.

Greens

#56 Light green. Generally used with #23 Red for nighttime effect. Good skin tones in day-for-night effects.

X-1 Light green. Lightens green foliage and darkens blue sky.

#58 Green.

Darkening the Sky (Color and Black-and-White)

If the sky is not blue, a red filter cannot make it darker on black and white film. On color film in any situation, a filter colors the whole scene. In these situations, there are two possible courses of action:

1. Use a graduated, neutral density sky filter.
2. Avoid showing the sky in the scene.

A neutral density filter reduces the amount of light transmitted to the lens without changing any of the color values. ND filters are just what their name implies: they are gray (or neutral) in color, and range from a minimum density (which allows most of the light to pass through it) to a high density (which transmits very little light). They can be used with either black-and-white or color film since they filter all colors equally. The main purpose of a neutral density filter is to reduce exposure without correction.

A graduated, neutral density filter may be used to darken a sky by reducing its exposure. The top half of the filter is of a given density, while the bottom half is clear. The two areas blend into one another across the center of the glass, eliminating a sharp line division. Use this graduated filter so that the upper part filters only the sky in your scene. This reduces its exposure and darkens it. Of course, you cannot let your actors, or parts of them, move into the sky area because they will be correspondingly reduced in exposure and destroy the scene's visual credibility.

Lighting (Color and Black-and-White)

To achieve the most pleasing effect in day-for-night shooting, try to stage the scene so the actors are lighted from behind and to the side. Light directly from the front, that is, from the camera side of the scene, flattens out the scene and nullifies the directional effect of moonlight. It looks fake because we think of night scenes as having light coming from above and from the side in little shafts and pieces. Flat front lighting destroys this effect.

Since the main source of light in exterior day-for-night shooting is the sun, the nature of the location and the staging of the scene are vital to the final effect. Obviously, since the sun cannot be moved around, try to stage the action so that the sunlight hits it advantageously. Set the action, if possible, so that the sunlight strikes the actors on the side and at the rear (Fig. 7.31).

Light hitting the back of an actor rims him from behind and makes him separate, or stand out, from the background. Side lighting gives shape and depth to his facial features. Back light alone leaves the actor in silhouette with no features visible. Just as in normal lighting, it is helpful to fill in the shadowed side of your subjects to

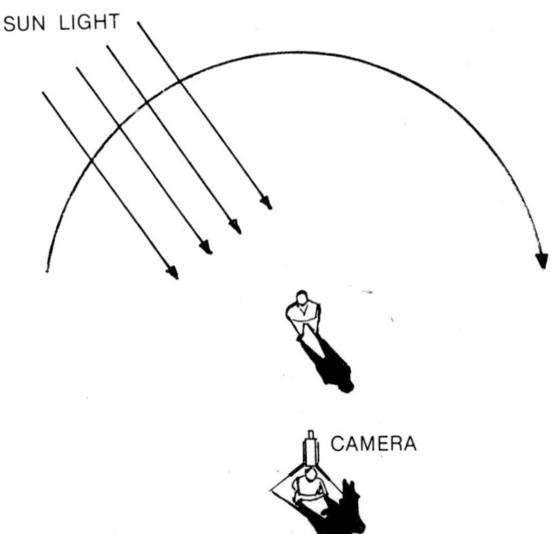

Fig. 7.31 In day-for-night lighting, stage the action so that the sunlight strikes the actor or subject from the side or rear.

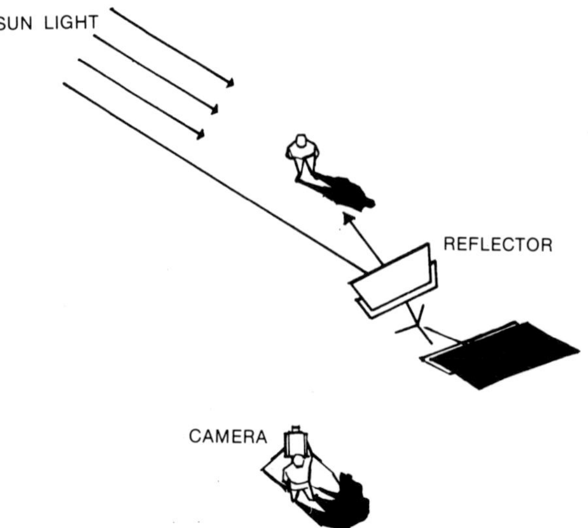

Fig. 7.32 Day-for-night. Actor backlighted by the sun, with reflector lighting the face so that features are visible.

provide more realistic detail and to eliminate the stark contrast (Fig. 7.32).

Try to get at least some back light and some cross light. Back light makes the subject stand out from the background, but by itself it creates a silhouette. Sidelight alone creates modeling and contrast, but without back light the subject blends into the background. Front light alone, or prominently, flattens the scene and makes it look false.

Sometimes it is neither desirable nor possible to stage your action to fit the best sunlight position. You can "rearrange" the lighting with reflectors and sunlight (Fig. 7.33). For example, if only direct cross light is possible, use reflectors to build up the backlighting and the fill.

There may be situations that require the sun to be completely blocked out and the use of a reflected key light from some other direction. This could occur, for example, when the sun is directly overhead, casting heavy shadows beneath the actor's eyes, cheeks, and chin; or when the sun's direction does not suit the staging and the action. The sun can be blocked with a butterfly scrim, which is a scrim net stretched on a large frame. Stands hold the scrim over the scene and cut out the overhead sun. You may then build a new key light and fill lights with reflectors (Fig. 7.34). The overhead scrim kills the strong downward directional quality of the sunlight, yet lets light through as general diffused illumination. By this method sunlight in medium and close shots can be controlled closely.

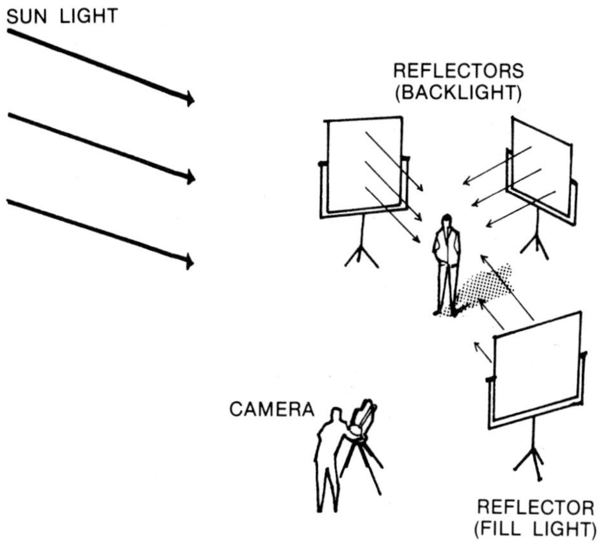

Fig. 7.33 If the sun is not in the "correct" position, rearrange the lighting with reflectors.

For tight closeups, rather than setting up a large butterfly scrim, a reflector on a stand may be used to block the sun (Fig. 7.35). There are many subterfuges to resort to to get the effects you want. Constantly examine situations, scenes, and setups, and put your boundless ingenuity to work at every opportunity.

Exposure (Black-and-White)

The exposure for day-for-night shooting is derived from the *normal daytime meter reading.* For an exterior scene, let us examine ways to determine the exposure for each of the following conditions:

1. Daytime—long shots.
2. Day-for-night—long shots.
3. Day-for-night—closeups and medium shots.

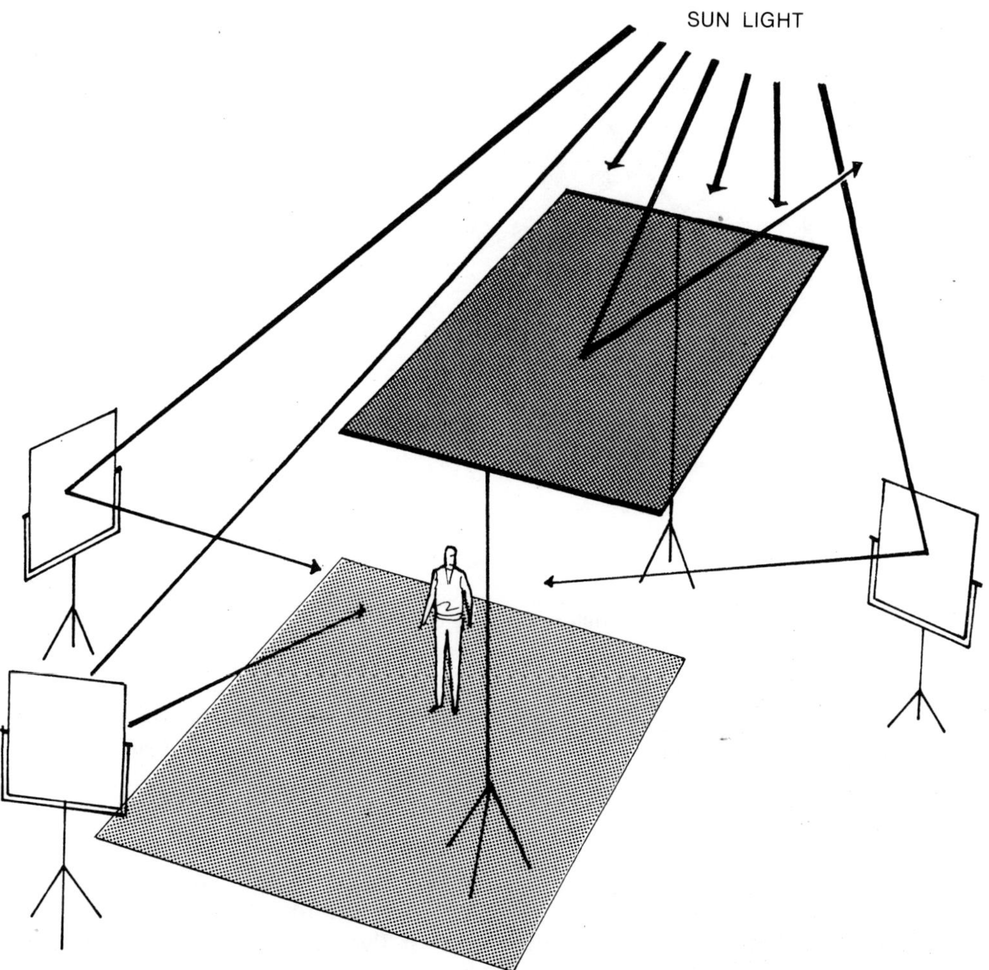

Fig. 7.34 The sun may be blocked off completely with a solid butterfly, and new key, fill, and back lights may be built up with reflectors. Fewer or additional reflectors may be used, depending on the situation.

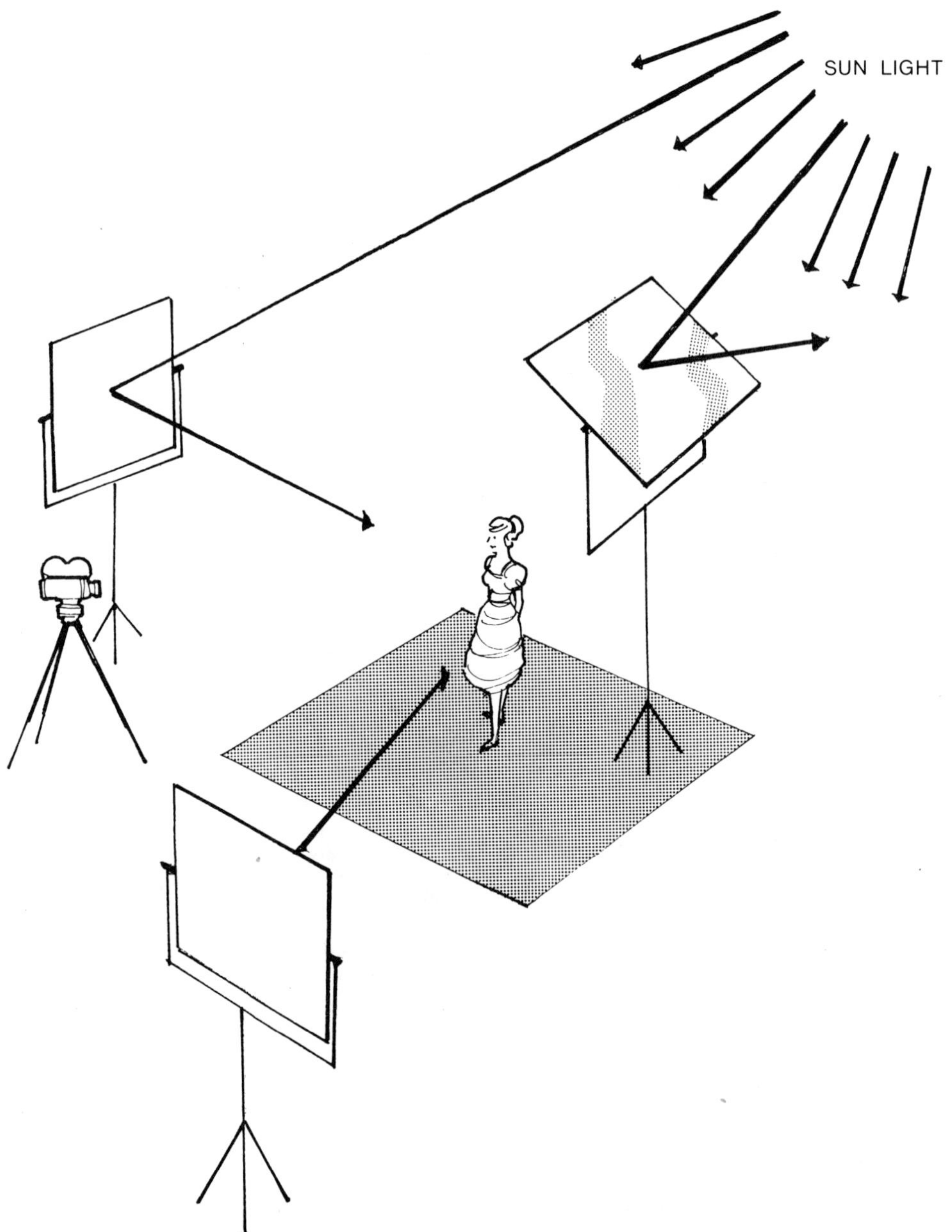

Fig. 7.35 In close shots, a reflector may be used instead of a large butterfly.

Our hypothetical scene is exterior on a sunny day. The sky is blue, pleasingly set off by several full-bodied columns of white clouds.

Daytime—Long Shots

This is to be a normal daylight effect. You want the clouds to stand out against the darker sky, but this they won't do very well on film without a filter. Select a #23A red filter to darken the sky and increase contrast, and proceed as follows (see Fig. 7.36):

1. Take the daytime meter reading. Suppose it calls for a lens diaphragm setting of *f*/16.
2. Apply the filter factor. The #23A Red has a factor of five, which means that the lens must be opened 2¼ stops from normal to compensate for the light loss caused by the filter itself.

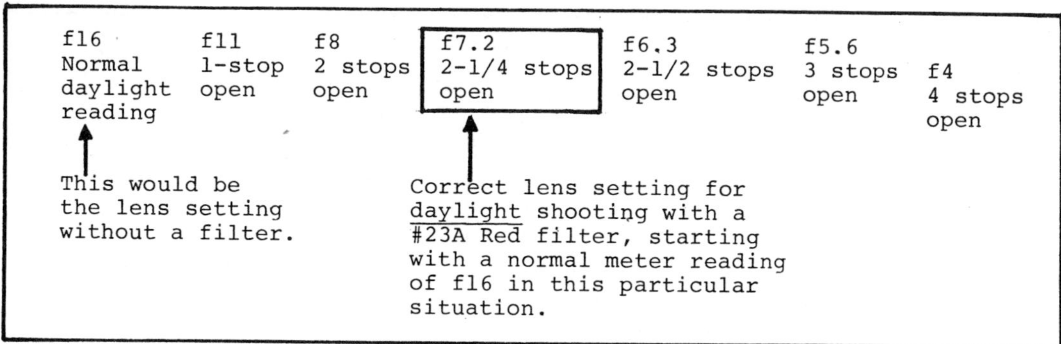

Fig. 7.36 *f*-stop setting for normal daylight scene, using a red filter to darken the sky (BW).

3. Set the lens at *f*/7.2 and shoot. Since the full filter factor has been applied, the scene will appear on film as daylight with white clouds against a darkened sky.

Day-for-Night—Long Shots

In shooting the same situation as a night scene, use the same filter, #23A Red, and underexpose the shot. Then proceed as follows (see Fig. 7.37):

1. Take the normal daylight meter reading. Again, in this case it is *f*/16.
2. Disregard the filter factor. The #23A Red filter factor of five means that for daytime exposure the lens should be opened 2¼ stops. But since a nighttime effect requires 1½ to 2½ stops underexposure, if you do not make the correction, the daylight lens setting results in 2¼ stops underexposure.
3. Set the lens at *f*/16 and shoot. Since no filter factor has been applied, the scene will be underexposed the proper amount for a nighttime effect. The red filter will darken the sky properly for night.

Day-for-Night—Medium Shots and Closeups

Under the same conditions—exterior, sunny day, blue sky, white clouds—do the day-for-night closeups and medium shots the same way, but add a green filter to the #23A Red filter when human faces and skin are in the shot. The usual day-for-night filter combination is #23A Red and #56 Light Green. Use the following method (see Fig. 7.38):

1. Take the daytime meter reading. Once more, let us assume that it is *f*/16.
2. Apply part of the combined factor for the two filters. Remember that when you use two filters together, you multiply their factors. #23A Red (factor five) times #56 Light Green (factor four) equals total factor twenty. This equals 4½ stops. If you make no factor correction, you will be 4¼

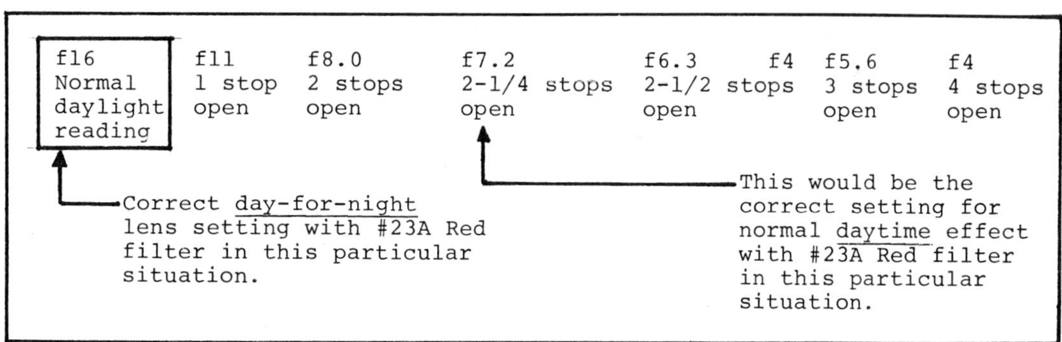

Fig. 7.37 *f*-stop setting for the daylight scene in Fig. 7.36 shot with a red filter as a day-for-night scene (BW).

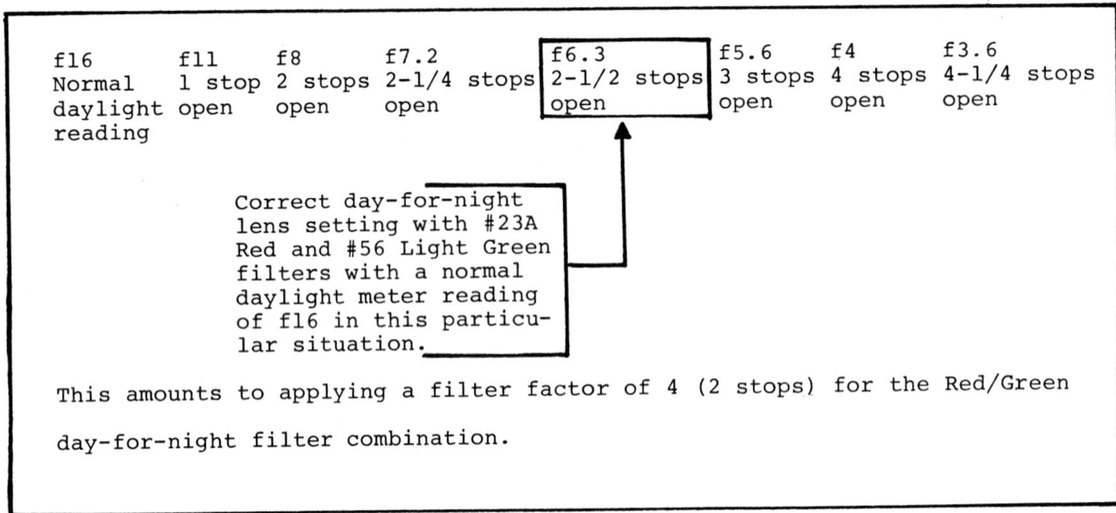

Fig. 7.38 *f*-stop setting for day-for-night medium shots or close shots of people, using both red and green filters (BW).

stops underexposed. But for night effect only 1½ to 2½ stops underexposure are needed. So open up only two stops, which will leave an underexposure of 2¼ stops.

Indoor House Lights (BW and Color)

When photographing houses or buildings day-for-night, show lighted windows, street lights, and signs. It is a strange looking night scene in which no lights are burning.

Generally, regular house lights are not bright enough to expose well in a day-for-night shot. So windows must be lit from the inside with strong lights. Again, observe an actual night situation on a bright moonlit night. Notice the brightness of lights in house windows relative to the illumination outside. Remember that in a day-for-night shooting, the sun represents the moon, and lights in windows must be correspondingly stronger to be seen. (Examine the scene through your viewing filter.)

Actual indoor house lights are quite visible on moonlit nights, but cannot be seen when the sun is up. Since the sun is taking the place of the moon, the intensity of house lights must be brought up to the point where the sun does not overpower them. They should be visible after the filters have been placed and the lens has been set for underexposure.

If convenient, stage the action so that the sun backlights or crosslights the house, as was discussed earlier. Windows will show up better on the shadow side and the flattening effect of stark front lighting will be avoided (Fig. 7.39).

Sometimes you can shoot at dusk just after street and house lights are turned on and there is still enough daylight to get an exposure. By choosing the right location and planning carefully, remarkable results may be obtained in this way. You are, of course, at the mercy of the quickly fading daylight and of people who turn lights on at twilight.

Under certain conditions it is possible to make effective long shots by combining a day scene with a night scene. Say you want to take a high panoramic shot of a city at night. The lights will expose satisfactorily, but there is not much detail. To get a more balanced picture, mount the camera rigidly and immovable and shoot the city in early evening while there is enough light to show details. Without moving or shaking the camera, wait until darkness sets in and all the lights go on. Then shoot the scene again. These two shots may later be superimposed to give you daylight detail with nighttime lighting. Obviously this method is limited to long shots, since any moving persons or objects will appear in the final result as ghost images.

Day-for-Night in Color

In the days of silent film, night scenes were often tinted blue, and even today it is a convention

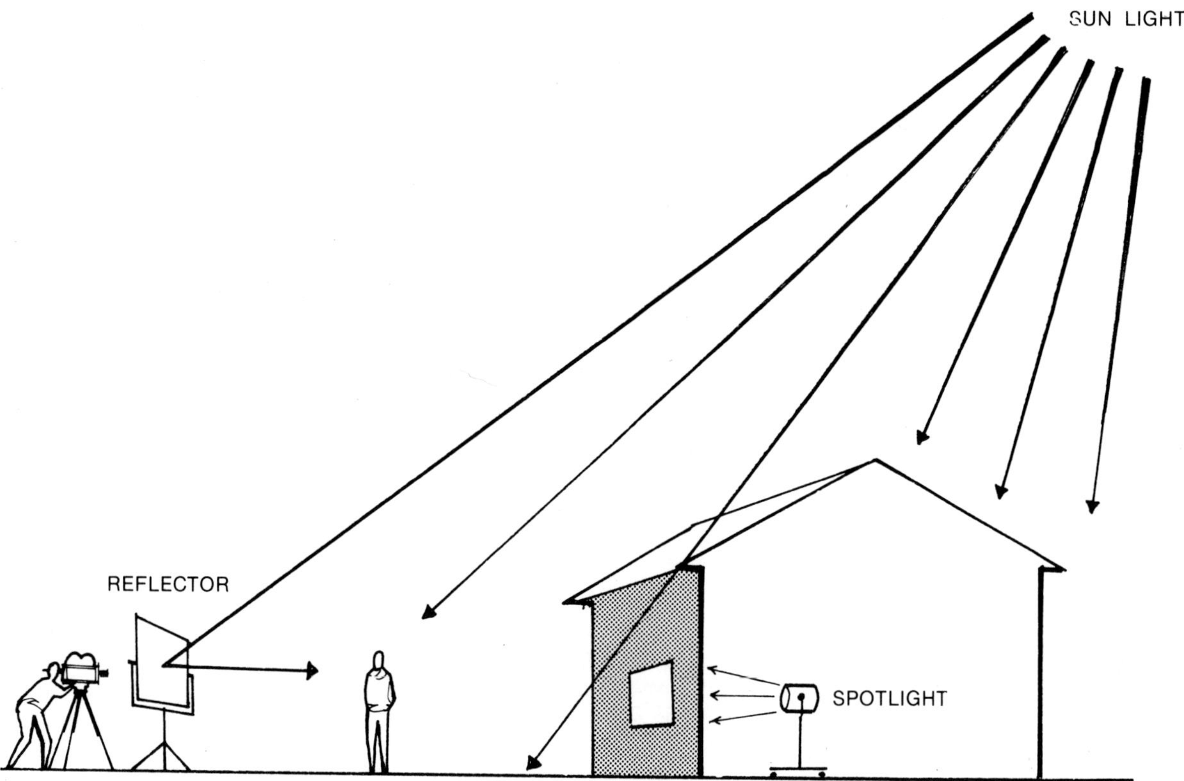

Fig. 7.39 Day-for-night setup. The sun strongly backlights both house and actor. The reflector bounces fill light into the actor's face. The spotlight is directed at a translucent curtain to make the window appear as lighted at night.

that night shots be bluish. Day-for-night scenes in color, as in black-and-white, assume the moon as the main light source even though real moonlight is gray, not blue. Some cinematographers will not make night shots blue, but will light and shoot scenes according to how they see night.

Professional 16mm color film, like professional color film of all widths, is designed to give normal color rendition when exposed in light whose color temperature is 3200°K. Motion picture incandescent lights are designed to produce light at 3200°K for interior shooting. Since daylight, at close to 6000°K is a great deal bluer than incandescents, a #85 or a C-4 filter must be used to shoot professional 16mm color reversal in daylight. If you shoot in daylight without the orange filter, the resulting picture has a decidedly blue cast.

Color Principles

The principles of color day-for-night shooting are basically the same as for black-and-white: darken the sky and underexpose the scene. In color, however, the scene may be given a bluish cast by leaving off the orange filter. The following are possible steps for shooting color day-for-night:

1. Remove the orange filter to give a bluish tone to the picture. (This is optional, since you may not want a night scene that is blue.)
2. Darken the sky with a pola screen or a graduated, neutral density filter, or both. Remember that in color a red filter will not darken a blue sky—instead, it will make the whole scene red.
3. Underexpose 1½ to 2½ stops.

There are some precautions to take when using a pola screen (also called a polarizing filter), since it darkens only the sky that is at right angles to the sun. If you stand facing the direction of sunrise, the pola screen is effective when the camera is pointed either to your left or to your right. Look through a pola screen and move it

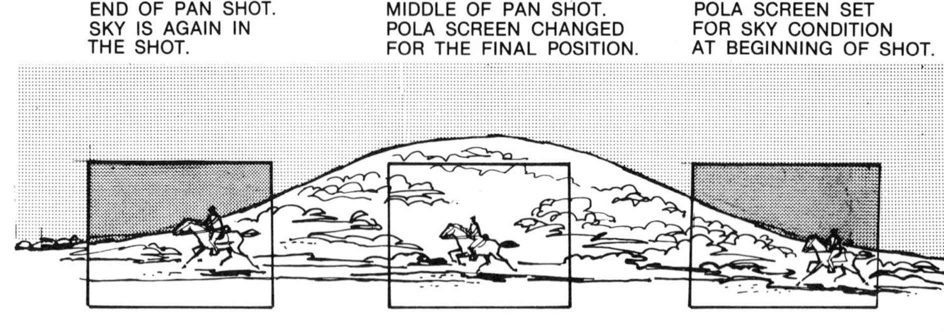

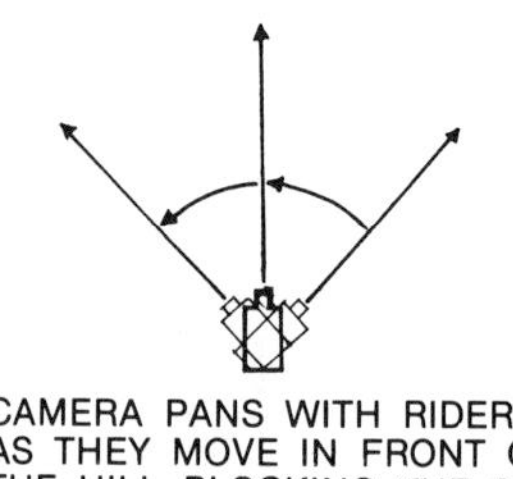

Fig. 7.40 A shot planned so that the pola screen can be changed during the shot to accommodate differing conditions at the beginning and end of the shot.

around, to get used to its effectiveness relative to camera angle and sun angle.

Because of the variable effectiveness of a pola screen, it is generally impossible to maintain a consistently darkened sky if the camera is panned to any extent. One cinematographer worked out a system for using the pola screen in an action picture whose director often called for pan shots of up to 180°. He used a camera angle in which the initial framing took in an area of sky. He set the pola screen so that the sky was darkened properly at the beginning of the pan shot. When he followed the action in the scene, he tilted down so that the sky was out of frame. This allowed him to readjust the pola screen for the sky that would be visible at the end of the shot (Fig. 7.40). Such techniques work quite well but require careful planning.

Studying a technique or art goes far beyond merely reading what someone else has said about it. Mastery comes with experimentation, involving failures and successes. Observe all kinds of night scenes and conduct as many tests and experiments as you can afford. This will provide a backlog of good usable experience.

DAY-FOR-NIGHT HINTS

Applicable to Both Black-and-White and Color

1. The basic method for shooting day-for-night is to darken the sky and underexpose the shot.
2. Whenever possible, shoot in full sunlight under a blue sky.
3. When the sky cannot be darkened by contrast or by neutral density, keep the sky out of the shot.
4. Arrange the scene and the action, wherever possible, so that actors and subjects are lighted from behind and from the side. (See Figs. 7.31, 7.32, 7.33, 7.34, 7.35, 7.39, 7.40.)
5. Fill in front shadows on faces with reflectors or lights.
6. Use reflectors or lights to backlight subjects when it is not possible or feasible to stage the scene for the best sunlight position.
7. If the action calls for it, scrim off or block out the sun and create new lighting with reflectors, lights, or both.

8. Light-colored clothing helps to separate the actors from the background. Dark clothing blends into the background, leaving only the faces visible.
9. Polarizing filters and neutral density filters may be used to darken the sky.
10. Since a polarizing filter eliminates reflections, it can make faces appear flat and lifeless looking because it destroys the highlights.
11. Check with your laboratory for suggestions and special requirements in exposing and shooting nighttime effects.
12. Be sure to tell the laboratory that the film has been shot day-for-night, so they will not compensate for the underexposure you worked so diligently to achieve.

Applicable to Color Only

1. To give the scene a bluish cast for night, shoot without color-correcting filter.
2. Darken the sky only with polarizing filters or neutral density filters. Do not use color filters, since they will color the scene.
3. When shooting without color-correcting filter, light from a gold reflector will give nearly white light for faces.

Applicable to Black-and-White Only

1. Red filters darken a blue sky, increase contrast, and lighten skin tones.
2. Green filters darken a blue sky slightly, decrease contrast, darken skin tones, and lighten green foliage.
3. For long shots, use a red filter only and underexpose 1½ to 2½ stops.
4. For medium and close shots of faces and skin tones in a scene, use a red filter combined with a green filter and underexpose 1½ to 2½ stops.
5. The standard day-for-night filter combination for black-and-white film is red plus green. Both the YL-7 filter and the Harrison 76-U filter are a combination of red and green.
6. When using a Harrison 76-U or a YL-7, a filter factor of six gives the correct underexposure for nighttime effect.
7. When the sky is gray or white, use a graduated, neutral density sky filter to lower its exposure. Use this together with whatever red or green filters you would normally use for day-for-night effects.

EIGHT

Some Aspects of Sound Recording

The distinguishing feature of motion picture sound is that it must be "in sync," or synchronized, with the picture. In recording a person speaking, the words must fit the lip movements and not be heard early or late. Sound effects, though not always recorded in sync, must be heard in sync in the final version of the movie. Everyone has seen out-of-sync scenes in which the lips move silently for an instant and then the voice follows, or a slam is heard and then the door shuts. It is not enough for sound and picture to be *almost* synchronized; if they are not precisely in sync, the desired effect is lost or an unwanted comic effect is produced.

PICTURE AND SOUND SYNCHRONIZATION

Most of the machinery and procedures in moviemaking are designed to ensure that picture and sound are always in sync. This is the function of sprocket holes in film and of sync pulses recorded on quarter-inch tape. The sprockets, or little teeth, on the wheels of cameras, sound equipment, projectors, optical printers, and laboratory equipment fit into a film's sprocket holes and maintain the film in an exact position while running, whether the machines are slowed down or sped up. Several rolls of film on different pieces of equipment may be kept in perfect synchronization if their sprocketed wheels turn at the same speed.

Up until the final print of the completed movie, both sound and picture are on separate rolls of film. In editing, projection, mixing, and printing, when a roll of picture is run, its corresponding roll of sound track must be run along with it on another machine. To project a reel of your picture at some stage in the editing to see how it looks on a screen, put the roll of picture on the the projector and the roll of sound on the playback machine, or "dummy." Both projector and dummy have sprocketed wheels on which both the picture film and the sound film are threaded. Then "lock" the two machines together electrically by throwing a switch. After being interlocked, both projector and sound dummy will start up at the same instant and run at exactly the same speed. The sprocketed wheels in the machines keep the two pieces of film always in the same relative position so that neither can get ahead or behind the other. Thus sound is heard in perfect synchronization with the picture. Film editing machines such as the Moviola, for example, are equipped with sprocketed wheels so that the picture may be threaded in one side and the sound in the other and they may be run simultaneously at the same speed.

Interlock Magnetic

There are three methods of simultaneous sound and picture projection: interlock magnetic, magnetic composite, and composite optical. In *interlock magnetic,* picture and sound are on separate rolls of film. The projectionist threads the picture film over sprocketed wheels in the projector with the picture start mark in the aperture of the projector. He then threads the magnetic sound film into the sprocketed playback machine with the start mark of the sound directly on the magnetic playback head. When "locked" together electrically, both projector and dummy start up at the same time and run at exactly the same speed. Thus the picture is projected while its separate sound track is played back in exact synchronization.

Magnetic Composite

The second method of sound and picture projection is *magnetic composite,* in which the sound is contained in a thin strip of magnetic emulsion that has been striped along the edge of the picture print. As the picture runs through the projector, a magnetic sound head picks up the sound from the magnetic stripe and channels it into the sound system. Magnetic striping is used for stereo sound in movies and is usually restricted to high-budget, hard-ticket productions. Although the sound is superior, the striping of release prints is costly and not economically feasible for normal release movies.

Composite Optical

The third method of projection, *composite optical,* is standard for both theatrical and nontheatrical motion pictures. The sound track consists of a photographic image within a narrow band running the length of the film along its edge. This photographic, or optical, track is a photograph of sound vibrations converted to light vibrations. As the film runs through the projector, the sound track passes over a small, intense *exciter lamp* that shines its beam through the film onto a photoelectric cell. As the film runs, the variations in the optical track that act on the beam of the exciter lamp cause varying amounts of light to hit the photocell. The photocell in turn converts these variations of light to electrical variations, which are then reconverted into sound by the amplifier.

The end result of motion picture production is the *composite release print,* either optical or magnetic, on which are printed both the final version of the movie and its accompanying final sound track. This print goes through the projector in the theater, classroom, home, office, or on TV, and the quality reaching the screen depends on the care that has been taken in all work up to that point. At the time of the original recording, the sound should be as good as can possibly be obtained since it undergoes many procedures before the final track. Sound is transferred to magnetic film from quarter-inch tape and goes through the editing ordeal. During the mixing session, it is altered if necessary by equalizing and filtering to reduce noise, eliminate sibilance and boominess, and sometimes to change its tone. What is left is transferred to photographic film as an optical negative that is then printed on the positive release print. It is easy to assume that if the original sound is noisy or boomy, or the volume is too high or too low, it can all be corrected and smoothed out later. Up to a point, it can. Often, however, when some unwanted element is removed from sound, something that should be kept is eliminated. Also, in the optical stage, sound undergoes all sorts of strange stresses. Since a photographic track cannot handle the wide volume range that magnetic film can, the sound must be compressed, that is, the peaks of volume are reduced in the transfer to keep the volume range within the limits of the film medium. Then, both the negative and positive optical tracks must be precisely exposed and developed by the laboratory to achieve the best possible sound reproduction in the projector, It is important that sound be recorded originally at the best possible quality so it may reach the projector in reasonably good condition, since it is possible to lose a certain amount of the original quality with each additional step.

SPROCKETED MAGNETIC FILM

Most synchronous recording today is done on quarter-inch magnetic tape. Recording synchronously on sprocketed magnetic film although obsolete, is still done occasionally, the major drawbacks being that the equipment is too heavy and the large amount of magnetic film required is expensive. When recording on quarter-inch tape, unwanted shots and NG material may easily be eliminated when transferring the good takes to the more expensive magnetic film. The sound for an entire production on quarter-inch tape may be carried in a small box or package, while the same amount of sound on magnetic film would require a hand truck. The mechanism required to maintain sprocketed magnetic film at a constant speed involves large synchronous motors and heavy flywheels for film stabilization. In this type of sync recording, both camera and recorder are equipped with synchronous motors designed to run at a constant speed when both are powered by the same A-C current, which they will be if they are plugged into a wall socket. Since the film in the camera and the magnetic film in the recorder are both sprocket-driven, if the two motors are running at a constant and equal speed, both camera film and recording film must always remain in sync with each other. Before the invention of the quarter-inch tape sync-pulse system, all recording was done with sprocketed film recorders. Today, sprocketed sound recording equipment is confined solely to the rerecording studio, while the quarter-inch recorder with its light weight, portability, low cost, and high quality is used for almost all synchronous production recording (see Figure 8.1).

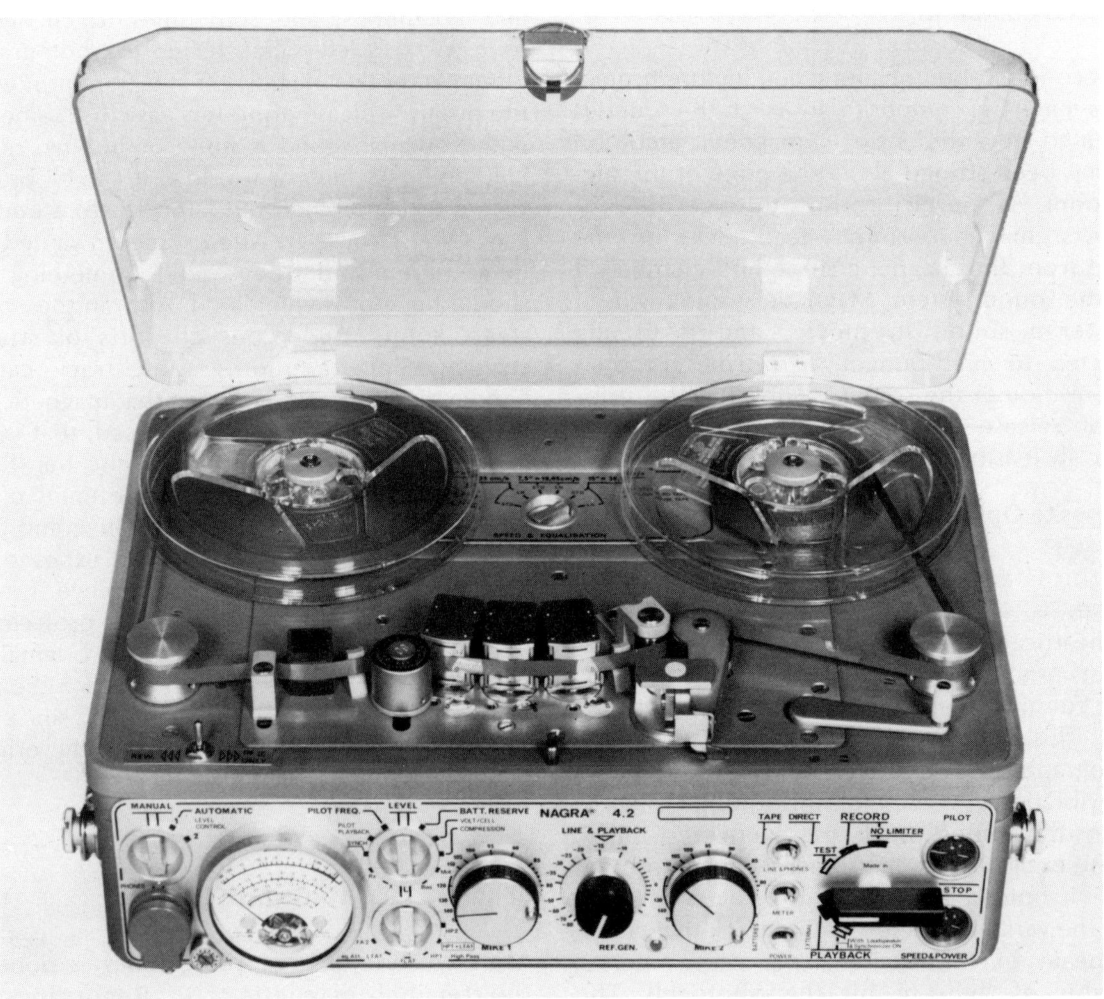

Fig. 8.1. Nagra synchronous ¼-inch tape recorder.

SINGLE-SYSTEM SYNC SOUND

A single-system camera contains the sound recording system as an integral unit, and is used mainly in news filming and in some documentary work. Most single-system cameras are 16mm and are designed to accomodate single-perforated film. Before exposure, the film is sent to the laboratory for *striping,* in which a magnetic emulsion is laid along its length on the unperforated edge. During shooting, the sound is recorded directly onto the magnetic stripe. Since the distance between the camera lens and the magnetic recording head is constant, the sound is perfectly in sync and is integral to the picture. Single system would seem to be an ideal way to shoot, since it is quite compact and no clapstick slates are required. But the integral sound system makes the camera heavy, and the sound quality is not as good as that on tape. In double-system shooting, as soon as the shot has been made, the quarter-inch tape may be put away and not touched until it is transferred to magnetic film. Then the tape may be stored as a protection copy against anything that may happen to the transfer. This cannot be done in single-system shooting because, the sound on the magnetic stripe has to go through the film developing machines along with the film to which it is attached. A protective transfer may be made after development, but by then the critical danger is past. If the sound were to be erased or damaged in the laboratory, the film would be worthless. Double-system shooting is used principally in one-time news and documentary work.

Quarter-inch magnetic recording tape, like film, stretches and contracts depending on the stresses it is subjected to and on temperature and humidity. Unlike film, tape cannot normally be held to a constant unwavering speed in the recorder. In the film camera this is not a problem because it is driven by a constant speed motor and the film is held to a constant speed by the sprockets that fit into the camera's sprocket holes. The problem, then, is to be able to record sound on tape that is always in perfect synchronization with the film in the camera.

During shooting, the requirements are different for synchronization than afterward. In shooting, a recorder that is simple, light, and reliable is manditory. Although it must be easily synchronized with the camera, it is not necessary that the camera and the recorder be in sync from the start. The two must, however, run in sync after a short period of getting up to speed. Only in the later phases of editing, sound cutting, mixing, and interlock projection must picture and sound be run in sync from the start, and this requires heavier studio equipment.

QUARTER-INCH SYNC TAPE

Quarter-inch tape recorders are used almost universally in shooting sync motion pictures (See Fig. 8.1.) They are lightweight and simple to operate, as well as being relatively inexpensive and reliable. Keeping the *sound* in sync with the film in the camera, regardless of the tape's stretching or shrinking or the recorder's speeding up or slowing down, is possible with a sync-pulse synchronization system in which electrical impulses at the rate of 60 per second (60 Hz) are recorded on the quarter-inch tape so that they aren't heard when the tape is played back. These sync-pulse signals may be generated and transmitted to the recorder by the following pulse systems:

1. Cord sync. In this arrangement, the camera runs on a battery-operated motor that is mechanically governed to run at 24 frames per second. Actually the speed of a governed motor may fluctuate a little above and a little below 24 fps; but as long as the fluctuation does not exceed one percent, or ¼ frame, the sound may later be resolved so it is in sync with the picture. On the governed motor, a small pulse generator puts out low-voltage electrical impulses at the rate of 60 per second (60 Hz) when the camera is running at 24 fps (Fig. 8.2*A*). At faster or slower speeds, the pulse rate varies proportionately. These sync pulses are carried through a wire from the camera to the recorder and recorded on the tape. No more than one camera and one recorder may be operated together in sync using this system.

2. Crystal sync. In this system, camera speed is maintained at an exact 24 fps speed by a crystal-controlled battery-operated motor (Fig. 8.2*B*). It is characteristic of a crystal (quartz, rochelle salt, etc.) that it oscillates at a precisely constant rate when an electrical current is applied to it. The control unit of a crystal-controlled motor con-

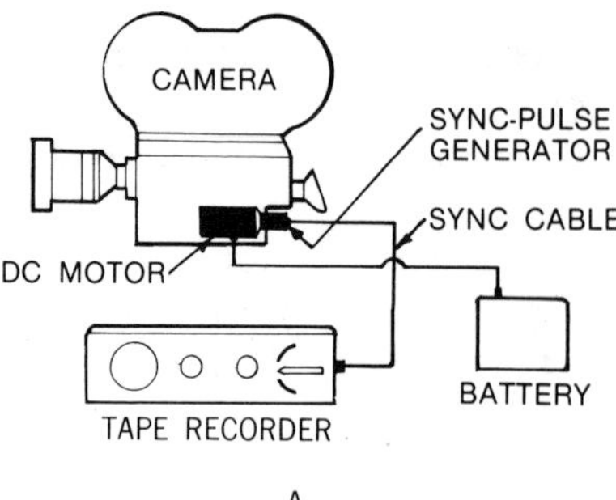

Fig. 8.2*A*. Synchronous recording with ¼ in. magnetic tape. Both camera and recorder operated by direct current from respective batteries. The sync pulse generator on the camera motor sends a 60 Hz sync pulse to the recorder through the sync cable.

tinually compares the speed of the motor to the frequency of its integrally mounted oscillating crystal. Variations in motor speed are automatically corrected at millisecond intervals so accurately that the speed of the camera may be considered constant. At the same time in the recorder an unvarying sync-pulse signal is supplied to the tape by a crystal device either installed inside of or attached to the recorder (see Fig. 8.2*B*). This device, called a *crystal time-sync generator,* consists of a tone oscillator whose output is precisely maintained at 60 pulses per second (60 Hz) through electronic reference to an oscillating crystal. Crystal control is so exact that there is no need for a cord between camera and recorder, which provides greater mobility in documentary and difficult dramatic situations. The sync-pulse signal is the same as that of a cable-carried sync pulse. The tape may be transferred and resolved in the normal way. Unless a radio-transmitted slate is used, slating must be done conventionally with clapsticks, since no connection exists between camera and recorder, there is no way of conducting the audible sound of an automatic slate to the recorder. With crystal sync, any number of cameras and recorders may be used simultaneously and they will be in sync.

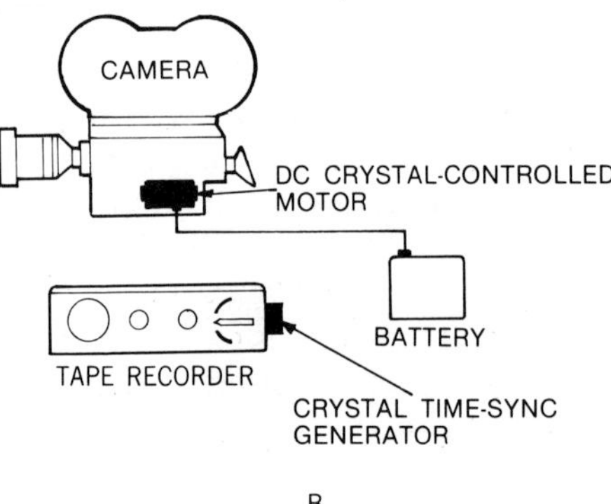

Fig. 8.2*B*. Synchronous recording with ¼ in. magnetic tape. The camera, equipped with a crystal-controlled motor, operates on direct current from its battery. The recorder, equipped with a time-sync generator that produces a 60 Hz sync pulse signal recorded on the tape, also operates on direct current from its own battery. No cable or wire connection between camera and recorder is needed to record sync sound.

3. Mains ac sync. The 60-cycle pulses in household alternating current, also known as *mains* current, may be used as a sync pulse when fed to the recorder through a small portable *synchronizer,* or *resolver.* When the recorder is used in conjunction with a camera powered by a *synchronous motor* that is in turn powered by the same household ac current, the picture and sound will be in sync (Fig. 8.2C).

4. Ac power supply sync. A sync-pulse signal may also be taken from a portable battery-powered ac power supply. This device converts battery direct current dc into alternating current ac for the operation of synchronous motor cameras on locations where there is no regular ac current available. By means of a resolver, this ac current may also be used to supply a sync-pulse signal to the recorder.

The following are some camera/recorder com-

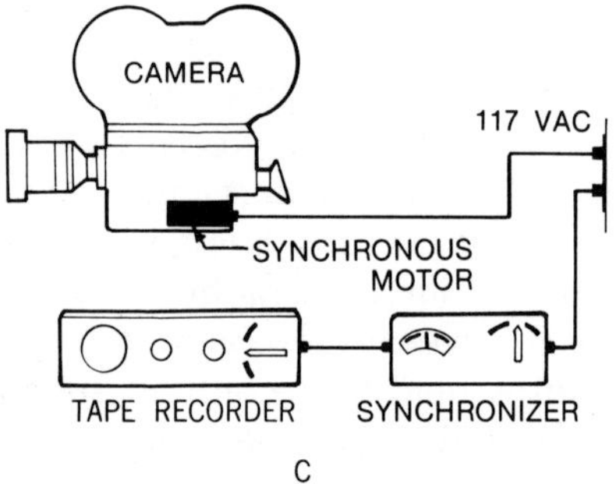

Fig. 8.2C. Synchronous recording with ¼ in. magnetic tape. Both camera and recorder plugged into household 60 Hz alternating current, which runs the camera's synchronous motor at a constant speed and also supplies the recorder with a 60 Hz sync signal. Since both camera and recorder are using the same current for reference, they will record picture and sound in sync.

binations for shooting sync sound:

1. Camera with crystal-controlled motor. Recorder with crystal time-sync generator. Both camera and recorder are battery operated.	Any number of cameras and recorders may be used.
2. Camera with synchronous motor powered by ac (mains). Recorder receiving sync pulse from ac (mains) through a resolver or converter.	Any number of cameras and recorders may be used.
3. Camera with governed motor equipped with sync-pulse generator. Recorder receiving sync-pulse signals through cord from camera. Both camera and recorder are battery operated.	Only one camera and one recorder may be used.

When camera and recorder run at a constant speed (in sync) the 60-cycle impulses will all be the same distance apart. If camera or recorder speed fluctuates, the impulses will be either farther apart or closer together on the tape. Later, when the sound is transferred from the quarter-inch tape to sprocketed magnetic film, the resolver measures the spaces between impulses and slows down or speeds up the recorder during transfer (see Figure 8.3). These sync pulses, then, act as "magnetic sprocket holes" during transfer from unsprocketed tape to sprocketed magnetic film, maintaining the sound on the magnetic film in the same relative position to the picture film as it was at the time of shooting. Clapsticks must be used to provide synchronization reference points. The usual sequence during shooting is for the director to call, "roll it," as the signal for the camera and recorder to start. When both the camera and recorder are up to "speed," the camera operator calls, "mark it," which is the signal for the slate person to slate

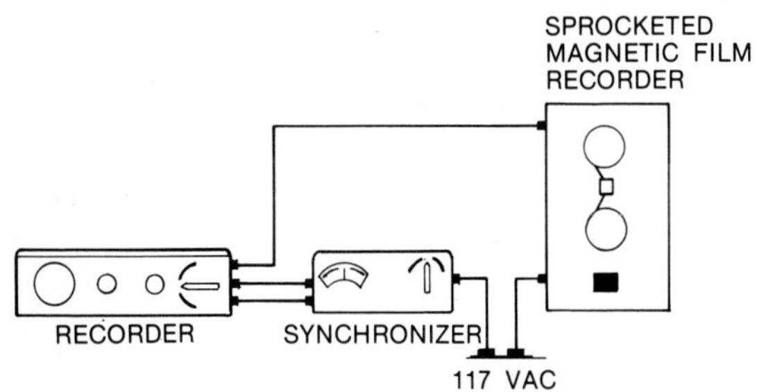

Fig. 8.3. To transfer sync ¼ in. tape to magnetic film; both the synchronizer (resolver) and the magnetic film recorder are plugged into the same 60 Hz household current, which becomes the reference signal for the tape recorder and the driving control for the film recorder. The resultant sound on the magnetic film will be in sync with the picture.

the shot. The slate then provides a visual sync reference at the head of the picture take and an audible reference at the head of the sound take to be used later in synchronizing the film with the sprocketed magnetic track. (See Syncing Dailes Chapter 10.)

Sync-pulse quarter-inch tape recording is used universally with all film widths, including 65mm, 35mm, and 16mm film production as well as in shooting movies on videotape. Most good quality super-8mm home-movie cameras are equipped with a pulse generator that may be used with the Nagra, Tandberg, and Stellavox recorders and other similar systems (see Figure 8.4).

Sync pulse is not an interlock system since the camera and the recorder cannot be started simultaneously and maintained at the same speed. Both must be started and allowed to build up to full running speed—one or two seconds—then clapsticks or some kind of sync signal must be used to establish the initial point of sync.

Shooting to Playback

In shooting musical numbers, singers and dancers are photographed as they mime or dance to prerecorded music played back over a loud speaker. Only by shooting to an exactly repeatable sound tack can you shoot successive takes and different camera angles in sync with music. Before shooting such scenes, all music (including vocals) must be recorded on ¼ in. tape simultaneously with a sync pulse. Each prerecorded playback tape should begin with a rhythmical voice countdown—"three, two, one"—followed

Fig. 8.4. Arriflex 16mm camera with crystal-controlled motor and Arrivox-Tandberg recorder with crystal time-sync generator make cordless-sync shooting possible.

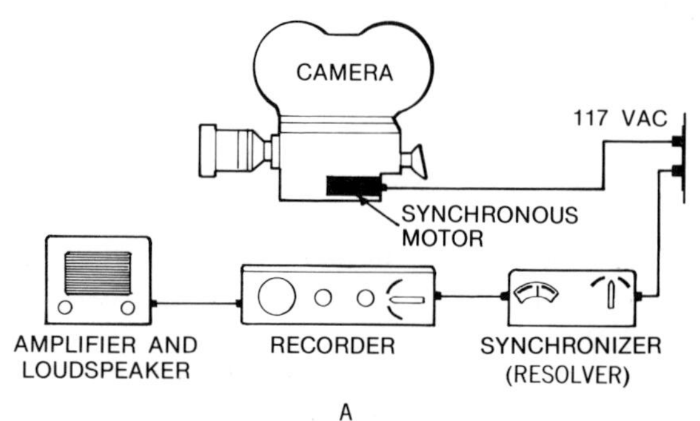

Fig. 8.5*A*. The camera, with a synchronous motor, operates on household alternating current at a constant speed. The recorder, playing a prerecorded tape with a sync pulse on it, operates on its own batteries, but takes a 60 Hz signal from household alternating current through the synchronizer, or resolver, as a reference signal. Sound played back will be in sync with the picture.

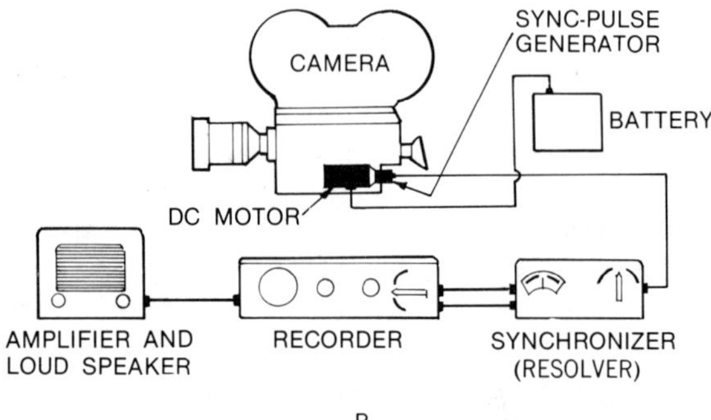

Fig. 8.5*B*. Synchronous playback with ¼ in. magnetic tape. The signal from the sync pulse generator on the battery-driven camera motor goes into the synchronizer as a reference signal for the playback tape. The synchronizer then controls the speed of the playback recording so that it is in sync with the camera.

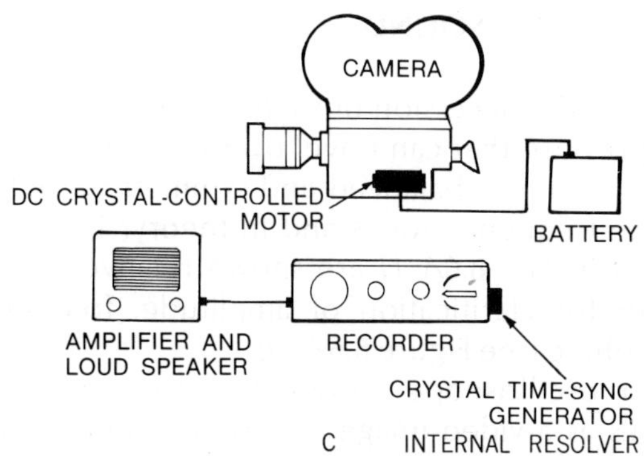

Fig. 8.5C. Synchronous playback with ¼ in. magnetic tape. With a crystal-controlled motor on the camera and a time-sync generator and internal resolver on the recorder, no connection between camera and recorder is necessary for playback synchronization.

by a slate clap. This countdown allows the camera assistant on the set at the beginning of each shot to synchronize his slate's clapsticks for the camera with the prerecorded clap on the playback tape. (See Syncing Dailies, Chapter 10.) Figure 8.5*A, B,* and C shows three types of synchronous playback with ¼ in. magnetic tape.

The aim of sound recording is to record desired sounds and eliminate extraneous ones. So many different sounds surround us constantly that if we were to listen attentively to each one, we would be too preoccupied to do anything else. To survive in such a sea of sound, human beings have a kind of internal psychological filter that either rejects or subdues unwanted sounds and allows only selected ones to reach the mind. Say you are engaged in a quiet conversation with a friend in a city park. In the background you hear an occasional bird, a shout or two of children playing nearby, and maybe a few footsteps as someone passes. It is all very pleasant and you and your friend converse easily at a comfortable voice level. Now, make a recording of your conversation and play it back. What is the result? The ambient sound is louder than you expected. Birds nearly drown out the conversation. The playing children sound like a gang fight. Water sprinklers you had not noticed earlier hiss insistently to the steady explosive accompaniment of a power lawn mower. Traffic on nearby streets makes strange shooshing sounds at irregular intervals, and it is apparent that the Air Force is conducting manuevers overhead. What has happened? It is the same scene you found so pleasant to chat in; yet it is not the same when recorded because a microphone does not have that peculiar human ability to select and subdue sounds according to their momentary importance. The microphone records everything and anything at just the volume it "hears" it, with the result that real sound does not always sound "real" at all. In motion pictures good sound consists only of those sounds that people hear after their internal psychological filter has eliminated or subdued all the unwanted sounds.

SOUND RECORDING

Production sound recording is the recording of sound intended for use in a motion picture. It includes the dialogue of actors recorded synchronously with the picture, the synchronous recording of sound effects, and the "wild," or nonsynchronous, recording of both voices and sound effects. The principal recording tools are the microphone, the quarter-inch magnetic tape recorder, and assorted related equipment and supplies. The task of the sound crew is to get the best possible sound under whatever conditions may prevail.

SOUND CREW

A sound crew may consist of one person or many, depending on the size and type of production being done. One person alone may handle the sound on a documentary-type shoot, carrying the recorder slung by a strap over the shoulder and hand-holding the microphone. Some productions may require a crew of two, one to operate the recorder and one to handle the microphone. On feature pictures, a crew of four or more may be necessary, but usually a sound crew of two can handle most productions where one microphone is used and the conditions do not call for extra equipment. The basic jobs of a sound crew are mixer, boom operator, and cable handler.

Mixer

The mixer, or sound director, is the head of the motion picture sound crew, who is in charge of and responsible for the ultimate quality of the recorded sound. The job involves analyzing the shooting situation, selecting the crew, ordering all equipment and supplies, supervising the recording, making all decisions, and delivering the final tapes and sound reports to the producer. The mixer's effectiveness depends largely on a knowledge of sound principles, the ability to use the tools available, an understanding of each step of the motion picture sound process from original recording through release printing, and keeping abreast of new techniques and tools. On the shooting set or location, the mixer has the following tasks:

1. Decides on microphone choice, placement, and movement.
2. Listens to rehearsals through the headphones.
3. Handles the microphone volume controls during shooting.
4. Determines whether the sound is good or bad.

Boom Operator

This is the crew member who handles the microphone. The name originated in the early years of feature films, where the microphone was usually mounted on a boom. Today, however, the microphone is frequently either hand-held or mounted on a fishpole. (See The Tools of Sound) It is the boom operator's responsibility to become familiar with the action being photographed and to keep the microphone always in the proper position relative to the actors. He operates the microphone boom, holds the fishpole, or holds the microphone, as the case may be. He is responsible for assembling and operating any kind of boom, fishpole, or microphone support that may be used on a production. Keeping the microphone correctly placed during a shot is so important that many mixers, or sound directors do this job themselves and assign an assistant to control volume levels.

Cable Handler

This sound crew member moves equipment, cables, and supplies as needed. On smaller crews this job is usually done by the mixer and the microphone handler.

THEORY OF SOUND

Sound is a succession of slight, rapid variations in air pressure that can travel over a distance. These waveforms are balanced and symmetrical only in single-frequency tones and in theory. The waveforms in Fig. 8.6*A–H* are shown relative to each other for clarification of amplitude, frequency, and phase (see Figure 8.6*A-H*).

An oscilloscope shows a picture of sound waves as a video image of sound vibrations. This waveform of a single tone—not speech or music—looks like a continuous letter *S* laid on its side and represents the vibrations in air that are emitted in all directions from its source. As it travels through the air, this sound wave acts like a billiard ball in that once it is set in motion it travels in a straight line until it hits something—a wall, a chair, a person—and then bounces off and continues in a straight line until it hits something else. Often, the way sound bounces off the walls, ceiling, and floor of the shooting location determines the resulting sound quality. Say dialogue is being recorded in a square room with hard walls. The sound will bounce back into itself from the walls, and the microphone will record the sound going and coming. The same sound will then be recorded twice, the second time occurring a split second after the first. This results in echo, or boominess, and the dialogue sounds as if it were "recorded in a barrel." To correct this,

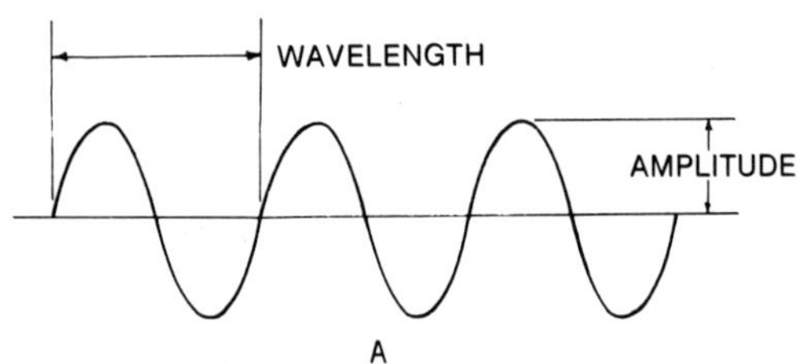

Fig. 8.6*A*. Pure sine wave. Wavelength is the distance from any point on the wave to the next same point, in other words, a cycle. Amplitude, or volume, is represented by the height of the wave. Frequency is the number of waves in a given space. Phase is the relative position of any point on a wave to another.

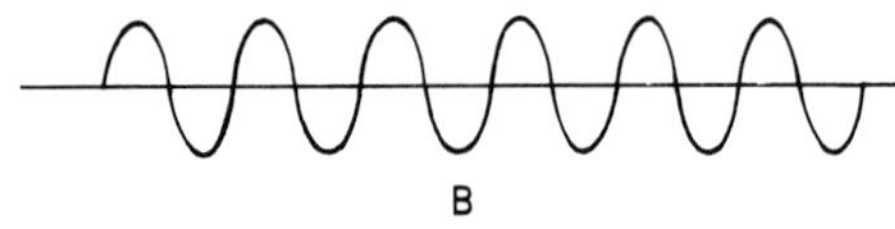

Fig. 8.6*B*. A higher pitch, or frequency, than the wave in *A*.

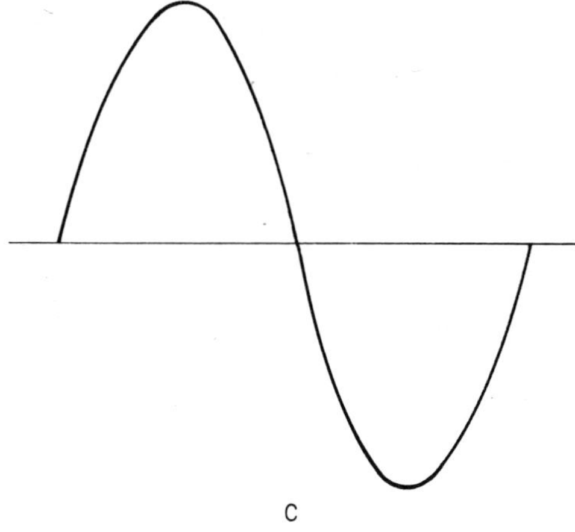

Fig. 8.6C. Low pitch, or frequency, as compared to *A* and *B*.

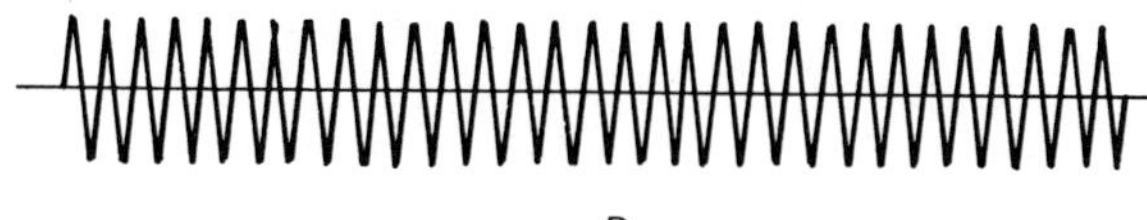

Fig. 8.6*D*. Quiet high-pitched tone.

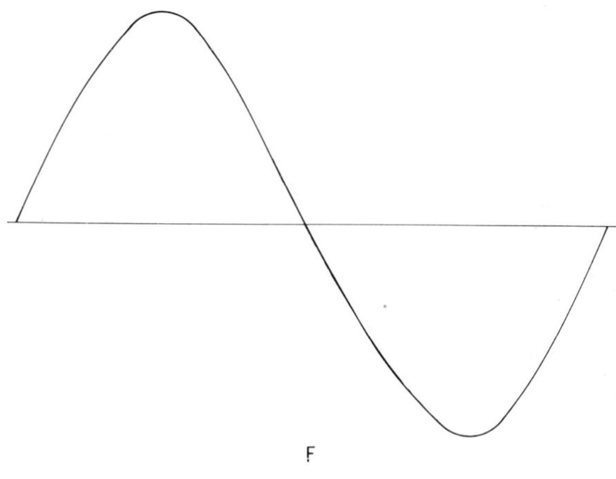

Fig. 8.6*F*. Loud low tone.

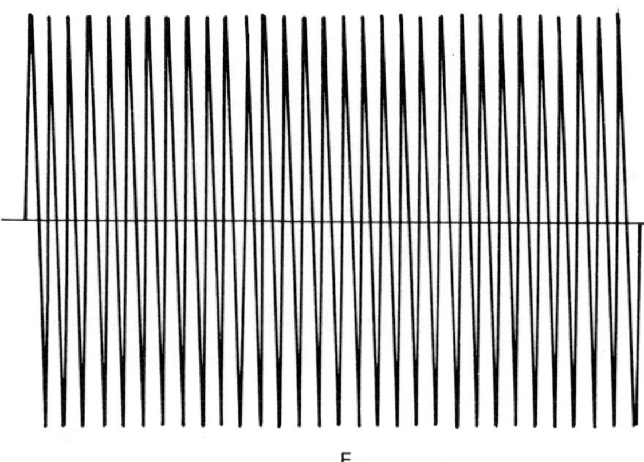

Fig. 8.6*E*. Loud high-pitched tone. Same frequency tone as *D* only louder.

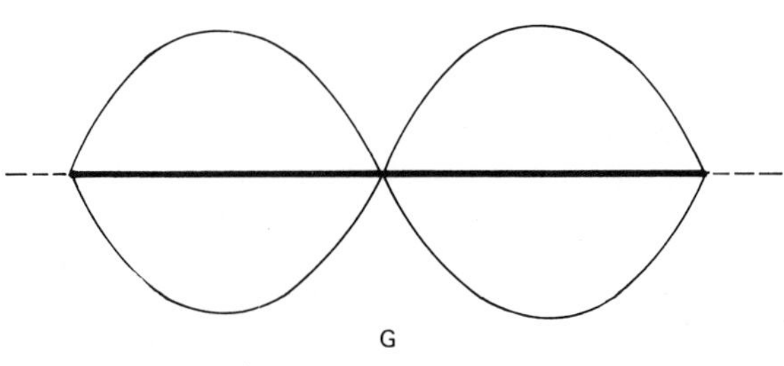

Fig. 8.6*G*. Two waves 180° out of phase. Such waves result in cancellation, or reduction in volume and distortion, depending on the degree they are out of phase.

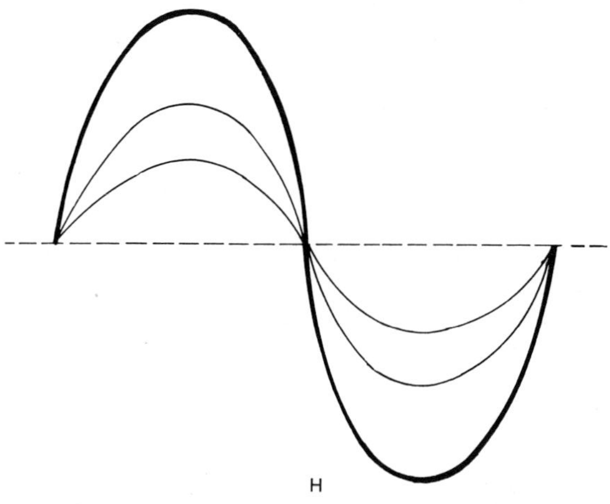

Fig. 8.6*H*. Two waves in phase. The result here is augmentation. The waves combine to give a third wave of greater amplitude.

such things as changing the angle of the walls (as on a set), placing absorbent pads or blankets on the walls or floor, using a lavalier microphone, or keeping the microphone close to the speakers would be considered. Analyze what the sound is doing and try anything and everything to obtain the desired sound quality.

As a filmmaker, you are concerned with three characteristics of sound: amplitude, frequency, and phase. *Amplitude* is volume and refers to the loudness of a sound. *Frequency* is the number of vibrations per second and determines the pitch or tone of a sound. *Phase* is the position of any part of a sound wave at any instant. The oscilloscope trace of a high-pitched tone shows many waves close together horizontally, while it shows a low tone as fewer waves in the same horizontal space. Low tones, then, are low frequency, and high tones are high frequency, with the whole range of tones lying in between the two. Amplitude, or loudness, is indicated by the vertical height and depth of the waves: the louder the sound, the higher the peaks.

Sound Waves

Unfortunately, the recording of sound for motion pictures is not the recording of single tones but of speech, sounds, and music, each of which is a combination of many tones, amplitudes, and frequencies that are called complex waveforms (Fig. 8.7). Notice that the complex waveforms for speech and music, while following the general pattern of a single tone alternating above and below the center line, are actually combinations of many different tones and degrees of loudness that result in these particular wave patterns. Every sound, be it syllable, note, word, chord, or noise, has its own peculiar complex waveform. Each little peak and valley represents those particular tones and amplitudes that make up a specific sound.

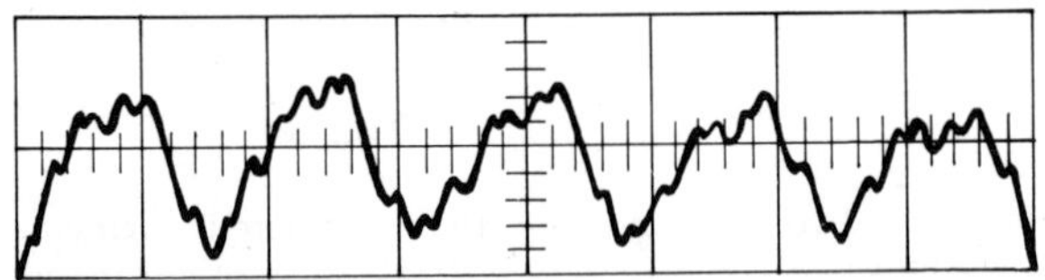

Fig. 8.7. A complex waveform for a musical sound.

Good Sound

Good sound is clear and distinct. It has no fuzzy or ragged sounds in it, and noises in the background are low enough not to interfere or even intrude slightly. Dialogue is clearly heard and understandable and does not echo or sound "boomy" unless that is the effect desired. Perspective, or apparent distance, is believable, that is, the sound of something close sounds close, and something at a distance sounds as if it comes from that distance. Bad sound, on the other hand, is characterized by distortion and noise.

Distortion

Distorted sound has a definite harshness to it. Musical tones are rough and ragged instead of clean, and voices have an unpleasant edge. Individual sounds do not stand out but seem to merge together discordantly, and the total effect is raspy and disturbing. The main cause of distortion is overloading, or overmodulating, which is simply recording at more volume than the system being used is designed for. Basically, all recorders work the same way. A microphone sends its small electric impulses into a preamplifier, where they are made stronger and sent into a larger amplifier. In this large amplifier the sound impulses can be increased or decreased manually by turning a knob that controls a device in the recorder, called a *potentiometer.* This is actually the familiar volume control, known in the profession as a "pot." It is the main control used during a recording, and by turning the pot one way or the the other, the volume (amplitude) is turned up or down.

Every recorder and playback machine has a limit to the amount of volume it can handle without distorting the sound that goes through it, and while recording the volume must be kept within the limits of the machine. Consider the waveform of a chord of music played through a recorder (Fig. 8.8); As the chord's volume is increased, it retains its characteristic shape, but its peaks extend farther above and below its center. There is an upper and lower limit to the distance the wave can expand before becoming distorted. This limit, called the envelope, represents the limit of the machine's ability to record or reproduce sound without distortion.

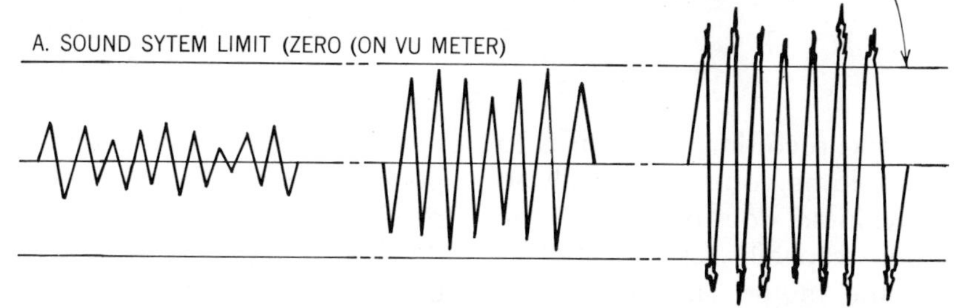

Fig. 8.8(*A*). The volume of a sound waveform (*A*) is held relatively low, well within the capability of the system. The same sound (*B*) at a higher volume, up to the limit of the system. Note the VU meter reads exactly zero. The same sound (C) at a volume higher than the system can handle. Note the distortion of the wave above the zero line. Note the VU meter above zero in the red.

Zero on the VU meter nominally represents the point at which the sound system goes into distortion. If you increase the volume so that the wave goes beyond the envelope limits, the wave still retains its original shape to some extent, but the shape of some of the peaks and valleys is altered. The chord is now distorted and will sound that way. You can control distortion by controlling the recording volume. There are two ways of doing this: one is to move the sound farther away from the microphone, and the other is to lower the pot, or volume control. Although moving the sound farther away from the microphone lowers the volume, it also changes the perspective of the sound and makes background sounds louder and more intrusive. Wherever possible, control the volume initially at the volume control on the recorder.

VOLUME INDICATION

A volume-indicating meter is an integral part of every recording machine. It shows the recording volume level and indicates the level at which distortion occurs. The meter measures and indicates the change in *decibels* of volume for speech, music, and sound effects. When the volume is increased, the needle on the meter moves across the scale to the right. Decrease the volume, and it falls back to the left. The decibel, or *dB* as it is referred to, is the standard unit of sound volume, and is the smallest amount of change in volume that can be detected by the human ear. The *volume unit,* or VU, is a unit measurement to indicate a change of 1 dB in volume for speech, music, and sound effects (see Figure 8.9.).

The meter on any piece of equipment is usually set so that 0 dB indicates the upper volume limit of that equipment's ability to handle sound without distorting it. When the needle is below zero, the sound is undistorted. The scale is calibrated in plus dB's above zero, and minus

Fig. 8.9. VU meter. The upper scale is in dB's from −20 to +3. The lower scale is in percentage of modulation from zero up to 100 percent, the nominal point of distortion. It measures peak averages.

dB's below zero. While recording the aim is to operate the pot, or volume control manually so that modulation, or volume, does not exceed the limits of the recorder's capability as indicated by the zero point on the meter. However, some recorders are designed to record undistorted sound up to + 4 db. The meter is a guide to avoiding distortion during recording and playback. It indicates the volume level at all times, and allows necessary adjustments to be made to keep the volume within the limits that the recorder can handle.

Two kinds of meters are of concern to the filmmaker: the *VU meter* and the *modulometer*. Most tape recorders used in film production are equipped with modulometers, while the VU meter is used mainly in studio consoles. Since the filmmaker is involved both in tape recording during shooting and studio recording during transfer and mixing, an understanding of each meter's distinguishing characteristics is necessary.

VU Meter

Examine the illustration of the VU meter. Starting at the left, there is an upper scale and a lower scale, The upper one starts at less than –20 dB and goes up to 0 dB, at which point the scale begins to indicate plus dB's up to 3. A heavy red bar extends from 0 dB to +3 dB. Whenever the needle is in the red line area, the sound is distorted. The lower scale is marked off in percent, and divides the range of acceptable recording in increments from zero percent to 100 percent. Either scale may be used, but it is important to know the meaning of the needle's position with regard to volume and distortion. The modulometer face is the same but it lacks a percentage scale.

There are certain limitations to the VU meter that affect the way it is used. It indicates only the average of the peak values of volume. Thus many peaks in the sound are not indicated on the meter because the meter movement cannot follow small, instantaneous peaks that change in both volume and frequency simultaneously. Although this has been compensated for partially by a built-in reduction in the response of the meter that prevents a certain amount of overmodulation on the part of the operator, keep in mind that individual peaks of volume are not indicated by the VU meter. A good, usable recording level ranges from –6 dB to –10 dB, depending on the material being recorded. Some professional studios record consistently at –12 dB, and others claim that –14 dB is the best recording level; but levels as low as this may be best only in studios and under completely controllable conditions. Although most sound has peaks of volume in it that cannot be anticipated, if it is recorded so that the VU needle falls between –6 dB and –9 dB, the peaks will usually hit at about zero, staying below the distortion level. An occasional quick peak into the red cannot be anticipated and usually does no harm.

Modulometer

Professional motion picture tape recorders are equipped with modulometers rather than VU meters. The dial and needle action is the same as on the VU meter and it is used the same way, except that the modulometer is a fast peak-reading instrument. It indicates the peak volume levels in whatever is being recorded, while the VU meter shows only the average of the peaks. If the modulometer needle does not go into the red, it is a sure sign that no distortion is occurring. If the VU meter needle does not go into the red, there is *probably* no distortion taking place.

Overmodulation and Overrecording

Overmodulation and *overrecording* both mean recording at too high a volume level. This is the cause of most distortion and bad sound. Recording too low is not necessarily a problem, but recording too high always creates a problem. As long as the needle is barely deflecting during recording, the volume may be increased later during transfer; although this will also increase background and system noise, these can be dealt with in other ways. In recording too high, however, the sound will be permanently distorted and nothing can be done to correct it.

Preamplifier Distortion

The preamplifier of a recorder receives weak signals from the microphone and amplifies them to a point where they can be further amplified for recording by the main amplifier. Extremely loud sounds or sounds coming from a high-output microphone that is too close to the source may cause the preamplifier to go into distortion. Since the meter is not normally set to read the volume of a recorder's preamplifier, it is possible to record with the recorder pot turned way down and the needle showing low volume yet still be getting distorted sound. In this situation, the distortion can be identified only by listening to it through earphones. If the sound is coming from some uncontrollable source, such as a jet airplane, the only solution is to wait until conditions are better. If preamplifier distortion is caused by a high-output microphone too close to the source of the sound, the microphone may be moved farther away. If the microphone cannot be moved farther away, a change to a lower output microphone may be necessary. For example, the Sennheiser 804 has a –21 dB output while the output of the Electrovoice 642 is lower at –48 dB, referring to the strength of the voltage going from the microphone to the preamplifier. High output is not necessarily good, or low output bad. A high-output microphone may be used farther away from the source of sound than one with a lower output, and the resulting quality will not necessarily be better or worse.

Recorder Head Tone

The peaks of speech—the instantaneous volume increases that the VU meter is not able to indicate—are about 10 dB above the average level of human speech. Therefore it is helpful to record a –8 dB or –10 dB tone at the head of each roll of tape. Professional recorders for motion pictures are equipped with a button or switch that records a tone on the tape when pressed. To record the head tone, thread the tape on the recorder and run it a few turns. Then make the voice slate with identifying information:

"Roll number one . . . Jane Doe Productions . . . *It's Only Tuesday*. . . . The following is a –10 dB head tone."

Then, with the recorder still running and recording, press the button and quickly adjust the pot until the meter reads –10 dB. Record at least twenty seconds of head tone. Later, when the ¼-inch tape is transferred to magnetic film, play the head tone into the film recorder and set the film recorder's pot so the –10 dB head tone is at 0 dB on the film recorder's VU meter. This sets into the film recorder compensation for the volume peaks in speech not indicated by the VU meter. Then transfer the whole roll of tape at that volume setting.

MICROPHONES

There are many different kinds of microphones and much technical information about them, the filmmaker need only know what a few microphones do and which one to use for the job at hand. Every microphone is a *transducer*, which is a device that changes one form of energy into another by picking up acoustical energy in the air and converting it to electrical energy.

The sequence of all sound recording starts with something that sets up vibrations in the air—a voice, a gun, an orchestra. The vibrations strike the microphone diaphragm causing it to vibrate, which in turn generates electrical impulses in an identical pattern to that of the air vibrations. These electrical impulses go into an amplifier, where they are made strong enough to be recorded on magnetic tape or film. Of the many types of microphones available, only three are generally used in motion picture production: the dynamic microphone, the condenser microphone, and the ribbon-velocity microphone.

Dynamic Microphone

In a dynamic microphone the vibrating diaphragm is attached to a small coil that vibrates within the magnetic field of a permanent magnet, producing voltage by induction. This type of microphone is generally more rugged and less expensive than the condenser type. It has good high-frequency response, can be screened successfully against wind noise, and can be panned rapidly without creating noise.

Condenser Microphone

The diaphragm of a condenser microphone is one of two plates in a two-plate capacitor. When the diaphragm vibrates, the capacitance changes in proportion to the vibrations, providing electrical impulses that can then be amplified and recorded. The condenser microphone has an extremely good frequency response and is excellent for maintaining high-frequency sounds. It has low distortion and little internal noise. It is a high-output microphone, which means that it can be used farther away from the source of sound than a dynamic microphone. Its disadvantages are that it tends to be less rugged than the dynamic microphone, is susceptible to moisture damage, and is difficult to screen against the wind. The condenser microphone requires an outside power supply and a preamplifier of its own.

Ribbon-velocity Microphone

The ribbon-velocity microphone consists of a light metallic ribbon suspended in a magnetic field. Sound-actuated vibrations of the ribbon generate voltages that are amplified. This type is more delicate than either the condenser or dynamic microphone, and is more susceptible to the *proximity effect,* distortion occurring when the microphone is within a few inches of the sound source. Unless the ribbon-velocity microphone produces the desired sound quality, condenser and dynamic microphones should probably be used for most motion picture recording.

The basic problem in motion picture voice recording is that the microphone must be outside the picture and must, therefore, be some distance away from the actor or speaker. In other kinds of voice recording such as stage singing, narrating, radio announcing, and platform speaking, the microphone may be placed very close to the speaker's or singer's mouth to eliminate the intrusion of ambient sound. In motion picture recording, however, keeping the microphone out of frame moves it away from the actor and allows the ambient sound to intrude. The skill of the motion picture sound recordist lies in his ability to deal with microphone distance and still obtain acceptable sound.

The two most important microphone design characteristics of concern to the filmmaker are *sensitivity* and *directionality.*

MICROPHONE SENSITIVITY

Sensitivity refers to microphone's ability to pick up sound frequencies. *Frequency* is the number of sound vibrations, or cycles per second. One

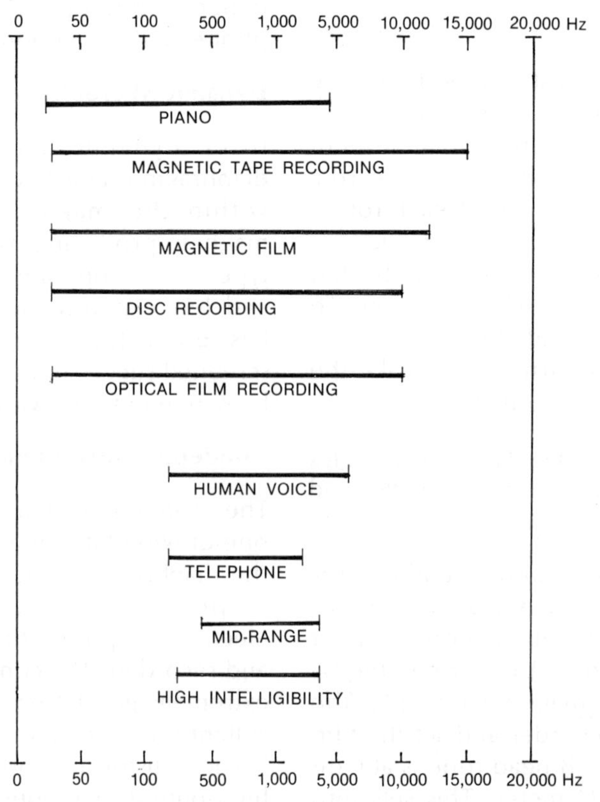

Fig. 8.10. Audible frequency range.

cycle per second is called 1 Hertz (1 Hz), and the frequencies of all sounds are stated in Hertz. The audible spectrum, the range of frequencies that can be heard by the human ear, ranges from a low of 15 Hz to a high of 20,000 Hz. Normally, every sound contains a certain range of frequencies, and eliminating or adding frequencies to a sound changes the way it sounds to the ear (see Figure 8.10). Music on a cheap radio with a small speaker sounds bad because some of the high and low frequencies are chopped off both ends of its frequency range. Voices sound strained and thin over many intercoms because such sound systems are not designed to carry the full range of frequencies of the human voice. In motion picture sound tracks, when we want a voice to sound as if it were coming over a telephone, we filter, or take out, certain frequencies from a normal voice to give it its peculiar telephone sound.

The normal frequency range of the human voice is from 200 Hz to 4000 Hz. There are, of course, lower and higher frequencies in the human voice, depending on the individual and whether the voice is male or female. The mid-range frequencies of the entire spectrum are considered to be between 400 Hz and 3500 Hz; so the human voice extends a little below and a little above the mid range. Every sound—voice, music, and noises—consists of its own particular range of frequencies; and for a recording of a sound to be a faithful reproduction, or of high fidelity, most or all of the frequencies in the original sound must be picked up and recorded. All microphones are not equally sensitive to all frequencies, so that one microphone may record speech that sounds a little high-pitched, another may record speech that sounds low and boomy. For this reason, microphones should not be mixed in a scene. Whenever possible, use the same type of microphone throughout. This is not always feasible, however, since microphones may have to be changed to accommodate various conditions. For example, you may have to switch to a lavalier microphone during a scene to eliminate strong, objectionable ambient sounds in a long shot. The difference in frequency response between the two microphones can often be corrected later by *equalizing* in the mixing session; occasionally, however, the difference is so great that the two cannot be matched exactly. So try to use the same type of microphone throughout a scene. Listen to sound recorded under similar conditions with different microphones and learn the sensitivity of each. Not only will you learn what to expect from a given microphone, but you will also develop aesthetic preferences for certain microphones over others.

MICROPHONE DIRECTIONALITY

Directionality is the second microphone characteristic of concern to a filmmaker. This refers to the ability of the microphone to pick up sounds better from one direction than from another. In making films extraneous sound should not intrude on the principal sound. The microphone should pick up the desired sound strongly and subdue unwanted sounds.

Pickup Patterns

Microphones are classified by the pattern in which they pick up sound. An *omnidirectional* microphone picks up sound equally from all directions. A *bidirectional* microphone picks up sound best from two directions, usually 180° from each other. And a *unidirectional* microphone picks up the strongest sound from one direction only (see Figure 8.11 *A* and *B*). Microphones for motion picture recording are mainly unidirectional, that is, they are more sensitive to sound coming from the front of the microphone, while subduing or eliminating sounds coming from the sides and back. A unidirectional microphone is essential in filmmaking since it frequently must be placed at some distance from the actors to be outside the picture. The farther any microphone is from a speaker, the more ambient noise and boominess it will pick up. But a microphone with a directional pickup pattern, because of its narrower acceptance angle, reduces unwanted noises from the sides and back. Microphones are classified for use according to their type of pickup pattern.

Cardioid Microphone (See Fig. 8.11*A*)

This is a directional microphone having a roughly heart-shaped pattern (cardioid) with an acceptance angle of approximately 150°. It is the standard studio microphone pattern and should be used whenever the ambient noise is not too loud.

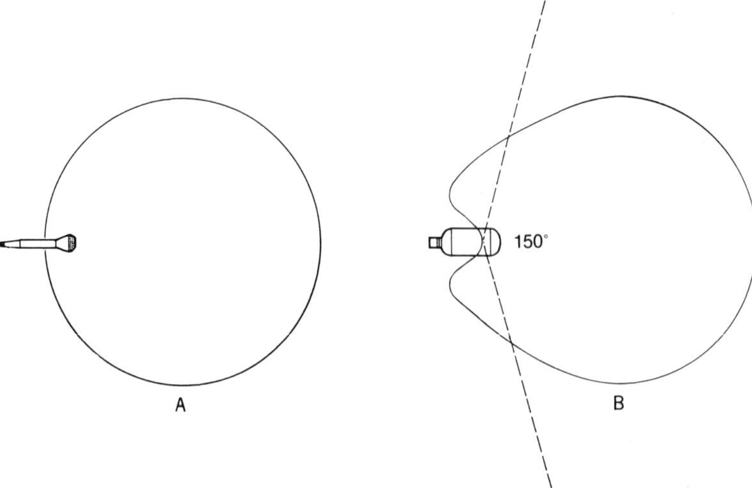

Fig. 8.11(*A*). Omnidirectional microphone picks up sound equally from all directions. (*B*) The pickup pattern of a cardioid microphone is roughly heart-shaped. It is most sensitive in an arc of about 150° to the front of the microphone. Sounds behind the microphone are picked up at a much lower level. A cardioid is a directional microphone.

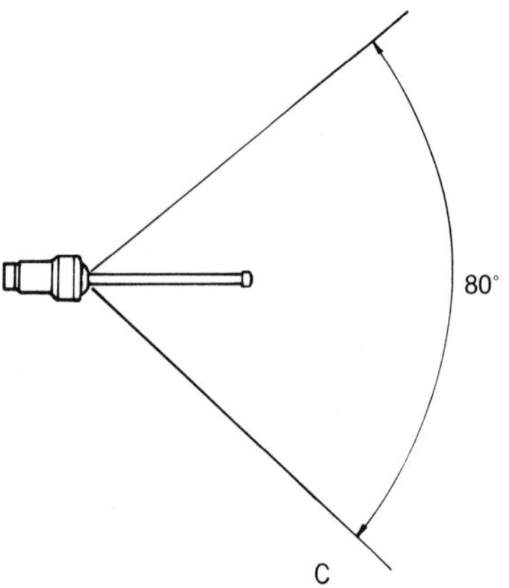

Fig. 8.11C. The in-line microphone has a cardioid pattern but is only about 80°. Sounds behind the microphone outside the 80° acceptance angle are suppressed.

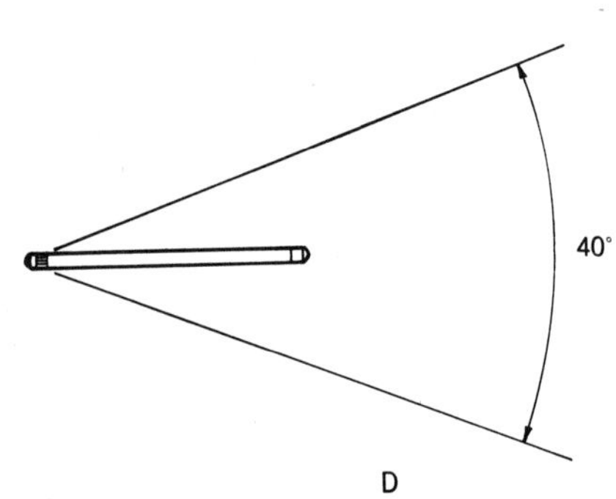

Fig. 8.11*D*. The super in-line microphone is highly directional and has an acceptance angle of about 40°. Its cardioid pattern is very narrow.

Cardioid In-Line Microphone (See Fig. 8.11C)

This is a directional microphone with a narrower acceptance angle than the cardioid, about 80°. This type of microphone should be used where the ambient noise would be objectionable with a cardioid. The more limited acceptance angle of the cardioid in-line microphone subdues much of the ambient noise from the back and sides, and records the actor at whom it is pointed at a greater volume.

Cardioid Super In-Line (See Fig. 8.11*C* and *D*)

This is a microphone with an acceptance angle of 30 to 40°. It enables work with the microphone farther from the speaker than is possible with the cardioid or the cardioid in-line.

Omnidirectional

An omnidirectional microphone is one with a pickup pattern of almost 360° that picks up sound equally well from all directions, and is therefore not suitable for general motion picture sound recording. Using an omnidirectional microphone in the same manner as a cardioid allows ambient noise to intrude on the principal sound. *Lavalier microphones* are omnidirectional and are used extensively in film production under certain conditions. A lavalier is usually quite small and, conventionally, hangs by a cord around the actor's neck. For most film recording it is taped to the actor's body or hidden in his clothing. Although the lavalier is omnidirectional, it is so close to the source of sound, the speaker's mouth, that little or no ambient noise is picked up. A lavalier should be used when it is impossible to get a boom-mounted or hand-held microphone close to the actors.

There are other, more directional types of microphones such as the rifle and varidirectional microphones and microphones fitted with reflectors to concentrate the sound. Generally such ultradirectional microphones are little used in filmmaking, being employed mainly for nature sounds or in special documentary situations.

The cardioid pattern (which includes the in-line and super-in-line cardioids) is, as was indicated earlier, characteristic of microphones that are best for motion picture recording. With the front of a directional microphone pointed toward the speaker's mouth, much of the sound from the sides and the back will not be picked up. There is, however, no known microphone that will eliminate all sounds from the sides and the back.

The type of microphone selected will be determined by the conditions existing at the shooting site, which may range from the excellent acoustic control of the motion picture sound stage to the chaos of a noisy factory. In attempting to eliminate objectionable ambient sounds from a scene, try to record only those sounds coming from the direction of the actor, and choose a microphone that will not pick up sounds coming from other directions.

MICROPHONE SELECTION

To select a microphone suitable for motion picture recording, first become familiar with the microphones produced by the various manufacturers for numerous uses. The manufacturers will send catalogues on request that contain polar-field patterns and complete descriptions of each microphone made. These catalogues often have much additional useful information on microphone placement and use.

Try to record with a directional microphone having the widest angle of acceptance. Although it is easy to assume that with today's high quality directional microphones it is best to record everything with the one that picks up the smallest area, this is not always desirable. In scenes where the actors have to move and must consequently be followed by the microphone, an actor may give a line "off-mike," that is, not speaking directly toward the receiving side of the microphone. Speaking off-mike causes a noticeable loss in sound quality, becoming muffled and lower in volume. It is the responsibility of the microphone handler to follow the actors and keep the microphone in a perfect recording position, but this is made more difficult as the acceptance angle of the microphone becomes narrower. When a 150° cardioid microphone is used, an actor can move farther from the centerline of acceptance angle before being off-mike. Also, the dialogue of two people can be covered easily with a cardioid because the microphone has to be moved only slightly to keep each actor in turn within the acceptance angle. The margin for error is greater with a cardioid (150° acceptance angle) microphone than with one having a narrow acceptance angle.

Procedure for Selecting the Best Microphone for the Job

Sound recording is relatively simple if conditions are ideal, but since they rarely are, the sound person is often forced to make compromises and adjustments to achieve acceptable sound. The following is a sequence of conditions and decisions to aid in determining the correct microphone for the situation.

1. Try first to record with a studio cardioid microphone in the optimum recording position, that is, three feet above and four feet in front of the actor's head. Conditions are usually ideal in the studio, where the acoustics are excellent and the ambient noise is extremely low. However, good conditions for using a cardioid in this position do occasionally exist outside the studio on

quiet streets, in some homes, on the desert, and in rural areas when the wind is not blowing too hard.

2. If the cardioid microphone, placed as mentioned above, picks up too much ambient sound, there are three alternatives:

(a) Move the microphone closer to the actor or the source of sound. This is the best solution for getting good sound but cannot always be done, since moving closer may put the microphone in the picture.

(b) If the microphone cannot be moved closer, try to reduce the ambient sound by using furniture pads to absorb reverberation, or by subduing the cause of the objectionable ambience.

(c) If the first two alternatives do not work, select a microphone with a narrower acceptance angle, say, an 80° in-line microphone. This reduces the volume of ambient sounds coming from the sides and back of the microphone. If the ambient sound is still too loud, use a super-in-line microphone with an acceptance angle below 80°. A working rule is to use successively narrower beam microphones the farther away from the actors the microphone is or the louder the ambient sound. The best answer to the problem of ambient sound is to keep the microphone close to the actor or speaker, but this cannot always be done.

3. Sometimes the action of the scene simply cannot be followed or reached by a conventional microphone. One solution to this problem is to use a lavalier microphone taped or clipped to the actor, with the cable hidden underneath the clothing and leading along the floor to the recorder. If it is not feasible or possible to run a cable from the microphone to the recorder, eliminate the cable by using a lavalier that has a miniature radio transmitter built into or attached to it. A radio receiver connected to the recorder picks up the transmitted dialogue or sound effects, which are then recorded normally. Scenes requiring a transmitting microphone would include those in which actors in a crowd must move freely, or two motorcyclists conversing as they are being photographed from a moving camera car, or two buggy drivers shouting at each other as they race side by side, or a situation in which the camera is so far from the actors that it would be impossible to use a cable from the microphone to the recorder.

Although it is not always possible, try to record all the film, or at least whole scenes, with the same type of microphone. Different microphones have different frequency responses and sound different. Passages of sound recorded with different microphones may be equalized later, but not always with complete success.

Equalizing

Equalizing here, refers to matching the frequencies of one sound to those of another. Say that part of a dialogue scene is recorded with a condenser narrow-beam microphone. Then, because the scene contains action that cannot be followed conventionally with the microphone, the remainder of the scene is shot with a lavalier microphone taped to the actor's chest. When these scenes are played back, the sound quality of the two microphones is discovered to be different even though the same voices were used. The dialogue recorded with one microphone sounds more high-pitched than the other, as if they had been recorded in completely different locations. Since audience credibility would be severely stretched by such a discrepancy, the two sections of dialogue must be equalized, that is, in the mixing session, the high, middle, and low frequencies may be selectively amplified, subdued, or removed from one or both of the recordings until they sound very much alike.

On some microphones it is possible to change the frequency response of the microphone by means of small patch plugs or a switch in the body of the microphone. This enables a change in the response of one microphone to be made to match that of another as closely as possible; or you may "roll off" (lower the volume of) frequencies below 100 Hz, to reduce room boominess and low rumbling sounds. Some recorders have roll-off switches that enable the reduction of low frequencies without changing settings on the microphone.

MICROPHONE PLACEMENT

The best placement for a microphone is about one to four feet in front of the actor and one to three feet above his head. We will call this the *most desirable position.* Point the microphone right at the actor's mouth, but if his speech is at all harsh or sibilant, reduce this by pointing the microphone slightly to either side of the actor's face. During dialogue and movement, maintain this position relative to the actor's head at all times. When two or more actors are speaking, move the microphone into the proper position from one to the other as each speaks (see Figure 8.12).

The person handling the microphone should become familiar with the scene and the dialogue so that all the actor's moves may be anticipated. Always keep the microphone close to the actor and do not let it get directly over or behind his head. Ambient noise such as boominess, traffic, airplanes, ocean, wind, footsteps, and crowd noises can be reduced by keeping the microphone closer than normal. A directional microphone helps, but is not as effective as close operation. However, placing a directional microphone too close to the actor or source of sound, generally two feet or less, may result in the *proximity effect,* an increase in low frequency response that causes what has been recorded to sound as if it were being played back through a recording needle with fuzz on it. In this case, it may be necessary to switch to a lavalier microphone, which is omnidirectional and not subject to the proximity effect.

Unfortunately, since the microphone cannot always be placed in the most desirable position, and the action and actors cannot always be followed precisely, the best possible compromise must be made.

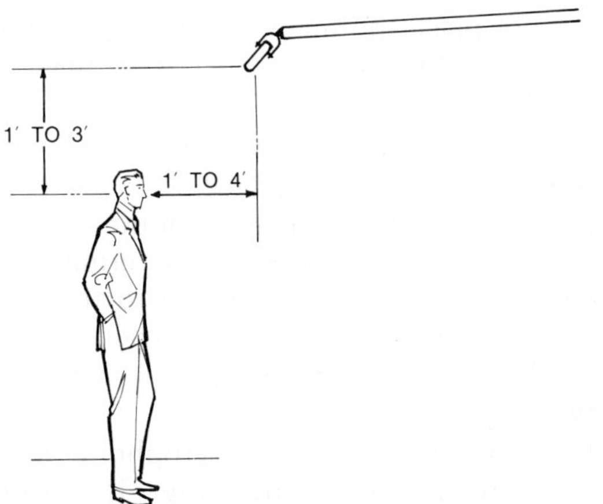

Fig. 8.12. The best working position for the microphone in motion picture dialogue shooting is about 1 to 4 feet in front of the speaker and 1 to 3 feet above. The final microphone position is always dictated by conditions.

If planning to record in a particular place, go there ahead of time, or while the camera setup is being made, and try the microphone in several different spots and listen over the headphones. Have one of the sound crew stand in as an actor and, as he speaks, try the microphone close to and far away, higher and lower, and to one side and then the other of the speaker. You can learn to determine the best mike position for any given spot very quickly. Do not be restricted just because the ideal microphone position is supposed to be in front of and just above the actor's head. Consider putting the microphone handler anywhere—on the floor, hanging from the rafters, hidden behind furniture—to get the microphone into a proper position to obtain acceptable sound. Regardless of where the microphone and handler are placed, however, point the microphone at the actor's mouth so that you get the same quality sound as would be obtained if the mike were in the most desirable position (see Figure 8.13*A* and *B*).

You may mount the microphone on a *boom* or on a *fishpole,* or hold it by hand. The boom is a relatively large piece of equipment primarily for use on a stage or a location where there is a crew large enough to haul it around and set it up. A *fishpole* is a lightweight pole about ten feet long. It allows the microphone handler to get into tighter spots than are possible with the boom, and is more convenient and less expensive to take on location.

For hand-holding a microphone, a number of pistol grips are available that may be attached to the mike mount. Some are efficient, others are not. If you plan to use a hand-held microphone, experiment beforehand, since it is disconcerting to get ready to shoot and find that the pistol grip for the mike is shaky, inconvenient, or noisy. The microphone should always be in a shock mount.

During a take, maintain the microphone in the most desirable position for each actor at all times no matter how the actors may move their bodies or heads. This may require ingenuity and agility whether using the boom, fishpole, or hand-hold. The microphone handler should wear headphones and should be familiar with the lines and who will be speaking them. When the actors rehearse, he should rehearse too, following with the microphone. Try to obtain the best quality possible because this is the first step in a long journey for the sound, and any off-mike speech

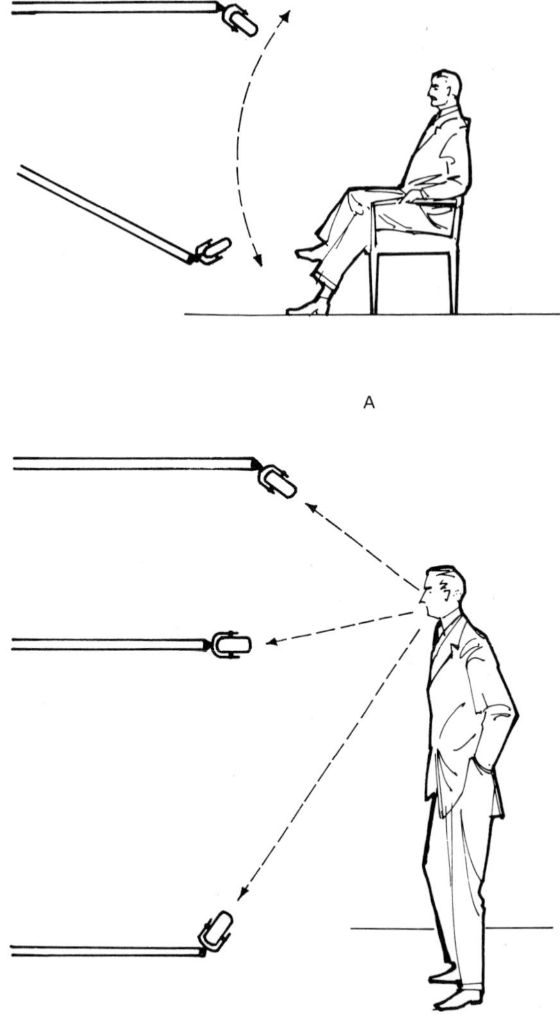

Fig. 8.13*A* and *B*. Depending on staging conditions, it may be necessary to try the microphone in many different positions. Try to keep the microphone pointed at the actor's mouth and as close as possible.

will sound off-mike forever. It is not enough to almost follow the actors with the microphone; its position must be exact by the time the actor speaks.

Another aspect of microphone placement is *perspective*. A voice at a distance sounds quite different from a voice close by, and believability in a film depends on the closeness of the voice being appropriate to the distance of the image on the screen. When a closeup is shown of a person speaking, his voice should sound as if it were as near to us as his picture indicates. Similarly, those at a distance must sound as if they are at a distance. This is accomplished by proper microphone placement, and is one way that the microphone "hears" in much the same way as our ears do. If the image is far from the camera, the microphone should be approximately where the camera is. If the image is close to the camera, the microphone should be close to the person speaking. This is not a hard-and-fast rule because the sound must fit the picture. This means that it may be necessary to experiment with the microphone at varying distances to get exactly the perspective that suits the image in the camera. Do not be misled, however, by the actual distance of the camera from the actor, since an actor may be far from the camera yet still be in a closeup by means of a long focus lens. The impression of distance you want the audience to feel determines the perspective.

The microphone handler is a very active participant who may have to make ingenious moves and assume strange positions to keep the microphone in the most desirable position. Merely pointing the microphone in the direction of the actors is not adequate. The microphone handler must always be ready to try many different positions quickly, without stopping the show or interfering with the director or the camera crew.

SUMMARY

1. Shock-mount the microphone on a stand, boom, fishpole, or support.
2. Do not place the microphone so that sounds bounce into it from a flat, reflective surface (e.g., floor, wall, building).
3. Do not place the microphone in the focusing spot of a curved wall or surface.
4. Be informed about the angle of the shot being made. The nature of a scene determines how close the microphone should be to the action. Long shots, medium shots, and closeups may be made by changing lenses without moving the camera.
5. Use the same type of microphone for the entire production if possible. If different microphones are used, try to match their frequency response.
6. Try to control frequency response by changing the microphone position. That is, if there is room

boominess, try to eliminate it by moving the microphone.

7. Any sound that is off-mike will be reduced. So try to keep unwanted sounds off-mike.

8. If the microphone is too close to the source of sound, the lows will become boomy and unpleasant. This is called the proximity effect.

9. The ideal microphone placement for dialogue is one to four feet in front of and one to three feet above the actor.

10. Do not pan the microphone too fast. This creates noise.

11. The person handling the microphone should keep it at a uniform distance through all moves so that proper quality and perspective are maintained.

12. For moves that cannot be followed with a boom or fishpole, hang or tape lavalier microphones inside the actor's clothing.

13. The microphone may be hidden on the set if the performers stay in a fixed position.

SYSTEM NOISE

Two kinds of noise are of most concern to the filmmaker: system noise and ambient noise. *System noise* is the hissing sound made by any recorder or sound-reproducing system; and even though much engineering time and money have gone into the design of sound systems to eliminate noise, every recorder has it to a certain degree. In a good professional recorder, system noise is not obvious unless the volume control is turned up quite high. On a good machine, system noise will not be apparent if the signal, that is, the voice or sound effect being recorded, is loud enough so that the volume control can be kept at a normal meter setting of −6 to −9 dB during recording. The strength of the signal is determined by the distance of the microphone from the actor's mouth or source of sound. The closer the microphone is to the actor, the lower the volume control setting, with consequently little or no system noise. As the microphone is moved farther from the actor, the volume control must be turned up to maintain the voice at its original level. In so doing, the system noise level is increased simultaneously. Every recorder has its rated signal-to-noise ratio. Professional recorders are designed with a high signal-to-noise ratio—the recorded sound will be much higher in volume than the system noise—so that under most conditions system noise is not a consideration.

AMBIENT NOISE

Ambient noise is the noise or sounds common to any environment. On the street, ambient noise is the sound of traffic; in an office, it is the sound of machines, air conditioner vents, and people talking. The general sounds surrounding us in any location comprise ambient noise; and even where no sound at all is apparent, such as in a quiet room or the desert on a windless day, there is actually a great deal of ambient sound. No such thing as absolute silence exists in the world around us; and even if there are no voices or noises, there is a sound presence that distinguishes each separate locality and place. For motion pictures to sound real and believable, the spaces between speeches and sound effects must contain at least some ambient sound or presence. When a sound track goes to absolute silence between speeches, the audience gets the feeling that a sound system is being turned on and off, which destroys the impression of reality. After a scene has been shot, no matter where it may be, the sound crew always records a few minutes of ambient sound or room tone to be used later by the film editor.

In any scene, the recording of sound is influenced by the quality and loudness of the ambient sound. Ambient sound should not overpower either the actor's voices or the sound effects of the scene. On a soundproof stage or in a very quiet location there is little or no problem. But when shooting on the street or in actual homes, offices, and other locations, ambient sound is frequently a problem because it is too loud relative to the voices or sound effects being recorded for the picture. If the microphone is placed very close to the actor, it is sometimes possible to record his voice without the objectionable intrusion of ambient sounds. However, if the microphone is moved away from the actor and the volume control is turned up to compensate, the ambient sound—traffic, footsteps, air conditioner, children playing, birds, crickets, whatever—becomes louder and more obtrusive. When recording in an area of fairly loud ambient noise such as a busy office, with the microphone close to the actor—three feet in front of and two feet above his head with the microphone pointed at his mouth—if the recording is made at a normal volume setting of –6 dB to –9 dB, the voice will be at normal volume and the ambient sound will be at a level low enough to sound as it should as a low background noise appropriate to the location. To move the microphone six feet away from the actor, the volume control will have to be turned up to maintain the voice at the original recording level; but the level of the ambient noise is increased because of the greater volume, and it becomes objectionably loud. If the microphone is moved farther away, and the volume turned up to maintain the voice level, the ambient sound becomes louder and more boomy. The farther the microphone is from the actor, the higher the volume level must be turned, and the louder the ambient noise becomes. Since reverberation is actually echo that is a part of ambient sound, as the microphone is placed farther from the actor's mouth, the reverberation also increases. Unfortunately, in motion pictures the microphone often must be placed at some distance from the actors to keep it out of the picture; making the compromise between microphone distance and the loudness of ambient sound is the principal problem of motion picture sound recording.

REVERBERATION

"Liveness," or reverberation, consists of a sound plus its reflection from walls and surfaces; the greater the reflected sound, the "livelier" a room is said to be. Liveness gives the impression of a large room or hall, an empty room, a basement, a prison cell, or the like. Although usually not much reverberation is heard in real life, it does exist, and the microphone picks it up. Too much liveness makes sound seem unnatural or inappropriate for most dialogue scenes and sound effects occurring in smaller rooms and locations. Liveness can be controlled or eliminated with proper microphone placement and by absorbing unwanted reverberation. The following techniques may help:

1. Use a directional microphone close to the speaker or sound effect if possible. This is the best remedy, and should always be tried first.

2. Be sure the microphone is not equidistant from two reflecting walls. The worst spot for a microphone is between hard, parallel walls, the same distance from each wall. Poor placement is also on a line bisecting the corner of a room or in the spot where sound waves are focused off a curved wall. Sometimes reflected sound is delayed long enough so that its up-and-down phases are the opposite of the up-and-down phases of the sound coming directly from the speaker. This is referred to as "180° out of phase," a condition in which the opposing sound waves cancel each other so that bits of words and sound are not heard at all. Sound waves less than 180° out of phase produce echo, or reverberation. (See Fig. 8.6*G–H*.)

3. Break up the reflective pattern of sound in a room by putting absorbent material such as furniture pads, Celotex, acoustic tile, or blankets on the floor and on the walls. Admittedly, it is difficult, but it sometimes helps to break up the sound reflected from the ceiling by covering it with absorbent material or by hanging absorbent objects.

In a sound stage where all is soundproofed against outside noises and all inside noises can be controlled or eliminated, it is a simple matter to get good, clean dialogue. Since not all shooting is done on soundproof stages currently, the best must be made of situations that are seldom amenable to good sound recording. To a certain extent, try always to recreate the conditions of a soundproof stage, that is, to reduce ambient noise to a minimum and control the conditions in the immediate shooting area to eliminate reverberation. Except in an exceptionally quiet location, traffic, airplanes, people, wildlife, machines, and local acoustics will all present problems. To reduce ambient noise, the most effective action is to use a directional microphone and keep it close to the speaker. The microphone should not be pointed toward the source of the ambient noise or toward a reflecting surface. If you cannot get close enough to the actor to bring the ambient noise down to an acceptable level, other measures will have to be taken, as follows:

1. Place furniture pads or some other absorbent material on the walls and floor so they are out of the picture. This may mean moving the padding around for every shot. Sometimes the furniture

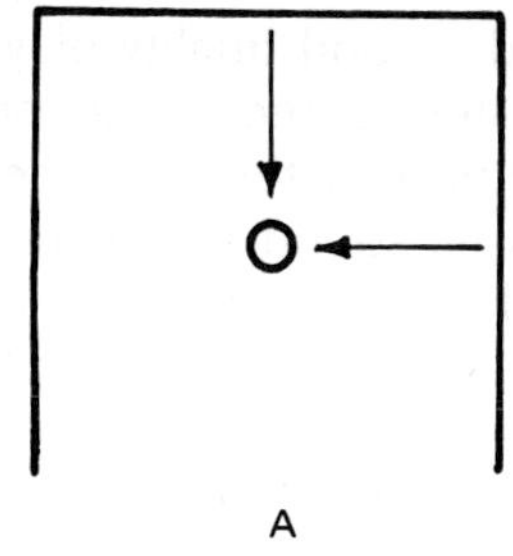

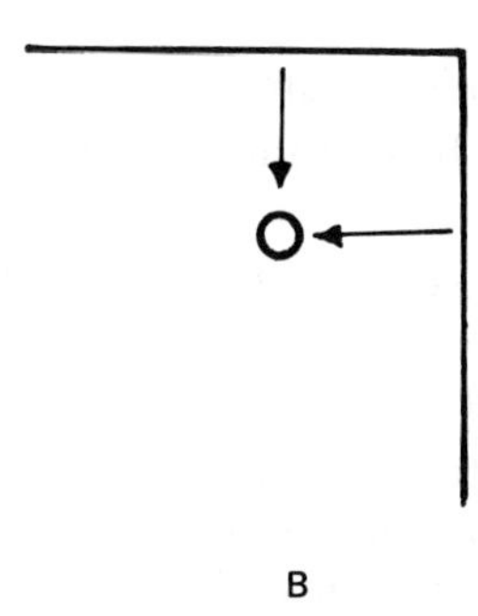

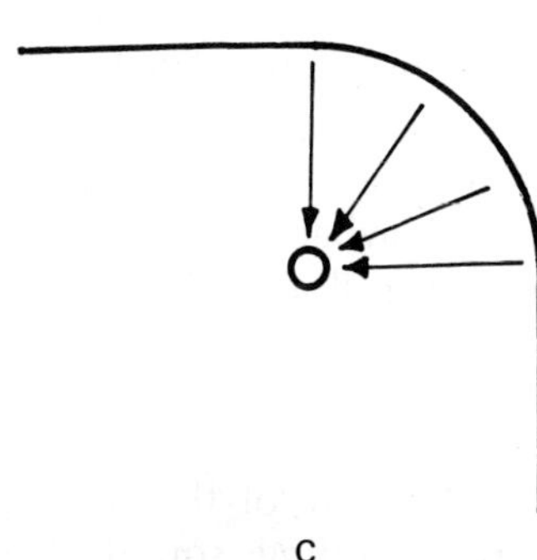

Fig. 8.14. Poor microphone placement causes serious reverberation and cancellation. Avoid the following: (*A*) Microphone equidistant from three or four walls. (*B*) Microphone equidistant from the two walls of a corner. (*C*) Microphone placed at the focal point of parabolic or curved walls.

can be rearranged so that it absorbs some of the sound. It may be possible to restage the scene for better sound; but remember that the important part of the film is the story or what you are trying to say. Do not try to rewrite the script merely to eliminate a boomy voice. Most important, though, is the nearness of the microphone to the speakers. Use a directional mike and do not point it at a reflecting wall or surface.

2. Street noise and people. These are the most usual ambient sounds you will encounter and there is not much that can be done about them except to use a directional microphone as close to the speaker as possible. Point the microphone away from background noise and away from a reflecting wall. Occasionally, when shooting on the street or in an area such as a lobby or a store with many people, you cannot get the microphone close to your actors, especially in medium to long shots. In such situations the following are alternate courses of action:

(a) Use a lavalier microphone on each actor and run the microphone cords, hidden in some way, to the recorder.

(b) Place a transmitting lavalier microphone on each actor and transmit the dialogue to the recorder.

(c) Record the scene as is with a boom microphone and let the ambient noise intrude on the sound. At a later date, replace the dialogue in a looping session, using the original unacceptable track as a cue track for the actors.

3. Airplanes. Although there is not much that can be done about controlling the flight of airplanes, you can determine the schedule for flight arrivals and departures in a given area. Air traffic in any area usually follows a pattern, always approaching and leaving the airport in the same corridors. Whenever possible, arrange sound recording away from airplane operating areas. Otherwise be prepared to replace most of the dialogue or spend many hours waiting for a few moments of plane-free skies to get a shot.

4. Machines. The principal mechanical offenders during recording are air conditioners, refrigerators, and heaters, but all types of other machines may be heard at inconvenient times. Often it is impossible to anticipate what kinds of machines may intrude. A location may have been scouted for noise and found suitable; then on the starting day, the public works department sends someone to dig a ditch. Or somewhere in the neighborhood a power lawn mower is turned on. A carpenter starts operating a ramset. The timed sprinkler system in the schoolyard across the street goes on. Since it is almost impossible to anticipate every kind of intrusive sound that may occur in any given location, the only solution

may be to use a directional microphone close to the actors and shoot in between bursts of noise.

Whenever possible, it is helpful to shut off air conditioners, refrigerators, and heaters. In a home it is usually simple to unplug whatever appliance is making the noise, but be sure to turn freezers and refrigerators back on after shooting. In a building other than a home the air conditioner is usually in a locked room in the basement, with air pumped to the rooms through ducts. If possible, get the main conditioner turned off for the shooting period, although sometimes this cannot be done without immobilizing the entire building. If the air conditioner in a building cannot be shut off, try taping pieces of cardboard over the inlet ducts in each room to eliminate the sound of inrushing air.

Indoor and Outdoor Sound

Most indoor sound has reverberation in it. Even though you try to cut down on excessive indoor reverberation during recording, a trace of it always remains, maintaining the illusion of indoor reality. Sound recorded outdoors has little or no reverberation, so if outdoor sounds are recorded indoors, keep the microphone close to the source of sound to cut down on reverberation. Conversely, if an indoor scene is shot outdoors, add a little reverberation, or echo, later in the mixing session to make it sound realistic.

SOUND TESTS FOR PRACTICE

Learning sound recording is convenient because many different situations can be set up easily and cheaply and recorded at little or no expense, since tape may be erased and used again. Before recording sound on your own or someone else's production, conduct experiments to increase your skill. It is helpful to make experimental recordings continually, since the situations and conditions under which recording may have to be done are almost infinite. Become familiar with most of the basic problems normally encountered in motion picture recording by doing the tests listed below. Essentially these tests consist of listening to a real sound, recording the sound, and then listening to the recording. You will need a recorder, tape, microphones, related equipment, and a good quality playback system. It is futile to listen to recordings on a cheap or low quality playback system because poor equipment degrades all sound no matter how well it was recorded. The following is a general procedure for conducting sound tests:

1. Select and set up the test (see below).
2. Make an equipment list and assemble the proper equipment and supplies.
3. Set up the recorder and equipment as if preparing for a scheduled motion picture shoot.
4. Thread the tape on the recorder and record the following:

(a) Roll identification (name, production, etc.).

(b) Minus 10 dB head tone: 20 seconds. (See p. 203.)

5. Voice slate each test, identifying it and describing the conditions and equipment used (e.g., "Sound Test #1—Traffic. . . .")
6. Record the test. Listen and watch: listen through the headphones and watch the meter needle. The headphones identify the sound of the recording, and the meter indicates the volume and whether distortion exists.
7. Keep a record of what has been recorded on a sound report form. List each test by its voice slate designation, and indicate any conditions or information that may help later. (See Fig. 10.6.)
8. Play the test back on a good quality playback machine and listen carefully and critically. To establish a uniform playback level, set the –10 dB head tone for each roll at 0 dB on the playback machine.

The series of tests listed below is designed to acquaint you with many of the basic problems encountered in recording sound. Conducting these tests, plus others you may devise, should provide a basic understanding of the central problems of sound recording.

1. Learn what distortion is and what it sounds like. Record some music from a radio or phonograph speaker directly into the microphone of your recorder. Record at several volume levels both above and below the 0 dB mark on the meter. (See VU meter.) Remember that for the recorder you are using distortion starts at 0 dB on the meter scale, so that sounds with a

volume level above 0 dB will be distorted. Also, make several voice and sound effects recordings at levels ranging from very low to very high, both undistorted and distorted. Play these recordings back through a good sound system and a good speaker and listen carefully. Do this until you are able to recognize distortion easily by ear and can accurately relate the position of the meter needle to the point and degree of distortion.

2. *System Noise.* In a quiet room, or preferably in a sound studio where the acoustics are nearly perfect for recording, place the microphone four feet in front of and three feet above an actor, which is theoretically the best microphone position for recording speech. Record a few lines at a level of about −9 dB, then move the microphone away from the actor at successive positions, recording a few lines at each position. Turn up the volume to maintain the same level (−9 dB) on the meter for each position. During playback notice that when you turned up the volume for successive microphone positions to maintain the actor's voice at the original level, the noise of the recorder system—usually a quiet hiss—increased. System noise in a good professional recorder at a normal recording level will scarcely be heard, if at all, if the recorder has a high signal-to-noise ratio. Cheap recorders have a low signal-to-noise ratio, but all recorders will produce system noise if the volume is turned up high enough. The implication for sound recording is to keep the microphone close enough to the source of sound to permit a low setting of the volume control, keeping system noise as low as possible.

3. *Ambient Noise.* Ambient noise is the normal sound of any location or place. It affects recording in the same way that system noise does but ambient noise is usually more intrusive. To study its effect, pick several sites with ambient noise levels ranging from low to high—a quiet room, a park, a busy street, a factory, a party, a construction site. At each place make test recordings of two people speaking. Start with the microphone close to the speakers, and increase the distance of the microphone from the speakers in each successive test. For each microphone position, turn up the volume control to maintain the level of the voices the same as in the closest position. Notice that as the microphone is moved farther away from the speakers and the volume control is turned up to maintain the same voice level, the ambient noise becomes louder. The microphone does not need to be moved very far from the speakers before ambient noise becomes unacceptably loud. In a home, office, or schoolroom the boominess, or echolike quality increases as the microphone is moved farther from the speaker. In these situations ambient noise consists mostly of the echo or reverberation of the speech off the walls back into the microphone.

4. *Sound Perspective.* Sound perspective is the apparent distance of a sound source as indicated by its characteristic sound. Simply put, noises at a distance sound far away, and noises nearby sound close.

Listen to sound perspectives in real life and observe what happens as the source of sound gets farther away. Start with a friend speaking up close to you, then move farther apart as you continue to speak, first in louder tones and then in shouts. First, voice quality changes because as you get farther apart the volume level is raised to project over a greater distance. Also, other noises intrude, making it more difficult for your words to be understood. Finally, there will be a point at which you and your friend are so far apart that the ambient sounds—the normal sounds of the environment—are dominant and you can only barely hear the other person shouting. Although ultimately, when you get far enough apart, you will not be able to hear one another at all, you will still hear the ambient sounds. Recreating the feeling of sound perspective is vital to the believability of a scene, so observe actual sound perspective about you, and learn to establish the proper perspective in the films you make.

5. *Reflecting Walls.* Set up the microphone in a room with parallel hard walls or in a spot where the sound from a curved wall comes to a focus, and make a recording of speech with the microphone equidistant from each wall. Then perform successive tests with the microphone in different positions, and try to find the one that eliminates or reduces the poor sound quality. Depending on the room, good quality sound may not be possible, but it can be altered enough to show some improvement. In such a situation, one or more of the walls may be made absorbent by hanging furniture pads or blankets on the walls outside the camera frame to absorb sound and prevent reflection. Since reflecting floors and ceilings act the same as walls, try put-

ting absorbent materials on these areas as well. Rearranging furniture sometimes helps to absorb sound in a room.

6. *Boominess.* Speech recorded in places other than studios often sounds as if it were "recorded in a barrel." Make voice test recordings in several different types of rooms: home, office, school. Start with the microphone close to the speaker's mouth, then make successive tests with the microphone farther away. As the microphone is moved farther away from the speaker, boominess increases. Also, it is probably greater if the microphone is pointing toward a hard surface floor. Point the microphone straight down, toward the floor then make tests its position changed to point upward.

The frequencies that cause most boominess are 150 Hz and below. This effect may be reduced by resetting the frequency response of the microphone so that it rolls off the low frequencies. A line filter does the same thing, eliminating the frequencies below 100 Hz. Make tests (1) with the microphone in different positions, (2) the frequency response changed, (3) and with a line filter. The most effective way to reduce boominess, however, is to place the microphone close to the actors.

7. *Proximity Effect.* This is an increase in the microphone's response to low frequencies when the distance of the microphone is less than two feet from the source of sound. It sounds like a recording needle with fuzz on it. Make successive tests of speech, moving the microphone closer until you get the proximity effect. Learn to identify it.

8. *Preamplifier Distortion.* A loud sound close to a condenser microphone will cause the preamplifier to distort even though the volume control is turned down and the meter indicates no distortion. Create preamplifier distortion by recording an actor with a strong voice close to a condenser microphone. This type of distortion can be identified only through headphones.

9. *Microphone Tests.* Record the speech of two actors, male and female, in a place that has good acoustics for recording. A sound stage or studio is best, but any place, interior or exterior, will do if the ambient sound is low and the reverberation is acceptable. Record the same exchange of dialogue on the following types of microphones in turn:

Lavalier microphone.

Dynamic and condenser microphones with about 150° acceptance angle.

Dynamic and condenser microphones with about 80° acceptance angle.

Dynamic and condenser microphones with a very narrow acceptance angle.

Make the test with the lavalier microphone suspended from the neck of one of the actors by a cord, or taped to the actor's chest inside the clothing. Only one lavalier microphone is needed for both actors if they stand close together. Mount each of the other microphones four feet in front of and three feet above the actors, with the front of the microphone pointing at their mouths. If possible, record this dialogue test under the same conditions, using several different brands of microphones in each of the types listed above. Play back all the tests and study the differences, to learn the characteristic response of each microphone and to help determine your personal preferences and dislikes. Microphones made by various manufacturers have different characteristics, and it is advantageous to know what each sounds like and how it responds. Also, whenever possible, make comparative microphone tests under as many different recording situations as possible.

10. *Sound Effects.* Recorded sound effects do not always sound the same as real sounds to the ear. If realistic sound were merely a faithful recording of ambient sound as it occurs in real life, it would be simple to make believable, realistic sound tracks merely by holding up the microphone and turning on the recorder. Unfortunately, it does not work out that way. In real life we are used to sound all around us, but most of the time we are not aware of just how much and what kinds of sound there are. The question, then, is what characteristic makes an effect sound like what it really is? The key to learning how to record good sound effects is first to listen carefully to real sounds and become skilled in identifying what makes them sound as they do. Next, record sounds, and try to reproduce or recreate distinguishing characteristics. Finally, listen to what you have recorded on a good playback system

and analyze what you have done. There are two basic requirements in recording sound effects: (1) record with as much volume as possible, and (2) keep ambient noise as low as possible. Again, this involves decisions about microphone choice and placement. If the microphone can be placed close to the source of sound, and the ambient noise is low, either an omnidirectional or a cardioid microphone may be used. If the microphone cannot be positioned close to the sound, or the ambient level is high, or both, one of the more directional microphones may be necessary. The following are some basic sound effects that appear simple to achieve yet often do not come out the way they are intended. Analyze these effects and record them so that they play back crisp and clean.

(a) Traffic. Record the sounds of street and pedestrian traffic in several different places. Traffic often sounds confused and not the way you think it should. Try the microphone in various locations, pointing in various directions. Learn to identify by ear those sounds that make for believable sound effects.

(b) Footsteps. Record a variety of footsteps—men's, women's, heavy feet, light feet, in sand, in dirt, on concrete, in dry grass, up and down stairs. Notice that men's footsteps often make a double sound as the sole touches down just after the heel, creating an effect that is often not as believable as single heel taps alone.

(c) Record automobile engines starting and running; automobiles starting, running, and stopping.

(d) Ocean. Record the sound of booming surf and the steady sound of rolling surf. To the microphone, the ocean often sounds like bacon frying. The problem is to analyze the sounds that make surf sound like surf and then record only that. You may have to mix two sounds to achieve the desired effect.

(e) Machines. One of the difficulties in recording machines is that the microphone often picks up the interior banging of parts rather than their external, characteristic sound. For example, the recorded sound of a striker hitting a bell is often more noticeable than the ring of the bell itself. Try recording several kinds of machines including a clock, a typewriter, a telephone dial, a garbage disposal, a mimeograph machine, a ditch digger, and any others available.

(f) Record specialized ambient sounds, such as the general presence of a summer night in the country, a schoolyard, a party, a quiet family group, a quiet (or noisy) day in the park, and so on. Although there will often be obtrusive sounds that destroy the believability of the scene you are trying to record, the aim is to try to get the desired sound without the intrusive unwanted sounds.

PREPARATION FOR THE SHOOT

Getting ready to do sound on a motion picture shoot requires three initial steps: (1) analyzing the location, (2) preparing a list of all equipment and supplies, and (3) assembling and testing the equipment.

Analyzing the Location

Before shooting, inspect the set or location for sound suitability. Listen to the acoustics of the area and decide whether the ambient level is low or high. Are the walls hard and reflecting? If the reverberation, or echo, is noticeable, would it be possible to damp the sound with furniture pads on the floor and walls? How much outside or traffic noises come through the walls and windows? What machinery—air conditioners, heaters, fans, water coolers, nearby elevators—adds to the ambient noise? Can machinery be turned off for the shooting period? If it cannot, is it possible to cover vents and air ducts to cut down on the noise? Try to ascertain what machinery goes on and off automatically and when. Is the location large enough to use a microphone boom, and is it possible to get a boom into the building or room? How can equipment be loaded and unloaded? Is there an elevator? How large? Is there a loading dock? How large is the stairwell? Such questions must be considered before the shoot begins. Inspection may indicate that you will need, say, a half dozen furniture pads instead of the two or three you usually carry. The layout may require longer microphone cables or special material to cover vents and ducts.

If there is noise nearby, such as lawn sprinklers, construction, or sound from other activities, try to have them postponed during shooting. Become aware of all activities that may make intrusive sounds and be sure that whoever is responsible for the film knows in advance what to expect. Do not get caught during shooting by an air conditioner or a ditch digger starting up unexpectedly. Make your inspection on a working day, when machinery in the area is normally operating. It may be advantageous in some situations to shoot on weekends and holidays, when all normal workday noise is absent.

Preparing a List of Equipment and Supplies

Based on the script requirements and your analysis of the sets and locations, prepare a list of equipment and supplies that may be needed. Refer to The Tools of Sound as a guide.

Assembling and Testing Equipment

Before going to the set or location, assemble all sound equipment. Put batteries in the recorder, plug in all cables and microphones, and make a test recording. Be sure that recorder, microphones, cables, and connectors are all in good working order. Do this far enough in advance that you can repair or replace any equipment that is not working properly before shooting starts. Adequate preparation is essential since many sound problems are the result of faulty or missing equipment, two conditions that can easily be prevented by forethought and preplanning. On the set or location, the problem is to record good usable sound with as little trouble as possible.

Checking Location

On arriving at the location, check the equipment and arrange it so that it may be set up and working quickly. As soon as you find out from the director or the person in charge where the next scene will be shot and what the action is, set up the recorder and load tape into it. Voice slate the head of the tape with at least the following: the name of the production, the date, and the roll number. Record a twenty-second head tone. Check the action areas for acoustics, space, and movement, and do whatever is necessary—run cables out of sight of the camera lens; place sound-absorbing pads where necessary; decide how to mount the microphone—boom, fishpole, or hand-held; and make a rough placement of the microphone and the microphone handler.

Recording

While the scene is being set up for the camera, and during rehearsal, watch the action and listen carefully. Be sure the microphone handler knows the action of the scene and practices following it during rehearsals. Set the volume level and practice maintaining or adjusting it as the rehearsal proceeds. When the scene is ready to be shot, let the director know that sound is ready. On the director's cue, start the recorder and call out "speed" when the recorder is running and you are sure there is a sync signal. If you hear intrusive noise when the recorder starts, or if there is no sync signal, call out "cut" or "no sync." If unwanted noise develops or the sync signal stops after the scene is under way, do not stop the take. Let the scene play all the way through, then point out the trouble, since the director may want the action regardless of sync or noise. Stop a scene for bad sound only before, or very shortly after, "action" is called.

Sound Report

Maintain an accurate, legible sound report that indicates every take of every scene with appropriate notes. (See Fig. 10.6.) Keep the sound report in triplicate: one copy to accompany the roll of tape, one for the film editor, and one for your record. Circle the take number of each good take and any others the director wishes to have transferred. When you are finished recording on a roll of tape, record the statement, "End of roll number ____." This indicates to the person transferring the sound that there is no more sound on the roll beyond that point. Do not rewind to the head. Put each completed roll of tape, tail out, in its box accompanied by one folded copy of the sound report, and mark on the outside of the box the name of the production, date, and roll number. At the end of the shooting day, give all recorded tapes to the person responsible for getting them transferred to magnetic film.

THE TOOLS OF SOUND

The tools of sound consist of all the equipment and supplies required to record sound for motion pictures. The following are the principal ones:

Quarter-Inch Tape Recorder

This is the main tool in recording sound. Any quarter-inch magnetic tape recorder may be modified for motion picture recording, but it is far more dependable and economical to use a professional recorder designed specifically for the purpose. Today, Nagra, Arrivox-Tandberg 3M, and Stellavox professional motion picture recorders are used universally to record almost all sound for motion pictures. The minimum characteristics necessary for a quarter-inch magnetic tape recorder to be used for motion picture sound recording are as follows:

1. Lightweight, portable, solid-state, dc motor powered selectively by internal dry-cell batteries or by an external ac power supply unit.
2. For synchronous motion picture production, the recorder must be able to put a sync-pulse signal on the tape along with the recorded sound to establish sync between the camera film and the recording tape. The professional recorder should contain, or be designed to accept, a crystal time-sync generator. There should also be an indicator to show when the sync pulse is on and recording.
3. Selectable tape speeds of at least 3¾ and 7½ inches per second. All professional voice and effects recording should ideally be done at 7½ ips, and music recording should be done at 15 ips, although all three speeds need not be available in the same recorder under usual production recording situations. It is possible to get acceptable dialogue at 3¾ ips and good sound effects at lower tape speeds, but 7½ ips is the professional standard and results in the best sound.
4. At least two microphone inputs with separate volume controls. The recorder should be able to accommodate both dynamic and condenser microphones.
5. A line input for recording from other sources besides the microphones, and a line output so that recorded material may be played back through a separate system or channeled into another recorder. It is convenient if the line input can also be used as an additional microphone input.
6. VU meter or modulometer marked in either dB's or percentage of modulation. With appropriate switching, the meter should indicate battery condition and volume levels for rehearsal and recording respectively. The meter dial should be illuminated and easy to read.
7. An output into which headphones may be plugged.
8. A monitoring system, so that testing, rehearsal, recording, and playback may be heard through the headphones or through an internal speaker.
9. Internal controllable filters that may be used to roll off low frequencies.

Mixer

This is a portable console containing input receptacles and volume controls for two or more microphones. It may be plugged into the line input of the tape recorder, making it possible to record with a greater number of microphones than the recorder normally accommodates.

Microphones

There are several kinds of microphones, each especially suited to specific motion picture recording situations. Since no one microphone is suitable for all situations, the ideal sound kit should include several different kinds. Many scenes and situations also call for more than one microphone.

Microphone Boom

A microphone boom is a wheeled dolly with a long arm, or boom attached, suitable for mounting a microphone on the end of it. Hand controls allow the operator to move the microphone in and out and from side to side to keep it always in the proper position while actors are speaking. A boom is usually used in studio shooting or on locations where there is enough crew to move it around and set it up; but it is not practicable on documentary shooting or other productions where the crew is relatively small and must move quickly.

Fishpole

A fishpole is a long, hand-held pole on the end of which a microphone may be mounted. Elaborate ones telescope to different lengths and have a swiveling mechanism on one end, so that by rotating the pole slightly the operator can quickly and easily turn the microphone from one direction to another. A fishpole is a light, portable, convenient, and relatively inexpensive way of getting the microphone into a scene.

Cables

Microphone cables are used to connect the microphone to the recorder. They consist of two main conductors surrounded by a shielding, all encased in a rubber or plastic covering. Sync cables connect the camera sync-pulse generator to the recorder. Cables should be handled with care because the delicate interior connections break easily, causing unwanted noise in the recording and even stopping it completely.

CABLE CONNECTORS

These are the fittings on the ends of cables that enable them to be plugged into equipment and into each other. There are two principal professional types: American-made Cannon fittings, and Tuchel fittings, made in Europe. Both are dependable, but the Tuchel fittings must be handled more delicately than the Cannons. Both should be treated with care and respect, since the soldered connections inside a plug or its receptacle easily break or become loose. Always carry a second set of cables complete with connectors, and be sure that all the equipment used at any one time has compatible connectors. Since motion picture equipment is often rented or borrowed, it is possible to have connectors and plugs that do not match. Before leaving for a shooting location, check to see that all cables and equipment can be plugged in correctly.

Shock Mount

A shock mount is a rubber or spring cradle to hang a microphone in for mounting on a boom or a fishpole. It absorbs shocks and vibrations that may be picked up through the microphone and recorded along with the sound. It also protects the delicate parts of a microphone from being damaged. Even though you hand-hold the microphone, put it in a shock mount.

Wind Screen

A wind screen, or wind gag, is a cover of light, porous material that is placed over the microphone when it is used outdoors or in situations where it must be moved rapidly during recording to follow the source of sound. It reduces or eliminates wind noise. The material should be on a wire frame surrounding the microphone, not on the microphone itself. Acoustifoam, marketed by the Electro-Voice microphone manufacturers, is effective for wind screens since it is easy to work with and does not affect a microphone's high-frequency response. A wind screen also protects against mechanical shock and the pickup of dust and magnetic particles.

Adapters

As indicated above, various pieces of equipment may not have plugs and connectors of the same type. A set of adapters makes it possible to hook almost any kind of incompatible plugs if they are wired the same basically. Adapter combinations include Tuchel-to-Cannon, Cannon-to-Tuchel, with male-to-male and female-to-female in each combination. Make up and carry any adapters you may need.

Line Pad

This is an electronic filter that plugs into the microphone line and cuts out some of the low frequencies that cause rumble, boominess, and wind noise. In some microphones this adjustment may be made on the microphone itself. A line filter may be of a fixed quantity to reduce preamplifier distortion when a highly sensitive microphone is being used.

Headphones

A set of headphones is essential for recording good sound. Although the meter on the recorder indicates the volume level of the recording, only by listening through the headphones during both rehearsal and recording can we identify whether the sound is right or if there is intrusive noise.

Both the mixer and the microphone handler must wear headphones during shooting to hear the sound the way it will be recorded. Without headphones, the human psychological filter causes us to hear how things should sound rather than the way they actually do. Since headphones used by many people are subject to rough treatment and consequent damage is done to their delicate connections, it is convenient to have a personal set of headphones in good condition for dependable use when needed.

Table, Chair, and Lamp

Make sure you have some place to put the recorder and the operator. It is not conducive to good sound recording to balance the recorder on any odd box with the mixer kneeling or standing awkwardly. Shooting sessions are often long and tedious, and recording under uncomfortable conditions can become quite miserable. A canvas director's chair and a strong folding card table are ideal; but if these are not practicable, arrange some way that the recorder may be placed solidly when in use. A shopping cart or something similar may be modified into a sound cart, and a folding canvas camp stool makes a good portable seat. A lamp is invaluable. If you are near an ac line, a regular desk lamp will work; in a location where there is no ac, use a flashlight, a necessary piece of equipment for many situations.

Sound Reports (See Fig. 10.6)

Most rental studios will supply regular sound report forms, or a printer will make them up for you. Even if you do not have printed sound report forms, have sufficient paper to keep the sound report plus whatever notes may be necessary. Maintain a complete, sequential, and readable record of each scene and take number and each sound effect. Be sure to have extra pens or pencils.

Batteries

Today, most battery-driven quarter-inch tape recorders use size D 1.5 volt or other type flashlight batteries. Generally one-time carbon-zinc flashlight batteries or the more expensive nickel-cadmium rechargeable batteries may be used. Be sure the batteries are fresh and that these are enough to last through the shooting period. A set of batteries lasts from one to three or four days shooting. Condenser microphones need an external power supply voltage, so be sure to have batteries if the recorder does not have a built-in power supply.

Recording Tape

Use good quality quarter-inch magnetic recording tape. For good recording, the *bias* rating of the tape must match that of the recorder, so be sure to use the correct type. If the appropriate type of tape to use is not known, check the specifications of the recorder or ask whoever rents or sells it. For sync-sound recording, it is convenient to have one roll of quarter-inch tape for every 10-minute roll of film, that is, one roll of tape for each 400-foot roll of 16mm film, or one roll of tape for each 1000-foot roll of 35mm film. Although a five-inch reel of quarter-inch standard tape will record for fifteen minutes, it is an advantage to have the sound for one roll of film on one roll of tape only. Tape is relatively inexpensive; so unless you are working on an extremely limited budget, the loss of five minutes of tape is well worth the convenience of having one sound roll for each picture roll. Do not carry or store recording tape near a dynamic microphone because the permanent magnet in the microphone will put unwanted noise on the tape. Be particularly careful of tapes on which sound has already been recorded. Be sure that both tape reels, supply and takeup, are in good condition because a bent or warped reel can cause flutter in the recorded sound.

Gaffer Tape

Gaffer tape is two-inch-wide cloth tape that is the indispensable tool of the motion picture industry. It is extremely strong and useful for taping cable connections, taping cable to floor and walls, mounting absorbent pads on walls, taping covers over air vents, and so on.

Paper Tape

Masking tape in widths of three-eighths inch, one-half inch, and one inch are useful for taping boxes, masking, and many other purposes during shooting.

Furniture Pads

Furniture pads are excellent sound absorbers. They may be hung on walls, draped over furniture, placed on the floor, wrapped around sound-reflecting objects, or used in any way necessary to absorb unwanted reflected sound. Usually two or three pads are sufficient, but the number carried depends on the area to be worked in. Other materials, such as blankets, space blankets, corrugated cardboard, and carpeting, are also good sound absorbers.

Grip Stands

These are the same stands used by the grip crew for holding camera diffusion, flags, and other items. They are excellent devices on which to hang pads and cables. At least two should be available to the sound crew.

Other Equipment

A six-foot stepladder is useful for mounting sound-absorbing material, hanging and routing cables, and as a platform for the microphone handler. Apple boxes are specially made, strong wooden boxes of various shapes and sizes used constantly on motion picture shoots for almost everything—for standing on, holding up objects, as temporary tables and chairs, braces, and so on. A grip crew usually has plenty of apple boxes, but the sound crew should have about three of its own. Rope and heavy twine are often useful; carry enough so that small pieces may be cut off separately. A large beach umbrella is indispensable for location work in direct sunlight. In the warmer seasons, direct sun can literally immobilize the crew and put the equipment out of commission. Be sure to have secure means for holding an umbrella upright over the working area. Driving the pole into the ground does not work well; some kind of stand, with sandbags or weights for sturdiness, is more reliable.

Hand Tools

Hand tools should be determined by individual technical skill and knowledge. If you are handy at soldering and repairing electronic equipment, you will probably already have personal tools to do the required tasks. If you are not, it is best to carry spare equipment and cables rather than attempting to repair broken equipment on the shoot. However, you should learn to replace connectors and to do general troubleshooting and repair. This is not too difficult to learn.

Obviously, if you were to take all of the above listed equipment and supplies on every shoot, you would barely be able to move. Use the list as a guide, selecting only what you need.

NINE

Basic Film Editing Operations

Before discussing actual editing procedure, certain basic operations and definitions should be understood. A firm grasp of the following essentials at the outset can make the physical job of editing easier:

1. Raw materials of film editing
2. Tools of editing
3. Splicing
4. Dailies
5. Synchronizing dailies
6. Start marks and leaders

THE RAW MATERIALS OF FILM EDITING

Your job as motion picture editor is to prepare, from certain raw materials, a completed composite motion picture. The whole job will be concerned solely with the manipulation of the following items.

Developed Original and/or Negative Film

The film exposed in the camera will be either a negative or reversal original. (See Film.) As editor, you must ensure that this "negative/original" is properly taken care of and stored. You may have to handle some of it during editing for inspection or for setting up optical effects. After workprint editing, you or the negative cutter will break it down and match it to the edited workprint.

Workprint

This is the positive print made from the camera negative or camera original. It is the film actually handled in editing. (See Dailies.)

Sound Tracks

The sound tracks used in editing are on sprocketed magnetic film and include the following.

Synchronous Sound

This includes all sound—usually dialogue, on-camera narration, and synchronous sound effects—that has been recorded synchronously to picture. It is referred to as "lip-sync" sound.

Narration

This is the voice of a speaker who is not seen in the picture. This kind of narration is sometimes called "voice-over" narration to distinguish it from on-camera narration in which the narrator is seen on the screen.

Sound Effects

These are all the sounds in a picture that are not voice or music, such as footsteps, doors opening and closing, whistles, birds, and so on. The two sources of sound effects are the sound effects library and live recording.

Music

The two kinds of music are that which is composed and scored specifically for a particular motion picture, and music that is prerecorded, or "canned." The latter type is available in the music libraries maintained by most studios.

Magnetic Composite Sound Track

This is the final, mixed magnetic sound track containing all the separate tracks combined into one. Also called the *mix track* and the *dubb track*.

Optical Negative Sound Track

This is the one sound track the editor handles that is not on magnetic film. It is a transfer of the composite magnetic track onto optical film and is used by the laboratory for printing the sound track onto the composite print of the picture. The editor or negative cutter often has to sync it to the negative/original for composite printing.

THE TOOLS OF EDITING

There is not much that can be done with film without the specialized tools for handling and manipulating it. Much editing time will be spent in handling film physically—winding it on and off reels, splicing it, running it through machines, putting it into and taking it out of cans, putting it on cores, rolling it up, rewinding it, and so on. This kind of activity is essentially unproductive, but it simply must be done in editing film. Thus, it is essential to develop manual skill in handling film and equipment to the point where it can be done rapidly and automatically. If you have to worry about the mechanics of getting a roll of film onto a reel, time and energy that are being wasted that otherwise could be spent on the creative part of the job. Learn to rewind film rapidly without injuring it. Learn to transfer it quickly from cores to reels and from reels to cores. Learn to read edge numbers that are illegible, to make splices neatly, to find a shot buried in a large roll, to put film rapidly into the synchronizer and the editing machine, to make up leaders in a few minutes, and to perform speedily and surely all the other manual operations that go into film editing. It is no accident that the best creative film editors are also the ones who are most adept at film handling.

Film Editing Tables

Everything from the top of a barrel to a kitchen drainboard has been used to edit film on, but for acceptable professional working conditions an editing table should meet a few simple but important specifications. Figure 9.1 shows a professional film editing table. Most professional editing tables are five feet long, two feet wide, and thirty-one inches high: this provides adequate working space under normal conditions, fits handily into almost any part of a room, is light enough to be moved, and is the proper height to sit at. You may work better with a larger area, like one filmmaker who works at two specially made eight-foot-long tables, thirty inches wide. One of these is thirty-one inches high for working seated; the other is thirty-seven inches high for working standing. A twenty-four-inch wide table may often be a trifle narrow, but a width of more than thirty inches is difficult to reach across.

An editing table should be mounted on a solid base or very sturdy legs since the rhythmic force applied when rewinding film quickly destroys a weak table. All commercially manufactured tables are mounted on frames made of welded and reinforced angle-iron or square steel tubing. The top of the editing table should be light-colored with a smooth surface, since a rough table top will scratch film, which is particularly undesirable for cutting negative. A light-colored top is essential because film seems to disappear on a dark surface. Some editors prefer white, but most use an off-white, with a linen or fine-line pattern to it. During editing, you will be working for long periods with light reflecting from the tabletop directly into your eyes; so the color of the top

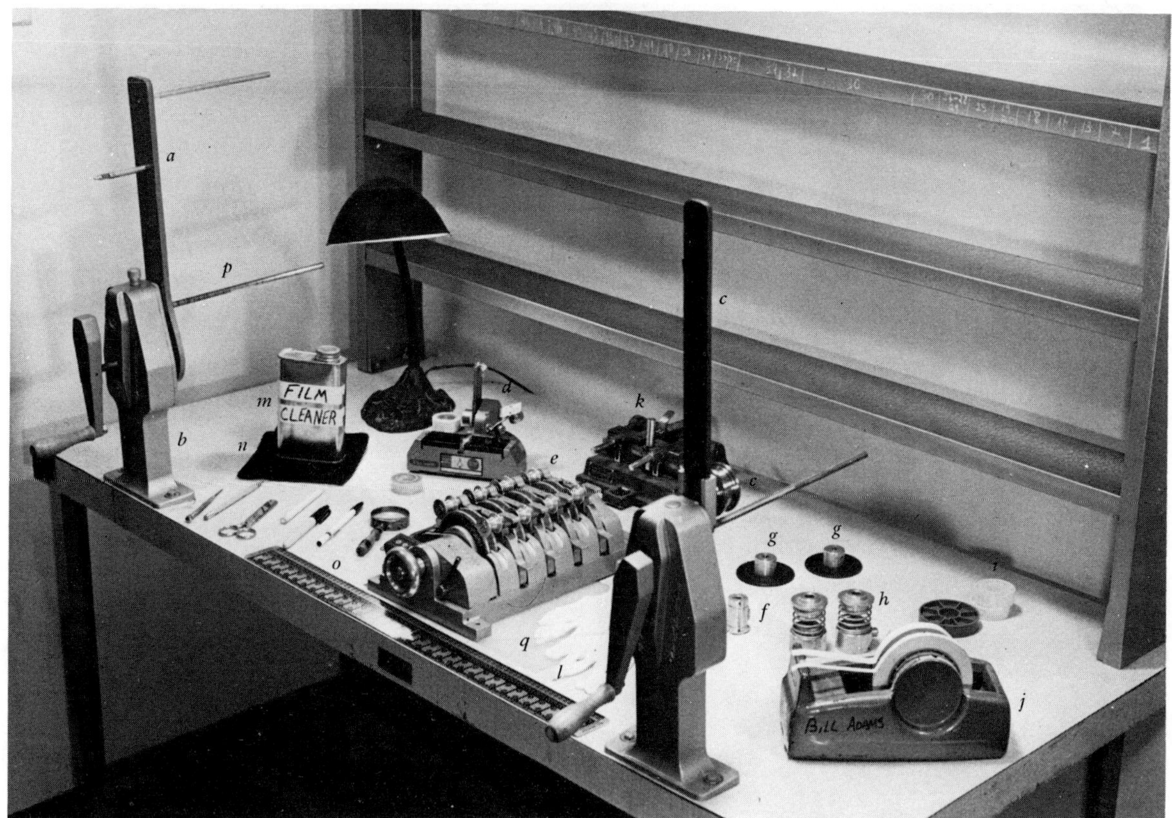

Fig. 9.1. Film editing bench and representative tools. (*a*) Leader stanchion; (*b*) rewind; (*c*) tightwinder; (*d*) tape splicer; (*e*) synchronizer; (*f*) core adapter; (*g*) spacers; (*h*) spring clamps; (*i*) plastic cores; (*j*) tape dispenser; (*k*) hot splicer; (*l*) cotton editing gloves; (*m*) film cleaning fluid; (*n*) film cleaning velvet; (*o*) frame counting ruler; (*p*) long rewind shaft; (*q*) light well.

should be a comfortable one for you to work with.

Lightwell

Mounted flush in the tabletop, a *lightwell* covered with translucent glass provides a readily available back light for inspecting film and locating edge numbers (Fig. 9.2). It is installed on the working side of the table between the rewinds and is sometimes offset either to the left or right of center, depending on the editor's preference. Do not leave the light on continually because the constant glare, even though a low-wattage bulb is used, is hard on the eyes. Use it only when examining frames in detail or identifying dark or partly obliterated edge numbers.

Shelves

Shelf space should always be available on or very near an editing table. A rack of shelves mounted right on the table is probably the most convenient; they need only be wide enough to hold rolls of film and small pieces of equipment and supplies. It is amazing how many small but necessary bits and pieces can be collected during editing, and a place to keep them is indispensable. Larger shelves, or racks to hold all the cans of film that are being worked on at any one time are also necessary.

Rewinds

These are the crank-operated shafts used to wind film back and forth on reels. Rewind shafts are removable and come in lengths that accommodate one, two, three, or four reels. Generally it is most convenient to have the long (four-reel) shafts, since you will handle as a matter of routine from one to four reels at a time. Edited film will have at least two sound tracks and probably three; and these, with the workprint,

Fig. 9.2. The lightwell in the editing table helps in film inspection and in finding edge numbers.

require a four-reel shaft to do most normal in-sync checking. A bent rewind shaft is a misery, making film handling difficult and sometimes impossible. Do not lean on rewind shafts, or hang or place anything on them except reels in the proper way.

At the outset learn how to work rewinds skillfully and speedily. Positive film may be wound safely from reel to reel at high speeds; the faster you can handle film the better. But exercise care, since it is of no advantage to rewind a reel at high speed and tear the film to bits in the process. Always wind from the left to the right, with the film on top (Fig. 9.3). Professional rewinds are geared so that the reel turns in the opposite direction from the way the handle is turned; so to rewind correctly, turn the right-hand rewind handle counterclockwise while the reel turns clockwise. Do not thread the film onto the bottom of the reel in order to turn the handle in the same direction the film is going. It should always be threaded to come off the top of the reel from left to right. And for a good reason: In a workprint the image can be seen correctly, that is, left is left and right is right in looking at the emulsion side of the film. This means that you will handle workprint emulsion up (out) most of the time, since almost all 16mm table viewers, synchronizers, sound readers, counters, and splicers are designed to handle film from left to right with the emulsion up. It is standard procedure in the 16mm film business to work film on the editing table from left to right across the top. This way, the reels and rolls of film will always be in the correct sprocket-hole and emulsion position for handling, which is especially important when two or more editors are working together. Thus, any one editor can pick up a reel that has been rewound by another and get to work without first determining how the film is wound (Fig. 9.4). In 16mm film with its single-perforation sound tracks and leaders, if the direction of wind on the reel is changed—say, threading it onto the right-hand reel at the bottom—the result will be a reel that must be rewound and flipped before it can be worked correctly. This requires additional time and energy that can be better used elsewhere.

Fig. 9.3. Rewinding film should be done from left to right, on and off the top of the reels. Note the long shafts.

Tightwinds

A tightwind is an attachment to a rewind that winds film onto *cores* instead of reels. Essentially it is a spring-loaded or weighted arm with a roller on it that holds the film on the core while it is being wound (Fig. 9.5). The core fits onto a *core adapter* that in turn fits onto the rewind shaft. Since the standard rewind direction is from left to right, the tightwind is generally mounted on the right-hand rewind. Motor-driven tightwinds are used in laboratories and sound studios, where it is necessary to put a large volume of film on cores (Fig. 9.6).

The tightness of film on the core can be controlled by the amount of holdback pressure applied. If you "core up" without any pressure, the roll will be so loose that its center will drop out, creating an incredibly complex tangle of film. If you hold back the film strongly while winding it onto the core, the roll will literally be rock hard, and the center couldn't be knocked out with a hammer. Since winding too tightly on a core scratches the film, a safe medium of hardness is necessary, depending on the film being cored. With workprint, cored rolls can safely be made quite tight; with negative or original, make the roll only tight enough to prevent it from falling apart easily.

When the amateur first sees a professional editor at work, he invariably asks why the editor keeps much of his film on clumsy cores instead of on handy reels. The answer is, of course, that keeping all film on reels in the editing room is most unhandy. Reels are bulky and take up more storage space than is usually available. When they are stacked, the pile becomes wobbly and usually falls over. As reels are handled, they get bent, and a bent reel is an editor's nightmare. Cored film, on the other hand, is light and convenient. Cored rolls stack extremely well on any flat surface and take up about one-fourth the space. Since film in laboratories and sound studios is handled almost exclusively on cores, any film sent out for lab or sound work must be cored up (Fig. 9.5).

Reels

A reel consists of a hub for film to be wound on with fixed flanges, or sides, to hold the film in place. The size of a reel indicates how many feet of film it will normally hold; thus, a 400-foot reel holds 400 feet of film. Motion picture reels are made of steel, plastic, and aluminum. Although the majority of reels are steel, inexpensive plastic 16mm reels are currently available. Aluminum reels are used for magnetic sound film because they are nonmagnetic and less likely to magnetize the film. The following are the reel sizes for 16mm and 35mm film:

16mm (feet)	35mm (feet)	
200	200	
400	1000	(Standard editing reel)
600	2000	(Projection)
800	3000	(Projection)
1200		
1600		

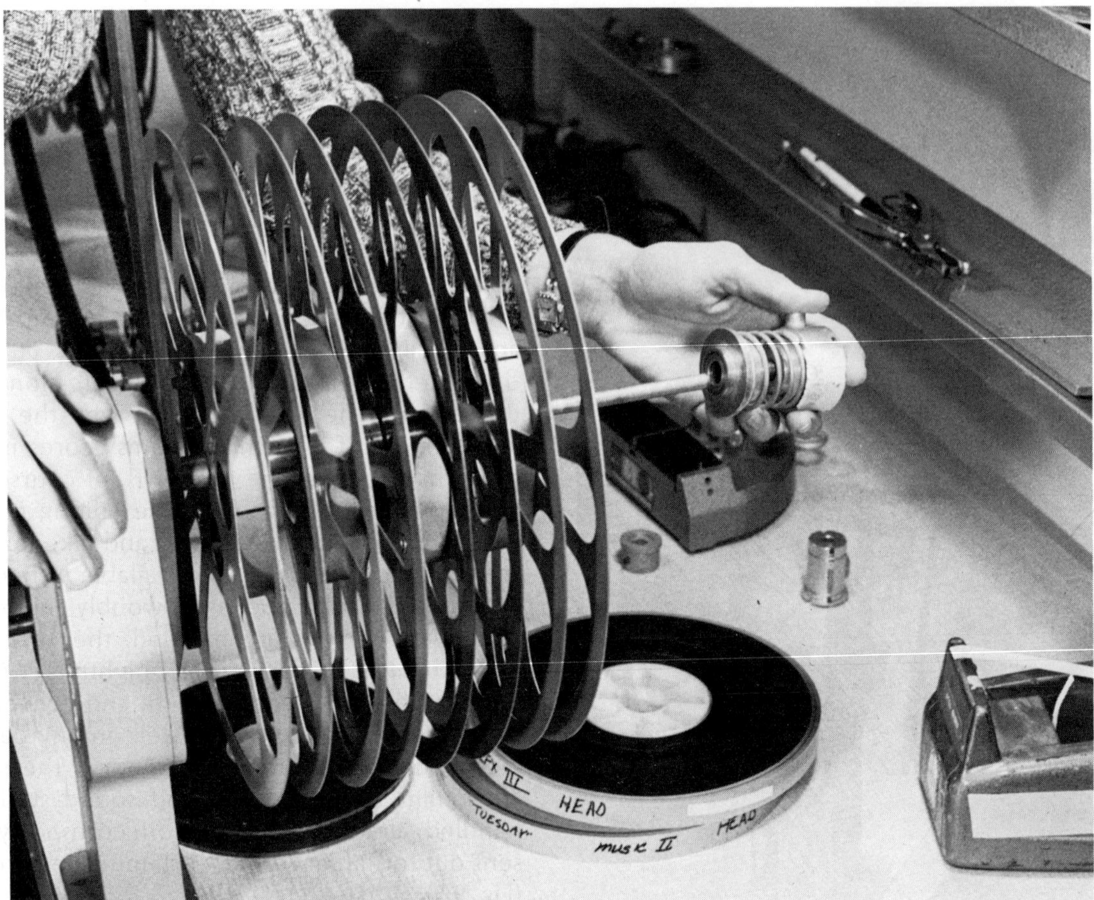

Fig. 9.4. A spring clamp fits over the rewind shaft to hold several reels tightly for rewinding.

In 35mm production, the 1000-foot reel represents a standard that is applicable to both 16mm and 35mm film. A *reel* in the movie business means *ten minutes of running time* and is based on the 35mm 1000-foot reel, which has been the standard editing unit for at least fifty years. Since 35mm film runs at a projection speed of 90 feet per minute, 1000 feet would actually be eleven minutes of running time.

In 35mm editing a 1000-foot steel reel is always used. If the picture is forty minutes long, it will be mounted on four reels; if it is ninety minutes long, it will be on nine reels; and these reels must be edited so that a change-over can be made unobtrusively between each reel. (See Appendix.) Larger sizes of 35mm reels are used only in theaters, where two or three reels are spliced together under special circumstances.

A 16mm film may be edited to almost any length in a single reel, so you will be using reels ranging from the 400-foot to the 1200-foot size. Rarely, if ever, in editing will you handle a 16mm film over 1200 feet in length. If the picture were this long, temporary breaks would normally be made in it, to work with shorter and more convenient lengths.

There are two kinds of 16mm reels: double-key and single-key. They are the same in construction and differ only in the shape of the spindle hole. The *double-key*-reel has a square hole on both sides, notched to fit onto a rewind shaft. Since the hole is the same on both sides (double-keyed), either side of the reel can fit onto the rewind. The *single-key* reel has a square, notched hole on one side only (single-keyed); the other side has a round hole that will slip onto the rewind shaft but is not slotted to fit the driving pin.

Single-keyed reels are made to fit on the shaft only one way and are intended for use on portable projectors in schools. With a single-key reel, the assumption is that an untrained operator can-

Fig. 9.5. Film may be wound onto cores by using the tightwind.

not possibly put the reel on the projector backward. Although this works well on projectors, single-key reels have no place in the editing room where reels are constantly changed from one rewind to another. Since they fit only one way, a great deal of time is wasted in rewinding to get the emulsion position to fit the reel. Some editors habitually throw away any single-key reels they encounter.

Bent reels make editing and projecting difficult. Even steel ones bend easily. Be careful not to bend working reels, although it doesn't pay to be so protective of the reels that nothing else gets done. It is helpful to keep a set of eight

Fig. 9.6. Sound tracks wound on cores. The core adapter fits into the center of the core so it may be handled on the rewind shaft.

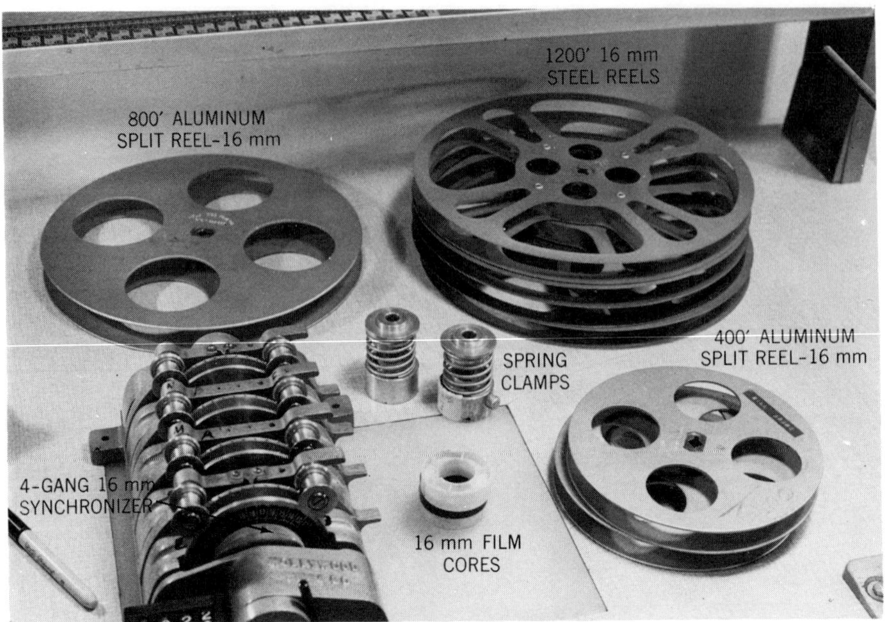

Fig. 9.7. Some basic editing tools.

reels, each in a can, to be used only when checking sound tracks, making out cue sheets, or cutting negative. Once a reel is bent, it is practically impossible to bend it back into its true shape.

Although some editors use aluminum reels that are nonmagnetic for sound track to protect them from becoming magnetized, steel reels are safe and are used for sound tracks more often than aluminum reels. If a steel reel becomes magnetized, it may be demagnetized by putting it in a cardboard film box and running it through the demagnetizer.

Split Reels and Flanges

A *split reel* is a reel whose hub is threaded so that the two flanges can be separated. Split reels provide a quick method of handling film on cores. With a split reel many rolls of cored film can be worked in turn, avoiding the necessity for many bulky reels of film that clutter the editing space (Fig. 9.8*A* and *B*.) A single, large split reel will enable you to handle cored rolls of many different sizes, but in 16mm work three sizes are convenient to work with—400 feet, 800 feet, and 1200 feet. If you have but one split reel, the 1200-foot size is best because it can handle all rolls up to 1200 feet. If you are limited to two split reels, the best combination is a 400-foot and a 1200-foot reel. In 16mm film production, most of the routine work can be done with a 400-foot split reel, which is handy, light, and small. The aluminum split reel is probably the best for all-around work, it is lightweight, yet strong enough to absorb rough treatment without bending. The steel split reel is the cheaper and lighter of the two but it bends more easily.

Flanges are actually split reels made of micarta, a strong, heavy plastic, Flanges come in two forms: The single flange, which consists of one side only with a full-size hub; and the companion flange, having two sides that can be separated as with a split reel. Because of their heavy material, micarta flanges are flat and will remain flat and rotate precisely without wobble. They do not nick when they are dropped, and are rugged enough to last for years.

Use companion flanges as you would split reels. A single flange can be convenient and fast for transferring cored rolls to reels, breaking down rolls, and coring up short pieces of film or individual shots. A single flange works better with 35mm than with 16mm film because the wider film does not slip off the roll as easily.

To transfer a cored roll to a reel, put a single flange on the left-hand rewind and place the cored roll on the hub. Hold the top of the roll against the flange with the left hand and wind

Fig. 9.8*A*. Cored roll of film fits onto keyed flange of the aluminum split reel.

Fig. 9.8*B*. One flange of the split reel screws into the keyed flange, holding a cored roll of film securely for handling.

the film onto the reel on the right-hand rewind. For winding short pieces onto cores, put the single flange on the right-hand rewind, put a core on the hub, and wind on the film, holding it on the core with the left hand. When breaking down a cored roll from a single flange or working so that you have to remove your hand from the roll from time to time, a vertical metal rod called an *upright,* mounted on a weighted base, will keep the film from falling off the roll. Even the movement involved in placing a cored roll on a split reel and screwing the loose side in place can cause enough slippage in a roll of negative/original to scratch it. An upright, therefore, is particularly suitable where 16mm negative/original must be handled quickly. Slipping a cored roll onto a flange that is already mounted on the rewind shaft and then sliding an upright into place involves very little manipulation of the roll.

Synchronizer

The *synchronizer,* also called *sync machine* or *sync block,* is the editor's indispensable tool. (See Figs. 9.9, 11.4.) It consists of two or more sprocketed wheels mounted on a central shaft so that a piece of film may be locked onto each wheel. Films locked into the sync machine are held precisely in the same relationship; they may be rolled forward or backward, always being held in sync. Observe how the synchronizer in Fig. 11.26 is being used to hold the workprint and the AB rolls in sync while a new scene is being laid in.

Synchronizers are made for 16mm and 35mm film. Each is equipped with a Veeder footage counter and a frame counter in the form of a marked circular plate on the face of the first sprocket. To set the frame counter, hold the synchronizer turning knob and move the knurled ring around the shaft until the correct frame number is in position. In Figs. 11.37*A* and 11.37*B*, the footage counter is being used to change *dead sync* to *printer sync.*

It is important to learn to use the sync machine skillfully and rapidly, for there is hardly an editing operation that does not require its use. In editing dialogue, the sync machine is used initially to sync up the clapsticks and sound bloop, and subsequently to check sync and establish new sync marks. Building sound effects tracks relies almost totally on the sync machine since many separate short pieces of sound track must be matched and synchronized to the picture. Leaders and start marks must be set up in

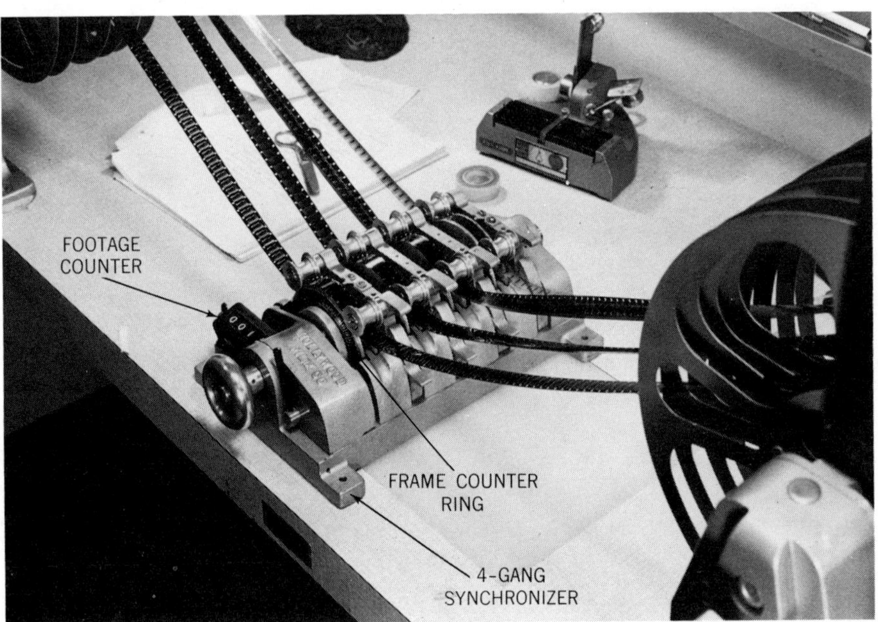

Fig. 9.9. The 4-gang synchronizer, or sync machine, can hold four rolls of film in sync with each other for syncing, marking, or checking.

the sync machine, and matching negative/original to the edited workprint would be impossible without it.

A common practice is to install on one or more of the sync machine sprockets a magnetic sound pickup head connected to a small amplifier/speaker, or "squawk box," on the editing table. With this arrangement, sound tracks may be listened to at the table while winding the film by hand. With a sound head, the synchronizer may be used in conjunction with a table film viewer to sync dailies, make up mixing cue sheets, check for sync, and edit sync dialogue, effects, and music. A motor may be attached to drive the synchronizer at a constant 24 fps speed. Although all the editing can be done on a synchronizer/viewer combination, timing, pacing, exact matching of action, accurate assessment of sound, or anything else requiring finesse must be done on one of the larger and more sophisticated editing machines.

Film Viewer

A film viewer allows viewing film quickly and easily while sitting at the editing table. It sits between the rewinds and as the film is wound through it from one reel to the other, the picture appears on a small glass screen. Some viewers are designed to run negative/original without scratching or otherwise harming it. Used in combination with a synchronizer equipped with a sound head, the viewer may be used for sync editing.

Miscellaneous Tools and Supplies

A variety of smaller tools and supplies will be needed to fully equip an editing room. When cutting a film in someone else's facilities, everything necessary will probably be supplied, but do not depend on it; freelancers often must work at home or in rented editing rooms; and as the filmmaker or producer, you should provide funds for such tools and supplies in the production budget. Whatever the situation, have a personal set of hand tools and bench supplies. (For a good list of these additional tools and supplies, see Tools and Supplies, Negative Cutting, Chapter 11, and Figures 11.2, 11.3.) With the obvious exception of those items pertaining solely to the process of negative cutting (breakdown papers, for example), you will need everything on that list plus the following items:

1. Film cleaner. The longer film is edited, the dirtier it gets. All extraneous marks and surface dirt should be removed from the picture before screening (especially for a client) to avoid confusion and clogging of the aperture.
2. *Cleaning velvet* to be used with film cleaner on the picture, or dry to remove surface dirt from the tracks (See Fig. 9.1).
3. Extra rolls of splicing tape to fit the type of splicer being used.
4. Frame counting ruler. This is usually two feet long for 16 or 35mm film, and is used to measure short lengths and mark effects precisely (Fig. 9.10).
5. Tool box or other suitable container for personal tools and supplies.

Special Hints

1. A *grease pencil,* or China marker, is designed to be used on the picture only. It makes visible, effective, but often messy marks that can be rubbed off easily. A grease pencil should not be used on the magnetic sound track because it will be deposited on the sound head of the editing machine or worse yet on the playback machine in the mix, causing the sound to become muffled. Use instead either an indelible marking pen, a ball-point pen, or a pencil. Most editors prefer a marking pen because the marks are easier to spot when rolling through a large quantity of film. These markers are also used to prepare leaders and to make permanent marks on the picture to indicate visual effects.
2. Make sure the scissors are demagnetized to avoid unwanted pops and clicks on the sound track. They should be blunt-nosed to avoid scratching or tearing sprocket holes in the film, or injuring yourself in times of stress.
3. Get used to wearing at least one cotton glove working with film, and two gloves always when handling negative/original. The greatest enemy of a clean sound track is ordinary body grease, and the negative/original can be damaged irreparably by one fingerprint. Even with the gloves, remember to wash your hands often.
4. To clean the picture, wet the velvet with just enough film cleaner to dampen it. Place the film reel on the left hand rewind. Fold the velvet over

Fig. 9.10. Ruler for frame counting is marked in both 35mm and 16mm frames.

the film, and apply a small amount of pressure while winding the film onto another reel on the right-hand rewind. Wind slowly to allow for drying time. To clean sound tracks, repeat the process using a dry velvet. Avoid using film cleaner on sound tracks because it will remove some of the magnetic emulsion. Occasional, heavy grease spots should be dabbed lightly with alcohol.

FILM EDITING MACHINES

Moviola

The *Moviola* (Fig. 9.11) is the traditional film editing machine. It has two motors, each operated by a separate footpedal. One motor is "wild," running at a variable speed that depends on how far down its pedal is pressed. The other, a constant-speed motor, runs only at 24 fps sound speed. Basically, the Moviola consists of a sound head on the left and a picture head on the right, both of which may be run either separately or locked together. To run a sync scene in sync, put the picture start mark or clapper frame in the aperture of the picture head, and put the sound start mark directly under the magnetic pickup in the sound head, then run them locked together. To make adjustments in sound or to try different combinations, unlock the heads and run either picture or sound independently. One way to work on a Moviola is to edit with the film coming from bins, one on each side of the editor's stool, while the edited film feeds out of the heads and into a cloth bag suspended on the rear of the machine. Film need not be on reels to be edited, and small pieces of film may be put into the Moviola, quickly, viewed or listened to, and then rapidly removed. The sound is heard from a small speaker mounted in the front panel; and although the sound quality is poor and the picture viewer is small, the Moviola is versatile, and is used universally for film editing.

Horizontal Editing Machines

Unlike the Moviola, horizonal editing machines, or "flatbeds" accommodate film assembled only on cores and in a horizontal position (Figs. 9.12, 9.13). The large picture viewers and speakers of these machines permit precise judgment and evaluation, particularly in music editing. They may be run both forward and in reverse at very high and very low speeds, enabling the film editor to rapidly perform all the nonproductive tasks that classically occupy so much of his time—tasks such as syncing dialies, winding forward and back to check sync or to reexamine a scene, setting up leaders, reading tracks in the preparation of cue sheets, and so on. The greatest asset of the horizontal editing machine is that it may have one, two, three, and sometimes more picture viewers, all of which may be run simultaneously in sync with one or more sound tracks. With two viewers, for example, all the closeups of a scene may be put on one viewer and all the medium shots on the other. Then, running each separately or together and reversing at high speed, you can experiment with the whole scene in several combinations without having to remove and replace many separate pieces of film. Also, film from as many as three cameras may be viewed simultaneously on the flatbed's three viewers, all running synchronously with a common sound track. For most routine editing, however, one viewer and one or two sound tracks are used. Interchangeable modules allow some makes of horizontal editing machines to be converted quickly to accommodate 8mm, 16mm, 35mm, and 65mm films.

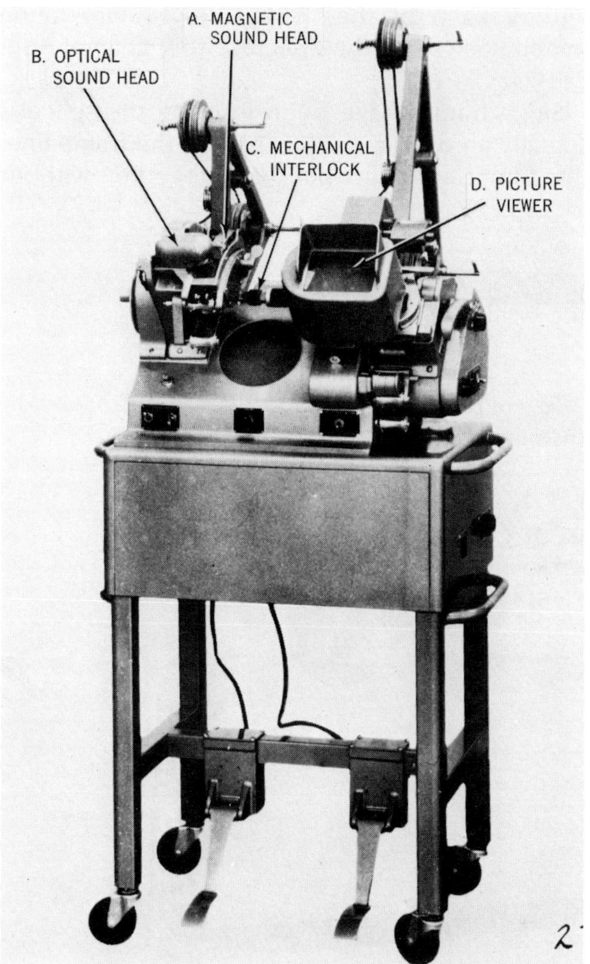

Fig. 9.11. The "green" Moviola has been the standard film editing machine in the film industry for 50 years. Sound and picture heads may be mechanically interlocked to run together in sync, or may be unlocked to run individually.

SPLICING

Splicing is simply joining together the ends of two separate pieces of film so that they become one continuous piece of film. Splicing one piece of film to another is probably done more often than any other task in film editing. This simple operation, should be done quickly and routinely and must result in a strong and relatively inconspicuous splice. The *splicer,* then, is one of the most used and necessary tools on the editor's table. Essentially it is a machine that can hold two pieces of film in precisely the correct position so that they maybe cemented or taped together. There are two basic types of film splices:

1. Tape splice. This is a butt splice used predominantly in workprint splicing and in repair splicing of negative originals.
2. Cement splice. This is a lap splice used in splicing negative/originals. Some editors, however, still use cement splices in workprint editing, and most projectionists repair projection prints and leaders with cement splices.

Tape Splicing

In a tape splice, (also called *butt splice*), the two ends of the film are butted up against each other and taped together with a short piece of special pressure-sensitive tape (Figs. 9.14, 9.15). For picture splicing, use transparent tape on both sides. For sound track splicing, use opaque tape on the base side only, since tape on the emulsion side of sound film blocks out the sound. The main advantage to tape splicing is that the cut occurs on the frame line and a scene may be reassembled into its original form without loss of frames. Thus, if a cut is tried and it does not work the way you want it to, reassemble the shots and try again.

There are two kinds of tape splicers: perforated and nonperforated. Different sized splicers of each kind accommodate 8mm, 16mm, 35mm, 65mm, and 70mm film respectively. Picture models make a straight-across cut in the film, sound track models make a diagonal cut, which sometimes results in a smooth transition especially in music cuts. A diagonal splice is supposed to eliminate the danger of an unwanted pop at the splice in the sound track. However, a straight-across splicer is perfectly safe with magnetic film if the cutting blade is nonmagnetic and care is taken not to let the splicer itself become magnetized. Both cement splicing and tape splicing can be done with nothing more than a pair of scissors, a razor blade, and cement, or with scissors and splicing tape, but splicers make the job less fatiguing and more precise (Fig. 9.16).

The *perforated* splicer uses splicing tape that contains perforations corresponding to those on the type of film that is being spliced. The nonperforated, or *guillotine,* splicer uses unperforated tape across the splice line and punches the proper holes in the tape at the time the splice is made.

Splicing tape for picture film is transparent, but will alter the density of the frames it covers if it is used in printing. Consequently, tape splices are not generally used in assembling negative or original AB rolls. Almost all workprint editing is currently done with tape splicing, but bear in mind that editing the workprint with tape may create a problem when you try to conform the negative to the workprint if you are not thoroughly familiar with the processes of both cement and tape splicing. A cement splice requires that one to two frames be lost from the end of each of the two pieces of film being joined (See Cement Splicing, this chapter, pp. 240–242).

Since frames have been lost and the splice is actually an overlap rather than on the frame line, the film cannot be put back together without

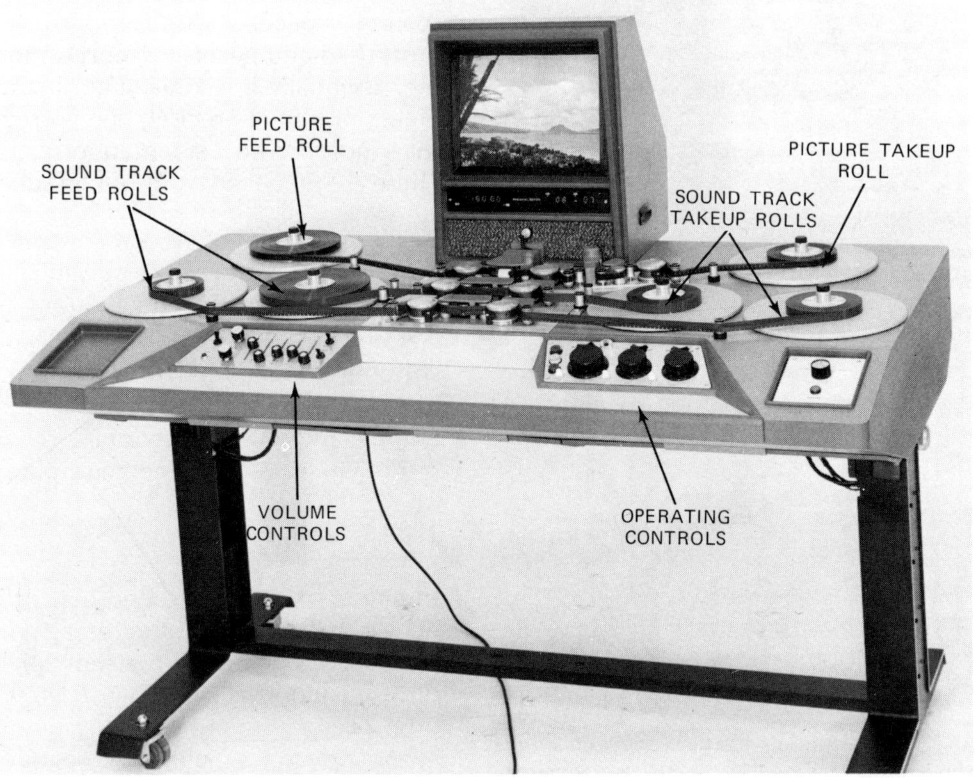

Fig. 9.12. Horizontal, or "flatbead," film editing machine. On the model shown here, two sound tracks and one picture may be run in sync or independently, backward or forward, at a wide range of frame speeds.

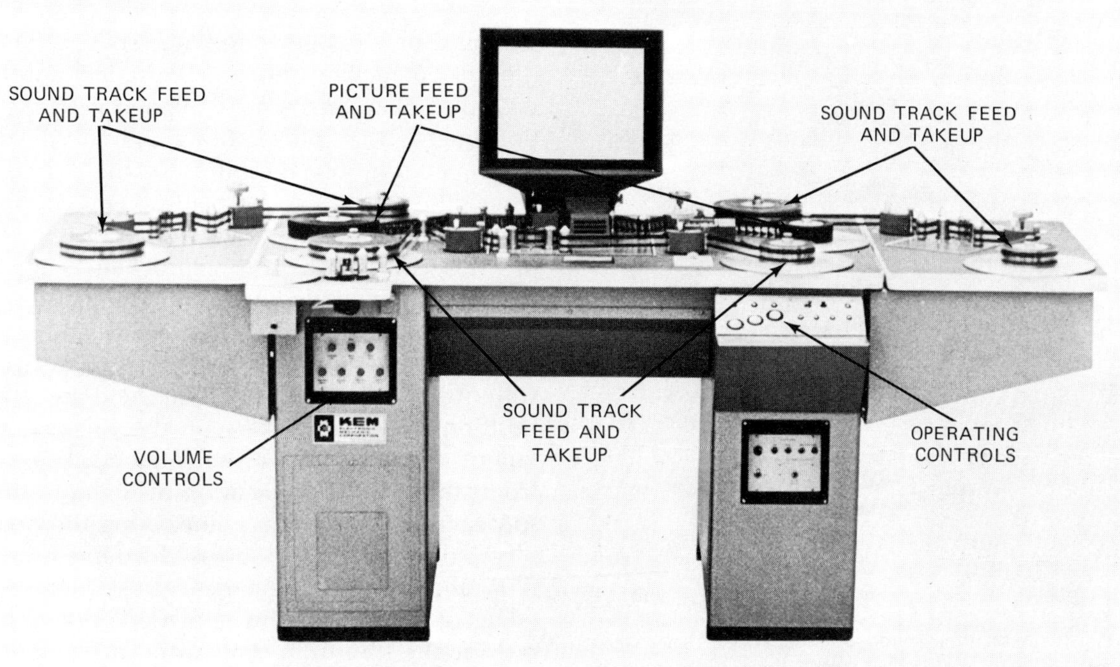

Fig. 9.13. An "eight-plate" horizontal film editing machine. Three sound tracks and one roll of picture may be run in sync or independently, backward or forward, at frame rates from 3 to 100 frames per second. Trial mixes may be made on this type of machine.

slugging, or replacing the lost frames with blank leader. If the workprint is edited with cement splices, however, the frames required to make the splices in the negative will be accounted for. In the tape splice the splice occurs between the frames, so that after making a cut the shot can be spliced together again without a loss of frames; therefore it is possible to tape-splice a workprint, using every frame of a shot without leaving extra frames to make the cement splices later in negative cutting. The negative may turn out to be shorter than the workprint because needed frames of negative will have to be cut away to make earlier cement splices. The only remedy is to recut the workprint to match the negative and

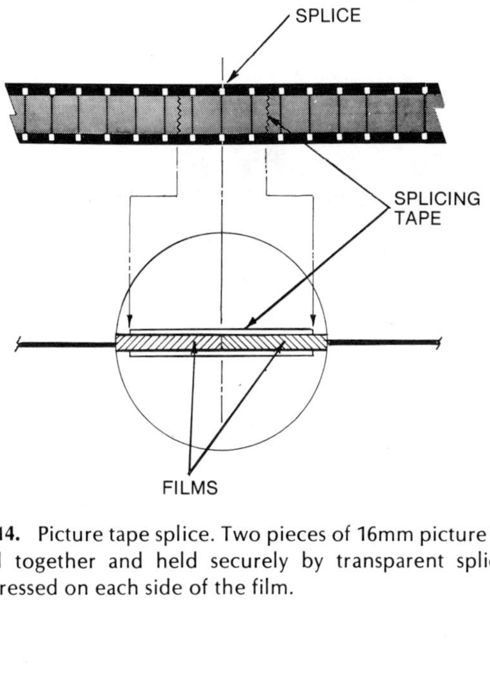

Fig. 9.14. Picture tape splice. Two pieces of 16mm picture film butted together and held securely by transparent splicing tape pressed on each side of the film.

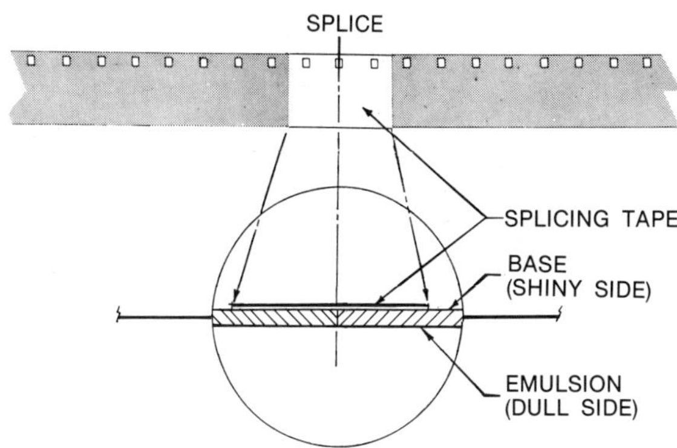

Fig. 9.15. Sound tape splice. Two pieces of 16mm magnetic sound film butted together and held securely by one piece of splicing tape on the base (shiny) side.

Fig. 9.16. 35mm diagonal sound tape splicer. The diagonal cut allows more precise cuts in sound and eliminates noise at the splice.

remix the sound tracks, an extremely costly procedure both in time and money. This is not to suggest that you abandon the tape splicer as a standard workprint editing device whose advantages far outweigh its disadvantages, but rather to caution that you remember the difference between the two kinds of splices to avoid problems in the negative cutting.

Perforated Splicer

To splice on the perforated tape splicer, position the tail of the one shot on the splicer sprockets with the splice line exactly aligned with the cutting line of the splicer. Bring the cutting blade down, cutting off the film on the frame line where the splice is to be made. Remove the unwanted portion of the film, and position the head of the second shot on the sprockets, again with the splice line aligned with the cutting line of the splicer. Bring the cutting blade down and remove the unwanted trim. The two ends to be spliced will now be butted together, held in splicing position by the sprockets on the splicer platen. Pull off about an inch of perforated splicing tape from the roll and position it lightly on the sprockets over the splice line. Bring the holding blade down firmly to press the tape onto the film, and tear off the tape against the serrated edges of the blade. Lift the blade and, before removing the film from the splicer, press down on the tape in the center to secure it. Then remove it from the splicer and rub the splice firmly from the center out so that all the bubbles and creases are smoothed out. Feel the edges of the film along the splice, and if any tape sticks out beyond the edge, trim it with scissors. Tape both sides of each splice in picture film to prevent jamming in the editing machine or projector. Splice sound film on one side only, the base side, and be sure the tape is bubble-free and securely bonded to the film (Fig. 9.17*A*–*G*).

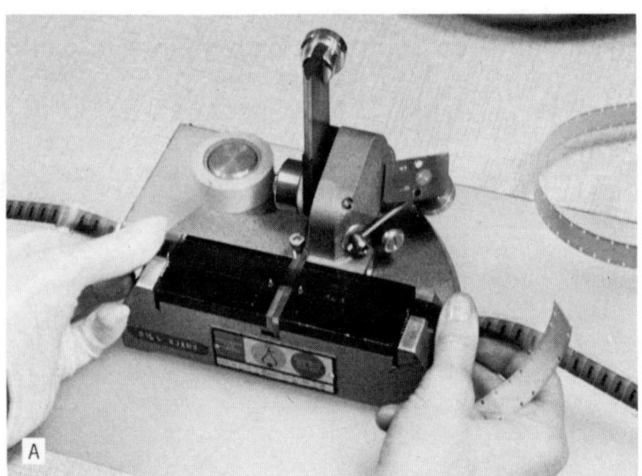

Fig. 9.17*A*. To tape-splice lightstruck leader to the head of a film scene, position the film on the splicer pins with the grease pencil splice mark positioned on the cut line of the splicer.

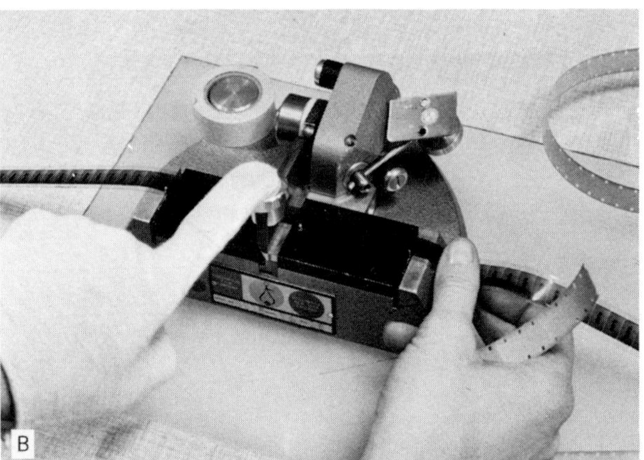

Fig. 9.17*B*. Cut the film with the spring-loaded cutting blade. Discard the right-hand piece of film and leave the left-hand piece registered on the pins.

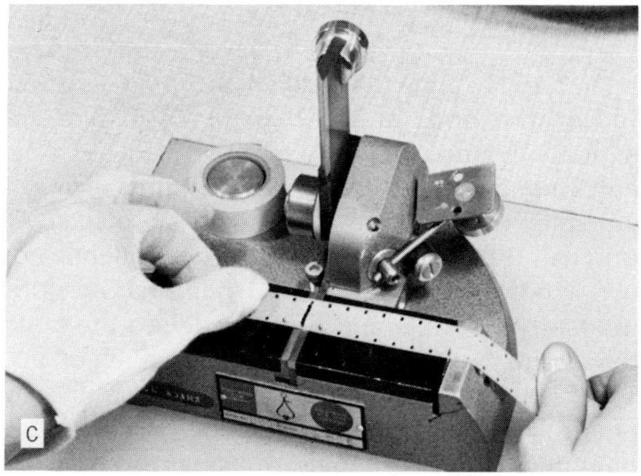

Fig. 9.17*C***.** Position the lightstruck leader on the registration pins with the marked splice line in position to be cut.

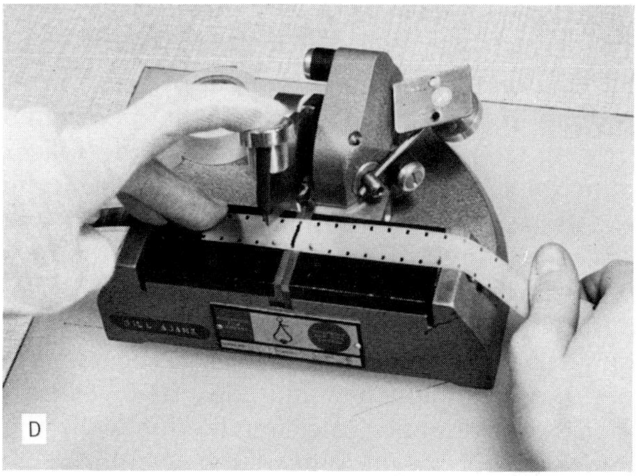

Fig. 9.17*D***.** Cut the leader and discard the piece to the left of the cut. Both leader and picture film are now registered on the splicer ready to be taped.

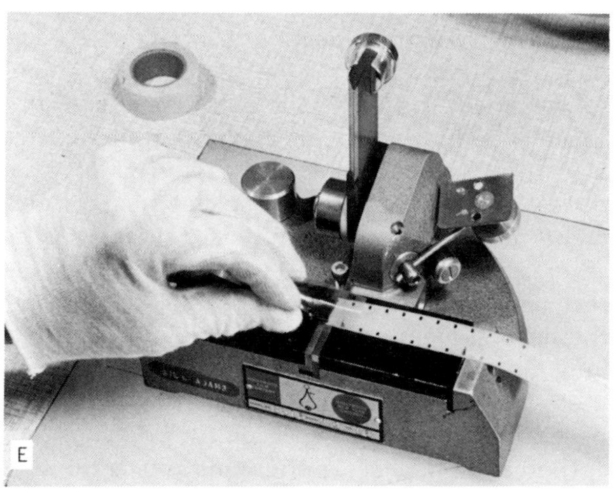

Fig. 9.17*E***.** Place a piece of perforated splicing tape on the registration pins lapping across both film and leader.

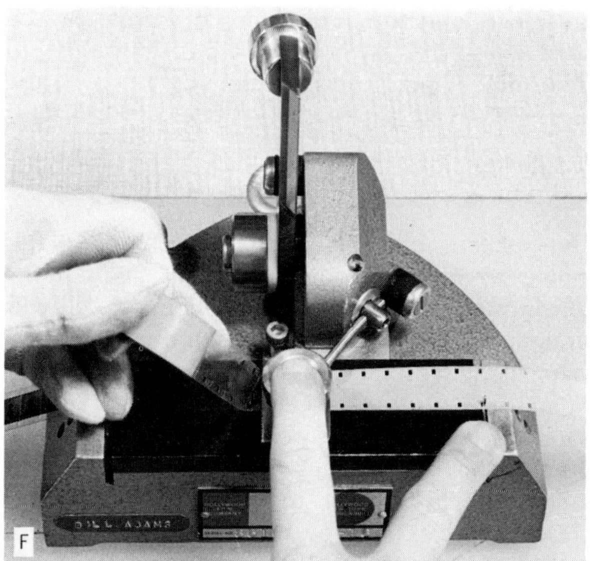

Fig. 9.17*F***.** Bring pressure blade down on the tape, and tear the tape from the roll on the serrated edges of the pressure blade.

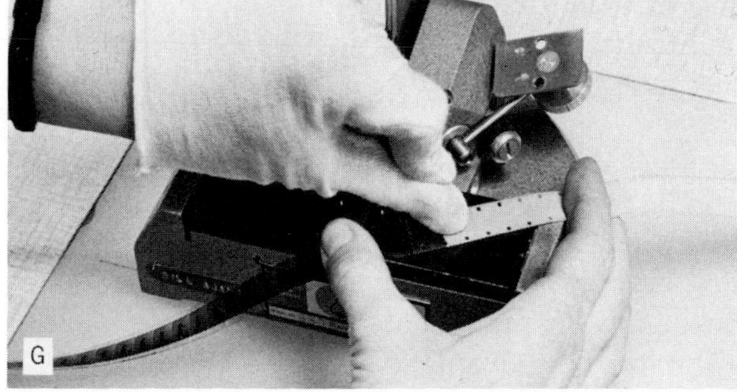

Fig. 9.17*G***.** Smooth out all creases and bubbles on the taped splice. (Tape both sides of a picture splice; tape only one side of a sound splice.)

Guillotine Splicer

Splicing on the guillotine (nonperforated) splicer is done in the same way, except that perforated splicing tape need not be used since the splicer punches its own sprocket holes and trims off the excess tape from both sides of the film in one operation. This type of splicer has the advantage that almost any kind of tape may be used, perforated or unperforated. It has two main disadvantages: the first is that in splicing single-perforated film, the film ends must be reversed if their sprocket holes are not in line with the punching dies of the splicer; the second is that the cutting blade is to one side of the splicer instead of on the splice line. This requires moving the film from the cutter to the splicing position on every splice, which is time-consuming and increases the probability of error. Before buying a splicer, try out both types thoroughly to determine which works best for you.

Splicing Block

The *splicing block* is a small machined plate, milled to hold two pieces of film aligned for splicing. Two slots across the splice line allow a straight-across or diagonal cut to be made with a razor blade. The splicing block is inexpensive and small enough to be carried in a pocket or handbag. Although it is neither as efficient nor as precise as a more expensive splicer, it will get the job done if it is the only tool available.

Good splices may be made in magnetic film without a splicer. Hold two pieces of film with their sprocket holes aligned and cut them simultaneously with unmagnetized scissors. Cut off a piece of perforated splicing tape about four frames long, press one end of it lightly on the tabletop, and slip the end of one piece of film under it with the sprocket holes aligned. Press the tape down firmly on the film, pull it up from the table, and slip the other piece of film under it so that it butts up against the first piece. Press the tape firmly and smooth out bubbles and wrinkles. This kind of splice is as good as those made on a splicer or a block, and with practice it can be done very quickly. The main disadvantage is that precision cuts cannot be made on the frame line, which is sometimes important if a shot needs to be put back together.

Cement Splicing

In a cement splice (also called *lap splice* and *wet splice*), the ends of the two pieces of film are overlapped and cemented together with a special film cement (Fig. 9.19). Today, cement splicing is generally used only in the assembly of negative/original rolls. Cement splicers are generally of two kinds: table models and pedestal, or floor models. Both table and floor model do the same thing and have the same functional elements. The blades of the table model are operated by hand, while the arms on the pedestal splicer are operated by foot pedals, making the splicing cycle faster and less fatiguing to the operator.

Cement splicing is speeded up if the temperature of the splicer is higher than the room temperature. All professional splicers are equipped with electrical heating elements to keep them at a constant splicing temperature. Table splicers with heating elements are called *hot splicers;* and even though the floor model splicer has a heating element, it is referred to as a *pedestal splicer*. Leave the splicer heating element turned on night and day, since it takes several hours to bring the splicer up to the correct temperature. Do not worry about the cost; the heating element uses very little power, lasts a long time, and can be replaced for a few cents. In the editing room, a splicer that is ready to use is necessary at all hours (Fig. 9.20).

The cement splicer, either kind, holds the two pieces of film and brings one down on the other in the proper relative position; but cememt splicing can occur only with the film base to base, since any emulsion or dirt between prevents the cement from working. Consequently, before the two are brought into contact, the lower piece of film must be scraped clean of emulsion in the

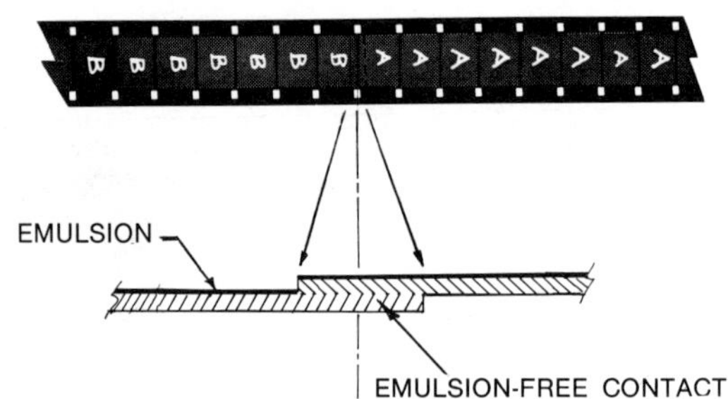

Fig. 9.18. In a cement, or lap, splice, the cement will adhere only when emulsion-free surfaces are in contact.

Fig. 9.19. Film-splicing cement bottle and brush cap.

area of the splice overlap. Cement does not glue the film together in the usual sense. Instead, it partially dissolves the two surfaces, which, on drying, actually become one solid piece of film. It is more like a weld than a glued joint (Fig. 9.18).

When the emulsion for splicing is scraped off or removed, no more than the emulsion should be removed. Adjust the scraper blade so that it removes only the emulsion without digging into the film. If the cutting blades are out of alignment or the pressure is incorrect, poor splices will result and even torn film. Theoretically, good splices can be made on any one of several inexpensive cold splicers. The main difference is time, since cement dries almost instantaneously in a hot splicer. Cold splices take longer to set, but taking them out of the splicer beforehand results in a weak splice. Since hand splicers do not have precision scrapers, be extremely careful to make a clean, even scrape. Emulsion comes off quite easily if dampened with a Q-tip or a little saliva on the finger. A razor blade or similar tool works well as a scraper, and a piece of emery board cut to fit the scraping surface may also be used.

Always use fresh, professional film cement, and keep cement in a small bottle with a brush on the cork or lid for daily use. Film cement quickly loses its effectiveness in a bottle that is being used; its more volatile elements evaporate, and as the cement becomes thicker, it loses its strength. Too much cement does not make a splice stronger and spreads to other parts of the film and dissolves the pictures. Just enough ce-

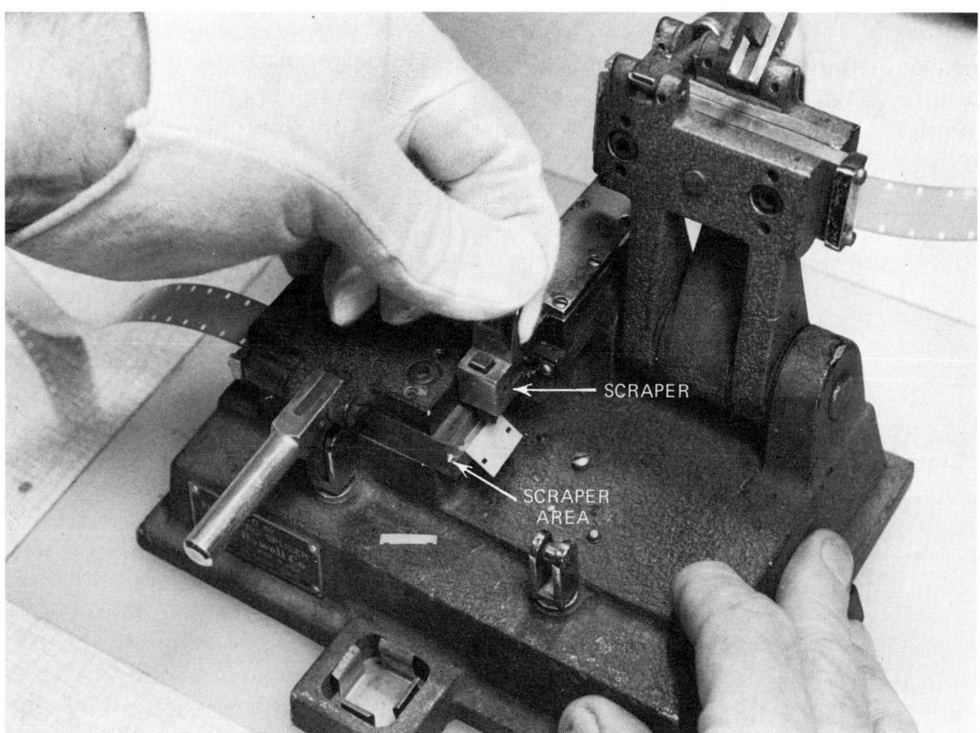

Fig. 9.20. To make a hot splice using film cement, draw the scraper back and push it across the film once or twice to remove the emulsion.

ment to wet the whole scraped surface is sufficient. The strength of a splice is not related to the force brought to bear in moving the blades of the splicer, so do not lower the blades with a bang. A splicer is a precision-made piece of equipment, and a fifty-dollar repair job is poor compensation for a splice that is not any stronger than one made gently. The best test of a splice is to try to tear it apart. If it has been made properly, it will be stronger than the rest of the film because the film becomes almost twice as thick at the overlap.

Negative/original material requires a different kind of cement splicer than positive workprint material. Splicers for negative/originals should be used for that purpose only. Since a negative splice is narrower than a positive splice, it must be near-perfect because too much is at stake to risk a break or a tear. Also, if a positive splicer is used on negative/original, there is the possibility that the frame lines will become visible as flashes in the print at every splice.

A negative splicer should be kept in fine, delicate adjustment. Keep the splicer scrupulously clean by applying acetone frequently, say, every fifty splices, to all the operating parts. This will dissolve the clogged pieces of emulsion, which can then be wiped out of the way. Do not use razor blades or paper clips to scrape operating surfaces, as they will make minute scratches even in hardened steel.

It is standard practice in 16mm splicing to uniformly lose 1½ frames from the end of each piece of film in a cement splice (Fig. 9.21).

In splicing 35mm film, two sprocket holes, or half a frame, are lost. Frames lost in splicing cannot be cement-spliced together again in their original form because in resplicing they would lose additional frames.

Slugging

Often in editing, a splice may not work or changes may have to be made. When the location of a splice is altered, or the shot is put back the way it was before you cut it, gaps in the shot may be created by lost or damaged frames. In this case, the standard practice in workprint editing is to *slug* the print, that is, to replace the lost or damaged frames with leader. Later this leader, or slug, will indicate the exact length of the shot to the negative cutter, who will splice in the corresponding undamaged negative/original. A slug, then, is a kind of place-holder for a piece of missing workprint. (See Fig. 9.22*A*,*B*.)

In slugging a workprint, the basic procedure for doing it with tape and cement splices is the same, except that the frames lost in the cement splicing must be compensated. The conditions in which a workprint would normally be slugged are as follows:

1. Reconstituting a shot
2. Repairing damaged film
3. Holding a place for film not yet shot.

Reconstituting a Shot

To reconstitute a shot, that is, to put it back together the way it was before it was cut, use leader to replace the frames lost plus the frames that will be lost when the film is cement-spliced back to its original length. Remember that frames

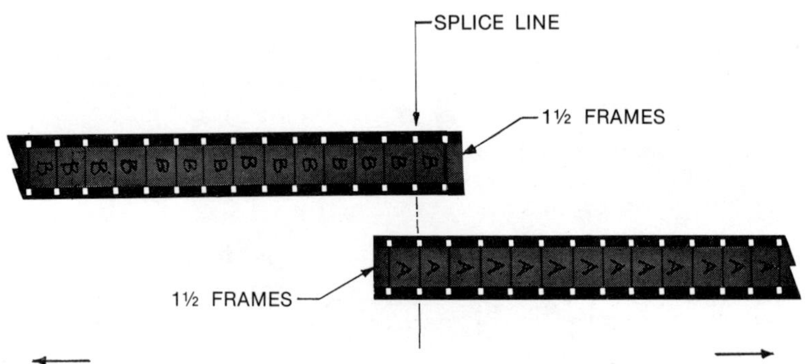

Fig. 9.21. Customarily, 1½ frames are lost in the hot splicing process. At least 1½ frames must remain beyond the splice line on each end of each piece of film to be spliced.

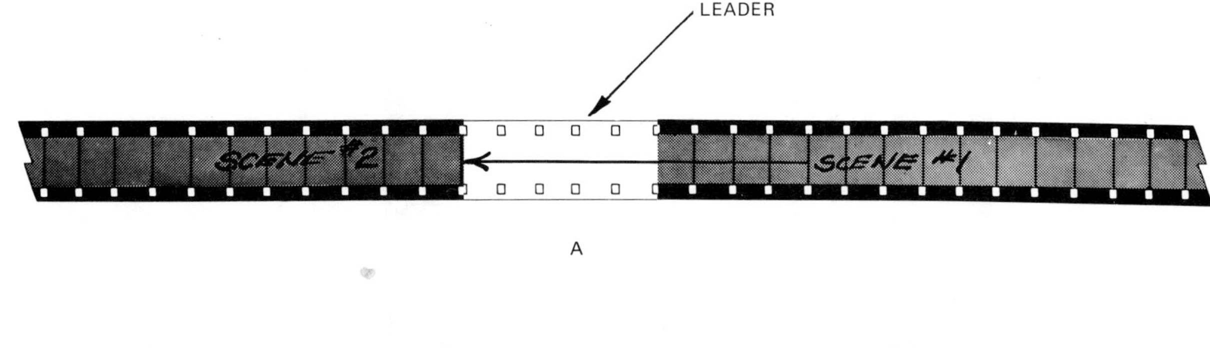

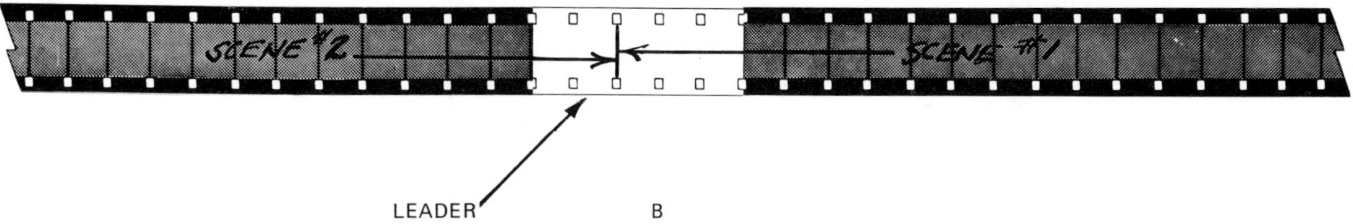

Fig. 9.22*B*. A leader slug replacing frames of two adjoining scenes. The arrows indicate the line where the splice is to occur.

are not lost on a tape splice if the splicer if used to cut the film. Since the cut is on the frame line, a shot can be reconstituted by butting the two pieces together and taping them. To show that the shot continues straight through the slug without a break in the action, mark it as shown in Fig. 9.22*A*,*B*.

Repairing Damaged Film

A section of film may be torn or broken in such a way that it must be replaced with a slug. If the damaged section is small, lay it out on the table and mark the limits of the damage. In a small break, the frame damage may be calculated at a glance and frames of leader can be spliced in quickly; in cement splicing, however, extra frames of leader will be needed because part of a frame at each end will be lost.

With a longer damaged section, rather than trying laboriously to count frames over several feet of film, use the synchronizer to establish splice lines on both film and leader. Put the damaged part of the film in the synchronizer and roll left until the first frame past the end of the damaged film is in the sync frame. Then, put leader in the sync machine and scribe splice marks in sync on both leader and film. After scribing splice lines at this point, roll the synchronizer to the right until the other end of the damaged film comes into the machine. In doing this, you will also be pulling the same amount of leader along with it. Mark splice lines at this end exactly as you did at the other. Thus, the correct amount of leader is measured out in the sync machine, and when you splice each end of your scribe marks, the leader replaces the damaged film.

Cement-Splicing Negative/Original AB Rolls

Primarily, 35mm and 16mm splices on a single roll differ in one respect: 35mm splices are not visible when the film is projected; 16mm splices are always visible. If a print is made from a single roll of 16mm negative/original, each splice will appear on the screen as a brief horizontal flash. The reason is that 16mm frames have no space between them, and when the film is scraped from the splice, the scrape extends into the picture. One of the advantages of 16mm AB roll printing is that the splices are invisible in the print. To achieve this, carefully follow the correct procedure for splicing.

Assemble 16mm negative/original with cement splices. Splicing tape is not really transparent, and it increases the density of the frames it covers and changes their quality when printed. Unless some advanced development in film splicing occurs (which is quite possible), cement splicing of

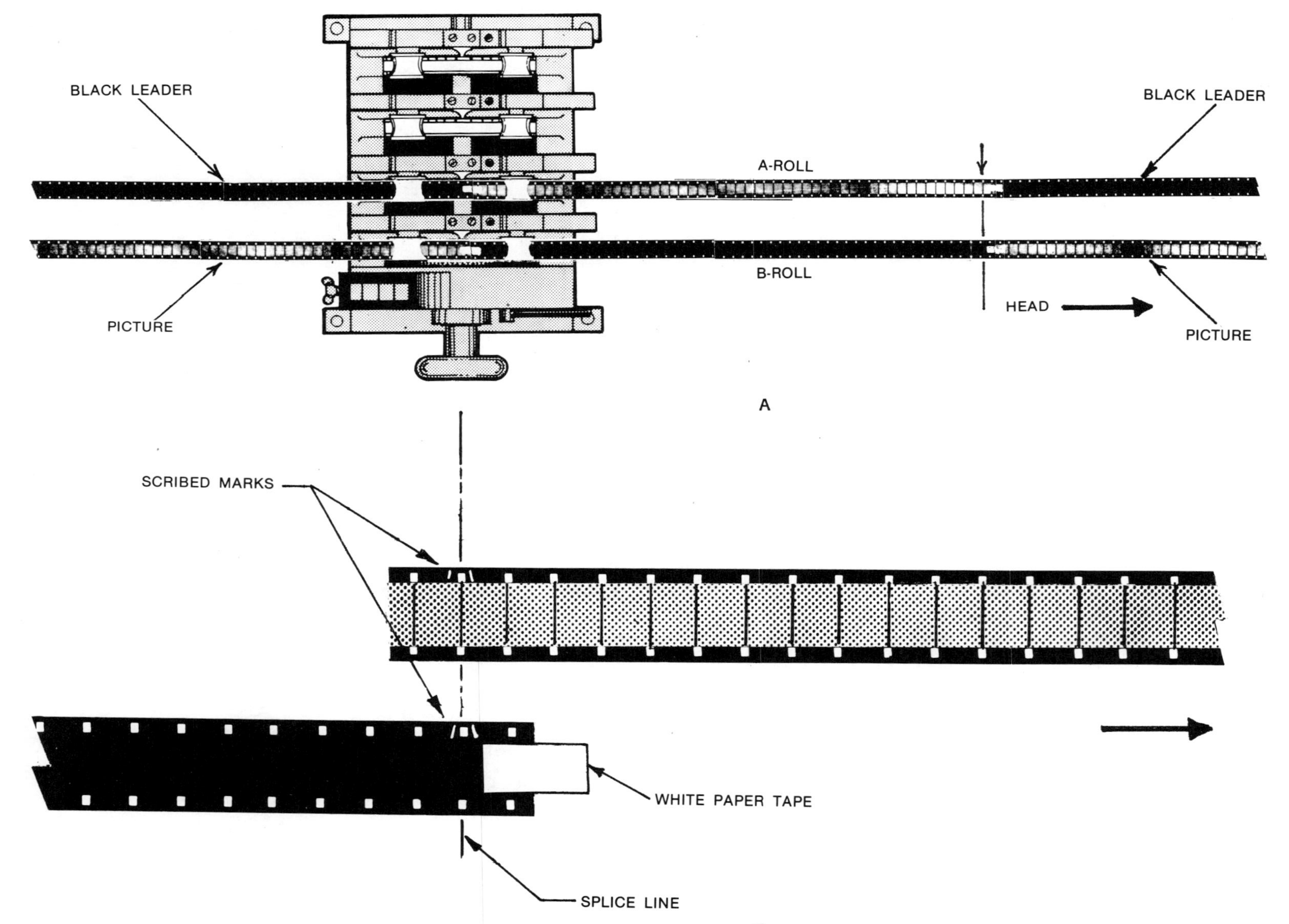

Fig. 9.23*A*. Negative AB rolls assembled with alternate pieces of black leader between each scene.

Fig. 9.23*B*. Diagram of cut and taped film ends of the A-roll, separated to show how they should be taped together temporarily before splicing.

negative/originals will remain the standard practice.

AB rolls are two rolls of negative/original that have been matched to the edited workprint. (See Negative Cutting, Chapter 11.) Each roll consists of negative shots alternating with lengths of black leader. During AB roll assembly, the negative cutter scribes the splice lines and tapes black leader and shots together so that the tail of each overlaps the head of the next. They are marked so that 1½ frames will be cut away in splicing (Fig. 9.23*A,B*). Notice that 1½ frames extend beyond the line where the splice is to be made. (Remember that any portion of a frame counts as half a frame) Actually the scribe marks are unnecessary, if you have made sure in negative cutting that every shot and piece of leader leaves 1½ frames (no more, no less) to be cut away in splicing. But scribe marks do reduce the chance for error since they are, in effect, sync marks.

Negative/original AB rolls must be spliced exactly as they have been set up without mistakes. Any error that changes the position of a splice by even one frame throws the picture out of sync with the sound track. In AB rolls such a mistake will result in a black frame between every other shot in the final print, so splicing AB rolls must be completely accurate. Thus, every splice must be made perfect on the first try. Perfect your splicing technique before attempting AB rolls. Preparation for AB roll splicing is as follows:

1. Be sure the room and the table are scrupulously clean.
2. Use a negative splicer that is clean and properly adjusted.
3. Wear clean, white editing gloves.
4. Start with fresh film cement in a clean bottle with a clean brush, and keep a supply of fresh cement available.

AB roll splicing procedure:

1. Put the roll to be spliced on the left-hand rewind. Thread the head leader onto a reel on the right-hand rewind. Wind until the tape that holds the leader to the first shot is in front of you.
2. Place the tail of the leader in the right-hand splicer head with scribe marks on the splice line.
3. Lock the blade down, lift the right-hand blade and cut off the end of the film.
4. Put the head of the picture shot in the left-hand blade of the splicer with the scribe marks on the splice line. Do not remove the tape, since it will be cut off with the extra 1½ frames when the right-hand splicer blade comes down. If the tape extends across the splice line indicated by the scribe marks, remove it because it will be in the way of the scraper.
5. Bend the end of the film down over the splicer blade.
6. Scrape off emulsion in one quick, sure movement. Avoid "sawing" the emulsion off.
7. Apply cement with one steady wipe of the brush. Too little cement will fail to moisten the film sufficiently; too much does not make a good splice and spreads to adjoining frames, partially dissolving their image.
8. Bring the right-hand splicer blade down immediately after applying the cement. The cement dries rapidly, and the two surfaces must be in contact before it begins to set. Let the blade set for 15 seconds before releasing it and proceeding to the next splice.

Never scrape the black leader in AB roll splicing, as this leaves a tiny opening at each splice that can print through as a flash. By scraping only the picture, any opening will be covered by black leader and will not show on the screen. Go through the roll, making splices only where the picture is on the left (every other splice). Then, without rewinding, put the roll back on the left rewind and splice through again. This time, since the roll has been reversed, only picture will be on the left side of the splicer and the film will thus be in proper scraping position.

DAILIES

The good camera takes are encircled and the bad takes are marked "NG" on the camera report during shooting. At the end of each day's shooting, the film from the camera is sent to the lab, where it is developed and only the circle takes are printed. These daily prints are called *dailies,* or *rushes* and, after being screened, they become the editor's workprint. (See Figs. 10.5, 10.6.)

For 35mm production, the laboratory customarily prints only the circle takes, but there are situations in which the lab is requested to print all takes, circle and NG. This generally occurs in 16mm shooting, when the cost of printing is worth having all the NG takes on hand. Also, printing everything precludes the additional physical handling of the negative/original entailed in the printing of circle takes. In a relatively short 16mm production, the additional cost may be almost negligible while in a 35mm theatrical production, printing all the NG takes may amount to many thousands of dollars. The decision to print or not to print everything lies with the person who pays the bills. To print only the good takes in 16mm, pick up the negative/original immediately after processing and remove the NG takes. Then splice the circle takes together and send them in for daily printing. (See Negative Cutting, Chapter 11, for procedure in pulling NG takes.)

When ordering daily prints of the camera negative/original from the lab, specify a timed daily or a one-light daily. The timed daily generally looks better because each scene in the roll has been printed at the light intensity which will yield the best print quality. The one-light daily is less expensive, but the photographic quality is often uneven throughout the roll. Any roll of camera negative/original sent to the lab for development and printing has many separate shots. The laboratory makes a one-light daily by printing the entire negative/original roll at a single printer light intensity. To arrive at the best light for one-light printing, the lab technician winds through the roll over his light table and keeps track of the preponderance of light or dark scenes. He then selects a printer light that will give the best exposure for the most scenes in the roll. If the cameraman's exposure were perfect on every shot, a one-light daily print would produce an entire roll of perfectly printed shots. Since the best of cinematographers is not perfect, however, almost every shot in a roll is either a little underexposed or a little overexposed. Thus, when a whole roll is printed with the light intensity set for an average, the rest of the shots will be either correct, overexposed, or underexposed depending on how accurately each was originally exposed in the camera. With a reasonably competent cameraman, exposures will be good enough so that a one-light print is usable in the editing room.

Timed Daily

In a timed daily, each shot in a roll is printed with its own proper printing light intensity. The *timer* is the laboratory technician who determines this intensity by first printing a test strip of eleven consecutive frames from each shot on a test printer. Here, each frame is printed with a light of a different intensity, the lights being numbered one through twenty-one to correspond to the twenty-one light intensities available on most motion picture printers. In making a test strip, only the eleven odd-numbered lights are used.

When the test strips have been exposed and developed, the timer sets them up in a row against a lighted panel and determines the correct light number for each shot. The numbers selected are then set into the control mechanism of the printer, and as the roll is being printed the preset control automatically changes to the proper light intensity for each shot. The resulting print is a timed daily. The test strips are also invaluable guides to the cameraman, who picks them up with the day's rushes, notes the lights his shots are printing on, and can judge their effect even when he disagrees with the timer's judgment. You might suppose that timing could be done automatically by some kind of photocell computer that records the total amount of light passing through the frame at any moment and sets the printing intensity accordingly. Such devices have been tried, but have not worked well in practice because of the psychological element involved in filmmaking. For example, a human face is often the object on which attention should be focused in a shot, even though this face occupies only a small part of the whole frame. An automatic device would time the shot for the average light intensity of the total scene. Only human judgment could then pick out the small wanted detail, the face, and time the shot to give it greatest prominence. Also, occasionally whole sequences of day-for-night scenes must be specially underexposed to produce a nighttime effect, and this too requires subjective judgment. Consequently there is no substitute for the timer's skill, and timers often work for many years to reach the top of their profession.

Usually a one-light daily is the best choice because it is the least expensive and serves as a guide to the camera exposure. The extra per-foot charge for timed dailies is worth it, however, when the edited workprint is to be used in screenings for people other than the editor. In this situation, you will want the best possible quality print obtainable particularly if approval of the picture or additional budget is at stake. (See Sponsor, Chapter 4.) Whether to order a timed daily or a one-light daily will depend on budget and circumstances. Although a timed daily is generally considered an expensive luxury, this will depend entirely on the circumstances of production.

Synchronizing Dailies

After the sync-sound scene has been shot, the picture negative/original is sent to the lab for developing and printing, and the quarter-inch sound track is sent to the sound studio for transfer to sprocketed magnetic film. The resulting sync-sound dailies, which consist of rolls of action and their corresponding rolls of sound track (most often dialogue), are then delivered to the editor. They are referred to as *action dailies* and *sound dailies.*

Since the picture and sound were photographed and recorded on two separate machines, each scene starts with the slate, clapper, and voice identification to provide reference points for synchronizing the two.

When starting to edit a scene, its sound and action slates and their sync frames are usually the first to be cut away. This leaves no way of syncing each shot as it is edited except by eye and trial-and-error in the editing machine, which is too tedious and time-consuming to be practical. So, before they can be screened or edited, they must be synchronized (synked) and sent back to the lab for coding. The coding machine prints an identical series of numbers along the edge of both action and sound. These numbers are printed serially every foot from the start mark to the end of the reel (Fig. 9.24). Effectively, code numbers become a foot-by-foot series of sync marks that enable the syncing up of sound and action even when they have been cut into small pieces. In large studios, these numbers are made to correspond to designations in the script, and are entered shot for shot in a log book maintained by the editor.

The picture slate at the head of each scene identifies in writing the production, the shot, and the take number. (Fig. 9.25) The slate assistant reads this information aloud, which records it on the sound track, and then slams the clapper board closed with a bang. This action is photographed on the film and is recorded on the sound track at the same time. The *first frame* in which the clapper touches the board (Fig. 9.26) is where the "bang" should be heard and is the *sync frame* for

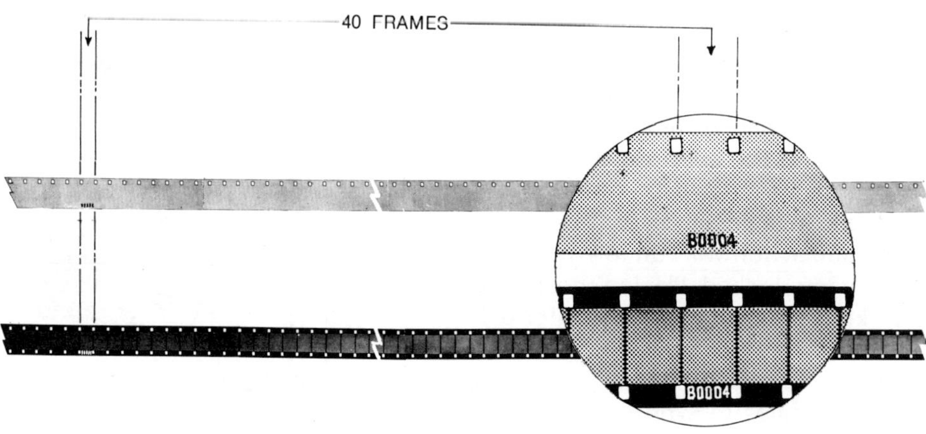

Fig. 9.24. Matching code numbers printed at either 40-frame or 20-frame intervals after sound and action have been synchronized provide sequential sync marks.

Fig. 9.25. The sound slate provides spaces for scene-to-scene information. The hinged clapper at the top of the slate is used to produce a loud bang at the beginning of each sync take.

the picture. The beginning of the bang on the sound track is the sync frame for sound, but since nothing can be seen on a magnetic track, it must be located by ear. Later, during negative cutting, when the final optical negative track is synked to the cut negative, the modulation of a *sync pop* will be visible.

To sync a shot, put the picture in the editing machine and run down to the sync frame—where the clapper first touches the board—and mark the frame with a grease pencil. Next, put the sound in the editing machine and run down until you hear the voice slate followed by the "bang." Stop the machine, back up ahead of the bang, turn up the volume, and move slowly forward by hand until you hear the very beginning of the sound. Stop and mark that point. The frames marked on the two pieces of film are the sync frames for that particular shot. If the picture sync frame is placed in the aperture of the editing machine picture head, and the sound sync frame in the sound pickup point on the sound head, the sound and action will run in sync when the two heads are interlocked. Placing these sync frames in any kind of double-system interlock will provide an in-sync playback (Figs. 9.27, 9.28).

Normally there is at least a full roll (and probably more) of dailies to sync up, a routine job usually assigned to an assistant editor. To sync dailies quickly, mark all the sync frames in the picture roll first, then mark the entire sound roll. After this, match them up in the synchronizer and mark for splicing. To sync dailies on the Moviola, proceed as follows:

1. Reel off the action film into a bin so that it is head out.
2. Put the head of the film in the picture head of the Moviola and run down to the sync frame of the first shot. With a grease pencil, mark the frame with a cross and write the scene and take number next to it.
3. Run through the whole roll, marking the sync frame for every scene and take.

Fig. 9.26. The sync frame of the slate is the first frame in which the clapper touches the board. It provides both visual and audible cues that may be used to put the sound track and the picture in sync.

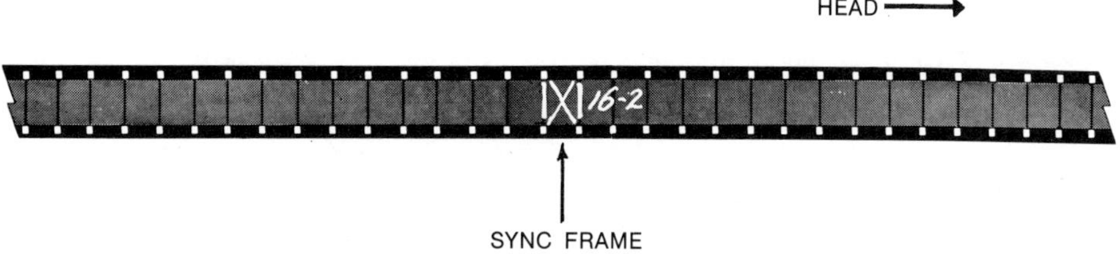

Fig. 9.27. The picture sync frame marked and identified as to scene and take number.

4. Rewind the film, head out, on a reel.
5. Reel off the sound film into a bin so that it is head out.
6. Put the head of the sound roll in the Moviola sound head and go through the roll, marking each sync frame with a felt pen.
7. Rewind the sound film, head out, on a reel.

Sync frames may be marked much more rapidly on a viewer and a sound reader than on a Moviola. To sync dailies on a viewer and a reader: Put the action reel on the left-hand rewind, thread it through the bench viewer and on to the takeup reel. Wind the roll through the viewer, stopping to mark the sync frames as they come up. Not being limited to the speed of the Moviola, you can wind rapidly between slates and thus speed up the whole job. Repeat the same process with a roll of sound film, using a sound reader or synchronizer equipped with a magnetic pickup head and speaker. Any kind of viewer and sound reader may be used for finding sync frames.

Syncing dailies on a horizontal editing machine proceeds about as fast as when done on the sync machine and viewer. Thread up the action and sound reels and go through each one inturn, marking and identifying each sync frame. Roll forward at high speed between slates.

Assembling Sync Dailies

After the sync frames have been marked on both sound and action for the entire roll, they should be assembled in sync and spliced with proper leaders for projection and sync-coding. The leaders and each scene, both sound and action, must be cut to exactly the same length (Fig. 9.29). This does not mean that all the scenes in each roll are the same length, only that the sound and action for any one scene must be of the same length. When they are spliced together, the whole roll of sound will be in sync with its corresponding roll of action.

Always set up the leaders first: double-perforated for action, and single-perforated for sound. Enough leader will be needed to allow for threading in the projector plus an ample amount for the interlock system to get up to speed by the time the picture hits the scene. (See Start Marks and Leaders.) Before sending film to the lab for coding, be sure to check for any special requirements the lab may have as to length of leaders and placement of start marks (Fig. 9.30).

Sync Coding

Code numbering machines are designed to print any four-digit number preceded by one or two letters. Any combination of letters or numbers may be specified. The leters available are *A* through *K*, with *I* and *J* omitted (Fig. 9.31) because they may easily be mistaken for the letters *J* or *I* or the number 1 when they do not print perfectly. This kind of error can create havoc in keeping track of many thousands of feet of film. For both sound and action, proceed as follows:

1. Pull off a little more than eight feet of single-perforated and double-perforated leader stock. Put them into the sync machine base up for sound, emulsion up for picture.

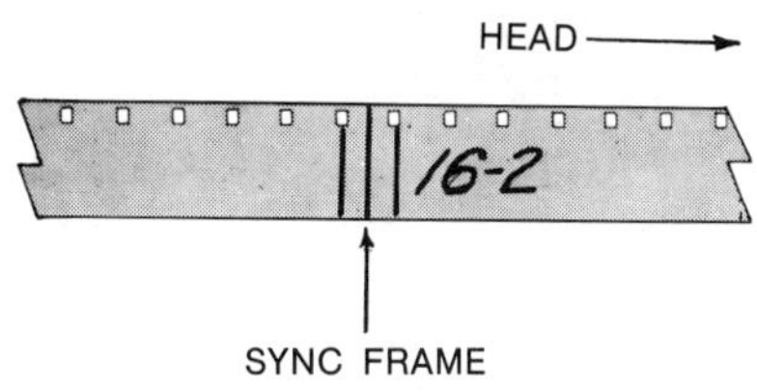

Fig. 9.28. The sound sync frame marked and identified as to scene and take number.

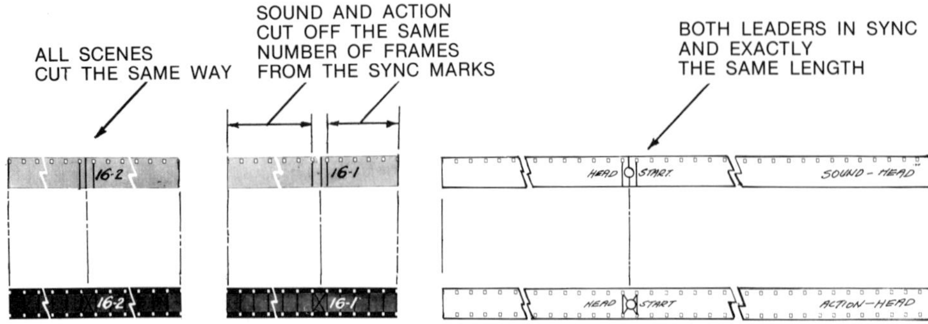

Fig. 9.29. For assembly, the sound and action for each shot must be in sync and of the same length.

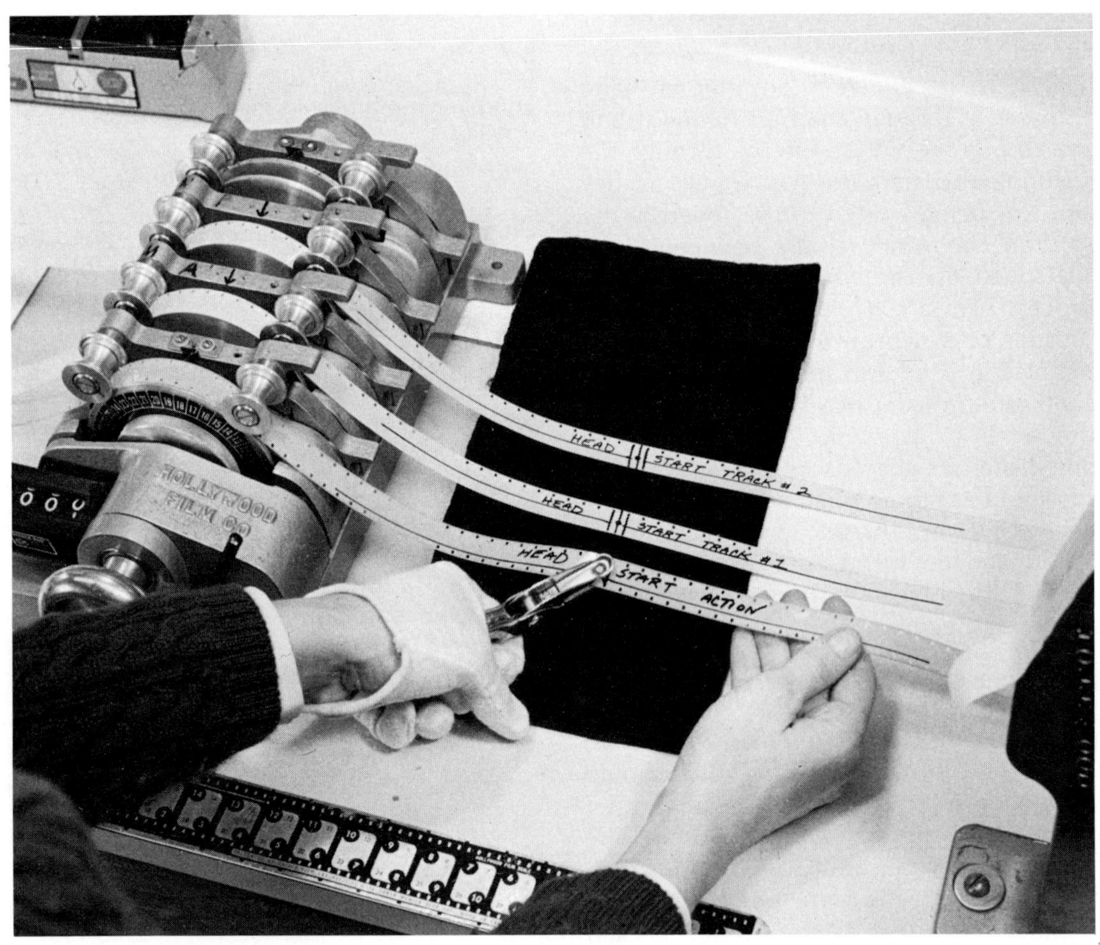

Fig. 9.30. Double-perforated picture leader and two single-perforated sound leaders synchronized, marked, and punched.

16mm	35mm
A 0000-9999	AA 0000-9999
B	BB
C	CC
D	DD
E	EE
F	FF
G	GG
H	HH
K	KK

Fig. 9.31. Code number combinations for 16mm and 35mm.

2. Mark identification at head of each leader.

3. On each put a code sync mark six feet from the head. Mark it *START CODE #A0001* (or whatever number and letter combination you choose).

4. Put splice marks two feet toward the tail from the START CODE mark. Splice marks must be the same number of frames from the START CODE, otherwise they will be out of sync after the splice. The leaders are now ready to be spliced to the assembled and synchronized sound and action dailies (Fig. 9.32).

To assemble the marked and synced dailies, put both sound and action reel heads out on the left-hand rewind. Put the synchronizer in the center, and two takeup reels on the right-hand rewind. Thread the heads of the two leaders on their respective takeup reels and roll them on to the reel as far as the tail splice marks. Put the sync frames of the first shot of action and sound into the adjacent rollers of the sync machine so they are locked in sync. Roll to the left to bring footage ahead of the sync frame into the synchronizer (Fig. 9.33*A*,*B*).

Mark the frame of picture and frame of sound that are opposite to each other in the synchronizer. These indicate where the splice with the leaders will be made. Cut off the film a few frames ahead of the splice marks.

Either make the splices, or tape each film to the tails of the leaders, but keep both films in the sync machine and wind the takeup reels until (at the end of the shot) the place where the director says "cut" comes into the synchronizer (Fig. 9.34*A*). A few frames farther, mark in-sync tail splice marks. Then roll down and cut the film off, leaving two to three frames (Fig. 9.34*B*). After cutting off the tails of the first shot even with each other, wind them up on the takeup reel so that they are off the bench and out of the way. Pull ahead the film that is still in the synchronizer until either a sound or action sync frame comes into the synchronizer. Since the footage between sound takes and action takes is never the same, the sync marks for this next shot will not be opposite each other (Fig. 9.35). Unlock the sprocket holding the film whose sync frame is not in the synchronizer and move the sync frame up into the machine. Make splice marks ahead of the sync frames and cut them off even exactly as was done at the head of the first shot. Continue through the rest of the rolls, cutting the heads and tails of each shot so sound and action are precisely the same length when their sync frames are in sync.

The shots and the leader may be spliced together as you go along, or the splicing can be done all at one time after synking and trimming.

Checking Sync

If splicing is done as you go along; the result will be two reels of spliced action and sound on the

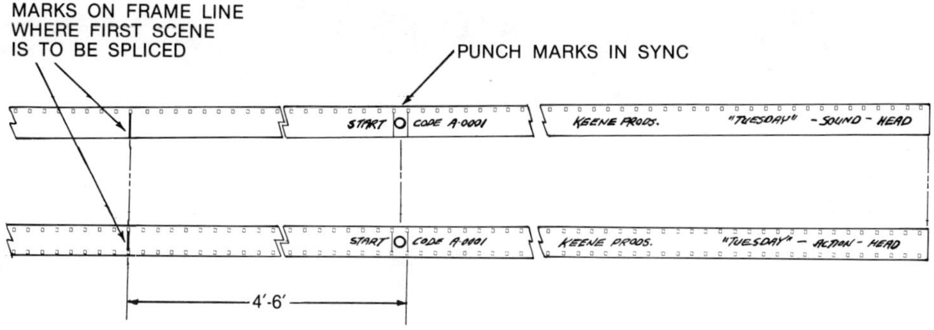

Fig. 9.32. Coding leaders in sync, marked with starting code number and marked for splicing.

right-hand rewind, tails out. Add tail leaders and make tail sync marks. Rewind the rolls through the sync machine to check sync. Make sure that all sound and action sync marks and sync frames are aligned with each other. Remember that if one scene is out of sync, all the scenes behind it on the same roll will probably be out of sync.

If the film is out of sync, check to see if a mistake was made in putting the film in the synchronizer by making sure that tail sync marks are aligned. If there was an error, correct it. If not, take the film out of the synchronizer, rewind both rolls to the head and place both start code marks in the synchronizer opposite each other. Roll down to the place where the rolls are out of sync. Then wind down past several sync marks to see if the number of frames out of sync is repetitive and constant. If it is, the removal or addition of the proper number of frames will bring the rolls into sync.

If only one shot in the roll is out of sync, readjusting or adding frames will only throw the other shots out of sync (Fig. 9.36*A*). To correct one shot without throwing the others out, remove the number of frames the shot is out of sync from one end of the shot and add the same number of frames at the other end (Fig. 9.36*B*). This moves your out-of-sync shot the correct number of frames in the direction you need, and leaves the shots on either side of it in sync (Fig. 9.36C).

Do not assume all is well because one problem has been corrected; check the whole roll.

Coding

After the dailies have been synked, spliced, and checked, put them on cores, heads out, emulsion up, then place them in a secure, adequately identified box or film can. Be sure that the lab

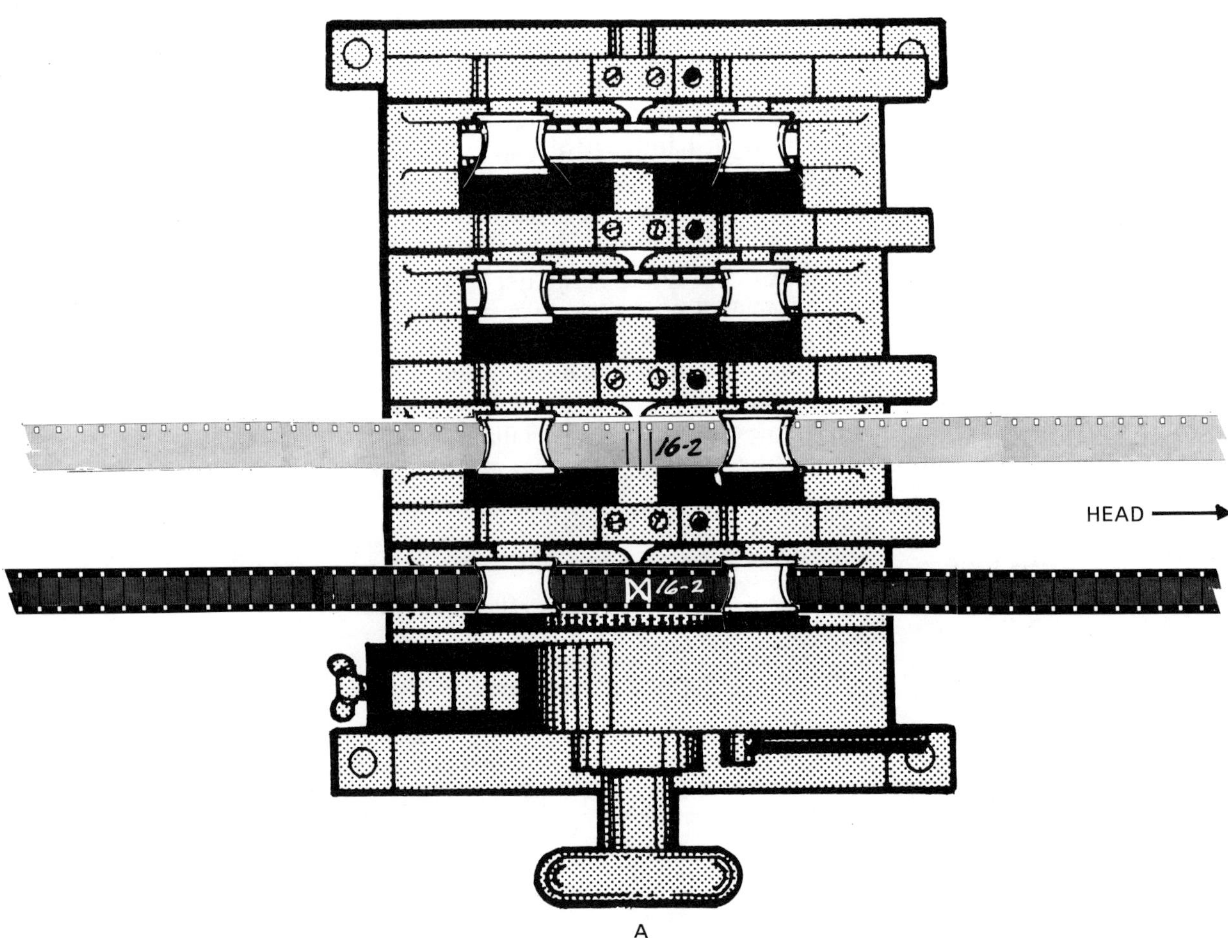

Fig. 9.33*A*. Sync frames of scene 16 take 2 picture and sound synchronized in the sync machine.

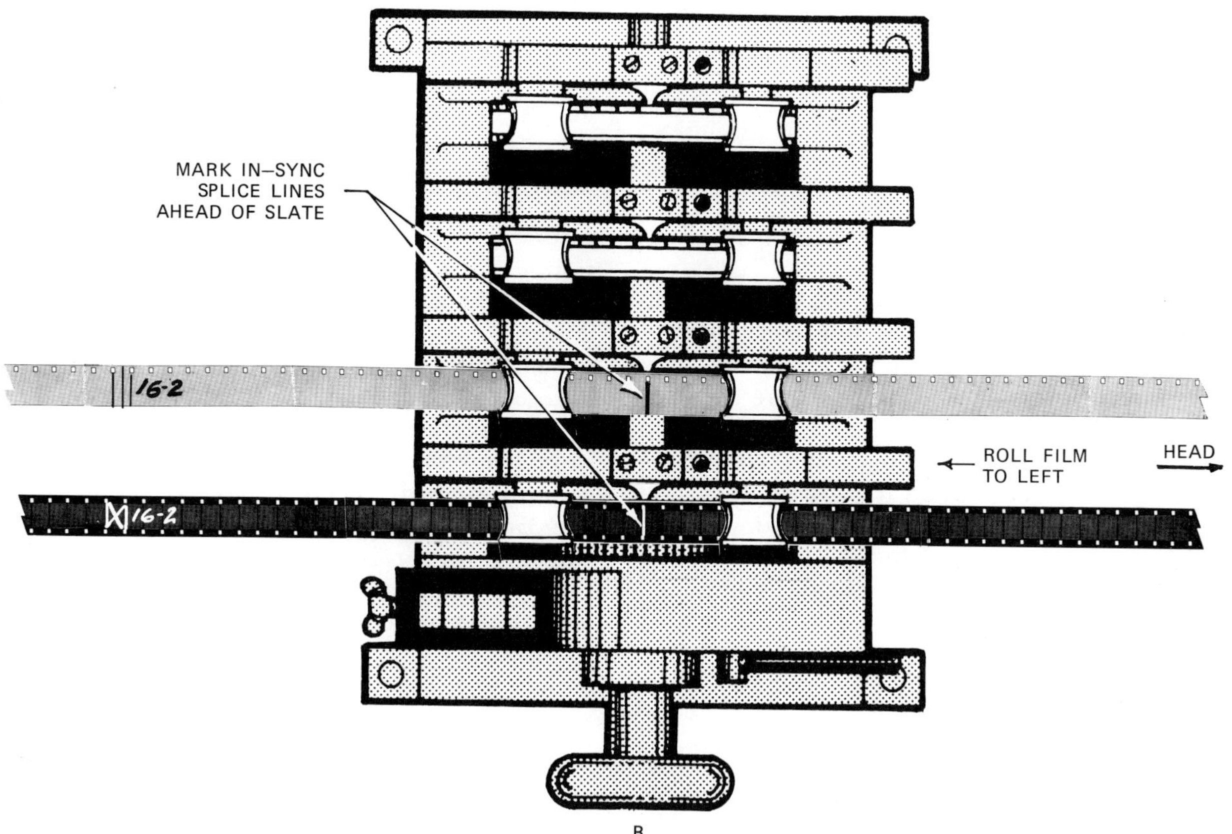

Fig. 9.33*B*. Scene 16 take 2, rolled to left in the sync machine so that splice marks may be made ahead of the slate.

order is in the can or attached to the outside. Keeping a log of code numbers is useful on small productions and essential on large ones. The form shown in Fig. 9.37 is representative of logs used in the film business. Scenes are not always coded in numerical script order, but rather in the order in which they were shot. This means that for large amounts of film the log must be arranged both by script sequence and by code number sequence. Devise a type of log that best suits your production and use it in the way that is most helpful.

Since the sole purpose of the many types of such paper work is to facilitate getting the job done, decide whether time spent in keeping logs and records is helping or hindering the production. This decision will depend on the kind of production, whether it is large and complex or short and relatively uncomplicated, and on the type of organization—large studio or individual filmmaker.

START MARKS AND LEADERS

Leader is blank film—film without a picture on it—used at both the head and the tail of action and sound workprints, cut negatives, and release prints. It is also used as a spacer between sounds in sound tracks, and between shots in conformed negative rolls. Properly prepared and marked leaders are essential in editing, interlock projection, coding, mixing, printing, and projection.

There are several types of leader stock, the most common being *lightstruck leader,* or the so-called "yellow leader," which is photographic film that has been exposed to light but not developed. Like film, it has an emulsion side and a base side. This is important to remember because leader emulsions must not come in contact with the sound head of the recorder or the playback machine. The base, or shiny side, of the leader must be spliced to the emulsion side of the sound film.

Clear, or "washed," leader is film from which all emulsion has been removed. It is transparent and is used primarily in negative AB rolls in fades and dissolves. Clear leader may be used as head and tail leaders on workprint and as filler in sound tracks, but it sometimes builds up static noise on the track and markings on it are difficult to read. Its main advantage is that it is inexpensive.

Black opaque leader is used to separate individual shots in reversal and negative AB rolls. During printing, this opaque leader holds back the printer light and prevents exposure between shots. Obtain black opaque leader only from a laboratory since its opacity must be quite precise for negative cutting. Since there is another kind of opaque leader used in laboratory developing machines that is not suitable for negative cutting, when buying black leader, specify its intended use.

SMPTE Universal Leader

The SMPTE universal leader, commonly known as *Society leader,* is a printed leader that is standard throughout the motion picture and television industries. There are two versions: one for the head of the picture and one for the tail. Society leader was designed jointly by the Society of Motion Picture and Television Engineers and the American Standards Association. During negative cutting, a negative or original of Society leader is usually spliced at the head of one of the rolls. It then becomes an integral part of the commposite print. Negative and prints of Society leader in both 16mm and 35mm are available at film laboratories. Since the 16mm version is a reduction of the 35mm, the two will differ in length but the number and relative location of frames is identical. Society leader provides certain information as well as space for other information

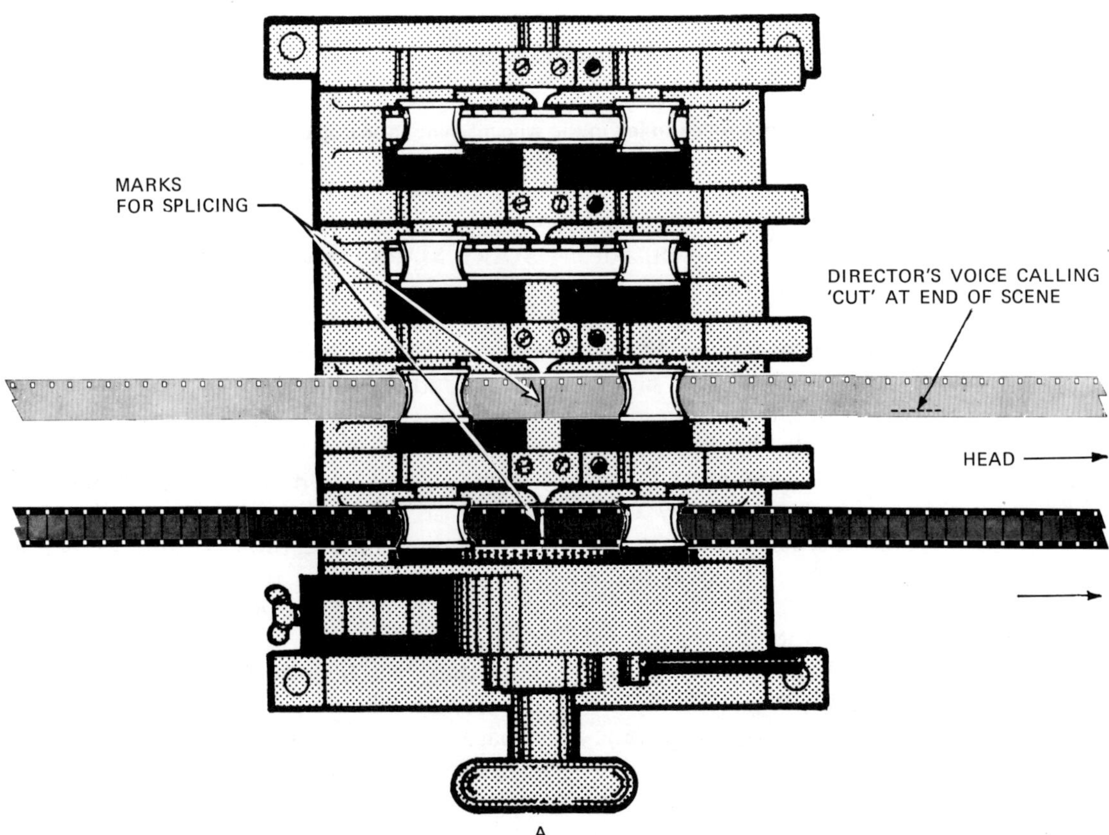

Fig. 9.34*A*. In-sync splice marks should be a few frames past the director's voice saying "cut." After marking splice lines, roll film to right.

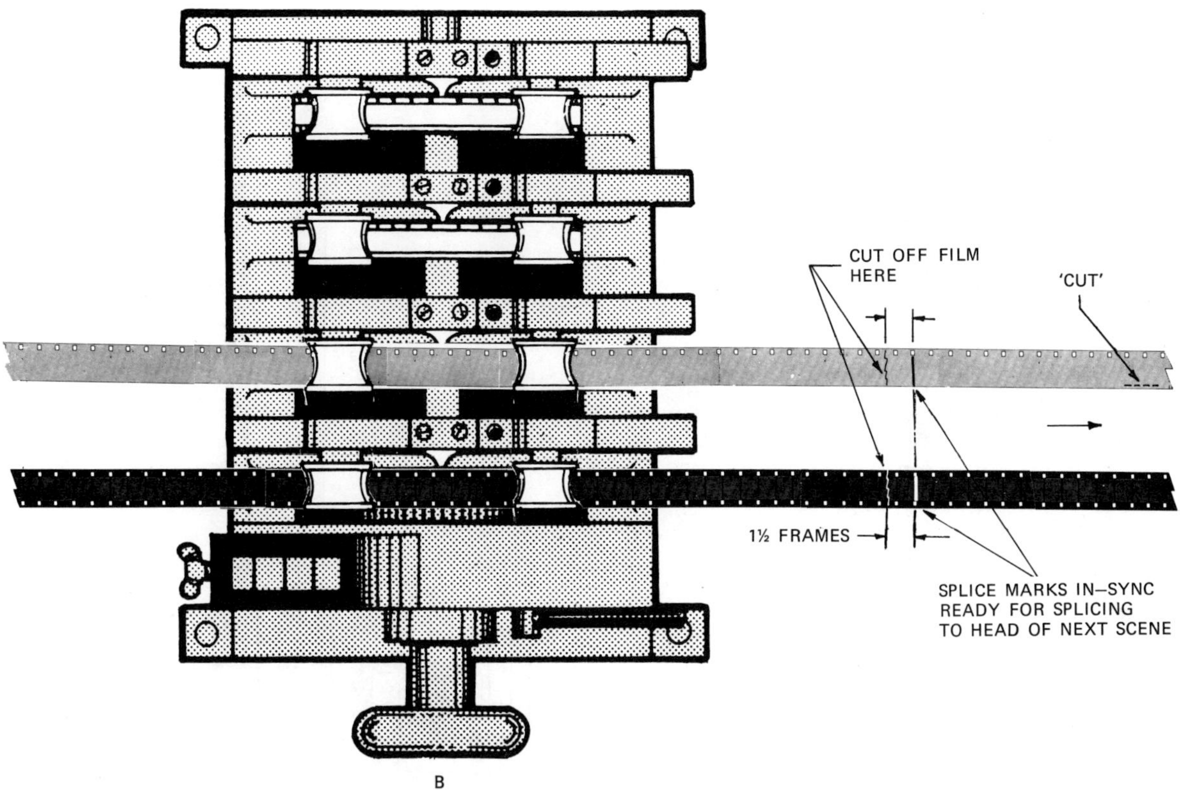

Fig. 9.34*B*. The scene rolled ahead, so that the tail may be cut off 1½ frames past the splice marks.

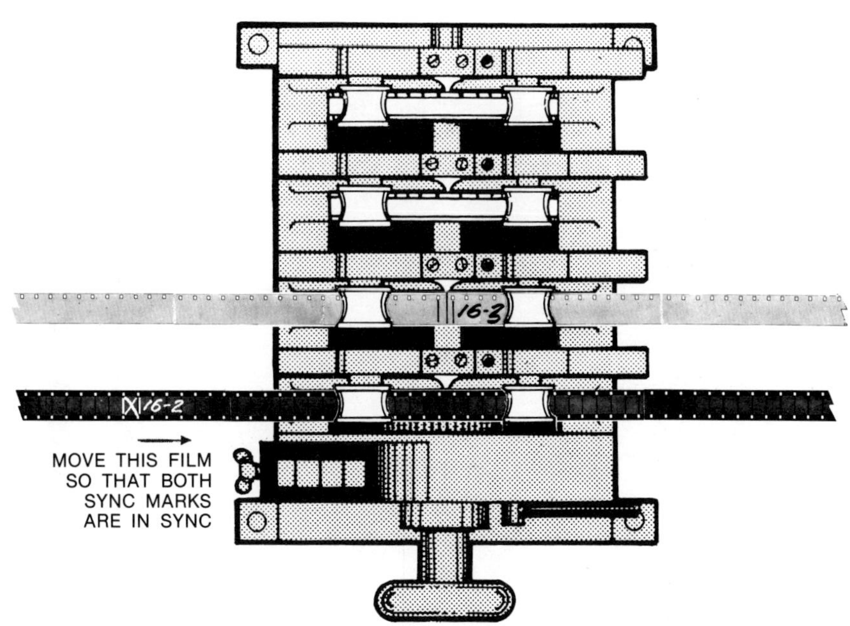

Fig. 9.35. Sync frame marks out of sync.

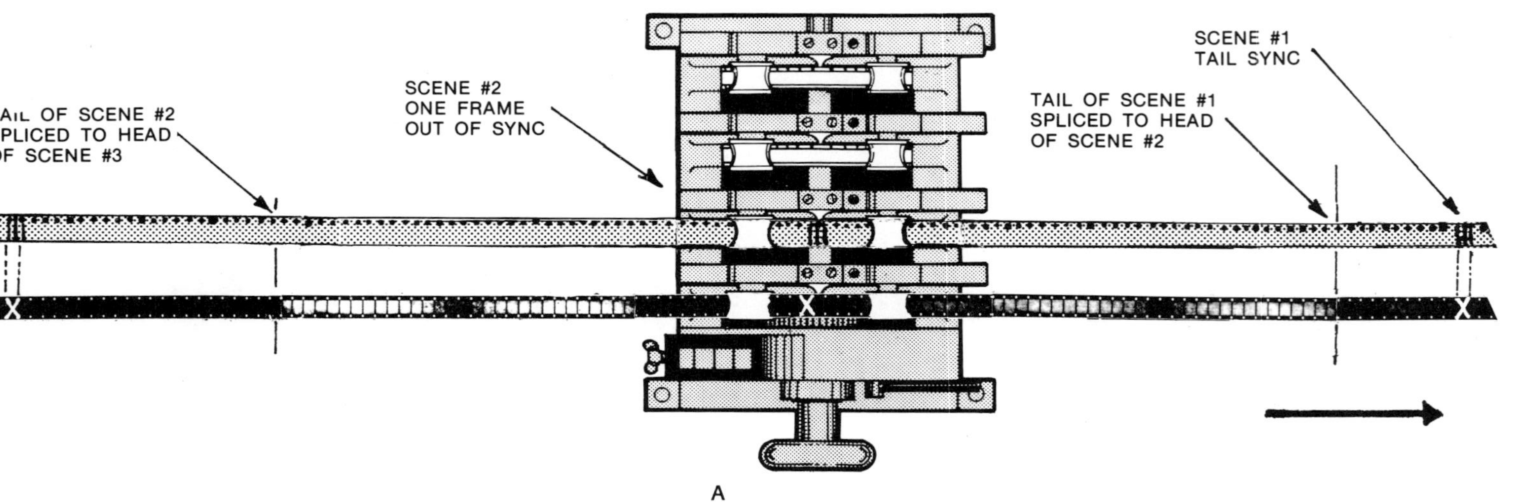

Fig. 9.36*A*. Scene #2 has one frame out of sync, while Scenes #1 and #3 on either side are in sync.

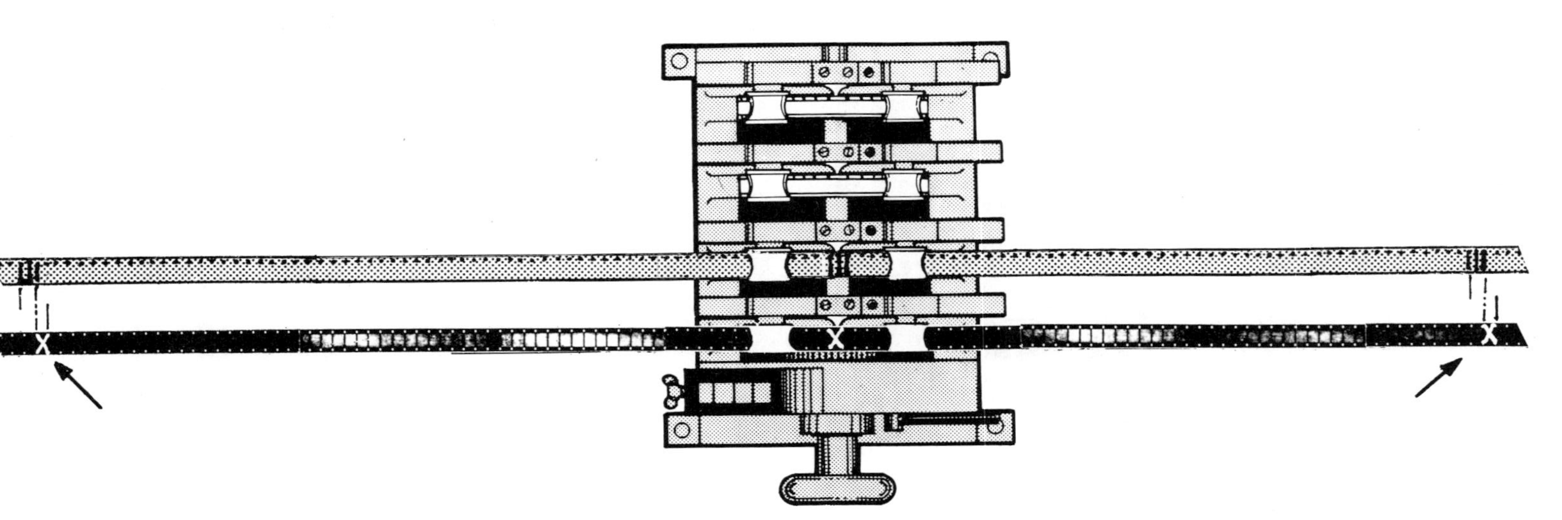

Fig. 9.36*B*. Correcting sync for Scene #2 throws Scenes #1 and #3 out of sync.

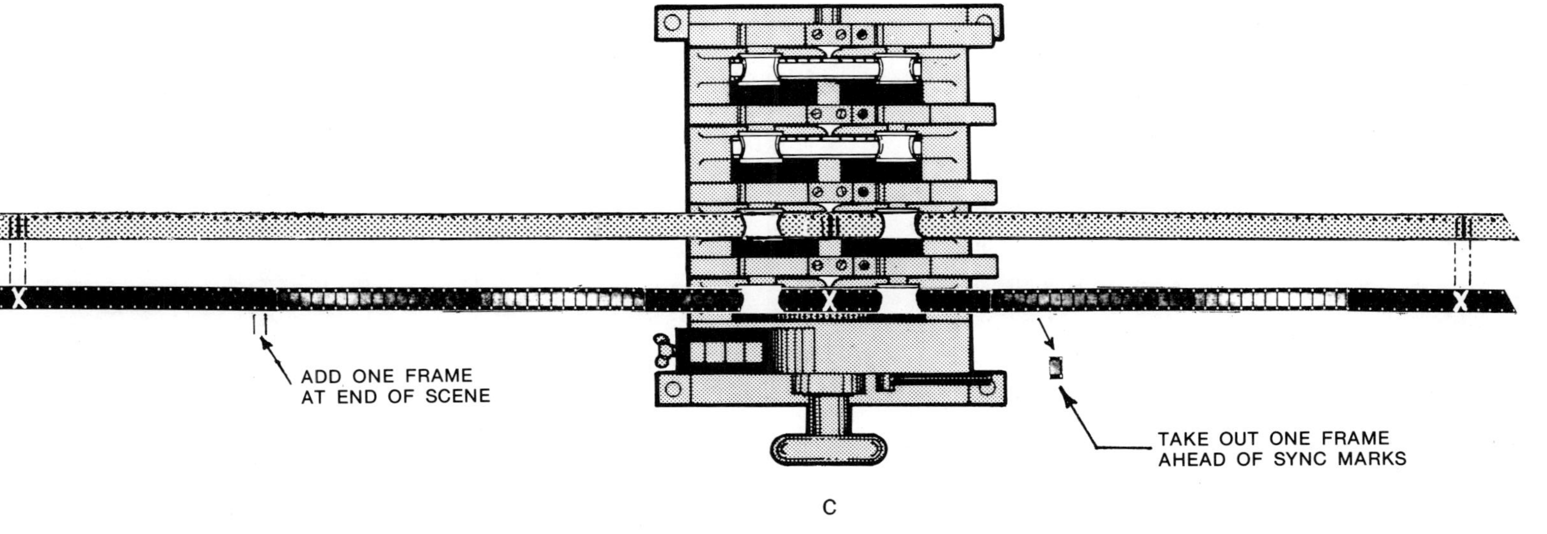

Fig. 9.36C. Sync may be corrected by taking out and adding an equal number of frames.

DAILY CODE LOG

PROD NO 348 TITLE "TOMORROW IS ONLY TUESDAY" DATE SHOT 12-17

SLATE NO.	CODE NOS. 1st & last	NEG ROLL #	NEGATIVE EDGE NOS.	NOTES
Sc3 T-2	B0004-0027	Roll #3	31/17 25 483 - 496	
Sc 21 T-1	B0028- 046	#8	31/11 13 245 - 287	
Sc 16-T-3	B0047-075	#2	32/17 21 152 -180	

Fig. 9.37. Typical code number log.

to be written in for printing on the composite print. The following describes the kinds of information included on the head of Society leader:

1. Marked frames on which to write the subject, length, reel number, aspect ration, and production name, all of which will be subsequently printed through to the composite print.
2. At the head, a printed arrow points to a frame line with the words "splice here." This is where the yellow head leader should be spliced. At the tail of the Head Society leader, at the end of the 48 black frames following the number 2, there is a frame line also indicated by an arrow and the words "splice here." This is where the first frame of picture should be spliced.
3. Frames 11, 12, and 13 are marked in this way:

[ ] [•] [ ]

These serve as a guide to threading up 35mm negative for printing in the darkroom.

4. Print-through cues for checking synchronization are provided by XXXX's and 0000's on opposite sides of the film.
5. Timing, or countdown. Printed numbers starting with 8 and going down to 2 represent seconds of time, each number being repeated 24 frames, or one second of screen time. Using these numbers as a guide, the projectionist may thread the Society leader in the projector so that he knows exactly the number of seconds it will take for the first frame of the picture to reach the aperture after the projector motor has been started. This is essential in cueing programs and in reel changeovers.

The formerly used "Academy leader," designed by the Academy of Motion Picture Arts and Sciences, is still found at the head of prints of older films. Its printed numbers start at 12 and go to 3, each number representing one foot of film. The 3 is followed by 48 black frames (two seconds) and the instruction "splice here" to indicate where the first frame of picture is to start. Academy leader is similarly used in cueing and reel changeover.

6. Between the numeral two and the first frame of the picture there are 48 black frames, so there will be two seconds of black screen just before the picture starts. The numeral one is accounted for but is not printed; if it were printed, it would occur in the black section. The frame line at the end of the 48 black frames is indicated by an arrow and the instruction "splice here," to indicate where the first frame of the picture should be spliced.
7. Control frames are marked with the letters C and F to indicate frames that may be removed and replaced by other frames for accurate framing information, technical checking, or duplicated test frames from the picture.
8. 35mm and 70mm magnetic cue positions are marked M 35 and M 70. Society leader may be obtained from the laboratory in negative original, or print. During negative cutting, a negative/original of Society leader should be included at the head of one of the printing rolls. It saves time and trouble to splice a print of Society leader to the head of the workprint at the start of editing when the head leaders are first made up. When starting to edit, assume that the Society leader is the first shot of your picture. (See Fig. 9.42.)

The Use of Leaders

The following are the kinds of leaders according to how they are used:

1. Protective
2. Editing and interlock projection
3. Coding
4. Mixing
5. Printing

Protective Leaders

During continuous routine projection, any roll of film will become worn. Sprocket holes tear, the film becomes brittle, and breaks occur. Most of this damage occurs on the first few feet at the head of the reel, since this is the part that is repeatedly threaded into reels, projectors, editors, and playback machines. To protect the head of any roll of film, splice on six to twelve feet of either lightstruck leader of special heavy-duty leader made explicitly for this purpose. Caution: If the film is 16mm, be sure to use single-perforated leader spliced so the perforations in the leader are on the same side as the perforations in the film. Replace this protective leader as it wears.

Editing and Interlock Projection Leaders

Leader at the head of a roll of film consists of three elements: the thread-up and identification section, the START MARK, and the run-up section.

THREAD-UP AND IDENTIFICATION SECTION

This is the part of the leader before the start mark that allows you to thread up the projector, editor, recorder, or playback machine with the start mark on the aperture or on the sound head. For both 35mm and 16mm film, the thread-up section should be at least six feet long. In 16mm, be sure that single-perforated leader only is used on sound tracks. Caution: If a reel of double-perforated 16mm picture contains any single-perforated film, the head leader for that roll must be single-perforated. The reason for this is that 16mm projectors, sync machines, recorders, editors, and playback machines are all single-sprocketed and can receive only single-perforated film in one position. Therefore, single-perforated film mixed with double-perforated film could easily be placed in a machine the wrong way and result in destruction of the single-perforated film when the unsprocketed portion hits the machine's sprockets. Single-perforated leader acts as a guide and ensures that a roll or reel is put into a machine in such a way that single-perforated portions are protected. Write identifying information on the run-up section of the leader. Include the following: HEAD or TAIL; Production name or number (Smith Prods. or Prod # ___); Reel number (R-1, R-2, etc.); Description of the roll (workprint, FX, Music, etc.).

The usual abbreviations used on leaders are as follows: Workprint: W/P; reel number: R-1, R-2, etc.; dialogue: Dial; narration: Narr; and sound effects: FX-1, FX-2 or FX-A, FX-B, etc. Mark the workprint and each sound roll with all identifying information.

START MARKS

A *start mark* is a marked or punched frame in a leader to indicate the starting frame for projection, printing, or synchronization. A start mark on the picture leader indicates the frame to be placed in the aperture of the editing machine or projector. A start mark on the sound leader indicates which frame is to be placed on the sound head for either editing or playback. Make a picture start mark by marking the outlines of the frame and making a cross. Make a sound start mark by marking three lines across the frame Fig. 9.38A,B. For positive visibility and permanence, most editors and laboratory technicians make a quarter-inch punch in the sync frame as well as marking it. Label each start mark with sufficient identifying information so that there is no doubt as to what it is. Remember, the start mark is six feet from the head of the roll, so some of the basic identification that has been marked at the head of the leader must be repeated at the start mark (see Fig. 9.39).

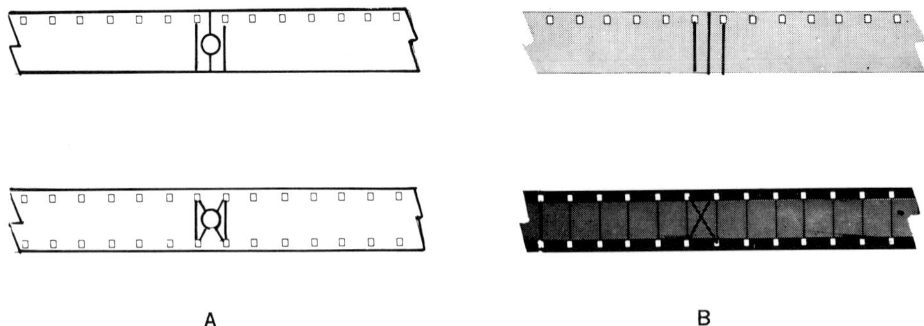

Fig. 9.38. (*A*) Punched start marks for picture leader and sound leader. (*B*) Sync marks on picture and sound film.

RUN-UP SECTION

The run-up section of the head leader is the part between the start mark and the first frame of picture. With the start mark in the aperture or on the sound head, the run-up section gives the projector or dummy time to get up to speed before the first frame of picture hits the aperture.

For editing and interlock projection, you should be able to thread the sound and action respectively in sync in the editor, the dummy, or the projector. For this, use a leader with six feet ahead of the start mark and at least six feet between the start mark and the first frame of the picture (See Fig. 9.39.) This arrangement will provide a set of working leaders to sync up sound and action in the editing machine and in the projection room during editing.

Coding Leaders (See Syncing Dailies, Chapter 9)

Picture and sound for dialogue or other sync-sound scenes should be coded before they can be worked with conveniently in the editing room. Coding is the in-sync printing of identical serial numbers on the edge of each roll of film, both sound and action. These numbers become sync marks at twenty to forty frame intervals. To set up for coding, first synchronize each shot as explained in the section on syncing dailies (Chapter 9). Splice all the shots in a roll with proper head leaders and send them to the lab for code number printing. Leaders for coding may be the same as editing or interlock leaders except that the desired code numbers must be marked beside the start mark. (See Fig. 9.40.) Six feet of

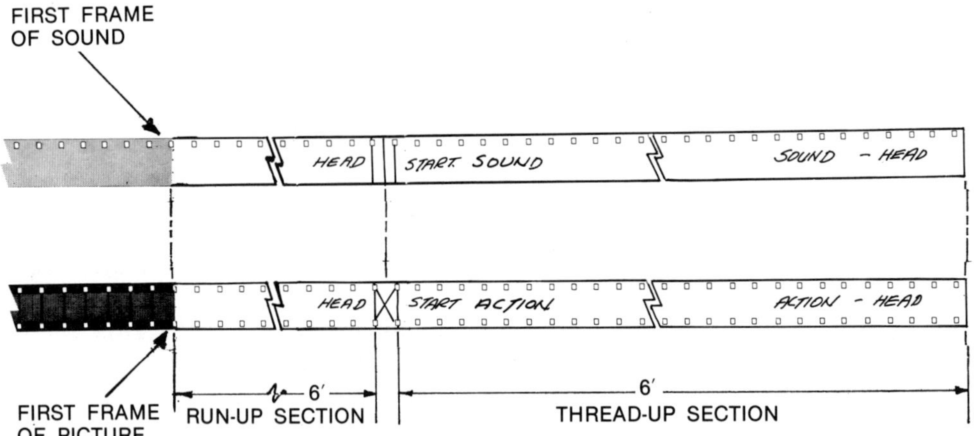

Fig. 9.39. Leaders should be long enough to allow threadup in the projector and runup to speed.

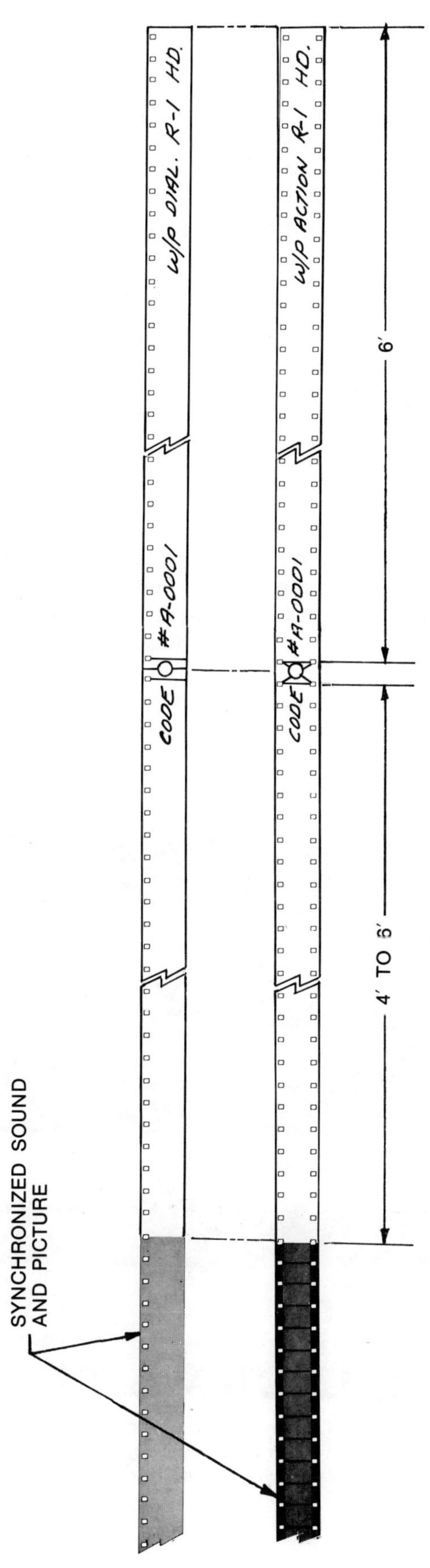

Fig. 9.40. Head leaders set up for sync coding.

leader ahead of the start mark and six feet following is sufficient. Some labs require only four feet from the start mark to the first frame of picture, but six feet is acceptable anywhere. Since the individual shots are usually broken down after coding, the leaders serve no further useful purpose.

Mixing Leaders

When ready to proceed with mixing, examine the condition and arrangement of the leaders on the workprint and all the sound tracks. At this point, you may wish to prepare the leaders so that no further leader changes have to be made and the picture can go right on through to final printing with the same leaders and start marks. Before making out the cue sheet for the mixing session, check the workprint and all the tracks for the following:

1. Splice a print of Society leader on the head of the workprint with sufficient yellow leader on the head of Society leader. (See Fig. 9.42.)
2. If a print of Society leader is not available, use an equal length of yellow leader in its place (260 frames). Mark the frame where the 2 would be if you were using Society leader.
3. Each sound track must have yellow leader equal in length to the workprint's Society leader and yellow leader combined. (See Fig. 9.44.)
4. Be sure that all start marks on the workprint and on all the tracks are in sync and are clearly identified.
5. Clearly and properly identify each leader.
6. Place sync pops on the leaders of the sound tracks in sync with the 2 on the Society leader. (See Fig. 11.38.)

The sync pop is a one-frame tone that produces a distinctive sound on the track. It is called by various names—sync pop, beep tone, sync tone, bloop—but they all refer to the same thing. The purpose of the sync pop is to put a visual mark on the optical sound track so it can be synced with the picture negative for printing the composite print. Recall that a mix is recorded onto a magnetic track, which must then be

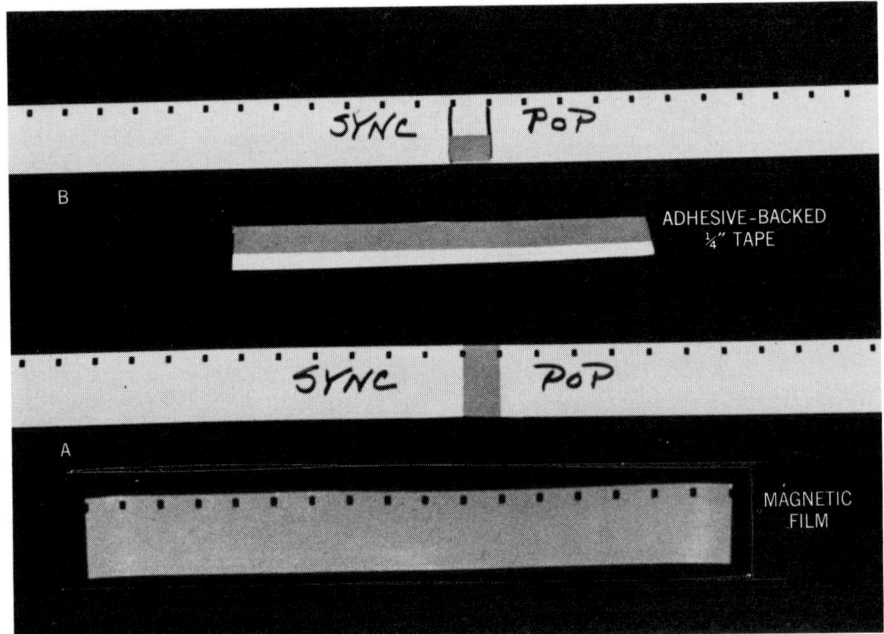

Fig. 9.41. Sync pop may be put on a sound track in either of two ways. (*A*) Remove one frame of leader and replace it with one frame of magnetic film sync pop in sync with the two on the Society leader. (*B*) Stick one frame of tape sync pop to the frame that is in sync with two on the Society leader.

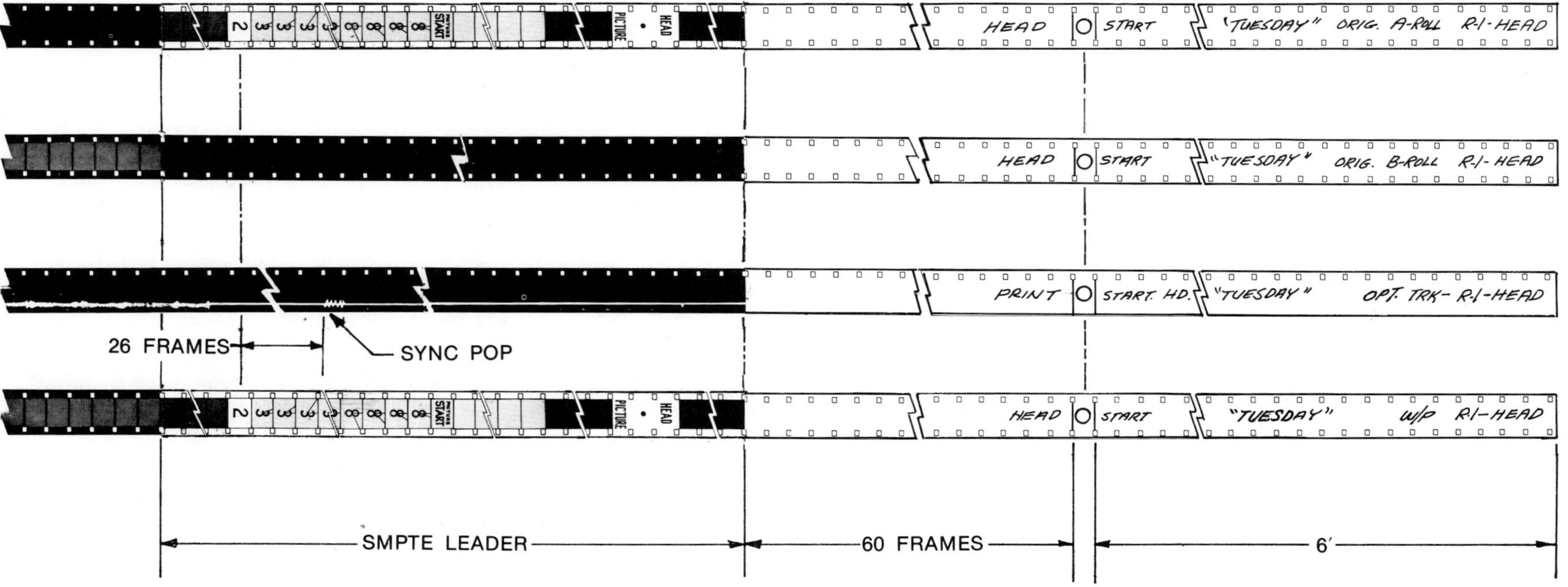

Fig. 9.42. Optical negative sound track and original 16mm AB rolls set up for printing in *printer sync* (workprint shown for orientation). The sound track start mark is made so that when it is in sync with the picture start marks, the sound is 26 frames ahead of the picture for printing. (Note: In edit sync, the sync pop is opposite the 2 on the Society leader.)

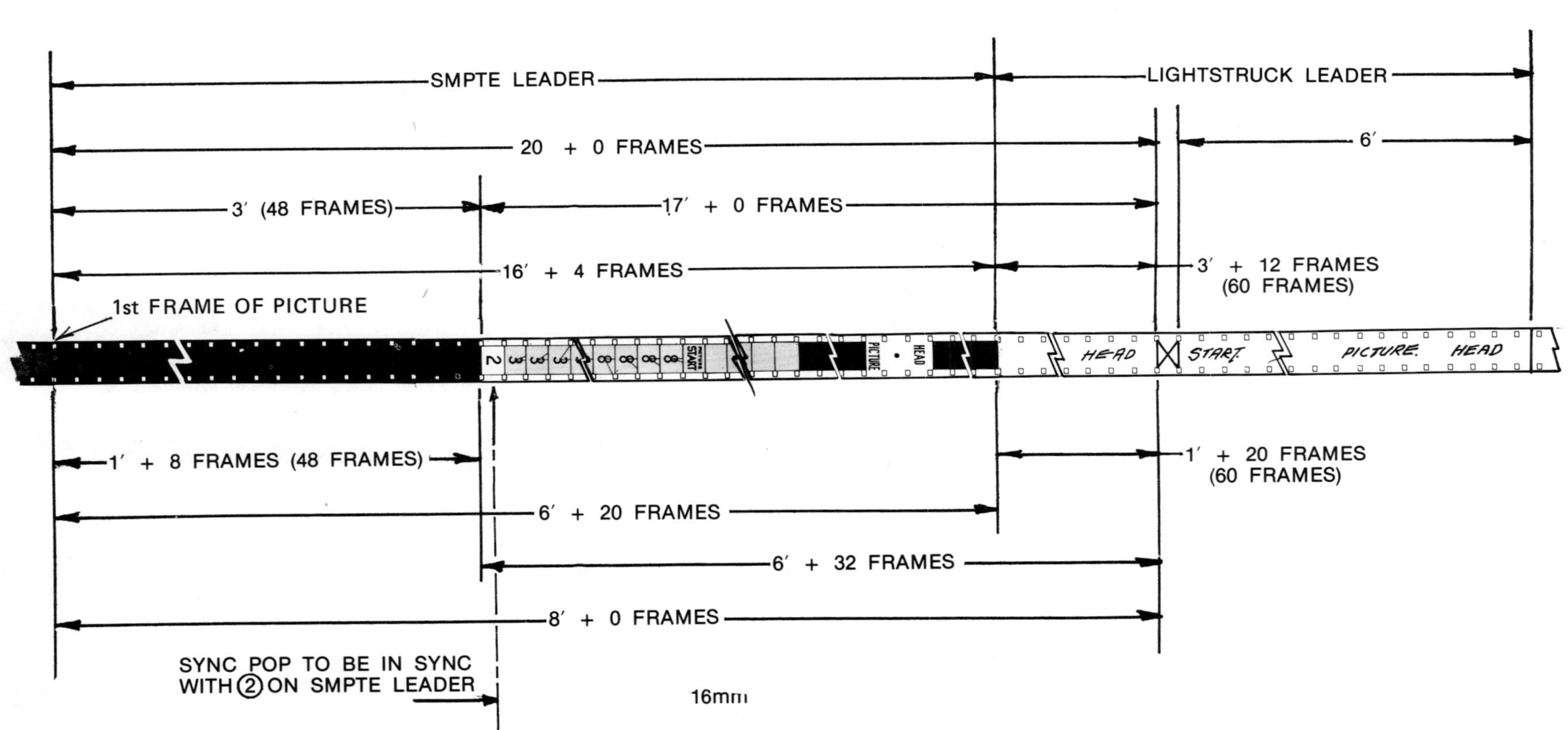

Fig. 9.43. A usable head leader standard (see Fig. 11.39) for mixing. The top figures are footage measurements for 35mm films; the bottom figures are footage measurements for 16mm films.

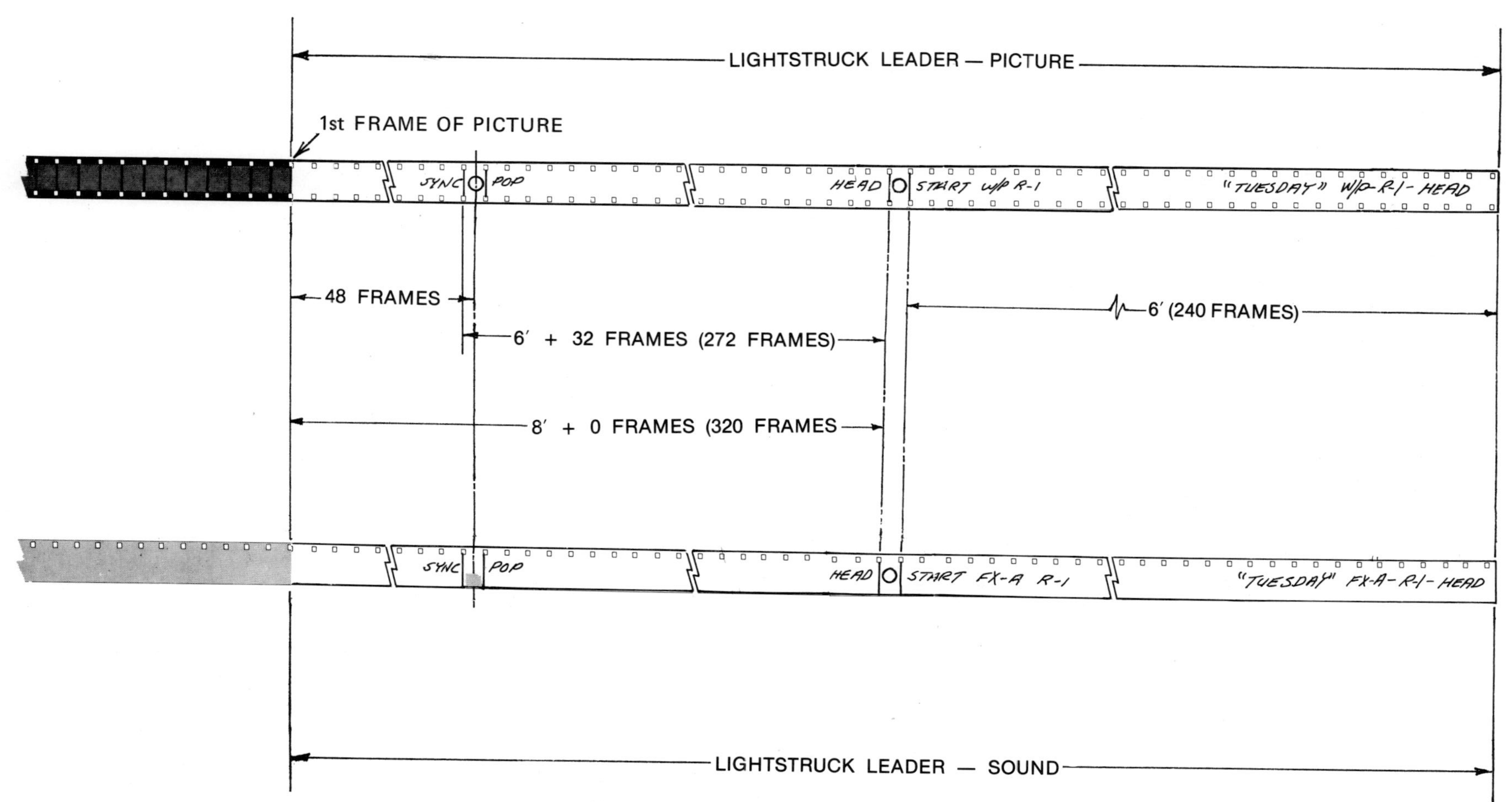

Fig. 9.44. 16mm mixing head leaders set up according to the standard shown in Fig. 9.43. The Society leader is not actually included in the workprint, but leader space has been allotted for it.

transferred to an optical track before it can be printed photographically on a composite print. The punched start mark on the magnetic track does not transfer optically, but the sync pop does and is visible as one-frame modulation on the optical track. If you have previously put the sync pop in sync with the 2 on the Society leader, the negative cutter merely has to sync the optical sync pop with the 2 on the picture negative roll, add a head leader, and mark it with a start mark to correspond to that of the negative picture. The negative and the optical track are then ready to be printed. Sync pop may be obtained from the sound studio on short pieces of magnetic film or on magnetic quarter-inch tape. It consists of a continuous 1000 Hz tone from which one-frame sections may be cut to be used as needed (Fig. 9.41*A* and *B*). To use sync pop that is on magnetic film, splice one frame of it into the sound track head leader so that it replaces the frame that is in sync with the 2 (Fig. 9.41*A*). Sync pop on quarter-inch tape comes with adhesive backing, so cut a piece of it the length of one frame and stick it to the leader in the sound track area of the frame that is in sync with the two (Fig. 9.41*B*).

Printing Leaders

At this point be absolutely clear about the distinction between *editorial sync* (also called *dead sync* and *cutter sync*) and *printer sync*. The two terms refer to the relative position of sync marks when sound and action are still on separate rolls of film. In editorial sync, the action and sound will be in sync when the sync marks are placed directly opposite each other in the sync machine (see Fig. 9.40). Thus, when the action sync mark and the sound sync mark are placed in the aperture and on the sound head respectively, the two will run in sync in interlock. Printer sync refers to the relative position of the action and the sound track as they will appear on the composite print of the film. A composite print is always projected on a projector in which the sound pickup head is a certain distance ahead of the picture aperture. In 16mm this *pull-up* is 26 frames; in 35mm it is 20 frames. That is, when a frame is projected on the screen, the sound for that frame is being played back from a point either 26 or 20 frames ahead of that frame on the film. The reason for this is that it is neither convenient nor desirable to design a projector in which the sound head and the picture aperture are at exactly the same location (Fig. 9.42).

Before sending the negative picture and optical negative sound track to the lab for composite printing, it is necessary to change the sync from editorial to printer sync so that the sound track will be printed the proper number of frames ahead of the picture. If you neglect to do this, or neglect to indicate on the lab order what kind of sync, editorial or printer, the negative and track are in, the first trial composite print may be printed out of sync. (For procedures in setting up printer sync, see Negative Cutting Chapter 11.)

TEN

The Mechanics of Film Editing

Motion picture editing is the process of selecting, rearranging, and assembling. Your job as editor is to select from many shots the ones you want and splice them together so that they say what you want them to say. It is bringing a new order to shots out of the random order in which they were photographed. Editing is the focal point of all motion picture production. As editor you will ultimately handle every foot of film produced. Initially you will work with large amounts of film from which you make selections and build a composite picture consisting of picture, sound, special effects, and titles. The job calls for a peculiar combination of mechanical dexterity and creative ability.

REQUIREMENTS OF THE EDITOR

The full extent of the movie editor's creative importance is not generally admitted. The editor is required to read the script and become familiar with it, to consult with the director, and to know exactly what the picture is supposed to do. He should understand nuances in meaning and be fully aware of the psychological implications of everything in the script. If the movie is a drama, he must understand the characters just as the writer and the director did, and he must try to steer them through their actions skillfully and sympathetically. If the movie is a documentary, the editor must understand the subject, and his feeling for it must be as strong as that of the writer and the director.

Since editing requires great manual skill, the editor is often considered merely a skilled craftsman rather than a creative artists. In fact, his role is consistently minimized by producers and administrators. Actually the editor is a creative contributor who is largely responsible for the excellence of the completed movie. Every good editor, at one time or another, has made a hero of his director or producer.

In editing you work with tractable individual shots. By intercutting, shots of a crying child, soldiers running and shooting, and a burning hut may be combined so that the audience thinks the child is a war victim. Yet the shots may be entirely unrelated. The shot of the child may be an isolated one made almost anywhere, that of the soldiers could be military maneuvers shot five years earlier in Australia, and the burning hut that of a peacetime accident in Tucson, Arizona. The way these shots are put together, along with the particular sound effects selected, determines what the audience will feel and believe. The power to create an illusion of reality out of nothing makes the motion picture possibly the greatest propaganda and story-telling device known to man. Through editing, you can, in spite of the truth, create the illusion of reality in stories, news reports, educational movies, documentaries, business movies, sales movies, political movies, and TV commercials. A well-stocked film and tape library will provide the raw material for any interpretation of world and human affairs desired, without regard to outward actuality or inner truth. This obvious characteristic of motion pictures—that putting two shots and their accompanying ideas together will result in a third, completely new idea—is the power of a film editor, who is really a kind of magician.

Some people, particularly scientists, claim that motion pictures can, and should, present reality as it is. This can be achieved in only a few situations, such as in static recordings of tests and the like. But actual reality has little to do with motion picture reality other than supplying visuals that look real. As movie director or editor, you must always be conscious of this: what actually is and what goes on outside of the frame are not pertinent to the editing. For some moviemakers, conscience dictates that they present things honestly. Others happily use the movie to make the most magnificant lies believable.

As editor, your job starts with a mass of raw material in the form of individual shots. But a medium with such immense capacities for building a new framework of reality is more than a mere assembly of scenes in the order in which they were shot. The last shot may have been made first, the middle section at the end, and the beginning shot in the middle. Editing consists of assembling and splicing these shots together in whatever order you choose to create the desired impression. Select shots, reject others, use only a few frames from a shot many feet long, insert parts of shots into other ones, reverse the order of things and ignore actual time, actual continuity, and actual reality.

GENERAL PRINCIPLES

Throughout the production of a motion picture, the sound and the picture are on separate pieces of film until editing is complete and the negative is ready for release printing. The picture is called the *action,* and sound is called the *track*. There are four kinds of sound—dialogue, narration, music, and sound effects. Some pictures will have all four, others one, two, or three in almost any combination. Dramatic movies usually have dialogue, music, and sound effects, and often whole sequences use only one type of sound. In one distinguished example, the French *Rififi,* there is a twenty-minute sequence accompanied only by sound effects as a team of thieves quietly cut their way through the concrete ceiling of a jewelry store.

EDITING PHASES

In editing, the task is to assemble the picture and its matching sound tracks. In cutting a narrated documentary, you will be working initially with only the action and the narration track. Later, music and sound effects in turn must be assembled to fit the action. Film editing entails the following five main phases or tasks:

1. *Picture editing.* Editing the workprint of the picture and its principal sound track.
2. *Sound effects editing.* Selecting and ordering sound effects and synchronizing them with the edited action.
3. *Music editing.* Selecting suitable music and synchronizing it with the edited action.
4. *Mixing.* Blending all the sound tracks—dialogue, music, narration, and sound effects—and recording them together on one track.
5. *Negative cutting.* Matching negative film to the edited workprint to arrive at a printing negative from which multiple release prints can be made.

How the major editing jobs are assigned and carried out depends on the kind of organization involved.

STUDIO ORGANIZATION

A film editor may work in any one of five types of organizations. In each the main task is the same—to complete a movie—but the working conditions, limitations, and rewards are entirely different. The following are the types of organizations:

1. Major studio production
2. Independent feature production

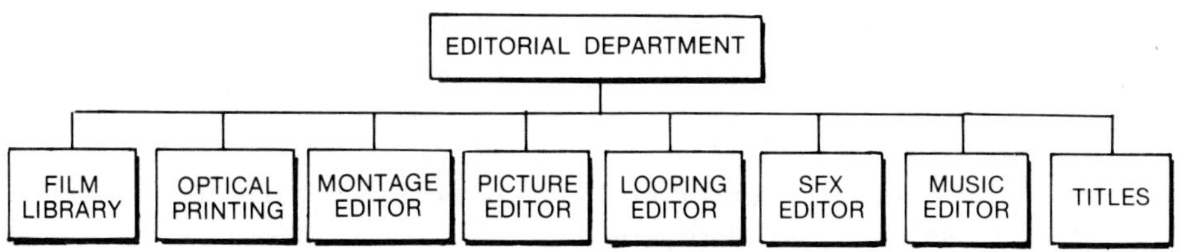

Fig. 10.1. Representative film editing department organization in a large studio or production company.

3. Small or documentary production
4. Animation
5. Individual filmmaker

Major Studio Production

In a large motion picture studio, editing is usually centralized in an editorial department, which in turn is broken down into smaller, specialized departments (Fig. 10.1). In this characteristic "big" setup, the editing process is conducted very much like a production assembly line. The editor is assigned a picture to cut. When he has finished, the music cutter and the effects cutter go to work on copies of the edited workprint. Simultaneously the looping department prepares picture loops for a dialogue replacement session; the optical department begins making dupe negatives for special effects; and the title department sets up and shoots the main and credit titles. The various elements are finally brought together, the sound tracks in the mixing session, the picture elements in negative cutting, and both sound and picture in release printing. The motion picture is a manufactured product, and each subdepartment performs its specialty without necessarily being intimately aware of what the others do. Large studios are really film plants, since they must operate with production-line efficiency for survival. Creative talent tends to be stifled under regimentation because the creative enthusiasm that usually exists in small independent units or in one-man productions is missing.

Independent Feature Production

In independent movie production, editing is less a departmentalized procedure and more of a creative process. Instead of being a member of an editing department pool, the editor works directly for the producer and hires his own effects editor, music editor, assistants, and apprentices (Fig. 10.2). This group becomes a more closely knit company and can operate at great speed unencumbered by departmental red tape and politics. Creative talent and enthusiasm have more opportunity for expression and are contantly encouraged.

Small or Documentary Production

In the small production company, the creative contribution of the editor often appears greater than in a large studio, especially when he is called on to put together a movie from existing footage before a script has been written. Many documentaries are made this way, using film from many sources—newsreels, expeditions, stock libraries, and so on. The editor on this kind of movie needs a certain sensitivity to be able to evaluate the individual scenes and arrange them in a continuity that is effective. The writer then composes narration to the edited footage. Often on this kind of documentary production, the editor and the writer or the editor and the producer work together as the movie is assembled. If the script has already been written, it is the editor's job to select suitable footage to fit.

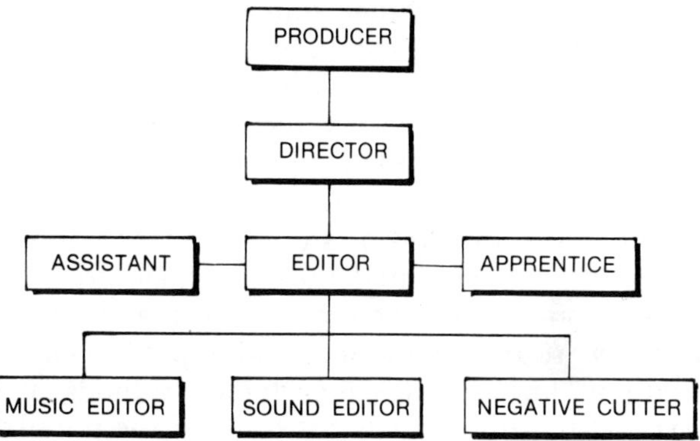

Fig. 10.2. Representative film editing organization for an independent producer.

Documentaries and movies for education, business, industry, and government are usually made by the smaller organizations known as "commercial" producers as distinct from "entertainment" producers. The people in such companies work together closely, usually with enthusiasm and cooperation. The editor may or may not have a music cutter, an effects cutter, and assistants, depending on the size and wealth of the organization.

Animation

The job of the animation editor is quite different from that of the live-action editor. Initially he "reads" the dialogue and music tracks and makes notations on bar sheets of the exact placement of each bit of sound. These sheets are used as a guide for animation. Since animated movies are photographed frame-by-frame according to carefully plotted exposure sheets, they are in a sense preedited. The animation editor functions more as a sound effects and music editor. After photography, he adds the sound effects, puts all tracks in sync, and prepares the tracks and cue sheets for mixing.

Individual Filmmaker

At the opposite pole from the big studio editor is the individual moviemaker who does everything himself not only because he has to but because he wants to. Most young moviemakers feel that they must do everything or it isn't their picture. This attitude is a necessary ingredient for the production of any work of art, but the length and scope of the picture determine just how much you can possibly do alone.

Regardless of whether editing is done in a big studio setup or by the lone artist-moviemaker, specific tasks must be performed almost the same way to arrive at a finished picture. Action has to be shot, sound recorded, and both edited. Tracks must be mixed, negative cut, and the release print made. In a major studio, all these operations have been fitted into a formal structure based on standardized procedures and terminology. You can be a fine motion picture editor without knowing specific studio methods and jargon, but the industry has fostered the popular impression that motion picture editing is an esoteric and complicated ritual available only to the few gifted editors in and around Hollywood. It is not. Almost the entire editing process is mechanical and can be learned by anyone, but it takes more than mere mechanics to turn out truly worthwhile pictures.

PICTURE EDITING

Preparation for Workprint Editing

When the dailies come back from the laboratory, leave the negative/original in the lab vault until you are ready for negative cutting. Do not keep the negative/original in the editing room or in a closet at home. Before actually assembling the workprint, several preparatory tasks are necessary. Tailor these tasks to fit your production. If there is no sync sound, you will not have to sync the dailies. If you are a lone filmmaker, the shot list may be eliminated. The following are preparatory steps to the actual cutting and assembly of your movie:

1. Logging negative edge numbers.
2. Synchronizing the dailies and assembling them in continuity.
3. Screening the dailies.
4. Preparing a shot list.
5. Reviewing the workprint critically.
6. Breaking down the workprint.
7. Making up head and tail leaders.

Logging Negative Edge Numbers

The daily rolls of workprint as they come from the lab will be exact duplicates of the negative/original from which they were printed. Consequently, all the negative edge numbers on the print will be identical to those on the rolls of negative/original. (See Fig. 11.7.) Writing down the first and last edge number of each roll provides a record of the numbers on the negative/original rolls without having to handle them (Fig. 10.3). However, this can be done only if no cuts have been made in the daily rolls. Once they have been cut or rearranged, they are no longer identical to the negative/original. Such a list becomes a negative roll list and enables you to determine the precise roll position of any shot in the dailies. Do not, however, confuse the

NEGATIVE EDGE NUMBER LOG

NEGATIVE ROLL NO.	
#1	J1/16 32 605 - 33005
#2	J4/13 27 500 - 27 900
#3	J1/87 15 322 - 15 422
#4	J5/78 14 644 - 15 045
#5	J1/17 21 073 - 21 472

Fig. 10.3. Negative edge number log.

designation "roll" with the actual roll returned from the lab. The roll number refers to the number assigned to the roll of film in the camera at the time of shooting. It should have been slated with a roll number, which should appear on the slate at the head of each camera roll. For convenience in printing, the lab often assembles two or more 16mm camera rolls into one large roll. Thus several individually numbered rolls of camera negative/original may be physically collected into one "roll." This means that two or more slated rolls must be identified out of a larger lab roll.

If roll numbers were not slated during shooting, lab rolls may be numbered arbitrarily and the inclusive edge numbers listed. It may seem tedious and unnecessary to record edge numbers by rolls, but it can save a great deal of time and trouble later as well as prevent too much handling of the negative/original. If a reprint of a scene or a duplicate for optical effects is needed, the proper negative/original roll can be located easily and quickly to pull the shot desired.

Normally the lab prints dailies with a full aperture so that the negative edge numbers, or key numbers, print through to the dailies. Occasionally, however, the numbers do not print through or are undecipherable. If this occurs and the dailies do not have key numbers on them, immediately set them up in sync with the negative/original and order the lab to sync-code the dailies and the negative/original together. (See Syncing Dailies.) Although this entails handling the negative/original, which is risky, lacking a method to match the negative/original to the workprint will cause serious trouble later. Without key numbers or negative-positive code numbers, you will be forced to match by eye, which can result in much unnecessary handling of the negative/original and is also expensively tedious, time consuming, and sometimes almost impossible to do.

Syncing the Dailies. (For a detailed account on how to sync dailies, see Basic Operations.)

Screening the Dailies

The creative job of the editor begins with screening the dailies. As soon as possible after coding, view them projected on the largest theater screen available. If the picture is sync sound, sync the sound and action before screening. On a large screen, defects are visible, a tentative mental image of how the scenes will look on the screen is possible, and certain shots may be eliminated at the outset. During the first screening of the uncut dailies, make tentative decisions and start editing the picture in your mind. You may wish to take notes, and may find it helpful to look at the dailies many times before going into the cutting room. Be sure to makeup proper leaders before screening dailies. (See Start Marks and Leaders.)

Preparing a Shot List

After viewing the dailies (workprint) on a screen, look at them on the editing machine and prepare a shot list that identifies each shot as to scene number, take number, description of the action, screen direction of the action, length of the shot, and any other pertinent information (Fig. 10.4). Even in a short movie, the number of scenes and takes can quickly become confusing. After breakdown it is easy to forget or mislay a shot, and a shot list is a ready reminder of exactly what has been done. Make a detailed description of every

SHOT LIST

Sc1 T-1	MS Motorcycle on highway PAN R to L 22'
Sc1A T-1	CU Rider on bike PAN R to L - Red helmet 16'
Sc2 T-1	CU HAND L to R 3'
Sc3 T-1	MS Rider picks up bike - policeman's feet
	enter L to R after bike is up.
Sc3 T-2	MS Rider picks up bike - policeman's feet LR

Fig. 10.4. A shot list is a record of all the individual shots the editor has to work with. It is usually prepared by the editor or assistant editor.

take of every shot and keep the list at hand as you work. It provides information about screen direction and exact action. Often, you can tell at a glance from the shot list that a shot is not usable where otherwise you would have to search for it and view it. Thus much cumulative time and effort can be saved. Without a shot list, it is quite possible to finish editing the picture and then discover that some of the best takes have been left out simply because you forgot you had them.

Reviewing the Workprint Critically

After compiling the shot list, further evaluate the footage again either on the screen or in the editing machine. Select good takes and possibles, and reject the obviously unusable ones. Make notes on your shot list.

Breaking Down the Workprint

Break down the workprint into individual shots. According to what is easiest for you, place each shot on a core, roll it up on the flange, or hang it on a hook in the film bin. The purpose of the breakdown is to make all the separate elements of the movie—that is, the shots—individually available in sequence. Mark the scene number and take number on each shot in grease pencil. For sync-sound shots, roll sound and action separately but mark them well. It may be convenient to combine your critical review with the breakdown by running the workprint through the editing machine. Place all the shots by groups into cans or boxes. As you edit any part of the movie, take the broken down shots for that part and arrange them at hand in sequence.

Be sure that the footage is broken down into individual shots. A shot extends from *camera start* to *camera stop*, which should be indicated by blank frames run off at the end of every shot. Occasionally, in a documentary or newsreel shooting, the cameraman does not have time to slate each shot, but he usually runs off a few blank frames, which make it easier to find where to cut, and sometimes prevents loss of valuable frames in later negative cutting.

Making Up Head and Tail Leaders (See Start Marks and Leaders).

Working Film Editing Materials

During editing, you will work with some or all of the following elements:

1. Picture
   (a) Master shots
   (b) Matching closeups and medium shots
   (c) Cutaways and inserts
2. Sound
   (a) Principal sound
   (b) Wild sound
   (c) Ambient sound
3. Paper work
   (a) Script supervisor's script
   (b) Camera and sound reports
   (c) Edge number log
   (d) Code number log
   (e) Shot list

Picture

The various types of shots have been grouped here because the way they are separated is usually the way they are arranged for each scene after breakdown preparatory to editing. Also, in setting up for editing on a horizontal editing machine, you will undoubtedly place each of the three types of shots on separate rolls.

MASTER SHOTS

A master shot is usually an establishing shot of a scene with a relatively wide angle to include all the participants and their dialogue for the entire scene. In dialogue movies and scripts, it is called the master scene. (See The Script.)

MATCHING CLOSEUPS AND MEDIUM SHOTS

These are the portions of the master scene repeated from different angles. Each shot overlaps the action of the master shot at both head and tail.

CUTAWAYS AND INSERTS

These are reaction shots of people, and closeups of hands, objects, bits of action, and surroundings that are pertinent to the action occurring in the master scene. Often, the reactions of people are in closeup. Cutaways and inserts are usually shot without sound.

Sound

The three kinds of sound are voice, music, and sound effects, but these can be placed into narrower categories for a clearer understanding of how the editor may use them.

PRINCIPAL SOUND

The normal sequence is to edit the action and the *principal sound track* simultaneously and later add the other sounds to the finished workprint. The voice track is usually but not always the principal sound, since the principal sound of a movie is defined as the most important sound relative to the visuals. In a dramatic movie, the principal sound would be the dialogue, and the picture would be edited along with the dialogue with secondary sound added later—in this case, the music and sound effects. In a narrated movie, the principal sound is the narration track; and in a picture such as Disney's *Water Birds,* which consists of visuals edited to music only, the music is the principal sound. Sound effects as the principal sound for entire movies are rare, but in parts or sequences of movies they are fairly common.

WILD SOUND

Wild sound consists of spoken lines and sound effects recorded without picture. They are recorded non-sync, and are available for the editor to use as necessary. Wild lines of dialogue are usually for off-screen action, but they can sometimes by used in sync situations, where the lines are short and can be synked by eye, or in action where it is impossible to identify the lip movements with the sounds.

AMBIENT SOUND

This is the sound of "silence" recorded on the set or location to be used by the editor between dialogue and sound effects, and is usually called room tone. Every room, hall, building, closet, or outside space has its own characteristic "sound" even when none of what we usually call sound exists. In a movie, when sound is recorded, this ambient noise is present even when people are speaking. To put completely silent spaces between speeches or sounds causes an abrupt and disagreeable stoppage of sound—there is no "presence," and we call it fake. Therefore room tone, or presence, should be put into all blank spaces in a sound track to maintain the proper ambient noise level of the site of the scene.

Paper Work

Certain written records are invaluable in editing. Depending on the complexity and scope of the production, all or none of the records described here may be necessary. Any production, however, would undoubtedly require at least an edge number log and a shot list.

SCRIPT SUPERVISOR'S SCRIPT

This is the director's script, which is held by the script supervisor on the set during the actual shooting. On it the script supervisor makes notations and markings as to exactly what was shot, how many takes, the different angles, length of each shot, changes, additions, and so on. Refer to the sections in the Production Unit chapter to learn how the script supervisor keeps a precise record of the production primarily for the editor.

CAMERA AND SOUND REPORTS

These are the logs of the camera crew and the sound crew respectively. They indicate the number and order of the scenes shot, the date they were shot, the footage of each, remarks, and the camera and sound roll numbers. There is one camera report and one sound report for each roll of picture and each roll of sound. Thus it is simple to locate by roll number any action or sound take. Notice the circled takes on the camera report (Fig. 10.5). These are the shots the director indicated as the ones he wanted to use. The same information may also be found in the script supervisor's notes. (See Figs. 3.1, 3.2, 3.3.) When the cameraman sends the film to the laboratory for development and printing at the end of the day's shooting, he sends a copy of the camera report along with it to be used as a guide by the laboratory, which prints only the circle takes. The sound man sends the sound reports with the master tapes to the studio, which also transfers only the circled takes (Fig. 10.6). The circled takes of both action and sound are then sent to the editing room. If a print of one or more of the NG takes is needed, the camera and sound reports for roll numbers should be checked and the indicated rolls sent back to the lab or studio for printing and transferring of the scenes needed.

EDGE NUMBER LOG (p. 270)

CODE NUMBER LOG (p. 253)

SHOT LIST (p. 271)

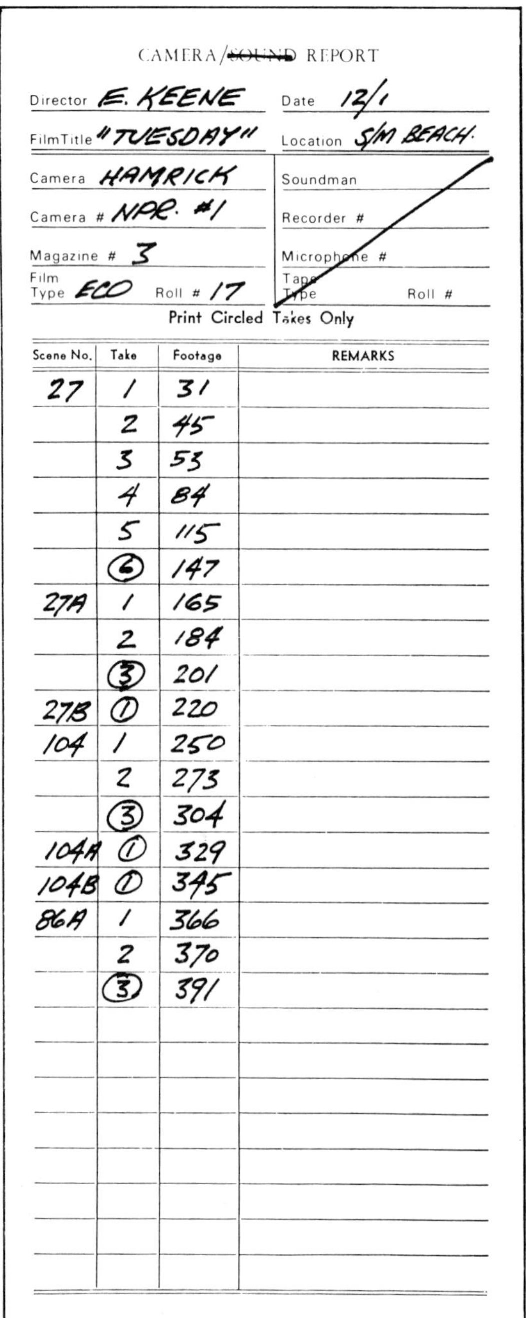

CAMERA/~~SOUND~~ REPORT

Director E. KEENE Date 12/1

FilmTitle "TUESDAY" Location S/M BEACH.

Camera HAMRICK Soundman

Camera # NPR. #1 Recorder #

Magazine # 3 Microphone #

Film Type ECO Roll # 17 Tape Type Roll #

Print Circled Takes Only

Scene No.	Take	Footage	REMARKS
27	1	31	
	2	45	
	3	53	
	4	84	
	5	115	
	(6)	147	
27A	1	165	
	2	184	
	(3)	201	
27B	(1)	220	
104	1	250	
	2	273	
	(3)	304	
104A	(1)	329	
104B	(1)	345	
86A	1	366	
	2	370	
	(3)	391	

Fig. 10.5. The camera report is a running record of shooting kept by the camera operator or assistant. At the conclusion of each shot, the scene and take numbers, footage, and explanatory comments are noted.

Workprint Assembly

After breakdown, begin editing the workprint by making up head leaders for both action and sound. (See Start Marks and Leaders.) At this point you may be more interested in starting out with the first shot of the picture, but preparing correct leaders initially will save much time and grief later on.

Separate all the broken-down shots into scene groupings. If you start editing with the first scene of the picture, set out all the rolls of that scene on the editing table. Put the other scenes into cans or boxes temporarily. Be sure to keep sound and action rolls together. If editing on a hori-

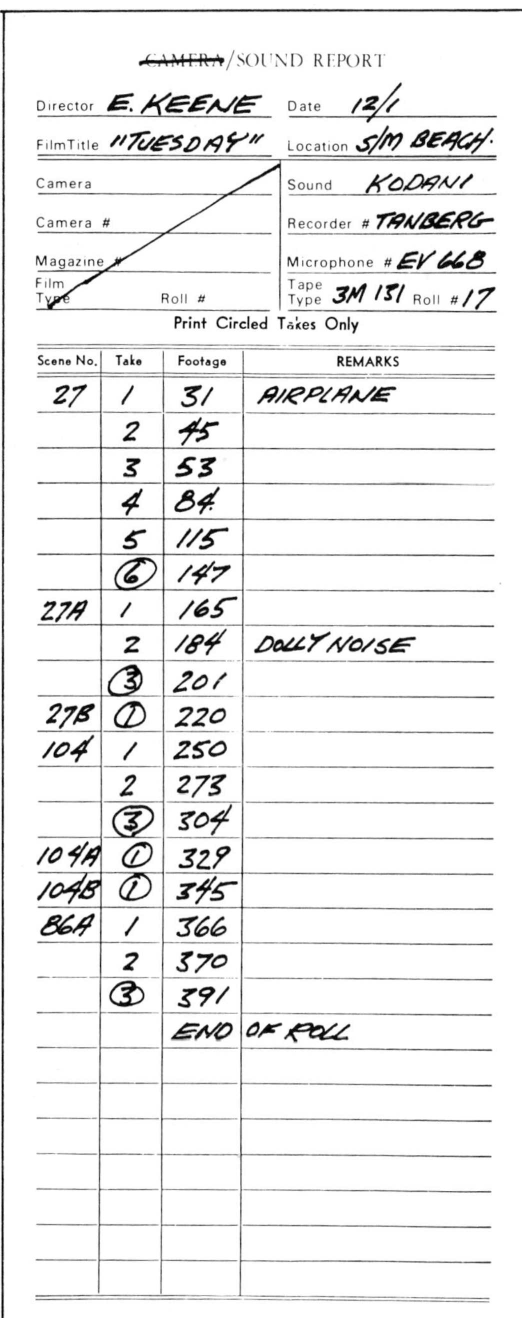

~~CAMERA~~/SOUND REPORT

Director E. KEENE Date 12/1

FilmTitle "TUESDAY" Location S/M BEACH

Camera Sound KODANI

Camera # Recorder # TANBERG

Magazine # Microphone # EV 668

Film Type Roll # Tape Type 3M 131 Roll # 17

Print Circled Takes Only

Scene No.	Take	Footage	REMARKS
27	1	31	AIRPLANE
	2	45	
	3	53	
	4	84	
	5	115	
	(6)	147	
27A	1	165	
	2	184	DOLLY NOISE
	(3)	201	
27B	(1)	220	
104	1	250	
	2	273	
	(3)	304	
104A	(1)	329	
104B	(1)	345	
86A	1	366	
	2	370	
	(3)	391	
		END	OF ROLL

Fig. 10.6. The sound report is a running record of sound takes analogous to the camera report.

zontal editing machine, reassemble the shots in convenient rolls—the master scenes on one roll, medium shots on another, and closeups and inserts on their respective rolls.

For movies without any synchronous sound material, decide which shot will open the movie by referring to the shot list, your notes, and your memory. Determine where you want the shot to begin and splice it to the tail of the Society leader at that point. Then run the shot through the editing machine down to the frame where you want to cut to the second shot. Mark this frame with a grease pencil, but do not cut the film off yet. Search for a second shot—you may wish to examine several—and view it in the editing machine several times to determine just where it should be spliced to the first shot. Again, mark the frame where the cut is to be with grease pencil, and make the splice.

If splicing with tape, make the cuts in the splicer rather than with scissors so that the scene may be put back exactly as it was should you decide to change the position of the cut. Since the tape splicer cuts on the frame line, a scene may be reconstituted to its original continuity no matter how many cuts have been made.

Continue to edit this way, working from one shot to the next, splicing as you go and letting the assembled picture feed into the editing bin or onto the editor's takeup spool. Assume that this first assembly is the final cut of the picture, although it won't be, because changes will have to be made, shots added and taken out, and the whole picture tightened up. Do not make a rough cut with the idea of going back later and making a fine cut. Edit the picture the way you want it the first time. Actually, it will be a rough cut, and you will undoubtedly have to go through it again. But if you approach the task initially thinking of it as a "rough," you will waste time and put yourself in a psychologically poor frame of mind. No matter how many times you must recut a picture, try to do it right each time. If the picture is assembled with the idea of doing a slipshod job first and then fixing it up on the fine cut, you may as well skip the first and start with the second.

Sync Sound Assembly

To assemble a sync-sound film, proceed in the same way but with the following considerations:

1. Put the sound and action of the master shot of the first scene into the editing machine in sync. Run this scene a few times to remember it.
2. View all the matching closeups and medium shots in sync.

3. Go back to the master shot, or whichever will be used as the first shot of the film, and mark the frame where you want to start. Be sure to mark the same frame for both sound and action.
4. Splice the heads of both sound and action of the selected first shot to the tails of the leaders that have been made up. Be sure they are spliced in sync. To be in sync, the splice on both sound and action must be the same number of frames from the start marks on the leaders and the same number of frames from the closest code numbers on both picture and sound.
5. With the first shot of the movie spliced on the head leaders, run the shot in sync down to a point where you wish to cut to the second shot. Mark the frame on both action and sound, then take the two out of the editing machine and lay them aside.
6. Examine other shots until you find the one you want. Mark the frame, both sound and action, where you want to splice it to the first shot and make the splices. The leader and the first two shots of the movie are now assembled. Continue in this way until the movie is complete.

Master Scene

Understanding dialogue editing requires a basic comprehension of the master scene and its composition. In editing dialogue, you work almost exclusively with the master scene and its accompanying medium shots and closeups, the fundamental raw materials of scene-building in a continuity film. Conventionally, the master scene establishes the situation while the closeups and medium shots are devoted to more detailed and intimate looks at what is going on (Fig. 10.7).

A director usually shoots medium shots and closeups so that they repeat and match portions of the action in the master scene. This gives the editor a master scene with matching angle shots to assemble in the best way possible. A rule of thumb is to start with the master scene to orient the audience, then go to closeups of the scene in the order that best tells what is happening. The editor has great latitude. If the scene plays best in its entirety from one angle, that is the way to edit it. But you will probably find that most scenes played from one angle become dull. Closeups tell the audience more about the inner thoughts and feelings of the characters, are more intimate, and generally reveal more emotional details.

Examine the script page in Fig. 10.7. It depicts an action in a psychologist's office. The therapist, Ellen, and the patient, Mrs. Tyler, are sitting and talking. This is the master scene, in which the basic situation is established and all the dialogue is indicated but no varying camera angles are required. Consider how such a scene might be directed. First, the director would shoot the scene in its entirety, showing both characters in a single shot going through all the dialogue. Then he would shoot several parts of the scene, dialogue and all, in medium shots and closeups, repeating the dialogue and action of portions of the master scene in each shot. This gives the editor a selection of shots, and he may edit them using whole shots or parts in any combination.

Look at the page of this scene from the script actually used by the director (Fig. 10.8), as marked by the script supervisor. Each vertical line on the page represents an individual shot from a different camera angle, indicating where the shot started and where it ended. In this master scene, six shots were made that cover one page of dialogue from several different angles. No matter how many shots were made, however, the edited scene must run only the approximate length of the master scene. Thus much unused footage remains after the final version has been put together. Actually, the scene may be edited any number of ways: It can be played in the master shot alone; but this would not allow the audience to examine Mrs. Tyler's distress closely, and would probably be dull. Or the scene can start briefly with the master shot and then cut to any one of the other shots. Or it can begin with the closeup of Mrs. Tyler's hands with Ellen's voice over and then cut to any one of the other shots as long as the continuity and meaning of the dialogue are maintained. The combination and sequence of shots used depends on the way the editor sees the scene and on his decision as to how it will be most effective.

Figure 10.9 shows the master scene described above and its matching medium shots and closeups as they were actually edited. Parts of Scenes 8, 8A, 8B, and 8C were used. Not used were the over shoulder shot of Mrs. Tyler, the closeup of her hands, and the medium 2-shot of the two women. Even though this is a simple scene with two characters sitting in the same spot

```
INT PSYCHOLOGIST'S OFFICE   DAY   SECOND SESSION

8.        MEDIUM VIEW    ELLEN AND MRS TYLER

          ELLEN and MRS TYLER are seated in comfortable
          chairs.  Between them is a small coffee table
          on which there are coffee cups and a plate of
          cookies.

                         ELLEN
                 Did Jennie come with you?

                         MRS TYLER
                 No.

                         ELLEN
                 Did you ask her?

                         MRS TYLER
                 I was going to, but it
                 wouldn't do any good.

                         ELLEN
                 Well, did you talk to her
                 about your finances?

                         MRS TYLER
                 I've been so tired and worried.
                 I wanted my husband to talk to
                 her, but he wouldn't.

                         ELLEN
                 I thought your husband was on
                 a trip.

                         MRS TYLER
                 He came home early.

                         ELLEN
                 How long will he be home?

                         MRS TYLER
                 He's going out again next week.

                         ELLEN
                 Did you ask him to talk to
                 Jennie?

                         MRS TYLER
                 I started to but he got mad
                 at me.

                         ELLEN
                 What was he mad about?
```

Fig. 10.7. A one-page master scene. The director will shoot several different angles of this scene, each repeating certain parts of the action from varying points of view.

throughout, the principle of the master scene with its matching medium shots and closeups applies to all continuity directing and editing no matter how complex. Having a variety of medium shots and closeups to support the master scene means that you control the pace, tone, and length of the scene. Through your choice of shots, the scene can be made to move rapidly, moderately, or slowly. Staying with longer shots tends to make action move slowly; going into closeups, particularly cutting back and forth between shots, speeds up the tempo. There are no hard and fast rules for cutting master scenes, there is only the requirement that they work the

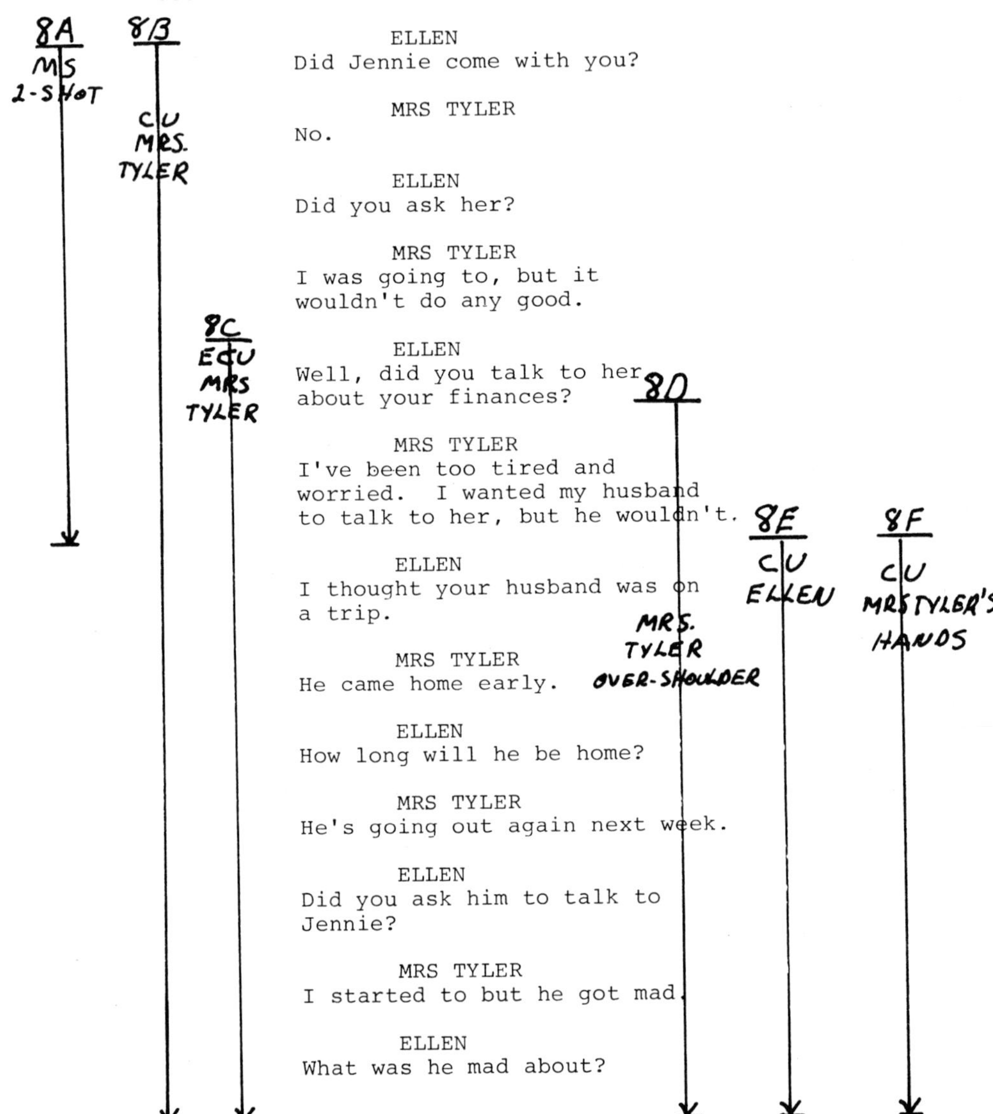

Fig. 10.8. The same master scene in Fig. 10.7, with the script supervisor's notations telling how the director actually shot the scene.

way you want them to. This means that you, as editor, must study the scene and all the shots, understand what is happening, and manipulate the shots to achieve the desired effect.

Code Numbers

Mechanically, the problem in dialogue cutting is handling the strip of action film and its corresponding strip of sound film to keep them together in sync. Coding provides sync marks at regular intervals on both sound and action. (See Syncing Dailies.) Consider the physical composition of the sync-sound shot: It consists of two lengths of film, sound and action. When they come back from being coded at the lab, these films still have the camera and sound slates on

1. 2-SHOT MASTER

2. CU MRS TYLER

3. CU ELLEN

4. ECU MRS TYLER

Fig. 10.9. The final version of the master scene (Fig. 10.8) as assembled by the film editor.

them, are the same length, and each strip of film has corresponding, identical code numbers at regular intervals along the edge. If the two pieces of film are placed in the editing machine with the sound slate in the sound head and the picture slate in the picture aperture, and the machine is then run in interlock, the picture and sound will be in sync. At any point, corresponding code numbers on sound and picture will be in sync, and voices and words will match the lip movements. Although the shot will now run in sync for its full length, you do not necessarily want every shot to run its full length on the screen. Editing means selecting, cutting, and rearranging. Thus the scene must be cut somewhere, possibly several times; and each time it is cut, the sound should accompany the picture. When cutting the picture, cut the sound at the same point. Keep any part of a shot and its corresponding sound track together and make them the same length.

Although dialogue scenes often seem to have many different forms, all dialogue editing consists of variations of two basic techniques: straight-across cutting and overlap cutting.

Straight-Across Cutting

This is the simplest arrangement for cutting dialogue and consists of cutting back and forth between one or more characters at the end of each one's speech. For example:

Character #1 Speaks. When he finishes, CUT TO
Character #2 He answers. When he finishes, CUT BACK TO
Character #1 Speaks. When he finishes CUT BACK TO
Character #2 And so on.

Figure 10.10 depicts graphically how straight-across cutting looks on the edited sound and action relative to the visuals. To edit this scene, start with the woman and run her shot in the editing machine down to the frame where you want to cut to the man. At this frame, make a mark on the picture and a mark at the same point on the sound track. This is where you will splice the head of the man's answering shot. Be sure that the splice marks of both sound and picture are in sync, that is, the exact same number of frames from the nearest code number. Cutting straight-across scenes is a matter of keeping sound and picture the same length.

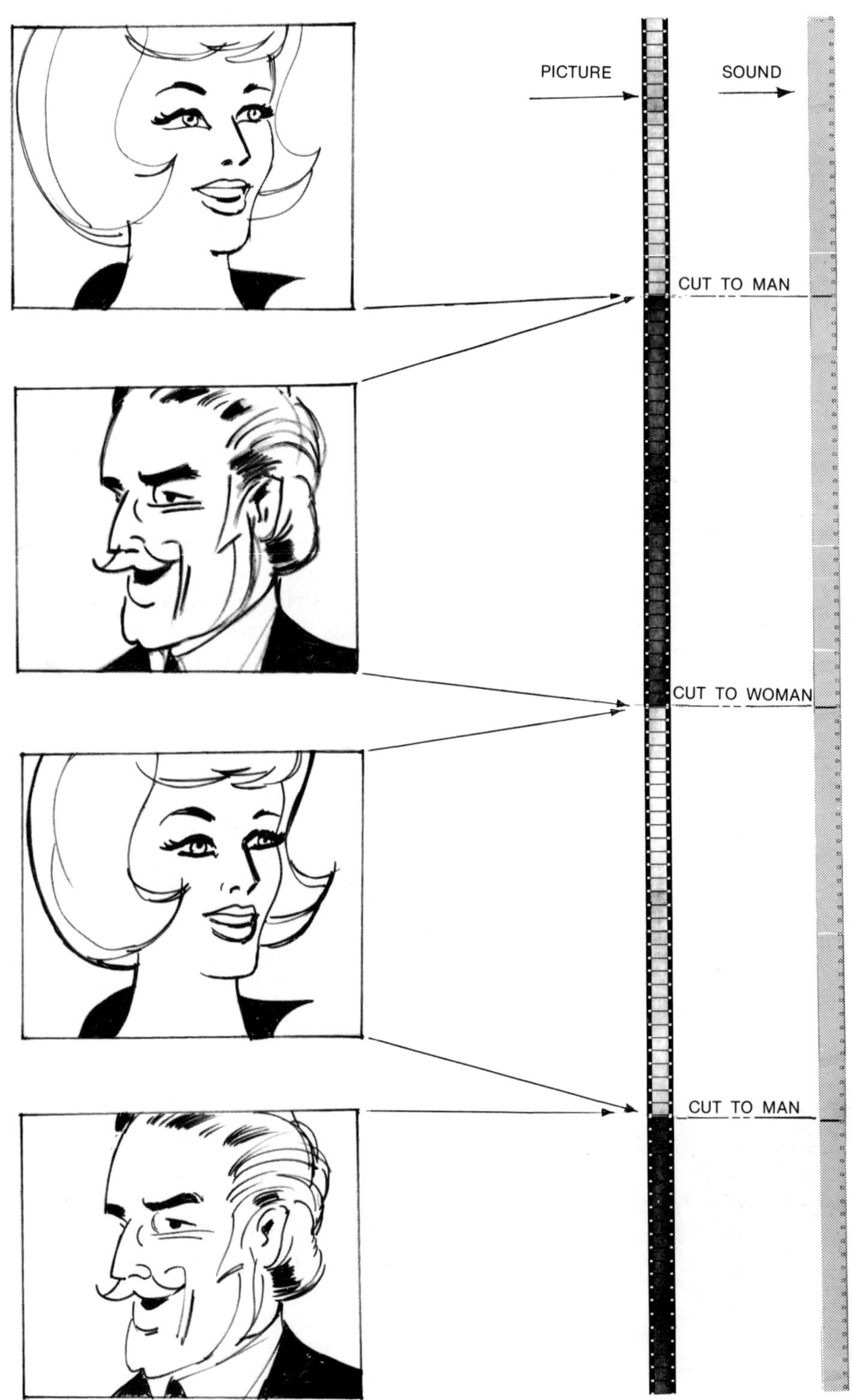

Fig. 10.10. Straight-across cutting. The voice heard is always that of the character seen on the screen.

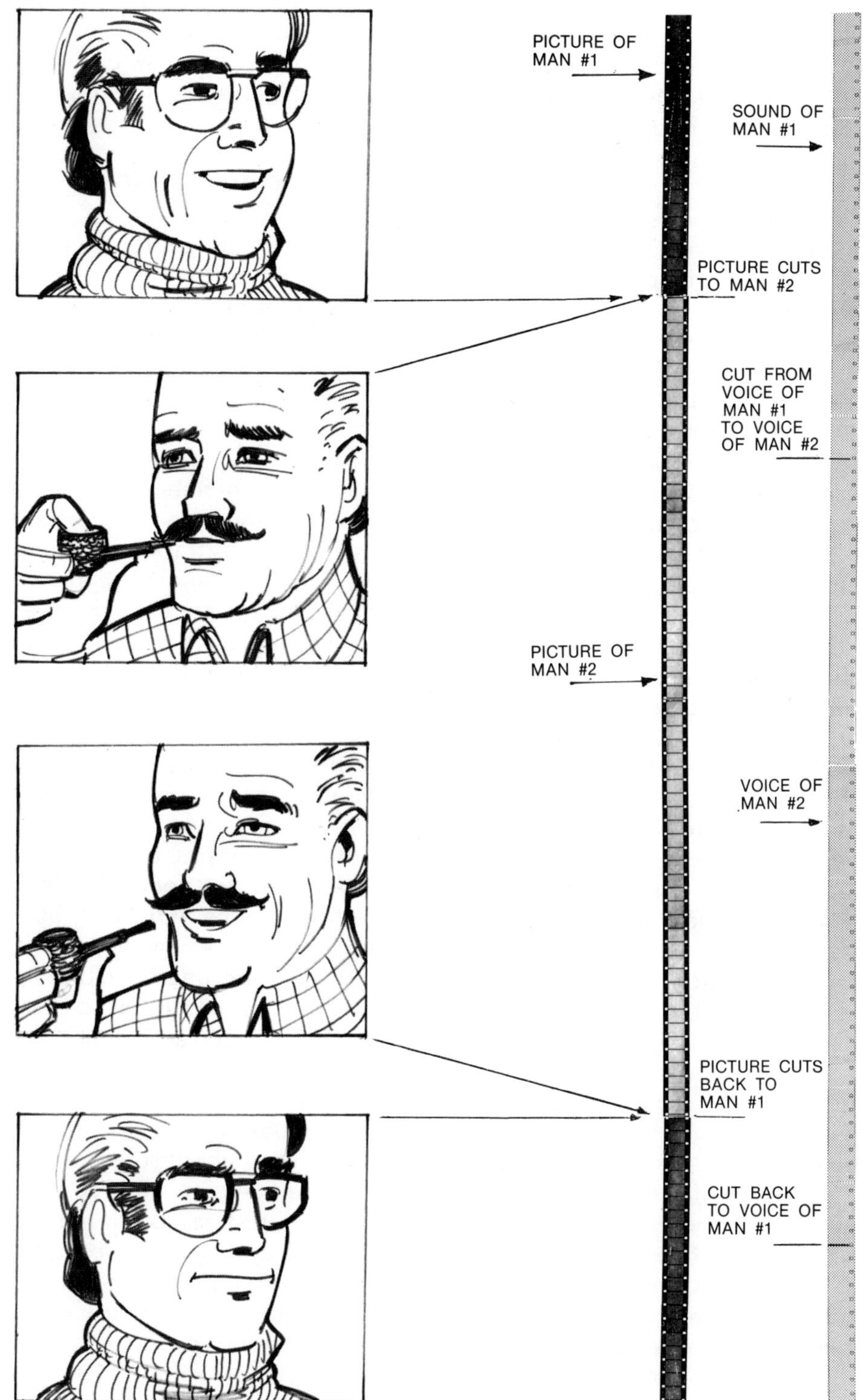

Fig. 10.11. Overlap cutting. The voice of one character is heard while another character is seen on the screen.

Overlap Cutting

In overlap cutting, the character who is speaking is not necessarily seen on the screen all the time he is talking. The speech of one character may overlap the picture of other characters, as in Fig. 10.11.

Varying the length and position of dialogue overlaps makes possible a wide range of meanings and inferences that can be put into a scene. As editor, you have almost complete control of how the scene will turn out and what its meaning will be. There are no absolute rules, but again the way straight-across and overlap cutting are used determines the pacing, timing, mood, and suspense of a scene.

To speed up a scene: use closeups, shots of short duration, and straight-across cutting.

To slow down a scene: use medium to long shots, shots of longer duration, and overlap the dialogue.

In overlapping dialogue, you are not limited to showing only the person being spoken to. You may cut to shots of anyone or anything that will help the scene. Overlapping can break the monotony in dialogue scenes, and you have the capability of controlling pace and connotation so that the scene is developed to its best advantage.

Always listen to the dialogue you are cutting and try to understand internal rhythm and pace. Straight-across dialogue tends to become both monotonous and rough simultaneously; for as one person speaks, we often want to see the reaction of the other person. Sometimes it is more important to see the reaction of the listener than it is to see the speaker. At other times, it is more important to hear the reply before we see the person who is replying.

To assemble dialogue, use the script as a guide. It provides the sequence of what is happening and indicates what coverage of the scene has been made—which is the master scene, how many closeups and cutaways, and so on. In editing, use any and all shots that will enhance the scene. Often a shot or piece of sound from some other, unrelated part of the movie may be used in a scene as an effective cutaway. Do not be afraid to change the order of dialogue and picture if it seems to make the scene play better, but make sure not to violate the entire meaning of the script by doing so unless that is your specific aim. With all the diverse pieces of a scene at your disposal, it is often possible to rearrange them in a way that completely changes their basic meaning; sometimes this may be desirable, and the result much better than the original scene.

SOUND EFFECTS EDITING

Sound effects cutting is the preparation of one or more rolls of sound effects in sync with the edited workprint. At this point in the editing process, the picture is in its final form. The edited workprint is now up to your specifications, or has been approved by the director and the producer. After sound effects and music are added, it should be ready to go into mixing and final printing without further changes. Your job is to build sound effects tracks that fit the edited workprint. Each sound effects track must be the same length as the workprint and must begin with a head leader having a start mark in sync with the workprint start mark. This is in preparation for the mixing session in which these sound effects will be mixed in with the principal track and the music.

In a film there is no such thing as sound "just happening." Every sound is there because someone deliberately and intentionally went to the trouble of putting it there. Sound effects are used not only for footsteps, telephones, cars, bells, crowd noises, and so on, but for all normal sounds that are missing or have been removed because they are unacceptable. Also, sound effects must be added to all scenes in which dialogue has been replaced, since the replacement voice recorded in the studio does not have the background effects that were present in the original shooting.

Start thinking about sound effects, referring to the completed script before any of the picture has been shot. Break down the script (see Script Breakdown) and make a scene-by-scene list of sound effects you think you will need. Most of the sound effects you will use will be "wild," that is, recorded non-sync separately from the picture and added to the sound track after the film has been edited.

Give copies of the sound effects list to the director, the sound mixer, and the script supervisor so that they will know what sound effects are to be recorded during the shooting of the film. If you are a lone filmmaker or have a small crew, be sure the list is handy at all times. Because of all the distractions on the set, if you haven't made a list you will probably forget and miss the advantage of recording when what has been shot is fresh in your mind. Usually, sound effects recorded during shooting are the best quality and are cheaper since the sound crew is on staff.

When screening rushes, make notes about what additional sound effects you want. Ordinarily, the sound effects editor will be collecting sound effects from the time the script is finished until the final tracks have been edited. These notes, plus the sound reports indicating what has been recorded during shooting, will help you compile a new list of sound effects.

The four general situations to work with in editing sound effects are as follows:

Sync Dialogue Recorded on a Sound Stage

On the dialogue track only those sounds of the actors as they carry out the scene are heard—footsteps, moving of props, breathing, doors opening and closing, and the dialogue. Some of these effects may be usable, others may not. Occasionally these real sound effects will record satisfactorily enough so that they may be used as they are. Body movements and footsteps may often be used; but sometimes they do not sound right, so sounds must be made. It is difficult to predict which of the sound effects that occur during shooting will be usable. You can judge only when you hear the dialogue track.

Sync Dialogue Photographed and Recorded on Location

If the location is isolated, the sound may be much like sound recorded on the stage, as described above. But if the location is populated and busy, along with the actor's lines, the ambient sounds that were going on at the time of shooting will be heard. Again, some may be usable and some may not be. Consider the following scene:

A girl is standing on the curb in a city street. Traffic is going by in the background, and some kids are playing on the sidewalk across the street. A car pulls up to the curb. The girl opens the door, looks at the driver, and says, "You're twenty minutes late." She gets in the car and slams the door. The car pulls away, tires squealing as it goes.

What sound effects do you want to hear in this scene? You want believable traffic noises, maybe a horn or two, kids playing, a car pulling up and stopping, the girl's voice, the car door opening and slamming shut, and the car pulling away accompanied by a skidding tire sound. You may choose to get a good sync recording of all the environmental sounds in the scene and replace the voice later if it can't be distinguished in the noise. In this case you will undoubtedly have to "sweeten" the track by adding specific needed effects such as the tire squeal, which is very difficult to record on city streets. Usually, the most important sound is the voice. So if this scene were shot on a real city street, the scene would probably be miked from inside the car with the mike pointed at the girl's mouth. It is also probable that most of the ambient effects would be unusable in the final sound track. The traffic might not sound like traffic. The kids playing would be either too loud or too soft, or would not sound like kids playing. The door slam might be too loud, and the car start and stop and the tire squeal would have the wrong perspective. As sound effects cutter, you would have to take out the unusable sounds and obtain good clean sound effects for, say, the traffic, the kids playing, a car start and stop, and the tire squeal. You would then assemble these new effects on separate rolls in sync with the action they are supposed to be coming from and move the door slam to one of the effects tracks so that its level could be controlled. Later in the mixing session, all these sounds will be mixed together into one track, each effect at the proper volume relative to the others.

Sync Sound Without Dialogue

This would be a scene in which you try to catch the live sounds of the action you are shooting. Shoot sync sound when you can in case the effects are usable. Some examples of this would be horse races, auto races, a close shot of a lock being picked, close shots of handwork such as machining, woodworking, or any scene with sound-producing action without dialogue. Since this type of shooting is planned primarily for the camera and not the sound, the effects are not always usable.

Silent Sequence Effects

The silent sequence is silent because it was shot without sound. Here, sound effects will have to be made up and added to the entire scene.

To begin sound effects cutting, you need the edited workprint, that is, the edited picture and its corresponding edited principal sound track. The task is to assemble sound effects tracks that enhance but do not obscure both the principal sound track and the overall meaning of the picture.

The following is a workable way to proceed:

1. Remove all unusable effects and noise from the dialogue (or principal) track.
2. Analyze the edited workprint for needed sound FX.
3. Obtain sound effects.
4. Assemble sound effects tracks.

Remove all Unusable Effects and Noise from the Dialogue (or Principal) Sound Track

These may be anything from "uh's" and "ah's" to unintelligible traffic noise. If the background noise is consistently bad, it may have to be removed by cutting it out, even between words or dialogue, and substituting new background effects. This is tedious, but can sometimes save what is otherwise an unacceptable track. If the dialogue is acceptable, poor background noise under the words will not be noticed if the unacceptable sound is removed from between the words.

On any dialogue or narration track, the silence between words consists of the ambient noise, or room tone, of the place where the sound was recorded. Every set, location, and studio has its own particular "sound" of silence. Always have plenty of room tone for every scene. If anything is taken out of the dialogue or narration track, fill in the resulting spaces with exactly the same amount of room tone. To some degree this will probably have to be done for every scene because there are always unusable sounds that must be removed, and there will often be usable sound effects that you will take out to put on another roll. (See Fig. 10.12.)

The sound track and the picture in a sync scene must always be the same length. If frames are removed from the dialogue track, replace them with the same number of frames to maintain sync with the picture.

Often during shooting, particularly on location and in documentary situations, background noise may be so loud that the dialogue is almost unintelligible. Noises such as airplanes, traffic, crickets, birds, air conditioners, running streams, and the shouts of children are usually the most troublesome. The ideal is to shoot under conditions where there are no unwanted background

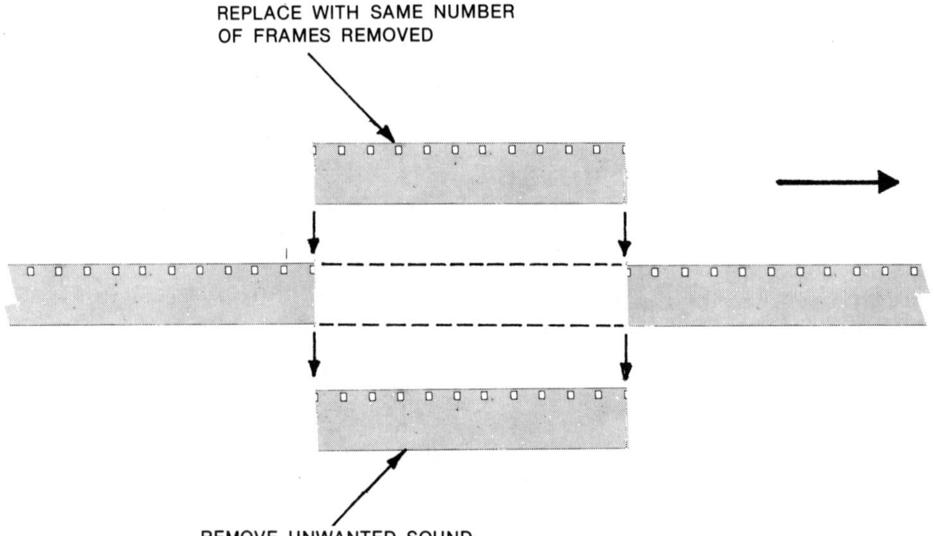

Fig. 10.12. Removing unwanted sound and replacing it with exactly the same number of frames of room tone or ambient presence.

	EFFECT	FOOTAGE	LENGTH	SOURCE	ROLL NO.	TRACK
1.	12-YR old Kids Playing Keepaway ball on Playground	100'-6x-130'-36x	30'-30x	Record	3	FX-2
2.	LIGHT neighborhood auto traffic	100-6x-130-36x	30'-30x	STOCK	3	FX-2
3.	Tire squeal-sports car takeoff	128'-10x-129-30x	60x	Record	3	FX-2
4.	Cheering baseball crowd-wild	131-0x-138-21	7'-21x	STOCK	3	FX-2
5.	Auto running-inside car	138'-22x-160-30x	22' 8x	stock	3	FX-2
6.	Car radio-announcer calling baseball game	138-22x-160-30x	22' 8x	Record		

Fig. 10.13. A sound effects list helps to gather and keep track of needed sound effects.

noises, but this cannot always be done. When objectionable sounds make the dialogue unacceptable or marginal, you can take the following corrective measures:

1. Reshoot the scene, correcting the condition. This usually gives the best result, but is the most expensive in both time and money. Often it may be impossible to get all the same people together a second time. In this case you would have to resort to one of the other measures.
2. Replace the dialogue.
3. Use the scene as is and remove as much unwanted sound as possible from the track.

Perhaps filtering during the mixing session will improve it further. To remove all of an unusable background noise, do exactly as shown in Figure 10.12, only do it more often because the sound must be taken out between every word. This means that you will sometimes be removing and replacing as few as one or two frames at a time. Be aware that sound studios have highly specialized equipment designed to eliminate or reduce background noise; they are even able to isolate very narrow bands of frequency if there is an objectionable noise that is not eliminated simply by dropping out the backround. When the track is very bad, the job of making it usable often involves eliminating unwanted noise with a judicious combination of manual removal by cutting and electronic modification.

Analyze the Edited Workprint for Needed Sound Effects

Project the edited workprint or run it through the editing machine and note every spot where a sound effect should go. Make a sound effects list, noting where footsteps should be, where doors open and close, where objects are moved or put down, keys jangled, money handled, barking dogs, birds, cats, kids, everything that makes noise or could conceivably make noise. Take detailed notes and indicate the following:

1. Description of the effect.
2. Where does each effect occur? Measuring from the head start mark on the workprint leader, indicate in feet and frames where the effect begins and ends.
3. Length of each effect. How long is it on the screen in feet and frames?
4. The sound perspective of the effect. Is it far away or close?
5. Any other peculiarities or requirements.
6. Availability. Is the effect available in your stock library, or can it be purchased, or do you have to record it?

Keep a constant log of all the above information throughout the production. With experience, you will find your own best way to log this material, but here is one workable way to do it (Fig. 10.13).

Good sound effects are never fortuitous. Think in terms of the final result you want to achieve. You are actually reconstituting reality by structuring an entire environment of sound effects and noise. Not only can sound effects create the feeling of extreme believability, but they can also create moods and convey meanings that are not indicated by the picture alone. Sound effects can give the audience a mental image of whole scenes and actions occurring outside the frame.

Obtain Sound Effects

Before assembling your sound effects tracks, you must gather together all the effects. Start collecting effects as soon as possible, even before shooting begins. There are two sources: original recordings and the sound effects library. Try to get as many effects as you can from "stock," as library material is called, since it is considerably cheaper and immediately available. Every studio and every filmmaker has, or should have, a stock library of some kind of both film and sound effects. If you don't have such a source, start building one. Gather effects wherever and whenever possible. When you buy effects from a stock library, transfer a copy. Whenever you are on a shoot, have the sound man record as many sound effects as he can of any and all kinds. Rig your FM and AM radio so they can be tied into a recorder. Many good effects are available from radio, sounds that may be hard to find or to make on short notice. You can also buy complete sound effects libraries on both discs and tape. This is expensive, but if your organization is well-funded, the investment is worth it.

In gathering effects for the picture, roll each one up by itself and put it with others in a marked film can or box. Be sure to identify what each effect is and where it goes. Also, keep a list or index of effects so you can easily pick out any one you want at any time. Even a small picture has many sound effects, and confusion escalates rapidly without some way to keep track of things.

Identify the cans containing sound effects by groupings: FX-Living room sequence, or *FX-Reel #1*. Grouping and marking effects saves much time and trouble later.

Assemble Sound Effects Tracks

Since the sound effects track is a buildup, you will undoubtedly end up with effects overlapping, that is, two or more effects occurring at the same time. This means that two or more FX tracks will have to be made, since two single effects cannot occupy the same place at the same time until they have been mixed together on one track. And this is what you are aiming at when you build sound effects tracks—the mixing session. Remember that during the mix, a human being must control the volume of each of your tracks, and avoid making up tracks that cannot be mixed because of sheer complexity and disorganization. Plan effects placement for the minimum number of tracks to get maximum mixing control. The easier a set of tracks is to mix, the better the outcome will probably be. A set of complicated, unorganized FX tracks hurts only you, and the result is mediocre.

Do not cram all the effects onto one track. Put similar effects on the same track, that is, those that are close to the same level. Ideally, the mixer should be able to set the volume for a track once and never have to touch it again. Theoretically this is possible, although not probable or usual, but try to plan your tracks so the mixer doesn't have to make frequent changes in level on any one.

How many sound tracks, or rolls, should you have? It depends on the nature of the film. Some movies may consist of only a principal track—voice, or music, or sound effects alone—but usually a one-track movie sounds incomplete. Sounds in combination such as voice, FX, and music, create a feeling of believability; so basically this means three sound tracks. But if certain sounds must overlap—such as music fading into music, or two effects occurring simultaneously—each must be put on a separate roll. When the sound quality of a section of dialogue does not match the rest of the dialogue, it must also be put on a separate sound roll so that the mixer may record it at its own equalization setting (see Mixing).

Building sound effects tracks involves the following:

1. Preparation of leaders.

2. Transferring good sound effects from the voice track(s) to another track.

3. Syncing and marking individual sound effects.

4. Splicing the synced and marked effects into the FX rolls.

PREPARATION OF LEADERS

Preparing adequate and proper head and tail leaders at the outset is important. If the leaders on the head and tail of the edited workprint and its principal sound track are not correct at this point, correct them. (See Chapter 9, Start Marks and Leaders.) The leaders for all sound tracks—voice, music, and effects—should be the same length as the leader on the workprint picture with all start marks in sync. Before beginning to assemble any track, make up the head leader.

In assembling tracks and making up leaders, be sure to maintain correct emulsion positions. A built-up sound effects track consists of individual effects on magnetic film joined together on one roll with leader in between and at head and tail. Leader and magnetic film should be spliced emulsion to base to prevent emulsion buildup on the recording head during mixing or interlock screening sessions. The reason for this is that the sound magnetic pickup head of a playback and recording machine ride heavily on the iron oxide emulsion of the sound track. When leader passes over the pickup head, if the emulsion side is toward the sound head, emulsion will be scraped off the leader and deposited on the sound pickup head. This distorts the sound reproduction or cuts it out altogether. If you go into a mixing session with the leader emulsion in the wrong position, the leader will have to be changed before the mix can continue. And changing the leader means more than just flopping it over, since it must be done throughout the roll. If you are paying an hourly fee for a mixing studio, a flopped emulsion can be expensive.

TRANSFERRING GOOD SOUND EFFECTS FROM THE VOICE TRACK(S) TO ANOTHER TRACK

Usually some sound effects on the dialogue track will be usable, but they should not be left on the dialogue track. Cut them out of the dialogue track and splice them in sync into a separate FX track. (See Fig. 10.12.) For example, two characters in a scene are sitting in a patio talking. One of the characters opens a beer can. As he pulls the top off, it sounds as loud as a pistol shot since the recording volume was set for the lower level sound of the voices. Assume the beer can sound to be usable but too loud. If it is left on the dialogue track, during the mixing session the mixer will have to quickly lower the sound level at this point and then quickly raise the level before the next word of dialogue. If effects such as this are taken from the dialogue track and put in sync on a separate FX track, the mixer can control the volume effectively. For best results, he should not be asked to control dialogue and effects on the same track. Occasionally it may be literally impossible. If both dialogue and many sound effects are close together and at different volume levels, the result will undoubtedly be disastrous.

The first step in removing effects is to go through the dialogue track and mark the beginning and end of each effect that must be moved over to the FX track. (See Fig. 10.12.) This can be done on a sound reader, on the sync machine with a magnetic pickup, or on the editing machine. Play the track, and when you come to an effect, mark its beginning and its end. Make your marks so that when you cut the effect out of the track, there is enough space to cut without snipping off any part of the sound. On the exact frame line, mark where the cut is to be made, and identify the effect on the magnetic film on which the sound effect is recorded inside the cut marks. *Caution:* write on the sprocket-hole half of the film only. *Do not use grease pencil.* After you have gone through the entire dialogue track and marked each effect, cut them out and splice them into the FX roll.

To remove effects from the dialogue track and splice them into the FX roll, you will need a three-gang sync machine, a roll of single-perforated lightstruck leader, a roll of room tone, and a splicer. This operation may be done on the horizontal editing machine instead of the sync machine, but not as conveniently. Proceed as follows:

1. Put the following two reels of film on the left-hand rewind sprockets facing away from you:

one reel of single-perforated lightstruck leader, base side up; and one reel of the edited dialogue track, magnetic film emulsion up.

2. Lock the first foot of the head of each roll into the sync machine. Turn the sync machine knob to the right until enough leader is on the table to mark it HEAD FX-1.

3. Thread the head of each film onto its respective takeup reel on the right-hand rewind, and wind the film to the right until the HEAD START mark of the dialogue track comes into the sync frame of the sync machine. Lock the sync machine at this point, and put a start mark on the lightstruck leader in sync with the start mark on the dialogue track. Identify this new start mark as HEAD ⌱ START FX-1.

4. With the two start marks still in the sync frame of the sync machine, set the footage and frame counters to zero.

5. Wind the two films, dialogue and FX-1, onto the takeup reels until the first sound effect (which you have previously marked) comes into the sync machine. Position the head splice mark in the sync frame, and make a similar mark on the FX track (leader) at exactly the same point.

6. In the third sprocket of the sync machine, lock a length of room tone that is a bit longer at both ends than the effect marked on the dialogue track. Put splice marks on this piece of room tone in sync with the beginning and end splice marks on the dialogue track. You have now marked a length of room tone that is exactly the same number of frames in length as the sound effect which you are going to remove from the dialogue track.

7. Roll the sync machine to the left so that the marked sound effect clears the left side of the sync machine. With the splicer, cut the sound effect from the dialogue track on the splice marks and splice its head to the splice mark on the lightstruck leader. As you make the splice, the splicer cuts the leader leaving an unspliced end hanging from the reel on the left. Splice this loose leader end to the tail of the sound effect.

8. With the splicer, cut the room tone on the splice marks and splice it into the space left in the dialogue track in place of the removed sound effect. (This is the same operation as is performed in removing unwanted FX from the dialogue track, Fig. 10.12.) Caution: Be sure leader and sound track are spliced together with reversed emulsions.

9. Wind the two rolls down to the next marked sound effect and repeat the process until all of the effects on the dialogue track have been moved over into the FX roll. Caution: Perform all these splicing operations on the left-hand side of the sync machine. This will keep both rolls in sync all the way through. If cuts or splices are made on the right-hand side of the sync machine, the tracks will be thrown out of sync.

10. Put correct tail leader on the FX roll. Rewind and set aside until later. (See Start Marks and Leaders.)

SYNCING AND MARKING INDIVIDUAL SOUND EFFECTS

The next step in building your sound tracks is to sync each wild effect to the picture and make sync marks for each on both the effect and the workprint. From the effects box, take the individual rolls of sound effects for the section or reel you are going to do. Set these effects out on the editing table in front of you in order.

Put the workprint in the editing machine and run down to the point where the first effect is to go. Put that effect in the editing machine with the picture and run them together. Juggle their relative positions until the effect sounds right. Maintaining this relative sync position, back up to the head where the effect is to begin, put sync marks on the effect and on the workprint, and put the same number on both so you can later assemble the effect of sync. (See Fig. 10.14.) Set this first synced effect in a can marked "Synced Effects," and proceed to the next. Continue doing this until you have synced and marked all the effects to the picture.

At first, not all stock sound effects will fit the picture. Often it will be necessary to juggle, shorten, lengthen, change, and combine effects to get the desired result. Stock footsteps often have the proper sound but the wrong cadence. The only solution to this problem is to remove or add frames between each step until they fit the steps of the person walking in the picture. This is tedious work, but it has to be done. Occasionally the sound of an automobile driving off is too long and has to be shortened. Usually, the best way to do this is to shorten it in the center. All sounds have a definite beginning buildup and a winding

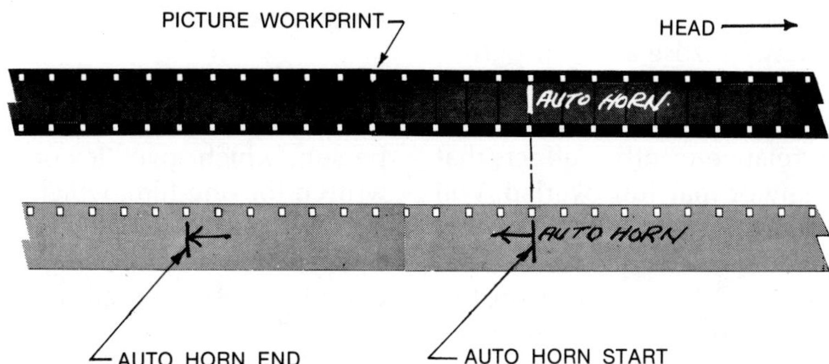

Fig. 10.14. A sound effect for a scene in the workprint marked in sync and identified so that the effect can later be assembled on an FX roll.

down at the end. If these beginnings or endings are cut off, it might change the sound so it is no longer believable. But a piece can be removed from the center and the two ends pulled together, and often no one will notice.

Sound effects cutting requires ingenuity. Try everything. You may find that sounds you have collected for one thing may be used for something else. For example, the sound of a paint scraper used at a very low volume may work perfectly as the sound of a man shaving. One brilliant editor had some thunder effects he wanted to use, but each clap started off weakly, building up finally to a good thunder roll without much drama. He spliced a cannon shot to the head of each thunder clap so that you couldn't tell where the cannon shot ended and the thunder began. This turned them into magnificent, exploding thunderclaps. No one detected or suspected the cannon shots.

Make every effect meaningful. Too many effects, result in a meaningless and distracting cacophony. The object is to use a minimum number of effects to create maximum interest and believability. Avoid inserting some noise that approximates the real thing; select sound effects that will do what you want them to. When you have finished synking and marking the effects, you are ready to assemble them into one or more tracks.

SPLICING THE SYNCED AND MARKED EFFECTS INTO THE FX ROLLS

This is the actual assembling of the sound tracks. You will need the sync machine, a roll of single-perforated lightstruck leader equal in length to the workprint, and a splicer. Proceed as follows:

1. Put the roll of lightstruck leader on the left-hand rewind along with the workprint picture. Remember that the picture should be emulsion up and the leader should be shiny side, or base up.
2. Put the sync machine on the table between the rewinds. Lock the first foot of the head of each roll into the sync machine and turn to the right until enough of the leader is clear of the machine to identify it as FX #___ HEAD.
3. Thread the head of each film into its respective takeup reel and wind until the start mark of the workprint comes into the sync frame of the sync machine. Lock the sync machine at this point, and put a start mark on the lightstruck leader in sync with the start mark on the workprint. Identify this new start mark as HEAD I|I START FX #___.
4. With the two startmarks in the sync frame of the sync machine, set the footage and frame counters to zero.
5. Wind the two films, workprint and FX track, onto the takeup reels until you come to the mark on the workprint indicating the first sound effect. Splice the sound effect in at this point in the leader roll in sync with the workprint. Use the sync marks you made earlier as a guide. *Caution*: Do all splicing to the left of the sync machine. If splices are made in the film after it has come out of the right-hand side of the sync machine, it will throw the rolls out of sync.
6. Continue this way until you have spliced in all the sound effects in sync.

You will probably not cut the sound effects rolls in precisely this way because as you progress, your own methods and sequence of doing things will develop. When splicing an effect into a track, consider its position relative to other effects that may run simultaneously or may just overlap. Will that other effect fit easily in the first effects track, or will you have to build a third track? What about the effect after that? If you put it on this track, will it follow too soon after this effect to be handled well by the mixer? The mental gymnastics required to juggle more than one FX track can sometimes be confusing. There will be times when you will have to work back and forth between two or more effects tracks to get the feel of how the two will mix together. Other times, portions of your picture may be done at widely separated points. There is no one way to describe how every editor edits or should edit. Thus the method described above is only a guide.

MUSIC EDITING

When you finally reach the stage of putting music to the picture, a kind of magic occurs. With the discriminating choice of music and its placement a film suddenly comes to life. Tense scenes become unbearable, sentimental scenes become tear-jerkers, and funny scenes are hilarious. If, like many filmmakers, you are tired of working on the film, adding music and seeing the transformation often has a rejuvenating effect that enables you to see the picture through its final phases. Remember, music is very powerful. Too much of a good thing can render your film ridiculous just as too little care can diminish the effectiveness of your picture.

Music, like everything else in motion picture production, does not happen fortuitously. It must be meticulously tailored to fit the picture it goes with, and its composition and selection must be undertaken carefully. There are two sources of music for motion pictures: an original score, and library music. There are advantages and disadvantages to both kinds of music depending on the circumstances. The choice you make depends on time, budget, aesthetics, and availability.

Original Score

An original score is the optimum complement to a motion picture. It is usually written by one person, which gives it continuity. It is expressly written for one film, which makes it unique. And each section is usually handled as a whole so there is very little editing to be done once it is complete. Almost all features and theatrical movies have original scores, and some have become more famous than the pictures themselves. Many believe the only valid movie music is an original score.

Although with a competent composer and orchestra the result is usually superior to that obtained using prerecorded music, it is far more expensive. In fact, all the problems related to the choice of having an original score composed for a film are a function of time and money, mostly money. If you are operating in a nonprofessional status, and have a friend who dreams of scoring your picture just for the experience and is willing to play his own instruments (which he does expertly), it is possible that your expenses will be reasonable since you will only have to secure a sound studio and the services of an engineer. Generally, however, if you are operating on a moderate budget, the comparative costs of an original composition versus a prerecorded library score put original music out of your range.

Consider what having an original score entails. First, there is the selection of the composer. There are plenty available, but the best ones are expensive. Since not everyone is able to recognize a competent composer by listening to his work, you may have several false starts, which will be time consuming, and you may have to hire expert advice, which will be costly. Although there are many good composers available who are not world-famous, the trick is to find one. There is also the question of revisions. The original contract usually stipulates how much rewriting the composer is expected to do for the fee; beyond that there will be an additional charge. Once the score is written it must be performed and recorded. Copyists, musicians, studios, and recording technicians can cost a great deal of money, and the organization of this work force can consume the valuable time of an independent filmmaker.

If you can afford an original score, start the

process early. The composer should be involved in the production as soon as possible. He cannot compose to a definite time limitation until he sees the edited version of the workprint and has timing sheets at hand. Before this he may read the script, have discussions with the director, and see rushes and portions of the picture as it is being edited. From these, he can begin to develop themes and generally start working out what he wants to do.

The editor assists initially on an original score by providing the composer with cue sheets to work from. This entails measuring the entire picture sequence by sequence and making cue sheets that indicate exact minute and seconds timing of all the action and moods. If the music is to fit the picture, it must be composed and conducted to a very precise timing schedule.

Library Music

There is a large and varied body of stock, or "canned" music readily available in music libraries. Stock music is constantly being composed and recorded by various companies whose business it is to provide music for motion pictures, radio, and television. Almost every sound studio in the United States has a complete library of every stock recording company, and any individual may purchase duplicates of all the various collections. Many studios have a listening room where any recording is available to be heard. Catalogues list each selection with its running time and a brief description. Although the descriptions are usually not very reliable, they do indicate the general style. In working on a moderate to large scale, you may find it advantageous to buy complete music libraries to keep in your studio. The cost of a library is that of the materials and transfer. You pay royalties on the music used only after it appears in the final motion picture.

The three main advantages to using library music are as follows:

1. Library music is less expensive. Costs include those for search time, transfer, editing time, and royalties. The total cost can range from thirty percent down to about five percent of what an original score may cost.

2. Library music is more convenient. After the picture is edited, the music can be selected and editing started in a relatively short time. This method is usually faster than a composer can write the music and record it with a live orchestra. Although speed does not guarantee a good score, it can be advantageous in regard to costs and deadline time.

3. Changes are easier to make with library music. To make changes in an original score, you must get the composer to rework the existing material or compose new music. Again, it has to be recorded by a live orchestra. This takes time and usually a great deal of money. With library music, changes can be made by merely selecting new music and reediting it. Also, the decision to make changes is not as traumatic since not so much money and time are at stake.

The use of stock music in movies has an unsavory reputation because of its undistinguished quality and mediocrity. Yet this is not always the case, for library music can sometimes be as good as, and even better than, original music. In years past, if a music track were criticized because it was canned, there might be some validity to the criticism because early music libraries did not contain very inspiring material. Today, however, if a motion picture score made up of library music is bad, it is probably the fault of the editor and whoever chooses the music. Music libraries currently offer a wide range of excellent music of all kinds from which to select. People are working continually to renew and enlarge these libraries, and the best composers and musicians are hired to augment this growing collection.

A good music editor can synthesize a track so skillfully that few viewers ever suspect the music was not composed especially for the picture. This does not mean that music from libraries is ready-made to lay in alongside the edited workprint. Much searching, hard work, and sensitivity are required to edit canned music into a functioning artistic score.

Another criticism of canned music is that the same pieces appear in many different pictures and are therefore not unique to a particular movie. Although this is possible, the wide range of music available today makes it unlikely that carefully selected music will appear in several pictures. Many people who use library music have little imagination and generally choose stereotyped selections, but an imaginative producer avoids musical clichés and choses music that is appropriate yet different. If you are even slightly sensitive and can project mentally what might be done with music, your selection and the final result will probably never be heard in any other film. Of course, it is possible for a theme or a melody to be heard occasionally in separate films, but if the music has been edited and applied creatively, your version will still be unique.

It is both unnecessary and undesirable that you use library music just as it is. You may use a portion of a selection, shorten it, put spaces in it, change the beat, and use it in any way you wish. Follow one basic rule, however: do not let a piece of music determine the length of a scene or sequence. Most novices and many professionals are unaware that they can shorten music to fit their needs, that they do not have to let music run on until it has reached its own stopping point. This alone results in numerous long, dull scenes. Control your music, and you will be surprised at how much you can accomplish.

The main disadvantage of library music is that it is not composed expressly for the movie in which it is used. The library score, no matter how skillfully it is done, is still basically a makeshift. Nevertheless, an artistically edited library score is a great complement to your picture and can be as effective as an original composition. In selecting music for a motion picture, proceed as follows:

1. Analyze each sequence of your film and note the mood or tempo that would be suitable. The perfect piece of music may not always be available in the stock library, so be prepared to make compromises. Be willing to change your thinking about what is suitable for a particular scene.

2. Make out a requirement sheet listing all the sequences that will need music. Indicate running times for each section if that information is available. If you have not yet decided what the length of the sequences are to be, make an estimate on the long side.

3. Go to the studio and select music, working from your sequence list. You will probably be stimulated into different channels by the music you hear. Sometimes a selection may suggest a whole new way of approaching a sequence musically.

4. Make more selections than you require. Although you must pay the transfer cost for any music you take, this is quite small relative to the final royalties and the benefit of having a wide selection to work with. When you select library music, the studio may charge an hourly search fee. You will be charged for transferring your selections and for the stock onto which you specify they are to be transferred. A workable way is to have the studio transfer the musical selections to magnetic film—either 16mm or 35mm, whichever you are working with—and then use these to do your editing. If you damage a piece or need more, call the studio and have them make another transfer. But when you order a retransfer of a section of music, be careful that it is in sync with the piece it is replacing. If, for example, you damage a section of music track after it has been edited to the picture, it is a simple matter to obtain another transfer from the original source and lay it in to replace the damaged section. But if the music originally came from a disc or non-sync quarter-inch tape, a retransfer may not be in sync with the damaged piece, consequently it will not fit the picture and will have to be reedited, which may not be possible. The reason for this is that a turntable or a non-sync tape playback does not play back at exactly the same speed every time, and subsequent transfers of a piece of music may not be the same length as the first transfer. To prevent this, the original transfer should be made onto quarter-inch tape with a sync-pulse synchronizing signal. Then, all transfers to magnetic film should be made from the sync tape. If this is done, you will have a quarter-inch sync tape master from which to make any number of transfers that will all be exactly in sync with each other and with the master.

Library music is usually added to the picture after it has been edited into its final form. Some very fine tracks have resulted from this method, but for the best track, the music and the picture workprint should be edited together simultaneously. In this way, the action and music proceed together, each being modified to fit the other. The music is still cut to fit the action, but there is the advantage of being able to adjust the picture to the music if necessary. In a large studio or on a high-budget picture only the music cutter is allowed to do this work, and he may edit the music only after the picture is in its final form. The small producer or lone filmmaker can profit by simultaneous music and picture editing.

It is possible to cut music satisfactorily, but it takes time and concentration and is often excruciatingly tedious. If attention is paid to musical phrases, notes, chords, and pauses, the score will work; if not, it will sound clipped and abrupt. You do not have to read music to be able to hear it. Pick out the strongest moments in the sequence to which you are setting music; these are the elements to accentuate. By juggling the selection of music with the picture in the editing machine, you can find the parts that best complement these moments. Try to manipulate the music through editing so that these parts match up with the picture, then let the rest of the music play where it falls. Try to strike an intelligent balance between making every little nuance fit the picture and having all the heavy accents in the wrong places. Too little editing defeats the purpose of the music; too much destroys its integrity.

A musical beginning that coincides with the start of a picture sequence and a musical conclusion that ends precisely as the sequence ends are important aspects of good music cutting. They help convey the feeling that the music has been made especially for the film. However, since sections of the music you choose rarely are the same length as the film sequences you intend to put them to, they are either too long or too short. A way to deal with this is to sync up the head and tail of the music so that they fit the head and tail of the visual; then either remove or add music to the midportion of the sequence as necessary. This involves careful listening and cutting to make the deletion or addition flow smoothly and fit the picture, but it can be done quite effectively. Here are some ways to make cuts in music:

1. Cut in a pause or break in the music. There are usually many small breaks in music that are not detected in normal listening. But if a music track is run very slowly in the editing machine or sound reader, breaks and pauses become easily identifiable. Although such pauses may be as small as one or two frames, this is enough space in which to make a cut.

2. Any drawn out tone or chord can usually be cut into, a portion removed, and the ends spliced together without its being noticeable.

3. A quiet or weak piece of music can usually be cut directly to a strong piece or to a heavy accent. However, it will not sound right if the cut is made the other way, from strong to weak or loud to quiet.

4. The middle of a passage that has a definite rhythm or beat can be shortened by cutting just before the beat and eliminating repetitions. Theoretically the overall rhythm is thrown off, but in most cases it will not be noticed if the passage is carefully selected.

5. A passage that is nondescript rhythmically may be cut into or shortened. If there are no rhythmic expectations set up by the music, a cut or removal of a section is generally not noticeable.

6. Listen for head and tail phrases of a piece of music, since these can often be spliced onto a smaller section of the same piece to give it a finished quality.

7. Cover bad cuts. Sometimes it is impossible to make a cut from one piece to another sound right. If this happens, try to cover the cut with some other music or sound effect—a bell, a horn honk, a gong, a gunshot, a cough, a chair scrape—just as long as what you use is appropriate to the picture.

8. A passage of music can be lengthened or shortened by varying the speed of the tape recorder when transferring from tape to magnetic film. Professional speed variers are available for use with standard motion picture production tape recorders. Although the speed variation alters the pitch of the music slightly, even a relatively major pitch change that is uniform throughout a whole passage cannot be detected by an audience.

Caution: Listen to each cut you make. If your ear tells you it works the first time you listen to it, the cut is good. But if you have to think about it and formulate a rationalization as to why it will be satisfactory, abandon the cut and try again. Be demanding with yourself.

In experimenting with music, you will find things that will and will not work. In addition to the points described above, you can do more in the mixing session to make the music succeed. At points where direct cuts and the rearrangement of music do not work the way you wish, make segues, or dissolves, from one music track to another. Or fade a piece out and immediately fade another in. In a musical segue, two pieces of similar orchestration and rhythm work well, but perhaps it is better to go from a quiet or slow piece of music to a faster or more dominant one. Although it is good to know that on occasion bad music tracks have been improved by ingenious mixers, you should always build the quality into the tracks themselves. A good rule of thumb is to avoid the imprecision of segues unless there is visual justification for the effect—a picture dissolve, for example—or unless you can find no other way to make the musical transition. It is always cleaner to make each piece of music fit its sequence perfectly; and if possible, each piece should have a definite beginning and a good ending. Always strive for that goal.

If the film is to have music "wall to wall," or all the way through, make sure there are no spaces between the different musical selections. Either the beginnings should follow immediately and rhythmically the endings of the previous pieces or there should be a segue between the two.

In setting up music tracks for mixing (see Mixing), follow the same procedure as previously described in the Sound Effects Editing section. Try to splice together on one roll as many pieces of music as you feasibly can. As long as the transitions between selections are unobtrusive mechanically, and as long as their respective volume levels are close, as many pieces as desired may be put on one roll. But if there are difficult transitions or widely varying volume and equalization levels, two or more music rolls will be required for mixing. If there is even one such difficult transition, take advantage of the extra roll by spacing out the rest of the music to make the mixer's task easier.

Music is least effective when it runs unvarying and unbroken under the visuals. At its best, music changes with the mood of the visuals, intensifying and sometimes even guiding them. At all costs, avoid innocuous music that merely fills the background while the picture progresses. Edit music as you would sound effects; that is, for each visual or sequence of visuals, insert music that does something appropriate to the visuals themselves. If a passage of music is too long, shorten it. Use only a few bars if the situation calls for it. Rearrange, repace, and reshape the music until it is an integral part of your film. But there will be times when no matter how many different pieces of music you try and no matter how you manipulate them, music simply will not fit the sequence. Generally, a sequence of film that cannot be set to music is badly edited; but if the picture cannot be changed, find some music that, if not perfect, is at least not destructive to the scene. Another possibility is that the sequence should stand without music, which is what it was trying to tell you all along. Do not assume that because music enhances most scenes, it should be applied indiscriminately.

MIXING

Mixing, rerecording, and *dubbing* all have the same meaning. They refer to the procedure in which all the edited sound tracks of a movie are combined into one *composite sound track.* The mixing session is conducted in a sound studio where the mixer, seated at a console, watches the film and controls the volume of individual tracks while they are being recorded. *Cue sheets* serve as a guide for the mixer. It is tempting to conclude that mixing information could be programmed and the mix controlled by a computer. As neat as this may appear to the scientific mind, it does not produce a track as good as one mixed by a person; for a fine quality mix results from the mixer's talent and "feel." Two competent mixers separately doing identical tracks will both produce final tracks of equal quality, yet both will be different in interpretation. In working with sound studios, you will quickly discover the mixer who does the best job for you.

The mixer, in trying to produce the best track possible, is concerned with three things: volume, equalization, and the physical possibility of achieving what you desire. First, he listens to the individual tracks and determines what sounds and voices must be equalized—to what extent must he alter the bass and treble components of certain sounds to make them sound as if they were recorded in the same place simultaneously. Next, he must control the volume of all the tracks so that they sound believable. Third, he is concerned with the way all the sounds have been assembled on their respective rolls because his successful control of volume and equalization depends on whether or not he can physically manipulate the controls to meet your demands. Two sounds may have been spliced together in one roll, making it mechanically impossible for the mixer to do what you wish. For example, if one sound effect immediately follows another on the same roll, the mixer cannot change volume on cue to the exact frame, and he cannot instantaneously change equalization settings in the same roll. When making up tracks for mixing, during picture editing, be guided by what you will require later in the mix.

Reels and Rolls

To avoid confusion in referring to the various elements involved in editing and mixing, be clear about the meaning of reels and rolls.

Reel

A *reel* is a unit of time—ten minutes—based on the length of the 35mm printing roll, which is 1000 feet, or ten minutes running time. The running time of movies is conventionally stated in "reels": a ten-minute picture is a one-reeler, a three-reel picture is thirty minutes. When a picture must be divided into sections because it is too long to handle in one piece, it is usually divided into reels of ten minutes each. Thus a picture thirty minutes long would be on three separate reels numbered R-1, R-2, and R-3. In 16mm production, however, pictures may be assembled into "reels" that are longer than ten minutes, sometimes as long as thirty minutes, because 16mm recording and printing equipment can accommodate reels of this size. In 35mm production, the division of pictures into ten-minute reels is still the standard.

Roll

A *roll* is also a section of film, but it always belongs to a particular reel. For example: Reel #1 of a picture has three sound tracks—dialogue, sound FX, and music. Each one of these is referred to as a roll—the dialogue roll, the FX roll, and the music roll. They are identified as R-1 Dialogue Roll, R-1 FX Roll, and R-1 Music Roll. If there is more than one of a roll, say FX, the first roll is designated R-1 FX Roll A, the second is R-1 FX Roll B, and so on.

Preparation for the Mixing Session

Although sound mixers sometimes come close to being magicians, the quality of the mix they can produce depends on how the tracks have been edited and prepared. If the tracks and cue sheets have been casually or carelessly prepared the mixer can rarely provide the quality you desire. Thus there are several preliminary tasks that must be done preparatory to a mixing session, as follows:

1. Arrange tracks for mixing.
2. Make sound rolls the proper length.
3. Prepare leaders.
4. Use suitable filler in sound rolls.
5. Remove extraneous sounds.
6. Make up cue sheets.
7. Clean workprint and sound rolls.
8. Assemble workprint and sound rolls.
9. Select raw stock.
10. Screen the picture and all tracks before the mix.

Arranging Tracks for Mixing

Be sure the sounds on each track are placed so that they can be physically manipulated. Put only one kind of sound on a roll. Do not combine dialogue with music, dialogue with FX, or FX with music on any one roll. In sync dialogue, where the sound effects have been recorded live on the same track, separate the sound effects onto a separate roll if possible. (See Sound Effects Editing.) To dissolve from one piece of music to another, have the two pieces on separate tracks—Music A and Music B—with enough of an overlap so the mixer can make a smooth transition from one track to the other. If such a transition is to occur at the same time as a 48-frame picture dissolve, do not expect the mixer to make the music dissolve in exactly 48 frames. Give him a few extra frames on the tail of the outgoing piece of music and on the head of the incoming music. If one sound follows another immediately on the same track, the mixer cannot change volume on cue to the exact frame. And he cannot make three or more simultaneous volume changes on one cut since he has only two hands. In editing, additional tasks may be added as needed, so do not try to cram everything into the least number of tracks.

Go through all the sounds, particularly voice, and look for sections that require equalization.

That is, sounds whose treble and bass levels are different and will have to be changed to similar levels. This occurs in dialogue or narration where different microphones were used, or where the acoustics differed on successive shooting days or locations. (See Microphone Sensitivity.) The mixer can balance, or equalize, these quality differences by changing the balance between frequencies. But generally he can only equalize sounds that are isolated on separate tracks. For example, if closeups are shot with a different microphone or under different conditions from those of the master scene, the voice quality of the two would not match. As editor, you will then have to put all the master scene dialogue on one roll and all the closeup dialogue on another. With this arrangement, the mixer can set the equalization ahead of time for each track. (For convenience during editing, you would normally assemble all dialogue on the same roll. But before the mix you would have to separate those sections that need to be equalized.) To separate dialogue into two tracks, follow the procedure for removing sound effects from the dialogue track, as explained in Sound Effects Editing. (See Fig. 10.12.) Also, any adjoining sounds that require volume changes should be put on separate tracks.

Dividing sounds onto separate tracks for ease in mixing does not mean that every sound has to be on a track by itself. What is required is sufficient space between sounds so the mixer can physically manipulate any required volume changes. Also, there should not be several volume changes simultaneously. Try to visualize the tracks as a constant flow: one track comes in as another goes out. Sounds are turned down low, others are made louder, and still others are turned out completely and brought in as the cue sheets indicate. Mixing is not a magical thing that just happens; it is a planned result that depends on the foresight of the editor and the skill of the mixer. Consider the requirements of mixing and arrange your tracks so they can be physically controlled.

Making Sound Rolls the Proper Length

Most professional sound studios conduct mixing on the basis of the 35mm reel, which is 1000 feet long. Often this means that only one reel can be mixed at a time. Therefore the editor must plan convenient breaks at one-reel intervals if any of the following apply to the picture: it is in 35mm; or it is in 16mm but is to be blown up to 35mm; or it is 16mm, but the studio can mix only in 35mm-reel lengths. If you do mix one reel at a time, do not make the mistake of putting a 16mm picture into 1000-foot rolls. Do put it into 400-foot rolls. In 16mm, ten minutes is 400 feet, but in 35mm ten minutes is 1000 feet. The running time, ten minutes, determines the divisions of reels for mixing.

Although some studios can handle 16mm mixing in rolls longer than 400 feet and even 35mm rolls up to thirty minutes, or 3000 feet, do not assume anything. Before preparing for the mix, check with the studio you intend to use and find out precisely its limitations and requirements. Caution: Each reel of sound and its rolls must have complete mixing leaders. (See Start Marks and Leaders.)

Preparing Mixing Leaders

Put mixing head and tail leaders on all reels of the picture and on all reels of the sound rolls before mixing. (See Start Marks and Leaders.) Properly organized and marked leaders ensure accurate sync, make the cue sheets intelligible, and make possible later in-sync assembly of mixed tracks for printing. It is extremely important to use correct leaders.

Using Suitable Filler in Sound Rolls

Usually a sound track consists of individual sound effects or passages of dialogue separated on the roll by lengths of film referred to as *spacer* or *filler*. The requirements of filler are that it does not foul up the magnetic heads of the playback machines and that it does not create static. The following are suitable for use as filler:

1. *Lightstruck positive film*. This is the well-known yellow leader, which is actually film exposed to light and left undeveloped. It has a base side (shiny) and an emulsion side (dull) just as film does. Be careful that it is spliced into the sound roll with its emulsion position the reverse of the sound stock emulsion. If the emulsion side of the filler touches the magnetic pickup head, emulsion will scrape off and pile up, distorting the sound or cutting it out altogether.

2. *Erased magnetic film stock.* This is perfectly suitable for filler, and its emulsion need not be reversed because the sound film emulsion is designed with sufficient hardness to withstand the scraping effect of the magnetic head. However, since magnetic film filler is the same color as the magnetic film used for the sound, it is difficult to tell visually where sound ends and filler begins. It is, therefore, convenient to reverse the emulsion of sound film used as filler.

3. *Processed film.* This may be any kind of picture film if you remember to reverse the emulsion position from that of the sound film. In 16mm sound rolls, use only clean, single-perforated film.

4. *Clear film stock.* This is film stock with no emulsion on it at all—it is base on both sides. It tends to build up static during long runs, causing cracks and pops on the track. It works well in a mix as long as the volume control is turned down while the clear film is running over the sound head. If you need to start a sound with an open pot (volume control), clear filler may result in static noise on the final track. Also, without an emulsion to give it body, clear film, particularly 16mm, is exasperating to handle. It forms loops and twists easily, and identification marks are difficult to locate.

Careful selection and assembly of spacer can prevent serious problems during the mix. Do not use stock that is badly shrunken or physically damaged by broken sprocket holes, tears, and torn edges. With 16mm film use only single-perforated filler for the sound rolls.

Removing Extraneous Sounds

Unwanted sounds on the various sound rolls can make a mix a long, miserable affair, so be sure to remove all sounds that are not part of the picture. Often the sound fidelity of the editing machine will be much lower than that of the mixing equipment, with the result that you will hear sounds you never heard before through the studio sound system. Unwanted sounds mean that the mixer cannot preset volume levels for tracks and leave them. He must keep all volume controls down and bring them up only on cue. This reduces the mixer's effectiveness, and in some cases may even result in an unusable track. If you go into the mix with noisy tracks, you will probably have to stop the mix and clean them up at an additional cost of time and money.

Making Up Mixing Cue Sheets

A cue sheet is a graphic description of a sound track. It is used by the mixer as a guide to where the sounds are and how they should be mixed. Keep the data on the cue sheets simple, direct, and brief (Fig. 10.15). Each cue sheet should contain the following information:

1. Where the sound is.
2. When the sound begins and ends.
3. How the sound comes in and goes out.
4. What the sound is.
5. Who is speaking.

Where the Sound Is

Identify each cue sheet as to reel number and roll number. Make a separate cue sheet for each sound roll, and number the sheets if there is more than one to a roll.

When the Sound Begins and Ends

This is the footage at which a sound actually comes in and the footage where it goes out. Make the cue only at the point where the sound is to begin or end, not at the splice. Do not ask or expect the mixer to make a cue on the frame. At 24 frames per second, on-the-frame cues simply cannot be made. If you want a sound to cue in precisely on a frame, edit the track so the sound begins on exactly that frame. Be sure you are thoroughly familiar with the number of frames per foot, feet per second, and frames per second for both 16mm and 35mm. (See Appendix.)

35MM FOOTAGE CUES

On 35mm cue sheets, indicate a cue only to the whole foot. Do not list half-feet or frames. (*Note*: 35mm film has 16 frames per foot.)

If an incoming sound does not occur on a whole foot, move the cue toward the head to the nearest whole foot. *Example*: 75 feet plus 9 frames should be marked on the cue sheet as 75 feet.

If an outgoing sound does not fall on the

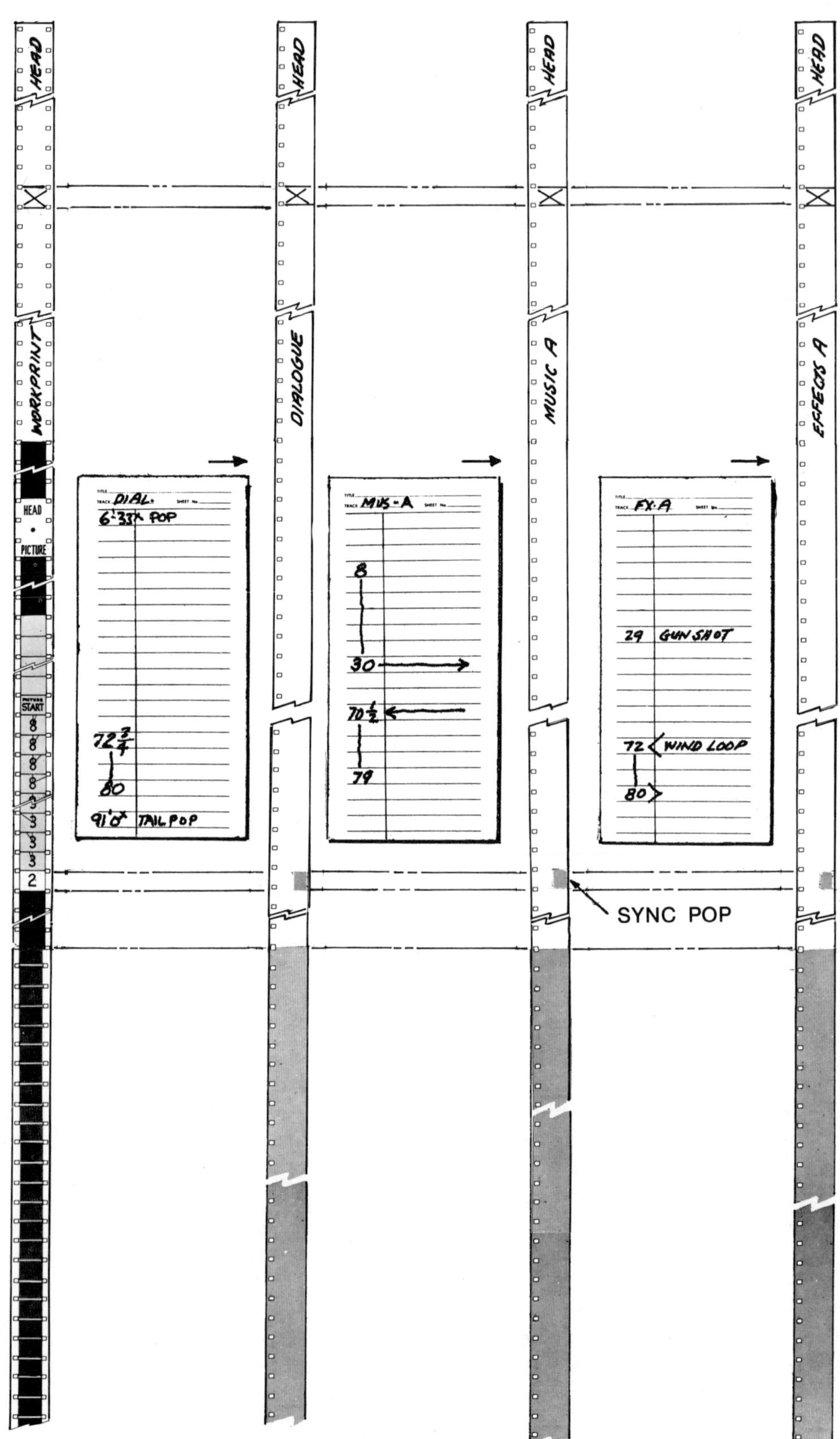

Fig. 10.15. A mixing cue sheet must accompany every sound track for a mixing session.

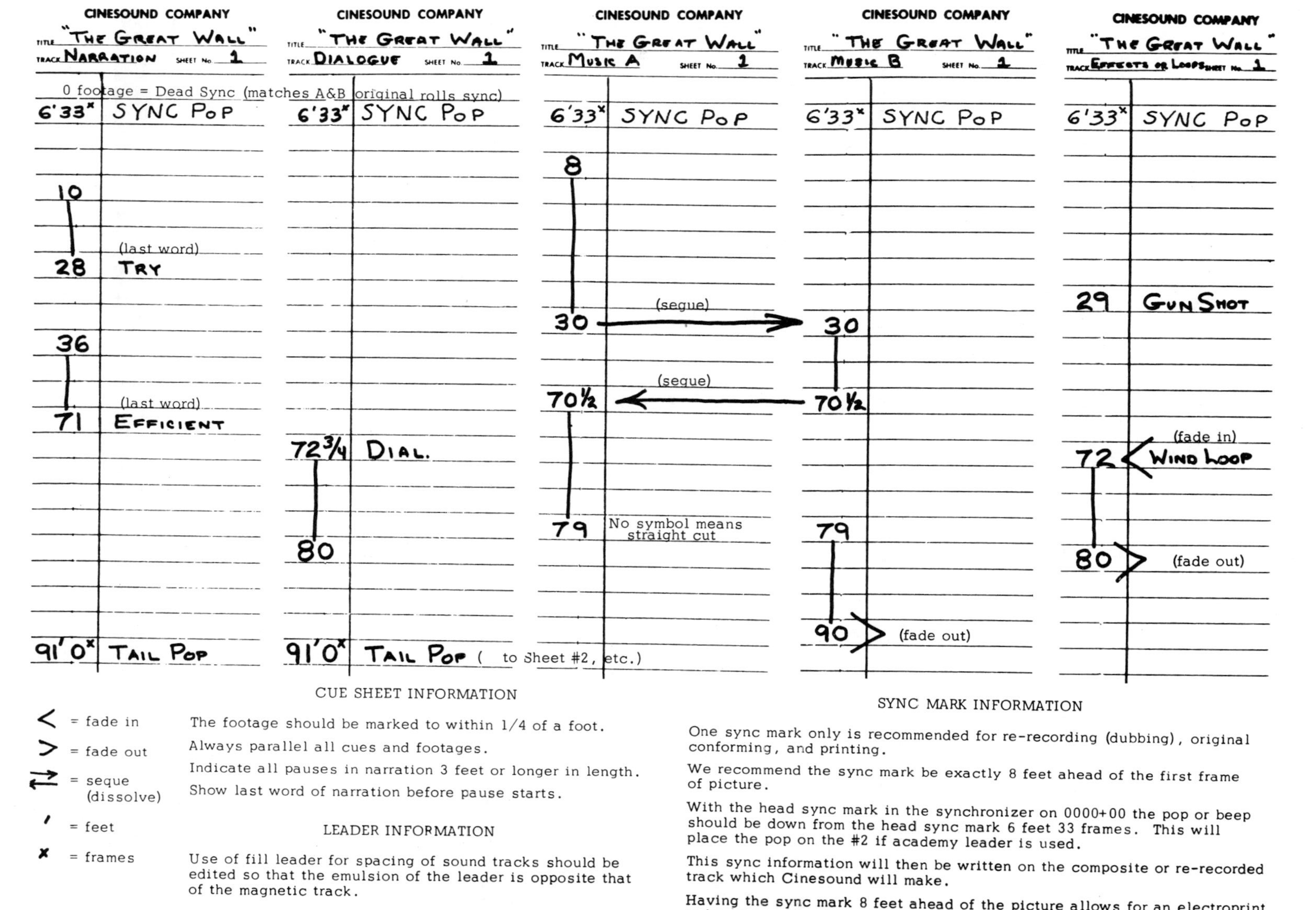

Fig. 10.16. Sample cue sheets issued by a studio to indicate its preferences as to markings and start marks.

whole foot, *delay* the cue to the next whole foot. *Example*: 130 feet plus 10 frames should be marked on the cue sheet as 131 feet.

16MM FOOTAGE CUES

In 16mm cue sheets, indicate a cue to the nearest half-foot or whole foot. (Note: 16mm film has 40 frames per foot.)

If an incoming sound does not fall on a whole foot or half-foot, move the cue toward the head to the nearest whole or half-foot. *Example*: 50 feet plus 33 frames should be marked on the cue sheet as 50½ feet.

If an outgoing sound does not fall on a whole or half-foot, delay the cue to the nearest whole or half-foot. *Example*: 74 feet plus 22 frames should be marked on the cue sheet as 75 feet. The reason for advancing incoming and delaying outgoing cues is that if you go to the nearest foot, it is possible to clip off part of the incoming or outgoing sound. Sometimes it is helpful to put visual cues on the workprint to guide the mixer. (See Fig. 10.17.) A common cue is a series of three or four punches at one-half or one-second intervals, the last punch being the cue. The first punches set up a rhythm that helps the mixer hit the last punch with great precision. Make punch marks with a one-hole, quarter-inch hand punch in the center of the frame on the workprint (Fig. 10.17).

Another visual cue is a *streamer,* a diagonal line scribed or marked on the film. On the screen the line appears to move from one side of the screen to the other. The cue occurs the instant the line touches the opposite side of the screen. 48 frames is the usual length of a diagonal streamer cue.

How the Sound Comes In and Goes Out

Indicate on the cue sheet how each sound is to come in and go out. First you need to know what the mixer can and cannot do for you during the mix. He normally has control of several elements for each track: on his console, for each sound roll there is a volume control, called a *pot* (for potentiometer), and controls for equalization, compression, noise reduction, and echo. During the mix, he manipulates the pots to control the entrance, volume, and exit of each sound. Before the mix, he makes appropriate settings of the other elements for each track, which normally remain at the preset level throughout the mix. The mixer can change the equalization during the mixing run, but only when two sounds are widely separated on one track and the other sounds are arranged so that the mixer is free at

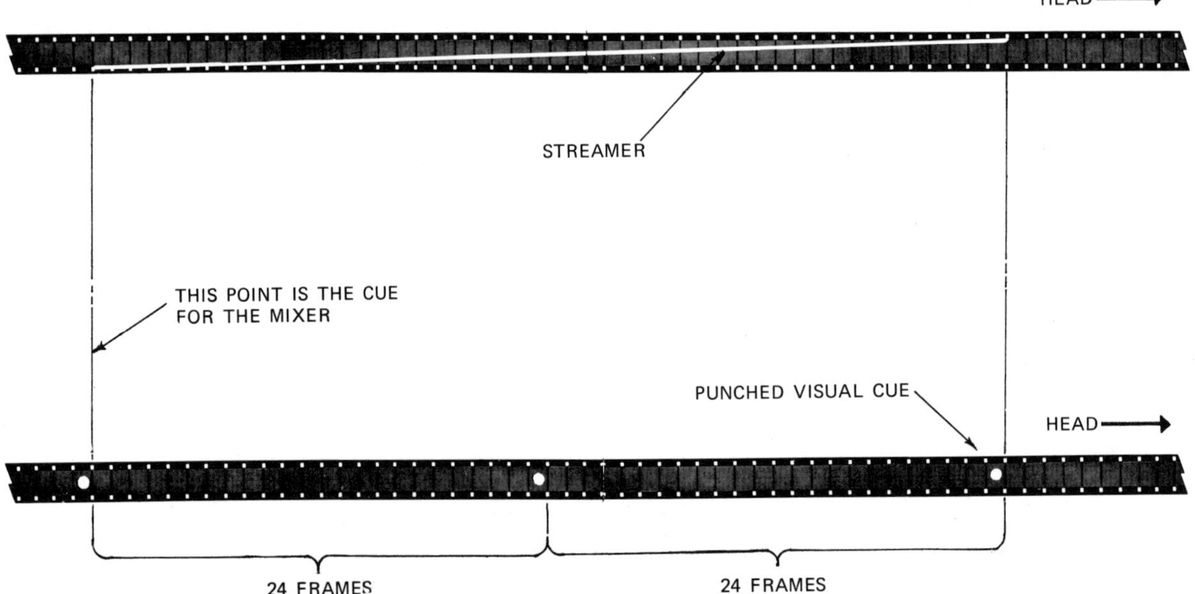

Fig. 10.17. Cue marks may be drawn, scribed, or punched on the workprint as visual cues for the mixer. Projected, punch marks occur rhythmically each second; a streamer appears as a vertical line crossing the screen.

some time during the run to make the change. Do not assume that equalization can be changed during the mix. Check with the mixer or the studio ahead of time.

Sound can come in and go out in three different ways: *fade, automatic,* or *switched.* During the editing you should try to build the tracks so that every sound comes in and goes out clean, that is, each sound has its own beginning and ending built into it. The mixer then has only to set the volume ahead of time for such sounds.

FADE

For a sound to fade in, the mixer turns down the pot ahead of the cue. On the cue, he gradually turns up the pot to increase the volume to the desired level. Indicate on the cue sheet the length of the fade and at what point it should be in or out. Remember that a fadein starts before the point where you want it to be in at full volume, so there must be sound on the track before the fadein begins. If a fadein of 48 frames is desired, be sure to have more than exactly 48 frames of sound ahead of the cue. A mixer may be extremely skillful, but he needs a little leeway. For a fadeout, there must be sound on the track at least up to the point where the fadeout ends.

AUTOMATIC

A sound comes in automatically when it begins on the edited track just the way you want it. All that is necessary is that the pot be set to the desired volume level in advance. Then the sound comes in clean, that is, without the mixer's having to control it with the pot. A sound goes out automatically when it does not have to be faded or switched out. The leader ahead of an automatic sound entrance and the leader following an automatic exit must be absolutely free of extraneous sound because the pot is open before the sound comes in and after it goes out.

SWITCH

During a mix, a track may be taken in or out instantly by means of a switch on the console. All tracks run simultaneously in sync during the mix, but a switch for each track determines whether it is in or out. The mixer can hold a track on OUT and then switch it to IN so that its sound begins instantly. Or he can switch a track out instantly. Do not normally expect a switched track to hit a cue exactly to a frame. If you require such exact cueing, edit the track in advance so that it hits the cue automatically. Switching-in might be used for sounds that begin at a preset volume or a preset equalization but not on an exact frame cue, such as background effects that enter during a picture dissolve or under some other overpowering sound such as an explosion.

What the Sound Is

Indicate on the cue sheet in one word or two what the sound is—traffic, footsteps, gunshots, and so on. Occasionally indications of equalization and volume level are put on the cue sheets, and in special situations note that a voice needs a telephone filter or a particular sound is required to be loud or soft. Generally, however, in the first run-throughs, the director and the mixer determine which sounds should be equalized or given special volume settings. It is better for the mixer to mark the sheets himself for these requirements than to have the editor mark them ahead of time by guesswork.

Who is Speaking

Note whether the sound is dialogue or narration. Sometimes you may want to indicate a particular character by name if, because of unusual loud or soft delivery, special control is needed.

Cleaning Workprint and Sound Rolls

Be sure that your workprint and sound rolls are clean before they go to the studio for mixing. Any of the following may cause bad sound or eliminate it altogether: grease pencil marks, felt pens, dust, fingerprints, adhesive from tape, scratches, poor splices. The best way to clean the sound track is to rewind it slowly, holding it in your hand with a glove, a piece of lintfree cloth, or a cleaning velvet. Do not use film cleaner or any other liquid cleaner even though both labels and salesmen tell you it is safe to use with magnetic film. Liquid cleaners tend to destroy the sound track. If the budget allows, have the laboratory make a cheap reversal black-and-white duplicate copy of the workprint to use in the mix. (Such a workprint copy is customarily called a *dirty dupe*.) Since the editing process has subjected the workprint to much wear, tear, and splicing, it often breaks or loses projection loops during the prolonged running of the mixing session. The dirty dupe provides a new, splice-free print that runs freely through the projector; and though its image quality is poor, it is satisfactory to mix by. If all markings are cleaned off the workprint before printing, you then have a clean dirty dupe that can be marked solely with cues for the mixer. Dirty dupes also made for FX and music cutting immediately following approval of the final version of the workprint allow sound effects and music to be edited while the workprint goes directly into negative cutting.

Assembling Workprint and Sound Rolls for Mixing

When entering the mixing session, the workprint and sound rolls must be ready to put on the projector and the playback machines. Place the clean workprint on a good, unbent reel wound for projection. Put the sound rolls heads out on cores or unbent reels. If not on cores, all 16mm tracks should be heads out on double-keyed, unbent reels. The hub diameter of reels used for 16mm sound tracks must be at least three inches.

Selection of Raw Stock

Although a sound studio will generally provide the raw stock for the mix at a price, it is usually cheaper to furnish your own stock. Be sure to select and handle magnetic film carefully. Use only high-quality, new magnetic film. Every studio adjusts its machines to handle certain types of magnetic film, so find out in advance what kind of stock your studio recommends. After you buy magnetic film, do not let it sit around. If you must keep it for any length of time, be sure to store it in a temperature- and humidity-controlled room.

Conduct of the Mixing Session

In the mixing session, the technicians in the machine room thread up the picture in the projector and the sound rolls on the playback machines. The mixer sits in the studio with the cue sheets arranged on the console in front of him (Fig. 10.18). When the machine room signals that

Fig. 10.18. Motion picture mixing studio. Note the footage counter and VU meter under the screen. (*Credit*: Glen Genn Studios, Hollywood, California.)

Fig. 10.19. The mixer adjusts volume controls for several sound tracks during a mix.

the picture and tracks are threaded and ready to go, the mixer punches a button and the machines roll. The picture is projected on the studio screen and all the sound tracks are played into the speakers. By means of the console pots, or volume controls, the mixer watches the picture and controls each track, making it louder or softer changing the equalization, or taking it out altogether.

Someone should be responsible for making final decisions in a mixing session. Usually it is the editor, who sits next to the mixer during the session. The mixer does the actual mixing, and the excellence of the final mix depends on his talent, skill, and taste. If you are the director or the one in charge of the mix, you may sit next to the mixer at the console or in a seat in front of the console. First, discuss the picture with the mixer. Explain how you feel the track should sound and what kind of overall impression you would like in the final track. Then proceed to the first run-through, in which the mixer gets his first impression of the tracks. On the first two or three run-throughs, the mixer and the technicians in the machine room will make adjustments and equalization settings and generally get the mechanics of the mix in order. Do not make suggestions until after the mixer has become familiar with all the tracks and has all adjustments and settings made. Watch carefully as the run-through proceeds and, with reference to the footage counter, note any suggestions or exchanges to be made.

Do not expect a finished sound track on the first few run-throughs because it usually takes many run-throughs to arrive at an acceptable mix. The mixer needs to practice with the picture and all the tracks until he is able to make a mix by "feel."

Since the mix is the culminating creative task in making a movie, there is generally quite a bit of excitement generated, and the producer, the backers, the clients, the sponsor, or other people involved always want to attend the mixing session. It is the first time the picture will be seen in its entirety with all the sound tracks, so it is a fairly auspicious event. Try to keep all such visitors out of the mixing session if possible. The mix is a hard-work session, and the picture shows up at its worst. The projection print at this stage is usually scratched and dirty, with the editor's markings and mixing cues on it. The first several trial run-throughs may sound unsatisfactory, even bad, and the entire movie will not be seen in uninterrupted continuity since only one reel at a time is worked on until it is completed. Usually uninformed visitors are quickly disenchanted. They are probably there only because it is a sign of status to be present at the mixing session. If backers are present, it is quite possible their reaction will be, "Is this what we spent all that money for?" Nonprofessionals are unaware that even the best movie in the world can appear uninteresting during the mix. Important people tend to make and receive phone calls in the studio, to walk in and out during run-throughs, and to provide unwanted and unnecessary distractions. Ideally, the only people present at the mix should be the mixer, the director, and the editor. You probably will not be able to keep others out, but try.

In most mixing studios, the projector, recorder, and playback machines can be stopped in sync and backed up ahead of any point where you wish to make a change or correct a mistake. Then the machines may be started again and the recording will be picked up at exactly the point where the change is to occur. This reversing ability of the mixing studio is extremely valuable in both time and money. Previously it was necessary when a mistake was made to stop the machines, rewind all tracks and picture, and start the run-through again, trusting that the job could be completed without making another mistake. In some studios without reversing equipment this may still be the case. Although automatic reversing may be a boon, it can also be a handicap because the best track comes from a smooth run-through in which the mixer has the "feel" of the tracks. If he has to stop, his mood is broken. No matter how many mistakes are made in a mix, a mistake-free track can be attained in one run-through with automatic reversing. But the finest track, the one that is the most artistic, can be made only when the mixer is free from many small interruptions.

ELEVEN

Negative Cutting

Negative cutting is the process of matching the negative/original footage to the workprint and synchronizing it with the final sound track so that composite release prints may be made. Since both *camera negative film* and *camera original reversal* film must be handled identically, the term *negative/original,* as used in this chapter, refers equally to both types of camera-exposed film.

Negative/original may be assembled either in a single roll or in multiple rolls called AB rolls. Originally, AB rolls were designed for 16mm negative/original assembly only because there is no space between the frames to make invisible splices; all 35mm and wider gauge films were assembled by the single-strand method because there is plenty of space between the frames and that is the way it had always been done. While it is still true that almost all 16mm assembly is done in the AB roll format, lately there has been a substantial switch in the wider gauge negative/original assembly from the single strand to this relatively new (twenty-five years) technique because filmmakers and studios have found they can get a less expensive and more satisfactory result by this method.

PRINCIPLE OF AB ROLL NEGATIVE ASSEMBLY

The principle of AB roll negative/original assembly is that alternate scenes of your negative/original film are spliced into separate rolls but still in exact workprint sequence. Black opaque leader between each scene in each roll fills in the spaces left by dividing the scenes into two or more rolls. Since AB rolls are assembled in conformity with the edited workprint, all the negative/original scenes, although alternately on separate rolls, follow each other in the proper order. (See Fig. 11.1.) To make the release print, the A roll is first printed onto the release stock. The black leader permits no light to pass through, so the release stock is unexposed wherever there is black leader. Then, before being developed, the B roll is printed onto the same stock, only this time the alternate scenes print into the unexposed spaces. The stock is then developed, and the result is one roll of film with all the shots printed onto it in the order of the edited workprint. Two principal advantages are gained by printing from multiple rolls: invisible splices, and an unlimited number of fades and dissolves.

Invisible Splices

In 16mm film the splice occurs on the frame line. Because of this, when the emulsion for the splice to be made is scraped off, a small part of the actual picture area is removed, leaving a narrow band of clear film. When spliced together in a single roll, these clear areas show through in pro-

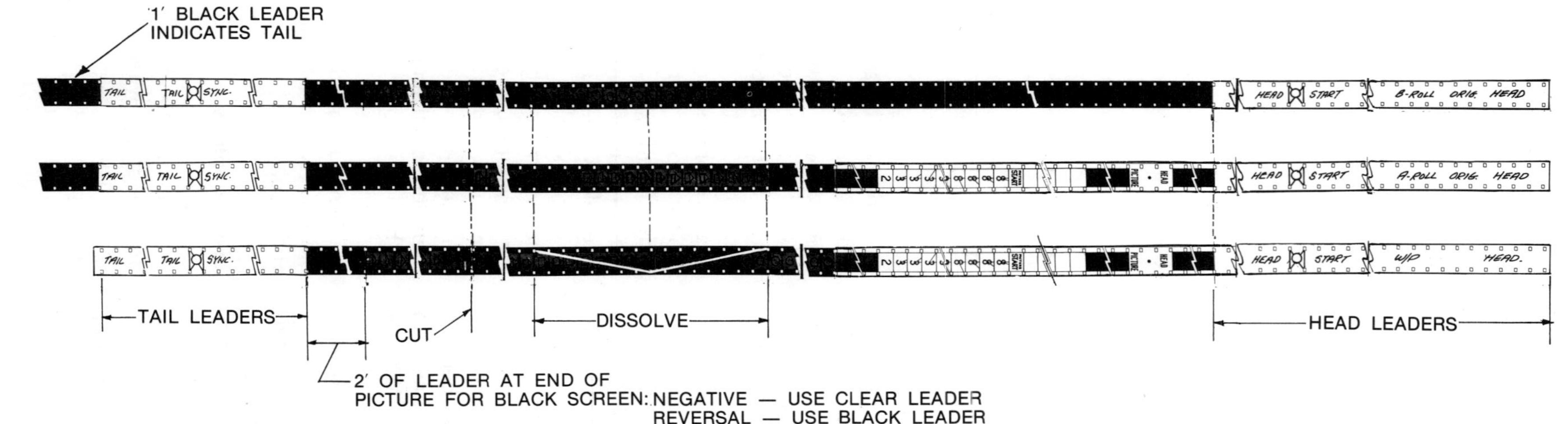

Fig. 11.1. Schematic diagram of negative/original assembled in AB rolls for printing. Scenes in the negative/original are matched to corresponding workprint scenes and assembled alternately on two rolls. Note the overlap of Scenes 1 and 2 for a dissolve effect.

jection in the form of frame line flashes. Film assembled in multiple rolls with black opaque leader between each shot does not produce these visible splices.

Unlimited Number of Fades and Dissolves

In AB-roll printing, dissolves, fades, and superimposures are made during printing directly from the AB rolls. This is in contrast to the single-roll method of cutting negative, where each effect dissolve, fade, wipe, and superimposition must be printed on a dupe negative in an optical printer and then spliced into a single negative printing roll. For each optical effect, laboratories charge a flat fee plus the regular per-foot rate for processing. Thus, it doesn't take very many dissolves, fades, or other effects for the cost to increase rapidly. Also, any duping process results in some loss of image quality; if the movie is to be printed from an intermediate film stock such as a dupe negative or color internegative, the effect on the image of duping the opticals can be critical. In AB-roll printing there is no loss of image quality and no additional cost per dissolve, fade, or superimposure because these simple effects are created automatically in the printing. The slightly higher cost per foot of printing from AB rolls rather than from a single negative/original is far less than the expense of having each effect made separately and generally results in a print with a more consistently precise image.

CLEANLINESS IN NEGATIVE CUTTING

Cleanliness is one of the most important considerations in negative cutting. Since the negative/original is unique and represents the total investment of money and labor, every effort to protect it is worthwhile. Aside from physical damage, the greatest danger to negative/original is dirt.

Dirt, as it applies to film, comes in many shapes and sizes. Dust is the most common and is ever-present. Minute particles of dust on the negative/original cause permanent scratches and specks. Such abrasions are immortalized in the film's emulsion and appear in all prints forever after like a congenital disease.

Dust collects on everything. It is carried into a cutting room on shoes, clothing, and other objects. Dusting with a cloth merely stirs it up so that it can settle again on everything in sight. Vacuuming picks it up, but blows greater amounts of finer particles out of its exhaust. The real solution to dust is an air-conditioning system with a dust filter. Unfortunately, such a system is very expensive, so do the best you can. Try to use an ordinary air-conditioned room that has smooth walls and ceiling. A room with lots of shelves and overhead fixtures is a storehouse for dust.

Vacuuming a room is a good way to start, but be sure and keep the exhaust end of the vaccum cleaner outside the room. Dusting and wiping with a damp cloth helps, but even this often smears the dirt so that when it dries it is dust once again. Do what you can until your negative cutting room is as clean as you can get it. Keep your synchronizer, rewinds, and other equipment spotless. Watch out for cigarette ashes and dandruff.

TOOLS; SUPPLIES, AND FACILITIES FOR NEGATIVE CUTTING

The tools, supplies, and facilities for negative cutting are not extensive, but they must meet certain qualifications to prevent damage or destruction to the irreplaceable negative (Figs. 11.2, 11.3). The principal requirements are as follows:

1. A clean, dustfree room.
2. A clean, sturdy editing table with a light-colored scratch-free surface equipped with the following:
   (a) A pair of long-shaft rewinds in good working condition
   (b) A tightwinder
   (c) Leader stanchion
   (d) Shelves
3. A comfortable chair or stool.
4. A desk lamp or other suitable lamp that can be set without glare.
5. A clean, well-adjusted, smooth running synchronizer. Check it carefully to be sure that it does not damage the sprocket holes or scratch the film. It should be at least a three-way machine, one sprocket for your workprint and one

sprocket each for the A and B rolls. More rolls require more sprockets (Fig. 11.4.).

6. Several unbent steel reels in good condition without nicks and burrs. All the reels should be the same hub size and overall size. They should be larger than the amount of footage in your film to prevent your negative from slipping off the reels as they become nearly full.

7. Two or more split reels.

8. A steel carpenter's or machinist's scribe for scribing marks on the film edges.

9. A pair of blunt-nosed, perfectly working scissors.

10. A magnifying glass for inspecting film, matching by eye, and reading illegible edge numbers.

11. A tape dispenser, preferably the double kind that dispenses from two separate rolls of tape.

12. A core adapter for accommodating a plastic core to the tightwinder.

13. A spring clamp to hold several reels tightly together on the rewind shaft.

14. Spacers to place between reels mounted on a single rewind shaft. Plastic cores make good spacers and cost little.

15. A single-hole hand punch (¼ inch) for punching start marks and sync pop marks in leaders.

16. Leader stock: Light-struck, double-perforated leader for AB roll head and tail leaders; Black opaque leader for AB roll assembly; clear leader, double-perforated (used only in negative AB roll assembly); and society leader negative/original.

17. Miscellaneous supplies: White editing gloves (enough pairs so that you work always with clean

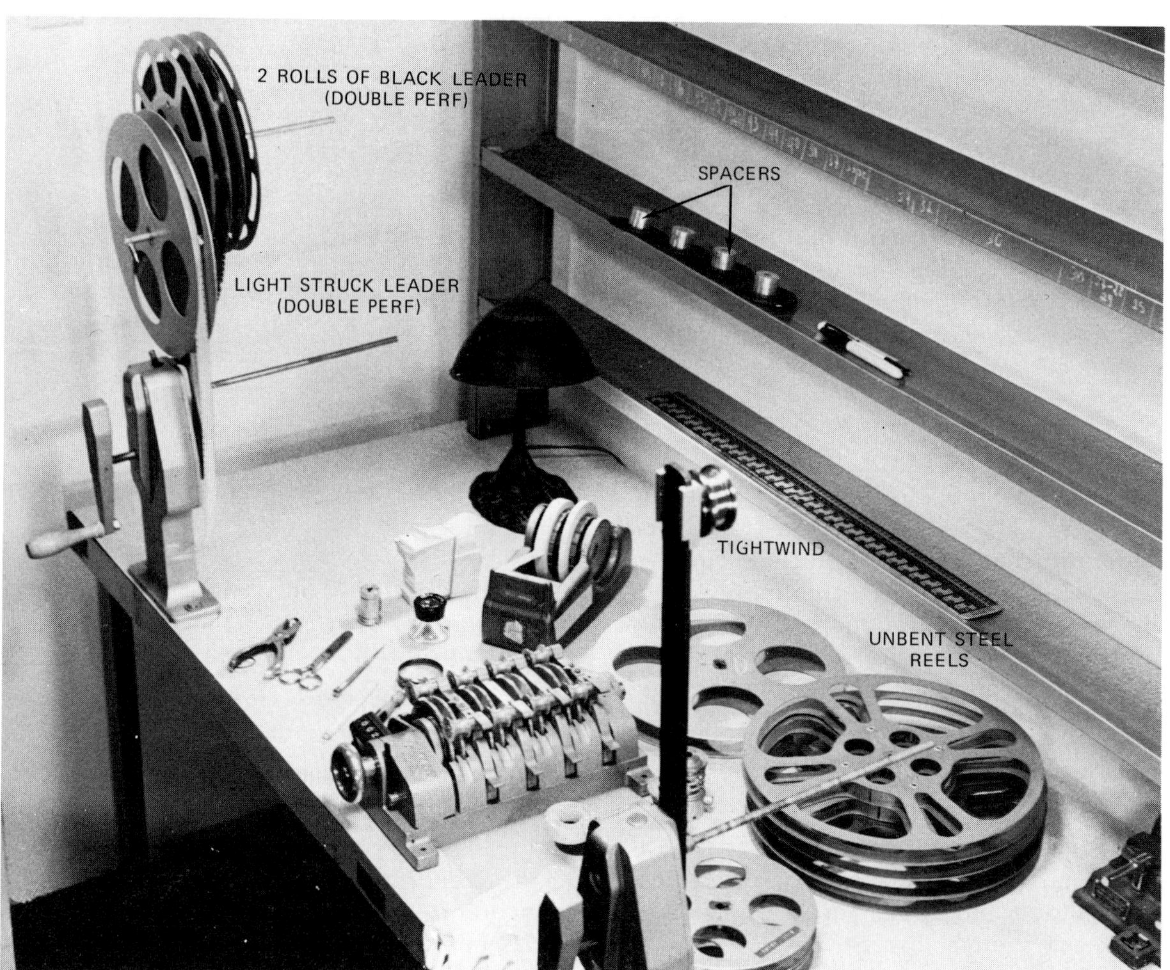

Fig. 11.2. Negative cutting layout, tools, and supplies.

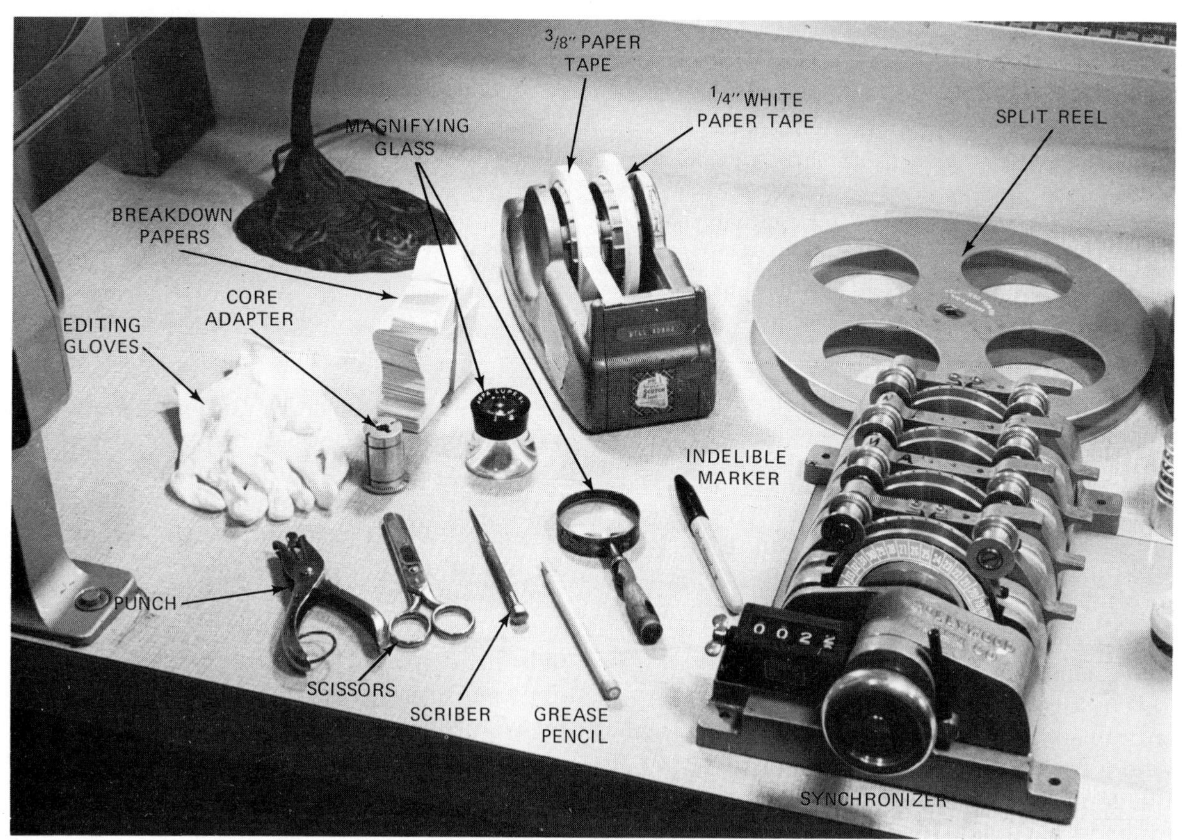

Fig. 11.3. Negative cutting tools.

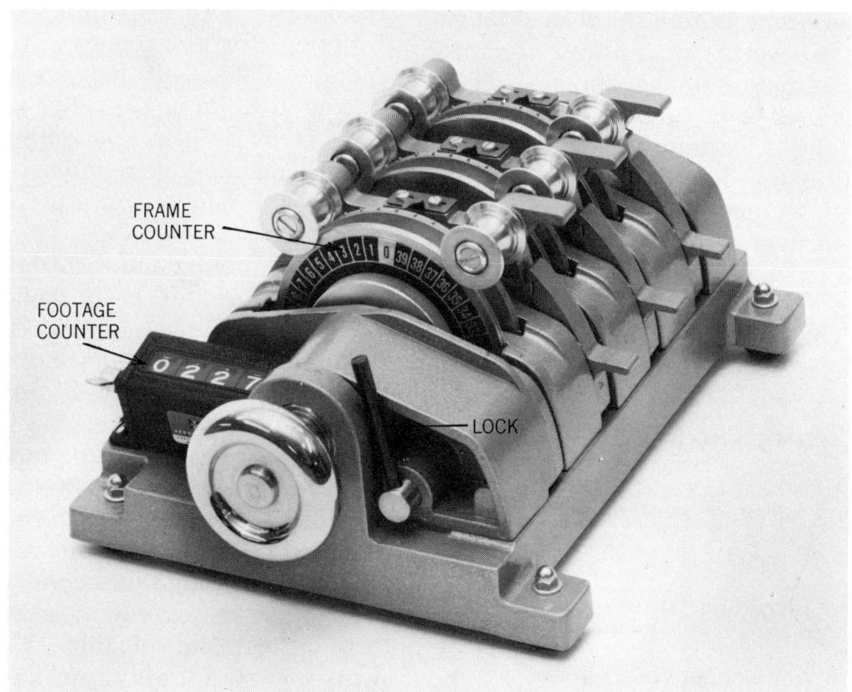

Fig. 11.4. 3-gang 16mm synchronizer. From Hollywood Film Company.

gloves; grease pencil—white, red, or yellow; tape—one roll quarter-inch white paper tape, one roll half-inch masking tape; negative breakdown papers; scratch paper; pen; pencil; indelible marking pen (fine point); tissue paper—several large sheets; film vault cans or 35mm 1000-foot cans for broken down negative rolls.

18. A radio. During the long, mechanical tedium of negative cutting, the creative spirit hungers for and needs aesthetic nourishment.

WORKPRINT MARKING

Negative cutting can begin only when you have a completed, approved, and properly marked workprint. The following effects must be indicated on the workprint in grease pencil: dissolves, fades, superimposures, extended scenes, unintentional splices, hold frames (freeze frames), and special optical effects (Fig. 5*A–F*).

In cutting the negative/original remember to use the splices in the workprint as a guide. Without some sort of mark, it is impossible to tell an unintentional splice from a deliberate one, and once a cut has been made in a piece of negative/original, it cannot be repaired. So be sure that all unintentional splices are clearly marked (Fig. 11.5*E*).

An extended scene is similar to an unintentional splice. In workprint editing, you may decide to have a shot run longer and its succeeding shot run shorter than you have actually cut it (Fig. 11.5*F*). In this case, draw an arrow from the existing splice to the point where the splice is actually wanted. This tells the negative cutter: do not cut the negative/original at the old splice A but extend the scene to B.

If the workprint is marked fully, correctly, and to length, the work may proceed smoothly.

NEGATIVE CUTTING STAGES

Negative cutting falls into seven distinct stages, as follows:

1. Reading and recording workprint edge numbers.
2. Breaking down the negative/original.
3. Selecting and numbering scenes of the negative/original corresponding to the workprint shot list.
4. Assembling AB rolls to match the workprint.
5. Splicing the assembled negative/original.
6. Marking the sound track for editorial and printer sync.
7. Preparing AB rolls for shipment to the laboratory.

Reading and Recording Workprint Edge Numbers

The first step in negative cutting is reading and recording the first and last edge numbers of each scene in the edited workprint. (See Fig. 11.6.) These numbers are essential since they are the means by which you can match each negative scene to the workprint (Fig. 11.6).

Place the workprint on the left-hand rewind, heads out, and thread it onto the reel on the right-hand rewind. Be sure the emulsion is up, since negative edge numbers on a print read correctly through the emulsion side. To backlight the numbers so you can see them, use a lightwell or a piece of white paper on the table with a light shining on it. Have a magnifying glass handy for hard-to-see numbers.

Wind down to the first shot in the workprint and locate the first edge number (Fig. 11.7). You need not count the frames ahead of the first number nor the frames following the last number. Often half the number has run off the edge of the film or a key digit falls into a sprocket hole. Don't despair. You will soon develop a skill for making out edge numbers.

Enter the number on a piece of paper, which will become your shot list. Go through the workprint, noting and recording the first and last edge number for each scene. Number these scenes consecutively on the shot list. The final result is a shot list of the scenes in your workprint listed in order of their appearance in the workprint (Fig. 11.8). Leave a space for remarks. For example, it is quite common for two or more shots in the workprint to be from the same negative/original scene. Note this so that the trims of that particular negative/original scene will not be filed before using the second, or third part of it. Also, indicate superimposures so that they will not be left out of the AB rolls. When the workprint shot list is complete, you are ready to break down the negative/original.

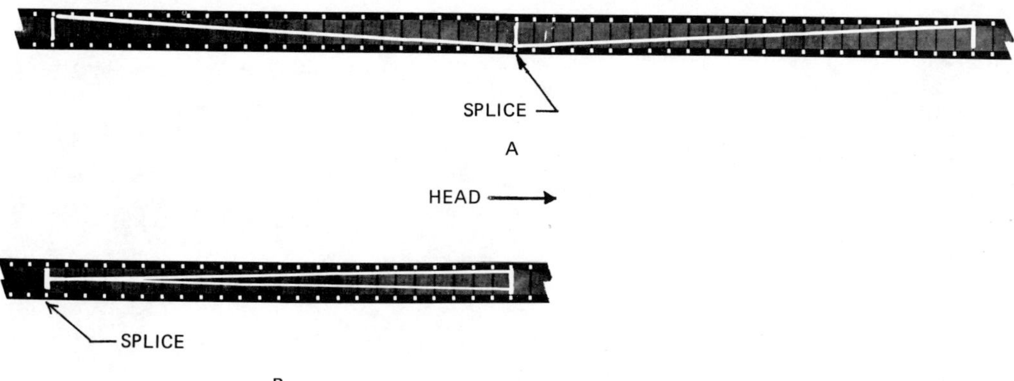

Fig. 11.5*A*. Workprint mark for a dissolve. (*B*) Workprint mark for a fadeout.

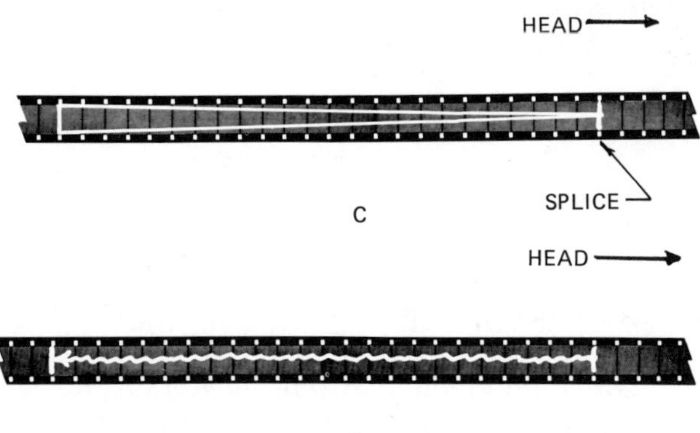

Fig. 11.5(*C*). Workprint mark for a fadein. (*D*) Workprint mark for a superimposure.

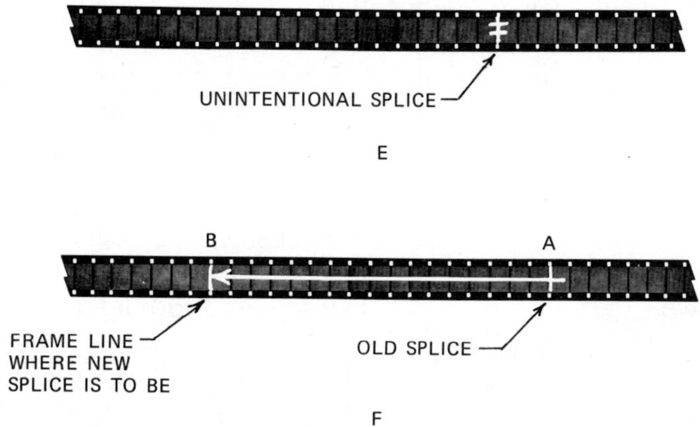

Fig. 11.5*E*. Workprint mark to indicate an unintentional splice to be disregarded by the negative cutter. (*F*) Workprint mark to indicate a change in splice position not physically made in the workprint.

Fig. 11.5. Workprint markings indicating instructions for the negative cutter.

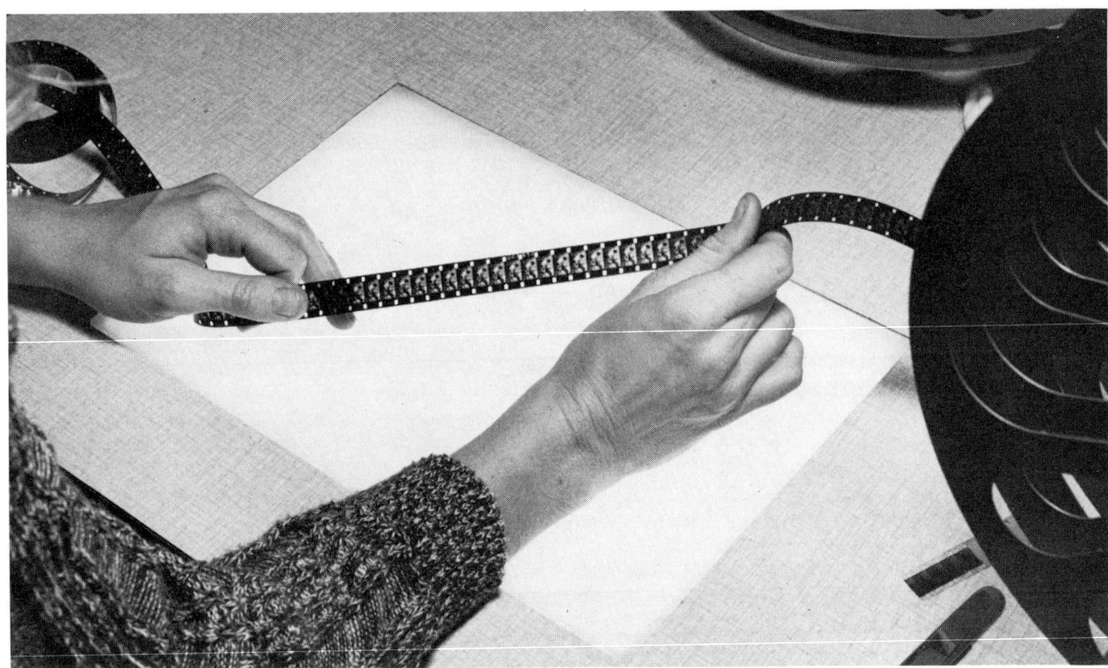

Fig. 11.6. Reading negative edge numbers from the workprint.

Breaking Down the Negative/Original

Breaking down the negative/original is the process of cutting each separate shot from the camera roll, winding it up on a core, and identifying it by edge number and by workprint shot list number.

In making the workprint from the camera negative/original, the laboratory usually splices several rolls together. Thus when the negative/original comes to you from the lab, it will probably be in 400- and 800-foot rolls. Each shot in these negative/original rolls must be removed from the rolls and cored up individually. You should have at hand the negative/original roll number list, which provides the inclusive edge numbers in each roll of negative/original (Fig. 11.9). Recall that this is the list compiled earlier from the workprint rolls (which are exact copies of the negative/original rolls) before you cut into them.

Fig. 11.7. Negative edge numbers, or key numbers, appear at either 20- or 40-frame intervals along the edge of original reversal and negative film.

Check the workprint shot list against the negative/original roll number list to ascertain which rolls contain no shots that are in your workprint. If there are any such rolls, leave them in the vault.

Before starting the breakdown, be sure the editing table and rewinds are clean. You will need the following items: a split reel, breakdown papers, clean gloves, magnifying glass, a pen or pencil, and a scratch pad.

Breakdown papers are pieces of paper 2½ inches long and twice the width of 16mm film that are used to hold a cored piece of film onto the core and to record edge numbers and other identification. They are safer for the film than either paper clips or tape, and provide a good writing area. To prepare papers for use, fold them in half lengthwise and pull each one over your finger to give it a slight curve. Breakdown papers are sold very cheaply by editing supply houses, but you can easily cut a large supply from

WORKPRINT SHOT LIST

1	J1/13 28 321 - 329	#24
2	J3/11 65 426 - 503	
3	J1/17 33 124 - 154	
4	J2/78 21 092 - 107	
5	J7/87 17 236 - 258	

Fig. 11.8. The workprint shot list is a sequential list of each shot in the workprint and its corresponding first and last edge numbers.

a few sheets of typing paper. Before starting to break down, fold as many as you may require (Figs. 11.10, 11.11, 11.12).

To install a breakdown paper, hold the cored roll in one hand and slightly separate the first two layers of film (Fig. 11.13). Then slip the folded paper over the two layers and very carefully pull the end until the roll tightens just enough to hold itself together. Pulling too tightly can damage the film. Leave a little tail sticking out since you can readily identify a shot, if you are familiar with the picture, by looking at one or two frames (Fig. 11.14).

Begin the breakdown by putting on editing gloves. Next, place a roll of negative/original on the split reel. Be careful not to let the center of the roll slip outward because this can cause scratches in the emulsion. Put the split reel containing the negative/original on the left rewind, unreel a foot or two, and inspect it. If it is heads out, carefully rewind it onto a core in another split reel or onto a new, clean steel reel. Break down a roll of negative/original beginning at the tail so that each shot ends up on a core heads out.

Start, then, with the tails out roll of negative/original on the left rewind. Put a core adapter on the right rewind and install a core so that the tightwinder roller fits down over it in alignment. Thread the end of the film into the slot of the core by folding back about one-half frame. Insert the fold into the core slot and wind a full turn on the core. Put the tightwinder roller down on the film. But before winding the shot onto the core, look for the negative edge number. Mark this number on a folded breakdown paper. Remember, you are breaking the roll down from the tail, so the edge number will be the last number in the series for that shot. Leave room on the paper for the first number (Fig. 11.15*A*). Wind the film onto the core until you reach the head of the shot, indicated by the slate (if distinguishable from the action) or by a camera stop. A camera stop consists of one or more blank frames made at the time of shooting by the cameraman covering the lens or pointing it at the sky and

NEGATIVE EDGE NUMBERS

ROLL NO.		LENGTH
1.	J1/16 25 625 - 027	400'
2.	J2/81 13 024 - 428	400'
3.	J1/13 06 104 - 206	100'
4.	J3/17 32 301 - 710	400'
5	J6/89 22 601 - 004	400'
6	J1/87 24 335 - 734	400'

Fig. 11.9. Negative edge number log.

Fig. 11.10. Negative breakdown papers before folding.

Fig. 11.12. Negative breakdown paper folded and curled to fit the outside edge of a roll of film.

running a few frames through the camera. This is more important than it may seem, for without camera stops it is often difficult to tell where one shot ends and the other begins.

When you have wound the complete shot onto the core note the first edge number on the shot and mark it on the breakdown paper (Fig. 11.15*B*). Cut the film off at the camera stop, remove the core from the rewind, and insert the breakdown paper as explained above. You now have one complete negative/original scene, wound heads out and secured safely on a core, properly identified, and ready for AB roll assembly. Place the cored film in a can or box beside you and proceed to break down every shot in the negative/original rolls in the same manner. As you break down, keep a *negative breakdown log,* which is a sequential record of the edge numbers of the shots in each negative/original roll. This may seem like an unnecessary step, but, if you become confused about where you are in the process, it can be vital to have an exact record of everything you have done so far (Fig. 11.16).

Break down every shot of your negative/original whether it will be used or not. At first it may seem unnecessary to break down shots that you are not going to use. But pulling out only certain shots often creates peculiar problems. For example, when selected shots are pulled from a roll, there must be a way to take up that part of

Fig. 11.11. Negative breakdown paper folded in half lengthwise is exactly the width of the film.

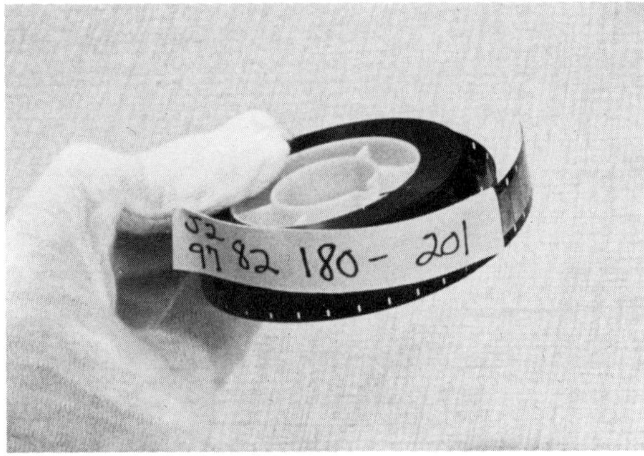

Fig. 11.13. Negative breakdown paper slipped over the two outside turns of the negative/original on a core.

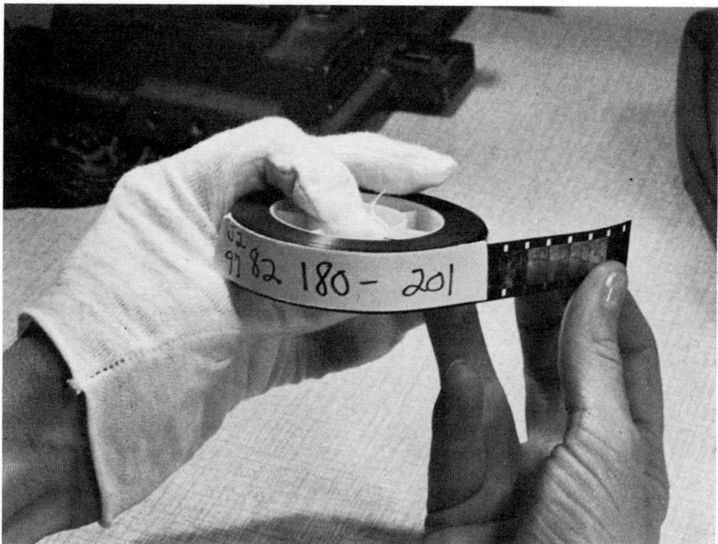

Fig. 11.14. Negative roll gently pulled only tight enough for the paper to hold the roll intact. The protruding end piece of film helps in identification.

the roll that isn't used. You would have to keep removing a takeup reel off the rewind and putting it back on. This entails more handling of the negative/original and consequently a greater possibility of damage. Also, if a shot is missing later on, you have to search for it by winding back through the partial rolls that are not broken down. If you have been at all careless, the time involved can be far greater than that originally required to break everything down.

Breaking Down Selected Shots Only

If you are determined to break down selected shots only from the negative/original rolls, you will need a list of workprint edge numbers arranged in numerical order. Since the order of shots in the workprint is random—two shots which may be next to each other in the negative/original roll may be separated by many shots in the workprint—all the shots selected from a given negative/original roll should be pulled in the order that they appear on that roll. To compile this list, rearrange the edge numbers from the workprint shot list into sequential order. Then, following this list, shots can be pulled as they come up without having to roll back and forth constantly according to the random order of the workprint.

Selecting and Numbering Scenes Corresponding to the Workprint Shot List

After all the negative/original shots have been broken down onto cores, the next task is to

Fig. 11.15*A*. Negative breakdown paper marked with the base number and the last edge number of a shot. Space is left in the center for the edge number at the head of the shot.

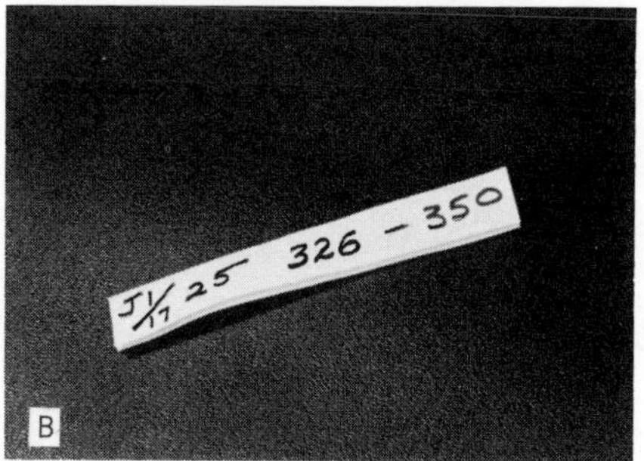

Fig. 11.15*B*. Edge number from head of negative/original marked in space previously left blank.

		NEGATIVE EDGE NUMBERS	
		NEGATIVE ROLL NO. 2	
J1/17 25	326-350	J1/78 14	121-136
	351-352		137-350
	353-365		351-451
	366-384		452-523
	385-402		
	402-423	J2/81 33	435-479
	423-445		480-503
	447-465		504-526
	466-486		527-545

Fig. 11.16. The negative breakdown log is a record of every shot broken down.

separate the cored scenes corresponding to those on the Workprint Shot List, and number them in workprint sequence. If number one on the workprint shot list is J1/13 28 321-329, look for the cored negative/original edge number that contains this number. Since a workprint shot is usually only a portion of the scene as shot, the workprint number will always be smaller than, but included in, the negative/original number.

As each cored scene containing a workprint edge number is pulled, mark it with the workprint shot list number and encircle it. When a cored negative/original scene contains two or more scenes in the workprint, mark these also (Figs. 11.17*A, B*).

After all the negative/original cored scenes called for by the Workprint Shot List have been pulled and marked, arrange them in numerical order either on the cutting table shelves or on small portable racks. Such racks are convenient since after the rolls have been arranged in numerical order, they can be stored in a cabinet, except for the ones being worked on. This saves space and prevents the rolls from gathering dust over a cutting period of several days. Put the outtakes, the scenes that will not be used, in boxes and return them to the vault.

Assembling AB Rolls to Match the Workprint

Before starting to assemble the AB rolls, make sure that the room, the table, and all equipment are clean. Lay out the broken down negative/original rolls in numerical order. Then set up the equipment. Place the reel of the workprint on the left-hand rewind, emulsion UP and feeding from the top of the reel. Put three reels with spacers on the right-hand rewind; one is for workprint takeup, the other two are for the AB rolls respectively. Put a spring clamp on the shaft

Fig. 11.17*A*. Broken down negative scene with its inclusive edge numbers on the paper. The encircled number 1 indicates that shot #1 on the workprint list is in this roll.

Fig. 11.17*B*. The encircled numbers indicate the workprint shots contained in this roll.

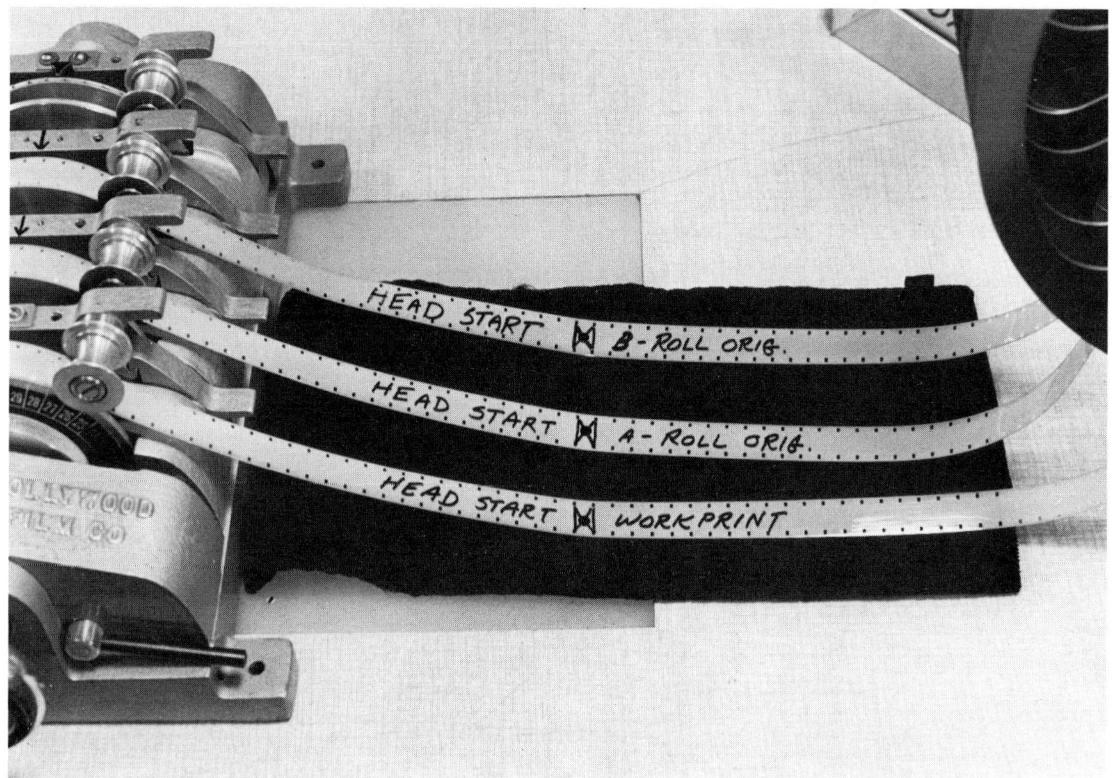

Fig. 11.18. Workprint leader and AB-roll leaders marked, identified, and punched in sync.

with a fourth reel for taking up trims on the shaft outside the spring clamp. Place the synchronizer in front of you between the two rewinds. (See Fig. 11.19.)

You will need a little more black opaque leader than the length of the workprint. A *leader stanchion*, either mounted on the left rewind or free-standing on the table, keeps reels of leader both instantly available and out of the way. (See Fig. 11.2.) Divide the black leader into two reels since you will be attaching black leader first to one roll and then to the other. If you do not have a leader stanchion, put the two black leader reels on the left-hand rewind shaft. This is slightly inconvenient because as the shaft turns the free reel turns and unwinds black leader on the table. This may be prevented by feeding one leader reel from the top and the other from the bottom. Thus, as the reel being used turns, the other reel winds itself up.

Lay out next to the synchronizer scribe, scissors, grease pencil, magnifying glass, and the tape dispenser loaded with a roll of quarter-inch white tape within easy reach.

Head Leaders

Prepare and mark the head leaders for both the A roll and the B roll. These leaders should correspond exactly in both length and start-mark position to the workprint leader (Fig. 11.18). (See Start Marks and Leaders.) Measure off two lengths of lightstruck double-perforated leader, emulsion UP and mark them to match the workprint leader. Place all three leaders in the synchronizer with their start marks locked at the sync frame position. Set the synchronizer footage and frame counters at zero feet, zero frames. All footage measurements are always made from HEAD START which is zero feet, zero frames (0′-OX). (See Fig. 11.18.)

Negative/original is generally double-perforated. Always request it when ordering film. If you have some single-perforated negative/original, use single-perforated head leader on each roll that any of it will fall in to prevent the timer from putting the rolls in the synchronizer the wrong way and tearing up your film.

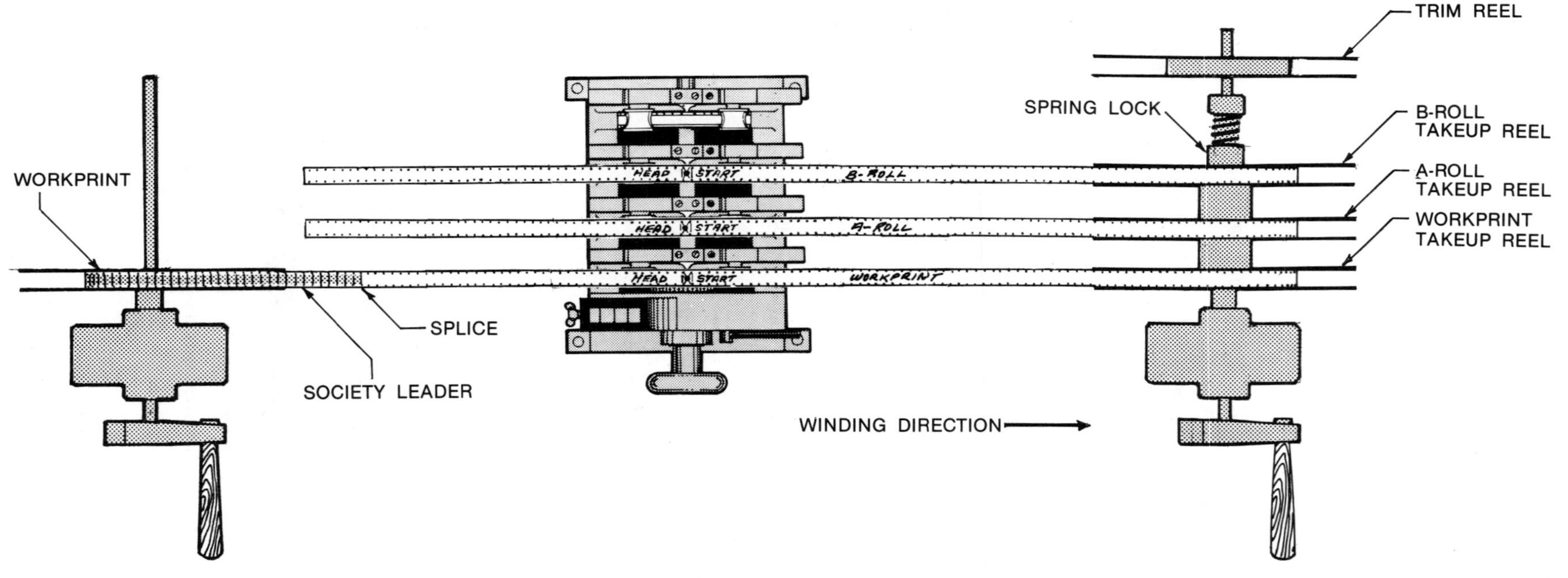

Fig. 11.19. Schematic arrangement of workprint, AB-roll leaders, takeup reels, and trim reel set up for negative cutting.

LAYING IN NEGATIVE ORIGINAL

The negative/original of Society leader is the first scene to be put into the AB rolls. It is not a part of the picture per se, but is a cueing guide for the projectionist in threading and starting the projector. To lay in the first piece of negative/original, wind down (to the right) to the splice where the first frame of Society leader in the workprint begins. Lock this splice in the sync position in the synchronizer. With a metal scribe, scratch a small mark in the emulsion on either side of the sprocket holes that are in sync with the splice in the workprint (Fig. 11.20). This is the point where the Society leader negative/original will start on the A roll; the black opaque leader will start at the same point on the B roll. When making scribe marks on the edge of the film, be sure to stay outside the picture area and not to tear the film (Fig. 11.21). Scribe on the emulsion side of the film; scratching a little of the emulsion away makes the mark clearly visible without digging into the film base.

The negative/original of the Society leader may be put into either the A or the B roll. Although it makes no difference which roll you start with, it must start at the splice line and be in sync with the workprint leader.

To lay in the Society leader negative/original in sync, wind ahead (right) until the HEAD frame of the workprint Society leader comes into the synchronizer sync frame. Next, take the core of the Society leader negative/original in your left hand and pull off two or three feet. With a piece of quarter-inch white paper tape, attach this end of the film to the trim reel. Turn the reel by hand until the HEAD frame appears on the cored negative/original (Fig. 11.22). Now lay the HEAD frame of the Society leader negative/original, emulsion UP, down on the A roll so it is exactly in sync with the HEAD frame of the workprint. Hold the negative/original (and the A-roll leader beneath it) in place on the synchronizer with your forefinger. (Be sure to wear editing gloves.) Press the lever that releases the synchronizer roller arm, and, while holding the negative/original and the leader beneath it in place, slip the negative/original under both rollers and clamp the arm back down with the other hand. The negative/original and the A-roll leader are now clamped one on top of the other in the A-roll channel of the synchronizer. Roll to the left to bring the workprint splice back into the sync frame on the synchronizer. (See Fig. 11.20.) At this point the head end of the negative/original and the tail end of the A-roll leader should be

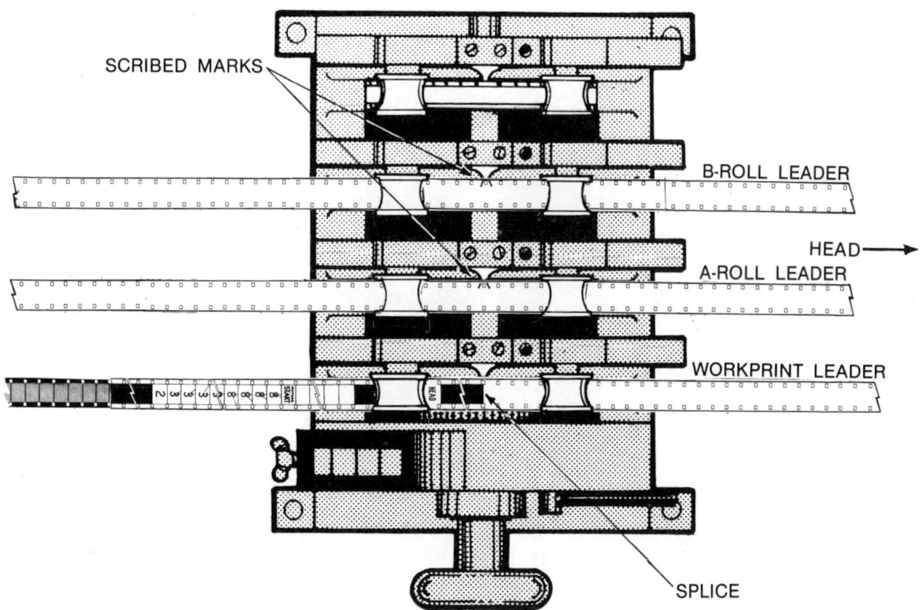

Fig. 11.20. Scribed marks indicating the frame line where the A-roll leader is to be spliced to the negative/original Society leader and where the B-roll is to be spliced to black leader. These scribed frame lines are in sync with the workprint splice.

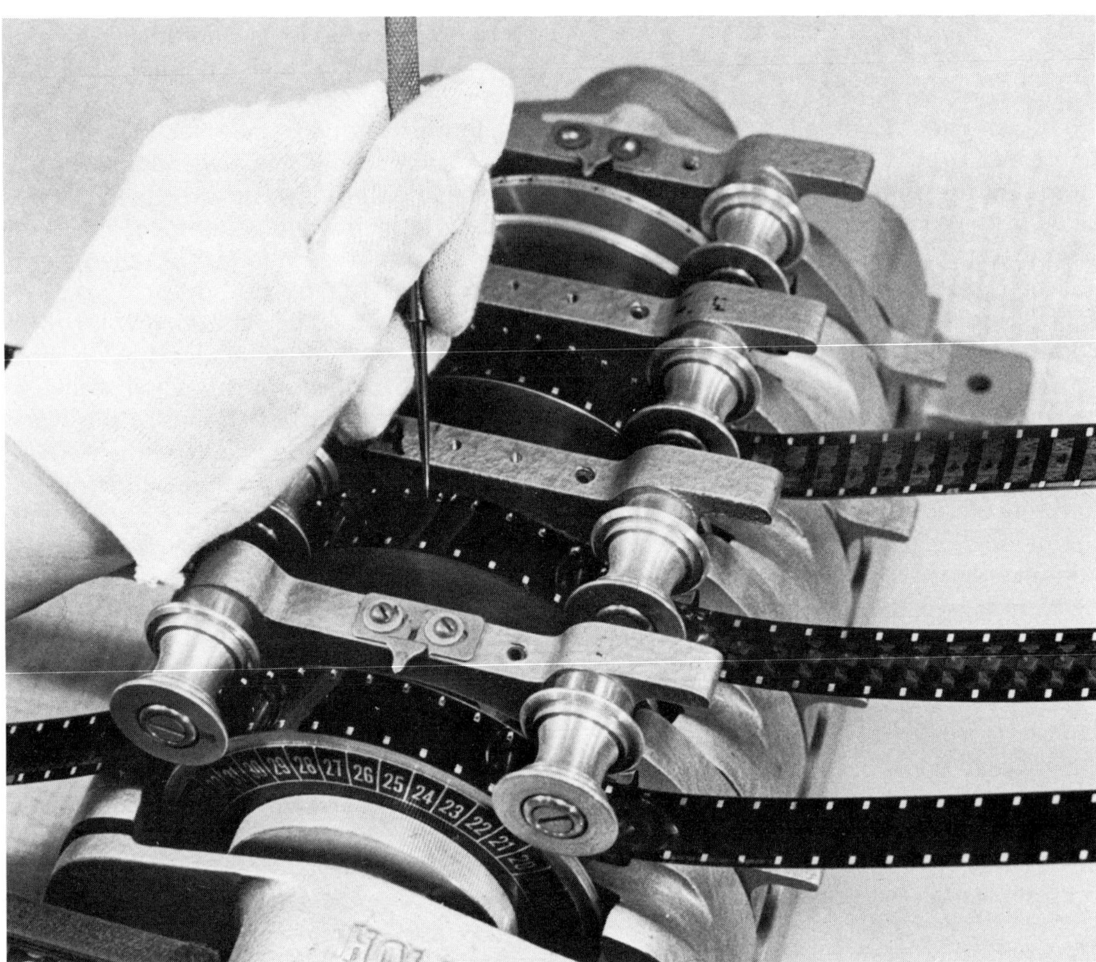

Fig. 11.21. Scribed marks should be on the emulsion side of the film outside the picture area.

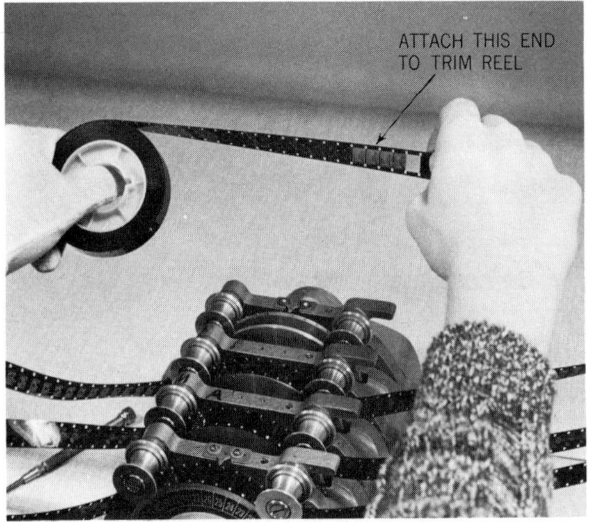

Fig. 11.22. Holding negative/original breakdown roll preparatory to laying it into the AB rolls.

trimmed. The two must be taped together for splicing. To do this, cut off the head end of the negative/original 1½ frames ahead of the scribe marks (Fig. 11.23). The splice will be made at the frame line indicated by the scribe marks, but always leave 1½ frames to be cut away when the splice is made. This loss is standard throughout the 16mm film industry (Fig. 11.24*A, B*). (See Splicing.)

Tape the negative/original to the leader beneath it using a short piece of quarter-inch white paper tape. (See Fig. 11.24*A*, 11.24*B*.) Do not let the tape touch the splice line. With the tape in place, roll the synchronizer to the left until the splice line clears the roller. Cut off the tail of the head leader underneath, again leaving 1½ frames to be cut away during splicing. With the Society leader negative/original laid in, trimmed, and taped, lay black opaque leader into the B roll following the same procedure:

1. Place the black leader on the piece of film locked in the synchronizer sync frame position.
2. Hold the two firmly together and unlock the roller arm.
3. Position the black leader under the rollers and relock the roller arm down.
4. Scribe the black leader on both sides of the sprocket hole corresponding to the splice in the workprint.
5. Roll ahead (right) a few frames and cut off the black leader, leaving 1½ frames toward the head from the scribe marks.
6. Roll back to sync position and tape black leader to the film underneath it (Fig. 11.25).
7. Roll back (left) a few frames until the splice line head leader clears the rollers. Cut off the head leader underneath leaving 1½ frames toward the tail from the scribe marks.

After the negative/original and the black leader respectively have been secured in the AB rolls, roll ahead (right), feeding negative/original and black leader through the synchronizer, until the next splice in the workprint.

In winding the workprint and the AB rolls through the synchronizer and onto the takeup reels, the black leader feeds itself from its reel on the leader stanchion. Let the negative/original feed directly into the synchronizer from the core held lightly in your left hand (Fig. 11.26).

When the next workprint splice comes into sync position in the synchronizer, prepare the rolls for laying in the next section of negative/original and its corresponding section of black leader. From here on, cutting the AB rolls

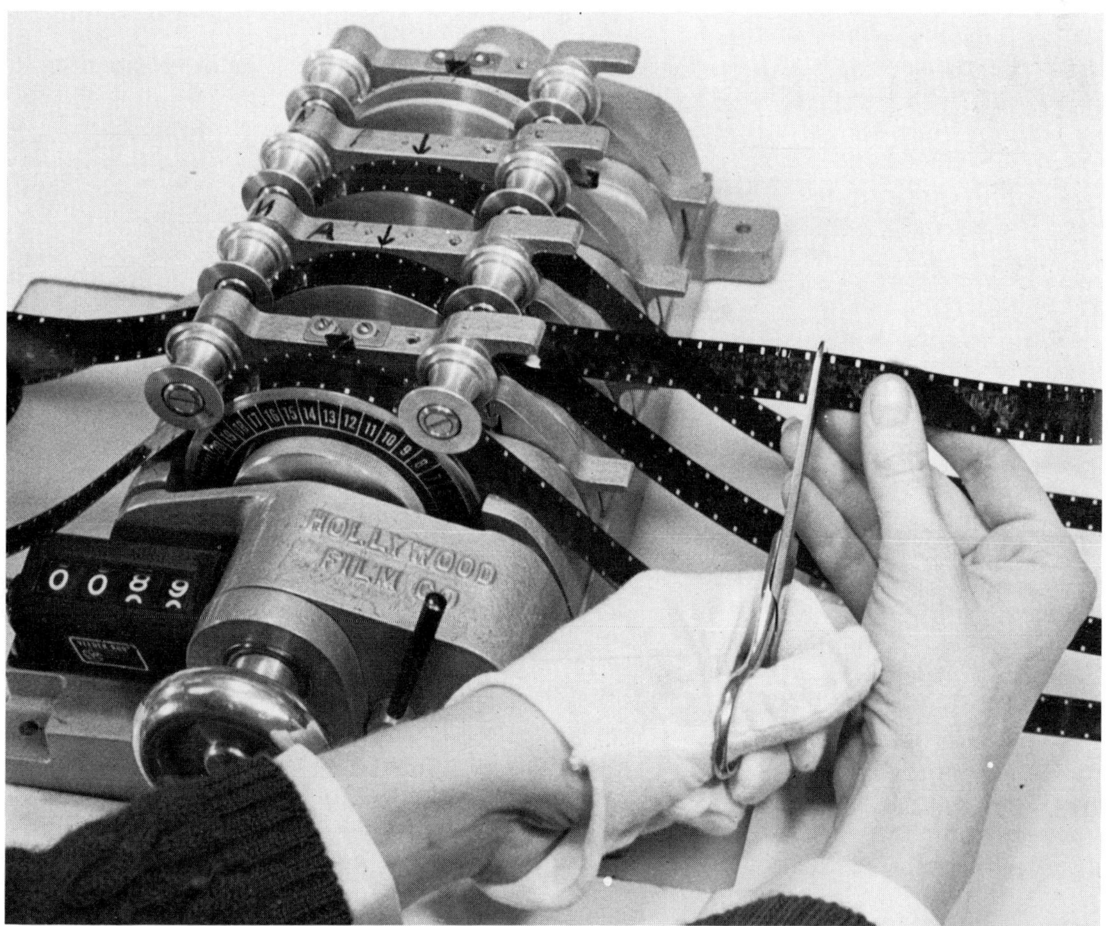

Fig. 11.23. The negative/original shown in rolled forward (right) to be cut off 1½ frames ahead of the scribed splice line.

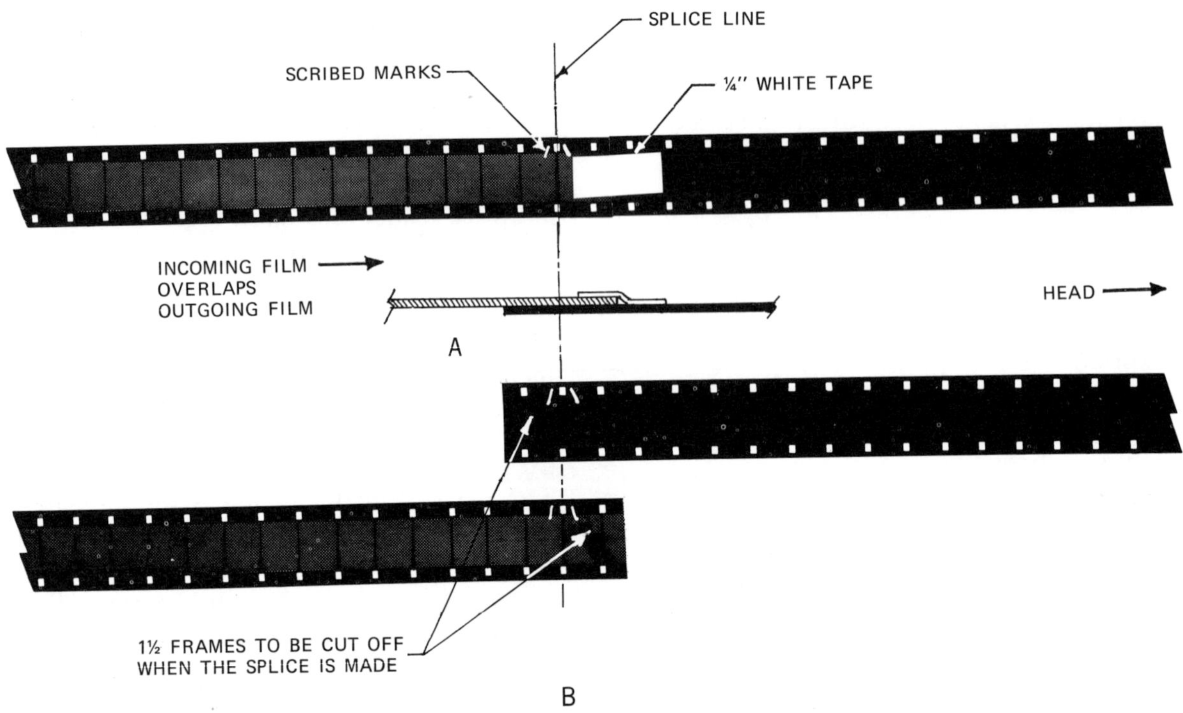

Fig. 11.24*A*. A cut that has been cut off and taped for splicing. (*B*) The same cut with the films separated to show the relationship of the splice line to the 1½-frame loss.

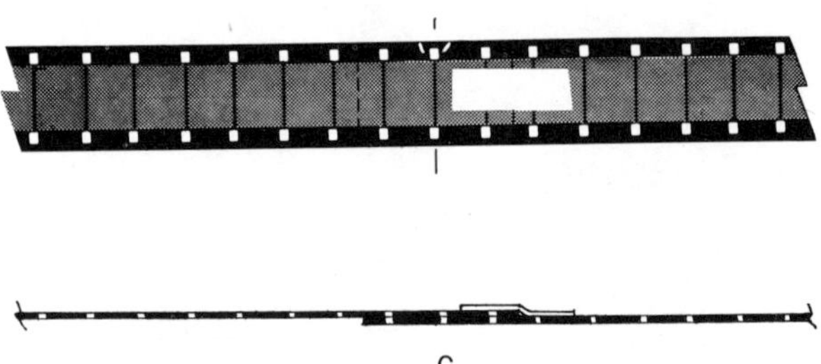

Fig. 11.24C. Section view of negative cut set up for splicing.

consists of putting each scene of negative/original alternately on the A roll and on the B roll with black leader between each scene.

LAYING IN PICTURE NEGATIVE/ORIGINAL

The procedure for laying in picture negative/original is the same as that described above except that edge numbers must be used to sync the negative/original to the workprint.

(a) When the splice to the first scene in the workprint appears, lock it in the sync frame and scribe both the A and B rolls.

(*b*) Examine the workprint closely. The negative edge number will be somewhere within one foot to the left of the splice. (See Fig. 11.27.) This number will extend over two or three frames. With grease pencil, mark the frame containing the three-digit portion of the edge number. Actually any frame the number touches can be used satisfactorily, but there is less chance of laying in a scene out of sync if you always use the same portion of a number for the reference frame. Roll the marked frame into the synchronizer sync frame position and lock.

(c) Select the proper negative/original cored scene from the rack by referring to the numbers marked on each cored scene.

(*d*) Remove the paper holding the cored roll together, and tape the head end of the scene to the trim reel.

(*e*) Turn the trim reel by hand until the key number corresponding to the one marked on the workprint comes into view.

(*f*) Lay the numbered frame, emulsion UP, on the black leader of the B roll so it is in sync with the marked frame on the workprint and lock it into the synchronizer.

(*g*) Roll to the left to bring the workprint splice back into the sync frame on the synchronizer.

(*h*) Scribe the negative/original on both sides of the sprocket hole corresponding to the splice in the workprint (Fig. 11.28).

(*i*) Roll ahead (right) a few frames to clear the synchronizer rollers and cut off the negative/original, leaving 1½ frames toward the head from the scribe marks.

(*j*) Roll back (left) to sync position and tape the negative/original to the black leader underneath it.

(*k*) Roll back (left) a few more frames until the black leader underneath clears the rollers. Then cut off the black leader, leaving 1½ frames toward the tail from the scribe mark.

(*l*) Scribe the black leader from the other reel on the stanchion 1½ frames from the head. Place these scribe marks directly over the scribed splice line of the Society leader on the A roll. Tape it down and lock the black leader into the synchronizer with the Society leader.

(*m*) Roll back (left) and cut off the Society leader underneath 1½ frames from the splice line.

(*n*) Wind ahead (right) feeding the negative/original from the core and the black leader from the stanchion. Continue to wind until the next workprint splice comes into the sync frame signaling the end of the shot.

(*o*) Scribe the negative/original on the B roll on both sides of the sprocket hole corresponding to the splice in the workprint.

(*p*) Also scribe the black leader on the A roll on both sides of the sprocket hole corresponding to the splice in the workprint.

(*q*) Scribe black leader and tape it on the negative/original on the B roll, matching scribe marks as described above, then lock the leader into the synchronizer.

(*r*) Roll back and cut off the negative original 1½ frames from the splice line.

(*s*) Tape the end of the remaining cored negative/original to the trim reel and wind it onto the trim reel.

(*t*) The B-roll is now secure, so proceed to lay the next negative/original scene into the A roll,

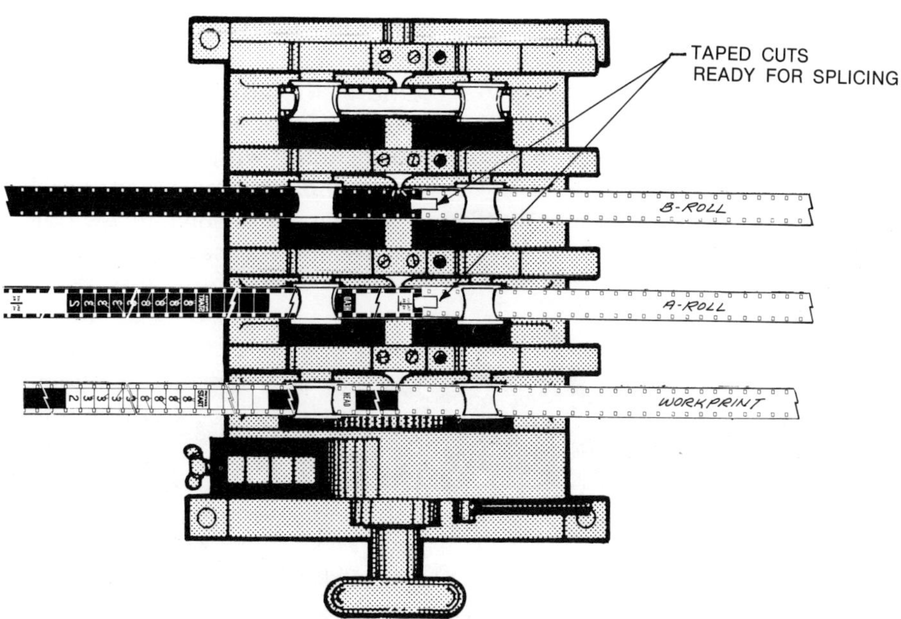

Fig. 11.25. Black leader laid into the B roll opposite the negative/original in the A roll.

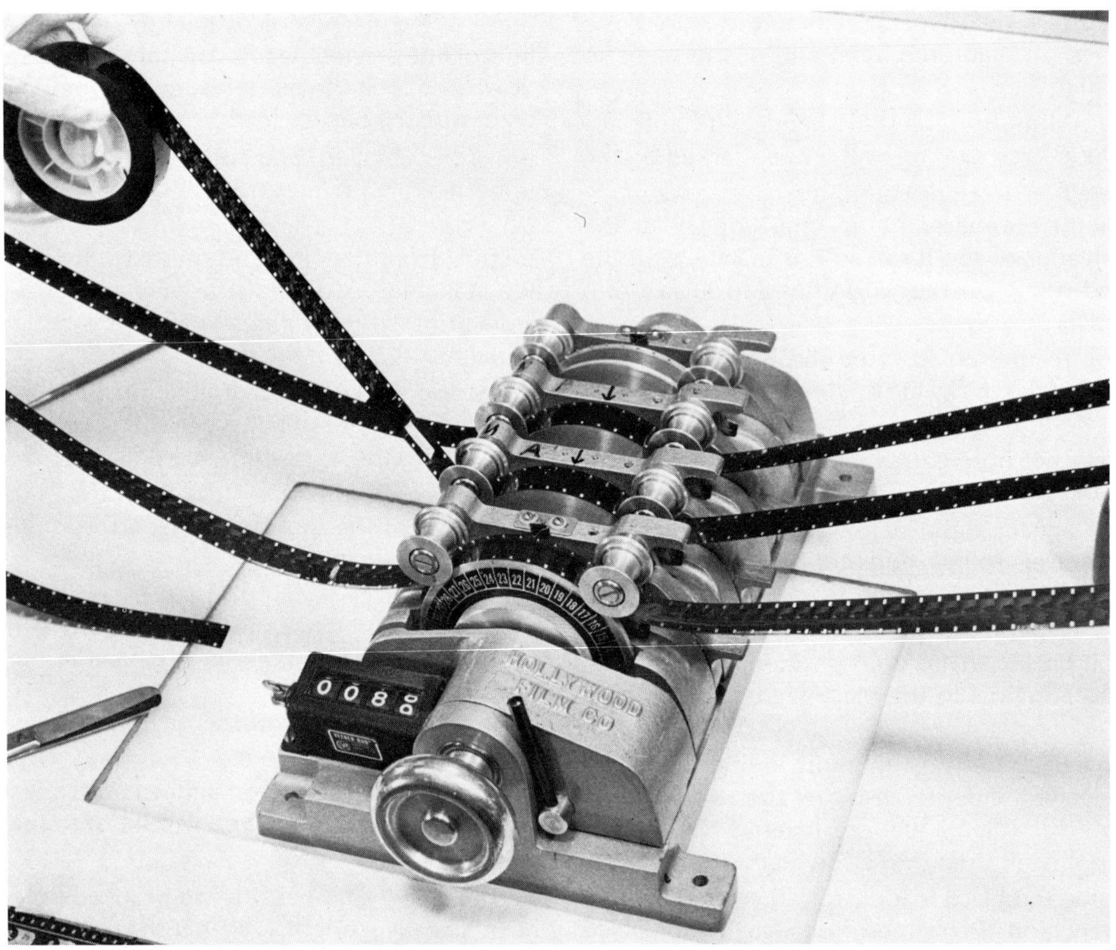

Fig. 11.26. Feeding negative/original into its respective roll after syncing, taping, and trimming.

repeating the procedure until all the scenes corresponding to those in the workprint have been assembled in the AB rolls. Always lay the incoming, left-hand piece of film on top of the right-hand piece. This makes all taped intersections uniform, which facilitates checking the AB rolls for accuracy when you are finished without damaging the negative/original.

AB-Roll Dissolves

One of the great advantages of AB-roll negative cutting is that as many dissolves as you wish may be included without making duplicate negatives and without paying a fee for each dissolve.

To make a dissolve in AB rolls, extend the tail of a scene on, say, the A roll past the starting

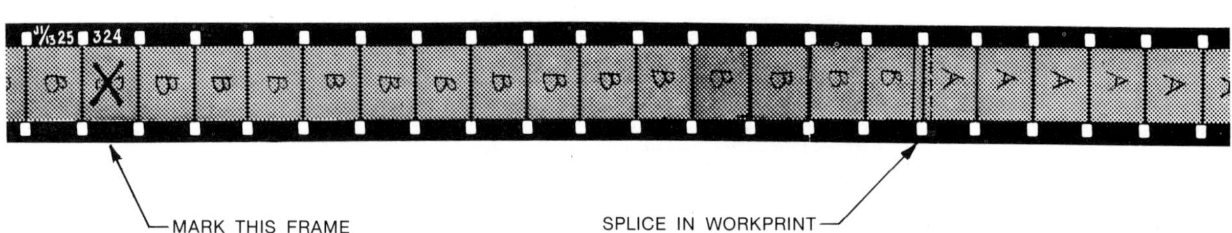

Fig. 11.27. The workprint negative edge number for each scene will appear within one foot past the splice.

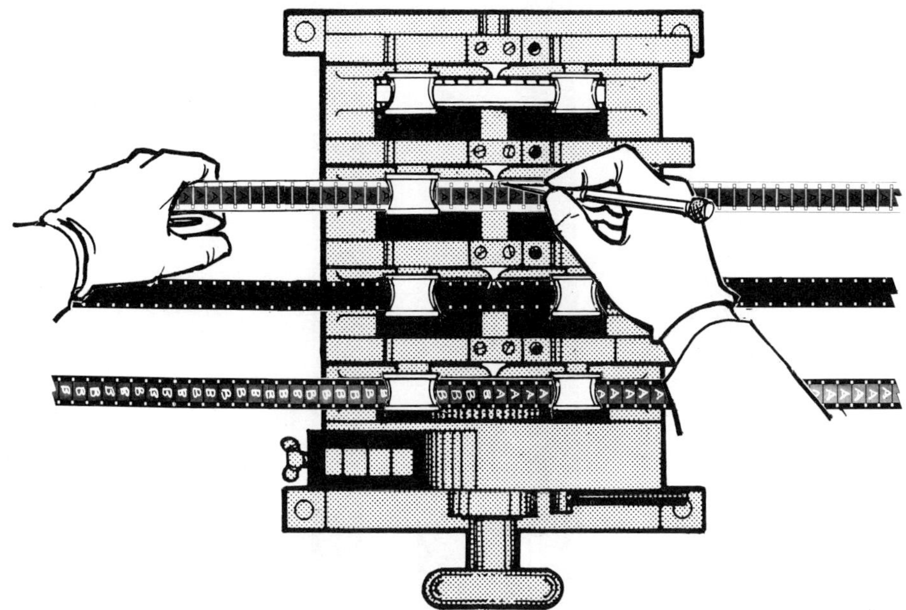

Fig. 11.28. The scribe marks on the A-roll black leader indicate the frame line where the next negative/original scene will start. The scribe marks on the negative/original B-roll indicate the frame line where the black leader will start.

point of the next scene on the B roll. Recall that in release printing the A roll is printed first onto the release-print stock, and then, before development, the B roll is printed onto the same stock. During printing the outgoing scene of the dissolve is faded out, and the incoming scene is faded in on top of it. The combination results in a dissolve, the center of which is indicated by the splice in the workprint. Since two workprint scenes overlapped together cannot be spliced, splice them at the center of the dissolve, cutting off the frames that are left over. In AB-roll cutting, these scenes can actually be overlapped since they are on separate rolls. The length of a dissolve is measured from its starting point to its end. Notice that in a 48-frame dissolve, the overlap is 48 frames for both the A roll and the B roll, which means there is a 24-frame overlap on either side of the splice line. This applies to a dissolve of any length. Although 48 frames is a good dissolve and should be considered a standard where possible, most labs are set up to make the following dissolve lengths automatically: 12, 24, 32, 48, 64, 72, and 96 frames. All dissolves should be of uniform length. If a special effect requires an enormously long dissolve or some other odd length, check with the lab to see if they can accommodate you and if there will be an extra charge (Fig. 11.29).

To lay in a dissolve, follow the same procedure for laying in negative/original except that the scribe marks indicating splice lines should be made opposite the beginning and the end of the dissolve markings (Fig. 11.30).

Procedure for laying in AB-Roll Dissolves

1. When the dissolve mark on the workprint comes into the synchronizer, lock the beginning of the dissolve in the sync frame.
2. Scribe the black leader of the B roll on both sides of the sprocket hole corresponding to the beginning of the dissolve (Fig. 11.31*A*).
3. Roll ahead (right) until the mark at the end of the dissolve is in the sync frame. Scribe the outgoing negative/original on the A roll corresponding to this mark (Fig. 11.31*B*).
4. Secure black leader to the tail of the outgoing scene matching scribe marks as before and lock it to the synchronizer.
5. Locate the first edge number of next shot on the workprint.
6. Lay in the new scene by edge number on the

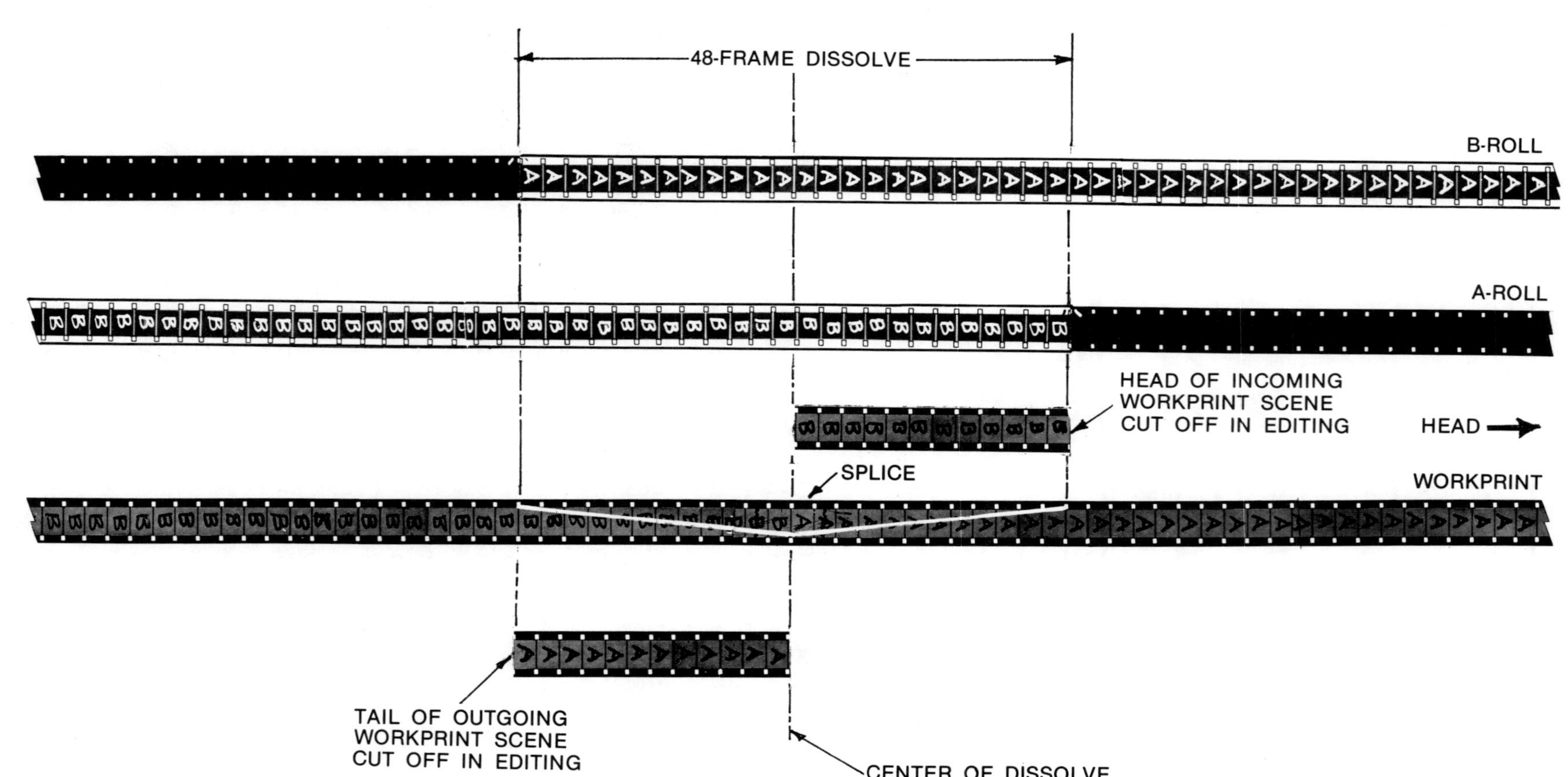

Fig. 11.29. Dissolve mark on the workprint indicates the actual beginning and end of the dissolve.

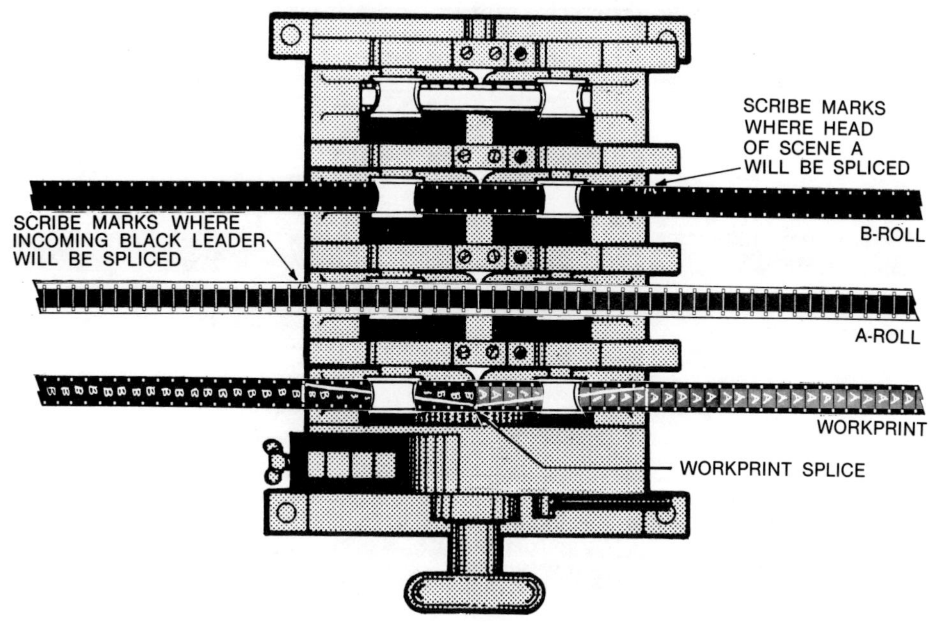

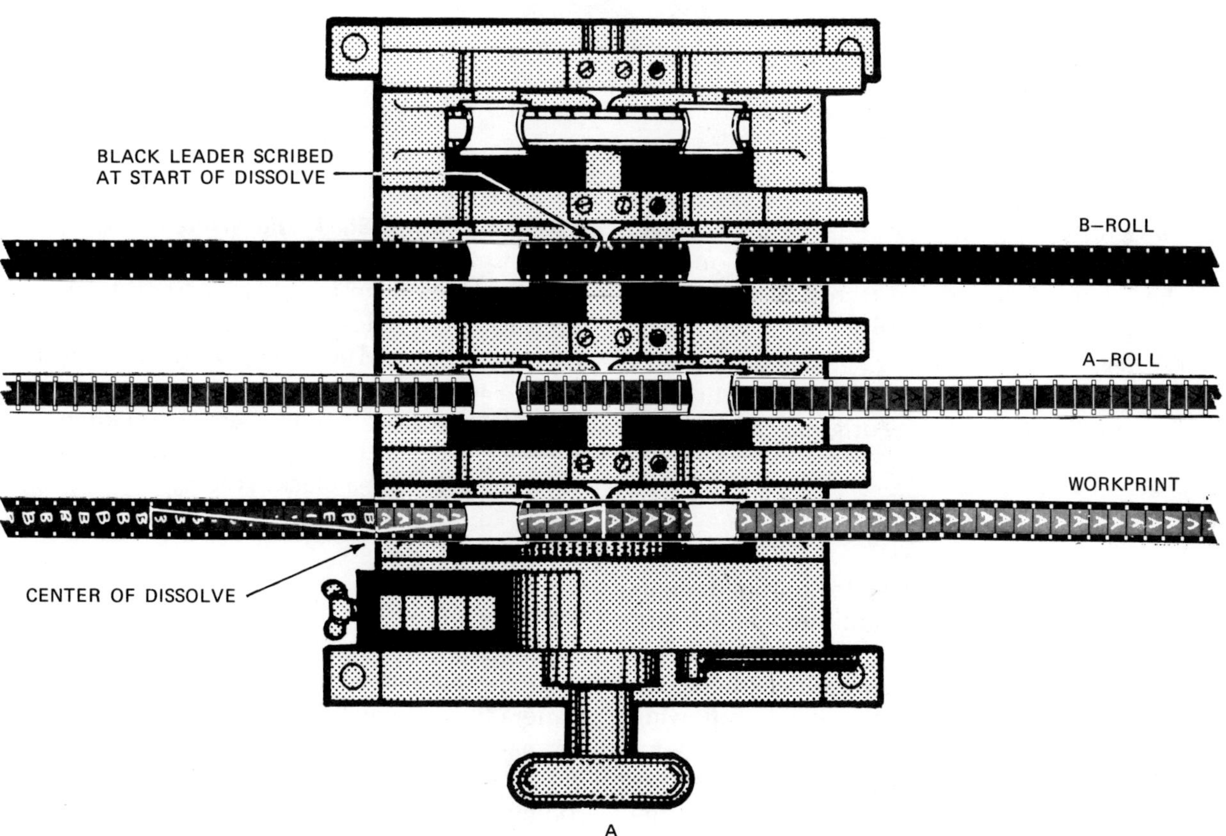

Fig. 11.31*A*. Incoming black leader is scribed in sync with the dissolve mark to indicate the splice line for the incoming scene.

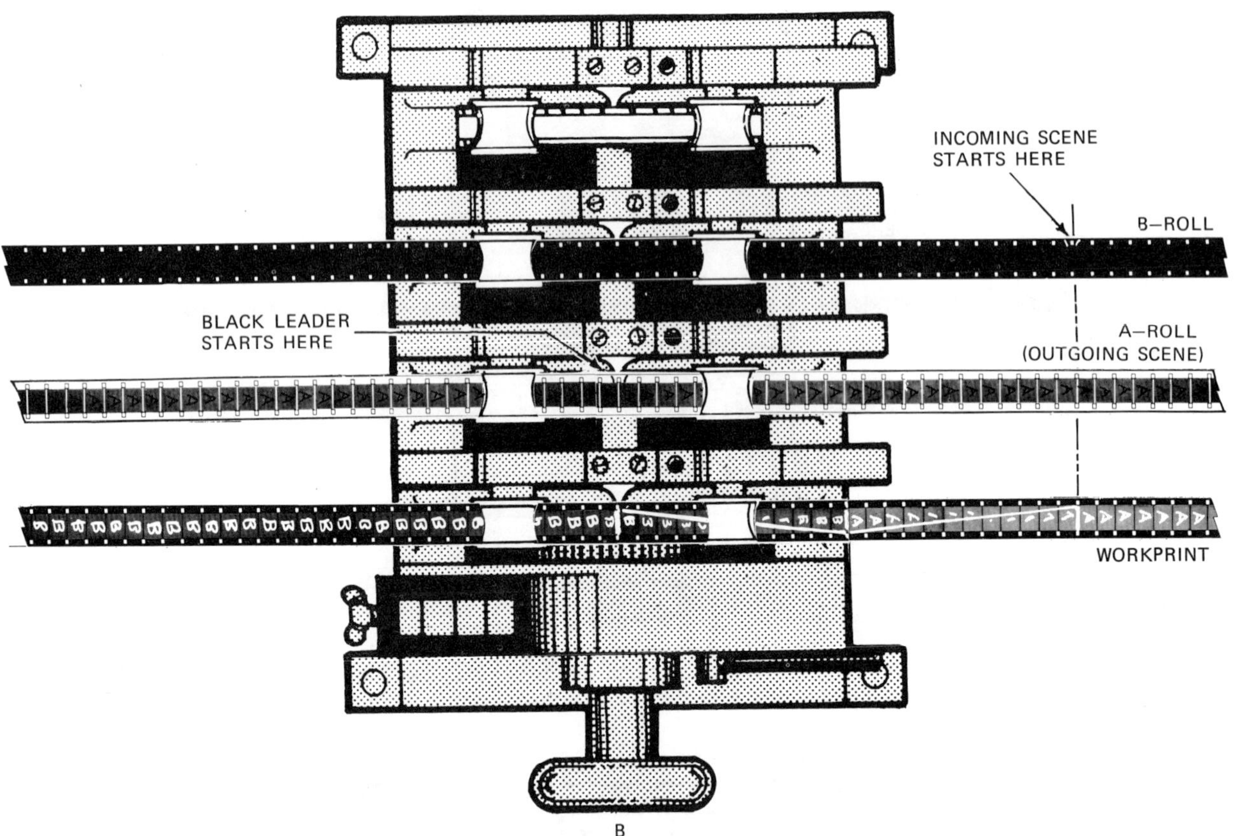

Fig. 11.31*B*. Rolled to the right, the tail of the dissolve mark indicates where the end splice line of the outgoing scene is to be scribed.

B roll following the standard procedure explained above, but don't scribe on the workprint splice line. Instead, roll back (left) to the beginning of the dissolve mark and make scribe marks there.

7. Follow the standard procedure for cutting off and taping the negative/original and black leader.

Fadeins and Fadeouts

There is no special procedure for putting fadeins and fadeouts in AB rolls. To indicate a fade, mark instructions on a small piece of tape and place it on the leader immediately preceding the scene you want to fadein, and immediately following the scene you want to fadeout. The following information should be on the tape: fade in or fade out, and length of the fade in frames. When the timer sees the notice indicating the start and the length of a fade, he will program his printing schedule accordingly.

Reversal Fades: Black-and-White and Color

A scene fades in from a black screen to normal intensity and it fades out from normal intensity to a black screen. Therefore, with reversal film (both black-and-white and color), always be sure that black leader comes before a fadein and follows a fadeout to ensure that the fade comes out of or goes into a black screen.

Negative Fades

The procedure for setting up fades in cutting negative differs slightly from that for reversal original. Negative here means the negative camera film on which light values are opposite to normal: dark areas are light, and light areas are dark. Thus each fadein or fadeout in a negative roll must have a piece of clear leader in sync with it on the opposite roll (Fig. 11.32). Reducing the printer light produces a light effect rather than a dark one. When this is done with negative, the

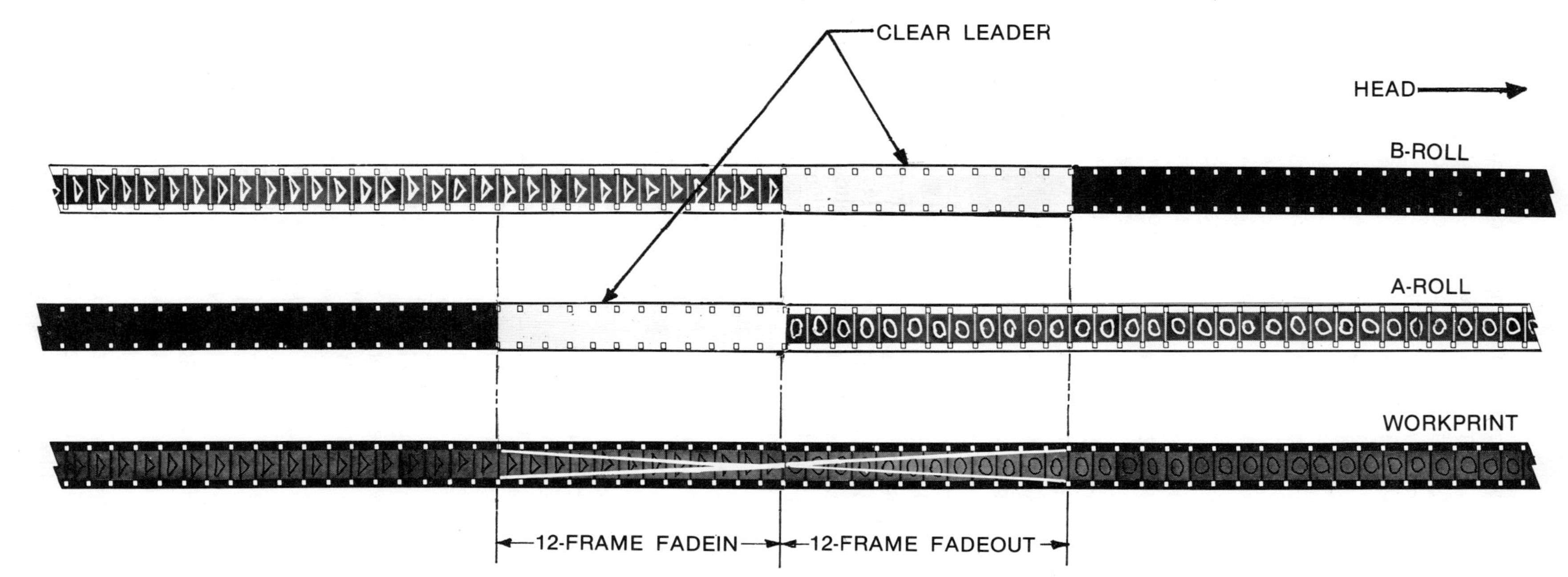

Fig. 11.32. Clear leader must be used opposite a fadeout or fadein in negative AB rolls.

effect is a "bright-out" instead of a fadeout. To counteract this negative effect, the clear leader on the opposite roll is actually dissolved into the bright-out area. The result is a normal-appearing fadein or fadeout. Lay this clear leader into the roll that is carrying black leader at the start of the fade just as you would a piece of negative/original, and run it only the full length of the fade.

End of Picture

When all the negative scenes have been layed into the AB rolls and taped, prepare the *blackout* leader and the *tail leaders.*

Leader should follow the last frame of picture so that the screen goes black when the picture ends. Since negative and reversal print differently, use the following respectively for blackout leader: For original (black-and-white and color), use black leader; for negative (black-and-white and color), use clear leader. Three feet of blackout leader will provide 4½ seconds of black screen, leaving ample time to shut off the projector. Follow this with at least six feet of lightstruck leader for identification and tail sync marks. Two feet of black leader at the end indicates the tail of the roll.

When the AB rolls have been assembled, check them before sending them to the lab. Catching a mistake at this point saves a great deal of time and money. Take the reels of black leader off the left-hand rewind if they were not on a stanchion and replace them with two good reels. Take the workprint and AB rolls out of synchronizer and rewind them, taking care not to bend back any of the 1½ frame overlaps. Then place the HEAD START marks in the synchronizer and slowly run through the rolls, checking to make sure that scribe marks and edge numbers match, that all dissolves and superimpositions are correctly set up, and that fadeins and fadeouts are properly marked.

ZERO NEGATIVE CUTTING

Zero negative cutting is the assembly of AB rolls so that each scene of negative/original remains uncut at its full length. Instead of cutting out and laying in the workprint portions of the negative/original, the whole scene is laid in and scribe marks are made on the edge of the film indicating to the timer the specific part to be printed. An accompanying cue sheet with detailed instructions for printing is also prepared (Fig. 11.33).

Zero cutting is tedious and expensive because more time is required and it may often result in as many as five printing rolls of negative/original. There are certain organizations and agencies—the U.S. Air Force, for example—that require all film produced for them to be zero cut. Also, certain research projects use film as primary data not to be altered or destroyed.

In zero cutting prepare head leaders and lay in the Society leader following the same procedure as in A-B Roll negative cutting described previously. Since the entire negative/original scene is to be laid into the roll, you may have to prepare a filler leader if the used portion of the scene is well into the roll. In the illustration, notice that when the portion of the negative/original that is to be used is placed in sync with the workprint, the scene extends ahead well into the head leader. Filler leader of the same length must be added to the tail of the head leaders of the negative/original rolls, the workprint, and the soundtrack so that the whole scene may be laid in uncut without disturbing the sync. Notice in Fig. 11.34 that negative/original scenes #1 and #2 run longer than the beginning of Scene #3. In this case the negative/original for Scene #3 would have to be put into a C roll, which calls for a new head leader and filler leader. (Filler leader is lightstruck leader that can be just an extension of the head leader.)

Scribe marks on the edge of the film outside the picture area indicate where cuts, fades, and dissolves should occur. A scribed "X" on the outgoing and incoming shot indicates a cut. In this method, a one-frame overlap is required on cuts: On the outgoing A-roll scene, scribe an X on the edge of the film one frame past the workprint splice. On the incoming scene in the B roll, scribe the X one frame ahead of the splice.

To indicate a dissolve, mark XX on the edge of the film at the center of the dissolve. The actual center of the dissolve is a frameline, but the XX scribe goes on the frame just preceding the workprint splice.

To indicate a fadeout or a fadein, scribe an arrow on the edge of the film pointing in the direction the fade is to go. Mark this arrow at the point you wish the fade to start.

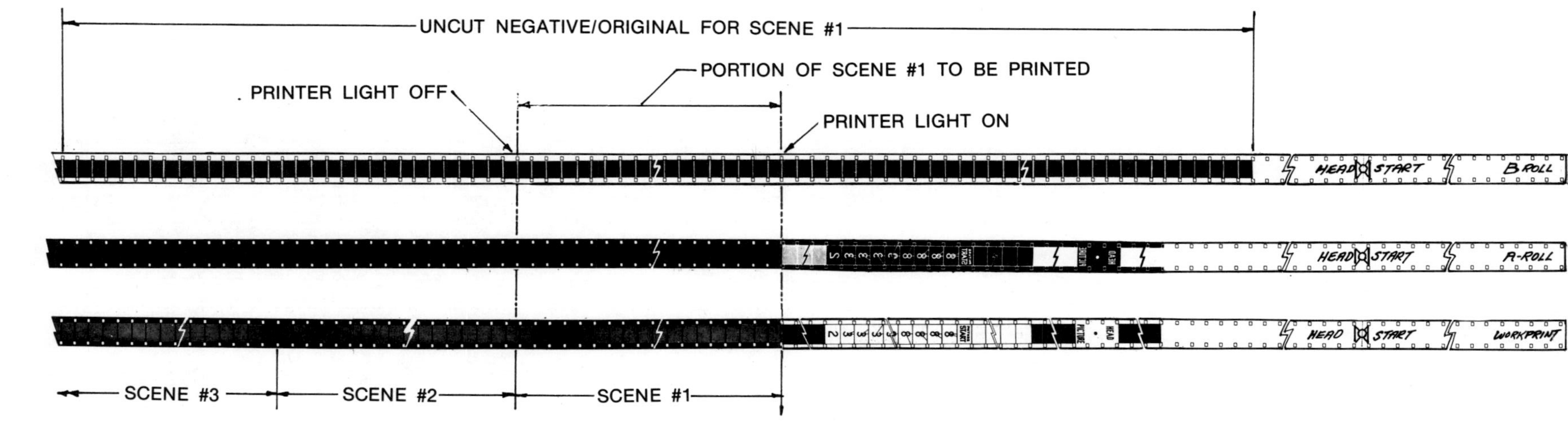

Fig. 11.33. In zero-cutting, a portion of a shot is used without cutting the negative/original. It is maintained at its original length.

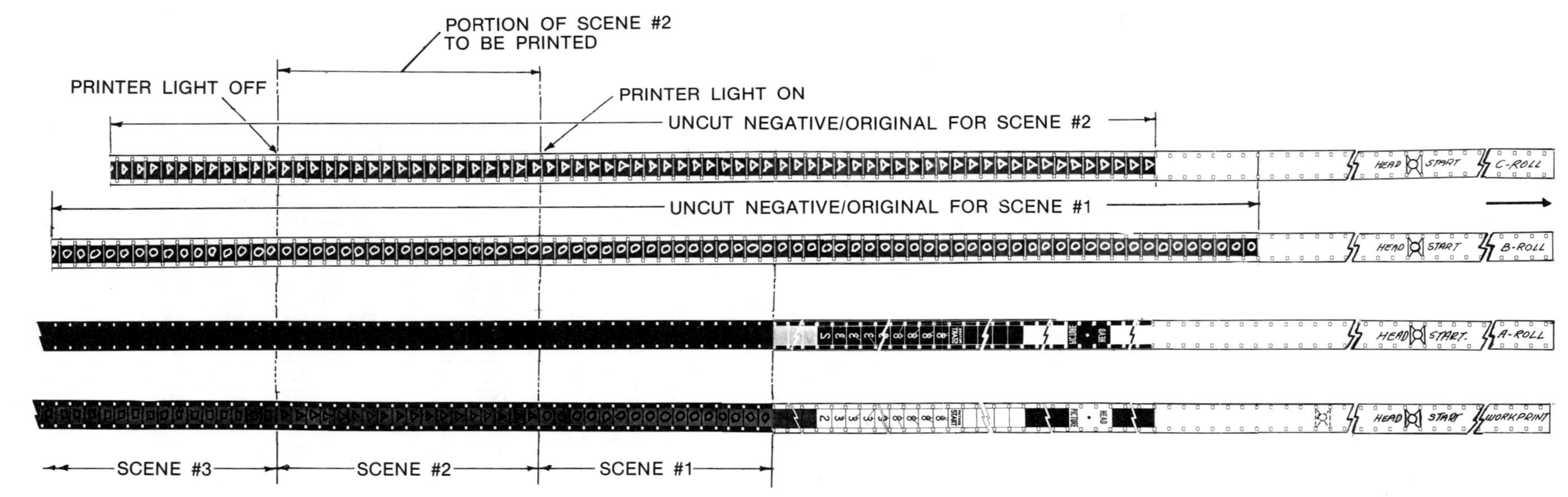

Fig. 11.34. Two uncut scenes assembled in zero-cut AB rolls. Filler leader lengthens the head leaders to accommodate the length of uncut Scene #1 negative/original. In this case, Scene #3 would have to be put on a C roll.

Feet & Frames from HEADSTART	EFFECT	LENGTH OF EFFECT	ROLL	NOTES
0'-0X	HEAD START			
13'-34X	START FADE IN	48X	A	
17'-26X	CUT		A TO B	
22'-21X	CENTER-DISSOLVE	48X	B to C	TITLES ON C-ROLL
26'-33X	CENTER-DISSOLVE	48X	C to B	
41'-10X	CENTER-DISSOLVE	48X	B to A	
47'-34X	CUT		A to B	
56'-00X	CUT		B to A	
61'-34X	START FADE IN	24X	C	SUPERIMPOSED TITLE
67'-23X	START FADEOUT	24X	C	
69'-32X	CENTER-DISSOLVE	48X	A to B	

Fig. 11.35. Printing cue sheet for zero-cut AB rolls.

Cue Sheets for Zero Cutting

Prepare the zero printing sheets after assembling, taping, and scribing the AB rolls. (See Fig. 11.35) Rewind the AB rolls and the workprint and rethread them into the synchronizer with the HEAD START marks in the sync frame position. Set the counter on the synchronizer at zero feet, zero frames (0'-OX). Wind through the picture, noting the footage and length of each effect in the cue sheet. It is easier to prepare cue sheets if two people work together: one person to call out the information and footage as he winds the rolls through the synchronizer, and the other to fill out the cue sheet accordingly (Fig. 11.35).

Several precautions should be taken during editing if you are planning to zero cut. Check with the laboratory first for printing limitations such as the minimum number of frames between the end of a dissolve and the following cut. If the laboratory machines cannot reset for a cut in the length you have provided, reediting will be necessary before cutting the AB rolls. Also, make notes ahead of time of multiple scenes derived from a single negative/original scene. Often two or more shots in the workprint will be parts of the same negative/original scenes. Such scenes will have to be cut apart and laid in separately.

SPLICING NEGATIVE/ORIGINAL AB ROLLS

It is best to let the laboratory splice the AB rolls, since its splicing equipment is designed especially for this type of work and is kept in perfect condition. The laboratory technician doing the splicing is highly skilled and works rapidly and surely, and the small cost is well worth the protection and careful handling your negative/original rolls receive.

If you prefer to splice the negative yourself, or if there is no laboratory nearby, refer to the section on splicing for the complete procedure.

MARKING THE SOUND TRACK FOR EDITORIAL AND PRINTER SYNC

During editing, the workprint and the sound track are marked in *cutter sync,* also called *editorial sync* or *dead sync.* That is, when both sync marks are aligned opposite each other in the synchronizer, the sound and picture are in sync. Cutter sync is used throughout editing and in interlock projection. However, when the sound track is printed onto the release print, it must be 26 frames ahead of the picture to be accommodated to the projector.

16mm projectors are uniformly designed so that the sound pickup head is 26 frames ahead of the picture projection aperture. Therefore, for the sound to be heard that belongs to the picture being seen, it must be 26 frames ahead of the picture. This is called the "26-frame pullup." If the release print sound track is to be made directly from the magnetic track, the 26-frame pullup will have to be made by changing the head start mark on the magnetic track (Fig.

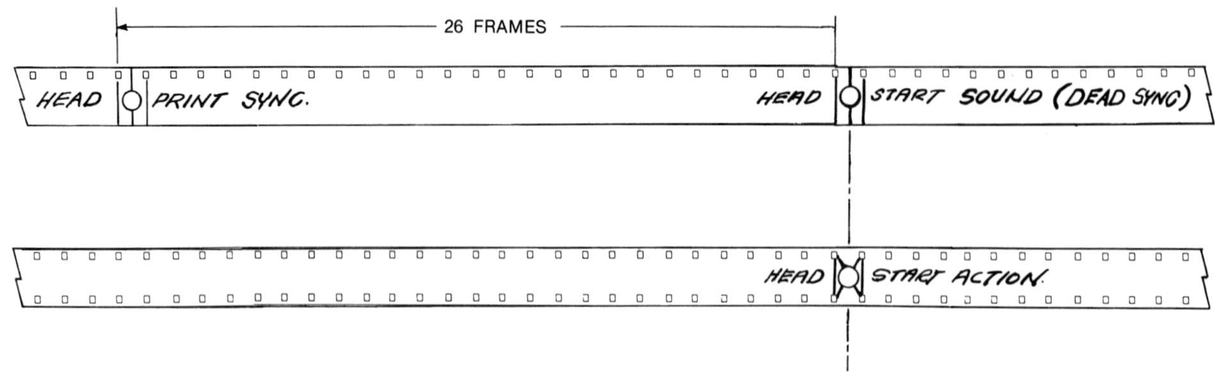

Fig. 11.36. To change dead sync to printer sync, the start mark must be moved 26 frames toward the tail.

11.36). To do this, move the cutter sync mark 26 frames toward the tail of the picture; it then becomes the *printer sync* mark, and the track is said to be in printer sync (Figs. 11.37*A*, 11.37*B*.) Proceed as follows:

1. Put the track in the synchronizer with head start in the sync frame position.
2. Set the frame counter at zero.
3. Roll the synchronizer to the right until the number 26 on the counter comes into the sync frame position.
4. Mark the 26 frame on the sound track leader and make it the new printer sync mark.
5. Cut off the old sync mark and add new leader to make up the loss.

SYNC POP

If the track on the final composite print is to be made from on optical negative, before it can be printed from the AB rolls the magnetic track must be transferred onto film as an optical image. If a sync pop has been placed on the track in sync with a known frame on either the A or the B roll, you can easily sync the new track to the AB rolls. The frame usually used as a sync point for

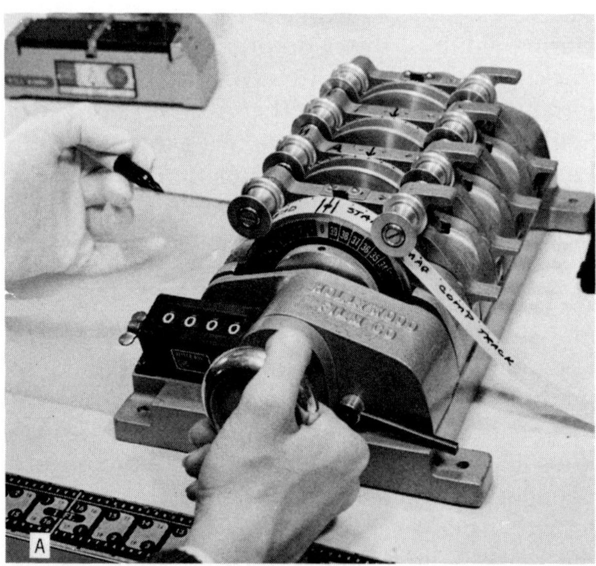

Fig. 11.37*A*. To change dead sync to printer sync, put the dead sync start mark in the sync machine and set the frame counter to zero.

Fig. 11.37*B*. Roll ahead (to the right) until 26 comes up on the frame counter. This frame is the printer sync start mark.

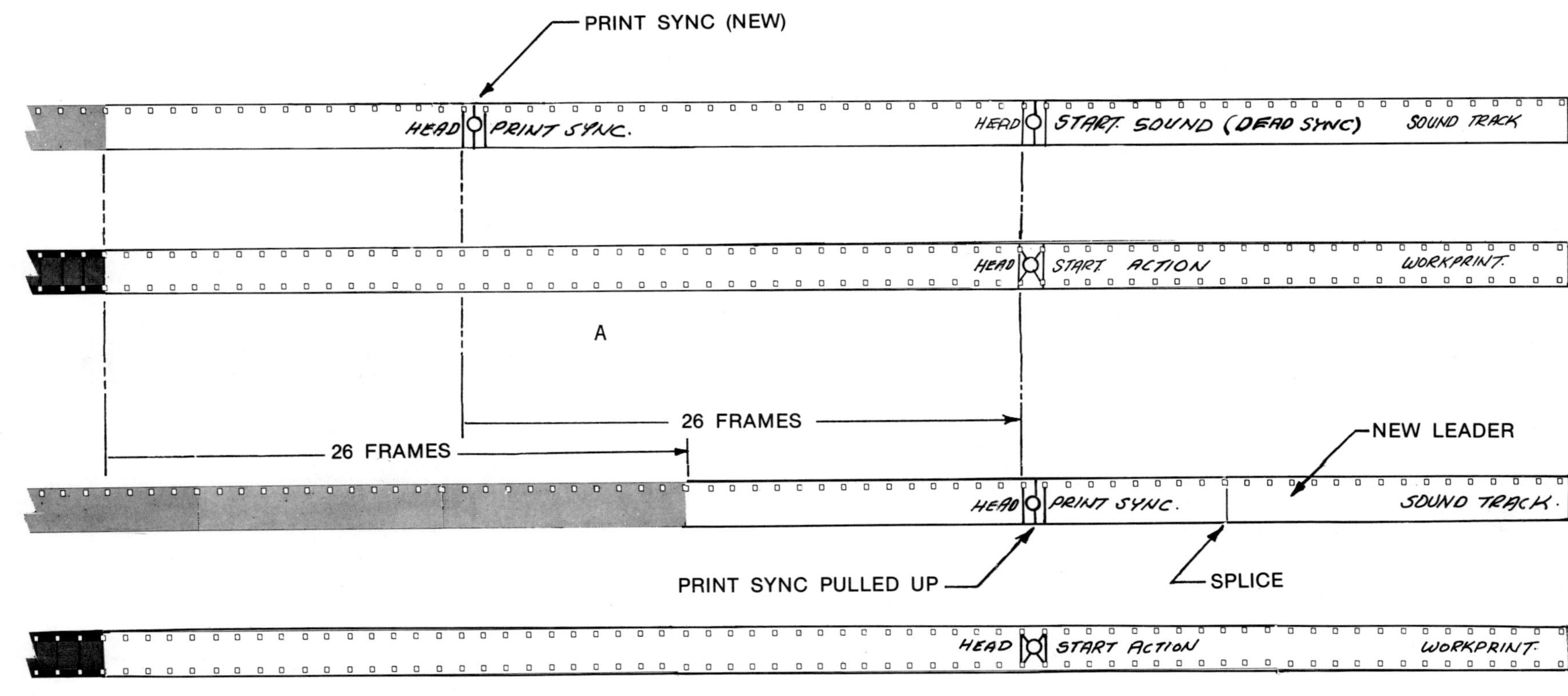

Fig. 11.38*A*. Printer sync mark made on dead sync leader. (*B*) Dead sync mark cut off and replaced with new leader.

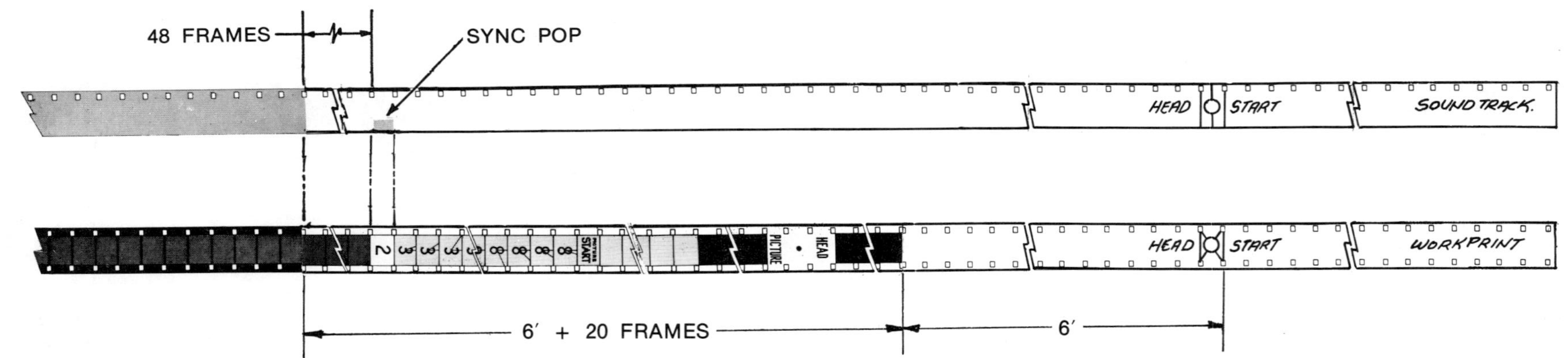

Fig. 11.39. Sync pop in dead sync with the two-frame on society leader.

the sync pop is the "2" on the Society leader. At the time of workprint editing the sync pop would have been placed on one of the sound tracks before mixing. (See Preparation for Mixing.) The sync pop, then, is usually in *cutter sync* (dead sync) with the "2" on the Society leader (Fig. 11.39). When the optical track comes back from the lab, to put the sync pop in *printer sync,* use the same procedure for putting the head start mark in printer sync, as follows:

1. Place the optical sync pop modulation in the sync frame of the synchronizer.
2. Set the frame counter at zero.
3. Roll to the right until the 26 on the frame counter comes into the sync frame.
4. Mark the 26 frame on the optical sound track, then put this frame in sync with the Society leader two on the workprint.
5. Roll to the head, and make a start mark on the optical track that is in sync with head start on the workprint. Identify this new start mark as printer sync. (See Fig. 11.36.) The type of sync, Printer or Cutter, need only be indicated on the sound track (Figs. 11.38*A, B*).

PREPARING AB ROLLS FOR SHIPMENT TO THE LABORATORY

Much grief can be avoided by making sure that all material is properly prepared and identified and instructions are explicit and complete before being sent to the laboratory. Most problems in the laboratory are the direct or indirect result of incomplete instructions and inaccurate information.

When AB roll assembly has been completed and checked for mistakes through the sync machine, prepare all materials for shipment as follows:

1. Wind each roll and the sound track carefully onto cores.
2. Wrap each roll in tissue paper and place it in a box or can for delivery.
3. Put tape on the outside of each container and write full identifying information on it: name of production, name of producer, material (A-roll negative, magnetic track, etc.), length in feet of each item, and can number.
4. Tape the lid on with two short pieces of tape. Do not tape around the perimeter of the can or box since this indicates unexposed film.
5. Prepare a complete and accurate laboratory order.

THE LABORATORY ORDER

Prepare the laboratory order (see Fig. 11.40) in duplicate, and keep one receipted copy for your protection. It should include the following:

1. Producer's name, address, and phone number
2. Material submitted
3. Type of material
4. Length of material
5. Work to be done
6. Special instructions
7. Date
8. Receipt line.

Laboratories may be reluctant to sign a receipt for material submitted, but insist on it. In the complex bowels of a laboratory many strange events can occur. If you have a signed, receipted lab order, there will be no question about what material was sent in and what is to be done with it (Fig. 11.40).

Use the printed order forms supplied by each laboratory, or type or write the order. Standard purchase order pads are available in any stationery store at a nominal price. Whatever you use, make sure it is explicit, complete, accurate, and legible.

CARE OF NEGATIVE/ORIGINAL FILM

The mechanics of negative cutting described so far gives little feeling of its peculiar flavor, which is derived from the irreplaceability of all original camera material. This negative/original film is your most valuable possession. In a very real sense it is your only possession. When the picture is edited, recorded, and ready for the first print to be made, there is nothing to show for the hundreds, thousands, or even millions of dollars you may have invested except a picture negative stored in one to twelve cans. A suitcase can easily carry a picture that may have cost as much as the

```
                    SAMPLE LABORATORY ORDER

TO: Slusho Laboratory                    FROM:  Joe Jones
    Address                                     Address and phone

        Material submitted:
           A-roll orig ECO - 400'
           B-roll orig ECO - 400'
           Mag comp sound track - 400'

        Work to be done:
           Splice AB rolls
           From mag com track make optical neg track
           From AB rolls and optical neg track make one
             1st trial color composite print.

        Special Instructions:
           Sync Pop is in Cutter Sync with 2 on Society leader
           Deliver on reel and can
           Needed by 9/24


                                         Received______________

                                         Date__________
```

Fig. 11.40. Sample lab order.

latest jet airliner. A match could destroy it in a few moments. The delicacy of the negative cutting process gives it a peculiar flavor; a kind of ritual surrounds it. There must be no haste, no short cuts. Carelessly winding up a roll of negative/original, followed by pressure on the edges to make it lie flat, produces cross scratches or *cinch marks* that cannot be removed. The same holds true for an accidental thumb mark on the emulsion surface, or a scratch made with a fingernail. Too much heat makes the negative soften and run. Rubbing one piece of film across another causes abrasions to the emulsion surface. A particle of dust pressed in by an adjacent turn of film leaves a permanent hole in the emulsion. Although all these blemishes are very small, when magnified in projection, they become very large indeed.

The preservation of the negative/original takes thoughtful planning and scrupulous care. Pay particular attention to the following important points:

1. Keep negatives and originals in two places only, the vault and the negative cutting room. In the vault, store them in cans or clean film boxes, and, if possible, at a constant medium temperature and humidity.

2. Confine handling of the negative/original to the negative cutting room. Dust is dangerous. Air conditioning is almost essential. Exclude other people as far as is practicable to avoid the continual coming and going that brings dust and disturbs concentrated work.

3. Dust or vacuum the surface or each cutting table frequently and keep it absolutely spotless. Carefully line the insides of bins and other difficult to dust areas with detachable covers or cover with soft tissue paper.

4. Wear white editing gloves when working. Wash them frequently.

5. Always handle negative/originals by the edges. When fitting them into and taking them out of the synchronizer, avoid rough contact between the films and metal.

6. Never assemble original film with metal clips unless paper is inserted both over and under the clips so that they are completely covered.

7. Avoid viewing negative/originals on projectors and moviolas since the most precise adjustment and expert maintenance cannot guarantee that they will not scratch the film. One time through the projector may be sufficient to put fine but permanent marks on the film that will be visible throughout the life of the finished picture. The practice of projecting negative/originals is harmful; do not tolerate it. The continuous motion film viewer is not, however, a potential

damager of film. It has fewer revolving parts and no intermittent motion. In operating it by hand, you can stop it instantly at the least sign of trouble.

The foregoing precautions for handling original films apply also to duplicating materials such as library footage and optical effects, because other negatives or positives will be printed from them to be intercut with the original film. Since they go through one or two additional processes, these secondary materials require even greater care than the originals if they are to show no visible deterioration.

While most other production activities modify or add to the film in some way, as negative cutter your chief concern is to add nothing and take away nothing, only to preserve untouched the irreplaceable image.

TWELVE

An Afterword

This is a guide for the would-be film producer, for the lone filmmaker, and for those somewhere in between. Whichever you may be, do not be intimidated; for there is no mystique, and in all kinds of motion picture production—high budget, low-budget, studio-made, or individually made, at any level of complexity or expense—the basic tasks are the same.

To make a film, it is not necessary to use a crew of seventy specialized technicians; it is only necessary to do the required work. With good reason, a large motion picture company may often use a large crew of technicians to shoot a movie; a smaller independent producer may use from five to fifteen people to do the same tasks; and a lone filmmaker may do them all himself. Who does a particular task and his title are immaterial. The job to be done is important.

Whatever kind of film you plan to make, the elements of production are similar. There are, of course, differences in every producing company: nomenclature may vary and the order of things may not be exactly as described here; one studio may use rubber bands instead of tape around rolls of film; another may underline rather than circle an entry in a script breakdown; and red grease pencil may be used instead of yellow. Although you will probably have to adapt what you have learned here to the particular situation you will be working under, the underlying process will be the same.

The newcomer to filmmaking is subjected to overwhelming intimidation both by the process itself and by other people. Every aspect has its own strange vocabulary; there are many strange new machines; and there seems to be a maze of complex procedures unlike anything found in more familiar forms of expression. Everywhere are self-styled "experts" who use professional jargon as weapons; and if you listen seriously to these experts, you are in danger of feeling too technologically naive to aspire to the making of films. But under no circumstances should you allow yourself to be intimidated by such talk or implications. Women are particularly vulnerable to the destructive talk of experts and their technical jargon since they have been bombarded from birth by big-man talk about the excruciating complexities of radios, automobiles, photography, and plumbing. Often they are initially disposed to accept the belief that filmmaking is just too complex. But intimidated people, when reminded that this is more of the same old, carefully administered mumbo-jumbo, often go far beyond their apparent capabilities and make stunningly effective films.

Many would have you believe that filmmaking consists entirely of technology. It does not. The motion picture is a vehicle of expression, just as writing and painting are, and the art of the motion picture begins not with photography and equipment, but with ideas and visualization. Eventually you will have to master one or another of the tools of film—cameras, recorders, film editing machines, or the like—but mastery of equipment is not useful for its own sake. Its sole purpose is to allow you to get your ideas on the screen. Because at first you do not know how to operate a camera or turn on a recorder or thread a projector or order a daily print, or because you do not even know enough to ask the right questions, don't allow yourself to be disheartened. The problems of filmmaking are not always simple, and dealing with them can be frustrating and discouraging. Their mastery may require hours of dedicated struggle, but they can be solved by ordinary human beings.

Even though filmmaking is the child of technology, you do not need to be, and should not be, an engineering specialist. Some of the worst films ever made have been done by people who thoroughly understood the technical and engineering aspects of film production; and, conversely, great films have been made by people who had not the slightest notion about what takes place inside cameras and amplifiers. Technical services are readily available in laboratories, sound studios, and specialized shops, so do not despair if you know nothing about photographic chemistry, physics, sensitometry, or other technical aspects of film production. Good films originate in the minds of creative people who can see; and you need only know how to use what is available to achieve what you want. This book is not a definitive manual, since the business of making films probably has as many ways of working and producing as it has people doing these tasks. Since each person eventually discovers his own best way of working, this material is offered only as a starting point—a detailed hint on how to go about learning your own way.

APPENDIX

Film Information

Projection sound speed. 24 frames per second for both 16mm and 35 mm film.

Frames per foot. 16mm, 40 frames per foot
35mm, 16 frames per foot

Ratio of 35mm to 16mm film. 2½ to 1

Edge numbers (key numbers). 16mm: appear at 20-frame intervals
35mm: appear at 16-frame intervals

Code numbers. 16mm and 35mm code numbers are printed at 1-foot intervals.

Sync pop. For both 16mm and 35 mm:

On SMPTE leader (Society leader), the sync pop should be in dead sync (cutter sync) with the 2 frame.

On the old Academy leader, the sync pop should be in sync with the 3 frame.

Sound track pull-up. On the composite print, the 16mm sound track is 26 frames ahead of the picture.
On the composite print, the 35mm sound track is 20 frames ahead of the picture.

1 reel is 10 minutes of screen time.

400 feet of 16mm film is 1 reel.

1000 feet of 35mm film is 1 reel ($2.5 \times 400 = 1000$).

Camera negative/original reads correctly through the base side of the film. Images and numbers are right side up and read correctly from left to right.

A print from a negative/original reads correctly through the emulsion side of the film. Images and numbers are right side up and read correctly from left to right.

Recommended Reading

Charles G. Clarke, *Professional Cinematography,* American Society of Cinematographers, Hollywood, 1964.

By far the best work on motion picture photography by one of the world's leading cinematographers. Its small size is misleading, for it contains much. It should be carefully studied by anyone seriously interested in cinematography.

Howard M. Tremaine, *Audio Cyclopedia,* Second Edition, Howard W. Sams, New York, 1969.

The definitive work on motion picture sound. It is highly technical and complete; but with diligence even the non-technical reader can find answers to most sound recording problems.

Alec Nisbett, *The Use of Microphones,* Hastings House, New York, 1973.

An excellent work explaining microphones and their use in motion pictures and television.

Loren Ryder, "How to Record Better Sound Tracks for Motion Pictures," *American Cinematographer,* October, 1967, pp. 721–724.

Six basic rules for getting good motion picture sound by one of the world's leading sound directors. Available in reprint from Ryder Sound Services, Hollywood, California.

Lenny Lipton, *Independent Filmmaking,* Straight Arrow Books, San Francisco, 1972.

A comprehensive book by an outstanding filmmaker on the mechanics and the tools of filmmaking.

Arthur Cox, *Optics,* Focal Press, Hastings House, New York, 1943.

A standard work on photographic optics.

American Cinematographer International Journal of Motion Picture Photography and Production Techniques, American Society of Cinematographers, Hollywood, California.

Known simply as the *American Cinematographer,* this monthly magazine is the contemporary reflection of what is happening in the film industry relative to cinematography and filmmaking. Each issue contains analyses of problems involved in the shooting of current feature and documentary films.

A. J. Reynertson, *The Work of the Film Director,* Communications Arts Books, New York, 1970.

Contains much highly concentrated and valuable information for the filmmaker.

Raymond Fielding, *The Technique of Special-Effects Cinematography,* Hastings House, New York, 1970.

An accurate, detailed compendium of the standard photographic effects of the motion picture industry.

John Alton, *Painting With Light,* The Macmillan Company, New York, 1949.

Although this work deals mainly with black-and-white photography and older studio methods, it contains much basic information on the cinematography of staged scenes.

Coles Trapnell, *Teleplay,* Hawthorn Books, Inc., New York, 1974.

Explains how to write screenplays for television and how to sell them. Contains examples of teleplay format.

Eugene Vale, *The Technique of Screenplay Writing,* The Universal Library, Grosset and Dunlap, New York, 1973.

A readable and valuable analysis of the dramatic structure of motion pictures for the writer of screenplays.

Wolf Rilla, *The Writer and the Screen,* William Morrow and Company, New York, 1974.

This book doesn't explain how to write, but it is valuable and should be read by anyone interested in film or television as a profession.

John N. Ott, *My Ivory Cellar,* Devin.

A definitive work on time-lapse photography by the acknowledged master in the field.

The *American Cinematographer Manual,* edited by Charles G. Clarke and Walter Strenge, American Society of Cinematographers, Hollywood, California, 1974.

Contains tables, charts, graphs, detailed data, and information indispensable to the motion picture photographer and camera operator. A must for the cinematographer's kit. Contains valuable articles on a wide range of processes and procedures in the film industry.

Association of Cinema Laboratories, *Handbook,* Third Edition, Virginia, 1972.

Contains recommended standards and procedures for motion picture laboratory services. Mainly for the use of laboratory technicians, but much of it is useful for the filmmaker.

W. Hugh Baddeley, *The Technique of Documentary Film Production,* Hastings House, New York, 1965.

A good, but not too detailed, explanation of the film production process. Gives a brief, easy-access summary of film production.

Raoul Pagel, *Hollywood Film Production Manual,* Raoul Pagel, Burbank, California, 1976.

Indispensable to the producer of theatrical films. It contains information that normally is gained through long expensive experience, such as dealing with unions and guilds, budgets, and information on equipment, facilities, and technicians throughout the world.

Ernest Walter, *The Technique of the Film Cutting Room,* Hastings House, New York, 1968.

A straightforward description of the mechanics of film editing.

SMPTE Journal, Published by the Society of Motion Picture and Television Engineers, Scarsdale, New York, a group of scientists and engineers involved in the technical and scientific advancement of film and TV.

Articles are mostly technical and specialized, but are sometimes of value to filmmakers.

Telephone Book.

The classified section, or "Yellow Pages," of the telephone directory is an invaluable and almost complete guide to all film and television services, supplies, and equipment.

Catalogs and Price Schedules.

Equipment manufacturers, rental houses, laboratories, studios, and film services publish catalogs, price schedules, and related material to aid and attract customers. A reference collection of such material is extremely useful to the filmmaker.

Index